CW00825700

Vice-Admiral Sir Bernard Rawlings

Frontispiece

Ministry of Defence

(NAVY)

WAR WITH JAPAN

VOLUME VI

THE ADVANCE TO JAPAN

London: HMSO

First published 1995

ISBN 0 11 772821 7

Contents

APPENDICES (*continued*)

ILLUSTRATIONS

Frontispiece. Vice-Admiral Sir Bernard Rawlings.

FIGURES

PLANS

(at end of text)

ABBREVIATIONS

AD	Destroyer Tender
AE	Ammunition Ship
AFD	Mobile Floating Dry Dock
AG	Air Group
AGC	Amphibious Force Flagship
AGD	Motor Torpedo Boat Tender
AGS	Surveying Ship
AH	Hospital Ship
AK	Cargo Ship, Auxiliary
AKA	Cargo Ship, Attack
AKN	Net Cargo Ship
AM	Minesweeper
AN	Netlayer
AO	Oiler
AOG	Aviation Fuel Tanker
AP	Transport
APA	Transport, Attack
APD	Transport (High Speed)
APL	Labour Transport or Barrack Ship
AR	Repair Ship
ARB	Repair Ship, Battle Damage
ARD	Auxiliary Repair Dock (Floating Dry Dock)
ARG	Repair Ship, Internal Combustion Engine
ARH	Heavy Hull Repair Ship
ARL	Repair Ship, Landing Craft
ARS	Salvage Lifting Vessel
ARV	Aircraft Repair Ship
ASR	Air–Sea Rescue
AS(W)	Anti-Submarine (Warfare)
AT	Ocean Tug : A, Auxiliary ; F, Fleet ; R, Rescue
AV	Seaplane Tender
AVD	Seaplane Tender (High Speed)
B–24	Liberator (Heavy Bombardment Aircraft)
B–29	Superfortress (Very Heavy Bombardment Aircraft)
BPF	British Pacific Fleet
CAPBRAX	Captain Barrack Ships and Small Craft
CGC	Coastguard Cutter
CINCAFPAC	Commander-in-Chief, U.S. Army Forces, Pacific
CINCPOA	Commander-in-Chief, Pacific Ocean Areas
COFT	Commodore Fleet Train
COMAT	Commodore Air Train
CVE	Escort Aircraft Carrier
DM	Light Minelayer
DMS	Minesweeper (converted Destroyer)
DUKW	Amphibious Truck
FAMG	Fleet Air Maintenance Group

FEAF	Far Eastern Air Forces
FOAC	Flag Officer, Aircraft Carriers
FONAP	Flag Officer Naval Air (Pacific)
GP	General Purpose
HF	High Frequency Radio
IFF	Identification, Friend, Foe ?
IX	Miscellaneous Unclassified
LCI	Landing Craft, Infantry: (G) Gunboat; (M) Mortar Ship; (R) Rocket
LCM	Landing Craft, Mechanical
LCS(L)	Landing Craft, Support (Large), (R) Rocket
LCT	Landing Craft, Tank
LSD	Landing Ship, Dock
LSM	Landing Ship, Medium
LST	Landing Ship, Tank
LSV	Landing Ship, Vehicle
LVT	Landing Vehicle, Tracked (' Amtrak '): (A) Armoured
MONAB	Mobile Naval Air Base
NSIS	Naval Store Issuing Ship
SEATIC	South-East Asia Translation and Intelligence Centre
SORNEI	Senior Officer R.N. Establishments, India
SP	Special Purpose
SRR(D) Ship	Special Repair Ratings (Dockyard) Ship
TBS	Voice Radio (' talk between ships ')
UDT	Underwater Demolition Team
USASTAF	U.S. Army Strategic Air Force in the Pacific
USSBS	United States Strategic Bombing Survey
VHF	Very High Frequency
VLR	Very Long Range
VS or V/S	Visual Signal
VSIS	Victualling Store Issuing Ship
VT Fuse	Variable Time Fuse
XAK	Merchant Cargo Ship
YC	Yard Craft
YDG	District Degaussing Vessel
YO	District Barge, Fuel Oil (Self-propelled)
YOG	District Barge, Gasoline (Self-propelled)
YP	District Patrol Vessel
YR	District Workshop, Floating
YRD(H)	District Workshop, Floating Dry Dock (Hull)
YRD(M)	District Workshop, Floating Dry Dock (Machinery)
YSD	District Derrick, Seaplane Wrecking
YSR	District Barge, Sludge Removal
YTB	District Tug, Harbour, Big
YTL	District Tug, Harbour, Little
YW	District Barge, Water (Self-propelled)

Preface

THE narrative opens in the Autumn 1944 with a description of the military situation of the Japanese. The production of war material had reached its peak and was beginning to decline owing to the diminution of stocks of raw materials and the inadequacy of the $3\frac{1}{2}$ million tons of merchant shipping, which were all that remained to Japan, to support both the economic life of the country and the requirements of the army and navy. The carrier-based air force had been destroyed, and the shore based naval air forces were resorting to suicide operating, an example which the army air forces soon increasingly followed. But the battle fleet was still powerful and the home army intact. The closer the Allies drew to Japan, the fiercer was the enemy's resistance.

In the United Kingdom the position as regards manpower, shipping and materials was rendering very difficult the formation of the Fleet Train to support the British Pacific Fleet which was soon to take part with the United States Fleet in the main operations against Japan : in fact, it was never possible to form an adequate Fleet Train, and as regards oilers and air and communications stores, in particular, there were serious deficiencies.

In this volume, the story of the war in the Indian Ocean is carried to its conclusion before that of the Pacific begins. The German and Japanese submarine campaigns were still a few weeks from defeat, but for the sake of continuity, these campaigns against our Indian Ocean shipping were described in Volume IV of this History right up to their final defeat. The same treatment was accorded in Volume IV to the history of the South-East Asia Area ; that is to say, to the strategy and to the amphibious and coastal operations conducted by the Commander-in-Chief Eastern Fleet under the control of the Supreme Allied Commander. The Commander-in-Chief still owed dual allegiance to the Admiralty and to the Supreme Allied Commander respectively. The present volume describes the operations by the Eastern Fleet and the British Pacific Fleet, under Admiralty control, the cutting of the supply lines of the Japanese Burma Area Army and the attacks on the Sumatran oil refineries. The importance of these refineries lay in the fact that with the abandonment by the Japanese of the convoy routes from Balik Papan and Miri the Sumatran oil was the only supply remaining available to Japan. After the British Pacific Fleet left for the Pacific at the beginning of 1945 the remaining ships on the East Indies Station, termed the East Indies Fleet, were occupied with operations to stop the supply of the beleaguered Japanese garrisons and their withdrawal and concentration nearer the centre, and with the clearance of the Japanese minefields.

Meanwhile in the Pacific the Americans were attacking the Philippine Islands and experiencing the first organised suicide air attacks. In the U.S. Seventh Fleet, in which Australian ships were serving, H.M.A.S. *Australia* was specially singled out as an objective, perhaps on account of the importance lent her in oriental eyes as the possessor of the most funnels. This extensive operation was still continuing when the Americans assaulted Iwo Jima, followed by the capture by the Australians with U.S. support of the oil producing areas of Borneo.

PREFACE

In March 1945 the British Pacific Fleet joined the U.S. Fifth Fleet (later to become the Third Fleet) in the long-drawn-out operation for the capture of Okinawa in which no less than 28 ships were sunk and 227 damaged by air attack. For weeks on end, until the shore airfields were in operation, the carriers had to abrogate their normal function and stand and give cover to the amphibious shipping and support to the troops under a hail of suicide air attacks. Here the Americans, who at first had been doubtful of the need for British help, came to appreciate the assistance of our ships.

From Okinawa the U.S. Third Fleet with the British Pacific Fleet serving in it as a Task Force proceeded to the final attack on Japan. The difficulties which Admiral Rawlings had experienced in keeping his ships in action at Okinawa with an inadequate Fleet Train were intensified in the air attacks and bombardments of the Japanese home islands in which we were to strike blow for blow with the amply supplied United States ships. The Americans were the great exponents of naval air warfare and it was known they would tolerate nothing but the best. But with these Allies lending assistance beyond their undertaking, and with great exertions and ingenuity on the part of officers and men, Admiral Rawlings was able to play his part and maintain his position in the right of the line to the moment of the surrender.

A short description is given of the attempts of the Japanese to end the war on their own terms ; and the volume closes with an objective appraisal of the war.

The full list of volumes of the Naval Staff History in which the war against Japan is described is as follows :—

Volume I. *Background to the War.*

Volume II. *Defensive Phase : Pearl Harbour to the Battle of Midway, with the Aleutian Operations.*

Volume III. *The Campaigns in New Guinea and the Solomons.*

Volume IV. *The South East Asia Operations and the Central Pacific Advance.*

Volume V. *Blockade of Japan.*

Volume VI. *The Advance to Japan* (this volume).

CHAPTER I

Situation in the Far East and Pacific in the Autumn of 1944

(Plans 1, 2)

1

BY the Autumn of 1944 the advance of the Allies had brought Japan to a position of grave danger. In September, the two lines along which the Allied advance in the Pacific was being conducted, by Admiral Nimitz in the Central Pacific and General MacArthur in the South-West Pacific, had converged at Palau and Halmahera ; and the Philippines lay wide open. The great war potential of the Allies was now nearly at peak, and the Japanese, overtasked and kept off balance by the rapidity of the Allied assaults, had been unable anywhere in the Pacific Ocean to offer more than local resistance to Admiral Nimitz's and latterly also to General MacArthur's advance. In the west their flank was crumbling under the pressure from which Admiral Mountbatten gave them no respite even during the terrible campaigning conditions of the monsoon. Japanese maritime strategy had always been dominated by the concept of a great fleet action to destroy the enemy naval power and secure their defensive perimeter. But the second Battle of Tsushima on which their eyes had been fixed since they broke the peace nearly three years earlier, had been denied them. Their fleet had twice been soundly beaten. At Midway, in June 1942, U.S. pre-battle intelligence, and at the Marianas exactly two years later American excess of strength, combined in both battles with superior American training and faulty Japanese dispositions, had neutralised the enemy's battleship strength and involved him in air battles in which American carrier based aircraft inflicted two crushing defeats.

But a further and more dangerous factor was now embarrassing the Japanese. For nearly three years, Allied attacks on their merchant shipping had been continuous. During the past 12 months shipping losses had been mounting at the rate of more than 250,000 tons a month, double the figure of current new construction. The merchant fleet which even at the outbreak of hostilities was inadequate, was by the Autumn of 1944 reduced by half. Introduction of a general convoy system in November of the previous year had served not at all to stem the losses, for the financial stringency and lack of skilled workers which in peace time had militated against the creation of a sufficient number of escort vessels in addition to both a battle fleet and a considerable merchant marine, operated even more adversely in 1944. The losses of merchant shipping were causing serious reductions in industrial output and consequently affecting the military machine. The production of war materials had reached its maximum in the Summer and Autumn of the year; but the inevitable decline from peak, a peak, in the case of Japan, far below that of the United States and the United Kingdom and one from which the Japanese no more than the Allies could prevent a decline, was accelerated where Japan was concerned through the shortage of war materials, legacy of the Western nations' trading embargoes in 1940 and 1941, which had become acute now that imports were further curtailed through the daily increasing difficulty of bringing in cargoes. In the last year of peace, ships of the civilian fleet excluding those under requisition by the Japanese Army and Navy, had carried nearly 49,000,000 tons of commodities. The figure for 1944 was little more than 17,000,000 tons. Only one thing now lay between Japan and economic strangulation, and that was possession of the Philippine Islands, Formosa, and the Ryukus. With the airfields of the Philippines in the occupation of the Japanese Air Forces and denied to the Allies Japanese convoys still passed along the transit route through the China Sea from the region which the enemy termed the Southern Resources Area: though with shocking losses. This route was Japan's lifeline. The slow alternative line of supply by railway all the way from Singapore to Fusan (Pusan) and from there by ferry across Korea Strait, was not yet available in its entirety, for there were breaks still unrestored in the line between Saigon and Pnom Penh and south of Hengyang. Loss of either the Philippines, Formosa, or the Ryukus would cut the route through the China Sea and reduce the country to dependence upon the economic resources of her Inner Zone of defence, that is, North China, Manchuria, Korea, Formosa, Karafuto and the Japanese home islands. Great efforts had been made to increase the output of raw materials in this zone, but production was still far from sufficient for the maintenance of the life of the country and quite inadequate to sustain a major war.

Japan's strategic position had, however, elements favourable to her, for she possessed interior lines of communication; whilst the shortening of her defensive perimeter was bringing the numbers of her diminishing merchant fleet and her convoy escorts more into line with the burdens laid upon them.

The Allies could now definitely look forward to victory and it was known that the thoughts of the Japanese were turning to means of ending the war but there was no certainty that the enemy could be brought to acknowledge defeat by sea blockade and air action alone.[1] In consequence, Allied strategy was based upon the expectation of having to invade Japan in order to bring about the unconditional surrender which at Cairo in December 1943 had been proclaimed as our intention. After the loss of the Marianas, Japanese strategy became entirely defensive. Preparations were being made for desperate resistance in the home islands. Numbers of suicide craft were building. A Home Defence Corps was being formed, to work in close co-operation with the Army; and in expectation of Allied air raids people were being evacuated from the large towns.

[1] The following entry appears in the report of the Far Eastern Section of the Naval Intelligence Division for 21st August 1944. 'The Japanese Foreign Office recently instructed the Japanese Ambassador in Moscow to consider the possibility of Russia intervening for peace between Japan and the Allies, in return for which Japan would use her good offices as between Russia and Germany. The Ambassador replied that there was not the slightest use his making such a suggestion, as the Russians were determined to destroy the Germans. He also aimed a shot at the Japanese Military by saying, "As the (Far Eastern) War was started without regard to the international situation, it can only be decided by force of arms and there is nothing which diplomacy can do".'

2

The Japanese main fleet was on paper still very powerful, despite the recent defeat in the Battle of the Marianas. Nine battleships, 11 aircraft carriers, 14 heavy and ten light cruisers[1] appeared a formidable fleet even when compared with the Striking Force of the U.S. Pacific Fleet. This consisted at any moment of some seven fast modern battleships, eight fleet carriers and eight light carriers, eight heavy and nine light cruisers. But the paper strength of the Japanese fleet was deceptive. Two of their battleships, the *Fuso* and *Yamashiro*, were old and with ineffective fire control radar, whilst two others, the *Ise* and *Hyuga*, had each had their after 14-inch gun turrets removed to make way for a flight deck ; and although these two last named ships had been recalled from Reserve on 1st May 1944 and included in the 4th Aircraft Carrier Squadron, they were found after conversion to be too slow for use as fleet carriers. The numerous heavy cruisers owed their existence to the Japanese cult of the offensive and to that end they carried torpedo tubes, in the employment of which however they had no success. Unlike the Allies, the Japanese did not employ all their armoured ships as floating A.A. gun platforms to defend their carriers. Consequently the chief practical use of their heavy cruisers was to carry long range reconnaissance aircraft, of which they had considerable complements and made use to obtain tactical intelligence. Until the present war had demonstrated the need for the Commander-in-Chief of a fleet in action to have at his disposal extensive communication facilities such as only a large ship could provide, it had been a Japanese tradition for him to fly his flag on board a cruiser. The commanders of the main groups of surface ships other than carriers in the complicated operational organisation of the Japanese fleet still did so. The present Commander-in-Chief of the Combined Fleet, Admiral Soemu Toyoda, flew his flag in the light cruiser *Oyodo*. Toyoda did not exercise tactical command of the striking force. This was still vested in the Commander of the carrier fleet, but a change was to take place before the next fleet action occurred in October, for in that battle Toyoda exercised a measure of operational control from headquarters in Tokyo.

The weakness of the Japanese fleet lay in its unbalance. Though the 11 carriers[2] had a total complement of some 500 aircraft, they had none on board. The losses of aircraft and, particularly, of pilots, at the Battle of the Marianas in June had been so heavy as temporarily to destroy the aircraft carrier squadrons as a fighting force. There were no relief air groups for Japanese carriers. Four months after the battle the Japanese were still engaged in rebuilding their air groups, though the training of a new muster of aircraft pilots was now approaching completion. Training was, however, so much less thorough than in the early days of the war, that the fighting ability of the Japanese air force was becoming affected. There were many obstacles in the way. Chief of these was the shortage of aircraft fuel which was to become critical within a few weeks. Fuel was indeed already so short that the number of attacks carried out by pilots on the single target ship available (an old battleship) had to be strictly rationed. Various other restrictions on training operated in sum to delay the rehabilitation of the air groups. Senior officers made representations about the poor workmanship in the aircraft supplied to them, such as badly machined

---

[1] These were the totals estimated by the Allies. The actual figures were :—Battleships 7, aircraft carriers 11, heavy cruisers 13, light cruisers 7.

[2] Excluding the pre-war light carrier *Hosho* which was attached to the Combined Fleet on 20th February 1944, but was non-operational and was reduced to Reserve, 4th Class, on 20th April 1945.

parts: a state of affairs not at that date, of course, confined to the Japanese; whilst the frequency with which aircraft became damaged during training was a subject of anxiety. When it came to actual battle not more than four of the 11 carriers were available to operate with the Japanese Striking Force. Of the remainder, two, the *Unryu* and *Amagi*, had only been commissioned in August and in the absence of air groups had had no opportunity of working up. Two more, the battleship-carriers *Ise* and *Hyuga*, as already mentioned, were useless as carriers; most of their air groups, with those of the *Junyo* and *Ryuho* in the 4th Aircraft Carrier Squadron, and those of the four carriers in the 3rd Squadron the fleet carrier *Zuikaku* and the light carriers *Chitose, Chiyoda* and *Zuiho*, were insufficiently trained to operate from carriers, and consequently were moved to shore bases in Formosa after a damaging air raid by the U.S. carriers of Task Force 38 in the second week of October.[1] But two more carriers, the *Katsuragi* and *Shinano*, the latter a battleship hull of 59,000 tons converted whilst building, were nearing completion for the 1st Carrier Squadron; and if air groups could be raised to man them the eight carriers of the 2nd and 3rd Squadrons would eventually constitute a formidable force. The ineffectiveness of the Japanese carrier air groups at that time was not known. Allied Intelligence on the eve of the assault on the Philippines reported that the Japanese Striking Force included six operational carriers with aircraft embarked.[2] The estimate of six carriers was perfectly correct; but the readiness date of their air groups had been indefinitely postponed.

The Japanese Navy was very short of destroyers, of which there were only 30 with the striking force of the Fleet. No less than 88 of the type had been sunk since war broke out. The 63 that remained included nine damaged during the past three months, eight classified as Second Class and several others suitable only for escort duty. The Japanese were trying to overcome the shortage of destroyers by building a large class of 1,260-ton vessels (*Matsu* class) originally designed as convoy escorts; in the prevailing shortage of fleet destroyers they were used for the latter purpose. In August 1944, the Commander-in-Chief of the Combined Fleet represented the severe shortage of the type in the Fleet and asked for another flotilla to be allotted. As there was no possibility of providing one, the vessels of the General Escort Command which had been formed in the previous November were placed under his orders; and Admiral Toyoda was consequently able to make operational use of the very few escort destroyers which were fit for fleet purposes. More than half the destroyers with the fleet were of pre-war construction.

By this date, probably all combat ships had one or two air warning radars, a surface search radar modified for fire control (for which there was no specially designed set) and a radar search receiver, whilst some had A/A or searchlight control radars. The efficiency of these radars was considerably lower than that of current Allied types.

3

The recent defeat of the Japanese Fleet in the Battle of the Marianas, and the destruction of the carrier based air forces, though it resulted in a change of government, had not sufficed to bring the military leaders of the nation to face realities. When appointing the new premier, General (retired) Kuniaki Koiso, the Emperor had laid upon him the ambiguous injunction to give the country's

[1] The pilots could take off from carriers but could not always land on them successfully (Admiral S. Toyoda, Commander-in-Chief, Combined Fleet, Interrogation Nav. No. 75).

[2] Far East and Pacific Intelligence Reports (Naval Intelligence Division) 23rd October 1944.

situation a fundamental reconsideration looking to the termination of the war. The new cabinet decided to prosecute the war with increased vigour and further sacrifices.

A month after the battle, Imperial Headquarters issued to the Commander-in-Chief, Combined Fleet a directive outlining the general operational policy he was to follow.[1] Refusing to recognise the seriousness of the strategic position, Imperial Headquarters enjoined Toyoda ' to maintain and make advantageous use of ' the situation. He was to draw up plans ' to destroy the enemy's strength '. This was to be accomplished by the land based air forces in conjunction with the Fleet. The Fleet was to be divided. The battleships were stationed in the South-Western Area (Singapore), to be near the source of oil supply, and were to be moved up as necessary to the Philippines or the Nansei Shoto, whilst the empty carriers were retained in the home islands during the period until the training of new air groups was complete. The submarines still had the main duty of operating against the Allied Fleets, ' by interception attacks in force or surprise attacks ', but part of the small remaining force would be ' assigned for reconnaissance of the enemy situation ' (in the course of which the submarines worked as far from home as the Indian Ocean and west coast of Australia) to cut the enemy's supply lines in the rear, and to transport supplies to ' our forward bases '—euphemism for bases by-passed by the Allies and cut off from all other methods of supply. The Japanese disposition list for 1st August 1944 shows 72 submarines (including those used for harbour defence). Actually, no more than 49 were still afloat : for some reason, possibly connected with morale, the list was swollen by the retention in it of boats sunk as long ago as May. Emphasis was placed on surprise by submarines and ' other types of surprise attack weapons ' at Allied advance bases (a reference to midget submarines and the type of human torpedoes called *kaitens*). In the home islands, defences were to be strengthened, for with the fall of the Marianas the main defence line had been ruptured. Most of the tasks were impossible of fulfilment. For example, in the Central Pacific Area, the whole of which was now in the hands of the Americans, if the latter attacked Toyoda ordained that they were to be crushed and their advance halted by the forces locally available, though these consisted of no more than the starving garrisons of the by-passed islands and a small and diminishing number of aircraft. The local defence craft had practically all been sunk by U.S. air attacks.

The most sensible injunction, but one impossible of fulfilment, was that the security of communications between Japan and the Southern Resources Area must be maintained : actually, the Japanese merchant shipping losses on the route were becoming almost unendurable. The only direction which in practice was followed so thoroughly as to cause the Americans real concern, was the prosecution of an air offensive against the new U.S. bases in the Marianas, constituting as these did, a direct threat to the Japanese home islands. We shall see in due course (Chapter XIII) what was the effect of three months' of enemy air raids on the airfields of the new American very heavy bombers (B–29s—Superfortresses) in Tinian and Saipan and the resultant damage and destruction of these valuable aircraft ; but it may be stated at once that the principal measure which put an end to the raids, namely, the capture of Iwo Jima which the Japanese bombers used as their staging base, had been decided upon even before they began. The raids, though troublesome, would not alone have justified the cost of capturing Iwo Jima.

---

[1] Imperial Headquarters Directive 431, 21st July 1944, General Policy for Urgent Operations, *see The Campaigns of the Pacific War* (USSBS), p. 292.

4

Since the Americans had won control of the entire central Pacific and were threatening the Philippines, the Japanese had to revise their war plans. Despite the danger of air attack on the home islands by the new U.S. very heavy bombers, to which the fall of the Southern Marianas had exposed them, the Japanese had lost so heavily in the battle of 19th–20th June, that it was hopeless to attempt to recapture Saipan. Until the carrier-based air groups were reconstituted, the area in which the fleet could operate was restricted to that which could be covered by their shore-based air forces. These by the early summer of 1944 had been badly battered. Many of the air groups had lost all their aircraft and the remnants of personnel and equipment were scattered all over the Pacific ocean. Small units of disorganised personnel which had been operating more or less independently, were drawn together and organised in Air Groups named after the areas in which they were to serve. The tactical responsibilities of these groups seem to have been limited to local defence, search, and patrol.

In the active operational areas of the Pacific from the home islands of Japan (exclusive) to the Philippine Islands there were at the beginning of September some 1,450 Japanese Army and shore-based naval aircraft. By the beginning of October, however, the U.S. Fast Carrier Force air raids on the Philippines had greatly reduced the numbers in the Archipelago, necessitating their reinforcement. When the Americans landed on Saipan in June, and with the Allies under MacArthur approaching the Philippine Islands, the Japanese had organised two new Naval Air Fleets, the Second and Third, making six in all. One further Air Fleet, known as the Fourteenth, which comprised little however beyond reinforcement aircraft passing through the staging base of Palau, had an existence of only two months, from 4th March to 5th May 1944. One complete air group was taken from the 27th Air Flotilla in the Bonin Islands, and for the rest, the new Air Fleets were formed from remnants of units withdrawn from the south as well as by raising new units. The headquarters of the various Air Fleets and the areas of operation of each were as follows :—

AIR FLEET	H.Q.	AREA
First ..	Davao ..	Philippines, region north of Australia.
Second ..	Japan ..	Western Japan, Formosa, Ryuku Islands.
Third ..	Japan ..	Eastern Japan, Bonin Islands, Northern Marianas Islands.
Eleventh ..	Rabaul ..	Micronesia (neutralised).
Twelfth ..	Kurile Islands	Northern Japan, Kurile Islands.
Thirteenth	Penang (later Singapore)	Malaya, Sumatra, western Netherlands East Indies.

The Thirteenth Air Fleet was largely a training unit. In the autumn of 1944 the Japanese were in the process of abandoning the airfields around the Java Sea and withdrawing all operational aircraft. Before the end of the year the Thirteenth Air Fleet moved from Penang to Singapore, which at that date was considered to be behind the lines. Its location was due mainly to the straitened fuel situation in Japan. There were about 400 training aircraft, and it included about 50 fighters for the defence of the Balik Papan and Tarakan oilfields and about 60 or 70 seaplanes for anti-submarine operations.

About this date (October 1944) the Japanese Army Command also regrouped the ten Army Air Divisions, the better to protect the Philippines and the Inner

Defence Zone. Two divisions in Manchuria (Second Air Army) and one in Indo China were withdrawn and stationed in the Formosa-Ryukus (one division) and the Philippine Islands (two divisions), the new dispositions then being as follows :—

AREA	NUMBER OF DIVISIONS	AIR ARMY TO WHICH BELONGING	HEADQUARTERS
Japan	2	First	Tokyo[1]
Formosa–Nansei Shoto	1		
Burma	1	Third	Singapore
Sumatra	1		
Philippine Islands ..	3	Fourth	Manila
Netherlands East Indies	1		
China	1	Fifth	Nanking

The Army Air Force had for some time been undergoing training in anti-submarine work.

5

The necessity of limiting the area in which the Japanese Fleet could give battle to that covered by their shore-based air forces, influenced future strategy and determined the line to be defended. This was drawn where it stood at the moment from the home islands of Japan through the Ryukus, Formosa and the Philippines, whilst in the south the perimeter ran through Timor, Java and Sumatra. The position of the fleet base was governed by the extreme difficulty which was being experienced in importing oil into Japan. In May, the Japanese had decided that if the Allies reached western New Guinea the fleet would use as anchorages Manila Bay and Brunei Bay in North Borneo, in preference to Tawi Tawi in the Palawan Islands which was unsuitable for prolonged occupation since it was not adapted to training purposes. The fleet anchorage at Brunei Bay had not yet been rendered safe as had been done in the case of Manila Bay long before the first heavy U.S. air raid took place in the fourth week in September 1944.

A decisive naval engagement in the south was unlikely, yet it was in the south, near Singapore, that the Japanese were compelled to base the battleship and cruiser strength of the Fleet, in order to be near the source of oil supply, the long vulnerable supply line for replenishment with ammunition and stores being perforce accepted. The ships used the anchorage at Lingga, 90 miles to the southward of Singapore. The carriers meanwhile remained in the Inland Sea, awaiting the completion of training of their new air groups. The other two components of the Mobile Force, the Fifth Fleet and the South-West Area Fleet, remained in the Ominato area in the northern part of Honshu and the Philippines respectively.

[1] Tokyo was also the headquarters of the Japanese Army Air Forces.

The expectation of the Japanese was that decisive action in defence of the new perimeter would take place near the home islands, Ryukus, Formosa or the Philippines. In defence of these regions the greatest possible co-ordinated effort by land, sea and air forces was to be made in a battle which the Japanese hoped would be decisive. Under favourable conditions a decisive battle might also be fought in defence of the Bonin Islands. Four alternative plans were drawn up for defence of the various areas, and were numbered ' Sho ' 1 to 4 in probable order of adoption, as follows :—

In ' Sho ' 1 the area to be defended was the Philippine Islands ; in ' Sho ' 2 Formosa, the Ryukus and southern Kyushu ; in ' Sho ' 3 Kyushu, Shikoku, Honshu and under certain conditions the Bonin Islands ; and in ' Sho ' 4 Hokkaido.

As ' Sho ' 1 and 2 were considered the most likely to be put into force priority was given to strengthening the defences in the area concerned. The plans were realistic in so far as they recognised that the backward state of training of the Japanese carrier forces rendered those for the time being almost impotent and it was unlikely rehabilitation would be complete before the Americans struck again. Only the fleet carrier *Zuikaku* and the three light carriers *Chitose, Chiyoda* and *Zuiho* of the third Fleet were to be used with the Main Body. Such aircraft as were available for employment in battle by the four carriers would, after striking, normally return to land bases if possible ; in the low state of training of the pilots they would land on carriers only in emergency. The carrier air groups might also operate from shore bases, and carriers without aircraft on board might be used in the ' decoy fleet ' (Second Diversion Attack Force) which at the time consisted of the two battleship carriers, three cruisers and a few destroyers.

The plans provided for the destruction by air, sea and land forces of the enemy when concentrated at the point of attack. The primary target would be carriers and transports, naval air forces taking as their principal target the U.S. carriers and Army air forces the convoys. The shore-based air forces were to be disposed in depth and were to conserve their strength until the enemy were on the point of landing. The more influential Japanese school of thought, drawing experience from the non-success of the recent defence of the Micronesian islands, saw that at all costs they must prevent the enemy from making a landing rather than attempt to destroy the invaders on the beaches which were their usual tactics. As the American fleet and amphibious forces approached sufficiently closely to their objective, air and surface torpedo attacks were to be made. A counter landing force was to be held in readiness for use if a favourable opportunity occurred.

The basic conception of the plans took into account the unreadiness of the carrier air forces and comprised exploitation of the main gunnery strength of the strong surface fleet and the land-based air forces. The specific operational plans were as follows :—

If the Philippine Islands, Formosa, or the Nansei Shoto were about to be attacked the 1st Diversion Attack Force (the heavy surface ships) would move to Brunei Bay or an anchorage in the north central Philippines, timing its arrival at the point where it could do most damage, that is, off the landing beaches, to coincide with that of the Allies. Avoiding attacks by the U.S. Fast Carrier Force and spearheaded by the 18-inch guns of the *Yamato* and *Musashi* it was to fight its way through any surface opposition and destroy the invasion convoys. The Second Diversion Attack Force would facilitate these operations by drawing off the U.S. striking force to the north-eastward and launching a flank attack on the carriers, and was also if possible to destroy the American supply force. The plan for 'Sho' 3 (attack on the main Japanese islands) was substantially the same, except that the Second Diversion Attack Force might join the First in the attack on the amphibious forces off the beaches. If Hokkaido were attacked ('Sho' 4) the First Diversion Attack Force would proceed to the north central Philippine Islands and stand by, whilst if circumstances called for it, the Main Body (the carriers) would proceed to the Sea of Japan or Sea of Okhotsk and there await events. If it was decided to use the fleet in defence of the Nanpo Shoto, the long chain of islands running southward from Honshu to the 24th parallel, the Main Body was to draw the U.S. Striking Force to the north and north-west of the Bonins, one of the sub-groups of the Nanpo Shoto, whilst the First Diversion Attack Force moved to the Inland Sea and awaited an opportunity to attack. The operations of all naval and air forces were to be co-ordinated. The Combined Base Air Force, as the Philippines naval air forces were termed, was to avoid attacking until the day before or the actual day of landing, when it was to attack in full strength. Its commander, Vice-Admiral Shigeru Fukudome, had no detailed information of the plans for the employment of the fleet in the Sho Operations: he knew only such as was contained in the orders issued to the air forces from the Combined Fleet.[1]

6

Unlike the Japanese Fleet, the Japanese armies had nowhere suffered more than local defeats. In China they were showing greater activity than at any time since the capture of Hong Kong, in an effort to obtain possession of the airfields from which the U.S. 14th Air Force operated against their China Sea convoys and to regain control of the railway corridor between the industrial north and south. In the South-East Asia Area commanded by Admiral Mountbatten, the Japanese Burma Area Army had staged an advance on India in the Spring of 1944; by the summer this had been defeated and the enemy were on the defensive.

The submarine menace in the Indian Ocean had also been overcome. The Japanese 8th Flotilla operating there had been almost completely destroyed by attrition and the Japanese were unable to reinforce it, and although several German U-boats continued to operate they did so under handicaps and with little success in face of the increasing number of escorts and anti-submarine vessels at the disposal of the Commander-in-Chief Eastern Fleet, Admiral Sir James Somerville. After the defeat of Italy, the Eastern Fleet had been reinforced and in April 1944 began operating against installations important to the enemy's war effort with a balanced fleet which by July contained three aircraft carriers, in the hope of drawing off some of the pressure on Admiral Nimitz's forces, a hope which however was not realised, for the enemy recognised the Pacific for the vital area.[2] It was not until December of the year, when our air strikes were canalised into operations against the Japanese oil supplies which will be described in Chapter III, that vital damage was caused to the enemy's war effort. Meanwhile, largely owing to the operations of our submarines and through mining by the Royal Air Force and the U.S. 10th Army Air Force operating from Indian airfields, the Japanese were having the greatest difficulty in maintaining the supply lines to their Burma Area Army. Their South-West Area Fleet, being now reduced to a small cruiser and destroyer force,

[1] Interrogation of Vice-Admiral Fukudome, Nav. No. 115.

[2] These operations were described in Vol. IV of this History.

was unable to operate successfully against our coastal forces backed by the East Indies Fleet, which were supporting the advance of our Army in Burma, or to challenge our control of the Andaman Sea and keep open the supply line to the garrisons in the Andamans and Nicobars. The airfields of Port Blair, formerly the eyrie of the Japanese in the Indian Ocean, now held few aircraft. The presence of the Japanese Second Fleet at Singapore was by that date rightly estimated by the Allies to be due to the difficulty of importing oil into Japan and was not considered by us to indicate any naval preoccupation on the part of the enemy with the South-East Asia Area.

CHAPTER II

Formation of the British Pacific Fleet
and Fleet Train

1

A BRITISH fleet was shortly to enter the Pacific and fight under American control. In the previous year, the British Chiefs of Staff had with some difficulty prevailed over the Americans on the issue that Britain demanded a full and fair place in the war against Japan from the time that Germany was defeated. Our Government felt that no opportunity must be given for critics to say that England, having taken all she could from America to help her to beat Hitler, stood out of the war against Japan and left the U.S.A. to fight alone.

When the surrender of the Italian Fleet in September 1943 set our ships in the Mediterranean free, Mr. Winston Churchill had taken the opportunity of making the offer of a detachment of our Fleet to proceed at once to the Pacific. The plan proposed by the Combined Chiefs of Staff at the Cairo Conference (' Sextant ') in November 1943 and subsequently approved, contemplated despatch to the Pacific of a detachment provisionally scheduled to become operational in June 1944.[1] It seemed to the Prime Minister that the American reply to his offer gave the impression that Admiral King did not need us very much.[2] The U.S. Naval Commander-in-Chief considered that his fleet really required no assistance in these waters, and he was anxious not to rob European operations for the Far East. He felt that British forces available after Europe was provided for, would be better employed against Japanese oil supplies and services in the Indian Ocean than in the Pacific.[3] But Admiral King was evidently prepared to accept British ships if necessary, for he outlined the logistic conditions on which they could be received and the extent of the facilities which the United States Navy would make available to them. His attitude is easy to understand. The American logistic set-up was heavily burdened, and additions to the fleet would merely increase the difficulties of supply. If a British force could be spared for the Pacific, Admiral King thought it might well be delayed until the late Summer or Autumn of 1944 ; whilst President Roosevelt thought it would not be needed before the Summer of the following year.[4] The proposal was, that the force, when sent, should operate in the South-west Pacific which was commanded by General MacArthur ; and it had been suggested that the British whose troops in October 1944 took over the fighting on land in New Guinea,

---

[1] CCS417(2), Annex II.

[2] Winston Churchill, *The Second World War*, Vol. V, p. 509.

[3] Telegram BAD 081939Z January 1944 and 222135Z January 1944

[4] Churchill, *op. cit.*, p. 511.

the Bismarcks and Solomon Islands, should take over entire control of the South-West Pacific Area, but Mountbatten was not at the time prepared to do so. This, however, by no means met the exigencies of the case ; the British Government felt it was essential for political reasons that our Fleet should take part in the main operations against Japan. Subsequently, Admiral King modified his proposal by agreeing that the operations of the British Pacific Fleet should be under the control of the Commander, Pacific Fleet, who was to conduct operations against the Japanese main islands prior to the projected invasion.

Meanwhile, though the part the ships would play in the strategy of the war against Japan was not settled, the Admiralty early in 1944 began preparations to send a fleet to the Pacific later in the year. A naval force sufficient to safeguard our communications and carry out minor amphibious operations in the South-East Asia Area would be retained in the Indian Ocean, all other available units, to the extent that they could be maintained, being concentrated in the Pacific towards the autumn or winter of 1944. This concept, if accepted, demanded that we should not be committed to any operation which would increase the scale of defence required for our communications in the Indian Ocean or entail an increase of our Eastern Fleet, since any such commitment must be at the expense of our effort in the Pacific. The Eastern Fleet, after the departure of the Pacific Force, would form a holding and trade protection force, undertaking such operations as were possible with the strength available, to deter the Japanese from withdrawing forces from South-East Asia.[1]

At the second Conference in Quebec (' Octagon ') in September 1944 Mr. Winston Churchill offered the British main fleet to take part in major operations in the Pacific against Japan under United States supreme command : an offer which President Roosevelt at once accepted. In the Final Report of the Conference, the Combined Chiefs of Staff agreed that the British Fleet should participate in these operations, with the understanding that it would be balanced and self-supporting. The probable deployment had been agreed[2] as being, by the end of 1944, of the order of :

2 Battleships
4 Fleet Carriers
2 Light Fleet Carriers
14 Escort Carriers
8 Cruisers
24 Fleet Destroyers
60 Escort Vessels

After the defeat of Germany it was hoped substantially to increase these numbers, and there would be based in the Pacific area :

4 Battleships
4 Fleet Carriers
7 Light Fleet Carriers
18 Escort Carriers
12 Cruisers
60 Destroyers
100 Frigates/A/S escorts
900 carrier-borne and 300 shore-based aircraft
24 submarines

with an assault lift for two amphibious divisions with one Training Brigade.

---

[1] Tel. Admty. 311944A March 1944 to Commander-in-Chief, Eastern Fleet.

[2] CCS428 (Revised), Annex III.

2

The number of ships would however be limited by the available facilities for their logistic support.

The plan to operate a British fleet in the Pacific involved a big problem of supply and maintenance. Distances in the Pacific were so great that logistics constituted one of the principal difficulties in operating. In the course of three years, the Americans had built up a great supply organisation and a network of bases. The U.S. logistic plan, though extensive, had been carefully worked out, and their bases had been assigned and their supplies estimated on a scale considered necessary to keep their fleet in operation but with little to spare. It was a condition that the British fleet should have its own supply organisation except in bulk oil supplies and be self-supporting, but the U.S. Navy would spare any excess facilities afloat and ashore in forward areas ; maintain harbour defences and minimum port facilities and personnel without prejudice to a movement forward if necessary ; render emergency and temporary battle damage aid to British units on the same basis as to U.S. units ; and make available its airfields in the neighbourhood of the fleet anchorage for British carrier aircraft, though it would not be prepared to support such aircraft for maintenance.[1] Any hopes inspired by the apparent lavishness of American logistic provision, that there would in fact be ' excess facilities ' in the Pacific, were however quickly dispelled in discussions between the British and U.S. Naval Staff representatives in Washington.

The logistics of U.S. task forces in the Pacific were examined by a naval mission which Rear Admiral C. S. Daniel in February took to the U.S.A. for preliminary consultations, with a view to making the best possible arrangements in the time available for the reception and maintenance of a British fleet in Australia which was to be the rear base. The mission later visited the U.S. Pacific Fleet. The two possible bases for a British fleet operating in the Pacific were India and Australia, but little consideration was needed to show the great advantages of Australia. For though India possessed some facilities for the immediate reception and accommodation of large forces, the state of the country and attitude of the population provided no such healthy basis on which to construct a policy as did Australia[2]. The date on which we could move the Fleet was actually determined by the time required to establish stocks in that Dominion and staffs to take over responsibility for naval stores.[3] The work of preparing bases, begun in 1944, went on throughout the winter and spring, together with the dredging of Torres Strait to allow the passage of battleships.

In November 1944 Admiral Sir Bruce Fraser who on 23rd August had succeeded Admiral Somerville as Commander-in-Chief Eastern Fleet was given command of the yet unformed British Pacific Fleet. He interpreted his instructions to be to operate and support the Fleet in company with the U.S. Fleet in their most advanced operations against Japan. It was the opinion of both Admiral King and Admiral Nimitz, Commander U.S. Pacific Fleet and Pacific Ocean Areas, that the U.S. fast striking forces were adequate to deal with the operations then in sight. This belief Admiral Fraser set himself to dispel when on 15th January 1945 he reported for duty to the Commander-in-Chief, Pacific and a conference took place at Pearl Harbour.

---

[1] Telegram BAD 081939Z/January 1944.

[2] COS(X) 44/1 Melbourne, 23rd August 1944.

[3] It was estimated that about 200 directing and clerical and 1,000 industrial staff would be needed for Australian stores depot, about 1,000,000 sq. ft. of storage space plus 300,000 for air stores. In addition, victualling stores would require about 100 directing and clerical and 600 industrial grades, 200,000 sq. ft. of storage space by the second quarter of 1944 and up to 800,000 by the end of the year.

The American attitude was based, not on any objection to the British Fleet in itself, but on apprehension lest part of the U.S. logistic effort would have to be diverted to support of the British. Apart from the strategical advance of bringing the largest possible force to bear against the enemy, there was little reason, from the U.S. point of view, why our fleet should be employed in the main operations when there were many less exacting tasks in the South-West Pacific and elsewhere to which it could have been assigned. Admiral Fraser was fully seized with the importance, from a national view point, of the British Fleet engaging in the most modern type of naval warfare yet evolved by fighting in company with its originators and prime exponents, enormous though the cost to the country would be. In no other way could we have learned the technical lessons which this type of warfare taught. Had we not operated our striking forces in this manner we should have finished the war with only second-hand knowledge of this revolutionary form of modern warfare. Fraser believed it would be nothing less than disastrous to our national prestige if the British Fleet, after being sent to the Pacific, had been relegated to a back area, as the Australians considered their own forces had been relegated, however well suited such operations might have been to the size and nature of the forces which we provided. It was quite clear to him that, in the intensive, efficient and hard striking type of war that the U.S. Fleet was fighting, nothing but the inclusion of a big British force would be noticeable and nothing but the best would be tolerated; and it says much for his personality and the cogency of his arguments that he eventually received from Admiral Nimitz a message which ran:

> 'The British force will greatly increase our striking power and demonstrate our unity of purpose against Japan. The United States Pacific Fleet welcomes you.'

Admiral Fraser's seniority would have made it difficult to command afloat, where he would have outranked Nimitz's immediate subordinates. Accordingly, Vice-Admiral H. B. Rawlings, Flag Officer, Naval Air Stations Indian Ocean, who had experience in fighting in the Mediterranean, was selected as second in command of the Fleet and to command at sea.

3

Our ability to operate in the Pacific where we were without adequate shore-based facilities for repair, maintenance and supply, depended upon the Fleet Train. This was an organisation new to the Royal Navy in war. Ever since the advent of steam, a British fleet had been accustomed to return to a shore base for replenishment of stores and ammunition. The establishment of new shore bases was considered to be too costly in men and materials and no doubts existed at the Admiralty as to the advantage over brick and mortar bases of mobile advanced operational bases such as the Americans used, capable of supplying practically every form of service which a Royal Dockyard or Supply Depot could provide. This led to the development of a new naval concept, that of the Fleet Train designed to enable ships to keep the sea for periods comparable to those of sailing ship days, under conditions of ceaseless expenditure of fuel, ammunition, and supplies of every description. The principle of the Fleet Train was the assembly at advanced anchorages, of ocean going shipping equipped to support the Fleet logistically during operations against the enemy, the actual supply of the Fleet being carried out by so-called Service Squadrons. These service squadrons were concerned with issuing replacement aircraft, fuel, stores, and ammunition, evacuating and replacing battle casualties. In addition, the Fleet Train included repair ships, store carriers, freighting carriers, amenity ships, harbour service craft, accommodation ships, hospital ships and the like.[1] The Train operated from a rear base at which major replenishments could be carried out. With the shortage of shipping under which we laboured, and the worn out state of several of the fleet auxiliaries and merchantmen after nearly five years of war, it was impossible to reach the standard of the ideal Fleet Train either in numbers or appropriate types of ships. Indeed, it was clear that assistance from the U.S.A. would be required. It had been agreed in the past that, in order to use our combined resources to the best advantage, the United Kingdom should concentrate on building naval ships and certain types of specialised shipping whilst the Americans would build normal types of merchant shipping and vessels not included in the British programme. This had naturally resulted in the unbalancing of the United Kingdom's programme. No provision had been made for the Fleet Auxiliaries considered necessary for the Fleet Train and there was no possibility of making this provision from British naval sources. These ships would have to come out of the United States merchant ship building programme.[2] Nine months later, however, at the second Quebec Conference (' Octagon '), in September 1944, Mr. Winston Churchill when making to the Americans his offer of a fleet, said that a Fleet Train had been built up of proportions ample to render the Fleet independent for a considerable time of shore-based resources.[3] The implications of operating a British Fleet in the Pacific were many and diverse. By September 1944 the Americans were on the point of beginning operations to reconquer the Philippines. To support a fleet in that area, with rear base at Sydney in Australia and no intermediate base, called for a very much more ample fleet train than was needed to support the Eastern Fleet in covering landings in Burma and then returning to Trincomalee for replenishment. In addition to the great distance of Australia from the Fleet's home bases, a prohibitive disadvantage lay in the undeveloped nature of the north and west parts of the continent. The harbour at Darwin could accommodate a fleet and its auxiliaries and serve as an advanced base, provided the approaches from the eastward and westward were dredged in places to permit the passage of capital ships, and better navigational aids provided. But neither Darwin nor any other region in the north and west was suitable for a main base or reception area. The Navy accordingly chose Sydney as the main base, whilst minor bases were to be established at Brisbane and Cairns in the north, Adelaide and Melbourne in the south, and Fremantle in the west. The harbour at Sydney was world-renowned. In the port, heavy cruisers could be refitted and there were docks for heavy cruisers, whilst a dry dock for capital ships was nearing completion. The despatch to Australia of floating docks was intended together with the construction locally of dry docks, but no floating docks could reach Australia before mid-summer 1945.

Allocation of shipping for the Fleet Train in the Pacific was begun early in 1944, but planning was handicapped by the uncertainties surrounding the employment of the Fleet and the area in which it would operate. The final report of the Combined Chiefs of Staff to the President and Prime Minister at the Octagon Conference went some way towards clarifying the situation.

[1] The state of the Fleet Train during the operations against Okinawa (March–May 1945) is given in Appendix T and during the final operations against Japan (July–August 1945) in Appendix U.

[2] *History of the Fleet Train* (MS) by Captain R. F. Leonard, Plans Division (Q), Admiralty, p. 36.

[3] *The Second World War*, Vol. VI, p. 134.

'The method of employment,' said the Chiefs of Staff, 'will be decided from time to time in accordance with the prevailing circumstances'.[1] The Americans by that time were operating from New Guinea and the Admiralty Islands, so that it could be assumed that the Fleet Train must be prepared to support the Fleet some 2,000 miles from its rear base. The size of the Fleet Train was limited by the decision that 24 million tons of imports into the United Kingdom for 1944 and for 1945, which dictated the size of the fleet we could send to the Pacific, were an irreducible minimum. For the Spring of 1944 the estimate of shipping required for the Far East was 262 ships totalling approximately one million gross register tons. The Navy were using 560 merchant ships totalling 2¼ million tons (including 1 million tons of tankers and colliers on single voyage charter), of which 573,960 tons were used on Fleet Train functions all over the world. It might seem at first sight that as the centre of gravity of the war shifted to the East, some of this tonnage should go East. But only 111 ships of 450,000 tons were suitable for employment in the East, and the new war would start before the old war ended and enabled ships to be released.

In November 1944 it became clear from the recent American successes in the Pacific, that by the time the British Pacific Fleet was operating in full strength the supply ships would have a haul of some 3,500 miles from the nearest Empire base, instead of 2,000 miles; consequently the estimate of ships needed had to be reviewed and more vessels added. At the end of the month the Admiralty's requirements for the Fleet Train were forwarded to the Ministry of Transport. Less than one-third of the ships needed were available at that date, and it was clear that many of the remaining two-thirds would be very difficult to obtain.[2]

During December Admiral Fraser, whose flagship the *Howe* had left Ceylon for the Pacific on the 2nd of the month, met the U.S. Commander-in-Chief, Pacific. Without delay, he sent a signal to the Admiralty, giving a brief summary of the U.S. organisation and methods of fighting. The British Pacific Fleet would be required to operate well in advance of the advanced base, remaining at sea for

[1] CCS680/2 (Octagon) 1619/44.

[2] The state of the Fleet Train (for British Pacific Fleet and East Indies Fleet) in September 1944 was approximately as follows:—Armament Supply Issuing Ships—13 required, two available, eight coming forward: it was thought this total of ten would suffice until July 1945. 'The Armament Store Carrier situation was worse'. Naval Store Issuing Ships—12 required, two available, three being built in Canada. Naval Store Carriers—16 required (eight for Pacific, eight for East Indies), one available, six had been recently allocated for conversion, the other nine 'were obviously going to be very difficult to obtain'. Distilling Ships—five required, one available. (At advanced bases in the Pacific no reliance could be placed upon shore supplies of fresh water, and there was a further complication that a peculiar contamination of many of the harbours of the East Indies and Northern Australia prevented full use being made of evaporators.) Air Store Issuing Ships—three required, one available, one building in Canada. Victualling Store Issuing Ships—22 or 24 required, nine likely to be available, three more refitting, two not altogether satisfactory might be released from the Mediterranean, at least seven more were needed. 'The Hospital Ship situation was an unhappy one'. S.R.R.(D) (Special repair ratings (Dockyard)) Accommodation Ships—four required, three in sight, one not yet in sight. Salvage Ships—'little anxiety at this stage'. Amenity Ships—two required (one for Pacific, one for SEAC), both being provided on highest priority. The procurement of Tankers took the form of drawing from a pool, for tankers did not require elaborate conversion before they could be used for servicing fleets and it would have been folly for the Admiralty to take tankers from other duties long before they were needed operationally. In February 1945 the Commander-in-Chief, British Pacific Fleet asked for the following additional ships—nine large and four small Harbour Oilers; three Harbour Water Tankers; four Water Freighters; four Armament Store Issuing Ships; eight Armament Store Carriers; four Victualling Store Issuing Ships; two Naval Store Issuing Ships; five Naval Store Carriers; six Bulk Issuing Ships or Naval Store Carriers in lieu. (Based on MS *History of the Fleet Train*). The state of the Fleet Train at the end of the war is given in Appendix U.

considerable periods. The Americans made it clear that the Fleet must be self-supporting in every respect, except as regards bulk fuels and W/T and radar stores. They were prepared to pool resources for the sake of efficiency, but it would be necessary for us to supply our correct quota, for they had no supplies to spare. Actually, when the British Pacific Fleet began operating, the Americans were far better than their word, and lent assistance quite outside their undertaking. 'I have found the American logistic authorities in the Pacific have interpreted self-sufficiency in a very liberal way', wrote Admiral Fraser, after our fleet had been operating in the Third/Fifth U.S. Fleet for some months. 'American authorities are most open-handed in allowing the British Pacific Fleet to draw surplus items'.[1] Admiral Fraser intended to operate the Fleet to the best possible effect, but from the information available to him he did not consider that the logistic support already planned was adequate to enable him to carry out prolonged operations in the new strategic situation involving as this did—(*a*) the institution of an intermediate base between Australia and the advanced base, (*b*) support at sea in advance of the advanced base, and (*c*) operations of a considerably more sustained nature than were previously contemplated.[2] This he followed up by an operations policy signal to the Admiralty.[3] His aim was to do as the Americans who kept their fleet at sea operating in the combat area for an indefinite length of time. This would entail logistic support on a scale not then contemplated. At first, the scope of operations would be limited, depending on the quantity of resources available. Later, when the pipe line had grown, he was planning to operate on the full American scale. There were no data in this signal on which the Admiralty could base any increase in the estimate of their requirements for the Fleet Train, though it was clear that some additions would be necessary.

It was not until some weeks after the Admiralty's estimated requirements had been forwarded to the Ministry of War Transport that the latter was in a position to make any definite move to provide the ships. Meanwhile, though Admiral Fraser's signal of 30th December had made it clear that the logistic support already planned was inadequate, the Admiralty considered it was likely to be wasted labour at that stage to make any substantial increase in the requirement which they were about to place before the Prime Minister; and, indeed, at the Anglo-U.S. Conference ('Argonaut') in the Crimea in January–February 1945 the Minister of War Transport stated categorically that he could only proceed on the assumption that no further ships beyond those specified in the Admiralty's estimate of October 1944 would be allocated to the Fleet Train.[4] The War Cabinet on 26th January discussed the Admiralty's requirements. They postponed any decision, decided that in view of the acute shortage of merchant shipping no fresh tonnage could be allocated to the Fleet for the present and invited the First Lord to bring up the proposals in two months' time, or earlier if in his opinion the situation justified. In February, however, Sir John Anderson who when the Admiralty's requirements threatened to stretch Allied shipping resources to a dangerous point had been appointed to inquire into the matter, produced his report. This was agreed by the Admiralty and the Ministry of War Transport; and the shipping position having eased somewhat the Admiralty's requirements were met. Rear Admiral D. B. Fisher had been appointed in October 1944 as Rear Admiral Fleet Train (RAFT).[5] On

[1] Commander-in-Chief's Despatches, November 1944 to July 1945, M.0406/46.

[2] Commander-in-Chief, British Pacific Fleet, 300330, December 1944.

[3] 100430 January 1945.

[4] C.O.S. (Argonaut) 4th Meeting.

[5] The duties of RAFT are given in Appendix Z.

1st December he left for Australia, visiting on the way ships building and converting for the Fleet Train in the United States and Canada; and at the beginning of January 1945 he began from temporary offices in Sydney the work of building up and co-ordinating the Fleet Train.

On 5th February, nearly three weeks after Admiral Fraser had sent from Sydney a telegram showing that a larger addition would be needed to the ships already allocated[1] the Admiralty learnt from him the details of the calculations on which the Commander-in-Chief's requirements were based. These showed that the total ration strength of the British Pacific Fleet in July would be 100,000, of whom normally 80,000 to 90,000 would require rations in the forward area.

The remainder of the story of the formation of the Fleet Train belongs to administrative rather than to operational history. It is sufficient to say here that the British Pacific Fleet began operating three or four months earlier than had been generally anticipated, whilst the Fleet Train was still in embryo. Up to the end of the war great difficulty was experienced, owing mainly to the inadequacy of the tankers. Nevertheless, the Fleet with generous U.S. logistic assistance fulfilled the exacting standards of the Americans with their more ample resources, though at the cost of great strain on the officers and men.

It was apparent to Admiral Fraser from the start, that quite apart from the Fleet Train, some form of advanced base would be needed if the British Pacific Fleet was to operate at the intense rate of striking usual in the U.S. Fleet. American experience had shown that it was uneconomical to operate the fleet more than 2,000 miles ahead of its foremost shore base, since beyond that distance the cost in Fleet Train ships became disproportionately high. For this reason, the progress of the Americans through the Pacific had been marked by a series of rapidly constructed vast temporary bases which, as the war moved on, were dismantled as rapidly as they were constructed, and moved forward to the next selected site. It seemed to Admiral Fraser that it should be possible to develop the comparatively small facilities required for the British Pacific Fleet, in at least a comparable time; and acting on this assumption, he asked for a base policy founded on the lines of an intermediate base and a number of advanced anchorages.

During the meeting between Admiral Nimitz and Admiral Fraser at Pearl Harbour in December 1944, an agreement had been signed from which Fraser had concluded that the intermediate base of the Fleet between Australia and the operating area would be at Manus in the Admiralty Islands, relying mostly on United States facilities until a British intermediate base could be established somewhere in the Philippines which it was expected would be by September or October 1945. By the term ' intermediate base ' was meant a storage base to which global bulk supplies were directed, with amenities for the Fleet. For major replenishment the ships would have to return to Australia. The main function of the base would be to act as a reservoir in the pipe line of supply, both of stores and personnel. There would be an advanced base or anchorage some 700 miles in advance of the intermediate base, from which the Fleet would operate, and a service area some 500 miles in advance of the advanced base at which the Fleet would meet the tankers and be refuelled at sea.[2]

It soon became evident that Manus would be too far back by the time a base had been established there. Though it was hoped to begin occupation in October, the base would not be complete until February 1946. Admiral Fraser

[1] Commander-in-Chief, British Pacific Fleet, 050604, February 1945. This addition is given at the end of footnote 3 on page 13.

[2] Commander-in-Chief, British Pacific Fleet, 240816, February.

informed the Admiralty that he intended to ask the Commander-in-Chief, Pacific to allocate some harbour in the Philippines, such as Subic Bay, but the Admiralty whilst approving the name H.M.S. *Pepys* for the projected Philippine Intermediate Base, decided to postpone further consideration of construction until the Commander-in-Chief British Pacific Fleet could report in the light of operational experience.[1] Admiral Fraser eventually found that the U.S. authorities were unlikely to agree to the establishment of a British base or shore facilities on any but a small scale in the Philippines, whilst by May it looked as though there might be an early end to the war against Japan. He came to the conclusion that the base could not be constructed in time to serve any useful purpose, and so advised the Admiralty.[2]

The absence of an intermediate base and the consequent need for the Fleet to return to its main base in Australia for periodical replenishment had some effect in reducing the length of time during which the Fleet could remain off the enemy coast. In practice, however, the amount of operating time actually lost was less than might have been expected, in view of the more rapid turn round achieved by replenishment at well equipped rear bases.

In the event, Manus was used as the main base for the Fleet Train, and for fuelling, provisioning and adjusting ammunition outfits of the ships of the British Pacific Fleet before sailing to join the U.S. Fleet prior to the two lengthy operations in which they took part ; and it was used after these operations for major replenishment of those ships for which there was no room in Australian harbours. During the first operation, in April 1945, the Task Force (T.F. 57) used Leyte in the Philippines as a replenishment anchorage between the first and second series of their strikes against the Sakishima Gunto. During the final operations against Japan the logistic support groups of the Fleet Train at first used Manus as an advanced anchorage instead of Leyte, though later the U.S. authorities delivered bulk fuel for them to Eniwetok in the Marshall Islands. Eniwetok was used as a terminal for the tanker groups, but Manus remained the main base for the Fleet Train and from it were sailed to and from the Fleet the Replenishment Aircraft Carriers, provision and ammunition ships, and destroyers with mails. The Fleet remained at sea throughout the final operations, an account which will be given in due course (Chapter XVI).

---

[1] A.M. 150530 March 1945.

[2] Commander-in-Chief, British Pacific Fleet, 050757Z May and 270156Z May.

CHAPTER III

Operations of the British Pacific Fleet
Against the Sumatran Oil Refineries

(Plans 1, 3, 4, 5, 6, 7, 8, 9, 10.)

1

On 22nd November the British Pacific Fleet was formed and Admiral Fraser hoisted his flag in the *Tarantula* as Commander-in-Chief. The flag of Vice-Admiral Sir Arthur Power, Vice-Admiral 2nd in Command Eastern Fleet, who now became Commander-in-Chief, East Indies Station, was struck in the *Renown* and hoisted in the depot ship *Caradoc*, at Colombo.

The organisation of the British Pacific Fleet was as shown below.

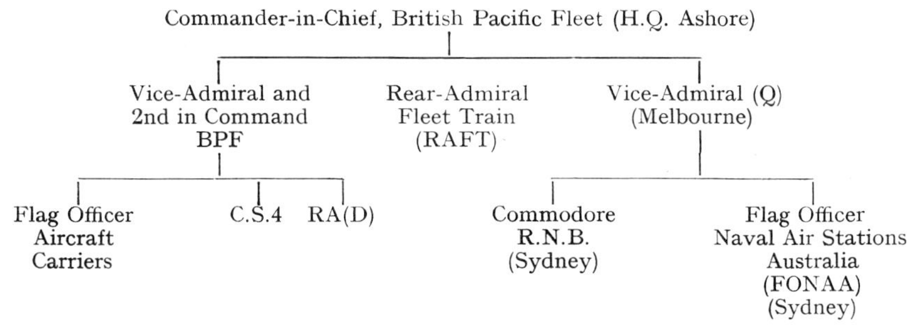

The ships detailed to constitute the Fleet were two battleships, the *King George V* (flagship of Vice-Admiral Sir Bernard Rawlings, Vice-Admiral Commanding 1st Battle Squadron and Second in Command, British Pacific Fleet) and *Howe*; the four fleet carriers, *Indefatigable* (Rear-Admiral Sir Philip Vian, Flag Officer Commanding Aircraft Carriers, British Pacific Fleet), *Illustrious*, *Victorious*, *Indomitable*; five cruisers; and three flotillas of destroyers.[1]

Three flotillas of escort vessels (minesweepers, frigates and sloops) comprised the Support Forces. The Fleet Train, at that date still much below full strength,

[1] The organisation of the British Pacific Fleet is shown in Appendix B.

consisted of forty-four ships. The remaining ships formed the East Indies Fleet: they were the three capital ships *Queen Elizabeth*, *Valiant*, and *Renown*, the 5th Cruiser Squadron (light cruisers), eight escort carriers, and thirty-four destroyers.[1]

2

Before leaving for Australia Admiral Fraser, in furtherance of the policy decided upon by the Chiefs of Staff, of destroying Japanese war potential, especially oil, arranged that the Commander-in-Chief, East Indies, should carry out with the ships designated for the British Pacific Fleet a series of operations designed to hit the enemy at one of his weakest points, his petroleum supplies. Lack of data rendered it difficult to estimate Japan's petroleum position, but it was known that the Japanese were extremely short of oil and aviation fuel, for the advance of the Americans in the Philippines had brought the China Sea under short range air patrol and the passing of tankers to the Empire was fast becoming too costly to be borne by the enemy. In the last quarter of the year the tonnage of tankers importing petroleum products into Japan reached a peak of two millions, but so heavy were sinkings and so depressive the effects of convoy delays, diversive routeing and other difficulties, that imports were no more than 217,000 tons—little more than one tenth of the tanker tonnage employed. This was in marked contrast to the previous year, when tankers had imported more than three-and-a-half times their own tonnage, despite the fact that imports slumped badly during the first three months of the year consequent upon teething troubles following the introduction of convoys on the Singapore run. Admiral Power planned to put out of action the most important of the Japanese oil refineries, those at Palembang in southern Sumatra, by attacking them with the maximum carrier forces as soon as possible, before the ships of the British Pacific Fleet left the Indian Ocean for the Pacific. An assurance had been given to the Australian Government that the British Pacific Fleet would reach the Pacific before the end of 1944. This date could not be kept if Palembang were attacked. But the carriers were not ready to reach the Pacific before the New Year, for they were in the process of changing over from Barracuda to Avenger bombers and could only have reached Australia in an entirely non-operational state. The code word for the operations against Sumatran oil was 'Outflank'. Owing to the state of training of the carriers being still incomplete, before attacking Palembang Admiral Fraser intended that they should carry out one or more operations against the Pangkalan Brandan refineries in northern Sumatra, in order to provide experience before undertaking the main operations.

Palembang was the centre of most important oilfields situated about 55 miles from the mouth of the Palembang River, 300 miles south of Singapore and about 150 miles inland from the nearest point on the west (Indian Ocean) coast. The two principal refineries were known as Pladjoe (Royal Dutch Shell) and Soengei Gerong (Standard Oil), both situated about five miles down stream from Palembang. Pladjoe was the largest and most important refinery in the Far East, whilst Soengei Gerong was second only to Pladjoe in importance and a large producer of high octane aviation spirit. Both refineries were confined in restricted areas and presented excellent targets for aerial bombing, given good weather.[2] When the Japanese attacked Sumatra in February 1942, the

[1] *See* Appendix C.

[2] The characteristic of an oil refinery at that date was a large insensitive area surrounding one or two small but vital objectives. Thus whilst insusceptible to area bombing, it provided targets for light but accurate carrier-based air attack.

Dutch and Americans fired the oil wells at Pangkalan Brandan and Palembang but time did not allow complete destruction of the refineries at Palembang to be carried out. The Japanese report that these installations were so advanced in design that had serious damage been done their technicians could not have repaired it ; but as it was, production was resumed within six months. The refineries were reported to handle nearly 3,000,000 tons of crude oil a year and with Pangkalan Brandan, to produce three quarters or more of the total aviation spirit required by Japan in addition to lower octane petrol, though the attempt to import this concomitant product had by the autumn of 1944 been abandoned on account of tanker shortage. At the end of 1944 when aviation spirit was in short supply in the Empire, the Japanese were doing their utmost to accelerate the flow from the Outer Zone in order to build up stocks for the defence of the country against the invasion which they well knew would come. The Sumatran refineries were of vital importance to the enemy and plans were being made to increase their output. By 1943, the concentration of defence against attack had made Palembang the most strongly defended area in South-East Asia, with Pangkalan Brandan only second in importance. Palembang had been bombed and mined on the night of 10–11th August 1944 by B–29 aircraft from Ceylon, resulting in the closing of the river. In consequence the oil from Pangkalan Brandan, instead of being sent overland to Palembang, had to be sent to Singapore from Belawan through the Malacca Strait where the tankers were exposed to attack from British submarines. A month later, the port of Belawan itself was closed for a time through mining, three Japanese A/S vessels being sunk by mines laid by the *Porpoise*.

3

The first preliminary operation in the ' Outflank ' series was to have consisted of an air attack on the oil refinery at Pangkalan Brandan (Operation ' Robson '). This refinery was situated about 50 miles north of Medan and 250 miles south-east of Sabang. Crude oil was piped to the refinery from the oilfields and the refined products exported from Pangkalan Soesoe, about eight miles north of the refinery and connected to it by pipelines ; and the Japanese were reported also to have laid a pipeline from the refinery to Belawan Deli, the port of Medan, for there was insufficient water at Pangkalan Soesoe for large tankers to top up to full capacity. There was tankage for about 30 million gallons at Pangkalan Soesoe, but the major installations were destroyed in 1942 when the Dutch carried out the demolition scheme.

Force 67, comprising the carriers *Indomitable* (Flagship of Sir Philip Vian) and *Illustrious*, the cruisers *Newcastle*, *Argonaut*, *Black Prince* and the destroyers *Kempenfelt*, *Whirlwind*, *Wrangler*, *Wessex* and *Wakeful* sailed from Trincomalee on 17th December. Force 69, the oiler group (R.F.A. *Wave King* escorted by the destroyers *Whelp* and *Wager*) was met on the 18th, and the *Argonaut*, *Black Prince* and destroyers fuelled between 1215 and 1545, when the carrier force proceeded to the flying-off position about 60 miles north by west of Diamond Point, Sumatra, arriving early on 20th December, undetected (Plan 4). Flying-off was delayed twenty minutes by intermittent heavy rain squalls, but at 0636 the strike was ordered to proceed. One Avenger crashed in the sea shortly after being airborne, but the crew were rescued uninjured.

The striking force of 27 Avengers escorted by 12 Corsairs and 16 Hellcats took departure at 0715 (Plan 5). Four Corsairs each armed with two 500-lb. bombs in addition to long range tanks were flown off later to catch up the main

1. Attack on Pangkalan Brandan, 4th January 1945.

[*Facing page 22*

2. Attack on Palembang, 24th January 1945.

3. Attack on Palembang, 24th January 1945.

strike. This was the first time Corsairs had taken off from a British carrier with long range tanks and 500-lb. bombs. These four aircraft were unable to locate the target, and returned without making an attack. The weather was poor, with low clouds, intermittent rain, and a squally wind from east-north-east, force two to four. The main body of the strike when some 14 miles from the coast encountered an insurmountable barrier of cloud ; finding it impossible to go round it, they descended through a gap to sea level, to find the target area still completely obscured by low clouds and rain. ' After some pardonable confusion among the clouds,' says the report, the aircraft proceeded to attack the secondary target, port installations at Belawan Deli. Owing to the weather, results were largely unobserved. The Avengers bombed the quay from 1,500 feet, and the fighters exploded a petrol tank. Three sheds were set on fire. Surprise was achieved. No enemy fighters were encountered, and both heavy and light anti-aircraft fire were moderate in intensity and inaccurate. All strike aircraft were landed on by 1050.

At 1630 that day eight Corsairs from the *Illustrious* and eight Hellcats from the *Indomitable* were flown off to make a low level attack on airfields in the Sabang area and Oleelhoe harbour, the port of Kota Raja, at the north end of Sumatra. No aircraft were seen on the airfields. This strike also took the enemy by surprise.

All wing leaders and squadron commanders reported that the R/T discipline of the force as a whole was poor. The orders of the striking force leader were delayed in transit. This, combined with bad flying conditions over the area caused the force to get split up during and after the attack. All aircraft made rendezvous after the attack at the same height, but fortunately, the spectacle of 55 aircraft orbiting at the same height, remained unobserved by the Japanese fighters.

4

As the second rehearsal for the attack to be undertaken later on Palembang, another raid was planned on the oil refinery at Pangkalan Brandan (Operation ' Lentil ') on 4th January 1945 (Plans 6, 7). Force 65 consisting of the carriers *Indomitable* wearing Admiral Vian's flag, *Victorious, Indefatigable,* with *Argonaut, Black Prince, Ceylon, Suffolk* and eight destroyers sailed from Trincomalee at 1030 on 1st January 1945 and arrived at the flying-off position north-east of Simalur Island early on the 4th. The operation coincided with a full moon period and as it was considered undesirable for the striking force to remain inside Malacca Strait, a flying-off position was adopted which though it entailed a more difficult flight across mountains, would allow the force to remain longer in the area if necessary. The weather was excellent, visibility being nearly 50 miles, and photographic reconnaissance was made of port installations at Belawan Deli, Pangkalan Brandan and Pangkalan Soesoe.

A fighter sweep of eight Hellcats from the *Indomitable* and eight Corsairs from the *Victorious* was flown off at 0610 to attack airfields near the oil refinery. The main strike of 16 Avengers from the *Indomitable* and *Victorious*, each armed with four 500 lb. bombs, escorted by 16 Hellcats from the *Indomitable*, 16 Corsairs from the *Victorious* and 12 Fireflies from the *Indefatigable* took departure at 0740.

The strike aircraft met no opposition on passage, but during the final approach there was accurate heavy anti-aircraft fire at Pangkalan Soesoe. Over the target area there was inaccurate light A.A. fire. About 12 miles from the target,

Fireflies were detached to carry out rocket strikes ; they report having set on fire a small tanker.[1] Avengers then came in to attack. The target was obscured by flame, but the bombing was accurate : considerable damage was inflicted and oil tanks were set on fire. Enemy fighters reported east of the target were engaged by the escort and five Oscars (Japanese army fighters) were shot down. One Avenger was damaged by an enemy fighter and one force-landed 12 miles offshore with engine failure, but the crew were rescued. One Firefly ran out of fuel and landed in the water near the *Indefatigable.*

A fighter sweep attacked Medan airfield and reported destroying seven out of the 25 Japanese aircraft found on the ground and shooting down two others. Belawan was also attacked. Too many of the escorting fighters were detached to strafe ground targets and four more chased and destroyed an Oscar, leaving the bombers very weakly covered whilst making for their rendezvous after the raid, though fortunately they were not attacked. The strike landed on by 1022 and the force withdrew south of Simalur Island, arriving at Trincomalee at 0830 on 7th January.

5

The small scale attacks on the oil refineries in Operations 'Robson' and 'Lentil' provided useful experience, and towards the end of January the British Pacific Fleet turned its attention to the plants at Palembang. After a full scale rehearsal at sea off Ceylon, on 16th January Force 63 left Trincomalee in poor weather with frequent rain squalls, with the object of putting out of action the Pladjoe and Soengei Gerong refineries at Palembang (Operation 'Meridian I').

Force 63 with a total complement of 238 aircraft, was constituted as follows :—

Indomitable (F.O.A.C., B.P.F.). 857 Squadron—21 Avengers II ; 1839, 1844 Squadrons—29 Hellcats and four Avengers, and six Corsairs as spares for the *Illustrious* and *Victorious.*

Illustrious. 854 Squadron —18 Avengers II ; 1839, 1833 Squadrons—32 Corsairs ; 1700 Squadron—two Walrus (A.S.R.).

Victorious. 849 Squadron—19 Avengers II ; 1834, 1836 Squadrons—34 Corsairs II.

Indefatigable. 820 Squadron—21 Avengers II ; 887 Squadron—22 Seafires F.111 ; 894 Squadron—18 Seafires L.III ; 1770 Squadron—12 Fireflies.

King George V, Argonaut, Black Prince, Euryalus, Grenville (Captain 5th Destroyer Flotilla) and three destroyers.

Kempenfelt (Captain 27th Destroyer Flotilla) and five destroyers.

The oiling force (escorted by *Ceylon* and one destroyer) was met on the 20th, and Force 63 oiled that day. During the night 21st–22nd, the force approached the flying-off position 35 miles from the west coast of Sumatra and 70 miles east of Engano Island, but the weather was bad and the forecasts unfavourable, and Admiral Vian decided to postpone the attack for 24 hours. On the following night, the weather was no better ; but by the night 23rd–24th conditions had improved and the flying-off position was reached at 0615. The intention was to make a heavy attack on Pladjoe refinery and a photographic reconnaissance of the airfields and the main target, whilst fighters raided Mana airstrip and swept

[1] Not listed in the *Japanese Report.*

over the airfields from which opposition might come. There was a lack of information of the enemy fighter strength and preparedness, but it was finally decided to neutralise the airfields at Lembak, Palembang and Talangbetoetoe.

The aircraft were organised as follows :—

Pladjoe strike	10 Avengers (849 Squadron) from *Victorious.*
	10 Avengers (820 Squadron) from *Indefatigable.*
	12 Avengers (854 Squadron) from *Illustrious.*
	11 Avengers (857 Squadron) from *Indomitable.*

The above were armed with 4 × 500 M.C. bombs.

Top cover	11 Corsairs (1834, 1836 Squadrons) from *Victorious.*
Strike and bow close escort	11 Fireflies (1770 Squadron) from *Illustrious.*
Stern close escort ..	8 Corsairs (1833 Squadron) from *Illustrious.*
Middle cover	8 Corsairs (1830 Squadron) from *Illustrious.*
	16 Hellcats (1839, 1844 Squadrons) from *Indomitable.*
Mana strike	4 Avengers (857 Squadron) from *Indomitable.*
Escort	4 Hellcats (1839, 1844 Squadrons) from *Indomitable.*
Airfields sweeps	12 Corsairs (1834, 1836 Squadrons) from *Victorious.*
	12 Corsairs (1830, 1833 Squadrons) from *Illustrious.*

Four Avengers, two Fireflies and one escorting Corsair became unserviceable shortly after take-off.

The main striking force began flying-off at 0615 and took departure at 0704. Landfall was made at 0718 and the aircraft began the climb over the mountains. The weather was good, with visibility about 60 miles. Thin 10/10 cloud at about 20,000 feet enabled the pilots to look into the sun while very low 10/10 stratus covered large areas. When some 20 miles from the target, balloons were seen flying over the target at 3,000 feet, a most unusual form of protection and a measure of the extreme importance which the Japanese attached to the Palembang refineries. The Fireflies which had been flown off in the second range and had caught up a few minutes earlier, were asked to shoot down the balloons, but owing to R/T interference they did not get the order. At 0808, the enemy opened anti-aircraft fire on the main strike whilst it was still out of range, and almost immediately afterwards about 25 Tojos (army fighters) engaged the escort from above, just as the Avengers were deploying into circular formation. These remained, however, almost unmolested and about six minutes later they began a 35° glide attack from about 8,000 feet. Bombs were released from an average height of 3,500 feet, some from above, some from below the balloon barrage. Thick oil smoke and fires from oil tanks struck by the first group of bombs impeded later aiming. As the Avengers completed their attacks they made for the rendezvous, 15 miles west of Palembang. They ran into heavy anti-aircraft fire and encountered numerous fighters, apparently lying in wait for them. For, owing to the necessity of flying-off, in the second range, the 24 Corsairs for the airfields' sweeps, these were too late entirely to achieve their object of minimising interference with the main strike. The fighter cover here was inadequate: two flights of Corsairs and one of Hellcats were covering the rendezvous whilst the Fireflies patrolled the lane from the target, the remaining fighters being engaged in air fighting south of the target. Several Avengers were here badly damaged before the enemy, having lost at least 11 fighters with several others damaged, disengaged at 0825 and the striking aircraft left the rendezvous, landing on their carriers by 1023 without further molestation.

Meanwhile, the *Indomitable*'s Avengers had dropped 16 × 500-lb. M.C. bombs on Mana airstrip. The airfields' sweep, though not entirely successful, by destroying 34 enemy aircraft on the ground and damaging numerous others prevented sustained attacks on the main strike and any counter-attack on the Fleet. The anti-aircraft defences were found to be alert, particularly at Talangbetoetoe, and five Corsairs were lost; but the Japanese aircraft made only half-hearted attempts to protect their airfields.

Six Corsairs, two Avengers and one Hellcat failed to return. One Corsair and one Seafire pilot had to bale out over the Fleet and were picked up uninjured. As soon as landing-on was completed the force retired to the south-westward at 22 knots. During the afternoon, several enemy aircraft were detected, only to fade from the screen before the combat air patrol could gain contact. The Japanese report that as the result of the raid the productive efficiency of the refinery was reduced by half.[1]

6

Force 63 oiled on 26th and 27th January. The fuel situation allowed only one more strike on Palembang. As the result of experience gained in the previous operation the fighter sweep was flown in two parts, timed to arrive simultaneously at the two main enemy airfields. The fighters were to establish patrols over the airfields on completion of the sweeps. The route from the target area to the rendezvous was altered to pass south of the target, thus avoiding the heavy concentration of anti-aircraft fire north of Palembang. The standing air patrol which was to be furnished by the *Indefatigable,* was to be backed up by four fighters each from the remaining three carriers; for it was a reasonable inference that as only one of the two refineries at Palembang had been attacked, the Japanese would anticipate an attack on Soengei Gerong, and although they would have found it difficult to bring in reinforcements of aircraft to Palembang, an attack on the fleet was an obvious possibility.

Force 63 arrived at the flying-off position at 0600 on the 29th to find heavy rainstorms in a belt 30 miles off the coast, though the Sumatran mountains seemed to be clear of cloud. H hour was postponed to 0640, when the carriers found themselves in a clear patch between rainstorms and the strike was flown off as follows:—

Soengei Gerong strike ..	12 Avengers (849 Squadron) from the *Victorious.*
	10 Avengers (820 Squadron) from the *Indefatigable.*
	12 Avengers (854 Squadron) from the *Illustrious.*
	12 Avengers (857 Squadron) from the *Indomitable.*

[1] SEATIC Publication No. 248 (N.I.D. 02477/47).

Close escort	12 Corsairs (1836 Squadron) from the *Victorious.*
	9 Fireflies (1770 Squadron) from the *Indefatigable.*
Midcover	16 Hellcats (1839, 1844 Squadrons) from the *Indomitable.*
Top cover	12 Corsairs (1830, 1833 Squadrons) from the *Illustrious.*
Airfields sweeps	13 Corsairs (1834 Squadron) from the *Victorious.*
	12 Corsairs (1830, 1833 Squadrons) from the *Illustrious.*
Mana armed reconnaissance	2 Fireflies (1770 Squadron) from the *Indefatigable.*

Bomb arming was as before, 4 × 500-lb. M.C. bombs.

The form-up was somewhat prolonged, and delayed departure until 0734, four minutes late. The Fireflies were flown-off in the second range and joined up shortly after departure. As soon as the strike was clear of the Fleet the two airfield sweeps and Mana reconnaissance took departure, the *Victorious*'s aircraft (Force Yoke) setting course for Palembang and those of the *Illustrious* (Force X-Ray) for Lembak Island. One of the *Victorious*'s aircraft was forced down in the sea through damage, and one of the *Illustrious*'s Corsairs was lost shortly after take-off, the pilot baling out. Of the main sweep, three Avengers fell out on the way to the target owing to unserviceability. Both sweeps were on the target by 0830, but unfortunately most of the enemy aircraft were already airborne. At Lembak, only three Tojos were seen: they were destroyed. At Palembang one aircraft was set on fire and two damaged. When the aircraft were over the mountains they found the weather had deteriorated and at 10,000 feet the top cover was considerably embarrassed by being forced into cloud. The target was sighted at 0840, when the Fireflies were sent to shoot down balloons which were seen flying at 4,000 feet. Almost immediately, deployment was carried out and the strike ran into anti-aircraft fire. Five miles from the target, several Japanese fighters attacked the rear of No. 1 Wing (849 and 857 Squadrons), damaging one Avenger. At 0845 the dive began from 7,500 feet through balloons going down in flames. Two aircraft were lost through striking cables. Bombing was more accurate than in the attack on Pladjoe, though burning oil tanks again made it difficult to see the target. The strike aircraft withdrew south of Palembang, then east to the same rendezvous as before. In the prevailing cloud the rendezvous, an island in the river, was not easy to find and the covering fighters had difficulty in spotting the bombers as they came out of the target area in ones and twos. Sporadic enemy air opposition was encountered. Seven Avengers were surprised by six to nine Oscars and Tojos, and all received damage. One Avenger followed a Tojo down to a height of 50 feet and destroyed it. At 0901 the strike aircraft were able to leave the rendezvous, landing-on by 1100 without further molestation.

Whilst the strike was in progress the Japanese made efforts to find the Fleet, which was under low cloud. The first enemy aircraft was picked up at 0900 but escaped in cloud. Seafires intercepted a small raid approaching from the north at 0939 and shot down one Dinah (Japanese army reconnaissance aircraft). One Corsair was lost when a force of Corsairs and Seafires was vectored out at 1026 to attack a group of 12 or more of the enemy. Ten minutes later, a group of Japanese passed 40 miles to seaward of the Fleet, but was allowed to proceed without attack. At length, shortly before noon, the enemy found our ships. A small raid, consisting of seven Army two-engine bombers was broken up by the combat air patrol, but most of the Japanese reached the main body of the Fleet and made low level bombing attacks on the *Illustrious* and *Indefatigable*. They were all destroyed before they could cause damage to the ships, but the *Illustrious* was hit by two of our own anti-aircraft shells and had 33 casualties, including 12 killed. Enemy aircraft did not finally quit the neighbourhood of the Fleet until 1910.

Losses of aircraft on both sides were heavy. We lost 16 through enemy action and 25 from other causes. In the air, at least 30 Japanese were shot down, a further 38 being destroyed on the ground. Damage to Soengei Gerong refinery stopped production until the end of March when both plants were producing at one-third capacity, which had improved to no more than half capacity by the end of May, although the Japanese had in stock materials for repair and these escaped damage in the raids.

In the Meridian Operation 32 British aircrew personnel were lost. Nine survived when their aircraft were shot down, and were made prisoners by the Japanese. Some months later, probably after the surrender of Japan, these nine airmen were murdered by their captors. Three junior Japanese officers admitted responsibility for the murders and anticipated the course of justice by committing suicide. There was lack of evidence to implicate other, senior, officers.[1]

[1] The papers on the subject are in Record Office Case ' Cabinet Committee 727 ', Vol. II.

CHAPTER IV

Japanese Attempts to Withdraw their Outlying Garrisons

(See Plans 1, 2, 3, 11, 12.)

ON the formation of the British Pacific Fleet in November 1944 the remaining ships in the Indian Ocean were (19th November) constituted the East Indies Fleet under Admiral Power. The Fleet included the 3rd Battle Squadron (Vice-Admiral H. T. C. Walker), 5th Cruiser Squadron (Rear-Admiral A. D. Read), escort and assault carriers and a ferry carrier, and more than 30 destroyers.[1] The Netherlands ship *Tromp* served in the 5th Cruiser Squadron.

On 8th January 1945 Admiral Sir Geoffrey Layton relinquished the post of Commander-in-Chief, Ceylon. He was succeeded by Lieutenant-General A. E. de R. Wetherall as General Officer Commanding-in-Chief, Ceylon.

On the appointment of Vice-Admiral Sir Bernard Rawlings as Vice-Admiral Commanding 1st Battle Squadron and Second-in-Command, British Pacific Fleet, the duties which he carried out as Flag Officer, Naval Air Stations, Indian Ocean were assumed by Rear-Admiral Clement Moody, who had been Rear-Admiral (Air), Eastern Fleet since December 1943. Admiral Moody now became Flag Officer (Air) East Indies Station,[2] and was placed in command of all Royal Naval shore air establishments on the station and all aircraft carriers and escort carriers belonging to the East Indies Fleet. The Commander-in-Chief, Vice-Admiral Sir Arthur Power, continued to operate escort carriers whilst employed on escort duties.

---

[1] *See* Appendix C.

[2] Short title F.O. (Air) E.I.

The organisation of the East Indies Station was as follows :—

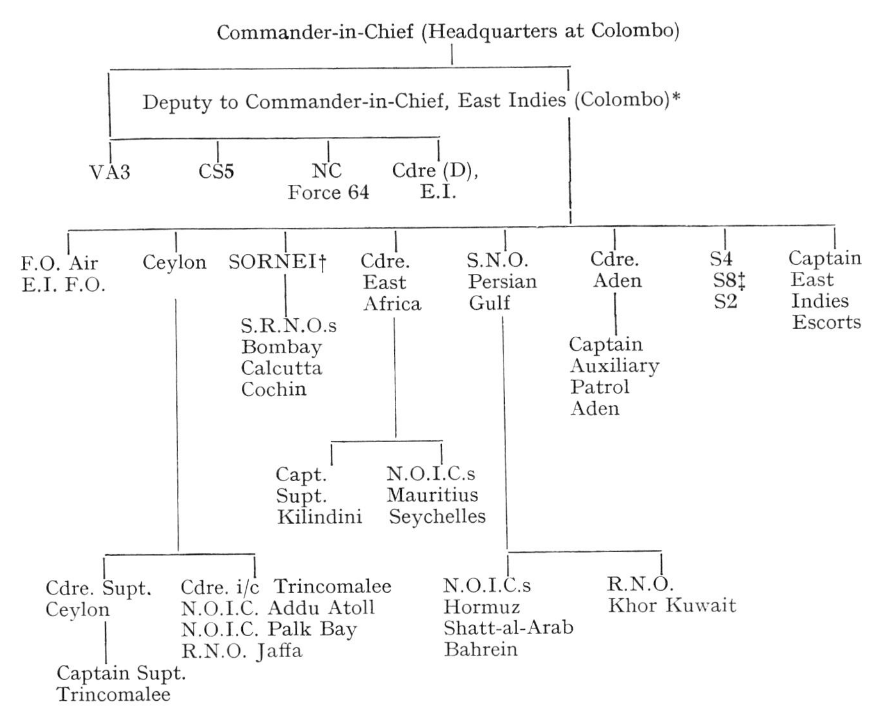

* Combined with F.O. Ceylon.
† Senior Officer, Royal Naval Establishments, India.
‡ Detached to Fremantle, under operational control of (U.S.) Commander-in-Chief, South-West Pacific Area.

During January, the two main squadrons of the East Indies Fleet were stabilized as follows :—

Third Battle Squadron ..	*Queen Elizabeth.* (Flag of Vice-Admiral Commanding Third Battle Squadron, Vice-Admiral H. T. C. Walker.) *Renown.*
Fifth Cruiser Squadron ..	*Newcastle.* (Flag of Rear-Admiral Commanding Fifth Cruiser Squadron, Rear-Admiral A. D. Read.) *London.* *Cumberland.* *Suffolk.* *Nigeria.* *Kenya.* *Phoebe.* H.M.N.S. *Tromp.*

The objects of the East Indies Fleet were threefold : the denial of the Indian Ocean to the Japanese and cutting the supply lines to their Burma Area Army and to such garrisons as existed in the Andaman and Nicobar Islands: destruction of enemy war potential, especially oil, and shipping, shore and harbour installations: close support of our army in Burma in that part of the campaign, namely the fighting in Arakan, where the conditions rendered such support both eminently possible and desirable.[1]

Our major operations in the Indian Ocean, as far as possible were co-ordinated with those of our Allies in the Pacific. The East Indies Fleet was, however, constantly occupied with numerous secondary operations called for by the strategic situation, as well as air operations and submarine patrols.

2

In February 1945 the Japanese began to withdraw their outlying garrisons in the south-west Pacific and concentrate them within a reduced perimeter. Their plan was to evacuate troops from the Moluccas, where General MacArthur was established at Morotai, and the scattered islands of the Banda and Arafura Seas, and to stand on the line of the Celebes, holding Borneo, Java and Sumatra as long as possible, with Indo-China and Malaya as the centre of resistance. On 5th February the zone of jurisdiction of the Japanese South-West Area Fleet was limited to the Philippines and it was replaced in the south-west Pacific by a new unit known as the Tenth Area Fleet with headquarters at Singapore. Vice-Admiral Shigeru Fukudome, formerly commander of the recently disbanded 2nd Air Fleet in the Philippines, was appointed Commander-in-Chief. Included in the Tenth Area Fleet was the 13th Air Fleet. This consisted nominally of two Air Flotillas, the 23rd and 28th, but at that date these comprised no more than a few airfield units and one Air Group (the 381st), though four air groups[2] were attached. The total strength was about 50 fighters, five night fighters, and 17 carrier torpedo bombers. The backbone of the Tenth Area Fleet was the Second Diversionary Attack Force, consisting of the battleship carriers *Ise* and *Hyuga* (4th Carrier Squadron), and the heavy cruisers *Ashigara* and *Haguro* (5th Cruiser Squadron). The *Oyodo* was included from 5th to 20th February. The *Isudzu* joined on 25th March, but lasted barely a fortnight, for she was sunk on 7th April by a co-ordinated attack group consisting of the U.S. Submarines *Charr* (Commander F. D. Boyle), *Gabilan* and *Besugo*. While patrolling off Makasar, this group picked up the *Isudzu* and four escorts proceeding towards Sape Strait. For three days, the Japanese force operated around Soembawa Island, moving troops and continually shadowed by the submarines when not forced down by aircraft. The *Besugo* expended all her torpedoes, repeatedly missing the cruiser but sinking one of the escorts, Minesweeper No. 12, whilst returning through Sape Strait on 6th April with a deckload of troops.[3] On the morning of the 7th the *Gabilan* made one hit on the *Isudzu* with torpedo which stopped the cruiser; and while the escorts were hunting the *Gabilan*, the *Charr* sank the cruiser in 7° 38′ S., 118° 9′ E.

---

[1] T.S.D.3183/45.

[2] The 11th, 12th, 13th and 31st Air Groups.

[3] The *Besugo* (Lieut.-Commander H. E. Miller), after reloading torpedoes at Fremantle, spent the remainder of her patrol in the Java Sea. At 1350 on 23rd April, while submerged on patrol between Surabaya and Borneo, she sighted a surfaced submarine at 14,000 yards, which was identified as a German U-boat flying Japanese colours. This was *U-183*. At 1427 the *Besugo* reached attacking position and fired six electric torpedoes at a range of 1,500 yards, at the still unsuspecting German. One torpedo hit, and the U-boat sank in four seconds in 4° 57′ S., 112° 52′ E.

Admiral Fukudome on 7th February was placed under the operational control of the Commander-in-Chief of the Southern Area Army, Count Terauchi, whose headquarters were at Saigon. Count Terauchi without delay issued a plan calling for the concentration of all forces of the Southern Zone in the Malaya and Indo-China regions, mainly the former. The garrisons in Timor, the Lesser Sunda Islands and Ceram were to move to Malaya, and forces stationed in other areas were to be drastically reduced.

The *Ise* and *Hyuga* were recalled to Japan and sailed from Singapore on 10th February with three destroyers,[1] carrying aviation spirit and other material. In view of the importance of their cargoes the Japanese took most careful measures to protect the movement, which was made with reliance on an accurate long range forecast of bad weather. Allied Intelligence discovered the timing of the movement. The ships were sighted off Singapore on 10th February by a long range search aircraft and at 1340 next day, by the British submarine *Tantalus*, on patrol in the South China Sea between the Anamba and Great Natuna Islands, but the submarine was forced down by aircraft of the escort and unable to make an attack. That day, aircraft attacked without success, and no better fortune attended an attempt to attack on the 11th off the coast of Indo-China by the U.S. submarines *Blower* and *Bergall*. As the enemy ships followed a coastwise route to Japan they were shadowed by army and naval aircraft, and a strike was planned for 1100 on the 13th, when the force would come within range of heavy bombers at Leyte and medium bombers and fighters at Mindoro. But on the 13th, almost unbroken cloud prevailed at all levels, and blind bombing was prohibited as submarines were co-operating. A strike arranged for the following day was also rendered abortive by the weather and the ships reached Moji without further molestation on the 19th.

Their departure left the *Ashigara* and *Haguro* and the old destroyer *Kamikaze* as the only components of the Tenth Area Fleet. Admiral Fukudome employed these ships on the protection of the troop evacuation operations which continued into June, with immensely heavy losses from Allied surface, submarine and air attacks.

The evacuation operations were four in number :—

' Sho (Akiraka) ' ..	Evacuation of troops from the Andaman and Nicobar Islands to Singapore.
' Chi '	Movement of troops from Singapore to Indo-China via Saigon.
' Transportation No. 10 '	Evacuation of about 15,000 men of the 48th Division.
' Ho '	Evacuation of troops from Borneo to Surabaya.[2]

The ships of the East Indies Fleet, particularly the destroyers, were kept busy preventing these movements.

---

[1] The destroyers were presumably sent from Japan. They are not shown in the (Japanese) organisation of the Tenth Area Fleet.

[2] No details of this operation are known. It is not described in Japanese Monograph No. 115, *Borneo Area Naval Operations* 1945 and is believed not to have been carried out. Captain T. Ohmae, I.J.N., who was on the Staff of the South-East Area Fleet, June 1942 to December 1943 and Chief of Staff, First Mobile Fleet, December 1943 to January 1945, stated in interrogation that the Japanese moved two army divisions from the Celebes-Borneo area to Malaya. (Interrogation Nav. No. 95.)

3

Up to the end of 1944 our operations for the control of the Andaman Sea had been conducted chiefly by submarines and aircraft. By the early summer of 1944 these had been so successful that the Japanese abandoned the use of large vessels for the supply of Port Blair, the base from which they carried out aerial surveillance of the Andaman Sea and Bay of Bengal. The withdrawal of the outlying garrisons towards the centre brought again some larger enemy ships into the Andaman Sea ; and towards the end of February 1945 Admiral Power arranged a series of anti-shipping sweeps of those waters by destroyers.

On 21st February, Force 68 consisting of the *Rotherham* (Captain 11th Destroyer Flotilla), *Roebuck, Rapid* and *Rocket* sailed from Trincomalee to carry out the first sweep (Operation ' Suffice '). The force was off the Andamans on the 24th. From 1310 to 1315 Z–6½ that day the *Roebuck* and *Rapid* bombarded the radar station on Great Coco Island, but the bombardment had to be discontinued on the approach of apparently hostile aircraft.[1] The whole Force later returned to Great Coco Island and all ships carried out a bombardment between 1405 and 1450.

On the 25th Force 68 went into Akyab which had been captured by us at the beginning of January. Sailing again on 27th February (Operation ' Training ') it operated inshore between Tavoy Island and Heanzay Basin during the night of 1st–2nd March, destroying three sailing coasters ; and on the 3rd bombarded Port Blair, returning to Trincomalee next day.

A further bombardment of Port Blair was carried out on the 19th (Operation ' Transport ') by the *Saumarez* (Captain 26th Destroyer Flotilla), *Volage* and *Rapid,* comprising Force 70. The force had sailed from Trincomalee on the 14th, passing through the Ten Degree Channel on the night 15th–16th, and sweeping towards Penang, but without result. Sigli in Sumatra was bombarded on the 17th. Two days later, the destroyers entered Stewart Sound on the south-east coast of North Andaman Island. There they found and destroyed a junk but came under fire from a gun, reported to be 6-inch or larger. The *Rapid* was hit and stopped. The *Saumarez* towed the ship clear, covered by the fire of the *Volage.* This ship, too, was hit, losing three men. On board the *Rapid,* casualties were heavy, one officer and ten ratings being killed and a further two officers and 21 men wounded. The Force went into Akyab on 20th March so that the ship might be temporarily repaired, but she had to be sent to Simonstown for permanent repairs.

Reconstituted with the *Saumarez* (Captain M. L. Power, Captain D.26), *Volage, Virago* and *Vigilant,* Force 70 sailed from Akyab on 25th March for a further sweep (Operation ' Onboard '). Entering the Andaman Sea by Preparis North Channel the Force had radar contact with a target at 21,000 yards and at 1047 Z–6½ on 26th March sighted a Japanese convoy of two naval auxiliaries escorted by two submarine chasers in position 10° 36′ N., 94° 56′ E., in the middle of the Andaman Sea. They were no doubt engaged on an evacuation operation. Mindful that a British destroyer had once been stopped by a lucky shot from a short range weapon fired by an inferior antagonist, Captain Power made the decision to fight outside the range of the Japanese short range weapons. At 1059½ the *Saumarez* opened fire, taking as target the smaller of the two auxiliaries, the *Teshio Maru,* range 14,000 yards. The remaining destroyers closed the *Saumarez* and opened fire as they came within range. The Japanese

[1] The times kept by the East Indies Fleet in the various areas of the stations are shown on Plan 3.

escorts, submarine chasers 34 and 65, paid no attention to their convoy, but kept away, making occasional smoke for their own protection. The *Virago* fired four torpedoes at the larger auxiliary the *Risui Maru,* at a range of 2,000 yards : all four missed. The *Volage* also fired four torpedoes : these, too, all missed. By 1129 the enemy ships appeared unharmed and all the destroyers were low on ammunition, except the *Virago* which was late in getting into action ; and Captain D.26 called on two Liberator aircraft to sink the enemy. One Liberator was armed only with depth charges, but the other sank the *Risui* with bombs. In making the attack this Liberator hit the ship's mainmast and crashed. Two survivors were rescued. The *Volage* eventually sank the *Teshio Maru* with gunfire. The *Vigilant* fired eight torpedoes at one of the escorts ; one torpedo hit and sank the target. The other escort was sunk by gunfire. In all, 18 torpedoes and 3,160 rounds of 4·7-inch ammunition were expended in this unsatisfactory action.[1] Our ships sustained only superficial damage. Prisoners taken comprised five officers, 45 men and seven women. None of the enemy ships was able to get off a distress message.

A sweep of the Tenasserim coast between Mergui and Amherst by Force 62 constituted of the *Rotherham* (Captain 11th Destroyer Flotilla), *Racehorse, Redoubt* and *Rocket* (Operation ' Penzance ') on the nights 1st–2nd April and the following night resulted in the sinking of a small auxiliary coaster and a junk. A reconnaissance of Narcondam Island was carried out on 2nd April, to investigate its suitability as a fuel and ammunition dump for coastal forces ; and on the 4th the radar station on Great Coco Island was again bombarded. On the 7th, the Force, which had gone into Akyab two days previously, sailed again and between the 9th and 11th carried out an anti-shipping sweep off the Burma coast, between the Moulmein River and Mergui, sinking several sailing craft. Liberators of 222 Group early on the 11th sank the net tender *Agata Maru* and her escort Submarine Chaser 7, north-east of the Nicobar Islands in position 9° 00′ N., 93° 40′ E. ; and that afternoon Force 62 picked up 62 Japanese and six Sumatran boys in Japanese uniform, survivors of these two ships. The Japanese, evidently as the result of these further disappearances without trace, ordered that exercises should be undertaken by all ships to ensure a distress message being sent off when attacked.

On 27th April Force 62 (the *Roebuck* wearing the Broad Pennant of Commodore A. L. Poland, Commodore D, with the *Racehorse* and *Redoubt*) sailed from Trincomalee, and on the evening of the 29th established a patrol in the Gulf of Martaban with the object of intercepting small craft between Rangoon and the Tenasserim coast (Operation ' Gable '). In the early hours of the 30th the force destroyed ten small craft which were proceeding from Rangoon to Moulmein carrying about 750 Japanese troops. These refused to be saved and were left in the sea.

4

On 22nd February, the day after the sailing of Force 68 to carry out the first sweep of the Andaman Sea, Force 62 sailed from Trincomalee to carry out the first of three photographic reconnaissances of the coast of Malaya, Operation ' Stacey '. Less than a month previously Admiral Mountbatten had reopened the land route to China, and had received directions from the Combined Chiefs of Staff, after completing the liberation of Burma, to proceed to liberate Malaya and open the Malacca Strait.

[1] Minute by the Director of Tactical and Staff Duties, Naval Staff, M.04434/45.

Twenty photographic reconnaissances were to be made as follows :—

On 26th, 27th, 28th February from positions inside the Andaman Sea :—

(a) Kra Isthmus from 7° N. to 9° 40′ N. and the off-lying Islands to the west.

(b) Phuket Island. This was required in detail ; for although the decision to seize the island had not at that date been taken, and, indeed, in the end was countermanded, the favourable strategic position of Phuket as a forward air, naval and general supply base for the assault on Singapore and Malaya, was obvious.

(c) Penang.

(d) Langkani and Butong Islands.

(e) Victoria Point, Hastings harbour and adjacent islands.

On 4th March, from off Simalur Island :—

(a) Areas in the coastal belt of north Sumatra from Sabang, position 3° N., 99° 45′ E.

(b) Part of Simalur and Nias islands.

(c) Penang.

Force 62 was composed of the assault carriers *Empress* and *Ameer*, in the former of which Vice-Admiral H. T. C. Walker hoisted his flag, the cruiser *Kenya*, and destroyers *Volage, Virago, Vigilant*, and frigates *Spey, Swale* and *Plym*. The tanker *Echodale* escorted by the frigate *Trent* constituted the Tanker Force (Force 61). The *Vigilant* returned with defects almost immediately after sailing, and rejoined at 1900 next day. The *Spey* was detached with defects at 1900 on the 26th, and changed places with the *Trent*.

The Force spent from the night of 25th/26th February to the night 28th February/1st March in the Andaman Sea, apparently without being discovered by the enemy. The weather was bright and the moon full, and it was important that the Japanese should not become aware that photographic reconnaissance aircraft were operating. Flying-off positions and times were as follows :—

26th February	7° 45′ N., 96° 22′ E.	0715
27th February	9° 11′ N., 95° 58′ E.	0800
28th February	8° 34′ N., 96° 43′ E.	0755
4th March	3° 51′ N., 95° 24′ E.	0739

Two strikes were planned but were abandoned, as photographs showed a complete lack of targets. For the last photographic reconnaissance there were no maps or photographs with which to brief Avenger pilots for a strike. On 1st March 804 Squadron shot down three Japanese aircraft, the first occasion, it is believed, on which aircraft from a British escort carrier had done this.

Weather conditions for photography were unexpectedly good, but winds were generally light or nil and catapults not entirely reliable. Moreover, there were some P.R. aircraft and camera failures.

The force returned to Trincomalee at 1000 on 7th March.

While the destroyer sweep of the Burma coast was still in progress Force 63 sailed from Trincomalee on 8th April under the command of Vice-Admiral H. T. C. Walker, to undertake photographic reconnaissance of the Port Swettenham and Port Dickson areas and to attack enemy shipping on the coast of Sumatra (Operation ' Sunfish '). Great importance was attached to this photographic reconnaissance, which was to complete that of the Kra Isthmus and Penang begun by Force 62 between 26th and 28th February (Operation ' Stacey '). The force consisted of the *Queen Elizabeth*, the French battleship

Richelieu,[1] the *London*, and three destroyers, the *Saumarez* (Captain D. 26th Flotilla), *Verulam* and *Vigilant*, with a carrier force comprising the *Emperor*[2] (Flagship of Rear-Admiral W. R. Patterson who had on 11th March succeeded Rear-Admiral Read in command of the 5th Cruiser Squadron) with 888 Hellcat P.R. Squadron, and the *Khedive*, with the *Cumberland* and the destroyers *Venus* and *Virago*. The original intention was to carry out the photographic reconnaissance, beginning on 12th April from a flying-off position west of Padang ; this was to be followed by anti-shipping strikes. The photographic reconnaissance had to be postponed for two days, owing to the breakdown of the *Emperor's* catapult. Accordingly, on 11th April the *Queen Elizabeth*, *Richelieu* and *London* bombarded Sabang, while the *Saumarez*, *Vigilant* and *Verulam* bombarded Oleelhoe.

No shipping was present at Sabang. The ships were subsequently attacked unsuccessfully by a force of ten enemy aircraft, two of which were shot down by our fighters.

On 12th April Force 63 fuelled from the Tanker Force (Force 70, the frigate *Lossie* and R.F.A. *Easedale*) and then proceeded to operate off the west coast of Sumatra. The photographic reconnaissance was carried out on the 14th and 15th as planned, with almost complete success. One of our aircraft was lost and our fighters shot down one enemy aircraft. An aerial strike was made next day on Emmahaven the port of Padang, in which one enemy aircraft was shot down and a 400-ton merchant ship reported damaged.[3] The *Venus* and *Virago*, meanwhile, made a sweep between the outlying islands and the mainland, from Ayerbangis Bay to Natal Road (Plan 3), sinking six junks. The force returned to Ceylon on 20th April.

Further successful photographic reconnaissances of southern Malaya (Operation ' Balsam ') were made on 18th, 19th and 20th June by aircraft of 888 Squadron embarked in the *Ameer* of Force 63. The force consisted of the *Royalist* (A.C. 21), *Stalker*,[4] *Khedive* and *Ameer*, with the *Suffolk* and destroyers *Rotherham* (D.11), *Racehorse*, *Redoubt*, *Relentless* and *Roebuck*. It operated from a flying-off position in the northern approaches to the Malacca Strait. On the 20th fighter strikes against the Sumatran airfields Lhokseumawe, Medan and Bindjai (Plan 3) were made by Seafires of 809 Squadron making their first strike against Sumatra, and Hellcats of 804 and 808 Squadrons. Runways at Medan and Bindjai were put out of action with 500 lb. bombs, aircraft were destroyed on the ground, and buildings, locomotives and rolling stock were effectively strafed, but no Japanese aircraft came up in opposition. One Hellcat was shot down by A.A. fire. Force 63 was apparently not detected throughout the operation.

5

The Supreme Allied Commander, South-East Asia, Admiral Mountbatten, had decided, on 22nd March, to launch a seaborne assault on Rangoon,[5] for it was doubtful whether the overland advance by the Fourteenth Army would reach Rangoon before the monsoon broke. The Americans had set a time limit

---

[1] The *Richelieu* rejoined the East Indies Fleet on 20th March, relieving the *Renown* which proceeded to the United Kingdom.

[2] The *Emperor* had joined the East Indies Fleet during March.

[3] Not listed in the *Japanese Report*.

[4] The *Stalker* joined the East Indies Fleet during March.

[5] This is the date given in Mountbatten Despatch. Commander-in-Chief, East Indies, in his War Diary for April 1945, says the decision was taken at the beginning of April.

for the use of their transport aircraft, which comprised 40 per cent of those which Admiral Mountbatten was using for the supply of the advancing troops. If we had not succeeded in opening the port of Rangoon by 1st June the withdrawal of these transport aircraft would force upon the Fourteenth Army a disastrous retreat to the nearest point at which the troops could be supplied by land. The date of the amphibious assault (Operation 'Dracula') was fixed for 2nd May, necessitating intensive work to mount the operation in so short a space of time.[1]

Dispositions were made to meet any threat to Operation 'Dracula' by enemy surface forces from Singapore. These consisted at that time of the heavy cruisers *Ashigara* and *Haguro,* together with the *Takao* and *Myoko.* Both of these last-named ships were out of action through damage caused in the previous October during the Battle for Leyte Gulf, but repairs were in progress. After the battle, the two ships had taken refuge at Brunei Bay and from there found their way to Singapore. The *Myoko* received further damage from the U.S. submarine *Bergall* on 13th December off the coast of Indo-China whilst proceeding to Japan for permanent repairs, and she therefore returned to Singapore. Both ships were non-operational, though it was believed at the time that the *Takao* might be effective or at least partially so. To prevent interference with the oversea expedition to Rangoon Admiral Power arranged that all available units of the East Indies Fleet should operate in the Andaman Sea (Operation 'Bishop') (Plan 11); the submarines *Scythian, Statesman* and *Subtle* established a patrol in the southern part of the Malacca Strait; and Royal Air Force Sunderland and Liberator aircraft based on the Arakan coast on 30th April began cross-over patrols from the south Andaman Islands due east to the Tenasserim coast.

Force 63 for Operation 'Bishop' was constituted under the command of Vice-Admiral H. T. C. Walker as follows: *Queen Elizabeth* (Flagship of B.S.3), *Richelieu, Cumberland* (Flagship of C.S.5), *Suffolk, Ceylon,* H.N.M.S. *Tromp, Rotherham* (D.11), *Tartar* (D.10), *Verulam, Nubian, Penn, Empress* (with 20 Hellcats of 804 Squadron embarked), *Shah* (with ten Avengers of 851 Squadron and four Hellcats of 804 Squadron). Admiral Walker had a free hand to plan and execute minor operations calculated to confuse and discomfort the enemy. He decided to interfere with any possible Japanese attempt to base aircraft on the Andamans and Nicobars and at the same time to destroy all shipping found in that area. The series of operations lasted 12 days. Force 63 sailed from Trincomalee on 27th April. Short endurance ships fuelled from the R.F.A. *Olwen* which had sailed from Trincomalee on the 26th escorted by the *Paladin* (Force 69). The force then proceeded via the south Batti Malv Channel, and at dawn on the 30th carried out a bombardment and fighter strike against the airfields of Car Nicobar. Port Blair was similarly bombarded in the afternoon. These strikes were followed up by a second bombardment of airstrips at Car Nicobar on the morning of 1st May and at Port Blair on the following day, after which Force 63 proceeded to their covering positions for the amphibious assault on Rangoon, in the north Andaman Sea. Aircraft of the force carried out strikes against shipping and airfields on 3rd, 4th and 6th May losing one Hellcat; and on the 6th the *Queen Elizabeth* bombarded the 6-inch gun position at Stewart Sound which had hit and damaged the *Rapid* and *Volage* on 19th March. The Japanese had recently laid anti-submarine mines in the Sound. No enemy air opposition was encountered throughout the operation, and the force returned to Trincomalee on 9th May.

[1] The Operation is described in Naval Staff History Battle Summary, No. 42, *Burma 1941–1945, Naval Operations.*

6

The movement of troops from Singapore to Indo-China (Operation 'Chi') began in March. In that month, the Japanese forces in Indo-China took over complete military control of the country from the Vichy French, placing the French Governor-General, Admiral Decoux, under protection. On 19th March Japanese troops placed garrisons in all important towns and executed a carefully prepared plan, seizing the electric power stations and communication and transportation facilities. The French troops in the country numbered perhaps 35,000 to 40,000, about a third of them being white soldiers. These attempted to hold out in a number of places, aided by the U.S. (China-based) Fourteenth Air Force which attacked the naval base and shipping at Saigon as well as various Japanese military centres, and dropped arms and equipment from its airfields in China, many of which had by that date been recovered from the Japanese after their capture during the latter half of 1944. But the French shortage of arms was acute, their few aircraft were obsolete, and their Resistance Groups could put up little more than a token fight. Before long, the French and Annamite soldiery melted away over the border into China and Siam, and before March was out the Japanese were in general control of all Indo-China. The troops who reached unoccupied China together with a number of French civilians, were granted permission to remain whilst re-equipping. The few French war vessels and merchant ships were either captured, sunk, or scuttled. Amongst the five ships seized by the Japanese was the submarine *Pegase,* whilst the sloop *Amiral Charner* and three other ships were sunk in attacks by the Japanese. Six or seven ships were scuttled by the French.

The transport of Japanese troops and supplies from Singapore to French Indo-China was carried out in three phases. The first convoy was wiped out by air attacks.[1] The second, consisting of three small tankers reached Réam safely, on the coast of Cambodia near the Cochin-China border (Plan 3). The third convoy, consisting of the 10,238 ton tanker *Toho Maru* escorted by the destroyer *Kamikaze* and a mine-sweeper, left Singapore on 12th June. The convoy headed for Réam but got no further than the south-east coast of Malaya, where American army aircraft attacked it on 15th June, sinking the *Toho Maru* and causing minor damage to the *Kamikaze.* Some 200 survivors were picked up by the Japanese escorting destroyer and minesweeper.

7

The fall of Rangoon on 3rd May and the thoroughgoing command of the Andaman Sea established by the destroyers and submarines of the East Indies Fleet and by the Royal Air Force, left the garrisons in the Andaman and Nicobar Islands in a precarious position ; and in an operation designated 'Sho' the Japanese began withdrawing these troops to Singapore.

Intelligence was received by the East Indies Fleet that the heavy cruiser *Ashigara* accompanied by the *Kamikaze* was due to sail on 10th May from Singapore for the Andaman and Nicobar Islands. Actually, however, the *Ashigara* did not sail but was ordered to proceed to Lingga for exercises with Army torpedo aircraft, beginning on 21st May.

On the 10th, the *Statesman* and *Subtle,* two of the submarines on patrol in the Malacca Strait, both reported sighting a Japanese cruiser of the *Nachi* class escorted by a destroyer, proceeding in a north-westerly direction. The ships

[1] No details of this convoy are forthcoming.

were the heavy cruiser *Haguro* and the destroyer *Kamikaze,* sailing loaded with food from Singapore to the Andamans ; two earlier attempts to throw supplies into the Andamans with small ships, had failed through the sinking of the ships by British air attacks. The *Haguro* and *Kamikaze* were to bring back troops. They were designated Force 1 to distinguish them from Force 2 consisting of the auxiliary supply vessel *Kuroshio Maru No. 2* escorted by Submarine Chaser *No. 57*, which was at sea at the same time running supplies from Singapore to Nancowry in Car Nicobar. The operations on which both these forces were engaged were termed 'Sho' (Akiraka).

Force 63 of the East Indies Fleet had returned to Trincomalee on the previous day, and at Trincomalee were also the ships of the Carrier Group which had been providing fighter protection for the Rangoon assault convoys and for ships in the assault area. The Group had been released from this duty on 4th May. Before returning to Trincomalee on the 9th, they carried out on the 5th and 6th air strikes against targets between Mergui and Victoria Point. When the report of the submarines came in a new Force 61 was at once constituted from the available ships in harbour at Trincomalee as follows :—

Force 61

Vice-Admiral H. T. C. Walker, Vice-Admiral Commanding 3rd Battle Squadron.

Queen Elizabeth (Flagship of B.S.3), F.S. *Richelieu.*

Royalist[1] (Broad pendant of Commodore G. N. Oliver, Commodore Commanding 21st Aircraft Carrier Squadron), *Hunter*[1] (24 Seafire, one Walrus), *Khedive* (20 Hellcat), *Shah* (four Hellcat), *Emperor* (15 Hellcat, nine Avenger[2]).

Cumberland (Flagship of Rear-Admiral W. R. Patterson, Rear-Admiral Commanding 5th Cruiser Squadron), H.M.N.S. *Tromp.*

Saumarez (Captain M. L. Power, Captain D.26), *Venus* (Commander H. G. de Chair), *Verulam* (Lieutenant-Commander D. H. R. Bromley), *Virago* (Lieutenant-Commander A. J. R. White), *Vigilant* (Lieutenant-Commander L. W. L. Argles), together with the *Rotherham* (D.11), *Tartar* (D.10) and *Nubian.*

The Force sailed on the afternoon of the 10th for the Ten Degree Channel to attack the Japanese force reported to be sailing from Singapore that day (Operation 'Dukedom'). A Japanese army reconnaissance aircraft sighted some of the units next day, west of the Nicobars ; and the enemy ships consequently turned back toward Penang. On the 12th, the *Statesman* and *Subtle* sighted them in Malacca Strait retiring south-eastward. The *Subtle* at 0705 made an unsuccessful attempt to attack in 3° 13′ N., 100° 39′ E. Admiral Walker appreciated that if he could avoid being sighted again by Japanese aircraft the enemy might make a second attempt to sortie, accordingly he steered for a position about 200 miles south-west of Achin Head, Sumatra, ordering the oiling force consisting of the destroyer *Paladin* escorting the R.F.A. *Easedale* (Force 70), which had sailed from Trincomalee on the 10th, to rendezvous with him for refuelling. He asked that all the available ships at Trincomalee should be sent to reinforce him, and on the evening of the 13th the *Nigeria, Roebuck, Racehorse* and *Redoubt* were formed into Force 62 and sailed, as well as a second Oiler Force (Force 67) consisting of the R.F.A. *Olwen*

[1] The *Royalist* and *Hunter* had joined the East Indies Fleet during March 1945.

[2] Not equipped with torpedoes, nor trained in night operation.

escorted by the *Penn*. The *Rocket* escorting a southbound troopship in approximately 2° N., 85° E., was ordered to leave her convoy and join Force 62 on the 14th.

That evening, the *Cumberland*, the 21st Aircraft Carrier Squadron and the 26th Destroyer Flotilla were detached and proceeded so as to reach a position about 50 miles west of the Six Degree Channel at 0700 next day, Rear-Admiral Patterson being ordered at 0325 on the 15th to take command of the operation. Admiral Walker himself in the *Queen Elizabeth* remained to the westward to refuel.

The second Japanese supply force (the *Kuroshio* escorted by *S.C. 57*) reached its objective, Nancowry, that day, and was returning to Malaya with 450 Army troops on board. The two ships were sighted on the morning of the 15th and attacked (contrary to orders) by an Avenger of No. 851 Squadron (H.M.S. *Shah*) operating from the *Emperor* since the *Shah*'s catapult was defective. The Avenger was one of an armed search of four flown off at 0730 that morning with orders, that the first aircraft to sight the enemy was to report and shadow, the remaining aircraft to close and attack with bombs. The Avenger which made the attack was hit and came down in the sea ; and in consequence of an error in the position given, the search failed to find the machine. The crew survived however, drifted ashore on the coast of Burma and were made prisoners-of-war. The attack caused no damage to the enemy supply force. A second armed search of four Avengers was flown off to attack, but was not able to find the enemy. One Avenger searched for the ditched crew, one turned back with engine trouble and the other two encountered the 26th Destroyer Flotilla and spent an hour trying to identify whether they were friend or foe, after which being short of fuel they returned to their carrier. The two Japanese ships reached Penang safely. On the 18th however, in the south channel of Penang whilst the ships were on onward passage to Singapore the submarine chaser exploded a mine, but was only slightly damaged.

Meanwhile, the *Haguro* and *Kamikaze* had left One Fathom Bank in Malacca Strait (3° 11′ N., 101° 13′ E.) on 14th May. At 1050 next day, in position 6° 55′ N., 96° 50′ E., about 15 miles to the south-eastward of the scene of the attack on Force No. 2, an Avenger of the *Shah*, operating from the *Emperor*, sighted them. At the time, the enemy ships were steering south-eastward at high speed. A strike of three Avengers which had been flown off from the *Emperor*[1] at 1335 made an unsupported bombing attack on the two ships at 1500, causing slight damage to the *Haguro* from near misses. After the attack the enemy turned to an easterly course.

At 0237 that morning Admiral Walker had detached the 26th Flotilla to intercept the second of the two Japanese Forces. When the news of the sighting of the enemy heavy cruiser was received the flotilla was diverted to the more important target and proceeded at high speed to intercept. The destroyers were organised in two divisions, the *Saumarez, Verulam* and *Vigilant* constituting the 51st Division, and the *Venus* and *Virago* the 52nd. Captain Power formed the flotilla on a line of bearing 020°, the 52nd Division spread five miles apart to port while the 51st was kept in open order to starboard to avoid closing within radar range of the coast of Sumatra.

Course 90° at 27 knots speed was maintained with the intention of gaining a position between the enemy and his base. As the afternoon wore on aircraft reports by carrier-based and R.A.F. aircraft of the position of the Japanese

[1] During the whole operation the enemy were out of range of the Hellcats.

ships differed considerably, and it remained uncertain whether contact would be made in daylight or after dark. No enemy aircraft came out from the Sumatran or Malayan airfields to attempt to interfere and support their two supply forces. At 1300, when the position of the enemy was approximately known Captain Power altered course to 110° and brought the flotilla into line abreast. By 1900 it was estimated that the enemy was still 75 miles to the north-westward and in the expectation that the Japanese would maintain a course of about 140° at 20 knots, the flotilla was spread four miles apart on a line of bearing 295°–115° in the sequence from west to east: *Venus, Virago, Saumarez, Verulam, Vigilant.* The enemy maintained a steady course. At 2245 the *Venus* obtained a radar contact bearing 045°, 34 miles, a range so great that there were doubts as to its authenticity. By 2322 the behaviour of the echo showed it to be a surface target. At 0003 on the 16th the *Saumarez* gained radar contact bearing 010°, 14 miles and Captain Power formed the flotilla into a star formation and ordered the destroyers to attack at 0100.

The destroyers were closing in to attack when at 0054 the larger echo reversed course abruptly, followed shortly afterwards by the smaller. This led the enemy straight towards the *Venus* which was cruising at maximum speed to reach her attack position. The *Venus*, taken at a disadvantage by the enemy's manœuvre, failed to fire torpedoes, the torpedo firing officer being unable to see the target which passed on an opposite course less than a mile distant. The *Haguro* turned back to the south-westward to comb the tracks of the torpedoes which she supposed the *Venus* had fired and in so doing headed almost directly towards the *Saumarez*. Captain D.26 had already signalled that he was unable to attack at the time given.[1] He now found himself in a favourable position, except that the torpedo tubes were trained to starboard and angled left, and he had first to deal with the *Kamikaze* which was close to starboard.

Captain Power had to alter course violently to starboard to pass close under the destroyer's stern, at the same time engaging her with main and close range armament, first in radar and then in visual fire, at point blank range, as she crossed from starboard to port and close down the port side. Meanwhile, the cruiser, though hampered by supplies stacked on deck,[2] had simultaneously opened fire on *Saumarez* with her 8-inch and 5-inch batteries illuminating very effectively with star-shell. At 0108 *Saumarez* shifted target to the cruiser, engaging her with main and close range armament. At 0111 the *Saumarez* was hit by a 5-inch shell in the boiler room, and almost simultaneously by a 8-inch shell on the port side of the forecastle and a hit on top of the funnel. Speed at once fell off and the wheel was put over to bring the sights to bear before the ship stopped, a full outfit of 8-inch torpedoes being fired at 0113 at a range of 2,000 yards from broad on the beam of the cruiser. Meanwhile all communication between bridge, steering and engine room in *Saumarez* was temporarily severed. About a minute or two later the *Verulam* on the port bow of the *Haguro* made an unmolested attack. The situation was now somewhat confused. The *Saumarez* withdrew to the north-west to examine damage, further than Captain Power had intended, because the telegraphs had been inadvertently left at 'full', and communications inside the ship took a few minutes to restore. Captain Power still attempted to continue to exercise control of operations. The *Haguro* altered course drastically but at each manœuvre found herself confronted

---

[1] 'An extremely silly signal to make' (D.26 *Report*).

[2] Interrogation of Vice-Admiral Fukudome, Commander-in-Chief 10th Area Fleet, under whose orders the *Haguro* and *Kamikaze* were operating. *See* Interrogation Nav. No. 115.

with a destroyer. These continued their attacks, a high measure of synchronisation in firing torpedoes being obtained by two pairs of destroyers: *Saumarez* 0113—*Verulam* 0114–0115; *Venus* 0125—*Virago* 0127. At 0209 the *Haguro*, overwhelmed, sank in position 5° 0′ N., 90° 30′ E. about 45 miles south-west of Penang. The *Kamikaze* received only slight damage from shellfire. She ran for Penang, but later returned to rescue the survivors of the *Haguro*. As enemy airfields were within easy range Captain Power, whose ship was found not to be badly hit, quitted the scene and concentrated with the fleet north of Sumatra. His ships had steamed 330 miles at 27 knots since they were detached by Admiral Walker on the previous day. 'The sinking of the *Haguro*,' wrote Admiral Mountbatten, himself a former destroyer captain, in his report to the Chiefs of Staff, 'is an outstanding example of a night attack by destroyers'; but Captain Power was very dissatisfied with his own conduct of it.

At daylight on the 16th the Japanese made reconnaissance flights from Phuket southwards into Malacca Strait. Some five enemy fighter-bombers made several air attacks on the fleet. The attacks were not pressed home, but at sunset a near miss on the *Virago* caused damage above her waterline and casualties of four killed and eight seriously injured. Forces were redisposed on 17th May in view of a possible attempt by the enemy to evacuate the Andamans. Half the Fleet and Force 67 returned to Trincomalee, the other half remaining at sea in approximately 30° N., 90° E. until 19th May, when they left for Trincomalee, arriving on the 21st.

8

Since 12th May the *Phoebe* had been patrolling off the coast of southern Burma, refuelling periodically off the China Bakir River entrance (15° 47′ N., 95° 30′ E., *see* Plan 3). On the 16th she established a patrol half way between Port Blair and Mergui to deal with any attempt by small craft to evacuate the Andamans towards the Tenasserim coast. Our blockade of the Andamans was causing great privation there; from natives in intercepted craft it was learnt that the food situation was acute. The *Phoebe* was subsequently reinforced by H.M.I.S. *Sutlej* and *Cauvery* from Rangoon. These ships formed Force 69, and were given the duty of attacking shipping between the Andamans and the Tenasserim coast and on the latter coast between latitudes 10° N. and 15° N. (Operation 'Adoption'). South of them, in the south Andaman Sea No. 222 Group of the Royal Air Force operated. On 1st June the *Ceylon* relieved the *Phoebe* as Senior Officer Force 69 and with two or three sloops maintained a patrol on the east coast of the Andamans and on the Tenasserim coast until 12th June. Force 69 lapsed three days later, and the patrol was subsequently maintained by a single sloop or frigate.[1] No enemy activity was observed.

On 5th June Force 65, comprising the 10th Destroyer Flotilla *Tartar* (Captain D.10), *Eskimo*, *Nubian*, *Penn* and *Paladin* sailed from Trincomalee to attack shipping between the Nicobar Islands and Sabang (Operation 'Irregular'). The R.F.A. *Olwen* escorted by the *Test* (Force 64) sailed from Rangoon to act as fuelling force. The *Paladin* was detached on the 7th to proceed to the Batu Islands, off the west coast of Sumatra, to carry out a special operation. Later, it was decided to maintain a destroyer on patrol near these islands until the 15th, and the *Penn* was detached. On the 12th, the *Penn* destroyed a Japanese landing craft containing about 20 men. On the morning of 11th June the submarine *Trident* patrolling off Diamond Point reported a northbound L.S.T., escorted by a submarine chaser.

[1] The sloops engaged on this duty were the *Cauvery, Godavari, Kistna* and *Narbada*. The frigate *Lossie* also carried out a short patrol of eight days.

Six Liberators of 222 Group, R.A.F. were ordered to begin a search at dawn, but before they could arrive, shortly after daylight on the 12th the *Tartar, Nubian* and *Eskimo* came up with the Japanese ships off Rondo Island about 20 miles north-west of Sabang, and destroyed both the enemy vessels. These were found to be the *Kuroshio Maru No. 2* with Submarine Chaser 57, the two vessels which had been engaged about a month previously in running supplies to Nancowry. Whilst retiring to the westward during the forenoon the destroyers were subjected to intermittent bombing attacks by a few aircraft, but suffered neither damage nor casualties. The patrol by Force 65 was abandoned on 15th June. H.M.S. *Test* and sloops of the Royal Indian Navy maintained a patrol of the Tenasserim coast between the latitudes of 10° N. and 14° 30′ N., until 27th July.

9

The sinking of the *Haguro* left the heavy cruiser *Ashigara* as the only ship in the 5th Cruiser Squadron, and indeed the only ship of fighting value in the Tenth Area Fleet. The transportation of troops from the Lesser Sunda Islands to Singapore via Batavia (Operation Transportation Nos. 10 and 11) continued in June, and on the 3rd of that month the *Ashigara* sailed from Singapore accompanied by the *Kamikaze,* to bring back troops from Batavia. The two ships left Batavia on the 7th to return to Singapore, with the *Ashigara* carrying about 1,200 troops. No air cover was provided, the Army arguing that it was a matter for the Navy,[1] a typical instance of the unwillingness of higher officers to co-operate which marked the operations of the Japanese Army and Navy throughout the war. Reconnaissance was flown from western Java covering Banka Strait. Beyond Muntok, at the western end of the Strait, the waters were considered safe from the incursion of Allied submarines, for the depths are small and the sinkings by submarines which had occurred there during the war could be numbered on the fingers of one hand. British submarines of the 8th Flotilla based on Fremantle and operating under the Commander Seventh (U.S.) Fleet, had since September 1944 been carrying out patrols in the Java Sea and the waters of the south-west Pacific and China Sea.[2] Enemy shipping was scarce and the utmost endeavours of the submarines resulted in the sinking of an average of no more than one sizeable ship a month. The *Trenchant* (Commander A. R. Hezlett) had sailed for patrol on 13th May and on the 25th sank Special Minesweeper No. 105 in the Java Sea. On 8th June Commander Hezlett had been ordered to shift station from the Java Sea to the coast of Malaya, but he had intercepted contact reports from the U.S. submarines *Blueback* and *Chubb,* that a Japanese heavy cruiser had entered Batavia ; and anticipating that the enemy would return to Singapore he obtained permission to patrol off Sumatra, and proceeded to the north end of Banka Strait, arranging that the *Stygian* which had sailed from Fremantle on the 29th May for the South China Sea, should carry out patrol a little north of the Strait.

In the early hours of 8th June the *Trenchant,* on patrol inside the Strait, received a contact report from the U.S. submarine *Blueback,* of a heavy cruiser and a destroyer northbound. Shortly afterwards, the *Trenchant* sighted a destroyer, but no cruiser, and closed the range to attack. She was sighted and fired on at close range. Commander Hezlett fired one stern torpedo as he hauled out at best speed. The torpedo missed. The *Kamikaze* was alone,

[1] Interrogation of Captain Yamanoue and Commander Ino, N.I.D. 0721/46.

[2] For details *see* Naval Staff History, *British Submarine Operations in the Second World War,* Vol. III.

for considering it safe for the *Ashigara* to proceed unescorted she had been sent on ahead to Singapore. Believing that now his presence was known the enemy cruiser would hug the coast Commander Hezlett closed to within two miles of the shore.

About noon the *Trenchant*, through her periscope, sighted the *Ashigara* coming up the Strait from the south on a steady course. An unlooked for choice of course in a narrow part of the channel on the part of the Japanese navigator, left the *Trenchant* in a bad firing position 30 degrees abaft the enemy's beam, with a torpedo run of 4,700 yards. Commander Hezlett fired his full broadside of eight torpedoes, including the two forward deck tubes. The *Ashigara* sighted the torpedo tracks, but in the restricted waters the navigator had no choice but to turn towards the torpedoes in order to comb the wakes, since a turn-away would have run the ship ashore. Her decks were crowded with troops watching helplessly during agonising seconds as the torpedoes approached. Before the ship could complete the 120 degree turn the first torpedo hit her. A few seconds later four more followed. Smoke and flame enveloped the cruiser, but as she listed to starboard she fired her anti-aircraft guns at the *Trenchant's* periscopes. In half an hour she sank, in position 1° 59′ S., 104° 57′ E. Amongst those on board who lost their lives was Vice-Admiral Hashimoto, commander of the 5th Cruiser Squadron.

With the sinking of the *Ashigara* Japanese naval power in the Southern Area was at an end. The Tenth Area Command remained in being under Vice-Admiral Ichise, to administer the minesweepers, submarine chasers and other small craft. Naval forces in the area had been reduced to the single destroyer *Kamikaze*, a few flying boats and some float planes.

10

In July, the East Indies Fleet began the operation of sweeping mines laid by the Japanese off localities which we expected to occupy before long. The Allies had been little troubled by enemy mines up to date. Apart from the shortage of money, materials and skilled labour in Japan the employment of passive forms of defence such as minefields, was less congenial to the Japanese temperament than activity. In place of mines, the enemy preferred such devices as midget submarines, human torpedoes, suicide boats, floating booby traps and swimming limpeteers ; and much misplaced ingenuity and labour were applied to developing such methods of damaging Allied ships. The Japanese mining plans for the Southern Area, drawn up before the war, made provision for a small number of mines, little more than 3,000 in all, to be laid during First Phase Operations.[1] In the Central Pacific, the first mine was not encountered by the Americans until 17th February 1944, when sweeping brought to light one at Eniwetok in the Marshall Islands ; and in the south-west Pacific mines caused little annoyance. As the Allies approached more closely to the main islands of Japan, however, more mines were found, and on the Burma coast the minesweepers were kept busy as our troops and coastal forces forced the enemy to give up one port after another.[2]

On 2nd July Force 62 (the 6th Minesweeping Flotilla) sailed from Trincomalee to sweep mines off Car Nicobar. The Force comprised the *Melita* (Commander D. L. Johnson, Senior Officer 6th Minesweeping Flotilla), *Gozo, Lennox, Pelorus,*

[1] In addition to mines which were to have been laid off Darwin and other Australian localities and at Rangoon, Colombo and Bombay.

[2] Volume V of this History contains a general plan of the Japanese minefields.

Persian, Postillion and *Lightfoot,* with the *Immersay* and *Lingay* as danlayers. Force 61 was in support—the *Nigeria, Ameer* (with 896 Squadron of Hellcats embarked), *Emperor* (with 800 Squadron of Hellcats), *Roebuck, Eskimo* and *Vigilant.* Rear-Admiral W. R. Patterson, Rear-Admiral Commanding 5th Cruiser Squadron, who flew his flag in the *Nigeria,* conducted the Operation (' Collie ') which in addition to minesweeping included bombardment and air strikes directed against suitable targets. Destroyers and minesweepers fuelled from the carriers as necessary on passage and during the operation.

The minesweepers operated off Car Nicobar daily from 5th to 10th July inclusive, returning to Ceylon on the 14th. A total of 167 moored mines were swept, all to the eastward of the island. To cover the activities of the minesweepers, the *Nigeria* and destroyers bombarded gun positions and targets of opportunity on the island, while Hellcats carried out a series of strikes, during which radar stations were put out of action and all craft seen in the area rendered unseaworthy. The only enemy reaction was accurate anti-aircraft fire. Four of our aircraft were shot down, but all pilots were rescued inshore, one by a Walrus aircraft flown off from the *Emperor* and the remainder by destroyers at which the enemy directed ineffective machine gun fire. The Japanese, believing that we intended to make a landing, took precautionary measures, including staking the airfield runways. On 7th July, Force 61, operating in heavy rain squalls, subjected Nancowry to ship bombardment and air strikes. Two Hellcats were shot down by anti-aircraft fire. At first light on the 11th 24 Hellcats attacked Kota Raja and Lho Nga airfields in north-west Sumatra. No aircraft were seen on either airfield, nor any at Sabang, but runways and buildings were bombed and strafed. One Hellcat was hit by anti-aircraft fire and force-landed in the sea, the pilot being rescued by a destroyer. A single Japanese aircraft approached the force and was shot down by fighters.

After the capture of Rangoon, the next main object of Admiral Mountbatten's forces was the capture of Singapore. For the assault on Singapore and Malaya and subsequent operations against Siam and Sumatra, a forward air, naval and general supply base was required. Phuket Island, about half-way down the Malay Peninsula, was chosen. The need for mounting an amphibious operation against Rangoon, in consequence of doubts whether the overland advance could win the race against the monsoon, caused the Phuket Island operation to be postponed, and it had not been mounted when on 19th July Vice-Admiral H. T. C. Walker took out Force 63 from Trincomalee to sweep mines off the island (Operation ' Livery ') (Plan 12). The minesweeping group consisted of the 7th Minesweeping Flotilla, the *Plucky* (Senior Officer of the Flotilla), *Squirrel, Pincher, Vestal* and *Rifleman,* with H.M.I.S. *Punjab* and *Deccan* as danlayers. Admiral Walker flew his flag on board the *Nelson* to which he had on 12th July transferred it from the *Queen Elizabeth* which subsequently left for the United Kingdom. With him in support of the minesweeper group were the *Sussex, Empress* (896 Squadron Hellcats), *Ameer* (804 Squadron Hellcats), *Rotherham* (Captain D 11th Destroyer Flotilla), *Racehorse, Raider* and *Paladin.*

The force arrived off Phuket on the morning of 24th July and the area which had been given first priority was swept on the 24th, 25th and 26th. Twenty-four mines were found. The first day's sweeping was marred by the loss of the *Squirrel* (Lieutenant-Commander M. Buist) which was mined forward. Two-and-a-half hours later she took a heavy list and had to be sunk by our own forces. Seven ratings were lost. Aircraft of the force carried out strikes against targets on the Kra Isthmus. Three small ships were reported destroyed,[1]

[1] Not listed in the *Japanese Report.*

rolling stock was shot up and a camp bombed. Six or more grounded aircraft were destroyed on Sungei Patani airfield. One Hellcat was lost in the course of the operations.

On the morning of 26th July suicide aircraft launched attacks against ships of the force. This was the first time the Japanese had employed this type of attack against any ships of the East Indies Fleet though such methods had been ordered against the East Indies Fleet units hunting the *Haguro* in May.[1] A single enemy aircraft was first detected by the *Nelson* at 38 miles distance, height 8,000 feet. The *Empress* and *Ameer* were operating fighters at the time but the *Nelson* did not direct them, and no interception was made. The enemy were shortly afterwards reported as a group at 6,000 feet. The *Nelson* sighted two Japanese aircraft at about 4,000 feet, which disappeared into a cloud almost at once. No shadowers were seen. The two enemy aircraft, two Val Mark I naval dive bombers, were next seen by the ' sun lookout ' diving out of the sun. They were taken under fire by the *Nelson* and *Ameer*. The latter hit one which dived at her ; it burst into flames, dropped its bomb in the sea and crashed in the water. The *Sussex* shot down the other in flames some 50 yards from the ship ; the aircraft struck the ship's side after hitting the water, but no explosion occurred and only slight damage was caused. The *Sussex* also shot down a second aircraft but one hit the minesweeper *Vestal* (Lieutenant-Commander C. W. Porter). The ship caught fire and had to be sunk by our own forces. Fifteen ratings lost their lives.

Force 63 left the area of operations that afternoon and returned to Trincomalee. This was the last active operation undertaken by the East Indies Fleet in the war.

[1] *Far East and Pacific Intelligence Reports*, 13th May 1945, p. 6.

CHAPTER V

Operations Preliminary to the Landing on Leyte

(Plans 2, 13, 14.)

1

BY the Autumn of 1944, despite the enormous expansion of the U.S. Navy, the Americans had not found it necessary in the Pacific to make any essential change in the organisation of their forces. These still operated in the areas assigned to them early in the war, and under the same supreme commanders. In the Pacific Ocean Areas, Admiral Nimitz commanded all forces, naval and army. In the South-West Pacific General MacArthur had the same function of supreme commander. No precedent existed for such power as that of the combined forces of the Pacific Ocean Areas and South-West Pacific, operating in unison at points 7,000 miles from the United States. The naval striking force of Admiral Nimitz's Pacific Ocean Areas Forces was the Third/Fifth Fleet ; that of General MacArthur was the Seventh Fleet which was under the operational control of Vice-Admiral T. C. Kinkaid. The system, by which the Commander-in-Chief and staff of Admiral Nimitz's striking force were changed at intervals, was being followed : when Admiral Spruance commanded the fleet it was known as the Fifth Fleet, and when he handed over to Admiral Halsey and left to plan the next operation it became the Third Fleet. On 5th August, too, the Fast Carrier Task Force was reorganised into First and Second Fast Carrier Task Forces, Pacific. The ships and crews remained the same, only the command and staff changed according as Mitscher or McCain took control. The change from Fifth to Third Fleet had occurred on 26th August 1944. The system had the effect of reducing the interval between operations, and the advantage that each operation was carried out by the Command and Staff which had planned it. It is said to have consistently misled the Japanese into an exaggerated conception of U.S. seagoing strength.[1] If after ten months of continuous campaigning during which some of the crews had not set foot ashore there was a certain loss of personal efficiency, there was nevertheless sufficient reserve of power in this, the greatest fleet afloat, to have ensured the success of every operation undertaken up to date. To ease the

[1] *Admiral Halsey's Story*, p. 197.

strain on the air groups of the carriers, these at regular intervals were taken bodily out of their ships and replaced by fresh groups. In the Autumn of 1944, when this narrative of operations in the Pacific opens, the fleet was carrying out a regular docking programme. Some of the ships had been at sea continuously for four months.

In conformity with its principal present role as a covering force for amphibious operations the Third/Fifth Fleet was organised as a Fast Carrier Force together with auxiliaries comprising a Joint Air and Surface Anti-Submarine Group ; a Service Group of repair ships ; and a Fleet Oiler and Transport Carrier Group of 24 oilers, seven escort carriers and 22 screening vessels to provide fuel, replenishment and aircraft replacements.[1] The Fast Carrier Force whose complement was not far short of 1,000 aircraft, was organised for carrying out air attacks on enemy ships or shore objectives and providing air support for landings. It comprised four Task Groups. Allowing for ships away docking, each group usually consisted of two fleet and two light carriers, with battleship or heavy cruiser support and a destroyer screen. From these last-named types provision was made for the formation of a Heavy Surface Striking Force of battleships, light cruisers and destroyers when battle with the enemy fleet was imminent, as well as a Light Surface Striking Force of light cruisers and destroyers. Thus the organisation of the U.S. striking force was the exact opposite of the Japanese. Normally it was designed for air battle, its alternative organisation being for the less likely contingency of a surface encounter. Its outstanding characteristic was the high speed of the heavy ships. The battleships could keep station with ease at 27 knots : the carriers could, and on one occasion certain of them did, maintain a speed of 30 knots for several hours on end. The Fleet contained an amphibious force, the bombardment and air support ships of which formed an additional considerable fighting fleet, consisting as they did at that date of some six of the older battleships, four heavy and four light cruisers, 12 escort carriers and 23 destroyers.

The Fleet was supplied, maintained and repaired by the Fleet Train. This organisation kept the forward area bases supplied with everything required for replenishing the Fleet with fuel, ammunition, aircraft, and stores and provisions of every kind, and replenished the ships at forward bases and at sea with all those items. At the majority of advanced bases, supply installations were non-existent or had been destroyed by the exigencies of war, and issues had consequently to be made, as in the open sea, direct from the supply ships into ships of the Fleet Train. These numbered at peak, in the Ryukus operation in April–June 1945, a total of 206 ships and vessels, comprising tankers, repair ships, floating dry docks, hospital ships, salvage vessels, tugs, ammunition ships, victualling and other store issuing ships, ferry aircraft carriers, together with the very considerable number of destroyers and escort vessels needed to protect the vast flotilla from air and submarine attack.

MacArthur's fleet, the Seventh, was a very much smaller force commensurate in size and composition with the lighter naval opposition encountered during the operations in New Guinea on which the South-West Pacific Area forces had been engaged since July 1942. It consisted of cruisers and destroyers with a force of escort carriers screened by destroyer escorts, and an amphibious force which was formed on 1st August 1944. Most of General MacArthur's landing operations encountered little opposition, for in New Guinea the Japanese merely held a number of beachheads with a perimeter of a few miles' radius

[1] *See* Appendix D.

and it was consequently possible to land almost anywhere, the opposition developing on shore later. When however a greater weight of metal in bombardment was needed than the Seventh Fleet could deliver, or if aerial preparation was called for beyond the range or capacity of MacArthur's shore-based air forces, Admiral Nimitz would supply this from his Central Pacific Forces.

These Central Pacific Forces, in addition to a plethora of surface ships included the Shore-based Air Force Forward Area (Task Force 93) composed of both Army and Naval units whose duties, since the completion of the central Pacific campaign, were chiefly reconnaissance, the defence of forward bases, and the maintenance in a state of neutralization of the by-passed islands in Micronesia. Its task was thus mainly tactical ; and when on 6th December it was converted into the Strategic Air Force, Pacific Ocean Areas, under the command of Lieutenant-General M. F. Harmon, it was reinforced by five VLR escort fighter groups to carry out tactical missions in the landing operations to be undertaken later by Nimitz, in addition to providing escort for the B–29's attacking Japan.

General MacArthur's land-based air forces, flying mainly from Morotai in Halmahera and from airfields in New Guinea, operated both as strategical and tactical forces. They consisted of the Allied Air Forces South-West Pacific Area and the Far Eastern Air Force. Both of these were commanded by General G. C. Kenney ; and their staffs, with the exception of Intelligence, were identical. The Allied Air Forces South-West Pacific Area had originally consisted of the Royal Australian and New Zealand Air Forces and attached Netherlands East Indies units with aircraft of the Seventh Fleet, and the Fifth U.S. Army Air Force. As the R.A.A.F. and R.N.Z.A.F. became dwarfed by the rapidly expanding U.S. Fifth Air Force, and with the U.S. Thirteenth Army Air Force also assigned to the South-West Pacific Area, the Far Eastern Air Force Command was established as a component of Allied Air Forces South-West Pacific Area, to control the U.S. Army air force organisations whilst Allied Air Forces South-West Pacific Area dealt with Allied and Naval units. Gradually, the Far Eastern Air Force assumed more and more of the operational attributes of the Allied Air Forces South-West Pacific Area, until by September 1945 the latter was completely identified with its former component.

In addition to the territorial division of command in the Pacific there existed an air command operating across theatre limits independently of both Nimitz and MacArthur. On 1st April 1944 the Joint Chiefs of Staff had appointed General of the Army H. A. Arnold their executive agent in commanding the 20th Air Force. This organisation operated the new long range very heavy bombers, the B-29's or Superfortresses, destined for ' softening up ' Japan for invasion. These operated first from India and for a time from China, whence they could reach out as far as Kyushu and Korea ; later they moved to the Marianas. The force was given its independence to ensure flexibility of employment of aircraft whose range transcended theatre limits. But this independence applied, with few exceptions, only to operating : the theatre commanders in which the force operated were charged with its administrative and logistical responsibilities. Thus there was left untouched Admiral Nimitz's responsibility, when the force moved to the Marianas, for building and defending the bases from which its aircraft operated, and for its logistical support ; whilst Nimitz, as Commander-in-Chief Pacific Ocean Areas, had also jurisdiction over these bases and the right of establishing uniform administrative policies throughout his Command. Consequently, the 20th Air Force was subject to theatre controls and dependent upon theatre services and priorities ; and so it remained until July 1945.

2

In September 1944, Allied strategy in the Pacific was still governed by the Combined Chiefs of Staff directive of 12th March 1944 based on the specific operations for the defeat of Japan approved by them at the Sextant Conference in the previous December. The directive stated that the advance by General MacArthur along the New Guinea–Netherlands East Indies–Philippine Islands axis would proceed concurrently with Admiral Nimitz's operations for the capture of the Mandated Islands of the Pacific ; and that a strategic bombing force would be established in Guam, Tinian and Saipan, for bombing the home islands of Japan. At that date, Formosa was still the objective of the main attack, which was to be made by Admiral Nimitz from the Central Pacific. The directive issued by the U.S. Chiefs of Staff to implement the plan charged Admiral Nimitz, after the capture of the Southern Marianas Islands, to support with his fleet General MacArthur in occupying Mindanao, with the object of establishing air bases from which the Japanese forces in the Philippines could be reduced and contained preparatory to a further advance to Formosa, either directly by Admiral Nimitz, or via Luzon by General MacArthur.[1]

The landing on Mindanao was fixed for 15th November. Before that date however events occurred which brought about a radical recasting of plans. During the second week in September the U.S. Fast Carrier Force under Admiral Halsey had carried out air raids on the Philippine Islands to reduce Japanese power prior to Admiral Nimitz's assault on the Palau Islands.[2] The damage caused by these raids was so heavy that in the first flush of success Admiral Nimitz, basing himself on Halsey's reports, announced that his task forces had ' annihilated ' the Japanese air forces in the Philippines. These were indeed reduced to temporary ineffectiveness pending reinforcement, which the Japanese undertook without delay. The revelation of the enemy's weakness brought about an immediate decision to accelerate the advance to Japan in conformity with the universal desire to shorten the war. Admiral Nimitz decided to curtail the operations against the Palau Islands, by omitting the capture of Yap ; and he offered to make available to MacArthur the III Amphibious Force, and the XXIV Army Corps, then loading for that operation, so that they could be used to attack Leyte Island, where information obtained from natives by a shot-down U.S. aircraft pilot indicated that the enemy garrison was of negligible size—this, though, was contrary to fact. A proposal by MacArthur's headquarters, he himself being at sea keeping radio silence, to omit the planned landings on Mindanao and the Talaud Islands and instead to attack nearly a month earlier, on 20th October, at Leyte in the centre of the Philippines reached the Joint Chiefs of Staff whilst in conference (' Octagon ') with the British Chiefs of Staff at Quebec. Approval of the change of plan was given without delay.

Occupation of Leyte would secure airfield sites and extensive harbour and naval base facilities for subsequent operations by General MacArthur in the Philippines. The east coast of the island offered certain advantages for a landing from the sea. It had clear and undefended approach from the east, long sandy beaches suitable for landing on, sufficient area for anchorage, whilst its command of Surigao Strait gave it access to the remaining central islands

[1] It has not been possible to consult the U.S. Chiefs of Staff papers, and this summary of the relevant part of their directive is based largely on S. E. Morison, *History of the United States Naval Operations in World War II*, Vol. VIII and the U.S. Air Force Historical Division's *The Army Air Forces in World War II*, Vol. V.

[2] *See* Vol. IV of this History.

of the archipelago. By landing at Leyte, the large Japanese forces in Mindanao would be by-passed, but since the nearest Allied airfields were nearly 500 miles distant from the landing beaches it was a prerequisite of success that the U.S. fast and escort carriers, though their primary task remained the seizure of every opportunity presented or created of destroying a major portion of the Japanese fleet, should nevertheless be able to establish control of the air over Leyte and prevent reinforcement of the island by the Mindanao garrison and other forces until MacArthur's land-based Allied aircraft were established on the Leyte fields. There was however one serious disadvantage in a late October landing, for from October until March is the season of the north-west monsoon in which the country on the east side of the mountains experiences torrential rains which would both delay the preparation of airfields and impede the highly mechanised U.S. Army forces. This disadvantage was accepted. In the event, it proved greater than anticipated, and it was only by making use of the fast carriers to provide tactical air support for the troops, long after they should have left for their next assignment, that the delay in bringing the airfields into operation was compensated.

3

It was decided that the Australian troops under General MacArthur's command should not be used in the liberation of the Philippines. The 1st Australian Corps under Lieutenant-General Sir Leslie Morshead, on 1st October 1944 after taking the lion's share of the fighting in New Guinea since July 1942 and receiving the mouse's share of publicity, had assumed responsibility for the continuing operations against the large enemy garrisons in New Guinea and the clearance of the remaining islands of the Solomons, as well as undertaking the conquest of New Britain. The garrisons of Bougainville, New Britain and New Ireland amounted to 60,000 men under General H. Imanura. When the American troops withdrew from these regions they left behind them a task much more considerable than one of merely mopping up, for except in north-east New Guinea the considerable Japanese forces were still in far better case than in the Andamans and Nicobars, where our blockade was reducing them to near starvation. The considerable scope of the operations called for a great base, and in northern New Guinea, Hollandia had become the largest base of the South Pacific, the number of Allied servicemen stationed there being said to amount to approximately a quarter of a million.[1] In Bougainville in the Solomons, when the Americans handed it over to the Australians they occupied in that large island no more than a defensive beachhead eight miles long in which two divisions of troops and other details to the number of 65,000 were crowded, and it took the Australians seven months of hard fighting to clear the main portion of the island and contain the remnant of the Japanese troops, some 20,000 in number, at the north and south extremities. In New Britain, where the Japanese garrison of some 40,000 was concentrated in the north around Rabaul, a major operation was called for to clear the 300 mile long island.

Though Australian troops were not used in the Philippines, the Australian Navy shared to the full extent of its capabilities in the various operations. The ships suffered equally with the Americans from suicide aircraft attacks and had considerable casualties. The *Australia*, for example, after being badly damaged and losing her captain by suicide air attack at the first landing, on Leyte Island, had to be sent to base for repairs. Returning to active service, at the

[1] *Spearheads of Invasion*, p. 171.

landing at Lingayen, in the space of four days she was struck by four suicide aircraft and near missed by a fifth. The ship had over 100 killed and wounded, but on the other side of the account it is claimed that she shot down 18 Japanese aircraft. Several theories have been propounded to account for the singling out of this ship for attack by the Japanese *Kamikaze* pilots. The most probable were her Commodore's broad pendant and the importance lent her in oriental eyes by the possession of three funnels. 'The Australian Navy,' signalled General MacArthur after the first landing, 'has played a full and splendid part in the successful landing at Leyte. It was my great pleasure personally to see it in action.'

4

Halsey's belief that the Japanese air force in the Philippines was 'a hollow shell operating on a shoestring'[1] was unduly optimistic, as General Arnold, who commanded the U.S. Army Air Force, gave warning. There was no doubt in the minds of the Japanese in the archipelago that General MacArthur would make good the promise to return which he uttered when in March 1942 President Roosevelt called on him to quit beleaguered Bataan in order to take charge of operations in the South-West Pacific Area. Consequently, during the greater part of 1944 and especially since the fall of Saipan in July, the enemy had been reinforcing the Philippines. In April of that year, Field Marshal Terauchi, Commander-in-Chief of the Southern Area Army, moved his headquarters from Singapore to Manila; and on 5th October, General Yamashita, the conqueror of Singapore and one of the ablest of the Japanese Generals, was recalled from obscurity in Manchuria to which he had been relegated through jealousy, it is said, on the part of the Prime Minister, Tojo, to take command of the Fourteenth Area Army which carried the responsibility for the defence of the Philippines. The islands were detached from the South-West Area and given the status of a Special Defence Area. The garrison amounted to seven infantry and one armoured divisions and four independent mixed brigades. The Japanese held two conflicting opinions regarding a policy for defence.[2] A decision had to be made, whether to attempt to intercept the enemy when they came within range for pre-invasion bombardments, or to permit them to land and fight a decisive battle on shore. In the latter case, no special reliance would be placed on sea and air support. After discussion and study the Southern Area Army Command at Manila came to the conclusion that once the naval and air bases fell to the enemy, the ground forces would be unable to defend Luzon where the main importance of the Philippines Islands centred. Accordingly, Field-Marshal Terauchi prepared to hold on in the Central and Southern Philippines; the enemy was to be checked on the beachhead with the local garrison. This called for strengthening the defence of potential landing points throughout the islands, the defence of all naval and air bases, and reinforcement of the positions attacked. Immediate reinforcements could come from Luzon, but these troops would have to be replaced from China, Korea and Formosa. General Yamashita pointed out that the shipping necessary, estimated at 200,000 tons, was not available. He was in favour of postponing the decisive encounter until he could engage the enemy on Luzon, where he would have a greater concentration of troops and equipment, and room to manœuvre. The Navy could not support this

[1] Tel. Commander Third Fleet to Commander Seventh Fleet, Commander-in-Chief S.W.P.A., Cincpac 230428 September 1944, quoted in *the Army Air Forces in World War II*, U.S.A.F. Historical Division, Vol. VI, p. 342.

[2] This account of the Japanese policy for the defence of the Philippines, is based mainly on Japanese Monograph No. 114, *Philippine Area Naval Operations, Part IV*.

proposal, for it ran counter to the 'Sho' Operation Plan calling for decisive action by all forces with a naval battle taking place within effective range of land-based air forces. In the event, when the Americans landed on Leyte seasoned troops were brought in from Luzon with heavy loss to reinforce the 19,000 men under the command of Lieutenant-General N. Suzuki which formed the garrison, being replaced by units of less fighting value from Formosa and the mainland of China; to the detriment of the defence of Luzon when this island was attacked in its turn.

The local naval defence forces in the Philippines were under Vice-Admiral D. Okochi, former Commander-in-Chief of Maizuru Naval Station in Japan. Okochi had no jurisdiction over any main naval units operating in the area. He had no fleet and most of his men were fighting on shore.

5

The recent regrouping of the Japanese army and naval air forces had been designed to strengthen the defence of the Philippines and the approaches to Japan from Formosa via the Ryuku Islands. By August 1944 the Americans had identified 260 airfields and ten seaplane stations in the Philippines.[1] The majority of the airfields were allotted to the Army Air Force. The Navy used Nichols and its satellites near Manila; Legaspi in the long peninsula stretching south-eastward from the main island of Luzon which is known to the Americans as the Bicol Peninsula; Tacloban and Ormoc on Leyte; the airfields of Cebu; Zamboanga and four airfields in the Davao area of Mindanao; and Tawi Tawi in the Sulu archipelago. The Army used the remaining fields. These were organised in nine Air Sector Commands. There is little doubt that the Japanese tried to do too much, for they lacked the necessary maintenance, supply and airfield defence personnel for the whole of the Philippines airfields. In theory, the system of dispersal was excellent and it permitted the enemy air forces to continue operations in the Philippines for an extended period. But as units became scattered and communications destroyed control broke down and what had been an organized military machine ended by approximating more nearly to a guerilla force, dangerous to the last, but doomed to eventual extinction. The final stand was made in the airfields around Clark Field, north-west of Manila, where army and naval units used impartially such airfields as remained operational from day to day.

At the time of the Allied invasion of the Philippines, by emptying Manchuria of aircraft[2] the Fourth Air Army stationed in the islands had been reinforced up to a strength of about 400 aircraft; the disorganisation caused by the U.S. carrier attacks in September and the subsequent hurried reinforcement prevents any close approximation. Only half of these aircraft were operational at that time. The number of naval aircraft was about the same. Immediately after the American invasion of the Philippine Islands in October, most of the 450 aircraft of the Second Air Fleet (Vice-Admiral Shigeru Fukudome) were moved from Okinawa, Formosa and Kyushu to the Philippines on the 23rd of month and combined with Vice-Admiral T. Onishi's First Air Fleet which had lost heavily in the raids of September and October and had only some 100 aircraft remaining. The balance of the Second Air Fleet's aircraft were sent to the

[1] The principal airfields are shown on Plan 14. Of the 260 airfields 115 were landing grounds without all-weather runways or completely adequate facilities.

[2] Lieut.-General Kawabe, Commander of Air Army in Manchuria, May 1943 to August 1944, statement in interrogation (Nav. No. 98).

Manila area later. The two air fleets were combined under the command of Vice-Admiral Fukudome, who was under the control of Vice-Admiral D. Okochi, Commander South-West Area. The total strength in the Philippines about the time of the U.S. landing on Leyte was some 650 aircraft, of which, however, little more than 400 were operational.[1] The subordination of Onishi to Fukudome was unfortunate; for the former was an air specialist of long standing, whereas Fukudome was without such experience.[2] During the past Summer, command of the Japanese air forces in Hokkaido, Formosa and Hainan had been unified, the army units being subordinated to naval command, a change which resulted in an increase in operational effectiveness. But it was otherwise in the Philippines, where the army and naval land-based air forces remained each under separate command and operated by co-operation between General Yamashita and Admiral Fukudome. The Headquarters of the Army Air Force were at Manila, and its Chief of Staff at Clark Field co-ordinated operations with the Naval Air Force. Though relations are said to have been harmonious, co-operation was for various reasons difficult to attain: the organisation of formations in the two air forces differed as did the terminology used in orders, whilst army airmen were unable to navigate to a fixed rendezvous.[3] Consequently the system failed to stand up to its first test, at the Battle for Leyte Gulf.

COMMAND ORGANISATION OF THE JAPANESE AIR FORCES IN THE PHILIPPINES

23rd October 1944

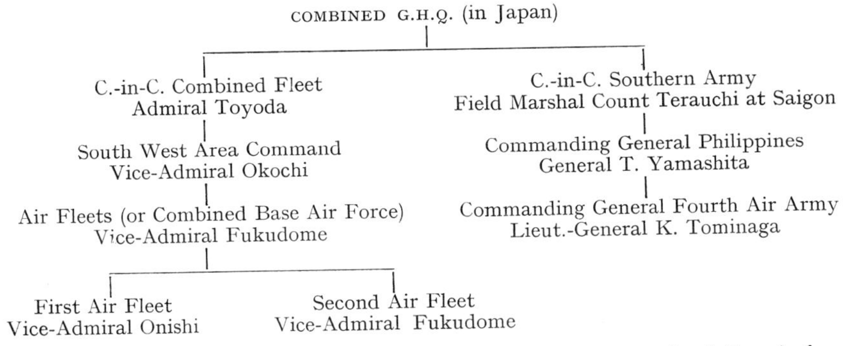

Until about the middle of December 1944 the total strength of the air forces in the Philippines, army and naval, was maintained by reinforcement at a level of 600 to 700 aircraft, naval aircraft preponderating somewhat.[4] The standard of training for reinforcements was usually not good and losses en route were heavy. By the middle of January 1945, the Second Air Fleet had been almost destroyed, for after the middle of December replacements failed to keep pace with the losses.[5] Accordingly it was dissolved and the remnant incorporated in

[1] USSBS estimate, see *The Campaigns of the Pacific War*, p. 319.

[2] Admiral Fukudome attributed his appointment to convenience and the fact that he happened to be available at the time.

[3] Admiral Fukudome in interrogation (Nav. No. 115).

[4] The same.

[5] Admiral Fukudome believed that one reason for the drop in the number of replacements might have been a change in policy at headquarters towards the Philippines operation when the prospect of success did not appear good. No notification of any decrease in the supply of reinforcement aircraft was, however, given to Fukudome.

the First Air Fleet the headquarters of which were then moved to Formosa, Admiral Fukudome himself being transferred to Singapore as Commander-in-Chief, Tenth Area Fleet. By that date, it is estimated that the losses of aircraft in the Philippines were in the neighbourhood of 3,000. Main causes of the losses were the bad weather of the season of the year, bad handling by inexperienced pilots, losses on the ground due to insufficient warning of U.S. attacks, and the fact that replacements had to be put into action as they arrived: there was no opportunity for training under local geographical and weather conditions. Moreover, the Japanese aircraft maintenance and supply techniques were by Allied standards extremely inadequate, a factor which may explain in part the scarcity of airborne aircraft in relation to the numbers manufactured. The special attack or *Kamikaze* aircraft constituted the nucleus of the Philippine force and were used only to attack ships, aircraft carriers and loaded transports having priority as targets, though no loaded transport was ever hit. Against land targets horizontal bombing only was employed.

6

With the nearest Allied airfields, at Morotai on Halmahera, almost 500 miles distant from Leyte, operations to secure control of the air over the landing beaches fell initially to Admiral Halsey's Third Fleet, whose Fast Carrier Force (Task Force 38) was commanded by Vice-Admiral M. A. Mitscher.[1] For the first time since the Battle of the Marianas in June all four groups of the Force operated together. At the beginning of October they were at Manus, Ulithi and off Palau. The nine fleet and light carriers of the force had an aggregate complement of more than 1,000 aircraft. They were supported by five battleships in one of which Admiral Halsey, Commander-in-Chief, Third Fleet, flew his flag, four heavy and ten light cruisers, and screened by 58 destroyers. It was the task of this force before the landing on Leyte took place, to establish air supremacy over the landing beaches. This necessitated destroying or reducing the enemy air forces in the Philippines, and attacking the bases through which the Japanese were passing air reinforcements from the Empire. At the same time, the primary task of the force was to seize or create opportunities to destroy the Japanese fleet. A secondary task was to obtain information on enemy installations. Admiral Mitscher's plan was to strike first the strongly defended aircraft staging bases in the Nansei islands and Formosa, following this by a repetition of the September air attacks on the Philippines[2] in preparation for the landings on 20th October. Principal targets were aircraft, aircraft facilities, and shipping.

The Nansei Islands form a chain 600 miles long running in a loop from southern Kyushu to Formosa. These islands, with Formosa, formed the inner defensive line for the East China Sea. They contained strongly defended naval bases and numerous airfields from which, as also from those of Formosa, the enemy could rapidly reinforce his air strength in the Philippine Islands. Every effort was made to ensure that the raid achieved surprise. Aircraft from the Marianas attacked Iwo Jima on the 8th, 9th and 10th October to hamper searches and Catalinas from Saipan flew patrols ahead of the carrier force. The ships followed the track of a typhoon which formed north of Yap and after moving north-west passed some 300 miles east of Okinawa on its route towards

---

[1] The organisation of Task Force 38 is given in Appendix D.

[2] These attacks are described in Volume IV of this History.

Japan. The strike by the fast carriers was arranged for 10th October. On the 9th Task Group 30.2 under Rear-Admiral A. E. Smith, consisting of the heavy cruisers *Chester, Pensacola,* and *Salt Lake City,* with six destroyers[1] made a diversionary attack on Marcus Island. Deception was attempted by smoke puffs dispersed over the horizon, floats with dummy radar targets, and pyrotechnics ; and the bombardment itself was so conducted as to create an impression that a landing was intended. The Task Group approached undetected in heavy weather, and bombarded the island at intervals from dawn until one hour after dark, expending 889 rounds of 8-inch and 1,933 rounds of 5-inch. The enemy return fire by coast defence guns was intense and the ships were straddled at ranges up to 18,000 yards, though none was hit. At the long ranges employed, the destroyers' 5-inch guns achieved no results ; but the 8-inch guns of the cruisers, using various fusings including air bursts, are reported to have silenced several of the enemy guns.

The fleet arrived off Okinawa undetected early on 10th October, having fuelled en route. There was at first no opposition. Fighter sweeps were made by two of the four Task Groups over the airfields at Yontan in central Okinawa (Plan 22) and on the nearby island of Ie. The U.S. fighters caught and attacked about 30 enemy aircraft on the ground at the northern Yontan field. A sweep by the other two Task Groups over the Naha airfields in southern Okinawa likewise encountered no resistance. The 20 or so aircraft on the airfield were dispersed in revetments and difficult to destroy. A second strike by Task Group 38.3 was met by about 16 enemy aircraft, including some of the new Japanese two-engined medium bomber called by the Americans ' Frances,' which was very fast and able to outdistance the U.S. fighters. The naval local defence and base vessels were attacked, the submarine tender *Jingei* and six minor vessels and two midget submarines were sunk. As the enemy had been taken by surprise, shipping had not been routed away, and approximately 60 small and medium merchantmen and a similar number of luggers and small craft were found in the anchorages and channels amongst the islands. In addition to numerous small craft seven merchant vessels aggregating 16,526 tons were sunk, in successive strikes throughout the day for the most part by means of a newly introduced U.S. aircraft torpedo. Miyako Island (Plan 23) 150 miles south of Okinawa, and other islands were reconnoitred. Harbour establishments and other military objectives were attacked, and the Japanese reported that the capital Naha, a town of 65,000 inhabitants, was completely destroyed. Target co-ordinators were kept over the targets all day. A total of 1,356 strike sorties was flown, 541 tons of bombs were dropped, 652 rockets and 21 torpedoes were fired. Eight U.S. aircraft were lost.

7

As soon as the last strike aircraft had landed on their carriers the U.S. fleet withdrew setting a course to the southward towards Luzon, with the intention of deceiving the enemy as to the plan to attack Formosa. The force began fuelling at 0730 next day and in the early afternoon a sweep was sent against the northern Luzon airfields (Plan 14). It was found that the Japanese had not as yet got these completely in operation. The carriers then moved to the attack on Formosa, the first made on that island during the war by carrier-based aircraft.

---

[1] The *Dunlap, Fanning, Cummings, Downes, Cassin, Chase.*

In his report, the Commander-in-Chief, U.S. Pacific Fleet, stated: 'An understanding of the operations off Formosa during the middle of October requires that the basic task assigned to the Third Fleet be kept in mind. That task was to create an opportunity to engage and destroy major portions of the enemy fleet.' A secondary object was the destruction of enemy aircraft and temporary neutralization of Formosa as a base for staging Japanese aircraft to the Philippines.

The island of Formosa, 190 miles long and 50 miles wide, with a population of nearly 6,000,000, was the strongest and best developed Japanese permanent base south of Japan. It was more strongly defended by anti-aircraft batteries and fighter aircraft than any area yet attacked. There were 30 widely dispersed operational airfields in the island and a large number of landing grounds situated in the west and south (Plan 15).

The U.S. problem was to prevent enemy aircraft based on Formosa or staging through it, from proceeding south to attack the amphibious operation about to begin at Leyte. This required both that the aircraft on the airfields should be destroyed and the air bases themselves put out of action. The cratering of runways, even when used against regions possessing few airfields had up to date proved only partially effective: it called for heavy expenditure of bombs, but it was a mere matter of hours for the enemy to fill the craters and render the runways again operable. In the attacks on Formosa, runway bombing was largely discontinued and effort was concentrated on destroying aircraft together with direct attacks on hangars, fuel dumps, workshops and other maintenance and servicing facilities of the principal airfields. About half the 772 tons of bombs expended was used in this manner, the remainder being directed against shipping, industrial targets, and harbour installations.

The approach of the force to Formosa was made during the night of the 11th/12th at high speed, and the opening strikes were flown off before dawn. The Japanese became aware of the approach of the force but the launching of the fighter sweeps was unmolested. The four Task Groups had each been assigned a sector of the island to attack. As the four fighter sweeps arrived over their respective areas they met strong enemy opposition. Large numbers of Japanese aircraft were over the target and anti-aircraft fire was intense. Enemy fighter opposition continued during the first bombing strike following the fighter sweeps, but fell off in a marked manner during the day. The Americans estimated at 259 the total number of enemy aircraft destroyed during the five days of operating. This is perhaps too high, but it is certain that the Japanese losses were very heavy,[1] and they facilitated the task of the American B–29's which made two unusually successful attacks on the Takao depots from airfields in China, on 14th and 16th October, in support of the fleet. Many of the aircraft destroyed were reconnaissance and anti-submarine types, and this had its effect on shipping in the China Seas. Attacks on merchant shipping by aircraft of the Fast Carrier Force were handicapped by the weather. Some 414 sorties were flown against shipping and 16 ships totalling 47,113 tons were sunk.[2] Only minor damage was caused to the extensive industrial areas of Formosa. Little was known of these and some of those attacked were not among the most important. The carrier force lacked experience in attacking installations of this

[1] The Japanese evidence as to their losses is not definite. The totals given in Admiral King's Second Official Report are too high, but that report was written before the war ended.

[2] Total taken from the *American Report*. The Japanese Report shows only 10 ships sunk by aircraft.

nature which differed from the types of targets attacked in previous operations. Bombs and fusings were sometimes not the most suitable for the purpose.

8

The air attacks on Okinawa and Formosa provoked the most violent Japanese air reaction thus far experienced during the war. The enemy at once rushed reinforcements to the threatened area. The whole of the air strength that could be made available was used to repulse the Allied intrusion into the inner defensive zone in the hope of inflicting a crushing blow. More aircraft succeeded in penetrating the American fighter screens and attacking the fleet, than had ever done so before. Two night attacks were attempted from Kyushu. The enemy even moved to Formosa half of the incompletely trained air groups of the four carriers of the 3rd Aircraft Carrier Squadron and the *Junyo* and *Ryuho* of the 4th Carrier Squadron. These included almost the whole of the naval air pilots upon whom depended the rehabilitation of the carrier air force as a fighting instrument. It had a far reaching result ; for the destruction of these air groups when they encountered the experienced American fighters, was so complete that the Japanese Navy never again succeeded in re-forming its carrier air force. In the fleet action which took place a few days later, there could be found in the whole of Japan little more than 100 pilots to man the carrier groups.

The enemy raiding tactics against the Third Fleet were good. They made a thorough reconnaissance of the fleet before sending off their aircraft attacks. These were made during dusk when detection was difficult, in the maximum strength as reinforcements were flown in to the Nansei Islands, Formosa and Luzon. Attacks came in low over the water from various directions, rendering radar detection difficult.

On 12th October more than 20 aircraft attacked Rear Admiral Bogan's Task Group (38.2). They were engaged by fighters at 25 miles distance, and caused no damage. A total of 43 enemy aircraft were engaged near the fleet that day, of which more than half were shot down. At 1730 on the following evening Rear-Admiral Davison's Task Group (38.4) was attacked by eight intruder aircraft which were not intercepted until they were over the force. All ships escaped damage, but an hour later the cruiser *Wichita* in Vice-Admiral McCain's Task Group (38.1) operating 85 miles east of Formosa, picked up visually 10 to 12 Japanese aircraft at ten miles' distance. It was after sunset and no protective fighters were up. Seven Japanese fast new medium bombers came in low beneath the overcast. An emergency turn was undertaken and the ships opened fire, shooting down all seven of the enemy ; but the heavy cruiser *Canberra* was hit by a torpedo launched by one of them. The explosion flooded both engine rooms and the two after boiler rooms and killed 23 men. The *Wichita* took the damaged ship in tow and a group of three light cruisers and six destroyers screened her on a slow withdrawal towards Ulithi. The Americans at that time made a practice of maintaining fleet tugs at sea within reach of any area where they were operating and the *Munsee*, which was standing by, proceeded to relieve the *Wichita* of the tow. The original plan had been to make air strikes on Formosa only on the 12th and 13th October, but the decision to try to save the *Canberra* instead of sinking her necessitated the fleet remaining nearby on the 14th, to defend her.

On the principle that offence was the best defence Admiral Mitscher continued to strike Formosa on the 14th with Vice-Admiral McCain's Group, whilst Rear-Admiral Davison carried out attacks on Luzon on that and the following day, to reduce the opposition coming from that island. Enemy air attacks from the Nansei Islands, Luzon and Formosa increased in violence that day, about 100 Japanese aircraft being engaged near the fleet. Between 1420 and 1820 four attacks were made. At 1516 the carrier *Hancock* was damaged by a near miss ; the A.A. light carrier *Reno* was hit and damaged by a suicide aircraft at 1707 ; and at dusk after the fighter screen had landed on their carriers, Japanese aircraft again attacked. Though the entire enemy group was shot down one of the attacking ' Frances ' succeeded in torpedoing the light cruiser *Houston* which had taken the place of the *Canberra* in Task Group 38.1. The ship's forward engine room was flooded and progressive flooding necessitated abandonment of the engine room and the two boiler rooms. The decks and longitudinals had begun to buckle and it was at first thought that the ship was breaking up, but ultimately it was decided to try to get her into harbour. The heavy cruiser *Boston* took her in tow shortly before midnight, the fleet tug *Pawnee* relieving the *Boston* at dawn on the 16th ; and screened by a force of light carriers, cruisers, and destroyers,[1] and covered by Task Force 38.1, another long slow tow to Ulithi was begun.

It had earlier on the 14th become apparent that the Japanese were making their maximum effort to destroy the U.S. Fleet by air attacks and that the reports of their aviators vastly exaggerated the damage they were causing.[2] To mop up the cripples, Combined General Headquarters ordered down from the Inland Sea the Second Diversion Attack Force consisting of the battleship carriers *Ise* and *Hyuga*, the two heavy cruisers *Nachi* and *Ashigara*, the light cruiser *Abukuma* and five destroyers. In anticipation of the move, Admiral Mitscher on the afternoon of the 14th detached Task Groups 38.2 and 38.3 to the eastward as a concentrated force to administer the *coup de grâce* to any enemy units which might attack the two towing groups now amalgamated as Task Group 30.3 under Rear-Admiral L. T. Du Bose.[3] Task Group 38.4 was sent to attack targets on Luzon on the 14th and 15th to reduce opposition from these ; and to replace the surface ships withdrawn from the Fleet to strengthen the towing group, cruiser and destroyer reinforcements were sent out from the Marianas. The fast carriers were due on the 20th to support MacArthur's landing on Leyte, and Admiral Halsey at first considered sinking the cripples. But his basic orders were, that if opportunity to destroy a major portion of the enemy that existed or could be created, this would become his primary task. Believing that this opportunity now existed, Halsey signalled to MacArthur the disquieting information that he must postpone his support.

On the 15th the Japanese air attacks on Task Groups 38.1, 38.4 and the towing group doubled in intensity, beginning early in the morning. All attacks were intercepted at 25 to 40 miles distance from the ships, but a few of the enemy aircraft got through and the carrier *Hornet* received some damage as did also the carrier *Franklin*, flagship of Admiral Davison's Task Group which was attacking airfields in the Manila area.

---

[1] Task Unit 30.3.2—Heavy cruiser *Wichita*, light cruiser *Mobile*, light carriers *Cabot*, *Cowpens*, destroyers *Burns*, *Charrette*, *Knap*, *Bell*, *Miller*.

[2] Excerpts from the Summary of First Diversion Attack Force in Operation ' Sho ' (*Campaigns of the Pacific War*, *Appendix* 89) gives the U.S. losses and damage as 12 or more carriers and many other ships, but there is reason to believe that these figures were for public consumption and that the Naval Command assessed the losses at a more reasonable figure.

[3] *Viz.* : Task Unit 30.3.2 and Task Unit 30.3.1 (light cruisers *Santa Fé* (Flag), *Birmingham*, *Houston* (damaged), heavy cruisers *Canberra* (damaged), *Boston*, destroyers *Caperton*, *Ingersoll*, *Cogswell*, *The Sullivans*, *Stephen Potter*, *Boyd*, *Cowell*, and the two fleet tugs *Munsee*, *Pawnee*).

The morning of the 16th found Japanese search aircraft shadowing the towing group. The U.S. protective fighters shot down two of them. At 1245 the light carriers *Cabot* and *Cowpens* in the group launched a combat air patrol of eight fighters, with four more to drive off shadowers, and an anti-submarine patrol. Shortly afterwards a large enemy raid appeared 80 miles distant, making for the crippled ships, and the *Cabot* and *Cowpens* each launched eight additional aircraft. The combat air patrol intercepted the enemy 45 miles from the ships and reported it to consist of 60 to 75 aircraft of all types, with fighter cover. From the composition of the force, which included five different types of naval bombers, this raid would seem to have been made up from the air groups of the 1st and 3rd Aircraft Carrier Squadrons which had been moved to Formosa. Against the U.S. fighters these partly trained pilots had little chance. The eight U.S. fighters made a violent pass at the Japanese top cover which immediately scattered, leaving the loaded bombers and torpedo aircraft below them without protection. On these, the American fighters went to work, while fighters were scrambled on board the carriers, and intercepted and shot down part of the raid which had broken off to the north. Nine Japanese naval single-engine bombers broke through but were all shot down by the *Cowpens*' fighters on a clean interception. No enemy aircraft got within ten miles of the *Cabot* and *Cowpens*, but three managed to penetrate to the ships in tow and one of them torpedoed the damaged *Houston*. The folly of committing air groups still under training, at so late a stage of the war, was amply demonstrated, for this torpedo hit cost the Japanese in all 24 single-engine bombers, nine medium bombers, and eight fighters, a total of 41 aircraft destroyed. A second afternoon attack cost the enemy nine more aircraft. The Americans' loss was a single fighter, whose pilot was recovered. But that evening it became clear that the Japanese search aircraft had located the two fast carrier groups lying to the eastward. The Second Diversion Attack Force, recognising that a trap had been set for it, quickly withdrew on the afternoon of that day without coming within range of Mitscher's aircraft; and Admiral Halsey was free to resume his mission of supporting the Philippine landing. No further attacks were made on the towing group, which by 20th October was out of range of enemy shore-based aircraft, and consequently able to dismiss its air cover. After skirting a typhoon, Ulithi was entered on 27th October.

The Japanese lost in the Battle of Formosa between 170 and 180 naval and about 100 Army aircraft.[1] The Commander-in-Chief, U.S. Fleet reported:—

> 'The strikes were of further importance from a strategic standpoint. They proved that the Fast Carrier Force could approach the strongest enemy air base outside Japan at a time when the enemy was aware of the approach; and could overwhelm the greatest aerial opposition which the enemy could muster there; could then deliver damaging attacks on Japanese ships and installations; and could follow such attacks with a successful defence against the heaviest counter-attacks which the enemy could mount against us. From this time forward, the enemy's strategic plan for control of areas south of Formosa was in jeopardy.'[2]

Halsey's fast carriers were not the only air forces engaged in working for control of the air over the Philippines. The land-based Allied Air Forces on

[1] Statement by Vice-Admiral Fukudome.

[2] *Operations in the Pacific Ocean areas during the month of October 1944.* A 16–3/FF12 Serial 002397. 31st May 1945.

Morotai and New Guinea were continuously engaged in neutralizing Japanese air bases in the Netherlands East Indies and the southern Philippine Islands, and their aggregate tonnages of bombs expended far exceeded those of the carriers.

Control of the air over the Philippines by the Allies was far from being won. The hulls of Halsey's carriers had scarcely disappeared over the horizon when the Japanese began to stage air reinforcements into Formosa and Luzon. Much hard fighting in the air had yet to take place, and for a time serious anxiety was felt for the success of the landing operation which began on 20th October.

The fast carriers during the six days of air fighting lost 76 aircraft in combat and 13 operationally. Air cover losses were 64. The number of sorties was as follows :—

Target	*Sorties*	*Bomb tonnages*
Formosa	1987	772
Luzon	152	25
Nansei Islands ..	26	1
Shipping	421	157
Interception ..	291	—

9

Immediately after the strikes on Formosa the Fast Carrier Force turned to action in more direct support of the landings on Leyte. For seven days, until the Japanese Fleet came out to challenge the invaders, one or more of the groups raided the Philippines.[1] Rear-Admiral Davison (Task Group 38.4) on the 17th attacked Legaspi and the Clark Field Area. During the next two days, Vice-Admiral McCain's Group (38.1) having fuelled on the 17th, after covering the towing group until it was out of the danger zone joined Admiral Davison in raiding the principal airfields in the Manila complex and shipping in harbour. Task Group 38.2 (Rear-Admiral Bogan) on the 18th attacked northern Luzon and shipping off the coast. On the 20th, McCain and Davison went south to support the landing made on that day on Leyte and to attack Cebu, Negros, Panay and northern Mindanao (Plan 13). Next day, while the other Task Groups were refuelling, replenishing and carrying out long-range searches Admiral Bogan continued the attacks on these islands. Good results attended the air attack on shipping, particularly in the Manila Area. Two submarine chasers, two tank landing ships and thirteen merchant ships over 500 tons were sunk. Considerable damage was also done to ground targets, principally at the more important airfields.

The U.S. losses of aircraft in the series of strikes between 17th and 23rd October were 36, of which all except 11 were caused on the first two days.

The heavy air attacks on the Philippines during September and the early part of October had for the time being greatly reduced not only the original Japanese air forces in the islands but the reinforcements flown in. The strikes on the Nansei Islands and Formosa on 10th–16th October and the heavy destruction they caused to enemy aircraft and installations at these staging bases prejudiced further reinforcement of the Philippines, with the result that enemy opposition in the air was temporarily exhausted after two days of

[1] The Philippines airfields are shown in Plan 14.

defending the airfields. On the 17th, 41 Japanese aircraft went up in defence, on the 18th, 118, and on the 19th, 25. The experience of the air forces engaged in maintaining the neutralization of the by-passed islands of the Central Pacific, were similar. A total of 98 four-engine naval bombers from Eniwetok were over Truk during October, meeting only 21 Japanese interceptors. The Marines made 817 combat flights over the Palaus and Yap, without losing a single aircraft in combat. On the 20th October, in the area of the Leyte landings enemy air opposition was negligible ; the work of the fast carriers, supplemented by the destruction of some 76 enemy aircraft by the escort carriers supporting the Amphibious Force had given the Allies for the moment complete air supremacy over the Philippines. Whilst no firm figure can be given of the Japanese aircraft losses in September and October, these are said to have been roughly equal to those of the Luftwaffe in the Battle of Britain. Their cumulative impact on the Japanese air striking power was decisive. They broke the Japanese Air Force as those of the Battle of Britain had broken the Luftwaffe.

' In retrospect the responsible Japanese Commanders with one voice blamed the loss of the naval Battle for Leyte Gulf and the consequent loss of the Philippines on their weakness in land-based aircraft, which in turn was the result of the United States carrier strikes.'[1]

The enemy's air forces were yet to give the Allies some of the worst moments of the war, and through the introduction of suicide operating (*Kamikaze*) to show themselves in the months to come capable of causing damage of a fantastic nature[2] but they operated as a wasting asset ' a sacrificial army of guided missiles '.

[1] USSBS in the *O.N.I. Review*, November 1946.

[2] The casualties to Allied ships in the Philippines operation from 21st October 1944 to 13th January 1945, from suicide attack alone were 22 ships sunk and 126 damaged, and in the Ryukus operation, 26th March to 21st June 1945, 27 ships sunk and 164 damaged,

CHAPTER VI

Liberation of the Philippines:

The Landing on Leyte

(Plan 13)

1

THE advance from Morotai to Leyte in one bound was a calculated risk. In taking it, General MacArthur, Commander South-West Pacific, in whose area the Philippine Islands lay, had perforce to abandon the traditional pattern of attack which had served him well in New Guinea, in favour of Central Pacific methods, in an area to which these were entirely unsuited. In the South-West Pacific advances had always been made within normal land-based, fighter-escorted bomb range. In the landings on Leyte, however, as in the Central Pacific, reliance would have to be placed on air support by carriers until airfields could be captured or constructed on shore, Leyte being outside the operational range of aircraft in New Guinea where MacArthur's Far Eastern Air Force under General Kenney was based. Even with the most rapid development of air facilities on Morotai—and they were completed nine days ahead of schedule—Leyte would remain outside the range of effective land-based air cover; for the Morotai airfields had been intended for the support of the invasion of southern Mindanao some 350 miles away, but Leyte was 300 miles further on. Even from Morotai, the Japanese air bases threatening southern Mindanao and Leyte (Plan 14) were outside the range of fighter-escorted heavy bombers and consequently Kenney could not completely neutralise them. The problem differed essentially from that with which Nimitz had had to contend in the Central Pacific. There, the enemy airfields were neither self-supporting nor mutually supporting. At Leyte, however, the Allied forces would be ringed round by land airfields and the carriers would be pitted against shore-based air forces capable of rapid reinforcement and owning all the advantage of staying power which the airfield possessed over the carrier.

The directive of the Joint Chiefs of Staff for the attack on the Philippines was issued in the middle of September to General MacArthur. The general concept of the operations entailed the seizure by amphibious assault by Army and Naval forces of strategic points on the east coast of Leyte Island and the adjacent islands, in the Central Philippines, and the control of the neighbouring waters. The purpose was to interpose Allied forces between the enemy in the southern and northern parts of the Philippines and to make possible the establishment of bases for further operations in the archipelago.

The tasks which General MacArthur assigned to Vice-Admiral T. C. Kinkaid, Commander Allied Naval Forces, South-West Pacific Area, were to transport and establish landing forces ashore in the Leyte Gulf–Surigao Strait area as arranged with the Commanding General Sixth Army, Lieutenant-General Walter Krueger.[1] This entailed providing air protection for convoys and naval task forces and direct support for the landing and subsequent operations, supplemented as arranged with the Commander Third Fleet (Admiral Halsey) who was not under MacArthur's control, and the Commander Allied Air Forces South-West Pacific (Lieutenant-General G. C. Kenney). Admiral Kinkaid had to arrange for direct air support and cover with carrier-based aircraft for the minesweeping operations and preliminary landings in the Leyte Gulf area during the period A–2 Day (A-Day being the date of landing, 20th October 1944), until the time when the airfields on Leyte island should have been put in a state to enable the land-based air forces to assume the mission of direct support. Kinkaid was responsible for transporting the troops and their supplies to the objective area, in naval assault shipping ; for preventing reinforcement by the enemy of the Leyte area from Samar, the islands to the west of the Visayan Sea, and north-eastern Mindanao ; clearing Surigao Strait of enemy naval forces and shipping ; and sweeping the strait to open it for naval operations and shipping in the Camotes Sea and adjacent waters, in conjunction with operations of the U.S. Sixth Army. Other duties were to provide submarine reconnaissance along probable routes of enemy naval forces and seaborne reinforcements and supplies ; to escort and protect shipping on the lines of communication to the objective area ; to provide a lifeguard (ASR) service ; and to establish in Visayan waters the naval forces required to support current and future operations.

The three principal task organisations of the Seventh Fleet which carried out these duties were : the Covering and Support Force (T.F. 77) under Admiral Kinkaid ; the Northern Attack Force (T.F. 78) under Vice-Admiral D. E. Barbey and the Southern Attack Force (T.F. 79) under Vice-Admiral T. S. Wilkinson.

The U.S. Sixth Army provided the troops. Kinkaid, as Task Force Commander, exercised operational control over all the support aircraft while in the objective area, whether these came from the Fast Carrier Force (which was not under his command but operated by co-operation), or from his own escort carriers, or from a land base. Long range sea patrol aircraft, aircraft on passage through the objective area and spotting aircraft not organic to ships or artillery units came under his operational control. Aircraft of Halsey's Fast Carrier Force detailed to support the operations, reported to his Commander Air Support Unit on arrival in the objective area, and remained under the tactical control of that officer until they left to return to their carriers. But in the Leyte operation neither the overall Attack Force Commander, Vice-Admiral Kinkaid, nor the Theatre Commander, General MacArthur, had any control over the movements of these carriers or the extent of the support which they furnished.

Admiral Kinkaid organised his forces as follows.[2] The Bombardment and Fire Support Group (T.G. 72.2) included six of the older battleships with heavy and light cruisers and screen, lent from the Central Pacific Forces. Admiral Kinkaid kept these under his own command. The Group was assisted on A-day by the Close Covering Group (T.G. 77.3) consisting of two Australian heavy cruisers, two U.S. light cruisers, and five U.S. and two Australian destroyers ;

[1] G.H.Q. S.W.P.A. Operations Instructions No. 70.

[2] Details of the organisation of the Amphibious Force are given in Appendix E and of the Tactical Forces in Appendix F.

and the Escort Carrier Group (18 escort carriers and their screen, lent by Admiral Nimitz), whose role was to provide cover and escort for the Task Force on passage to the objective and close air support and air cover during the operation. The Minesweeping and Hydrographic Group and the Beach Demolition Group were also under Kinkaid's direct control. The two Attack Forces were composed essentially of assault shipping and escorts. The duty of the Northern Force, Task Force 78, was to land an advance force on 17th October on Dinagat and Homonhon Islands and a raiding party on Suluan Island (*Figure* 1) to secure the approach to the main beaches so that the A-day assault forces would not be subjected to artillery fire from these points ; and on A-day to land and establish the U.S. 1st Cavalry Division on White Beach, between Tacloban and Palo, and the 24th Infantry Division (less the 21st Regimental

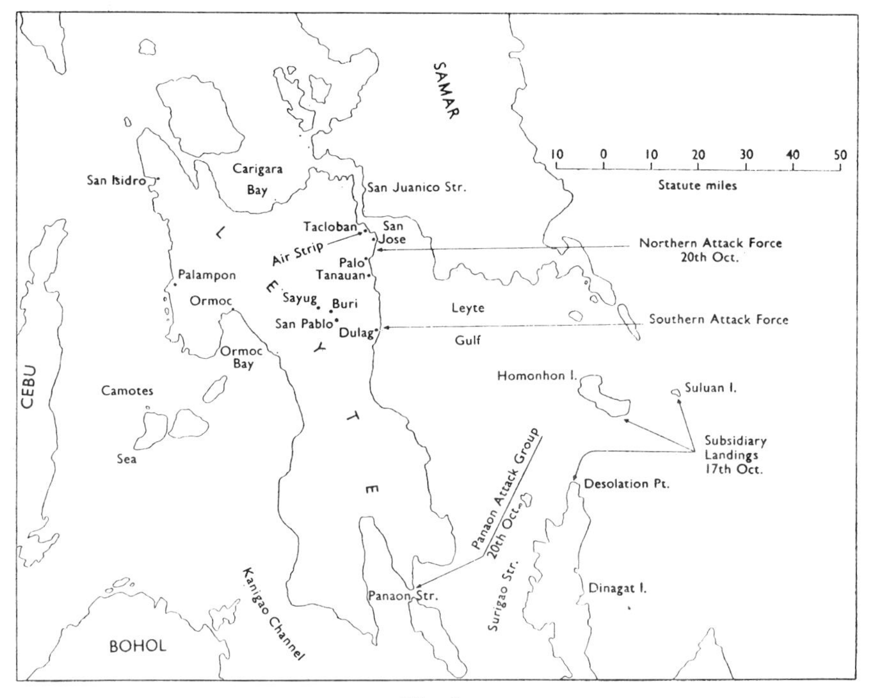

Fig. 1

Combat Team) about two miles to the southward on Red Beaches near Palo (*Figure* 2). An Attack Group consisting of the 21st Regimental Combat Team was to land nearly 20 miles to the southward in Panaon Strait (Green Beach). The Southern Attack Force was to land the XXIV Corps (7th and 96th Infantry Divisions) on two beaches Orange/Blue and Violet/Yellow at Dulag on the east coast of Leyte Island.

Despite the short time between the ordering and carrying out of the operation, the orders were very detailed. Some were received too late for adequate study ; and Vice-Admiral Wilkinson, Second-in-Command of the operation, did not receive the Operation Plan of the Seventh Air Force (Task Force 73), one of the air forces detailed to cover and support the invasion, until after his return to base.

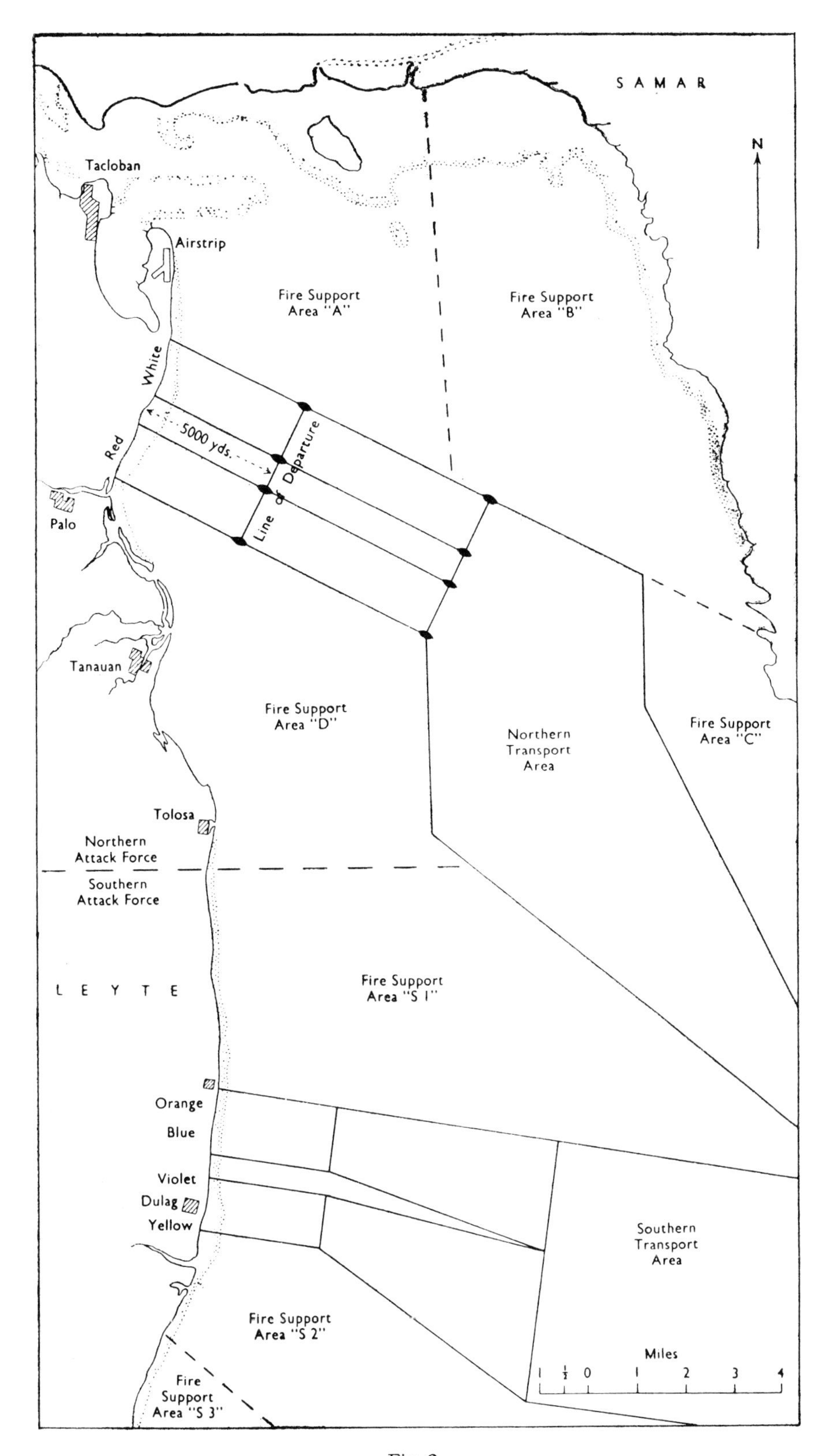
SAMAR
N
Tacloban
Airstrip
Fire Support Area "A"
Fire Support Area "B"
White
Red
5000 yds.
Line of Departure
Palo
Tanauan
Fire Support Area "D"
Northern Transport Area
Fire Support Area "C"
Tolosa
Northern Attack Force
Southern Attack Force
LEYTE
Fire Support Area "S 1"
Orange
Blue
Violet
Dulag
Yellow
Southern Transport Area
Fire Support Area "S 2"
Fire Support Area "S 3"
Miles
1 ½ 0 1 2 3 4

Fig. 2

2

The South-West Pacific Command did not believe that the Japanese fleet would fight for the Philippines, though fast task forces might strike at the Allied supply lines taking advantage of darkness, surprise and the support of land-based air forces.[1] This view was not entirely shared by the Third Fleet.[2] In order to meet the eventuality of a sally by the Japanese Fleet the Joint Chiefs of Staff directed the Commander-in-Chief, Central Pacific, to provide a fleet to cover and support Kinkaid ; for the Seventh Fleet, even though heavily reinforced from the Central Pacific forces, was incapable of disputing with the Japanese Fleet. Admiral Nimitz detailed the Third Fleet under Admiral Halsey, to perform this duty. In view of the situation which arose on the fifth day after the landing on Leyte the Commander-in-Chief, Central Pacific's Operation Plan No. 8–44 is important. The brief ran as follows :—

> 'The Joint Chiefs of Staff have directed that C.-in-C. Pac. furnish necessary fleet support to operations (including Leyte and Western Samar) by forces of the South-West Pacific.—Forces of Pacific Ocean Areas will cover and support forces of South-West Pacific.—Western Pacific Task Forces [Third Fleet] will destroy enemy naval and air forces in or threatening the Philippines Area, and protect the air and sea communications along the Central Pacific Axis.—In case opportunity for destruction of major portions of the enemy fleet offers or can be created, such destruction becomes the primary task [of all POA forces].—Necessary measures for detailed co-ordination of operations between the Western Pacific Task Forces and forces of the South-West Pacific will be arranged by their respective commanders'.[3]

It was arranged between the Commanders that the Third Fleet under Admiral Halsey should act as follows :—

> 'During the period A–10 to A–7 effect carrier strikes on Okinawa and Formosa and northern Leyte objectives. Selection of targets to be dependent upon Intelligence data and the strategic situations obtaining at that time.
>
> 'During the period A–4 and including A-Day, to effect carrier strikes on the Luzon–Bicol area, the Leyte–Cebu–Negros area, and in support of the landing in the Leyte area.
>
> 'Beginning on A+1 and thereafter to operate in strategic support of the operation, effecting strikes as the situation at that time required.
>
> 'It was assumed that the shore-based air forces, Central Pacific, would operate in the general Bicols area as soon as effective, from Palau'.[4]

---

[1] M.012980/44 Leyte (Philippines) Operation, *British Combined Operations Observer's Report*, p. 3.

[2] M.0237/45 *Battle of the Philippines, Action Report C.T.G.* 38.3, *24th/25th October* 1944, p. 2.

[3] *Operations in the Pacific Ocean Areas during the month of October* 1944.

[4] *Amphibious Operations, Invasion of the Philippines, October* 1944 *to January* 1945. U.S. Fleet, H.Q. of Commander-in-Chief, Cominch P.008.

3

The most difficult problem for the Americans to solve was logistical, for the operation was to take place at a distance of 6,000 miles from the main source of supply in the U.S.A. and the amounts of fuel oil, supplies, equipment and ammunition required were formidable.

For the Third Fleet ships lent to General MacArthur and for the assault troops, including those engaged in the operations in the Palau Islands which continued until nearly the end of November, 66,400 tons of ammunition were sent out from the U.S.A. Replenishment of the Third Fleet was undertaken by six ammunition ships and a similar number of auxiliaries carrying an average of about 6,000 tons of ammunition apiece. But by far the largest item was oil. In the month of October alone the Fleet received 643,000 tons of oil fuel; most of this came from the Caribbean, but some was brought all the way from the Persian Gulf, the first time that this source had been used in the Pacific War. The problem was complicated by the moving forward of base facilities in October more than 1,000 miles from Eniwetok in the Marshall Islands to Ulithi in the Palau Islands where a fleet anchorage was established as soon as possible after the occupation of the atoll on 23rd September.[1]

During the Leyte operation, the supply of the troops, Army air forces and the ships forming a regular part of General MacArthur's Seventh Fleet, was the responsibility of South-West Pacific Area agencies. The westward movement of the American and Australian forces in the South-West Pacific Area was followed by a re-alignment of naval servicing facilities. In Australia, Brisbane provided an operational base for all classes of ships, and a convoy assembly port. The Commander Service Force, Seventh Fleet, drew his supplies from the base. There was a naval supply depot at Cairns. At Darwin the mines were stored which the Royal Australian Air Force used in the minelaying campaign which it was carrying out far and wide in the South-West Pacific Area. The other function of Darwin was to carry out minor repairs to submarines. Fremantle–Perth was the base of a large part of the Seventh Fleet submarines and was a naval supply depot. There was at Sydney a U.S. naval supply base and a maintenance base for escort vessels. The principal functions of Morotai were to provide an operating base for land-based aircraft and seaplanes and an operating and repair base for M.T.B.s and landing craft. Many of the bases remote from the actual theatre of operations particularly in the Solomon Islands and Bismarck Archipelago, were being closed down and their establishments transferred to bases further forward. The principal naval and air base for advanced operations was situated at Manus in the Admiralty Islands. Manus had been occupied in March on a sudden, unpremeditated decision resulting from the discovery that it was lightly defended, but already in six or seven months the Americans had established three floating docks, and the naval supply depot was particularly well stored. By November there were nearly 35,000 naval personnel on duty. During the early part of the Philippines campaign the base was used also for repairs and supplies by the Third Fleet

[1] The main distances involved were:—

Manus to Leyte	1,500 miles
Saipan to Leyte	1,270 miles
Hollandia to Leyte ..	1,250 miles
Guam to Leyte	1,200 miles
Biak to Leyte	1,020 miles
Ulithi to Leyte	925 miles
Palau to Leyte	625 miles
Morotai to Leyte	600 miles

ships under Admiral Halsey's command and those temporarily transferred to the Seventh Fleet. By the end of November, Hollandia on the north coast of New Guinea was developed as the main base of the Seventh Fleet, and as already noticed the Service population of the base is said to have been a quarter of a million : there were 215 ships in harbour and a further 250 smaller vessels around the shores.

Three Service Squadrons provided for the needs of the Third Fleet. Squadron Two administered the fleet repair ships and tenders, hospital ships and mobile hospitals, mobile salvage, together with those important items from the point of view of U.S. morale, mails and motion picture exchange. Service Squadron Ten provided for battle damage, emergency repairs and upkeep of ships, besides assisting in furnishing supplies to fleet units. It had as a secondary duty the provision of emergency support to shore-based Army, Naval and Marine Corps Units, over and above that which could be furnished by shore-based supply organisations. In order to carry out these duties, Service Squadron Ten was set up as a mobile advanced base, comprising floating storage for provisions, fuel and general stores, together with ships, tenders and harbour craft necessary for rendering all service required at a fleet anchorage. It was also assigned vessels especially equipped for handling aviation supplies and was fitted to provide limited storage for emergency Army and Marine Corps stores. A system was developed of employing specially detailed naval vessels to transport and deliver freight consigned to ships of the fleet. Service Squadron Eight was responsible for the supply, transportation and distribution of fuel, diesel and lubricating oil, aviation fuel, provisions, general stores, and ammunition for the fleet and bases. All Service Force oilers, provision ships, stores issuing ships, ammunition ships, and certain miscellaneous auxiliaries were assigned to Squadron Eight, as well as chartered tankers and provision ships. Services rendered to damaged vessels by the service squadrons included the restoration of moderately damaged ships to fighting effectiveness, and temporary repairs to badly damaged ships to render them fit to undertake the long voyage back to Pearl Harbour or the west coast of U.S.A. in safety, and, where possible, under their own power. The ships and vessels of the Service Squadron dealing with damage were classed as repair ships, internal combustion engine ; mobile floating dry docks ; repair ships, battle damage ; submarine tenders ; salvage vessels ; ocean tugs ; floating workshops ; heavy hull repair ships ; floating derricks ; destroyer tenders ; and M.T.B. tenders. Some of these vessels remained at Manus, others were sent forward to Saipan, Guam, Ulithi and Kossol Road (Palau Islands).

Twenty-nine fleet oilers provided for the fuel requirements of the fleet, being organised with their escorts in Task Group 30.8. The group was several times attacked in a determined manner by enemy aircraft, but suffered only minor casualties and lost none of its cargoes. In order to expedite the turn round of fleet oilers and to ensure emergency reserve storage at the various advanced bases, tankers and floating storage tankers and barges were stationed at these points. The replenishment of the fleet with bombardment ammunition was on the basis of two-and-a-half to three extra outfits, with 20 rounds per gun of armour piercing shell for a possible fleet action. Three outfits of general purpose and one of armour piercing bombs were provided for the carriers.

In October, the base of the Fleet was moved forward from Eniwetok to Ulithi. It had originally been intended to support the main body of the Third Fleet at Manus but the advancing of the Leyte invasion date upset the logistic arrangements, as most of the supplies at Manus were diverted to the task of making ready amphibious elements for this operation, at the expense of other units. The unexpected consumption of supplies by one source was reflected in shortages elsewhere. The Carrier Groups caused particular disorganisation of the supply system at Manus when they shifted the base arranged for them at Manus to Ulithi, forcing shipping scheduled for the Admiralty Islands base to be split and re-allocated. The move of base facilities to Ulithi began in the first week of October by convoys moving in long slow tows. All through the month, the tactical situation remained in such a state of flux that it was never possible to make a firm decision as to the relative percentages of support required at Ulithi and Manus respectively. Ulithi was by no means an ideal anchorage. During the operation it was swept by a typhoon whilst the carrier *Bunker Hill* was replenishing. All her supplies were lost through the foundering of her boats and many other boats at the anchorage. Its strategic position, however, justified acceptance of its shortcomings.

4

Though Australian troops on 1st October took over from U.S. troops the responsibility for the remaining operations in the South-West Pacific, General MacArthur disposed of insufficient U.S. army troops and of but a fraction of the naval force required for the Philippine operations. Admiral Nimitz consequently transferred to his command various Central Pacific forces including the whole of the III Amphibious Force under Vice-Admiral Wilkinson which was diverted whilst *en route* to capture Yap, for which it had been detailed. The full list of forces lent by Admiral Nimitz to General MacArthur was as follows :—

(*a*) The XXIV Corps, a total of some 50, 250 men ;

(*b*) Garrison forces to the number of about 20,000 men.

(*c*) The 77th Division, as area reserve ;

(*d*) Four transport groups with associated escorts and landing, control and mine craft.

(*e*) A fire support group of six pre-war battleships, three heavy and three light cruisers, and screen.

(*f*) A support group of 18 escort carriers and their screening forces.

(*g*) Various service units.

The force employed comprised 157 combat ships (six battleships, five heavy and six light cruisers, 18 escort carriers, 86 destroyers, 25 destroyer escorts, 11 frigates), 420 amphibious vessels (transports, landing ships and craft), 84 patrol, minesweeping and hydrographic craft.

The Royal Navy was represented by the fast minelayer *Ariadne*[1] which had laid mines off Wewak in New Guinea, on the night 19th/20th June. In the Leyte operation she was to be employed as an assault troop carrier. Australian ships participating were the *Australia*[2] (broad pendant of Commodore J. A. Collins), *Shropshire*,[3] *Arunta*,[4] and *Warramunga*,[5] forming part of the Close Covering Group ; the *Gascoyne* (the first frigate to be built in Australia), *H.D.M.L.* 1074 and the Landing Ships, Infantry, *Westralia, Manoora* and *Kanimbla.* Commander R. B. A. Hunt, N.O.I.C. Port Moresby, was placed in charge of the Surveying Section.

---

[1] Captain Lord Ashbourne.
[2] Captain E. F. V. Dechaineux.
[3] Captain C. A. G. Nichols.
[4] Commander A. E. Buchanan.
[5] Lieut.-Commander J. M. Alliston.

South-West Pacific Air Forces under Lieut.-General G. C. Kenney protected the left flank and rear of the line of advance by attacks on enemy bases, aircraft and shipping in the area south of Latitude 20° N., including Mindanao, the Celebes, Halmahera and Netherlands East Indies. The 5th Air Force was responsible for the northern part of the area, including Luzon and the Gulf of Tonkin. The 13th covered the remainder of the Philippine Islands, Sarawak and the South China Sea as far as Sunda Strait. Air Command, North Solomons operated in the Solomon Islands and New Britain. The remaining large area including Borneo, the Netherlands East Indies except Sumatra and New Guinea was the responsibility of the Royal Australian Air Force. The northernmost Allied base at that date was Morotai. Air Forces, Central Pacific (Admiral Nimitz's mobile tactical 7th Air Forces in Saipan and Guam) gave support by attacks on similar targets in the area east of longitude 40° E., including Chichi Jima, Truk, Yap and Jaluit. The 14th Air Force in China and the new 20th Air Force also operating from airfields in China, for whose heavy bombardment aircraft great runways were being formed in Saipan, Tinian and Guam, operated over Formosa and the China Sea. Between them, all these air forces, together with those of the Third Fleet, searched the entire Pacific Ocean west of approximately Longitude 150° E. to the coast of China and from the Netherlands East Indies to the home islands of Japan.

The command organisation in the attack on the Philippines was as follows :—

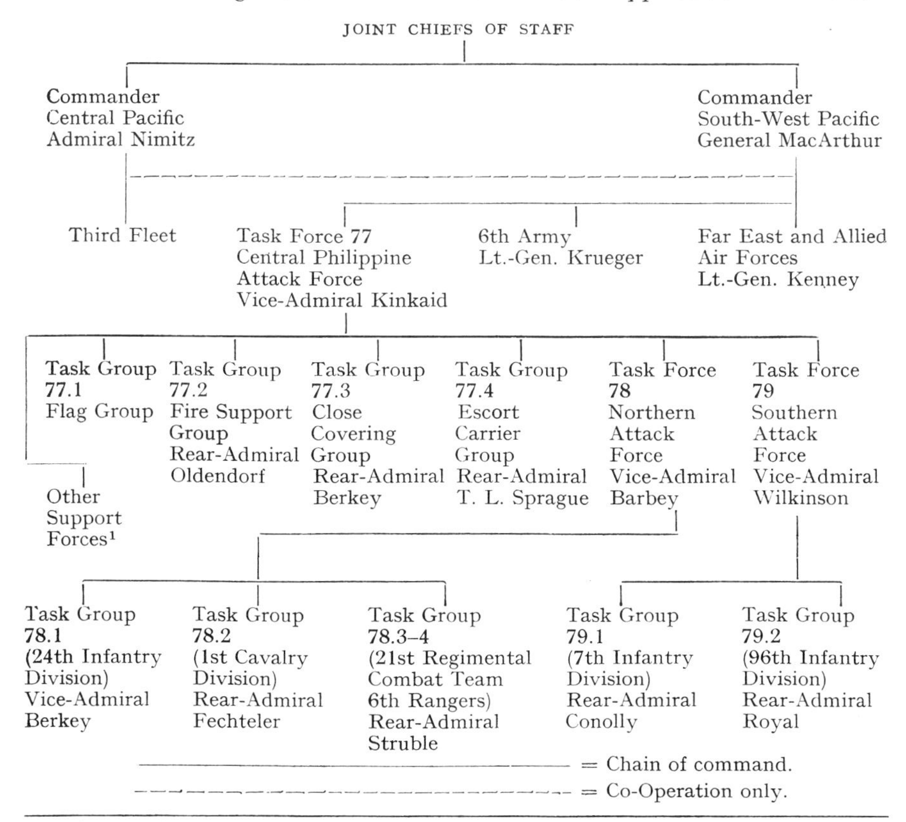

[1] Minesweeping and Hydrographic Group (77.5); Beach Demolition Group (77.6), Service Group (77.7).

The system of command of the forces engaged, as set out above, showed the same anomalous division of naval control as had been employed in the previous month at Morotai, where owing to the inactivity of the enemy it had not been tested. It provided for unified command only at the point of contact with the enemy on shore. The Theatre Commander General MacArthur had no control over the Third Fleet on which he relied for the protection of his transports against the Japanese Fleet.

Since the Leyte landings were to be made on two beaches separated by a distance of ten miles, two attack forces, Northern and Southern, were formed, composed respectively of the VII Amphibious Force (the amphibious force of the Seventh Fleet) and the III Amphibious Force (that which formed part of the Third Fleet). The naval commander of each of these attack forces retained command of his combined naval and ground forces until the commanding general of the troops had landed and was ready to take command, after which the Assault Task Force Commander had no further responsibility or authority over the troops ashore. In the assault on the Philippines, the Commanding Generals of the 1st Cavalry and 24th Infantry Division (Northern Attack Force) assumed command ashore at 1430 on A-Day, the Commanding General of the XXIV Corps (7th and 96th Infantry Divisions—Southern Attack Force) at 1200 on A+3-Day. The Commanding-General of the 6th Army assumed command of all army forces in the Leyte areas at 1400 on A+4-Day.

In view of the importance of air support to an amphibious assault, and the need to co-ordinate it closely with naval gunfire, artillery, and troop movement, Admiral Halsey employed in support of the operation the entire strength of the Third Fleet—four fast carrier groups with their covering and screening ships.[1]

Other Central Pacific forces in addition to the Fast Carrier Force and the 7th Air Force remained under Admiral Nimitz's command and were detailed to cover and support the invasion. The principal of these were the submarines, 26 of which Vice-Admiral C. A. Lockwood concentrated in the area between Japan and the Philippines. Rear-Admiral R. W. Christie, Commander Submarines South-West Pacific also stationed 14 at strategic points. The *Darter, Dace, Rock* and *Bergall* were in the Palawan Passage area, the *Blackfin* west of northern Palawan, the *Gurnard* off the oil port and Japanese fleet anchorage Brunei Bay, the *Cobia* at the north end of Makasar Strait, the *Batfish* in the Sulu Sea covering the inner end of Surigao Strait, the *Guitarro* and *Angler* were off Manila, and the *Bream, Cero, Nautilus* and *Cod* were strung out along the north-west coast of Luzon. Between them, these submarines sank three heavy cruisers during the sortie of the Japanese Fleet to repulse the American landing in the Philippines; and if the failure of the enemy fleet to accomplish its mission was due in some measure to loss of confidence on the part of the Japanese Commander-in-Chief, these sinkings no doubt contributed to the result.

5

The forces taking part in the operation assembled at various bases. The Northern Attack Force (Vice-Admiral Barbey) assembled at Hollandia and Manus. The Southern Attack Force (Vice-Admiral Wilkinson), originally detailed to capture Yap, sailed from Hawaii and was diverted to Manus whilst on passage. The Sixth Army Reserve assembled at Hollandia, Morotai and Guam. From these bases the forces sailed on 13th and 14th October.

[1] For organisation of Third Fleet *see* Appendix G.

The landing on Dinagat Island was made on A—3-Day (17th October) as planned, against light opposition, but bad weather necessitated postponing the landing on Homonhon Island until next day ; one small minesweeper was swamped, one destroyer escort dismasted, and some of the landing parties' boats broached-to. The raiding party landed on Suluan Island on the 17th, but could not be withdrawn that day, as planned, as its landing craft were damaged by the weather ; and it withdrew on the 18th. Casualties were insignificant.

It was known that a considerable number of minefields existed in Philippine waters and an extensive programme of sweeping was accordingly arranged. The minesweeping group sailed early with the bombardment and fire support group and the Dinagat–Homonhon attack force. Minesweeping was to have begun on A—3-Day under cover of naval and air bombardment, but it was considerably hampered until the weather improved next day.

The choice of A-Day for the main landings on 20th October was affected by the state of the moon and tide. Sunrise was at 0630 that day, but the late time of 1000 was fixed for the landing (H-hour), partly in order to allow the bombarding forces to carry out adequate preparation, but principally because of the strength of the current in the channel between Dinagat and Homonhon Islands. Here a tidal current flowing 270° and 090° respectively during the flood and ebb, runs as fast as six knots at spring tide, whilst eddies and whirlpools are not uncommon. With a large body of ships whose maximum station keeping speed was 8–8½ knots it was desirable to pass through at the most favourable time. High water was at 0942 on the 20th. The moon was three days old.

There was evidence that a landing on Leyte had not been expected so soon, and the island had few defences. South of Tacloban were four heavy, probably dual-purpose, anti-aircraft guns. For the rest, the Japanese depended on machine guns and light artillery such as 75-mm. field guns on the shore, as well as the general use of mortars covering the sea approaches and the beaches. The number of all these was inadequate. The underwater demolition teams found that there were no underwater obstacles. There were about 19,000 troops in Leyte at the time of the landing. This was opposed by part of the 16th Division, but there was no great enemy strength in the area selected for the landings. The ships' bombardment, which began three days before the assault, did much to minimize the amount of opposition experienced at the water's edge.

The two Attack Forces entered Leyte Gulf during the night of the 19th/20th. Landing ships, tank, in which the assault troops were embarked, proceeded to their lowering positions. These positions were so far—more than four miles—from the line of departure of the landing craft that several boat groups went off their route and reported in error to the wrong line of departure for their landing beach. For three hours before H-hour the beaches were subjected to very heavy naval and air bombardment. The *Shropshire* fired more than 1,200 rounds from her main 8-inch battery during these three hours.

Aircraft of the Escort Carrier Group (77.4) had been on station since 0630, bombing high priority targets pending such time as direct support of the landings was called for. Between 0800 and 0915 the target area was cleared for the attacks by the fast carrier aircraft. After this time, until the hour of landing, the beaches were under high angle naval gunfire and rocket barrage, air support being withheld.

The hour of landing the 21st Regimental Combat Team on Green beach was advanced to 0900[1] and the bombardment cancelled in order to avoid casualties

---

[1] This is the time given in Communication P.—008.

amongst the friendly inhabitants, who flocked to the beach on the appearance of the Allied ships. The elaborate defences were not manned and there was no opposition to the landing.[1]

There was no off-shore reef at Leyte Island. The Northern Attack Force assaulted in Landing Craft, Vehicle and Personnel (L.C.V.P.). When the attack on Yap by Admiral Wilkinson's force (the Southern Attack Force) was cancelled and the force was diverted to Manus, new orders were issued but the loading of the ships was not altered, and the troops assaulted in the Landing Vehicles, Tracked (LVTs or amtracks) with which the force had been equipped to cross the coral reefs of Yap. The presence of these amtracks was fortunate, for the southern beaches were backed by a marshy strip which could not be crossed even by DUKWs (amphibious trucks) but could be negotiated by LVTs. The Japanese fixed defences were constructed largely of logs, earth and sand. Little barbed wire was used and no concrete.

The main landings were begun on time. There was no opposition at White Beach, but at Red Beach enemy artillery and mortar fire sank one L.C.V.P. and damaged three landing ships. Enemy fire continued on the beach and interfered with the unloading of LSTs and the landing of artillery. Unloading of LSTs was also delayed by the water gap being greater than the report of the Underwater Demolition Teams had given reason to suspect ; and as the Northern Attack Force had no pontoon causeways, these and LCTs were transferred from the Southern Attack Force whose beaches were sufficiently steep—to allow for LSTs to beach and unload direct.

In the south, the landings of the XXIV Corps near Dulag on Orange/Blue and Violet/Yellow beaches were made against light opposition. A little mortar and light artillery fire was directed against boats and several LCIs were slightly damaged. It was considered that the general lack of opposition in the beach area was partly due to the effects of naval and air bombardments and rocket fire. Moreover, not being compelled to stand and fight as on the tiny islands of Micronesia, the enemy withdrew to the localities further inland where natural defences such as cliffs and caves existed.

The Japanese made sporadic air attacks on the ships throughout A-day, but the covering fighters prevented serious attacks, shooting down a number of enemy aircraft. Land masses blocked out radar coverage almost completely and in consequence visual sightings were passed to the protective fighters by the fighter director nets. Several enemy aircraft which eluded the fighters, were shot down by the ships' anti-aircraft fire. No night fighter protection was available, and with more than a hundred Japanese airfields within easy flying range a decision had to be taken whether the ships should get under way and take evasive action both to avoid discovery and to be free to manœuvre if attacked, or whether they should remain at anchor with smoke protection. The latter course was chosen because of the difficulty of manœuvring a large force in the limited water of Leyte Gulf and the possibility of mines in the unswept part of the area in which the ships would have to manœuvre when taking evasive action. An inner screen of LCI gunboats was stationed near the shore to prevent attack by enemy M.T.B.s, and an outer screen of destroyers was thrown around the entire Transport Lowering position for A.A. gunfire. General MacArthur, who had proceeded from Hollandia in the cruiser *Nashville*, landed on Leyte on the afternoon of A-day.

---

[1] The native inhabitants seem to have disposed of the Japanese in the neighbourhood.

4. The beach at Leyte Island : unloading supplies.

[*Facing page 74*

5. Sinking of the U.S.S. *Gambier Bay* at the Battle off Samar.

Despite minor counter-attacks and some interference from snipers the troops advanced steadily. Unloading of cargo continued all night at a reduced rate, the Navy being responsible for all work up to the water's edge and a divisional shore party inland.

At the Northern beaches the arrival early on A+2-day of the first reinforcement groups of transports, LST, LCI and Liberty ships, added to some misjudgment at the beaches, resulting in White Beach becoming a solid mass of oil drums and stores of all natures. In the south, the stretch of marshy land backing the beaches necessitated the building of roads across it, resulting in delay in unloading and sailing ships.

CHAPTER VII

The Battle for Leyte Gulf[1]

(Plans 16, 17)

1

SINCE the Battle of the Marianas in June 1944 the Japanese fleet organisation for battle had undergone various changes all directed towards strengthening the fleet for action against the U.S. Fleet in the Pacific. In order to form the most powerful possible striking force for the fleet action on which their eyes were fixed the Japanese had drawn almost every operational ship capable of lying in the line into the Mobile Force, as the striking force was termed. The Japanese had never adopted in full the organisation of their fleet in the model common to the Americans and ourselves, in groups of three to five carriers, each group being a self-contained unit with the carriers supported by battleships and cruisers and screened by destroyers. At the recent Battle of the Marianas the enemy had gone so far as to take the important step of placing all the forces engaged under the command of the Commander of the aircraft carriers ; but the main battleship and cruiser strength was still formed in one group separate from the two main carrier groups which were thus deprived of the powerful anti-aircraft protection which the battleships could have afforded them.[2] Owing to the unreadiness of the air groups of the carriers the main battleship and cruiser strength of the Fleet was, after the Battle of the Marianas, removed from the control of Vice-Admiral T. Ozawa who had commanded the Fleet in the battle. Termed the First Diversion Attack Force, the seven battleships, 11 heavy cruisers and two light cruisers, screened by a destroyer flotilla, were to operate separately under Vice-Admiral T. Kurita,

[1] A detailed description of this battle is contained in Naval Staff History Battle Summary No. 40, *Battle for Leyte Gulf 23rd–26th October 1944*, C.B. 3081 (30). This Battle Summary was, however, published before Admiral Halsey's autobiography *Admiral Halsey's Story*, became available. Halsey throws light on the much debated subject of his actions during the battle ; whilst the substance of certain signals regarding the role of the Third Fleet, which passed between MacArthur and Halsey, is given in *The Army Air Forces in World War II*, Vol. V, which publication also was not available when Battle Summary No. 40 was written.

[2] The operational organisation of the Japanese Fleet is shown in Appendix A (1) and the administration organisation in Appendix A (2).

at least until the carrier air groups should have been reconstituted. Until then, the shore-based air flotillas were to take their place, thus severely limiting the area in which the striking force could give battle. The carriers were termed the Main Body or ' A ' Force, legacy of their former importance as the main striking force. They remained under Ozawa's command and comprised the fleet carrier *Zuikaku* and the three light carriers *Chitose, Chiyoda* and *Zuiho*, with one heavy cruiser and a destroyer flotilla. Two further carriers, the *Junyo* and *Ryuho* formed a separate unit termed ' B ' Force, which however never operated with the Mobile Force after the Battle of the Marianas. Since the recovery of the Aleutians by the Americans in August 1943 the Fifth (Northern) Japanese Fleet under Vice-Admiral K. Shima had no longer any important function to fulfil. Accordingly, it was to operate in the Striking Force. With the addition of the two battleship carriers *Ise* and *Hyuga* it formed a fourth group in the Mobile Force termed the Second Diversion Attack Force. In the event of the Fleet becoming involved in an air battle it was intended that this group should operate with the carriers under Admiral Ozawa. Behind the Mobile Force there stood almost nothing except the two newly commissioned aircraft carriers *Unryu* and *Amagi* which were not yet worked up. Every possible ship had been gathered into the Mobile Force. The First (Battle) Fleet had been disbanded on 25th February 1944 and its ships included in the Second (Scouting) and Third (Blockade and Transport) Fleets: these fleets had changed their identity and were become respectively the Battle and Air Fleets. The Fourth (Mandates) Fleet, no longer contained any tactical units; only a few base forces lingered on shore, starving, among the by-passed islands of Micronesia, visited at rare intervals by a clandestine submarine. The Fifth Fleet had been brought in as we have seem. The Sixth, was the Submarine Fleet: on 15th September 1944 it comprised 42 submarines. A considerable number of the boats were now reduced to transporting to designated points of attack the piloted torpedoes known as *Kaitens*, or carrying supplies to bypassed bases. The Seventh (Escort) Fleet had as yet no existence: it was formed in April 1945. Such ships of the Eighth (South-West Area) Fleet as survived the fighting in the Solomons, Bismarcks and New Guinea were now included in the Mobile Fleet. The Ninth Fleet, which had never consisted of more than a very few anti-submarine vessels, had ceased to exist. As for the foreign stations, the Area Fleets, so called in the U.S. terminology, were mainly organisations which administered base, A/S and escort forces, and are more properly termed Commands. The only one of them which included any tactical forces was the South-West Area Command under Vice-Admiral S. Kawase[1] with headquarters in the Philippines but shortly to move to Singapore. This Command disposed of the 16th Cruiser Squadron consisting of one heavy cruiser (the *Aoba*), two light cruisers (the *Kitagami* and *Kinu*), and a destroyer division. These were included in the Striking Force, on paper, but actually never operated with it. The North-East Area Command in the Kuriles disposed of nothing heavier than escort vessels, since the removal of the Fifth Fleet which had been its striking force. The Central Pacific Area Command was dissolved on 18th July 1944 its base, Truk, having been lost and the Marianas being plainly doomed. The light craft, minor war vessels and landing craft which composed the China Area Fleet were still active, for the Japanese were securing the few possible landing places on the China coast not already in their possession. On 27th September they made a surprise landing near Foochow, and occupied the town a week later, thus temporarily bringing all the coast under at least loose control.

[1] Appointed August 1944.

2

On receiving news of the preliminary landings in the Philippines, Admiral Toyoda, Commander-in-Chief of the Combined Fleet, lost no time in alerting the Mobile Fleet for the 'Sho' Operation.[1] The order went out at 0928 on 17th October, a few minutes after U.S. troops landed on the islets at the mouth of Leyte Gulf to secure the entrance. The First Diversion Attack Force (I–YB) under Vice-Admiral T. Kurita, containing the main battleship and cruiser strength of the Combined Fleet, was ordered to advance from its anchorage in the Singapore area to Brunei Bay in North-West Borneo. On the 18th the Allied bombardment ships were reported entering Leyte Gulf and U.S. voice radio messages regarding the point of landing were intercepted.[2] Operation 'Sho' was accordingly activated at 1732.

At this juncture, it was not possible to adhere to the organisation of the Striking Force which had been planned for air action. None of Vice-Admiral J. Ozawa's three predominately carrier forces, namely 'A' Force (the main carrier force), 'B' Force (the carriers *Junyo* and *Ryuho*), and the Second Diversion Attack Force (the two battleship carriers with heavy cruisers in support) was in a position to fight an air battle. No more than 118 trained pilots in all could be found to man the air groups of the four carriers of 'A' Force,[3] whilst the aircraft of the two carriers in 'B' Force and of the two battleship carriers in the Second Diversion attack force had all been landed in Formosa and the Philippines and were operating from land bases. Consequently the following arrangements were made: 'A' Force was converted into a decoy force to draw the U.S. fleet away from Leyte and permit the heavy ships of Admiral Kurita's First Diversion Attack Force to penetrate into the Gulf and break up the landing; 'B' Force did not sail; the battleship carriers of the Second Diversion Attack Force, without aircraft on board joined 'A' Force to augment the anti-aircraft defence, whilst the cruisers and destroyers of Vice-Admiral K. Shima's Fifth Fleet operated, not with the Second Diversion attack Force of which they formed part[4] but in support of a detachment from Kurita's surface fleet, known as 'C' Force, which was formed by taking the two old battleships *Fuso* and *Yamashiro*, the heavy cruiser *Mogami*, and four destroyers out of the First Diversion Attack Force and placing them under the command of Vice-Admiral S. Nishimura. The complicated organisation of the Japanese forces is best clarified by describing the various components according to the area in which they operated, as the Northern (Ozawa's), Centre (Kurita's), and Southern (Nishimura's and Shima's) Force respectively.[5]

There was now no longer any question of the Japanese fighting a decisive fleet action. In its existing state the Striking Force, even when operating within range of the land-based air forces, could not expect successfully to engage the huge and highly trained weapon under Halsey's hand. All it was now hoped to do was to get the heavy ships of Kurita's First Diversion Attack Force into Leyte Gulf and break up the invasion shipping. To enable Kurita to get through without being attacked by the U.S. fast carriers, evasion would have to

---

[1] The organisation of the Japanese forces is given in Appendix H.

[2] USSBS analysis of the Philippines campaign printed in ONI Review, Vol. I, No. 13, November 1946.

[3] The aircraft complement of the force was 52 fighters, 28 fighter bombers, 25 torpedo bombers, seven bombers, four attack aircraft, total 116 plus two float reconnaissance aircraft aboard the *Oyodo*.

[4] *See* Appendix A (1).

[5] *See* Appendix H.

be resorted to ; and it was the duty of Ozawa's Northern Force to decoy Halsey's carriers away to the northward, since in the state of depletion of its air groups it was far too weak to act offensively. The Southern Force, composed of Nishimura's ' C ' Force and Shima's Second Diversion Attack Force (shorn of its battleship carriers), was to attack the invasion shipping from the South, via Surigao Strait, whilst Kurita with the bulk of the battleships and heavy cruisers came in from the Pacific. The operation was incompletely planned and the arrangements were equivocal. Air cover for the Centre Force, the first essential for ships operating within flying range of the American fast carriers, was neglected. It is true that the land-based aircraft had been much reduced through the Allied preliminary air operations ; but Vice-Admiral Fukudome, commander of the naval air force in the Philippine Islands, who alone was in a position to furnish the necessary air cover, was given no details of the plans of Kurita's force : he received only general instructions to employ his aircraft to repulse any attempt at landing by the enemy.[1] Nishimura and Shima, whose ships constituted the Southern Force, though their function was identical and it was intended that they should act in concert, were given no instructions for joint action. Neither Admiral was made subordinate to the other.[2] They were not even under the same supreme command, for Nishimura's ' C ' Force was part of the Combined Fleet, whereas Shima with the Second Diversion Attack Force when the operation began was placed under the command of Vice-Admiral Okochi, Commander-in-Chief, South-West Area. The two forces came from widely separated regions, Shima from the Ryukus and Nishimura from Singapore, and their commanders had no communication with one another either before or during the operation. Kurita himself could obtain no information of the position of any American forces standing between him and Leyte Gulf. The Japanese Command had no great expectation that the plan would succeed, and no plan to exploit any success. Admiral Toyoda reasoned that if the Philippines were lost the shipping lane to the Southern Resources Area would be completely cut. Consequently there was no sense in saving the fleet at the expense of the Philippines. Ozawa was prepared to lose his fleet in playing his part ; and Admiral Toyoda couched his orders to Kurita in such terms as implied that the Centre Force was to carry out its mission, even if this should entail the loss of every ship.[3]

3

The Japanese High Command had hoped to carry out the attack on the Allied amphibious forces on 22nd October ; but the loading of the few aircraft on board the four carriers of the Northern Force and the provision of fuel for the Second Diversion Attack Force which had retired to Amami O Shima, the most northerly of the Ryuku Islands, after its abortive sortie at the time of the Battle of Formosa, caused a series of delays. Finally, 25th October was designated as the date of attack.

The First Diversion Attack Force coming up from Singapore reached Brunei on 20th October. Here, Kurita detached the ships which were to form ' C ' Force. The two fleets sailed again on the 22nd. Nishimura proceeded eastward through the Sulu Sea.[4] Kurita with the Centre Force headed north-east along the west

[1] Interrogation of Vice-Admiral Fukudome, Nav. No. 115.

[2] Shima was the senior of the two Admirals.

[3] Interrogation of Admiral Toyoda, Nav. No. 75.

[4] *See* Plan 16.

coast of Palawan before turning eastward through the central Philippines to San Bernardino Strait where he intended to turn to the South for Leyte Gulf. His force comprised the five modern battleships, ten heavy cruisers, and two flotillas of destroyers. Shima with the Second Diversion Attack Force, leaving Bako in the Pescadores (*see* Plan 16) on the 21st whither he had proceeded from Amami O Shima, fuelled his destroyers at the Japanese anchorage in Koron Bay in the Calamian Islands. No tanker had arrived there, and the cruisers had consequently to supply fuel to the destroyers ; and when the force sailed on the 24th and came south to follow and support Nishimura, the ships were short of fuel. The Northern Force with Admiral Ozawa's carriers sailed from the Inland Sea on the afternoon of the 20th and shaped course for Luzon. With Ozawa came the carrier *Zuikaku* and light carriers *Chitose, Chiyoda* and *Zuiho*, with few aircraft on board, the battleship carriers *Ise* and *Hyuga*, three light cruisers and a flotilla of destroyers. ' I had not much confidence in being a lure ' said Ozawa. ' But there was no other way than to try '.[1] As we shall see, he was successful beyond his hopes, but the plan was ruined by circumstances beyond his control.

The available Japanese submarines in the Formosa area were ordered to proceed off Leyte. Seven were disposed in the sector between the north-east and south-east of that island, and three off Lamon Bay on the east side of Mindanao, dispositions which were in accord with General Yamshita's estimate of the probable Allied landing points. None of the submarines were able to reach their patrol positions before the 25th. The Second Air Fleet was ordered to move to the Philippines. From the neighbouring islands, Mindanao, Cebu and Panay, reinforcements of troops converged on Leyte ; and the first convoy of reinforcements from Luzon began to load at Manila. One tanker was sent to Koron Bay and two into the Sulu Sea. Nothing definite could be gathered from such of these movements as were sighted by the Allied reconnaissance aircraft.

Early on the morning of the 23rd reports came in from the U.S. submarines *Darter* and *Dace*, forming a co-ordinated attack group, of enemy battleships and cruisers proceeding up the Palawan Passage, the narrow channel between Palawan Island and the unsurveyed Dangerous Ground to the westward. These enemy ships were part of the Centre Force. Both submarines attacked within a few minutes of one another, the *Darter* sinking the heavy cruiser *Atago*, Admiral Kurita's flagship, and severely damaging the *Takao*, whilst the *Dace* sank the *Maya*. The *Darter*, manœuvring into position during the night for a further attack, went aground and could not get off. The *Dace* took off the crew, but every attempt to destroy the ship failed. The Japanese later boarded the abandoned vessel, but found nothing of value. The *Takao* eventually reached Singapore, where on 31st July 1945 she was attacked and further slightly damaged by the midget submarine *XE* 3 (Lieutenant I. E. Fraser, R.N.R.) towed by the submarine *Stygian* (Operation ' Struggle ').[2] An attempt by *XE* 1 (Lieutenant J. E. Smart, R.N.V.R.) towed by the *Spark* to attack the *Myoko* at the same time, was unsuccessful.

Almost simultaneously with the reports of the *Darter* and *Dace*, the submarine *Bream* reported a cruiser and destroyer force to the westward of Luzon, steering a course for the Verde Island Passage, the northern entrance to the Sibuyan Sea. This was Admiral Shima's Second Diversion Attack Force making for

[1] Interrogation of Vice-Admiral Ozawa, Nav. No. 55.

[2] *See* H. & A. 1277/45 and interrogation of Lieut.-Commander Utsunomiya, Japanese Navy Air Force, N.I.D. 01023/46.

Koron, to refuel. The *Bream* attacked one of the cruisers, but failed to cause any damage. Various other sightings were made during the day, from which Admiral Kinkaid formed the opinion that the Japanese intended to attack the ships lying in Leyte Gulf, approaching probably through the southern entrance, Surigao Strait.

4

Admiral Halsey also could make nothing more of the enemy sighting reports than that the Japanese were preparing to make a major effort. Vice-Admiral Mitscher who commanded the Task Force (T.F. 38) consequently sent out air searches from his carriers to discover their intentions.[1] The Third Fleet fuelled on the 22nd and at 1800 Vice-Admiral McCain's Task Group 38.1 which contained five carriers, left for Ulithi to replenish. At daybreak next day the three groups remaining with Admiral Halsey were lined up east of Luzon about 125 miles apart, Task Group 38.3 (Rear-Admiral Sherman) being in the northern position in about 15° N., 123½° E. (Plan 16), Task Group 38.2 (Rear-Admiral Bogan) in the centre, off San Bernardino Strait; and Task Group 38.4 (Rear-Admiral Davison) in the southern position, off Samar Island. The Fleet concluded that its position was known, for during the night single enemy reconnaissance aircraft were almost continuously in the neighbourhood of the northernmost Task Group, though night fighters which were kept in the air, held most of them at a distance. There was no sign of the Japanese fleet, and early on the 24th Vice-Admiral Mitscher sent out search and attack groups covering the western sea approaches to the Philippines which soon discovered the Japanese Centre Force. No search to the north or north-east of Luzon was ordered, consequently Ozawa's Northern Force which was coming down from Japan remained undetected until the late afternoon, though within aircraft range.

Contrary to American belief, the enemy aircraft from Luzon which had been on Admiral Sherman's radar screens throughout the previous night, did not sight his ships until 0700 on the 24th. Admiral Fukudome at once sent off strikes to attack. Most of the aircraft, of which 200 in all were despatched, together with 70 from the still undetected Northern Force, were types which had been landed from carriers to operate from shore bases, and their state of training was far from complete. Admiral Sherman sent up every available fighter to break up the attacks, and manœuvred to keep within shelter of the rain squalls which swept the sea, emerging into the clear only to launch and land on aircraft.

After an hour and a half there was a lull in the fighting. Suddenly a single aircraft, which had mingled with the returning friendly fighters, dived out from a low cloud on to the light carrier *Princeton* and put a small bomb through her flight deck amidships, which was full of torpedo aircraft armed and fuelled ready for strike. Fires spread fast, ammunition in ready service rooms and lockers began to explode. The *Princeton* lost all way, took a position across the wind, drifting to leeward. The light cruiser *Birmingham* and destroyers attempted to pour water on her fires. Owing to the different rates of drift, it was difficult to keep a ship alongside the *Princeton* on the windward (port) side without a line to keep the ships together and causing damage through the crashing of the carrier's projecting sponsons in the seaway. Fire hoses were ineffective

[1] The organisation of the Third Fleet is given in Appendix G. The fast carriers had on 5th August been reorganised as First and Second Fast Carrier Task Force. The reorganisation merely meant that the same ships were commanded by a different Admiral. Vice-Admiral M. A. Mitscher commanded the First Fast Carrier Task Force. Vice-Admiral J. S. McCain commanded the Second Fast Carrier Task Force when it began operating.

up-wind, for it was now blowing hard. Captain Inglis of the *Birmingham* who took charge, put his ship alongside the *Princeton's* port side. There were not enough men left aboard the carrier to handle the hoses, so volunteers from the *Birmingham* clambered aboard and led the ship's hoses down into the hangar. Suddenly, the *Princeton*'s after magazines exploded, blowing off her stern and the after part of the flight deck and causing heavy casualties.[1] Aboard the *Birmingham* the carnage was far more terrible. Her upper deck, crowded with men fighting the fire and manning the A.A. guns was raked from stem to stern. In an instant of time over half her ship's company were killed or injured.[2] Nevertheless, within the hour, when the *Princeton* asked the *Birmingham* for a tow the survivors prepared to rig their ship for towing. At 1604, however, threatened with a further explosion, the *Princeton* had to be abandoned and sunk. Her sinking cost the enemy over 100 aircraft shot down around Admiral Sherman's Task Group.

5

It was now late afternoon, and during the whole day aircraft from the carriers of Task Force 38 had been engaged in attacking the Centre Force as it threaded the islands on the way towards San Bernardino Strait (Plan 16). At 0810 on the 24th Admiral Kurita was in Tablas Strait, steering 015° at 18 knots when search aircraft from Rear-Admiral Bogan's Task Group (38.2) discovered him. This group and Rear-Admiral Davison's group (38.4) sent off strikes against him, whilst Rear-Admiral Sherman (Task Group 38.3) stood by the *Princeton*. Vice-Admiral McCain was ordered to reverse course and bring his group (Task Group 38.1) to a position from which he could launch a search to the north and north-west at dawn next day.

All day long aircraft from the two task groups battered the Japanese Centre Force as it crossed the Sibuyan Sea. The enemy put up no aerial opposition but anti-aircraft fire was intense, and the losses of U.S. aircraft caused were eight fighters, 20 bombers and 15 torpedo aircraft.

Admiral Halsey considered it important to slow down the enemy battleships and damage their fire control gear, and accordingly his aircraft directed their attacks against the battleships which were in the centre of a circular formation. The great new battleship *Musashi* was sunk. The heavy cruiser *Myoko* was damaged and returned to Singapore unescorted ; the battleship *Yamato* was hit by several bombs, and the light cruiser *Yahagi* and the destroyer *Kiyoshimo* also received minor damage.[3]

The Centre Force sustained these day-long attacks almost entirely without air cover. The standard protection for a Fleet was ordered for the Centre Force, but no more than a negligible number of aircraft reached Kurita, despite his repeated requests for cover. The weather was bad, the Japanese pilots inexperienced, and the distances from the Luzon airfields long. But the chief reason was that Admiral Fukudome was making his first experience of controlling naval air forces dispersed over various airfields. He found difficulty in providing support for a moving fleet. He was convinced that the best protection he could give Kurita was to concentrate his entire air force in attacking the American fast carriers, instead of weakening the fighter escorts of his strike groups by sending

---

[1] Total losses : Killed 7, missing 101, wounded about 190.

[2] Losses were : Killed 229, missing 4, wounded 416, half of them seriously.

[3] Japanese signals. None of the damage, except the sinking of the *Musashi*, is shown in the Japanese Report.

fighter cover to the Centre Force. The Army Air Forces gave no help, mainly because liaison with the Navy was not good, also the crews could not navigate over water.

At one time, about 1600, Kurita reversed course and retired temporarily to the westward, until the hoped for air cover should have reached him. The fact that he was sighted and reported during the short time he was on this westerly course, turned out to be important. Later, on Toyoda's orders, he resumed his course for San Bernardino Strait. Sunset was at 1805. The night carrier *Independence* shadowed the Centre Force until midnight when it began the transit of the Strait. This information failed to get through to Halsey for the shadowing aircraft were on the same frequency as the powerful Japanese nearby land wireless stations and their signals were jammed. However, sufficient enemy reports were received before midnight to make it clear that the Centre Force was continuing to steer for San Bernardino Strait.

6

Admiral Halsey's aircraft had discovered Admiral Nishimura's 'C' Force (part of the Southern Force) early that morning (24th), but the Commander-in-Chief, Third Fleet assumed that the Seventh Fleet could take care of this small detachment of two battleships, one heavy cruiser and four destroyers. At 0905 a reinforced search group from the *Enterprise* of Rear-Admiral Davison's group had discovered and attacked Nishimura's force in the Sulu Sea in 8° 55′ N., 121° 50′ E., south-west of Negros Island. The attackers thought they had done a deal of damage, but in point of fact, all they did was to cause minor damage to the battleship *Fuso* and the destroyer *Shigure*. Nishimura was reported again at 1240, close south-west of Negros Island, on a south-easterly course, after which he disappeared from sight for nearly 12 hours. Evaluation of reports up to 1240 was rendered difficult by the frequent omission of essential details, such as the enemy's course and speed. There were many failures to recognise correctly the class and even the type of ship sighted. However, Admiral Kinkaid was not long in making up his mind that the enemy intended a night surface attack on the Expeditionary Force shipping for whose safety he was responsible, and he sent orders to Rear-Admiral J. B. Oldendorf, who with his flag in the heavy cruiser *Louisville* commanded the Fire Support and Bombardment Group (Task Group 77.2), to make all preparations for defence. He reinforced Admiral Oldendorf with the Close Covering Group (Task Group 77.3) under Rear-Admiral R. S. Berkey, consisting of two U.S. light cruisers and five destroyers, together with H.M.A.S. *Shropshire* and *Arunta*. The *Australia* and *Warramunga* had originally formed part of this force but the *Australia* had been withdrawn on the 21st after having been hit and damaged by a suicide bomber; she was escorted back to Manus by the *Warramunga* (*see* page 97). Admiral Oldendorf disposed his force[1] on a line across the north part of Surigao Strait, on the parallel of 10° 35′ N., between longitudes 125° 16′ E. and 125° 27′ E., with M.T.B.s in the south approach to the Strait. He was handicapped by shortage of ammunition, since 70 to 80 per cent of his ships' outfits consisted of bombardment ammunition. For their main armaments in the event of action with the Japanese fleet the battleships engaged on bombardment duty carried no more than 20 to 30 rounds per gun of armour-piercing shell, of which they had already expended a proportion in bombardments. As regards 6-inch armour piercing projectiles there was not in the

[1] The composition of the force is shown in Appendix F.

entire force sufficient even for 15 minutes' firing by a single light cruiser. Admiral Oldendorf's intention was consequently to close rapidly and fight the action at moderate range. His freedom of action was hampered by the possibility that he might have to defend Leyte Gulf against an attack from seaward as well as holding Surigao Strait singlehanded, because at 1723 Admiral Halsey signalled that he intended to take the Third Fleet north-eastward during the night.

'C' Force was ahead of schedule, for Nishimura had advanced the time of his attack, informing Kurita too late for the latter to order him to adhere to the original plan of attacking about an hour before daylight. American M.T.B.s in the south approach to Surigao Strait attacked him at the entrance. Their action probably threw the Japanese off balance. He was attacked again at 0300 in the narrowest part of Surigao Strait, by destroyers of the Special Attack Group (Appendix F) whose primary duty was as an anti-submarine screen. Their attack had the effect of causing the enemy to separate into two groups through the heavy ships dropping astern, apparently as the result of torpedo hits. Twenty minutes later, the *Arunta* led a torpedo attack by the destroyers of the Right Flank Force. According to statements of Japanese prisoners-of-war this attack would seem to have been the most damaging of all. About a quarter of an hour after its conclusion, soon after 0400, Nishimura was attacked by the destroyers of the Left Flank Force in which the Japanese caused the only damage suffered by Kinkaid's force in the night action, the destroyer *Albert W. Grant* being disabled. The results of these attacks by Allied destroyers were disastrous for the enemy. The *Yamashiro* broke in two as the result of an explosion in a magazine and sank. The destroyers *Michisio* and *Yamagumo* were sunk; whilst the *Assagumo* retired, being pursued and sunk in the afternoon by cruisers and destroyers.

The surviving enemy ships then came under fire successively from the cruisers of the Left and Right Forces and the battleships. The Allied ships used full radar control, including the *Shropshire,* whose type of radar was not designed for main armament fire control. The Japanese radar was useless: it was unsuitable for fire control and ineffective for search in this engagement, close under the land. The Americans were using flashless propellant, and the enemy could do no more than fire a few rounds at the *Shropshire's* gun flashes. Under the drenching Allied fire the *Fuso* sank unseen by any human eye. The heavy cruiser *Mogami* turned away badly damaged by gunfire, and as she lurched down the strait, barely maintaining steerage way, the heavy cruiser *Nachi* of Vice-Admiral Shima's force coming up the Strait collided with her causing considerable further damage. She crept on, and got as far as Camiguin Island where at 0900 she was sunk by carrier-based air attack. Of the ships of 'C' Force only the destroyer *Shigure* escaped.

Admiral Shima with the Second Diversion Attack Force was about 30 miles astern of Nishimura when the latter entered the Strait. On his way up the Strait the light cruiser *Abukuma* was torpedoed by one of the American M.T.B.s and dropped astern with her speed reduced to ten knots. Visibility was poor, the night very dark, the flagship's radar was not working effectively for search, and the Admiral did not know what lay behind the dense smoke ahead of him. At 0420 the *Nachi's* radar picked up a group of ships; Shima swung to starboard and fired torpedoes. The collision with the *Mogami* occurred as the *Nachi* turned away after delivering her attack. All ships of Shima's force then retired. U.S. army aircraft from New Guinea sank the damaged *Abukuma* on the 26th; the remaining ships escaped.

There was no rest for Admiral Oldendorf's Task Group. Whilst his cruisers and destroyers were still deep down the Gulf pursuing the remnants of the enemy Admiral Kinkaid directed him to send immediate help to Rear-Admiral C. A. F. Sprague who had just reported that his escort carrier Task Unit 77.4.3 was in action with the Japanese Battle Fleet east of Samar ; and Oldendorf, with his ships exceedingly short of ammunition and fuel, prepared to do battle with Kurita's fleet to defend the amphibious shipping.

At that moment, a further large defenceless collection of miscellaneous craft was arriving from Hollandia. Consisting of tugs, barges, dredgers, small floating docks and small tankers it had left Hollandia 16 days earlier, accomplishing the passage to Leyte at four knots. Its entrance was more than dramatic to such officers as were aware of the seriousness of the general situation. The Operation Plan had provided for oilers and ammunition ships to be available at Leyte Gulf on 23rd October for resupply of the Fire Support Group, but the ships of the Group had taken up their positions to defend Leyte Gulf on the previous day, and there had consequently been no opportunity of replenishment. They were dangerously short of ammunition and many were short of fuel. A number of the destroyers had expended all their torpedoes in the night engagement, and there were no replacements available in the Gulf. Ashore, there were 150,000 men to be fed and supplied by the cargo vessels which for all the protection Kinkaid could give, were at the mercy of the Japanese battle fleet. The operation stood on the edge of disaster.

7

Despite the loss of the battleship *Musashi* and four heavy cruisers damaged or sunk by submarine and air attacks soon after sailing from Brunei Bay, Admiral Kurita with the Centre Force pursued his way towards Leyte Gulf. His presence in the Sibuyan Sea and probable approach to San Bernardino Strait were known to the Seventh Fleet escort carriers operating under Rear-Admiral T. L. Sprague east of Samar in support of the landings on Leyte. These forces belonged to the Pacific Fleet and had been temporarily transferred to the Seventh Fleet as Task Group 77.4. They consisted of 18 escort carriers organised in three groups of six each with screen of seven or eight destroyers or destroyer escorts (Appendix F). Their primary missions were to provide air support for the troops, protective air patrols for the transports, anti-submarine air patrols, in addition to their own protection from air attack. They carried about 30 aircraft apiece.

On the morning of 25th October, in the northernmost station east of Samar was Task Unit 77.4.3 (Plan 17) under Rear-Admiral C. A. F. Sprague, consisting of the *Fanshaw Bay* (flagship), *St. Lo*, *Kalinin Bay*, *White Plains*, *Kitkun Bay* (Rear-Admiral Ofstie) and *Gambier Bay*, with the destroyers *Hoel*, *Johnston*, *Heerman*, and destroyer escorts *Samuel B. Roberts*, *Dennis*, *Butler* and *Raymond*. Admiral Kinkaid assumed that the northern flank of his escort carrier force could not be exposed without ample warning. He had intercepted a signal made at 1512 on the previous afternoon by Admiral Halsey to the Third Fleet, saying that a force of battleships, cruisers and destroyers was being formed as Task Force 34, presumably to engage the Japanese First Diversion Attack Force. At 2024 Admiral Halsey advised him that the enemy Centre Force was moving in the direction of San Bernardino Strait and that he was taking three groups north to attack the enemy carrier force (Ozawa's Northern Force) which had been discovered. Since Halsey had removed the fast battleships from the carrier groups and organised them as Task Force 34, Admiral Kinkaid assumed that they were guarding the exit from San Bernardino Strait. Unfortunately, this assumption was due to misinterpretations of Admiral Halsey's signal timed 1512. The signal was designated as a Battle Plan and prescribed the composition of the force which ' will be formed as Task Force 34 under Vice-Admiral Lee, commanding the Battle Line.' It did not state when the force was to be formed or where it was to engage. Task Force 34 was not actually formed until 0240 on the 25th, that is, some hours after Halsey advised Kinkaid that he was taking three groups north. During the early hours of the 25th it was borne in upon Admiral Kinkaid that there was no definite assurance in Halsey's signals, that Task Force 34 was remaining behind. Accordingly, at 0312 he sent a signal asking Halsey if he was in fact guarding the San Bernardino Strait. Once again, the Americans' communication system betrayed them. The signal was not received until 0648—more than three-and-a-half hours later ; and when the reply, sent at 0704, was received, it was too late ; the escort carriers were already fighting for their lives against the enemy which had fallen upon them unexpectedly from San Bernardino.

Even so, the escort carriers would have been in a position to give a very good account of themselves in action against Kurita's fleet, had they received warning. Unfortunately, Kinkaid did not receive all the sighting reports of the Third Fleet search groups. Whilst under air attack on the 24th, the Japanese Centre Force had perforce wasted much time in taking avoiding action. Its speed of advance during daylight had been very low, and it was not until the evening that Kurita was able to continue on his course at speed. Halsey duly repeated to Kinkaid a sighting report of 2030 showing the Centre Force between Burias and Masbate Islands[1] but as far as is known, Kinkaid never received a sighting report timed 2145 (received by Halsey at 2320) giving the enemy's position as 12° 45′ N., 123° 22′ E., the furthest eastward yet reported.[2] If that is in fact the case, then the blame for the situation in which the Seventh Fleet escort carriers found themselves at daylight on the 25th would seem to lie at the door, not of any particular individual, but rather of American signalling.

Kurita was six hours late. It had been planned that he should pass through San Bernardino Strait at 1800 on the 24th, but the Third Fleet air attacks delayed him until midnight. On emerging into the Pacific he turned south according to plan. Rear-Admiral C. A. F. Sprague's carriers suddenly received warning of his approach in various ways, all more or less simultaneous, some by intercepting Japanese voice transmissions over the inter-fighter director net ;

[1] Commander-in-Chief Pacific in his report, *Operations in the Pacific Ocean Areas during the Month of October* 1944 (Serial 002397) states that the contact when plotted, showed the enemy to be making good about 24 or 25 knots a radically greater speed than his previous rate of advance, indicating that Kurita was determined to get through San Bernardino Strait. This is assumed to mean that Commander-in-Chief Pacific considered Admiral Kinkaid should have plotted the contact and been prepared for such an eventuality. The contact report stated however that the Centre Force was on various courses and trailing much oil, which does not give the impression of a fleet in a hurry ; and a qualifying signal sent by the same *Independence* night reconnaissance aircraft at 0010, saying that the enemy course could be south-east as well as the north-east previously reported, was apparently not received by Kinkaid. Commander-in-Chief Pacific's estimate of the enemy's speed is surely excessive. The *Nagato* could do no more than 24 knots, the *Haruna* 25, and the damaged *Yamato* 26 ; and these battleships proved themselves next morning unable to gain effectively on the fleeing escort carriers whose maximum speed was 17 to 19 knots.

[2] Commander-in-Chief Pacific, in his report, was unable to say whether Halsey repeated the signal to Kinkaid or not. Halsey's report is not forthcoming though certain extracts from it are contained in *Secret Information Bulletin No. 22—Battle Experience—Battle for Leyte Gulf, 23rd–27th October* 1944 (U.S. Fleet, Headquarters of the Commander-in-Chief, 1st March, 1945).

others by radar ; others again from hearing and seeing the anti-aircraft fire of Kurita's ships against the Leyte anti-submarine patrol which Admiral C. A. F. Sprague had launched an hour earlier. This patrol reported large groups of ships about 15 to 30 miles from the carriers : from the *Fanshaw Bay*, flagship of the northern carrier group (77.4.3) the radar range was 18½ miles.

At the time, this carrier group was in approximately 11° 50′ N., 126° 10′ E., about 40 miles east of Samar, on a northerly course, with the carriers in circular formation. Admiral C. A. F. Sprague at once ordered all available aircraft to be launched, increased to full speed and turned to a course of 90° which was sufficiently close to the light north-easterly wind to permit launching aircraft, whilst taking his ships away from the enemy who were now almost within gun range. The contact report which he broadcast at 0705 was the first intimation received by Commander Seventh Fleet that the Centre Force had passed through San Bernardino Strait. Admiral Kinkaid at once ordered all his surface forces to concentrate at the eastern entrance to Leyte Gulf preparatory to proceeding to the assistance of the escort carriers and all aircraft on troop support missions were recalled and despatched to attack the enemy fleet. The remaining two groups of escort carriers moved north in support : some delay was caused to Rear-Admiral T. L. Sprague's group (Task Unit 77.4.1), because just at that time he came under heavy suicide attack by enemy aircraft followed by submarine attack[1] whilst Rear-Admiral Stump's group (Task Unit 77.4.2), which was about 20 to 25 miles away,[2] did not hear that the northern escort carrier group was under fire until 0814 ; for although one of his aircraft sighted and reported the Japanese fleet at 0643, it took over an hour-and-a-half for the message to reach Stump.

When the masts of the American ships were sighted Kurita altered course from 200° to 110° in order to come up wind of the carriers and prevent them from launching aircraft. All his ships increased to their individual full speeds. They opened fire almost immediately, at ranges varying from 26,250 yards (the *Kongo*) to 35,000 yards (the *Yamato*). The range quickly closed but the U.S. screening vessels laid an effective smoke screen, and in the squalls and heavy rain storms which reduced visibility Kurita could not make out whether he was chasing fast carriers or escort carriers nor what was the strength of the force against him. His reconnaissance aircraft gave him no information. So instead of steering straight for the Americans, none of whose ships mounted a heavier gun than 5-inch, he wasted time in encirclement. The attacks of the American aircraft had the effect of making his ships scatter and lose time in evasive manœuvres.[3] At 0720, in a rain squall, Admiral C. A. F. Sprague seized his chance to turn towards the protection of the battleships at Leyte, and a bold alteration of course from 080° to 170° opened the range somewhat. The Japanese did not for a long while perceive the change, for the smoke, both chemical and funnel, largely obscured the vision of both forces. But the pressure of the Japanese heavy cruisers which by about 0800 had advanced up the port quarter of the U.S. force and were firing broadsides at ranges down to 12,000 yards, forced the American ships gradually off course.

---

[1] *See* page 80.

[2] The Action Report of the *Gambier Bay*, one of the ships of the northern unit, says that Stump's group was only 10 miles south of them at the time but this is surely an under-estimate.

[3] Kurita's report on the battle, excerpts from which are printed in *Campaign of the Pacific War*, Appendix 89 is typical of the bombast and disregard of realities which characterised the Japanese. Of the battle at this juncture he writes : ' All air units, over-coming the desperate defence put up by the enemy's aircraft and screening vessels, pressed on magnificently . . . in the spirit of " a sighted enemy is a dead enemy. . . ." '

At 0740 Admiral C. A. F. Sprague ordered the screen commander to launch a torpedo attack. In the low visibility co-ordinated attacks were not feasible, but six of the seven vessels made gallant individual attacks in which three of the six, the *Hoel*, *Johnston* and *Samuel B. Roberts* were sunk with heavy loss.[1] The attacks gained time for the escort carriers, and so reduced the speed of the heavy cruiser *Kumano* from a torpedo hit, that she abandoned the operation and retired. The Japanese destroyers made one or perhaps two attacks, but their torpedoes were fired at long range and did no harm.

Meanwhile, despite the number of enemy ships firing at them the escort carriers for a long while escaped damage. The Japanese fire was slow and their spotting poor. But at 0911 the *Gambier Bay* was overwhelmed and sunk with the loss of 133 officers and men, an enemy cruiser firing into her to the end at a range of 2,000 yards. The Japanese cruisers were threatening to turn the escort carriers to the northward, towards the enemy battleships. To try to prevent this, the destroyer escort *Raymond*, though she had neither smoke nor torpedoes left, closed an enemy cruiser, drawing the fire of the latter away from the escort carriers to herself, and at length, at a range of 5,700 yards causing the cruiser to turn away. The desperate expedient was also tried of ordering Avengers which had expended their bombs to make dummy torpedo runs on the enemy. But by 0830 Rear-Admiral C. A. F. Sprague's aircraft attacks dwindled. For the most part the machines had completed their attacks and were making emergency landings in a field alongside Tacloban airstrip which resembled a ploughed field rather than an airstrip[2] or on the escort carriers of Rear-Admiral Stump's group (T.U. 77.4.2), to be serviced before taking-off again. At Tacloban, U.S. Army aircraft crews, who knew nothing about naval aircraft, refuelled and bombed them up. Almost every Liberty boat and landing craft in the harbour shot at them coming and going.[3]

At 0814 when Rear-Admiral Stump received news that the Northern Escort Carrier Group was under fire he was steering almost directly away from the battle. He at once turned into the wind and began launching aircraft. His first strike hit Kurita as the enemy ships were passing the sinking *Gambier Bay*. In expectation of shortly being attacked from the air Kurita had just hoisted a signal to his ships to close and assume circular formation. The main weight of Admiral Stump's strikes fell on the Japanese between 0910 and 0930 and so damaged the heavy cruisers *Chikuma* and *Chokai* that they had to be abandoned and sunk.[4] A fourth cruiser was also in trouble, the *Suzuya*. She had left the formation at 0745, to stand by the damaged *Kumano*. Her subsequent movements are unknown, but she was damaged, apparently by air attack, and sank early in the afternoon.

There now occurred something which to Sprague's escort carriers, fighting with little hope of survival, must have seemed like a miracle. At 0925 the Japanese fleet fired torpedoes at long range, turned 16 points to port in succession

---

[1] Casualties :—
Hoel : killed and missing 253, wounded 19.
Johnston : killed and missing 184, wounded 40.
Samuel B. Roberts : killed and missing 89, wounded 50.

[2] Tacloban airstrip had been graded preparatory to laying the steel matting. Seeing that the naval pilots would be unaware of the danger of landing on the soft surface an officer seized a pair of signal flags and waved in more than 40 of the 67 aircraft which made emergency landings on the grass alongside. *Marine Aviation in the Philippines*, p. 23.

[3] *General Kenney Reports*, p. 460.

[4] The destroyer *Nowake* was later sunk by Admiral Halsey's carriers, whilst standing by the *Chikuma*.

and retired to the northward. By 0940 all firing had ceased: the battle was over. Kurita had given up the attempt to overtake the ships he was chasing. He was still uncertain of their type, for incredible though it seems, his cruisers, which were in easy visual range of the escort carriers, gave him no information,[1] and Sprague's fighters had prevented the *Yamato's* reconnaissance aircraft from finding out anything. The evasive manœuvres necessary to avoid the American destroyer and air attacks prevented Kurita from gaining ground. His losses since leaving Brunei Bay had been serious. He was drawing more heavily on his fuel supply than he could afford. Believing, from the reports of his ships, that he had disposed of his opponents, sinking three or four carriers, two heavy cruisers and some destroyers, he began to re-form his fleet before setting course for Leyte Gulf to carry out the now badly overdue attack on the invasion forces.

There was no rest yet for Rear-Admiral C. A. F. Sprague's force. About 1050 an attack by land-based suicide aircraft from Luzon developed. The escort carriers *Kalinin Bay* and *Kitkun Bay* were hit and the *St. Lo* was sunk.[2] The remnant of Admiral C. A. F. Sprague's group, all damaged with the exception of one ship, retired to the south-westward. They sailed for Manus next day with a borrowed screen. His aircraft had made 252 torpedo and 201 fighter sorties. About 105 aircraft had been destroyed in the battle. He had lost two of his six carriers and three of the seven destroyers and destroyer escorts of his screen. Personnel casualties were 1,572 officers and men. But their resolute defence had saved the Seventh Fleet and invasion forces from any damage which Kurita might have been able to effect.

8

Meanwhile, whilst the escort carriers were fighting for their lives, Halsey with the other three groups of the Third Fleet was 250 miles to the northward, attacking Ozawa's carrier force which had been discovered at 1640 on the previous day by aircraft of Rear-Admiral Sherman's group.

At day-break on the 24th Ozawa was in position 19° 0′ N., 126° 40′ E. Fukudome's shore-based aircraft reported the position of Rear-Admiral Sherman's task group to him at 0820, and at 1115 Ozawa's search aircraft sighted them bearing 120°, distance 180 miles. Half an hour later Ozawa sent off a strike of 76 aircraft, of which more than half were fighters. After the strike no more than three of the surviving aircraft returned to their ships and 30 or 40 landed in Luzon. U.S. aircraft reports of this Northern Force varied, but Admiral Halsey came to the conclusion that it contained at least 17 ships and possibly as many as 24.[3] The former figure was correct, for Ozawa had with him one carrier, three light carriers, two battleship carriers, three light cruisers and eight destroyers.[4] Halsey, unaware that the carriers were almost devoid of aircraft, came to the conclusion that of the three Japanese forces the

[1] 'We had poor communication with our cruisers and couldn't see what they were doing'. Interrogation of Commander Otari, Operations Officer on Vice-Admiral Kurita's Staff (Nav. No. 41).

[2] The attack is described in Chapter VIII, p. 98.

[3] The Far East Report of the 24th gives the following composition of the Northern Force, estimated from sightings: Two battleships similar to converted *Ise* class, two heavy cruisers, 11 other cruisers or destroyers. One hour later, three aircraft carriers (two *Shokaku* class, one converted cruiser type), three light cruisers, five destroyers (*GHQSWPA* 250855).

[4] The composition of the force is given in Appendix H.

northern carrier force presented the greatest danger. Flying his flag aboard a battleship as he did, he was not personally in a position to interrogate aircraft pilots. He came to the conclusion that the Centre Force had been so badly damaged that it could not win a decision against the Seventh Fleet, for even if he discounted considerably his airmen's reports it seemed reasonable to suppose that Kurita had suffered severe losses from the air attack on the previous day.

Three alternative courses of action presented themselves to the Commander Third Fleet. He might leave his battleships (Task Force 34) to block San Bernardino Strait and take the carriers north with light screens to attack the Northern Force ; or keep his fleet concentrated off San Bernardino Strait ; or take the entire fleet north to strike the enemy carriers. Division of his fleet he rejected as unsound. The second alternative he rejected because it would leave the Japanese carriers with freedom of action. The destruction of these carriers, potentially the most dangerous of the enemy's ships, would contribute most to the Philippines campaign, even if a temporarily hazardous situation were caused at Leyte through attack by the Japanese Centre Force on the Seventh Fleet. That Halsey was not altogether easy in his mind is clear. Between the Japanese battle fleet and the mass of defenceless shipping off the Leyte beaches there stood, first, Kinkaid's battleships which Halsey had cast for the role of taking care of the Japanese Southern Force, and secondly the 18 escort carriers. The success of the Philippines campaign required that these 18 little ships should hold the pass until the Third Fleet, having dealt with the enemy carriers, could return to rescue them. Halsey's decision was based on his interpretation of his function under the directive given to him by Admiral Nimitz, Commander-in-Chief, U.S. Pacific Fleet, which was as follows :

> ' Western Pacific Task Force (Third Fleet) will destroy enemy naval and air forces in or threatening the Philippines Area, and protect the air and sea communications along the Central Pacific Axis. In case opportunity for destruction of major portions of the enemy fleet offers or can be created, such destruction becomes the primary task (of all Pacific Ocean Areas forces). Necessary measures for detailed co-ordination of operations between the Western Pacific Task Forces and forces of the West Pacific will be arranged by their respective Commanders.'[1]

The role of his fleet, as Halsey saw it,[2] was to destroy the Japanese carrier fleet, once this had been discovered ; though to state as he does in his memoirs, that Ozawa's force ' gravely threatened not only Kinkaid and myself, but the whole Pacific strategy,' can only be regarded as an over-statement ; for Halsey had with him three full groups—11 carriers—whilst reports gave the enemy but three (actually four) carriers together with the two converted battleships, *Ise* and *Hyuga* which at best had but small aircraft complements.[3] Moreover in Admiral Nimitz's opinion he should have been able to deduce from the enemy reports that it was improbable Ozawa had with him any other battleships than the *Ise* and *Hyuga* and little if any strength in heavy cruisers.[4]

Clearly, there was misunderstanding between MacArthur and Halsey as to the role the Third Fleet carriers were to play. Halsey's directive from Nimitz

---

[1] *Operations in the Pacific Ocean Areas during the month of October* 1944, p. 56.

[2] *Vide* his memoirs, *Admiral Halsey's Story*.

[3] *Vide* Tel. GHQSWPA 250855 October 1944 already quoted.

[4] Commander-in-Chief Pacific, *Operations in the Pacific Ocean Areas, October **1944***, p. 69.

established the Japanese fleet as his primary objective. MacArthur considered that the Third Fleet's covering mission was its essential and paramount duty.[1]

His mind made up, Halsey steamed northwards, setting a low speed of advance in order to avoid passing the enemy during the night. At 0240 he directed Vice-Admiral Mitscher to form the Heavy Striking Force (Task Force 34) under Vice-Admiral Lee, and station it ahead of the fast carriers to provide for co-ordinated surface and air attack on the enemy. Formation in the darkness of so large a disposition as six battleships, two heavy cruisers, five light cruisers and 18 destroyers occupied nearly two hours.

Contact with the enemy was made at 0710 when the Japanese Northern Force was sighted in 18° 37′ N., 126° 45′ E. The American fast carriers had already launched their first strike ; it was orbiting 50 miles north of the Fleet, and only 85 miles from the enemy. The second strike arrived over Ozawa's force at 1010. Between them, these two strikes disposed of the *Chitose* which sank at 0937, and the damage to the remaining three carriers rendered at least one of them unmanageable. One destroyer, the *Akitsuki,* was sunk.

Meanwhile, calls for help had been coming in from Admiral Kinkaid. Admiral McCain's fast carrier group, which was fuelling some 350 miles away, intercepted the first call for assistance at 0725, more than an hour before Halsey became aware that Kinkaid needed help. At 0848 Halsey ordered McCain to proceed at best possible speed to the assistance of the escort carriers, a signal which he cancelled half-an-hour later (*see* page 93). Neither Kinkaid nor Sprague knew for some time after Kurita broke off the action, that the Centre Force did not intend to renew the action ; and at 1003 Kinkaid sent a desperate message to Halsey in plain language, asking for help. Almost at the same moment Admiral Nimitz at Pearl Harbour, evidently uneasy, inquired the position of the Heavy Striking Force.[2] Halsey was enraged. ' It was not my job to protect the Seventh Fleet ' he said.[3] Having received reports that his carriers had already badly crippled the Japanese Northern Force he decided about an hour later (at 1115) to take his battleships south. With them came Admiral Bogan's group of carriers, the *Intrepid, Cabot* and *Independence* and their screen.

The remaining two carrier groups continued their attacks on the Japanese Northern Force. The carriers *Zuikaku* and *Zuiho* were sunk by air attack during the afternoon ; cruisers and destroyers sank the damaged *Chiyoda* and the destroyer *Hatsutsuki* after a prodigious expenditure of ammunition, the *Santa Fé* alone firing 892 rounds of 6- and 5-inch ammunition at the destroyer in the space of 13 minutes—incidentally, a rate of fire much below her maximum. The light cruiser *Tama* was damaged and the U.S. submarine *Jallao* intercepted her that night and sank her with torpedoes. Both the converted battleships *Ise* and *Hyuga* were damaged, but to sink them was beyond the power of the American aircraft : the practical difficulty of crippling by air strikes alone heavy ships at sea and free to manœuvre was not at that date universally

---

[1] *The Army Air Forces in World War II,* Vol. V, p. 360, based on the following signals : Com. Third Fleet 190100 October 1944 and 210645 October 1944 to Commander-in-Chief South West Pacific, and MacArthur 212240 October 1944 to Com. Third Fleet.

[2] The story, vouched for by a U.S. official historian and by Halsey in his *Memoirs,* is that a cryptographer padded out Nimitz's simple inquiry into : ' The whole world wants to know where is Task Force 34 '.

[3] *Memoirs,* p. 219. But Admiral Nimitz's Operation Plan (*see* p. 67) specifically stated that ' Forces of Pacific Ocean Areas will cover and support forces of South-West Pacific '.

recognised and was one of the lessons of the Battle for Leyte Gulf.[1] Both battleships reached safety.

9

Ozawa had succeeded in carrying out the difficult task assigned to him, but his carrier fleet had been sacrificed to no purpose, for the Commander of the Centre Force had completely abandoned his object. After Kurita broke off the action with the U.S. escort carriers he did not at once proceed to Leyte Gulf, but spent some hours appreciating the fuel situation and preparing for action in the Gulf. The damage his battleships could have done to the invasion shipping and on shore, was enormous. Kinkaid, with his ships low on ammunition, could have put up little resistance ; whilst the 150,000 men in the beachhead and command posts ashore were all within gun range from the sea.

Meanwhile, Rear-Admiral Stump continued his air attacks making in all six strikes. These were responsible for sinking the destroyer *Nowake*. Kurita was in a position which called for greater resolution than he possessed. The nerves of his crews had been upset by the torpedoing of three heavy cruisers in Palawan Passage ; coming at the outset of the operation this was regarded as a bad omen. Since then he had lost the battleship *Musashi* and five more of his heavy cruisers, three sunk and two returned to base damaged. Intercepted signals indicated that American forces, both surface and air, were concentrating to attack him. But he could not discover the position of the enemy. Inability to obtain adequate intelligence had compounded the difficulties of the Japanese at sea throughout almost the entire war : it was now to be Kurita's undoing. He had had no information since the previous day when he learnt that the U.S. carriers were east of Luzon. He had sighted the masts of Rear-Admiral Stump's escort carrier group. He did not know what these ships were, but he suspected the presence in the neighbourhood of another carrier force besides Halsey's fast carriers. He sent off two reconnaissance aircraft from the *Yamato*. Both pilots landed on shore but neither of the two sent any information. Kurita had heard by now of the disaster to Nishimura's force, and he believed that in Leyte Gulf he would come under heavy attacks from ship and shore-based aircraft and be caught ' like a frog in a pond ' to quote his own words. He expected to be given no air cover himself. On the spur of the moment, at 1236 he signalled to the fleet that he was abandoning the plan to enter Leyte Gulf, and was proceeding north to search for the enemy task forces. In so doing he incurred no criticism from his Commander-in-Chief. His task of entering Leyte Gulf to destroy the expedition even if this entailed the destruction of his entire fleet had been indicated to him as a general aim, and it was left to his judgment as to how to carry it out. His argument was, that now the American landing was an accomplished fact it was of less importance to attack the invasion shipping ; and that, anyhow, the ships would by now have heard of the battle and begun dispersing out of the Gulf. Seaplanes stationed at San José in south-west Mindoro (Plan 14) had the responsibility of keeping him informed of the shipping situation in the Gulf. But the weather was bad, the range of the seaplanes small, and they sent no information. He hoped that by going north he would encounter the American fleet which he trusted was now hurrying south to help their compatriots whom he had been engaging that morning. In the open sea his battleships would have the liberty of manœuvre under air attack which would be denied them in Leyte Gulf.

[1] *C.T.G.* 38.4, *Operations in Support of Occupation of Leyte*, 23*rd*–31*st October* 1944 (1st and 2nd Endorsements), M.09953/45, p. 48.

Massive air attack arrived within the hour, from Vice-Admiral McCain's fast carrier group. At 0725 that morning, when McCain intercepted Admiral Kinkaid's call to Halsey for help—an hour and five minutes before it reached Halsey himself—his five carriers were fuelling 357 miles east-north-east of San Bernardino Strait. At 0848 Admiral Halsey sent him orders to assist the escort carriers under attack off Samar, by a strike against Kurita's force. It is doubtful if the signal was ever received.[1] McCain stopped fuelling at 0900. Half an hour later, inexplicably, Halsey changed his target, ordering him to 'strike as practicable' the enemy carriers (Ozawa's Northern Force) retiring northwards. Barely had this order been received before there came another call from Vice-Admiral Kinkaid, asking for Lee's battleships to proceed at top speed to cover Leyte and for a strike by the fast carriers. 'There was an ominous tone in the frantic calls for assistance,' says the Captain of the *Hornet*, and McCain reacted at once. Anticipating instructions (which duly arrived at 1001) from Vice-Admiral Mitscher, his Task Force Commander, ordering him to launch the earliest possible strike, he immediately altered course to 245° and steered for Samar at 30 knots. This great speed the task group maintained for five hours. The distance to the target from the point, 300 miles, where the earliest strike could be launched, was too great for the torpedo-bombers to carry torpedoes and return without refuelling, and McCain therefore sent a message to Kinkaid asking whether Tacloban airfield was fit for landing on. No reply was received, consequently the torpedo aircraft had to be loaded with bombs, which practically put it out of their power to sink Kurita's battleships or even to slow them until Halsey's fast battleships could come south to complete their destruction. Though the Commander Task Group 38.1 was unaware of it, it was possible as already described, to use a strip of grassland alongside Tacloban airfield and numerous escort carrier-based aircraft engaged in the battle off Samar landed there that day, though there were many accidents.

One hundred aircraft composed McCain's first strike, launched at the limit of range with bomb load, with small chance of survival unless the target could be located promptly and conditions were favourable for recovery. Rear-Admiral Stump's radar picked up the flight and his flagship, the *Natoma Bay*, at 1302 vectored it on to Kurita's fleet which was approximately on the parallel of 12° N., some 15 miles off Samar, steering 330° at 25 knots' speed. At 1225 McCain launched his second and last strike. There was still no reply to his query about Tacloban, so again the torpedo aircraft had to be loaded with bombs. No vital damage was caused by these strikes, though practically all the armoured ships were reported hit. But they could all still maintain 20 knots, increasing to 24 when aircraft appeared; and all were battleworthy. With his heavy ships trailing oil Kurita toiled northward all day. By evening he was off San Bernardino Strait, short of fuel. There was no sign of the American fleet. At 2130 he turned to port, entered San Bernardino Strait, and steered for his oilers at Koron Bay.

In the attempt to catch up with the enemy before they reached San Bernardino Strait Admiral Halsey at 1620 formed his two fastest battleships and a screen into Special Task Group 34.5 (Appendix G(3)) under Rear-Admiral O. C. Badger, who took the group on ahead at high speed. But they were too late. The night carrier *Independence* at 1825, half-an-hour after sunset, launched a long range search and attack group, but failed to find the enemy. During the night McCain made rendezvous with the three carriers of Rear-Admiral Bogan's

[1] Neither Vice-Admiral McCain's report nor that of his flagship the *Wasp* mention it, but the evidence that it was sent is incontrovertible.

groups which had come south with Halsey, and at dawn on the 26th these eight carriers began launching long range strikes at Kurita's retreating force. In all, 174 aircraft came up with the enemy fleet. They sank the light cruiser *Noshiro* and the destroyer *Hayashimo*. On the following day the destroyers *Fusinami* and *Shiranuhi*, the latter one of Admiral Shima's force, were found amongst the islands and sunk. U.S. army heavy and medium bombers also made several attempts to attack the remnant of the Centre Force. Attempts on the 25th with Liberators from New Guinea failed for lack of co-ordinated naval and army intelligence. Bombers from New Guinea found Kurita next day and sank the damaged light cruiser *Abukuma* and caused some topside damage to the *Yamato* by splinters ; the enemy ships met the aircraft with fire from their main batteries at ranges up to nearly 16,000 yards. On the 27th in order to deny Kurita's battleships facilities for repair 53 Superfortresses from Kharagpur (Calcutta) successfully bombed the King George V dock at Singapore, a round trip of 4,000 miles, putting it out of action for three months ; and on 16th November heavy bombers of the Thirteenth Air Force attacked the anchored fleet units at Brunei, but inflicted only light damage from near misses.

Five days of fighting had ended in victory over the Japanese Fleet, though not its annihilation. But the Japanese did not repair the whole of the damaged ships and from now on the fleet was reduced to raiding, blockade running, and escort status. In the first-named capacity the four modern Japanese battleships which remained, constituted a threat to MacArthur's operations in the Philippines when the old battleships lent to the Seventh Fleet from the Central Pacific should be withdrawn. For lack of trained pilots the Japanese naval air force suffered a steady conversion into a suicide weapon. As such, it was still to cause enormous damage to the Allied ships engaged in the Philippines operation, and indeed to place the attack on Leyte in jeopardy.

The Battle for Leyte Gulf, like both the other two great air battles of the war, was decided largely by the failure of intelligence. At Midway, in June 1942, the Japanese assumption that the U.S. carriers were two thousand miles away, and the consequent omission to carry out reconnaissance cost the enemy his entire carrier force. Just two years later, at the Battle of the Marianas, American inability to shadow the Japanese Fleet at long range enabled the latter to escape destruction. The Battle for Leyte Gulf was a tragedy of American lack of accurate information of the state of Japan's carrier-based air forces, and on the Japanese side, of failure to discover the whereabouts of the U.S. Pacific Fleet. As had frequently occurred in the past, signal communication showed itself to be the weakest part of U.S. fighting economy.

CHAPTER VIII

Liberation of the Philippines:

The Fight for Air Supremacy

(Plans 2, 13, 14, 15.)

1

IT soon became evident that the Japanese were employing new tactics in their air attacks. Faced with U.S. superiority in aircraft types, pilot training and fighter direction technique and inspired, it is said, by the crash, on 15th October, reportedly into a carrier but actually into the water alongside the ship, of an aircraft piloted by Admiral Arima, the enemy adopted in defence of the Philippines the *kamikaze* (suicide) tactics which had been under consideration since the heavy losses suffered in combat with the American fighters in the Battle of the Marianas in June. There had been occasional instances of this type of attack throughout the war. A pilot, for example, whose aircraft was badly damaged, would sometimes aim it at a ship. But the defence of the Philippines was the first operation in which suicide air attacks were organised. They were initiated by the 1st Air Fleet. The first *kamikaze* pilots were volunteers, later, they were detailed for the duty ; and it is known from airmen prisoners-of-war and from captured war diaries, that the order to immolate themselves was by no means always regarded with enthusiasm. From the Japanese point of view, once it had been decided that the loss of pilots could be borne, there were advantages in suicide operating. It gave terminal accuracy of the bomb, at that date difficult to achieve except by well-trained dive-bomber pilots, whilst incompletely trained pilots and obsolescent or obsolete aircraft could be used as *kamikaze*—in fact, any aircraft to which a bomb could be lashed was adequate. Moreover, it doubled the range or alternatively halved the quantity of fuel needed by the aircraft, since no return to base was provided for. The percentage of *kamikaze* aircraft which hit their target is not known[1]

[1] Admiral Halsey in his memoirs, p. 232, says the percentage of hits was one in 100 which is obviously far too low. Captain R. Inoguchi, Chief of Staff of 1st Air Fleet throughout the Philippines campaign stated in interrogation (Nav. No. 12) that the figure was approximately one in six for naval *kamikazes* and probably less for army machines ; this is believed to be near the mark.

but in the Philippines operation some 150 hits or near misses were made, sinking 23 ships and extensively damaging 72.

The attacks were difficult to counter if the enemy aircraft succeeded in eluding the protective fighters. In the early days, the *kamikazes* almost invariably attacked singly, the groups splitting up at a distance of about 30 miles from the target. These single aircraft were difficult to detect and to distinguish from friendly aircraft in the air. They could trail the U.S. aircraft back to the Fleet or keep within the nulls of the American radars, sometimes skimming the surface of the water so that radar could not detect them in time for the protective fighters to shoot them down. During the U.S. landing in Ormoc Bay, Leyte Island, on 7th December, however, the Japanese *kamikazes* adopted a new tactic of grouping up over a target with a dozen or more aircraft, and then carrying out a co-ordinated attack on one selected ship. This was usually an unarmoured vessel, if possible a destroyer on radar picket duty or a carrier with aircraft on deck, for the bombs had little terminal velocity and consequently little penetrating power, and no armoured ship was ever sunk in this manner. Against very steep dives though not against *kamikazes* approaching from a low altitude, high speed and the use of helm were sometimes effective. For though the pilot usually aimed his machine until the moment of crashing, Japanese aircraft in use at that date tended to become very stiff on the controls at high speeds : consequently, any manœuvre by the ship which necessitated the pilot altering his angle of dive, improved the ship's chances of avoiding the suicider, particularly if the attacking aircraft was badly damaged by gunfire, its controls destroyed, engine damaged or pilot killed. Even in such cases, however, inertia and the characteristics of the aircraft tended to make it continue on the same course unless a wing or other essential control surface was shot away ; and instances occurred where the aircraft continued in its dive with both wings shot away, becoming in effect a released bomb. It was thus very difficult to deflect by A.A. gunfire and the conclusion arrived at by the Americans was that nothing except heavy and accurate gunfire would stop suicide aircraft once the dive had begun. To combat that type of attack close mutual support was necessary, and no ship should be stationed in an outlying position if it could be avoided.[1] This was, however, a counsel of perfection and unattainable, for it was later found that amongst the measures to counter suicide attack the stationing of destroyers and destroyer escorts as outlying radar pickets was one of the most effective.

Vice-Admiral T. S. Wilkinson, in a report, pointed out the difficulty of hitting a *kamikaze* aircraft by anti-aircraft gunfire with the existing U.S. automatic sight.[2] From an attack position, outside automatic weapons range, the suicide aircraft could be expected to reach its target, if not stopped, in about 20 seconds. The automatic weapons' gunner had difficulty in leading the target, an essential when using the proximity fuze which the Americans introduced during 1944 for use with their anti-aircraft guns. The important feature of this fuze was an electronic device which detonated the shell at a specified distance in front of the target. Though the A.A. gunner might be following the target when the attack began, any large change of course by the evading ship would require the automatic sight to alter its generated lead. This took an appreciable time, during which the directed fire was considerably off the target. When the enemy aircraft dived towards the target at full throttle, as was usual, the automatic sight was unable to generate sufficient lead to bring the fire up to the target.

[1] *Amphibious Operations, Invasion of the Philippines October* 1944 *to January* 1945, p. 3/7.
[2] *ibid.*, Chapter III, p. 11.

The aircraft in its dive was constantly accelerating and the gunsight had no means of compensating for such acceleration. Admiral Wilkinson recommended that lead generating sights should be fitted with a control which would cause the sight rapidly to over-compensate for the speed of the target. The defect in generated lead also existed when an aircraft approached and passed a ship close aboard. An acute angle at first, the angle between the line of sight and the path of the target increased until it became a right-angle and then decreased. The angular rate of traverse of the guns was accelerating until the aircraft passed by, with the result that the generated lead lagged most when the target was within the most effective range. Under those conditions, the gunner, in order to hit the target, had to shift from sight to tracer control at some point in the aircraft's approach.

Under the threat of suicide air attack the U.S. and the British Pacific Fleet in its first operation (' Iceberg ') devoted from 40 to 60 per cent of their effort to defence.

The first Allied ship to be hit by a suicide aircraft was H.M.A.S. *Australia.* At 0646 on 21st October, off Leyte, whilst the ship's company were at dawn action stations, a low-flying enemy aircraft approached from the land. Hit by A.A. fire, the aircraft turned away, but turned back again and crashed into the *Australia's* foremast, setting the bridge on fire. Thirty officers and men lost their lives through the explosion and fire, including Captain Dechaineux, whilst Commodore Collins was amongst the many wounded. The ship had to be escorted back to Manus by the *Warramunga.*

The local airfields at Leyte were quickly captured, but time was required before they could be made operational and land-based air forces established ashore. Despite continued air strikes against enemy airfields in Luzon and Formosa by the Third Fleet, by the escort carrier aircraft, and by U.S. land-based air forces from Morotai, the reaction to the landings by the Japanese air forces was sharp and vigorous, and the Allies were far from holding control of the air over Leyte. Air preparation prior to the landing had been insufficient.[1] The neighbouring enemy airfields were too numerous, too close to the objective area, and too closely linked to the home islands of Japan to be readily neutralized as had been done during the Central Pacific campaign. It was evident that to bomb them intermittently caused negligible damage to their operating facilities and that daily sweeps in force over all fields that could be used for aircraft flown in from the enemy bases to the north and south was necessary.[2] The multiplicity of airfields (Plans 14, 15) was such that no attempt was made to bomb runways for the Japanese merely made good the damage. Revetments, dispersal areas, supply dumps and bivouac areas were bombed and strafed, but above all, aircraft were attacked on the ground, if they could be found. The Japanese went to astonishing lengths in their dispersal and camouflage, though to the prejudice of effective operating.

At 0740 on 24th October, taking advantage of the absence of the aircraft of the Fast Carrier Force during the Battle for Leyte Gulf, Japanese suicide aircraft began a series of attacks on Escort Carrier Group 77.4.1. The group had sent off all available aircraft early that morning, to support Admiral C. A. F. Sprague's task unit which was under attack to the northward, off Samar. Without warning, a Japanese naval fighter loaded with a bomb crashed on the

[1] *The Army Air Forces in World War II,* Vol. V, p. 677.

[2] Devices such as were employed by Rommel in North Africa for rendering the surfaces of airstrips unfit for use were not employed by the Americans.

flight deck of the *Santee*, exploding and causing a serious fire on the flight and hangar decks. A few minutes later the ship was torpedoed amidships by a submarine which was not detected.[1] Simultaneously, suicide aircraft narrowly missed the *Petrof Bay* and *Sangamon*: hit by anti-aircraft fire they plunged into the sea alongside, damaging the latter ship. A suicide dive bomber hit another carrier, the *Suwannee*, at 0759, causing a heavy explosion and fire and many casualties. Both the *Santee* and *Sangamon* were back in operating condition however by 1030, with their fires under control. Twenty minutes later the survivors of Admiral C. A. F. Sprague's task unit, their surface engagement with Kurita's fleet having just come to an end, were subjected to a series of suicide attacks by enemy aircraft. These went on until 1130, without a respite during which protective fighters could be sent up. An aircraft dived on the *Kitkun Bay*: hit hard, it lost most of the left wing while still about 200 feet in the air and began to spin. The bomb was released and landed on the *Kitkun Bay's* starboard bow, bounced off into the sea where it exploded, damaging the ship. The aircraft itself struck the ship's port bow. The *Kalinin Bay* was hit by two naval fighters which wrecked a section of the flight deck and caused other damage. At 1038 an aircraft dropped a bomb on the *St Lo* and afterwards crashed on board whilst the ship was loading and servicing aircraft. The aircraft itself went overboard, but its bomb penetrated the flight deck causing explosions. By 1100 it was clear that the ship could not be saved, and she sank at 1125 after seven explosions had taken place, 114 men being killed and missing and 394 wounded. It was two days before all the survivors were picked up. The enemy attacks continued. A low level attack by three aircraft was beaten off by the ships' gunfire and at 1220 an attempted suicide dive on the *Santee* was foiled.

Further considerable damage was caused on that day to the *Santee* by one of the Japanese submarines operating to the eastward of Samar. At 0752 a torpedo fired by one of these vessels struck the ship on the starboard side amidships, flooding one compartment. The *Santee* quickly regained steering control, however, corrected the list caused by flooding, extinguished the fires and was in operating condition once again by 0900. The submarine was never detected. To the northward, there was a submarine alarm at 0805 in Admiral C. A. F. Sprague's unit and a submarine was reported sighted. It was fortunate that no attack developed, for the escort carriers were at the time fleeing precipitately from the Japanese fleet, and their screening destroyers and destroyer escorts were fully engaged in trying to protect them from the enemy battleships and heavy cruisers.

2

In consequence of the losses and damage of escort carriers in these air and submarine attacks and the aircraft losses in the Battle off Samar U.S. air strength at Leyte was badly reduced. Half of Admiral Kinkaid's escort carriers were out of action, and taking advantage of the lack of fighter cover over the beachheads the Japanese on the afternoon of 25th October made 12 attacks, sinking two L.S.T.s and doing damage ashore. Next day, in a series of *kamikaze* attacks which began at 0900 the escort carrier *Suwannee* was badly damaged off Leyte, for the second day in succession. Admiral Kinkaid asked that fighters of the Far Eastern Air Force should be established on the island as soon as possible. But development of the airfields occupied longer than anticipated.

[1] *See* below, this page.

The landing strips were in bad condition when captured, and the heavy monsoon rains—35 inches fell at Dulag in the first 40 days of the operation—impeded the work of putting them in operable condition. The work was delayed too by shortage of construction materials resulting from congestion on the beaches.[1] The plans for the Leyte operation did not specify the exact date for the transfer of direct air support of the troops from the Navy to the land-based Air Forces. Under the operational instruction, the Commander Allied Air Forces, Lieutenant-General G. C. Kenney, was to assume this duty at the earliest practicable date after the establishment of fighters and light bombers in the Leyte area, as arranged with the Commander, Allied Naval Forces, Vice-Admiral Kinkaid, who was responsible until the land-based air forces took over.[2]

At 1600 hours on the 27th, with one airfield (Tacloban) in operation, General MacArthur announced that the Allied Air Forces would assume responsibility for the defence and support of the troops in the Leyte-Samar area, and he issued a directive that no air forces of the Third or Seventh Fleets should thereafter attack any land targets except after specific co-ordination with his Headquarters.[3] With MacArthur's concurrence all Third Fleet units were directed to withdraw to advanced bases at discretion. The fast carriers had been operating continuously for a fortnight. The ships needed replenishment and the pilots rest.

3

It immediately became clear that MacArthur's land-based air forces were unable to hold the enemy air forces in check. Barely had the Commander-in-Chief released the Third Fleet before Admiral Kinkaid was asking Nimitz to continue to maintain a strong combat patrol over the objective area at Leyte and to attack the Japanese airfields as practicable. He was not satisfied with the cover that the shore-based aircraft were providing for his fleet, and so many of his escort carriers had been crippled that he could not provide for his own defence. In a single night Japanese aircraft destroyed 27 U.S. fighters on Tacloban airfield.

The air situation was deteriorating rather than improving, and it was evident that if the Allies were to avoid further heavy losses and, indeed, if the campaign for the liberation of the Philippines was to be brought to a successful conclusion, the airfields from which the Japanese operated must be neutralized and the aircraft themselves destroyed. It was clear to Halsey that his carriers had no alternative but to continue operations against the enemy air forces until the Leyte airfields could support sufficient aircraft to take their place ; he prepared to respond to Kinkaid's request, and on 2nd November the Commander-in-Chief, Pacific, confirmed his decision and directed him to employ the Fleet so as most effectively to support the operations at Leyte. A series of air attacks on Japan arranged to begin in the middle of November on the assumption that the situation would permit the withdrawal of the fast carriers from Leyte, had to be

[1] The crowding and confusion caused by dumping cargoes on the narrow peninsula on which Tacloban airstrip lay was estimated by Sixth Army to have delayed completion of minimum airfield facilities by as much as two days. ' Kenney finally threatened to bulldoze the dumps into the sea '. (*The Army Air Forces in World War II*, Vol. V, p. 357.)

[2] *Marine Aviation in the Philippines*. Historical Division, H.Q.U.S. Marine Corps, p. 23.

[3] ' Kenney later assured Arnold that there had been no hard feelings about the matter '. (*The Army Air Forces in World War II*, Vol. V, p. 369.)

postponed. General Kenney sent forward such fighters as the airfields could support, and at Halsey's suggestion an experienced Marine Group was sent up from the South Pacific ; the Far Eastern Air Force in New Guinea and Morotai undertook attacks against the central and southern Philippines airfields through which the Japanese were staging their aircraft against Leyte, whilst Allied Air Forces struck also against the reinforcement routes. But Halsey himself was forbidden to strike, except in self-defence, against the central and southern Philippines where the majority of the Japanese airfields lay (Plan 14)[1] ; these were reserved for the Army Air Forces and Kinkaid's Seventh Fleet escort carriers. The 'fatal boundary line', as it is termed by Vice-Admiral J. S. McCain, who on 30th October succeeded Mitscher in command of Task Force 38 (the Fast Carrier Force), was apparently drawn about the parallel of 15° N. ; and because of it, Task Force 38 was not permitted to strike dangerous enemy air concentrations within range. McCain reports, too, that he was ordered to strike shipping as a primary target instead of first eliminating the threat of enemy air concentrations.[2] On 5th November, after four of his carriers had been hit, resulting in two of them being put out of action, Halsey obtained permission from MacArthur to attack the central Luzon airfields. It was one more instance of the failure of divided command which had enabled the Japanese Fleet to escape destruction only a week previously.

One of Halsey's four fast carrier groups had returned to Ulithi for replenishment after the Battle for Leyte Gulf, with food and ammunition almost exhausted. A second group fuelled on 27th October. The remaining two groups took over the heavy duty of keeping protection patrols over their own force and the amphibious shipping, supporting the troops ashore as far as possible, and as soon as permission was given, neutralizing the enemy airfields by fighter sweeps over the central as well as the northern Philippines which were beyond range of General Kenney's aircraft, whilst maintaining a covering position to guard against raids by Japanese surface forces on the amphibious shipping. On the 28th a second task group left for Ulithi and the fuelling group began a high speed return to Leyte, arriving next day in time to make a fighter sweep and three strikes against shipping and airfields in the Manila area.[3] The ten escort carriers of the battered Seventh Fleet which Admiral Kinkaid had succeeded in keeping in operation at Leyte, left on the same day for replenishment. On the 31st, the fourth fast carrier group left for Ulithi and there remained only a single group in support off Leyte until 3rd November, when two further groups returned.[4] Between that date and 27th November, when Task Force 38 was relieved, it made 6,282 aircraft sorties, of which 4,198 were offensive. The Fleet's aircraft losses were heavy, and the carriers suffered eight suicide crashes, six of them serious. On 28th October, interception of a

[1] *Admiral Halsey's Story*, pp. 230–31, 243.

[2] *Brief of Action Report, C.T.F.* 38 *Operations off Japan for the period from* 2*nd July to* 15*th August* 1945. M.0283/46.

[3] *Operations in the Pacific Ocean Areas during the month of October* 1944. Commander-in-Chief U.S. Pacific Fleet and Pacific Ocean Areas, p. 20. It is not clear how this squares with the reports of Halsey and McCain that T.F. 38 was not permitted to strike the central Luzon airfields until 5th November (cf. *Admiral Halsey's Story*, pp. 230–31).

[4] The foregoing are the movements of the carriers as reported by the Commander-in-Chief Pacific Fleet. They have been given in detail, because the official history of the U.S. Air Force *The Army Air Forces in World War II*, Vol. V, pp. viii, ix, gives a different account of their movements from which the inference seems to be that the Third Fleet failed to carry out its assignment and left Leyte unprotected for nearly a week. McCain appears to have believed that he could have done more, had Halsey permitted, for he reported 'only a part, instead of the whole Task Force, was ordered to strike' (M.0283/46).

raid by Japanese aircraft at dusk necessitated landing some of the aircraft at Dulag field whilst this was under attack, and several machines were wrecked. Bad weather at the Leyte fields about this time caused further operational losses.

On the 29th, off Luzon, whilst confined to a narrow area searching for aircraft pilots shot down on the previous evening, Admiral Bogan's group was attacked about noon by 23 aircraft. The combat air patrol shot down 21 of them and anti-aircraft fire destroyed another, but one got through and attacked the carrier *Intrepid* which took the first of the five *kamikaze* hits which put her out of action before the war ended. The blow was a glancing one and damage was slight. Admiral Davison's group was attacked next day whilst cruising about 100 miles east of Samar. Early in the afternoon, the protective air patrol shot down four Japanese naval fighters apparently attempting suicide crashes. At 1405 twelve additional fighters were launched to aid a tanker reported under attack. They had barely left the deck when the *Franklin*, which had already been slightly damaged by a bomb hit on the 15th, was subjected to suicide attack by six enemy aircraft. One dived into her flight deck abaft the island, whilst two others missed, one of them crashing into the *Belleau Wood*. The two carriers lost 158 men killed and 45 aircraft destroyed. Both ships were seriously damaged and had to be withdrawn and sent to Ulithi for repairs. During these three or four days the fast carriers lost in combat 34 aircraft. They engaged 250 Japanese aircraft, of which they claimed to have destroyed 114. The total losses in the air of Japanese naval aircraft during October were amongst the heaviest of the war, though they were to be exceeded during the following month whilst the struggle for air supremacy over Leyte raged.[1] These early attacks caught the American carriers with tired crews and depleted complements of aircraft. Since the end of August they had lost 220 aircraft in combat and some 50 further aircraft in accidents.[2] No less than 85 per cent of these losses had occurred in the last 20 days. The normal level of accidents was rising owing to pilot fatigue. The *Wasp's* Flight Surgeon reported for example, that of the ship's 131 pilots only 30 were fit to continue fighting. But it was not yet possible to rest them, for the situation was critical.

4

On passage from Ulithi to Leyte, for the first time since 1942, the Fast Carrier Force was successfully attacked by an enemy submarine. Though an increase of submarine activity had been anticipated, a Japanese submarine was able to penetrate the outer screen and make an effective attack on one of the ships of Task Group 38.3. On the night of the 3rd/4th November the task group was approximately 320°, 700 miles from Ulithi, proceeding at 15 knots, zigzagging, in bright moonlight, in a smooth sea with a low short swell. No night anti-submarine air patrol was airborne, and the formation was dependent for A/S protection on lookouts, radar, and the sound detectors of a more than generous destroyer screen.[3] These failed to give warning of the presence of the enemy submarine. At 2325 the light cruiser *Reno* was struck on the port side by a torpedo. The submarine which fired the torpedo, though hunted, remained

[1] The Japanese naval aircraft losses month by month during the war are given in Vol. III of this History, Appendix Q.

[2] *Admiral Halsey's Story*, p. 228.

[3] Comment by D.T.S.D. on N.I.D. 0051371/44—*Observers with the U.S. Pacific Fleet Reports : Report No.* 1, *dated* 10th *November ' Carrier Strikes on Luzon,* 5*th and* 6*th November* 1944 '.

undetected. The after engine room and after boiler room of the *Reno* were flooded, a considerable portion of the crew's quarters were opened to the sea, and steering control was temporarily lost. The ship took a list which soon reached 16°. Her displacement increased by about 30 per cent. Occasional small fires broke out. Three destroyers were detailed to escort the ship back to Ulithi. The difficulties of the passage were intensified by high winds and heavy seas from a nearby typhoon. Attempts were made to right the ship by filling starboard oil and water tanks, pumping fuel from the port tanks and shifting moveable weights from port to starboard. When the list to port had been reduced to 7° and was still decreasing, the ship suddenly started to list to starboard, and lurched to a maximum of 20°.[1] Electrical fires continued to break out in the forward engine room, from short circuited cables. It was necessary to stop the starboard engine, and the ship was taken in tow. Her people were eventually successful in reducing the free water surface by pumping out flooded compartments which could be made watertight and thus achieving an improvement in the reserve buoyancy. In spite of the bad weather the ship reached Ulithi safely on 11th November.

5

The torpedoing of the *Reno* marked a period of increased activity by Japanese submarines, undertaken in conformity with the plan to employ every military means in defence of the Philippines. The campaign began with the sinking on 29th October on the shipping lane between Hawaii and the west coast of the U.S.A. of the s.s. *John A. Johnson*, the first U.S. merchant ship sunk by a Japanese submarine in the Pacific during 1944. From 31st October to 6th December, with two days' intermission a U.S. hunter-killer group operated in the area without success. On 13th November, however, the frigate *Rockford* and the minesweeper *Ardent* escorting a convoy sank *I–38* in position 31° 55′ N., 139° 45′ W. approximately 155 miles from the point where the *John A. Johnson* was attacked. On the 12th, the destroyer *Nicholas* forming part of the anti-submarine screen of the light cruiser *St. Louis*, was *en route* from Ulithi to Kossol Passage, the U.S. anchorage in the Palau Islands (Plan 2) when she had radar contact with an enemy submarine at 21,300 yards. The *Nicholas* sank the enemy, which was found to be *I–37*, in 8° 4′ N., 138° 3′ E. On the 19th a netlayer engaged in laying a torpedo net across the western entrance of Kossol Passage sighted a submarine which surfaced and quickly submerged. After a hunt of six hours the submarine, *I–177*, was sunk by the destroyer escorts *Conklin* and *McCoy Reynolds*.

Ulithi was attacked on the 10th by midget submarines (*kaiten*) carried to the scene by *I–36* and *I–47*, which launched five *kaitens* between them. One of these torpedoed and sank the oiler *Mississinewa* loaded with over 14,000 tons of oil and 400,000 gallons of aviation fuel. Only two or three of the *kaitens* came to light and were destroyed by the Americans; of the remainder no trace was found.[2] The sinking of the *Mississinewa* was the only success achieved during the war by the *kaitens* upon which the Japanese expended a by no means inconsiderable effort.

[1] 'This sudden change in the situation was directly attributable to the free surfaces existing in the large flooded compartments, and the small margin of stability remaining. The ship at the time was undoubtedly in a condition of negative stability; and the shifting of weights resulted in the sudden switch from a port to a starboard list'. (*Operations in the Pacific Ocean Areas during the month of November* 1944, p. 77.)

[2] The attack is described in Vol. IV, Chapter XI.

The principal enemy submarine activity during the month was, however, in the area of the Philippine Islands, where Japanese submarines operated both as blockade runners and on offensive patrols. Ten contacts were made. Off the east coast, especially north of Leyte Gulf, submarines attempted, without success, to intercept the U.S. convoys to Leyte. Some of these convoys included 40 to 60 ships, screened by 6 to 10 escorts. A group of U.S. escort carriers and their escorts furnished anti-submarine support off Leyte Gulf, in addition to protection against air attack. For protection of the convoys, a hunter-killer group (Task Unit 70.2.1) consisting of the escort carrier *Anzio* and destroyer escorts, moved from Morotai to Leyte early in November. The group conducted an anti-submarine sweep around the Third Fleet fuelling area off the east coast of the islands, in the course of which the *Lawrence C. Taylor* on the 17th, after a night hunt, sank the submarine *I–26* in 12° 44′ N., 130° 42′ E., after aircraft from the *Anzio* had reported her.[1] On the night of the 27th–28th four destroyers of Division 43, after completing a bombardment of enemy installations at Ormoc Bay, conducted a sweep in the western part of the Comotes Sea in search of enemy barges which were engaged in bringing reinforcements to Ormoc. At 0115 an aircraft on patrol reported an enemy submarine approaching on the surface. The destroyers opened fire, which the submarine *I–46*, returned. She was hit and went down quickly in position 10° 48′ N., 124° 35′ E.[2] The sinking by the *Scabbardfish* of *I–365* on the 28th in the approaches to Yokohama in 34° 44′ N., 141° 1′ E. and *RO–100* by a mine in 7° S., 156° E. in the Solomon Islands brought the number of Japanese submarines sunk during November to seven, after which activity declined once more, the best of the Japanese boats being employed as midget submarine carriers on fruitless *kaiten* operations.[3] The German submarine *U–537* was encountered on the surface north of Lombok Strait on the morning of 9th November by the U.S. submarine *Flounder* patrolling as one of a co-ordinated Search and Attack Group with the *Guavina* and *Bashaw*, and was sunk by torpedoes in 7° 13′ S., 115° 17′ E. At the time, *U–537* was on the way home with important materials for Germany, the Germans having abandoned blockade running with surface ships, as entailing unacceptable losses.[4]

In areas further from the Philippines, merchant ships generally continued to proceed independently, although in the South-West Pacific Area Admiral Kinkaid gave escort to his convoys proceeding to the air base at Morotai.

For a very long time the Americans had largely discounted the enemy submarine menace in the Pacific. With the torpedoing of the *Reno*, it was now, however, to receive close attention. Admiral McCain considered that the defence of the Fast Carrier Force against enemy submarine attack constituted a serious problem which he anticipated might prove increasingly important in future operations. The protection inherent in a force of that type, namely speed and constant, unpredictable movement over a wide area, was largely nullified by the more or less stereotyped method of employment which the force was called upon to adopt in its strikes in support of the Philippines landing operations. Launching positions, routes to flying-off positions, and fuelling areas became standardized to a point where the element of surprise was almost wholly lost. The great size of the force, when several groups were operating together, might

---

[1] The operation is described in M.01405/45 *U-boat probably sunk by U.S.S. L. C. Taylor and aircraft from U.S.S. ANZIO.*

[2] *See* M.01934/45 *U-boat known sunk by U.S.S. Waller, Renshaw, Saufley, Pringle, off Davao Gulf.* The submarine is there erroneously called *I–362.*

[3] *See* Vol. IV, Chapter XI.

[4] *See* Vol. IV, Chapter XII.

result in a submarine finding itself in position to approach one group if it missed opportunity on another. The need to keep radar screens as free as possible of friendly aircraft in order to facilitate the detection and interception of enemy aircraft when attack was still the major threat, entailed almost entire elimination of air anti-submarine patrols during operations off enemy held territory. At best, too, such patrols by carrier pilots were of questionable value, due to lack of indoctrination, experience and training, together with inadequate anti-submarine equipped aircraft. Admiral McCain recommended an increase in the number of special A.S.W. groups assigned to hunter-killer operations in the area in which the force was operating[1] ; a specially trained A.S.W. team of destroyers to accompany the force, the speed of destroyer escorts being too low ; pilots specially trained in A/S warfare to be assigned to the force ; and training in at least the rudiments of A/S warfare of Air Combat Intelligence Officers and all carrier personnel responsible for or engaged in the conduct of air operations.[2]

6

Meanwhile, at Leyte *kamikaze* air attacks continued to cause serious damage. Little more than 48 hours after the retirement on 29th October of the battered Seventh Fleet escort carriers for rehabilitation, the Japanese made a heavy attack on the remaining ships of Admiral Kinkaid's fleet, sending down a strong suicide force. At the time, 1st November, the Allied support forces of the Seventh Fleet in the area consisted of three battleships, the cruiser H.M.A.S. *Shropshire*, three light cruisers, 12 U.S. destroyers and H.M.A.S. *Arunta*. At 0900 and again at 1340 determined attacks were made on destroyers of the screen by enemy torpedo bombers and suicide aircraft. The destroyer *Abner Read* was sunk by one of the latter and the *Ammen*, *Claxton* and *Killen* were also hit, sustaining considerable damage. There were few land-based aircraft at Leyte at the time. Those at Tacloban had been reduced by raids and operational accidents, but typhoon weather further south was preventing General Kenney from sending reinforcements. The airstrip itself was cratered. Consequently, when the Japanese attack developed the ships were without adequate protective fighter cover. Anti-aircraft fire shot down at least ten of the 15 enemy attackers and prevented any aircraft from reaching the heavy ships which were their apparent target. On 6th November, three groups of Japanese aircraft, by showing a U.S. IFF code, were able to make an attack on Seventh Fleet ships near Leyte, causing considerable damage.[3]

For nearly a month the ships of the support force had a respite from attack. On the forenoon of 27th November, however, in weather too bad for protective air patrols to be sent up, some 25–30 enemy aircraft made a raid. The battleship *Colorado* and the light cruisers *St. Louis* and *Montpelier* were hit, the two first-named receiving extensive damage. Two days later, suicide aircraft attacked the support force at evening twilight. The battleship *Maryland* and the

[1] We ourselves were convinced by experience of the superior tactic of compelling the enemy submarine to come to the A.S.V. protected convoy, rather than employing hunting groups. It is true that the Americans had considerable success with such groups formed round an escort carrier on the Biscay to Cape route, but it is questionable whether they would have been equally successful without special intelligence.

[2] *C.T.F.* 38 *Action Report* 30*th October* 1944–26*th January* 1945, M.03191/45 (behind M.06562/45).

[3] The authority for this misuse of the U.S. IFF code is the *U.S. Pacific Fleet and Pacific Ocean Areas Weekly Intelligence*, Vol. 1, No. 23, 18th December 1944. No details of the attack are given and no other mention has been found.

destroyer *Aulick* were hit and badly damaged, and had heavy casualties, whilst the destroyer *Saufley* received minor damage. Five enemy aircraft were destroyed in this raid.

Meanwhile, the enemy had been attacking the Tacloban airstrip with determination. Early on 2nd November, 25 to 30 single-engine enemy aircraft made on the airstrip eight strafing and five bombing runs with fragmentation and incendiary bombs, destroying or damaging 12 aircraft. When a second raid of 30 to 35 enemy aircraft attempted to follow up in the hours shortly after daybreak, however, they found themselves opposed by 15 U.S. fighters which shot down half or more of them before the raiders could make their escape. The attacks were repeated next day. More than 100 enemy aircraft were thought to have been engaged in low level attacks on Tacloban just before dawn and after dusk. They dropped GP, AP, phosphorous, and incendiary bombs which damaged or destroyed a few U.S. aircraft. On the morning of the 4th, 35 Japanese aircraft attacked the airfield, destroying or damaging 41 aircraft. Dulag airfield was also attacked on that day by some 50 aircraft. On the 10th the airstrip at Carigara Bay was temporarily rendered unserviceable. The enemy made daily raids on the Leyte area from 12th to 19th November losing in that period 74 aircraft, whilst between the 9th and 30th an additional 62 attackers were reported shot down.

7

On 5th November, General MacArthur having yielded to Halsey's arguments in favour of attacking the Japanese *kamikaze* aircraft at source, on their airfields on Luzon, Admiral McCain arranged an attack in which a different task was assigned to each of the three fast carrier groups taking part. Rear-Admiral Montgomery (T.G. 38.1) was to attack northern Luzon, including the Clark Field area, Aparri and the shipping in Lingayen Gulf and to the northward. Rear-Admiral Bogan (T.G. 38.2) was to raid southern Luzon south of 14° N., the Verde Island Passage, Mindoro airfields and the northern part of the Sibuyan Sea. Rear-Admiral Sherman (T.G. 38.3) would cover the area between 14° N. and 15° N., including shipping in Manila Bay. The attacks were each to consist of a fighter sweep at dawn followed by successive strikes in strength. To counter the enemy's suicide attacks much larger protective fighter patrols were provided than was usual. Instead of the defensive combat air patrol of eight fighters and an anti-submarine patrol of four fighters ordinarily employed the plan of attack on Luzon called for the maintenance of a combat air patrol of 20 fighters during daylight, with a further four fighters operating close to the ships at low level. This increase in fighter protection, the fighter sweeps, use of fighters for search and attack missions, cover for submarines on rescue service, photographic missions and radio relay aircraft rendered it difficult to furnish sufficient fighters to escort the bombers to the target, and thus reduced the number of aircraft which might otherwise have taken part in strikes.

Task Force 38 arrived at the launching point around 15° 30′ N., 123° 15′ E. at approximately 0615 on the 5th. The position was 80 miles from the coast of Luzon and nearly 160 miles from Manila. The carriers moved about 60 miles to the eastward during the course of the day. The dawn fighter sweep apparently surprised the enemy, and airborne opposition was light except over the Clark Field–Mabalacat area (Plan 14) where Admiral Montgomery's fighters reported shooting down 58 Japanese aircraft. Opposition in this region continued throughout the 5th and on the following day. Very large numbers of aircraft were on the airfields ; photographs showed numbers in the nature of 400 or more in the Clark Field area. They were thoroughly dispersed, the taxi-ways extending sometimes as far as two miles from the airfield, the aircraft being well camouflaged and mingled with dummy aircraft. For the most part, the enemy used satellite fields with grass airstrips rather more than the more obvious paved runways, rendering thorough photographic coverage essential for pilot briefing and damage assessment. Throughout the 5th and 6th the airfields and dispersal areas were persistently strafed and bombed, but after the early strikes of the 5th almost all enemy aircraft disappeared from areas other than Clark Field, and accordingly from 1100 on the 5th onwards Admirals Bogan and Sherman sent most of their strikes to attack the aircraft in that complex.

Early on the 5th, reports came in of 15 to 20 freighters of various sizes, a light cruiser and several destroyers in Manila inner harbour, whilst a *Nachi* class heavy cruiser and two destroyers were trying to proceed out of the outer harbour. Rear-Admiral Sherman (T.G. 38.3) sent strikes against these ships at 1100 and 1300. The *Nachi*, as the cruiser was found to be, after a large number of hits from the 46 aircraft torpedoes which were expended, in addition to bombs and rockets, broke in three pieces and sank.[1] The destroyer *Akebono* and destroyer escort *Okinawa* received damage, and patrol vessel *P.107* was sunk. The attacks on shipping in Manila Bay were renewed on the 6th. The strikes met intense anti-aircraft fire which under the prevailing condition of low cloud rendered successful attacks difficult. The only sinking was a 5,000-ton tanker.[2]

The Japanese reaction was not proportionate to the large number of aircraft on the fields, being no doubt affected by the constant carrier aircraft attacks. In the first enemy raid which approached the force on the morning of the 5th all the aircraft were shot down. At about 1300 however aircraft appeared on the radar screens closing rapidly from the west. Detection was difficult as the screen was choked with the simultaneous return of U.S. strike aircraft. In the almost unbroken cloud cover from about 3,500 to 7,000 feet, four of the enemy evaded the fighters vectored out to shoot them down ; and at 1335 these four began suicide attacks on Rear-Admiral Sherman's group (T.G. 38.3). Three were shot down, but the fourth crashed on board the *Lexington*, flagship of the Fast Carrier Force, causing damage and a large number of casualties, though the ship remained in action. About 50 miles to the southward, two isolated destroyers of Admiral McCain's group (T.G. 38.1), whilst engaged in anti-submarine operations, sustained four well co-ordinated torpedo attacks by two or three aircraft in each raid, the method being for one or two of the enemy to approach from one side and distract attention from another attacking simultaneously at low altitude from the opposite direction. Neither destroyer was hit, and the Commander-in-Chief was unable to account for the choice of these isolated and comparatively insignificant ships for attack, when the main force contained valuable targets. On the following day some 15 to 18 enemy aircraft approached the task groups, but did not succeed in making effective attacks, being driven off with heavy loss by the U.S. protective fighters.

---

[1] The *Nachi* was reported to have received nine torpedo hits, 13 × 1,000 lb. and 6 × 250 lb. G.P. bomb hits, and 16 rocket hits. *Action report of Manila strikes, 5th–6th November* 1944 (M.0857/45). It would appear from Admiral Nimitz's report, however, that he considered the number of hits claimed to be exaggerated.

[2] The considerably larger number of ships reported sunk and damaged on 5th and 6th November by Commander-in-Chief, Pacific in *Operations in the Pacific Ocean Areas during November* 1944 is not confirmed by the post-war *American Report* nor by the *Japanese Report.*

8

The Japanese, having made the decision to fight a decisive battle with the Allies, wherever the latter might land, had adopted reinforcement of the invaded area of the Philippines by troops as well as aircraft, as an integral part of the plan of defence. Until General Kenney's land-based air forces were established on the Leyte airfields it was not within his power to stop this traffic, and it fell to the fast and escort carrier forces to undertake the duty. The reinforcement (' Ta ') operations were conducted by the Commander-in-Chief, South-West Area, whose headquarters were at Manila ; and they began simultaneously with the sortie of the Combined Fleet which resulted in the Battle for Leyte Gulf. A Transportation Corps had been organised in February 1944 in Japan, under Rear-Admiral Akira Shoji ; its headquarters moved to Formosa at the time of the U.S. landing on Leyte, and subsequently to Manila.[1] The strength of the Corps at that date was about 30 defensively armed transports and cargo ships ; and it was these which, with others specially detailed, were employed on the reinforcement operations, together with destroyers or frigates, escorted by light cruisers, destroyers and other light craft. Later, when the build up of Allied air strength had made such methods unprofitable, the use of evasion by small craft was adopted. On one occasion, the battleship carriers *Ise* and *Hyuga* were used to bring troops and stores to Koron Bay in the Calamian group (Plan 13) where they were transferred to small ships for passage to Manila and thence onward in convoy. The enemy had an inland waterway via Verde Island Passage, the Sibuyan Sea, Visayan Sea, Samar Sea or Camotes Islands, by which his reinforcement convoys could reach the important supply base at Ormoc on the west coast of Leyte Island, which was chosen as the landing place for reinforcements. The waterway was difficult for the Allied surface forces to reach. It was easily protected by air from the many Japanese-held airfields within range in the Visayas, Luzon and Mindanao, into which the enemy continued to move air reinforcements. In the north-east monsoon which prevailed during the Leyte operation, weather moves from west to east, enabling the Japanese convoys to pass through the Sibuyan Sea to Ormoc under cover of cloud fronts. Five Army divisions and one independent brigade were despatched in all. But despite their advantages, the Japanese losses were heavy, and the reinforcements which succeeded in getting through proved insufficient to stem the advance of the U.S. troops on Leyte, and had the effect of seriously weakening the defence in the other islands and thus facilitating their subsequent capture.

The first reinforcement consisted of some 2,000 troops of the 30th Division carried on board three transports escorted by the light cruiser *Kinu* and the destroyer *Uranami*. The convoy was sighted and attacked on 24th October west of Luzon by U.S. Liberator aircraft and both the escorts received minor damage. The convoy reached Ormoc, however, where the transports unloaded successfully ; but on withdrawal it was encountered fortuitously and attacked on the 26th by Liberators attempting to find and mop up survivors of the Battle for Leyte Gulf and by Third Fleet aircraft, and both the *Kinu* and *Uranami* were sunk.[2]

---

[1] Interrogation of Rear-Admiral A. Shoji (Nav. No. 101).

[2] Subsequent investigation shows that the statement by the U.S.S.B.S. in their appraisal of ' Sho One ' (*ONI Review*, November 1946 (pp. 40, 41)), that two of the three transports also were sunk, is incorrect. None of them was damaged.

Taking advantage of the weakness of U.S. land-based air forces over Leyte the Japanese went on urgently with the 'Ta' operation. Their second reinforcement was more important. It coincided with the absence of the Seventh Fleet escort carriers replenishing and the unavoidable temporary reduction of the fast carriers stationed off Leyte to a single group. The convoy, which was commanded by Rear-Admiral M. Matsuyama, consisted of four large transports and cargo ships[1] carrying 12,000 men of the 1st Division, one of the finest Japanese formations, from the Tokyo area, escorted by six destroyers of the 1st Flotilla and four frigates of the General Escort Command under the Commander 1st Destroyer Flotilla.[2] This Division had been destined for Manila, but was sent on to Ormoc in conformity with the plan to fight the decisive battle on Leyte Island. The convoy was given air cover. It took the route via Verde Island Passage, the Sibuyan Sea, between Burias and Ticao Islands and the Camotes Islands to Ormoc Bay. Off Palompon, on the west coast of Leyte Island, U.S. army fighters attacked it late in the afternoon of 31st October, using machine-gun fire and small bombs. A little superficial damage was caused. The convoy reached Ormoc just before sunset. U.S. motor torpedo boats were sent to attack it during the night, but the destroyers of the escort kept them off. Next morning, shortly after dawn U.S. fighters again began attacking. In the early afternoon, Liberators bombed the convoy, sinking the army transport *Noto Maru*, but not before she had nearly finished unloading. The remaining three ships completed landing troops and supplies and sailed that evening. All the 12,000 men were successfully put ashore.

The three surviving transports with a fourth added, accompanied by the same escort augmented by two or three destroyers, sailed from Manila again on 7th November for Ormoc with the remainder of the 1st Division and the main strength of the 26th Division. It was joined *en route* by three or four armed transports which entered Ormoc Bay in company. Protected by a typhoon over Leyte, it was not until the evening of the 9th, while rounding the southern end of the peninsula west of Ormoc that the convoy was discovered and attacked by U.S. medium bombers escorted by army fighters. Only superficial damage was caused but this involved the deck equipment and unloading tackle of the transports ; and though the convoy reached Ormoc at dusk, the transports were unable to unload their equipment during the night as intended, owing to the damaged condition of their gear and lack of landing barges, for air raids on the 5th, 6th and 7th had destroyed most of the barges at the beaches. The troops were, however, landed successfully, ferried to shore, it is reported, by the four frigates of the escort. Fighter aircraft arrived at dawn and began to harass the convoy, which sailed about three hours later. American M.T.B.s attacked without success as the convoy left Ormoc Bay ; and off the southern tip of Ormoc Peninsula about noon B–25s (medium bombers) set on fire and sank the *Kashii Maru* and the *Takatsu Maru*, one of the new freighter-transports of 5,350 tons with heavy A.A. armament,[3] and so damaged the frigate *C.D.*11 that she had to be beached and became a total loss. Four destroyers and a

[1] *Kashii Maru, Kinka Maru, Noto Maru, Kozu Maru.*

[2] The First Destroyer Flotilla belonged to the Fifth Fleet and contained at the time eight destroyers, the *Sazanami, Usugumo, Hatsuharu, Hatsushimo, Shiranuhi, Kasumi, Ushio, Akebono*. The four last named had recently been engaged in the Battle of Surigao Strait. It is uncertain which were the six destroyers engaged in the reinforcement operation. The convoy is described in Interrogations, Nav. Nos. 37 and 57 (Interrogation of Rear-Admiral Matsuyama).

[3] This ship had presumably taken the place of the sunk *Noto Maru*. The translator of Admiral Matsuyama's Interrogation calls her the *Kozoma Maru*, but there was no such ship in the Japanese Merchant Navy list.

frigate stood by the damaged transports until they shortly afterwards sank. Whilst thus engaged, one of the four destroyers was hit by a bomb in an attack by U.S. army fighters in the early afternoon, but was able to reach Manila, down by the bows.

Meanwhile, another convoy—actually the third in sequence—had been reported late on the 9th heading for Ormoc Bay. This convoy, which was commanded by Admiral Hayakawa, consisted of four transports and cargo vessels[1] carrying the remainder of the 26th Division and supplies, escorted by five destroyers and a minesweeper. It was given fighter cover. At the time, three Task Groups (38.1, 38.3 and 38.4) of the Fast Carrier Force, which had been fuelling and replenishing, were about 400 miles west of Saipan, a position to which they had run from a typhoon on the 8th. At midnight on 9/10th November they received orders to destroy the enemy convoy, and they thereupon set course for Leyte at 26 knots. At 0600 on the 11th they launched searches from a point 200 miles east of San Bernardino Strait, and located the convoy between Cebu and Leyte Islands. Within 45 minutes, full air group strikes aggregating 347 aircraft were in the air proceeding to attack. The strike co-ordinator who arrived before the first strike ordered the four transports to be first attacked, and in a matter of minutes all four were sunk by bombs and torpedoes within a mile of the shore. As the later air groups arrived they were ordered to destroy the escorts. These manœuvered ceaselessly. In all, 264 aircraft attacked the six ships, sinking the destroyers *Naganami*, *Hamanami*, *Shimakaze* and *Wakatsuki* and the minesweeper *W*.30. The Japanese fighter cover, numbering some 25 to 30 aircraft, attempted to protect their ships, but after two-thirds of them had been shot down the remainder made off. Only one U.S. aircraft was lost in this engagement, but eight were shot down by the intense anti-aircraft fire of the convoy. The difficulty experienced by aircraft, of sinking destroyers free to manœuvre, was illustrated by the number of bombs, 377 and torpedoes, 19, expended.[2]

On completion of the strike, the carriers retired to the eastward. One enemy pilot picked up out of the water after one of the minor suicide attacks which were attempted on the retiring force informed his interrogator that he was no volunteer for *kamikaze* but had been detailed to immolate himself. He had no enthusiasm for his task.

The Japanese ran six more convoys of reinforcements to Leyte. On two occasions, 26th November and 6th December, the enemy attempted to protect his convoys by paratroop raids on Leyte airstrips occupied by the Americans : both raids failed. The enemy were harassed by American M.T.B.s based on Leyte and Samar Islands which ranged as far north as Masbate Island ; by the increasing number of Army and Marine garrison aircraft now being based on the Leyte fields ; and by destroyer sweeps ; whilst the strikes of the Third Fleet carriers against Luzon accounted for several vessels in harbour at Manila and elsewhere. Though Japanese aircraft tried desperately to protect their transports, this continual harassment rendered the unloading of any considerable amounts of stores and equipment most difficult. Landing craft, fishing vessels and barges were used for bringing troops from nearby islands, but could not be employed for the passage from more distant Luzon. One convoy of 28 barges heavily escorted, got safely through and landed 2,400 troops whilst the land-based air forces at Leyte were engaged in covering Leyte Gulf ; the inability

[1] *Seiho Maru, Mikasa Maru, Tensho Maru, Taizan Maru.*

[2] *See* Admiral Sherman's remarks in M.0640/45, *Task Group* 38.3 *Report of Ormoc Bay strike,* 11*th November* 1944.

of the U.S. aircraft to get back to their fields for refuelling and loading with bombs before darkness saved the convoy. On 25th November, Third Fleet aircraft destroyed two transports, the *Manei Maru No. 6* and the *Kasagisan Maru*,[1] off Lingayen. On the night of the 27th/28th, after Japanese minefields off the south-west coast of Leyte had been swept, a division of U.S. destroyers went up and bombarded the enemy held beachhead at Ormoc, in the course of which they sank the Japanese submarine *I*–46 near the entrance to the bay. On the following night, the destroyers carried out a sweep in the Camotes Sea, sinking a submarine chaser and Patrol Boat *Ch*.53, whilst army aircraft sank the transports *Shinetsu Maru* and *Shinso Maru* after heckling them all night to prevent their unloading. A third raid on the night 1st/2nd December proved barren.[2] But on the following night, the destroyers *Allen M. Sumner*, *Cooper* and *Moale* entered Ormoc Bay in the early morning hours to destroy five enemy ships reported present. The destroyers were almost continuously attacked from the air. The *Sumner* was slightly damaged by near miss bombs. The *Cooper* was hit by a torpedo which was not seen ; she broke in half and went down in less than a minute with the loss of half her crew.[3] But the destroyers, firing intermittently at surface targets detected by radar, and at enemy aircraft and land targets, sank the Japanese destroyer *Kuwa* and damaged a second, the *Take* ; and next day 250 Japanese bodies were counted at the beaches, in addition to large numbers in the water.

The two final reinforcement convoys arrived at Leyte on 7th and 12th December respectively. During the whole of the 7th, army and marine land-based aircraft attacked the first of the two, sinking high-speed *Transport No.* 11 and four other transports ;[4] whilst on the 12th M.T.B.s sank the destroyer *Uzuki*, and land-based aircraft the destroyer *Yuzuki*, *Tank Landing Ship No.* 159, and the transports *Mino Maru* and *Tasmania Maru*.

In the course of the ‘ Ta ’ Operation the Japanese succeeded in landing some 30,000 army troops and 10,000 tons of material. In addition, between 10,000 and 15,000 men were lost *en route*.[5] Half of the supplies sent from Japan were lost,[6] and the quantity landed was insufficient to enable the Fourteenth Army to stage an offensive on a scale large enough to drive the Americans out of Leyte. The light cruiser *Kinu*, nine destroyers,[7] a frigate and eight lesser war vessels were sunk either in Ormoc Bay or whilst escorting convoys, together with 16 transports and a large number of beaching craft ; whilst the losses of aircraft protecting convoys was severe, most of the 600 naval aircraft lost by the Japanese during November being thus accounted for. In addition the Japanese Naval Air Force reported the loss operationally during the month, of 700 aircraft.[8]

---

[1] From the *American List*. This sinking is not shown in the *Japanese List*.

[2] *In Operations in the Pacific Ocean Areas during the month of December* 1944, p. 40, a description is given of sinking by gunfire an escorted enemy freighter at 0245 on 2nd December. Neither loss nor damage is shown in the *Japanese Report*, nor is any ship listed as sunk in the *American Report*.

[3] Most of the survivors were picked up by Catalinas, one of which, in a single flight, carried 56 survivors in addition to her crew of nine.

[4] *Hakuba Maru*, *Akagisan Maru*, *Shinsei Maru No.* 5, *Nichiyo Maru*.

[5] Japanese Monograph No. 114.

[6] *The Effects of Strategic Bombing on Japan's War Economy*, *Appendix A*, *B*, *C*. Report No. B.I.O.S./J.A.P./P.R./1589, p. 51.

[7] In addition to the eight destroyers already described as sunk, the *Wakaba* was sunk on 24th October south of Mindoro Island.

[8] This was a lower ratio than usual. The average loss ratio of the war was 40 per cent in combat to 60 per cent operationally.

9

Very heavy sinkings were made by the aircraft of the Fast Carrier Force in three raids carried out against shipping and airfields on Luzon, on 13th–14th, 19th and 25th November. General MacArthur's air strength on Leyte was not yet sufficient to neutralize enemy air bases in the Philippines, and accordingly after fuelling on 12th November three of Admiral McCain's fast carrier task groups proceeded towards the central Luzon area to attack shipping and aircraft reported there. At the large Clark Field air base a precursor of the ' air blanket ' type of operation was employed, one fighter sweep arriving over the airfield as the previous one was departing. Enemy air opposition was generally light, the Japanese defence largely taking the form of camouflage and dispersal, but the Americans destroyed a number of aircraft both in the air and on the ground. Their own losses in two days of strikes reached the unusually high figure of 25, chiefly as the result of intense anti-aircraft fire experienced during attacks on shipping at Manila. The aircraft sank the light cruiser *Kiso,* destroyers *Akebono, Akishimo, Hatsuharu* and *Okinami,* and *Submarine Chaser No. 116.* Great execution was done amongst the transports and freighters in Manila Bay, 18 ships of 93,400 tons being destroyed, whilst Manila was put out of operation as a port of reinforcement for Leyte for a considerable time. The destruction of shipping, damage to harbour facilities, and obstruction of the harbour with sunken ships, all served to reduce the use of the harbour, so that San Fernando, on the north side of Lingayen Gulf had to be employed as an alternative convoy assembly port.

After fuelling on 18th November the Fast Carrier Task Force, consisting of the three groups 38.1, 38.2 and 38.4 returned to the Luzon area for further strikes next day against aircraft and shipping. The usual pattern of a fighter sweep to locate targets, followed by strikes, was employed. Air opposition over the airfields was light, the Japanese relying here too mainly on camouflage for protection of their aircraft. In this art they were masters, and at one airfield the U.S. pilots failed to locate a single aircraft where photographs subsequently showed that upwards of 70 were parked. Nevertheless, the airmen reported destroying a total of more than 100 enemy aircraft on the ground. Shipping was scarce and at Manila difficulty was experienced in distinguishing the few undamaged ships amongst the wrecks. Two ships, the transport *Seian Maru* and a tanker which has never been identified, were sunk at Manila, and the large freighter, *Esashi Maru* north of San Fernando. A strike group of 13 fighters from the *Wasp* loaded with 500 lb. bombs located the heavy cruiser *Kumano* beached off Santa Cruz (15° 47′ N., 119° 48′ E.). This ship had been torpedoed during the Battle for Leyte Gulf and had limped back to Manila. She had been torpedoed again on 6th November off Cape Bolinao, Luzon, whilst escorting a convoy, by the *Raton,* one of a wolf pack of four U.S. submarines of the Seventh Fleet, and had been escorted to her present position by the destroyer *Okinami.* The *Wasp's* strike group dropped eight bombs on the immobilised ship, but did not succeed in hitting her. In this raid on 19th November, Japanese retaliatory air attacks on the U.S. task force were the heaviest of the month. Beginning during the night before the attacks on Luzon they continued until the carriers left the area on the evening of the 19th. The Americans were employing destroyer pickets along the line of expected attack, 40,000 yards from the centre of the Task Force, and they received rapid and accurate information of the enemy's approach ; whilst the sunset combat air patrol was stationed, in accordance with a new defence doctrine, at several different altitudes, 30 miles from the force. All enemy raids were intercepted by the C.A.P. or additional fighters vectored out, and none got through to the ships. On the other hand, the increase in defensive patrols, and an increase which had newly taken place in the ratio of fighters to dive bombers in the complements of the carriers, had the effect of reducing the striking power of the force.

A further shipping strike, with the damaged *Kumano* as one of the primary objectives, was made on 25th November. Only two groups, 38.2 and 38.3, of the Fast Carrier Force, a total of four fleet carriers and three light carriers, were available.[1] The *Kumano* was found in the same position; temporary repairs appeared to have been made to her, which would indicate that salvage was under way. The *Ticonderoga* flew off a strike of eight fighters, 13 scout bombers, and nine torpedo bombers. Several bomb hits were made prior to a torpedo attack in which six torpedoes hit the ship on the port side. She capsized and sank within four minutes of the first hit. It was during this raid that, as already described, two ships of a small reinforcement convoy, the *Manei Maru No. 6* and the *Kasagisan Maru* were sunk west of Lingayen.

During the whole of the November raids the fast carriers had launched their aircraft from the same area, some 150 miles east of Manila, and only 60 to 80 miles from the east coast of Luzon; and moreover, the raids had each been made at a fairly regular interval of six or seven days. The Americans were consequently not surprised at being located by enemy aircraft on the 25th.[2] At noon, Task Group 38.2 was steaming on course 220°, speed 20 knots, with Task Group 38.3 about 35 miles away. Each group at the time had the usual combat air patrol up. Both groups were preparing to launch the third strike of the day and the aircraft of the second strike were returning, when enemy suicide attacks began. At 1226, with enemy aircraft reported at 25 and 30 miles' distance, three carriers of Task Group 38.2 began launching. With these and returning strike aircraft and protective fighters in the air the radar screens of the group became saturated within 30 miles, rendering it practically impossible to plot the approach of enemy aircraft, some ten to a dozen of which got through and attacked the ships. Two suicide aircraft hit the *Intrepid* and a third the *Cabot*, whilst the *Hancock* was slightly damaged by a near miss. Task Group 38.3 began launching aircraft two minutes after the attack began. Five minutes later, before flying-off was completed, the *Essex* was hit by a suicider. The enemy aircraft was not armed with a bomb; nevertheless damage and casualties were heavy, though the ship was able to remain at sea. In the other group the *Cabot* was extensively damaged and lost 34 men, but was able to land-on her aircraft about an hour later. Damage to the *Intrepid* was more serious and her casualty list was heavy.[3] With everything but her bow hidden in an inferno of flame and thick black smoke, rocked by explosions, with blazing aviation fuel cascading down her sides, she kept her station in the formation and within half an hour had restored her communications which had been destroyed, and resumed duty as flagship of her group, though she was unable to land-on the 75 aircraft which she had in the air when hit and these had to land at Tacloban Field or on other carriers. Seventeen were lost.

By the middle of November control of the air was beginning to pass to the Allies. By the end of the month the Third Fleet ships were in need of repair and

---

[1] T.G. 38.2. Carriers *Hancock, Intrepid,* light carriers *Cabot, Independence.*
T.G. 38.3. Carriers *Essex, Ticonderoga,* light carrier *Langley.*

[2] The foregoing are the reasons given by Commander-in-Chief, Pacific for the preparedness of the Japanese. Admiral Halsey in his Memoirs (p. 235) says the Japanese were forewarned by the pattern of the U.S. radio traffic.

[3] Fifty-four killed, 15 missing, 50 wounded.

replenishment and their crews of a change from the rigours of three months of almost constant operating. In the last month, Japanese *kamikaze* attacks had cost them 328 men, some 90 aircraft, and had put three carriers out of action. Moreover, the invasion of Mindoro was fixed for 5th December and the fleet was required to take part. Task Force 38 was accordingly withdrawn to Ulithi for a few days, the strike on 25th November being their last in support of Leyte. There were then 182 Army fighters based on the island's airfields: a fortnight later the number was 317. The first direct support of the ground troops by Kenney's aircraft took place on 26th November.

10

In addition to the *Nachi* and *Kumano*, the Japanese lost during November two further main units, the battleship *Kongo* and the 59,000-ton carrier *Shinano*, both sunk by U.S. submarines. After the Battle for Leyte Gulf, the *Kongo*, with other units, had returned to Brunei Bay which was a safe anchorage. The ships made their way back to Japan at various times, and on 21st November the *Sea Lion* (Commander E. T. Reich) patrolling north-west of Formosa, had radar contact, at the unusually long range of 44,000 yards, indicating either a very large target or the existence of a sort of radar mirage. The target was the *Kongo*, proceeding in column with another battleship and two cruisers, screened by a destroyer on each bow and a third on the starboard beam. The *Sea Lion* was on the port bow of the formation. The night was moonless, sky overcast and sea calm, with visibility about 1,500 yards. The enemy ships, which were not zigzagging, were heading about north-east at 16 knots. At 0256 the *Sea Lion* began firing electric torpedoes from her six bow tubes at the leading battleship (the *Kongo*) followed at 0259 by three stern shots at the second battleship. Three hits were made on the first battleship and one on a destroyer which blew up. Contrary to standing orders, the torpedoes had been set to run at eight feet, and the *Kongo*, far from being slowed, increased speed to 18 knots with the remainder of the formation. Two hours later, however, whilst the *Sea Lion* was trying to reach attacking position once more, the *Kongo* began to drop astern, and at 0524 she blew up and sank in position 26° 09′ N., 121° 23′ E. This was the only Japanese battleship sunk by a submarine during the war. The *Skate* on 29th December 1943, 150 miles north-east of Truk had made two hits with torpedoes on the *Yamato*, and the *Tunny* a similar number on the *Musashi* on 29th March 1944 off Palau, but both battleships reached harbour under their own steam.

The keel of a third giant battleship of the same class as the *Yamato* and *Musashi* had been laid, but during construction the ship had been converted to an aircraft carrier, named *Shinano*. At 2048 on 28th November the *Shinano* was carrying out trials south of the entrance to Tokyo Bay in approximately 32° N., 137° E. when the submarine *Archerfish* (Commander J. F. Enright) had radar contact with her at 24,700 yards. The sky was overcast, but a bright moon gave visibility at times up to 15,000 yards. The *Shinano* had four escorts and was proceeding at a speed higher than the maximum of the *Archerfish*, accordingly the latter sent off a contact report in the hope that some other submarine might be able to attack. Proceeding at full speed on the surface, at 0300 on the 29th Commander Enright was rewarded by a turn towards him of the enemy force, and at 0317 he began firing all six bow tubes, depth setting 10 feet, range 1,400 yards, from a position on the starboard beam of the

Shinano.[1] All six of the torpedoes hit the target, but after the second, with a destroyer 500 yards on the *Archerfish*'s quarter and the wakes of torpedoes she had fired betraying her position, Commander Enright went deep. The carrier's escorts made a half-hearted attack, 14 depth charges being counted, only one of which was near enough to cause damage. Loud breaking up noises continued for nearly an hour ; and at 0610, when the *Archerfish* surfaced, nothing was in sight through the periscope. The *Shinano* did not sink for some hours, however ; probably she went down about 1000 when a large and distant single explosion was heard. It was subsequently learnt that the ship was not in a good state of watertight integrity. Dockyard workmen were still completing her and openings existed in various watertight bulkheads. Her escorts rescued most of her crew. On 9th December the U.S. submarines *Redfish* (Commander L. D. McGregor), and *Devilfish* (Commander R. E. Styles), co-operating on patrol in the East China Sea, torpedoed the aircraft carrier *Junyo* in the approaches to Korea Strait. The carrier received only medium damage, but the Japanese did not repair her and she never operated again. Better fortune attended the *Redfish* on the 19th of the month while on patrol north of Formosa. That afternoon, running submerged, Commander McGregor sighted the newly commissioned carrier *Unryu* with an escort of three destroyers, ferrying aircraft reinforcements to the Philippines. At 1635, a fortunate turn of the enemy brought the carrier within range and Commander McGregor began firing the last four torpedoes remaining forward. One hit was obtained, right aft, which immobilised the *Unryu* and caused her to develop such a heavy list that the aircraft with which she was loaded began sliding over the side. Meanwhile the four stern tubes had been fired at close range at a destroyer charging down on the *Redfish*'s periscope. Directly another tube could be got ready the submarine fired a torpedo at the carrier, at 1,100 yards' range. The torpedo hit just abaft the amidships structure ; tremendous explosions ensued, and the *Unryu* began to capsize. The *Redfish* delayed overlong taking photographs of the sinking ship, and in the depth charge attacks made on her in the shallow water which prevails in the East China Sea, she received severe damage. She had a crack in the forward torpedo room pressure hull plating, 12 broken battery jars, steering gear jammed on hard left, bow planes jammed on a 20° rise, all hydraulic power lost, and sound gear out of action. However, she made port safely. The *Unryu* sank in position 28° 59′ N., 124° 03′ E.

11

The inability of the Japanese to move reinforcements and supplies into Leyte otherwise than in small craft by evasion was in significant contrast to the freedom of movement at sea of the Allies. General MacArthur was planning further landings. By the beginning of December, the U.S. troops had cleared the enemy from most of eastern Leyte and were working westward through the central range of mountains. The Japanese still held the western part of the island with an estimated 35,000 troops.

During November, General Krueger's transportation problems on shore at Leyte had been greatly complicated by the wet weather. The Commanding General proposed that a division of troops should be moved through Surigao Strait and the Camotes Sea and put ashore near Ormoc, the port through which the Japanese were being re-supplied and towards which U.S. forces were advancing in an encircling movement to cut off the Japanese 26th Division.

[1] An account of the attack is given in *United States Pacific Fleet and Pacific Ocean Areas Weekly Intelligence*, Vol. I No. 24, 25th December 1944.

Admiral Kinkaid considered the operation too hazardous to undertake until better air cover was available. Moreover, invasion of Mindoro was projected on 5th December, and there was insufficient assault shipping for both operations to take place simultaneously. On 30th November, however, the decision was taken to postpone the Mindoro landing, shipping consequently became available, and it was decided to land the 77th Division less one regimental combat team (=brigade) on 7th December in Ormoc Bay, between three and four miles south-east of Ormoc. Unknown to both antagonists the date coincided with the arrival of a Japanese reinforcement convoy in the bay.

The attack groups sailed from Leyte Gulf and crossed the Camotes Sea under cover of darkness.[1] Minesweepers preceded the remainder of the expedition and cleared a passage through Kamigao Channel on the 6th. The expedition was off the landing beach at 0600 next day, and at dawn fighter cover arrived. After 30 minutes' preliminary bombardment by destroyers and rocket craft, beginning at 0640, to which the enemy made little reply, the troops began landing without opposition at 0707. By 0900 all vessels were unloaded, with the exception of two stranded on a reef. Forty minutes later, heavy enemy air attacks began, the Japanese adopting the tactics of grouping up over individual vessels for co-ordinated suicide attacks. The U.S. fighters provided what Admiral Kinkaid described as the finest support seen in the South-West Pacific Area. But nine enemy suicide aircraft made a co-ordinated attack on the destroyer *Mahan*, following each other in rapid succession, giving the ship barely enough time to develop effective fire against each successive aircraft.[2] The *Mahan* and a second destroyer the *Ward*, were badly damaged by suicide crashes and had both to be sunk by gunfire. At 1100 the attack group, excepting five which had been unable to retract, was formed up for return to Leyte Gulf. Suicide attacks continued. At 1302 the fast transport *Liddle* was hit but was able to proceed. About two hours later, the destroyer *Lamson* was hit and severely damaged, and had to be towed back to Leyte Gulf. The enemy continued to attack until 1745; four landing ships were hit or near missed, one of which had to be abandoned. Meanwhile, the Japanese were attempting to unload a convoy about 35 miles north of Ormoc, under continuous air attacks in which no less than 153 U.S. aircraft were employed. Almost the entire convoy was sunk,[3] but most of the troops swam ashore, though they lost nearly all their equipment.

The first re-supply echelon for the troops at Ormoc, consisting of 13 L.M.S.s and L.C.I.s, screened by the destroyers *Reid*, *Conygham*, *Smith*, *Caldwell*, *Coghlan* and *Edwards*, left Leyte Gulf to arrive off Ormoc about 2300 on 11th December. The formation was attacked by suicide aircraft at about 1700 that day, when the *Reid* was crashed by two aircraft and sunk, whilst the *Caldwell* suffered minor damage from a near miss. During the retirement of the force next day the *Caldwell* was again attacked by a group variously estimated to number 23 to 30 enemy aircraft. She was hit and severely damaged, but was able to proceed under her own power.

The effect of the U.S. landing at Ormoc was to reduce the Japanese to attempt to run their reinforcements for Leyte in small landing barges into minor ports in the north-west part of the island. On Christmas Day the Americans made

[1] The group comprised one destroyer (flagship); nine high-speed transports, 27 landing craft, infantry; 12 landing ships, medium; four landing ships, tank; nine minesweepers; four landing craft, infantry, rocket; one rescue tug; two submarine chasers; screened by 12 destroyers.

[2] *See C.T.G.* 78.3 (*U.S.S. Hughes*), *Action Report, Ormoc Landing, 7th December* 1944. M.01790/45.

[3] *See* p. 110.

further shore-to-shore landings on the west coast of Ormoc Bay and further north at Palompon, the only port of consequence remaining to the Japanese on the west coast of Leyte. By the end of the month Leyte was practically overrun. The remaining Japanese formations had disintegrated and were compressed into a few isolated pockets in the mountains where the difficult terrain rendered mopping up troublesome, though the final result was merely a matter of time. Organised enemy resistance ceased on 20th December. By 2nd January 1945, a total of 60,809 unburied enemy dead had been counted, and 434 prisoners taken. Mopping up continued for nearly five months, and by 8th May a further 25,000 Japanese had been killed or captured. American forces ashore numbered over 240,000. Their task in capturing the island had been rendered unduly difficult through lack of information of the terrain and climate of Leyte. The advancing of the target date for the operation had cut down the time available for study of the subject ; and the difficulties encountered in the preparation of airfields and movement of troops ashore came as a severe disappointment to almost everyone. Experience at Leyte was a vindication of the traditional methods employed in attacks in the South-West Pacific Area ; that is to say, the advance of army and naval land-based air forces in co-ordinated moves, with new beachheads kept always within range of fighter-escorted bombers.

CHAPTER IX

Liberation of the Philippines:

Seizure of Mindoro

1

BY early December, the Far Eastern (land-based) Air Force held an incomplete and precarious control of the air over the Central Philippine islands. To advance this cover, in anticipation of the projected landing in Lingayen Gulf for the capture of Luzon General MacArthur planned to seize lightly held Mindoro and develop airfields in the south-west part of the island near San José. From the point of view both of topography and weather Mindoro was well suited to form an advanced air base for the assault on Luzon. Lying on the southern flank of that island and separated from it by the Verde Island Passage, a strait eight miles in width, Mindoro had the advantage that its mountainous central range, running from north to south, sheltered the south-western portion of the island causing its dry season to coincide with the north-east monsoon which lasted as a rule from December to the end of May. That part of the island was relatively isolated from the remainder, it had good roads and a narrow gauge railway, and the cane fields provided more suitable land for airfields than the rice paddies of Leyte.

Though the garrison of Mindoro was small, comprising less than 1,000 men scattered in small detachments throughout the island, whilst friendly guerilla forces were known to be armed and operating, the operation presented a hazardous venture deep into waters over which the Japanese still retained air control. When the date for the assault (U-Day) had originally been fixed at 5th December, it was expected that the Allied land-based air force would be in firm control of the central Philippines and southern Luzon before the operation began and would be able to provide effective cover for the assault forces. As we know, this expectation was not fulfilled but Admiral Halsey was prepared to co-operate by making neutralizing strikes on the Luzon airfields. When on the 25th November however four of his carriers were damaged by suicide air attacks, both he and Admiral Nimitz (who was not best pleased at this injury to his carriers in a role for which they were unsuited and an operation of which he was not in charge) urged ten days' postponement of U-Day; and accordingly the date was changed to 15th December. This provided further time for the Fast Carrier Force of the Third Fleet to make their neutralizing strikes. It also gave time for further attacks by the fighter-bombers established on Leyte and heavy bombers from Morotai to reduce the enemy's air strength in the central Philippines, and thus improve their control of the air; and it enabled the shipping position to be improved. It was decided to send the Seventh Fleet escort carriers into the Sulu Sea to support the landings whilst the fast carriers maintained what the Americans termed a blanket over the Luzon airfields from the east. To protect the attack force from surface and air raiding formations the ships detailed to participate were given additional support in the form of a Heavy Covering and Carrier Group (Task Group 77.12), consisting of three battleships, three light cruisers, six escort carriers, and 18 destroyers under Rear-Admiral T. D. Ruddock, Jr. (*See* Appendix K). Thus South-West Pacific Area Forces instead of advancing behind a land-based aerial bomb line, were to rely upon a combination parallel to that commonly employed in the Pacific Ocean Areas. The innovation is reported to have been highly successful.[1] The battleships and light cruisers acted as anti-aircraft batteries and provided gun power for protection against surface forces, and the escort carriers furnished air cover. The maximum speed of the old battleships and the escort carriers was approximately equal, and they were thus suited for mutual co-operation. Land-based aircraft were responsible for cover at dusk each day and during the passage of the ships through restricted waters of the Mindanao Sea. The Attack Force, under Rear-Admiral A. D. Struble in the light cruiser *Nashville* consisted of 116 landing ships and craft, many under tow, protected by 12 destroyers. Close cover was given by Rear-Admiral R. S. Berkey with a group of cruisers and destroyers ; whilst 23 M.T.B.s accompanied the flotilla. The 19th Regimental Combat Team (reinforced) of the 24th Infantry Division, and the 503rd Parachute Regiment under Brigadier-General W. C. Dunckel, were detailed to carry out the landing, with service troops to establish airfields and other facilities. To conserve the air cover available, Admiral Struble decided to combine his U-Day and U + 1 Day convoys, even though this would entail leaving some landing ships off the Mindoro beaches overnight.

2

By 15th December when the landing on Mindoro took place, attacks on the Japanese air forces in the central Philippines had so reduced these that they consisted of little more than 30 aircraft based on Negros.[2] The enemy aircraft on the airfields of Luzon were, however, estimated at some twelve times this number, and the route to the landing beaches remained a perilous one ; it passed through waters within range of numerous enemy airfields, where space for evasion was limited and the proximity of land hindered radar detection of enemy aircraft. The blanketing of the Luzon airfields by the Third Fleet, however, adversely affected the reinforcement of the airfields of the central Philippines by the enemy.

The Japanese had early intelligence of the passage of the convoys and sighted them as they entered Visayan waters on 13th December, but they anticipated the landing not on Mindoro but on Luzon where the establishment of shore-based air forces would threaten the China Sea life-line.[3] That day, they attacked with a total of 150 aircraft and also ordered out from Saigon Admiral Shima's Second Diversion Attack Force (Appendix A), less the sunken light carrier *Abukuma* : but the U.S. Fast Carrier Force was sighted in the Sulu Sea on its way to attack the Luzon airfields and the force retired without attacking.

---

[1] *U.S.S. Denver, Action Report,* M.01813/45.

[2] *The Army Air Forces in World War II,* p. 396.

[3] Japanese Monograph No. 114. The Naval Analysis Division of the U.S.S.B.S. in an article in the *ONI Review,* November 1946, says the Japanese believed the expedition was bound for Palawan.

The first enemy attack on the convoys came at about 1500 on the 13th when a single suicide aircraft unobserved by the lookouts, came from behind an island and crash-dived the light cruiser *Nashville*, flagship of the Attack Group. The ship was struck on the superstructure, with a tremendous explosion. Communications were badly damaged, 175 officers and men were killed, and a further 100 wounded. Admiral Struble was unhurt and transferred his flag to the destroyer *Dashiell*, while the *Nashville* was escorted back to Leyte Gulf. The transfer was made without either ship reducing speed. During one of a number of dusk attacks, the destroyer *Haraden* in Admiral Ruddock's Heavy Covering and Carrier Group was crashed by a suicide aircraft and also had to be sent back to Leyte. But the enemy's attempted attacks next day failed, apart from one which severely damaged the oiler H.M.A.S. *Bishopdale*. The escort carriers of Admiral Ruddock's force claimed to have shot down a large number of enemy aircraft, some of them in the course of sweeps to neutralize enemy airfields considered to lie too close to the track of the convoy for safety.

Mindoro was reached during the night of the 14th–15th and the landing began at 0730 next morning in the bay south of San José. Opposition was negligible, but during unloading two L.S.T.s were hit and set on fire by suicide air attacks and the destroyer *Howorth* was damaged. In Admiral Ruddock's Group, the escort carrier *Marcus Island* received minor damage. A working party of some 1,200 troops had been brought along for the sole purpose of unloading, and the operation was completed before dusk. The Attack Group began its return passage to Leyte at 1900, the troops quickly captured their objectives ashore, and the immediate construction of airfields and roads began. By 22nd December San José field was operational for fighters and heavy bombers. An M.T.B. base was established by 16th December.

The first re-supply echelon for Mindoro, consisting of 11 destroyers[1] with 14 L.S.T.s, six freighters, four L.C.I.s and an Army supply vessel had left Leyte during the evening of the 19th. Air attacks began on the morning of the 21st, and one L.S.T. was sunk and a second L.S.T. and a freighter damaged. In the late afternoon of the 26th a patrolling Catalina sighted the Japanese Second Diversion Attack Force approaching Mindoro from the South China Sea. The force consisted of the heavy cruiser *Ashigara*, light cruisers *Oyodo* and *Kashii*, and destroyers *Kiyoshimo*, *Kasumi*, *Kashi*, *Asashimo*, *Kaya* and perhaps the *Sugi* and *Hinoki*. The slow battleship carriers *Ise* and *Hyuga* were left behind at Cam-ranh Bay. Army aircraft from Leyte attacked at low level soon after dark in very bad weather and sank the destroyer *Kiyoshimo*, in a wild night engagement in which no less than 26 U.S. aircraft out of a total of 105 which attacked, were lost. Despite the damage his ships had suffered Admiral Shima bombarded the Mindoro beachhead an hour before midnight, sinking one and damaging other merchant ships and destroying some stores and equipment on shore. That the loss was not higher was ascribed to the damage to the Japanese main batteries and casualties to guns' crews caused during the air attacks in the early part of the night. By that time aircraft of the U.S. Fifth (Army) Air Force were established on the Mindoro fields, and next day, during his retirement, Shima was attacked by medium bombers and fighters. All three cruisers, the *Ashigara*, *Oyodo* and *Kashii*, and four of the destroyers, the *Kasumi*, *Kaya*, *Asashimo* and *Kashi* were damaged. When the initial sighting of the enemy was reported, a force of four Allied cruisers and nine destroyers left Leyte Gulf

---

[1] *Ausburne, McGowan, W. D. Porter, Converse, Stanly, Foote, Kimberley, Newcomb, Lowry, Bryant, Young.*

at high speed to attack it, but despite the damage they had suffered, the remnant of the Japanese force escaped towards Cam-ranh Bay without being brought to action.

During the remainder of the month the enemy made repeated air attacks on the shipping and beachhead on Mindoro. In the second re-supply convoy on the 28th an ammunition ship was blown up and an L.C.M. was sunk in persistent and vicious air attacks.[1] Mines were dropped in the path of the convoy. It was not until the enemy had a more serious landing on Luzon to contend with that air attacks ceased.

3

During a brief period of replenishment which the Third Fleet spent at Ulithi after their air strikes late in November, countermeasures for defence against suicide air attacks were worked out. The Fast Carrier Task Force was re-organised in three instead of four groups, to enable more battleships and cruisers to be assigned to each group for anti-aircraft protection (*see* Appendix L). In one group, composed of three carriers and two light carriers, one of the air groups was used for the most part at night. The additional number of destroyers helped to meet the demand for strike pickets (' Watchdogs '). These were destroyers with aircraft homing devices, stationed on each side of the target bearing on strike days. Their duties were to assist in control of strike aircraft and to give advance warning to the force of approaching enemy aircraft. Returning friendly aircraft were confined to specified lanes and had to identify themselves to specified pickets (' Tomcats ')—' delousing ', as it was termed—in order to put a stop to the Japanese practice of following the strike aircraft back to their carriers. The new method was also designed to keep radar screens clear of friendly aircraft on the line of most probable enemy approach. A third defensive measure consisted in a substantial increase in the fighter complements of the fleet carriers. In place of 36 fighters, 36 bombers and 18 torpedo bombers these carriers now carried 73 fighters, 15 bombers and 15 torpedo bombers : for the last-named type the Americans were now finding little use, whilst the new fighters could also be used as bombers. The increased number of fighters permitted a type of operation in which constant combat air patrols could be maintained over enemy airfields throughout the day and night to prevent the take-off or landing of any enemy aircraft during a specified period, in this case, the three days required for the approach of the attack force to Mindoro, the landing and unloading.[2] This superseded the former practice of a dawn fighter sweep followed by three or four successive attack groups. There were between 90 and 100 known or suspected enemy airfields in the area of Luzon assigned to the Third Fleet for neutralisation (Plan 14). Information of these fields was inadequate, and complete coverage was essential to success, accordingly pilots were instructed to photograph each airfield. Since the Japanese practised wide dispersal and clever camouflage of their aircraft, orders were given to cover thoroughly the area within five miles of each field. In addition to neutralizing the airfields, the Third Fleet had the duty of denying the use of harbours in Luzon to enemy ships. Target priorities were, in order : enemy aircraft, installations whose destruction would immediately affect adversely the operation

---

[1] Reports of the attacks are in M.01807/45 and M.03224/45.

[2] The method employed is described in detail in *Operations in the Pacific Ocean Areas during the month of December* 1944, para. 48.

of enemy aircraft, and enemy ships so far as attacks on these did not adversely affect the accomplishment of the primary mission.

The Third Fleet groups sortied from Ulithi by 11th December. Wireless deception was used.[1] From 14th to 16th December, the fast carrier aircraft carried out strikes on Luzon. Every known or suspected airfield was covered ;[2] 36 were found to be operational, 32 non-operational, and 23 non-existent. With so large a number of fields to be attacked or observed, round-the-clock coverage was of course very thin ; whilst the great increase in the proportion of fighters to bombers and torpedo aircraft in the carriers complements reduced the tonnage of bombs dropped to less than one-third of the average. Air opposition was slight at the outset and there was little evidence that the enemy made any large scale or persistent effort to bring in reinforcements of aircraft. Out of a total of 272 enemy aircraft reported destroyed in the three days of operating, 179 were destroyed on the first day ; 208 of the total were destroyed on the ground. No enemy aircraft penetrated the defensive patrols of the force and no American aircraft was lost in combat, but 27 were lost operationally and a similar number was brought down by anti-aircraft fire, for some of the airfields were very heavily defended ; at the Clark Field complex for example, it is reported that 74 heavy, 237 medium and 174 light A.A. guns were mounted.[3] Anti-aircraft fire caused the loss of about 75 of the 100 aircraft lost during each of the months November and December by the U.S. Army. The losses of the carriers were little less.

4

At the conclusion of the strikes on 16th December the fast carrier force began its withdrawal. Admiral McCain intended to appoint a fuelling rendezvous to the eastward, and to return with his force to Luzon on the 19th for a further three-day series of strikes. These plans were nullified by a typhoon which struck the fleet on the 18th, east of Luzon.[4]

As the result of high-speed steaming during the recent operations, many of the destroyers were low on fuel, some having only 15 per cent remaining. Attempts were consequently made to refuel on the 17th in increasingly heavy weather. The fuelling rendezvous was changed to one which it was estimated would be clear of the track of the approaching storm. Information available to the fleet of the location and path of the storm was meagre. Early warnings were delayed. The typhoon followed a path considerably further north than anticipated, and the northernmost units of the task force were almost directly in its path. The centre of the storm about 35 miles away was clearly shown on the radar PPI scope of the *Wasp*. Wind speeds were from 50 to 75 knots, and considerably higher in gusts. Mountainous and confused seas built up, and barometric pressure as low as 28·15 inches was recorded. Visibility varied

[1] The Commander-in-Chief Pacific Fleet reported that tactical surprise was achieved, but the British Naval Liaison Officer reported that the Japanese intercepted U.S. R/T messages which warned them of the attacks.

[2] Report of Commander Fast Carrier Force.

[3] *The Army Air Forces in World War II*, p. 408.

[4] The following papers give a good description of the Typhoon: M.01645/45, M.0116/45, M.01267/45, M.0961/45. A critical appreciation is in Pacific Fleet Confidential Letter 14CL–45 of 18th February 1945, which is reprinted in U.S. Naval Institute Proceedings, January 1946. Numerous reports from ships are in *Operations in the Pacific Ocean Areas during the month of December 1944, Annex B.*

between 0–1,000 yards, in consequence of flying spume and rain. Ships attempted to maintain fleet course, speeds and formations. Commanding officers and subordinate commanders failed to appreciate that dangerous weather conditions existed, until it was too late to make preparations for security which might have been helpful.

Some of the destroyers caught in the worst part of the storm found themselves unable to alter course by use of any combination of engines and rudder. In certain destroyers which were eventually lost, water was taken in quantity through ventilators, blower intakes, and every kind of opening. Switchboards and electrical machinery were short-circuited and drowned out. There was free water up to two or three feet over engine and boiler room plates and in other compartments. This apparently came in from above, as there was no evidence of ships' seams opening. Steering control was lost, power and light failed, the main propulsion plants stopped, and all ability to communicate was lost. Wind velocities carried away upper deck gear and made it impossible to secure gear which had gone adrift, or to jettison or strike below top weights, for men could not stay on deck. Rolling in excess of 70° was reported by various ships ; the *Dewey*, with port tanks filled to give her a list of 20° to port, reported rolls of 75° to starboard and on several occasions the lee wing of the bridge scooped up green water. The *Aylwin* hung for about 20 minutes between 30° and 70°. Such rolling exceeded the stability range of the lightly ballasted destroyers. The *Hull* though well above the point where ballasting was required, unfortunately decided not to flood her tanks and capsized ; and the *Spence* and *Monaghan* were also lost. Typical motion before capsizing was that the ship would take a heavy roll of 50°–80° to leeward, hang for a little while, then roll completely over, floating for a short time before going down. All these ships manœuvred up to the time of sinking in the attempt to maintain station. The *Dewey* which gave up the attempt after altering course to avoid collision with a carrier, attributed her safety to the fact that whilst she was borne down by the wind one of her funnels was blown overboard, thus reducing wind pressure. She reported that the needle-like spray removed paint from metal surfaces like a sand blaster. The light aircraft carriers and escort carriers also suffered considerably. A total of 146 aircraft were lost, the replacement carriers losing 86 of this total from their decks. Fires broke out in the light carriers *Monterey*, *Cowpens* and *San Jacinto* as the result of damage to aircraft fuel tanks in which some residual aviation fuel remained after degassing. The damage to radar and radio equipment in various ships created a serious situation in view of impending air strikes. These were abandoned. The force fuelled on the 22nd and returned to Ulithi two days later.

As the result of extensive searches, 92 officers and men from the sunken destroyers were picked up, but nearly 800 were drowned.

CHAPTER X

Liberation of the Philippines:

The Lingayen Landings

(Plans 13, 14, 15)

1

BY the end of December all of Leyte was under U.S. control, except for mopping up of isolated and disorganised enemy groups. On Mindoro, naval as well as air units were firmly established, giving the Allies a base on the China Sea to attack shipping and support landings on Luzon. Manila Harbour was interdicted and Japanese transports bringing supplies from Formosa were forced to utilise such ports as San Fernando and Aparri for disembarkation points.

Amphibious landings in Lingayen Bay, Luzon were originally scheduled for 20th December, but on account of the enemy resistance on Leyte had to be postponed to 9th January (S-day). The object of the operations (' Musketeer ' or ' Mike One ') was stated to be the prompt seizure of the central Luzon area; destruction of the principal defence forces; denial to the enemy of the northern entrance to the South China Sea; and the provision of bases for the support of further operations against the Japanese. Strategically, only the third of these objects was cogent. It is true that some use was made of Subic Bay, on the west coast, chiefly as a submarine base from which British as well as U.S. submarines later operated; but destruction of the principal defence forces and seizure of the central Luzon area was merely a triumph for MacArthur's advocacy and a concession to the American belief that the liberation of the Philippines was an obligation on their honour.

Apart from the central plain, almost the whole of Luzon is mountainous. There are two main entrances to this plain from the sea: at Manila Bay and at Lingayen Gulf. The entrance to Manila Bay was blocked by defences on Corregidor Island, at Cavite (Plan 13) and on the shores of the bay. From undefended Lingayen, however, good roads and a railway ran to Manila via the airfield complex around Clark Field, with vulnerable points only at the crossings over the swamps to the north of Manila Bay. Luzon's other large airfield complex east of Manila Bay could be approached from the south-west part of the island where there were several good landing beaches. In 1942, the Japanese had made subsidiary landings at Legaspi in the extreme south-east and Aparri in the extreme north of Luzon. General MacArthur did not propose to land at either of these points. These were airfields near Legaspi, but the Bicol peninsula was mountainous and isolated from Manila. As for a landing in the north, at Aparri, in view of the large Japanese garrison there was the risk when driving southward, of being held up in the Cagayan valley. The Bataan peninsula, where in 1942 the Americans had fought their delaying action, could be cut off by a landing in Subic Bay.

The main landing was to be made in Lingayen Gulf (*Figure 3*) a generally rectangular area almost 20 miles wide and 30 miles long, exposed to the north-west, with unlimited anchorage area at the inner end. The entire inner end is

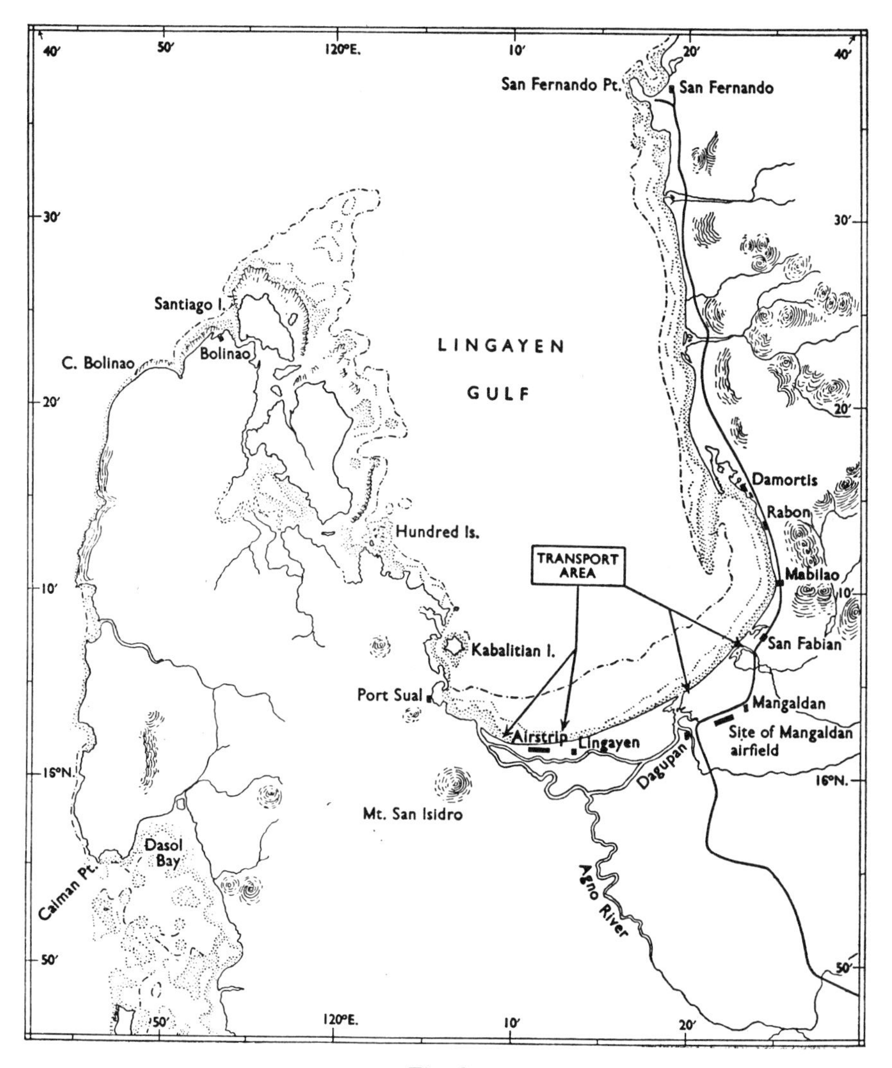

Fig. 3

bordered by sandy beaches whose slopes in most places are so gradual that pontoon causeways were necessary for LSTs to unload. In general, photographic coverage was inadequate and failed to give accurate information to supplement the old charts.[1] Contrary to expectation, however, certain of the San Fabian beaches were found to be suitable for dry-ramp beaching of LSTs, which contributed materially to the speed of unloading. The daily tidal range is 12–18 inches, the terrain inland of the beaches was compartmented by lagoons with fishponds, backed by rice paddies ; but in January, the driest season of the year in the Luzon plain, it offered no serious obstacle to passage inland. Enemy defences were weak throughout the area ; there were neither off-shore obstacles nor beach positions, and contrary to pre-assault intelligence, the waters, though suitable for mining, held very few mines. The beaches selected for the landing were distributed over most of the south and south-east shores of Lingayen Gulf, one group being generally opposite the town of Lingayen and the other on both sides of San Fabian town.

2

The Japanese had continued to send reinforcements to Luzon during December at an accelerated pace, but it had become progressively more difficult to transport them from Luzon to the Central and Southern Philippines, and as a result, an increasing number were stranded in Luzon. There were in the island about 135,000 troops (14th Area Army) of which more than 15,000 were naval ; including reinforcements, however, the Japanese are said to have employed 23 divisions in the defence of Luzon. Their plan was to hold on to Corregidor and Manila to the last.

The Allied Luzon Attack Force (Task Force 77) was under the command of Vice-Admiral T. C. Kinkaid (Commander Seventh Fleet) in the Amphibious Force flagship *Wasatch*. The troops were under the command of Lieutenant-General W. Krueger. The landings on the San Fabian beaches were to be made by the 6th and 43rd Divisions of the U.S. Sixth Army, and those on the Lingayen beaches by the 37th and 40th Divisions of the Sixth Army.[2] Vice-Admiral D. E. Barbey commanded the San Fabian Attack Force (Task Force 78) which comprised a total of 209 vessels, in addition to nearly 100 miscellaneous small craft.[3] The Lingayen Attack Force (Task Force 79) under Vice-Admiral T. S. Wilkinson, comprised 134 vessels, including the landing ships, infantry, H.M.A.S. *Westralia, Manoora* and *Kanimbla*, together with miscellaneous small craft. The two units, for San Fabian and Lingayen respectively, of the Bombardment and Fire Support Group (Vice-Admiral J. B. Oldendorf) (T.G. 77.12) included six of the older battleships, five heavy and one light cruiser and 19 destroyers. In the Close Covering Group (T.G. 77.3) under Rear-Admiral R. S. Berkey were H.M.A.S. *Shropshire* (Captain C. A. G. Nichols) and *Australia* (Captain J. M. Armstrong). Seventeen escort carriers and their screen under Rear-Admiral C. T. Durgin provided air support ; and an additional escort carrier with five destroyer escorts, accompanied the force as Hunter-Killer Group. Minesweeping and Hydrographic, Screening, Salvage and Rescue,

[1] Report by British Combined Operations Representative (Pacific) on the Lingayen Operation, M.03737/45. ' The latest hydrographic data possessed by MacArthur and the High Command was that available from worksheets of the U.S. Coast and Geodetic Survey of July 1903 ' (*Spearheads of Invasion*, by W. N. Swan, p. 184).

[2] The Sixth Army in Leyte and Mindoro was relieved by the Eighth on 26th December.

[3] The organisation of the Luzon Attack Force is given in Appendix M.

Reinforcement and Service Groups brought the total of ships to more than 600, apart from landing craft and small craft. Eleven Royal Australian Naval ships were included.[1]

As we have seen, the U.S.Third Fleet still had the duties of destroying any enemy naval or air forces threatening to interfere with the operation, and of preventing reinforcement of air units via Formosa. Several land-based air forces supported the operation. The Fourteenth and Twentieth, elements of the latter being now based in China, carried out strikes on objectives within range and reconnaissance in the China Seas and Singapore areas before and during the operation. The XXI Bomber Command (part of the Twentieth Air Force) and the Seventh Air Force, operating from the Marianas, performed similar duties to the northward. The Far Eastern Air Force, operating from Leyte, Mindoro and Morotai, attacked the Japanese lines of communication and airfields in Luzon and other islands in the Philippines. Fighter aircraft of this force augmented the air cover for the convoys during the passage from Leyte to Lingayen Gulf.

3

The various components of the Luzon Attack Force began leaving Leyte on 2nd January. The Minesweeping and Fire Support Groups, and the Escort Carrier Group (less those carriers with the amphibious convoys) proceeded well ahead of the Attack Forces, arriving and beginning operations at Lingayen Gulf on S minus 3 Day. All groups used the same general route for approach to the objective area ; through Surigao Strait and the Mindanao Sea northward through the Sulu Sea, passing to the westward of Negros, Panay and Mindoro, thence well off shore to the westward of Luzon, entering Lingayen Gulf on south-easterly courses. The reason for choosing this route, though it ran in part through restricted waters and was likely to lead to early discovery by the enemy, were that it was shorter, the weather was better than in the open Pacific, and better protection by land-based aircraft was possible. The advanced forces made the passage in two main groups, each of which contained six escort carriers and an equal proportion of the heavy ships and screen. The two groups normally remained within supporting distance of one another, and were preceded by the Minesweeping Group.

Surigao Strait was passed in daylight on 3rd January. That evening, enemy air attacks began. A Japanese fighter made an unsuccessful suicide dive on the escort carrier *Makin Island*, crashing in the water alongside. In the Minesweeping Group the oiler *Cowanesque* received minor damage from a suicide attack and minesweeper *YMS* 53 from a near-miss bomb. Early next morning enemy air reconnaissance located the flotilla in the Sulu Sea, and from then onwards maintained contact. Attacks began in the late afternoon, whilst the ships were off the west coast of Panay. A suicide aircraft was seen approaching the escort carrier *Ommaney Bay*. At the time, a long routine transmission was in progress over the TBS circuit, and the ship could not be warned. Land masses rendered radar detection difficult. No heavy ship was in a position to supplement the light fire protection provided by the escort carriers. The aircraft crashed on board the *Ommaney Bay*, which had her aircraft fully fuelled and armed and nine torpedo warheads stacked on the hangar deck. Explosions and fires followed, and the ship had to be abandoned and sunk. Another escort carrier, the *Lunga Point*, was near-missed by a suicide aircraft.

[1] *Shropshire, Australia,* destroyers *Arunta, Warramunga,* frigates *Warrego, Gascoyne,* H.D.M.L. 1074, fleet minesweeper *Benalla,* L.S.I.s *Westralia, Manoora, Kanimbla.*

The ships cleared Mindoro Strait safely in the early morning of 5th January, and the combat air patrols intercepted and successfully turned back two raids at 0800 and 1200. A third raid, at 1645, was not intercepted. Anti-aircraft fire shot down some of the enemy but six aircraft succeeded in crashing on board ships. The heavy cruiser *Louisville* and H.M.A.S. *Arunta* in the van group, and the *Australia* and the escort carrier *Manila Bay*, the destroyer *Helm* and destroyer escort *Stafford* in the rear group were hit, but all except the last were able to proceed with their groups. H.M.A.S. *Shropshire* received minor damage. Forty miles ahead of the Bombardment and Escort Carrier Groups, six or seven suicide aircraft attacked the Minesweeping Group at 1740. *LCIG 70* was hit and slightly damaged and two other vessels received slight damage from near misses. A Japanese destroyer force approached the group west of Manila Bay ; two destroyers came close enough to be sighted, but retired at high speed when the destroyer *Bennion* approached. Aircraft flown off from the escort carriers attacked them, sinking the *Momi* and slightly damaging the *Sugi*. The *Momi* was not seen to sink, and accordingly, in order to prevent her from effecting repairs at Singapore, on 11th January the King George V dry dock was bombed, together with the Admiralty IX Floating Dock, by Fortresses from Kharagpur, but no damage was done. On the night 25/26th January, as Japanese ships damaged in the Philippines operations were moving into Singapore, and also as part of the blockade, Superfortresses mined the approaches to the harbour.

4

The Minesweeper, Escort Carrier and Bombardment Groups reached Lingayen Gulf early on the 6th. The Japanese, who expected the landing to be attempted around Manila Bay or further south, were taken by surprise. The minesweepers entered the Gulf at 0700 to begin sweeping, whilst the escort carriers operated to the north-westward. The fire support ships conducted some bombardment of targets at the entrance to the Gulf, entering at 1555, on receipt of word from the minesweepers that no moored and only two floating mines had been found. The Australian cruisers carried no aircraft and they consequently used U.S. and Australian land-based aircraft spotters, with whom the *Shropshire* reports communications were chaotic, for hurried conditions prior to the operation prevented thorough understanding between the ships and the spotters. The *Shropshire* fired nearly 10,000 rounds of ammunition during four days in the Gulf. The intention to carry out a short bombardment of the actual landing beaches was abandoned on account of heavy enemy air attacks.

Fighting had been going on all day between the combat air patrols and enemy aircraft, a number of the latter being shot down. At 1153 suicide aircraft penetrated the defence and attacks began on the ships with a near miss on a destroyer, followed shortly after by successful crashes on the battleship *New Mexico* (on board which Admiral Fraser, Commander-in-Chief, British Pacific Fleet, was embarked) and the destroyer *Allen M. Sumner*. It was estimated that during the day more than 50 enemy suicide aircraft attacked the ships. Four more destroyers, the battleship *California*, the heavy cruiser *Louisville* and light cruiser *Columbia*, were hit.[1] The damage to the *Louisville* from this second crash rendered it advisable to withdraw her from the Gulf, and she was sent to join the escort carriers outside. Three of the destroyers were so seriously damaged that they had to retire on the 10th for repairs. The *Australia* was hit

[1] The list of damaged ships is given in Appendix J.

again and received further extensive damage. Meanwhile, the minesweepers had also been heavily attacked. The *Long* was hit twice and sank later, the *Brooks* was hit and had to be towed to the rear area for repairs; and the *Southard* was hit but continued in operation. In all, on the 5th and 6th, 26 ships were damaged and two sunk by suicide aircraft attacks. It was clear that even the ring of Allied land-based air forces that encircled Luzon, from China through Morotai, Mindoro and Leyte to the Marianas, could not keep the Luzon airfields neutralized; whilst the escort carriers were not available for the task, being fully engaged in trying to protect the ships. The situation appeared so serious to Admiral Oldendorf that he thought plans might have to be reconsidered, failing drastic measures; and on his recommendation, Admiral Kinkaid requested the Fast Carrier Task Force to cancel its strikes on Formosa and instead to cover the Luzon airfields to prevent further damage to the Bombardment and Minesweeping Groups. The heavy ships retired out of the Gulf for the night, whilst the minesweepers remained near the entrance. Here they were attacked during darkness in the early morning of the 7th and the *Hovey* was sunk by an aircraft torpedo, whilst the *Palmer* was sunk during the afternoon by bombs. Under cover of the fire of the Bombardment Group underwater demolition operations were carried out that day: no beach defences or underwater obstacles were found. The fire support ships carried out a bombardment all next day, finding few targets. The *Australia* was again extensively damaged by a suicide craft and was relieved of bombardment duties for the remainder of the day.

5

Next day, 9th January, was S-Day for the landing. The Attack Force arrived in Lingayen Gulf in the early hours, having sailed from Leyte in two convoys. The first of them, the San Fabian Attack Force, passed through Leyte Gulf on the evening of 4th January. On the afternoon of the 5th, not far from Apo Island off the south coast of Negros, where the Japanese had a midget submarine base, the light cruiser *Boise* reported two torpedoes fired at her unsuccessfully by a midget submarine which was depth charged, rammed and probably sunk by the destroyer *Taylor* after being attacked by an aircraft of the A/S patrol. Two torpedoes, which also missed, were fired later at an LST but hunter-killer operations failed to locate the submarine. At 2136 on the 7th the Commander Destroyer Squadron 23, stationed with four destroyers five miles on the starboard beam of the Assault Convoy, had surface contact with an enemy destroyer at a range of 15,000 yards. Though charged with the specific duty to attack and destroy enemy forces approaching the convoy, he asked permission to investigate before proceeding to attack. Hampering orders were received from the Task Group Commander specifying a distance beyond which he was not to proceed without permission. After some indecision how to fight the battle, he decided to engage at long range rather than attempt a surprise torpedo attack; and at 2227, with the range at 10,000 yards the target was illuminated and engaged. Two minutes later, the enemy destroyer altered course 180°, giving her every opportunity of firing torpedoes. Fortunately, she did not do so, presumably being taken by surprise, for Comdesron 23 took no avoiding action but continued on a steady course.[1] The enemy was eventually reported sunk,[2] but in actual fact escaped.

---

[1] *U.S.S. Braine. Action Report—Night destroyer action off Manila Bay, 7th January* 1945. M.03199/45.

[2] *Operations in the Pacific Ocean Areas during the month of January* 1945, p. 55.

At dawn next day, air attack developed on the convoy. The combat air patrol shot down or damaged several of the enemy, but one crashed on board the escort carrier *Kabashan Bay*, and a transport was also hit, though both ships were able to remain with the convoy. The Lingayen Attack Force forming the second convoy, proceeded at high speed through Leyte Gulf in the early morning of 6th January and escaped attack until about 1900 on the 8th when the escort carrier *Kitkun Bay* was hit by a suicide aircraft. Serious underwater damage was caused and the ship was taken in tow until able to proceed under her own power. A little later, a suicide aircraft dived on H.M.A.S. *Westralia*. Hit hard, it dived into the sea astern of the ship and disintegrated. The two bombs which it carried fell one on each side of the ship and exploded, causing only minor damage.

6

On the morning of the 9th, the Bombardment Groups preceded the Assault Groups to their fire support area off the landing beaches in Lingayen Gulf. The scheduled bombardment began at 0700, and at about 0930 the first wave of landing craft beached. The beaches had also been bombed, machine-gunned and rocketed by aircraft from the Escort Carrier Group. Beach positions were found not manned. At Lingayen beaches opposition was negligible ; at San Fabian sporadic mortar and artillery fire which began about 1000 caused some damage and casualties to landing craft until silenced by the ships' fire. General unloading was under way by 1100. The surf on S-Day was only four feet high, but conditions next day were bad and slowed up unloading ; though they improved on the 11th. LVTS, DUKWs, and self-propelled pontoon barges were employed to unload the larger transports, most of which were ready to depart at the end of S-Day, in a fast convoy. On each of the succeeding days, a fast and a slow convoy sailed until the assault shipping completed unloading on 12th January. The Reinforcement Groups began to arrive on the 11th.

Meanwhile, the Japanese Philippines Air Force continued to attack as fiercely as ever, though the Allies could not know that it had almost reached the point of self-destruction. On S-Day the light cruiser *Columbia* was hit, for the second time, by a suicide aircraft which came in suddenly out of the sun. Early in the afternoon, the *Australia* received her fifth hit, the fourth in five days, a Japanese suicide aircraft diving out of a cloud and striking her foremast and foremost funnel almost before the ship had time to fire a shot. The battleship *Mississippi* was hit almost simultaneously but both ships continued in action. Heavy casualties were caused on board the battleship *Colorado* by an anti-aircraft shell hit from one of the Allied ships. The *Columbia*, the *Australia* (with 44 killed and 65 wounded), the *Louisville* and H.M.A.S. *Arunta* all extensively damaged were ordered to rear areas in the late afternoon for repairs. The *Shropshire* hoisted Commodore H. B. Farncomb's broad pendant. Three destroyers badly damaged on the 6th had to follow them to Leyte next day. On that day, the Lingayen Defence Force was constituted under Admiral Oldendorf, from the remaining ships of the Bombardment and Fire Support, Escort Carrier and Covering Groups. The force provided cover for the convoys of assault shipping sailing from Lingayen, during the first part of their passage, whilst for added protection seaplane patrols were also established in the Gulf. After the 10th, the position of the Fast Carrier Force which was operating in the South China Sea, also afforded protection. Several of the ships in the return convoys were attacked by suicide aircraft on passage to Leyte, but none received serious damage.

At the landing area however, suicide aircraft succeeded in damaging a number of the exposed destroyers and destroyer escorts engaged in screening the transports with smoke. In protecting them, 'H.M.A.S. *Shropshire* was particularly valuable to the Bombardment and Fire Support Group because of her excellent search radar equipment and her accurate and complete reports on air contacts', reported Admiral Oldendorf. 'Within land-locked areas H.M.A.S. *Shropshire* was able to report bogies (unidentified aircraft) when radars of all other ships were blocked by land echoes'.[1] In the early hours of the 10th the Japanese adopted fresh measures and several enemy assault demolition (*hayabusa*) boats, probably from Port Sual (Figure 3, page 124) carrying depth charges, made suicide attacks on ships in the transport area, sinking two LCIs and damaging two destroyers, a transport, and three tank-landing ships. An expedition of LCI(G)s and LCI(M)s was organised and searched along the coast, but found no further suicide boats.[2]

The four Divisional Commanders took command of their troops ashore before dusk on S-Day; and on 11th January the two Corps Commanders assumed command in their respective areas (I Corps: San Fabian, XIV Corps: Lingayen) and the Advanced Headquarters of the Commander-in-Chief South-West Pacific Area were opened at Dagupan (Figure 3, page 124). On the 13th Lieutenant-General Krueger assumed command of all Sixth Army Forces ashore and General MacArthur went ashore to his Advanced Headquarters at Dagupan.

General Yamashita had abandoned his original plan to fight a decisive battle in the central Luzon plain. The Combined Fleet was in no condition to afford support, and by 13th January the air forces in the Philippines had been shot to pieces and thereafter made no further successful suicide attacks on the ships. The new policy of the enemy aimed at inflicting heavy casualties on the U.S. troops and postponing as long as possible the loss of the island. For this purpose, Yamashita disposed the main strength of the 14th Area Army in the central mountainous region of Luzon, with some forces in the eastern mountains. The defence of the naval and air bases was considered to be of secondary importance. Sporadic air attacks against the invading troops continued until 18th January, though after the 12th most of the aircraft came from Formosa. Few reinforcement aircraft reached Luzon, and within a few days no more than the ruins of the enemy air organisation remained in the island. The remnant of the Philippine air forces, hoarded to repulse the invaders of Luzon, had destroyed itself in suicide attacks, though it had given no uncertain testimony to the effectiveness of this form of attack. The Second Air Fleet was disbanded on 8th January, and Admiral Fukudome retired to Singapore a week later. What was left of his air fleet was incorporated in the First Air Fleet; and with the few remaining fighters of this fleet Admiral Onishi retired to Formosa where the main concentration of enemy aircraft outside Japan was located. On 22nd January the U.S. Fifth Air Force began a series of strikes against Formosa which, though Admiral Nimitiz considered them to have failed him during a critical period in his next operation against Okinawa, never, however, entirely ceased until the war ended.

---

[1] M.06463/45. H.M.A.S. *Shropshire*, Action Report—18th January 1945, Lingayen. Covering letter by C.T.G. 77.2.

[2] These boats first became a serious menace during the Ryukus Operation. A description of them and their tactics is given in Naval Staff History, Battle Summary No. 47, *Naval Operations in the Assault and Capture of Okinawa, Operation 'Iceberg'—March–June* 1945.

7

After the typhoon of 18th December the Fast Carrier Force had retired to Ulithi to repair its damaged ships and replace lost aircraft. Whilst there, some internal changes were made.[1] The dive bombers in the *Essex* and *Wasp* were replaced by fighters, bringing their complements to 91 fighters and 15 torpedo aircraft. Two Marine fighter squadrons were placed aboard the *Essex*, making the first use of Marine fighter pilots with the Fast Carrier Force. On 5th January, when the night carrier *Enterprise* joined up, she formed with the light night carrier *Independence* a separate group (T.G. 38.5) under Rear-Admiral M. B. Gardner, within the task force organisation, as had been recommended by Admiral McCain.[2] Normally, the two carriers and six destroyers of this group were assigned to Task Group 38.2 (Rear-Admiral G. F. Bogan), which contained three carriers (the other two groups containing each two carriers and two light carriers), and operated independently when directed by the Task Force Commander. Prior to this, there had never been more than one night carrier, the *Independence*, with the force. It had been the usual procedure for this ship, with escort of two destroyers—all that could be spared—to operate as a detached unit of Task Group 38.2, in a position permitting freedom of manœuvre for air operations yet if possible within TBS range, and taking care always to keep to windward of the Task Group, no matter what manœuvres the latter should carry out. Routine operations by the night carrier group comprised keeping aircraft airborne or in readiness at all times for protection of the force from dusk, night or dawn attack ; covering the withdrawal of the force by a flight, termed the ' Zipper ' Flight, which bridged the gap between the departure of of the final day C.A.P. and the arrival of the night ' hecklers ', these latter being also drawn from the aircraft complement of the night carriers. On the night before a strike, night fighters with half bomb bay tanks, searched the approaches to the enemy harbours for shipping or war vessels. On days when visibility was zero, night fighters might be used for regular search missions.

8

The Fast Carrier Force under Vice-Admiral McCain sortied from Ulithi on 30th December with the primary mission of destroying enemy aircraft in Formosa.[3] The launching position, east of the southern part of Formosa, 140 miles from the nearest airfields, was reached undetected on 3rd January. Targets were southern Formosa and the Pescadores Islands (Task Group 38.2), central Formosa, Okinawa and the Sakishima Gunto (Task Group 38.3), northern Formosa (Task Group 38.1). The weather was bad and frustrated efforts to keep continuous air patrols over the targets, moreover the strike ranges were too long to enable this type of operation to be carried out successfully. Many strikes had to be cancelled, but more than 800 offensive sorties were made. U.S. losses were 32 aircraft and 22 pilots and aircrew men and were actually slightly larger than the Japanese losses during the two days, a most unusual state of affairs at that period of the war. A considerable volume of shipping was found in harbours along the west coast of Formosa, and though the U.S. claims of damage and sinking were not substantiated in full, the Japanese admitted

[1] The organisation of the Fast Carrier Force in January 1945 is given in Appendix N.

[2] *T.F.38, Action Report, Formosa.* M.03191/45.

[3] The Formosa airfields are shown on Plan 15.

to several ships damaged, including four frigates and some other minor war vessels, whilst three merchant ships were sunk.[1]

9

Early on the morning of 5th January, General MacArthur asked Admiral Halsey to carry out strikes to the southward of the dividing line between the strike areas of the fast carrier and land based air forces[2], in order to cover Clark and Angeles Fields (Plan 14). At dawn on the 6th, the Fast Carrier Force having refuelled at sea, was in launching position 115°, 120 miles from the north-east tip of Luzon (Cape Engano), approximately 250 miles from the principal objectives. Flying conditions continued unfavourable, and certain early strikes had to be cancelled. This, together with Japanese dispersal and camouflage reduced the effectiveness of the attacks. It was not possible to keep continuous combat patrols over the Luzon airfields to prevent Japanese aircraft from taking off, and the ships in Lingayen Gulf suffered accordingly from suicide attacks as we have seen. Air opposition was light, but again the Americans had many operational casualties. Photographs taken at the end of the day indicated that 237 enemy aircraft were apparently still operational in Luzon, about 150 of which were concealed near the Clark Fields. At Admiral Kinkaid's request, Admiral Halsey cancelled the strikes against Formosa arranged for the following day and arranged to give special coverage to the enemy airfields in the Lingayen area, previously ordered to be reserved for the escort carriers, to assist in preventing further damage to the bombardment and minesweeping forces in the Gulf. Weather on the 7th continued bad in the launching area but better over the targets, and a large number of enemy aircraft was destroyed. But Task Force 38 lost 28 aircraft, 18 of them from operational causes, and in the bad weather the rescue of airmen from the sea was difficult and 25 were lost. The following day was S-Day for the Lingayen landing for which Admiral Halsey had been asked to provide direct air support. Admiral Kinkaid had asked whether he would consider moving the Third Fleet to the westward of Luzon to give direct air support to the Lingayen operation during the period the loaded transports were off the beaches. But Halsey's conception of carrier warfare rejected passive defence of an area in favour of stifling the opposition at its source.[3] In this case, the source comprised the southern Formosa landing fields within 400 miles of Lingayen, whose aircraft constituted a direct threat to the invasion. These fields were out of range of General Kenney's South-West Pacific land-based aircraft, and Halsey considered attack there preferable to giving direct support in the Lingayen region. From a point over 100 miles from the nearest part of the coast of Formosa, distances to objectives varied from 140 miles to the nearer southern Formosa airfields, to over 300 miles to Okinawa. As many strikes as possible were sent to Formosa. Several were weathered out, but the U.S. losses were light, a total of nine aircraft, six of which were lost from operational causes, for air opposition was slight. A Japanese frigate, two submarine chasers, two tankers and two cargo vessels were sunk and a further considerable number of aircraft destroyed on the ground.

---

[1] *Iwato Maru* (auxiliary), *Kinrei Maru*, *Shinshu Maru* (aircraft ferry).

[2] *See* p. 126.

[3] *Admiral Halsey's Story*, p. 243.

CHAPTER XI

Fast Carrier Sweep of the China Sea

(Plans 2, 13, 15)

1

EVEN before Admiral Kinkaid made his request that the Third Fleet should come west of Luzon to support the Lingayen operation it had been in Halsey's mind to carry out a sweep in the China Sea. For three years no Allied ships other than submarines had entered those waters, but Japanese surface control was now to be challenged (Plan ' Gratitude '). Through the China Sea passed trade routes which were absolutely indispensable to Japanese war economy. Development of the resources, natural and artificial of Formosa, North China, Manchuria, Korea and the home islands, by means of which the enemy had striven since before the war to render the country independent of imports from the south, had not gone far towards rendering Japan self-supporting, and she was still dependent upon raw materials brought by long hauls through the China Seas, for her ability to make war. Losses of ships on these routes, from submarines and latterly from air attacks, had been terrible. It was not unknown for entire convoys, escorts and escorted alike, to be sunk. But the traffic had to go on. Ships must continue to essay the passage by taking diversive routes or by hugging the Asiatic shore, here anchoring by day and moving only at night, there acting conversely.

If the Japanese could not protect their own ships, they were still not without the ability to render hazardous any American incursion into the South China Sea. Whether the Third Fleet were to enter via Luzon Strait or through the inland waters of the Philippines a close approach to enemy held territory was unavoidable. Surrounding the Sea were a large number of enemy air bases, so placed that a U.S. force could be both located and attacked at almost any part of this enclosed region. While the Allies knew the positions and relative importance of the various airfields, detailed information was incomplete. The Formosan airfields (Plan 15) normally held about 300 aircraft and were capable of rapid reinforcement. China, Hainan and North Indo-China were estimated to contain 500, South Indo-China, Burma and Siam 170, and the Netherlands East Indies 280.[1] Most of these were Army aircraft, which were considerably less effective against ships than their naval compatriots. There was no shortage of aircraft, it was the pilots that were lacking, and hence the

[1] This is the estimate of the Commander-in-Chief U.S. Pacific Fleet. The Admiralty Intelligence Report gives Malaya–Sumatra 209, Philippines—N.E.I 1026 on 8th January.

introduction of *kamikaze*, which could be operated by incompletely trained airmen. This was not the only hazard to an American force penetrating into the South China Sea. Bad weather was to be expected, for during January the region is subject to frequent typhoons. In view of the distances to the nearest U.S. bases these conditions constituted a considerable hazard.

One of the advantages of entry by the Third Fleet into the South China Sea was the cover it would afford to the shipping in Lingayen Gulf. Two heavy naval defeats in 1944 had not altogether eliminated the menace of the Japanese Fleet which, though incapable of fighting a fleet action, could still muster sufficient ships for a raid. The effective ships were now estimated to consist of five carriers with total complement of 180 aircraft, two battleships, two battleship carriers, 15 cruisers and about 45 destroyers—the two last types being somewhat over estimated. Of these, the two battleship carriers, two escort carriers, seven cruisers and some 13 destroyers were believed to be in the Singapore–Indo-China area. Actually there were in the south no escort carriers and only three cruisers, the *Haguro* and *Ashigara* at Singapore and the *Isudzu* in the Netherlands East Indies. None of the carriers had any air groups on board, for there were no trained carrier air pilots available : training of carrier airmen had been abandoned. If Halsey could locate and destroy the ships in the south he would eliminate the threat from these to the Seventh Fleet traffic passing from Leyte to the west coast of Luzon. The Americans considered that the psychological effect on both the Japanese and Chinese of the entry of the Third Fleet into the South China Sea would be no less important from a strategic standpoint than the cover afforded to the Lingayen shipping.[1] In addition, Admiral Halsey expected to find concentrations of merchant shipping at the principal ports of the Asiatic mainland, as well as convoys which should offer valuable targets for attack. He had already prepared plans for the operation. The order was given to execute them on conclusion of the air strikes on 9th January.

2

After landing-on the strike aircraft the Third Fleet set course for Luzon Strait, passing through at high speed during the night of the 9th–10th. Task Force 38 used the Bashi Channel to the northward near Formosa, whilst part of the Service Group (T.G. 30.8) followed the Balintang Channel to the south (Plan 13). This Service Group which provided fuel and replacement aircraft, consisted of 25 oilers with a light screen of seven escort carriers, nine destroyers and 18 destroyer escorts ; but only six of the oilers with two escort carriers and screen entered the China Sea.[2] With the Fleet there was also an escort carrier hunter-killer group which acted as an anti-submarine force in support of fuelling groups whilst en route to rendezvous with Task Force 38, and during fuelling. For 16 hours these forces, spread over 30 miles of ocean, were within 100 miles of enemy airfields on the northern coast of Luzon or the southern coast of Formosa, but they were neither discovered nor attacked, the only enemy seen being three unsuspecting transport aircraft flying from Luzon to Formosa, engaged in evacuating the Operations Section of the Philippines Air Command ; these were shot down by night fighters of the *Independence*. On the morning of the 10th the fleet turned to a south-westerly course, maintaining this for nearly 48 hours. During these two days, a total of 686 aircraft were flown-off on

[1] *Operations in the Pacific Ocean Areas during the month of January* 1945, p. 12.

[2] The organisation of the Fleet is given in Appendix N.

searches, most of which proved negative, the pilots having instructions to avoid detection. Weather was bad and hindered both flying and fuelling which took place on the 11th. On completion of this Admiral Bogan's Group (38.2), with the night carriers, and reinforced by two heavy cruisers and a destroyer division went on ahead at high speed towards the coast of Indo-China. It was believed that enemy heavy units including the *Ise* and *Hyuga* would be found at Cam-ranh Bay, and it was hoped to destroy them. Night and daytime searches alike however, failed to discover the battleship carriers, which actually were at Singapore.

The enemy were taken completely by surprise. Convoys were at sea. Eleven Japanese aircraft on a training mission were intercepted and destroyed without putting up a fight. Throughout the 12th, fighter sweeps blanketed enemy airfields from Saigon to Quinhon, finding little air opposition but claiming the destruction of nearly 100 aircraft on the ground. Shipping and waterfront installations from Cam-ranh Bay to Saigon were attacked. Despite the handicap of poor weather a large amount of shipping was destroyed. The dismantled French cruiser *Lamotte-Piquet* was sunk at Saigon. Several convoys were found off the coast of Indo-China and were attacked. Twelve tankers and 21 cargo or passenger ships, a total of 142,235 tons, the training cruiser *Kashii*, seven frigates and some minor war vessels were sunk, and numerous other ships damaged. The Americans lost 23 aircraft, including one army heavy bomber which was shot down in error, not having its IFF switched on. One hundred strike sorties were flown for every 70 defensive sorties. Sorties per aircraft reached the high figure of 1.7. Ninety per cent of bombs expended were aimed at shipping targets. One ship was sunk for every 12 sorties and seven-and-a-half bombs or torpedoes.[1]

3

On completion of the strikes of 12th January the fleet ran to the north-eastward at high speed to avoid a typhoon in the south. While the typhoon centre was avoided, fuelling was rendered slow by the heavy weather, and occupied most of the 13th and 14th. The oilers were completely emptied by the time fuelling was finished. On the morning of the 15th, from positions 70°, 155–170 miles from Takao (Formosa), and 110°, 215–260 miles from Hong Kong, strikes were launched against Formosa and the China coast from Amoy in the north through Swatow to Hong Kong and Canton in the south. One task group attacked targets as far as 450 miles apart, from northern Formosa to Canton. Little shipping was found on the China coast, and few aircraft on the airfields ; and on account of deteriorating weather, attacks on these targets were abandoned by noon. A fighter blanket was attempted over Formosa where a considerable number of valuable targets were found at Takao and Toshien (Plan 23). Attacks on these were pressed home until bad weather caused them to be diverted to Bako harbour in the Pescadores. The destroyer *Hatakaze* and a high speed transport were sunk at Takao and the destroyer *Tsuga* at Bako, but the only merchant ship sunk was the 10,564 ton tanker *Mirii Maru.* At Pratas Reef, aircraft from the *Enterprise* destroyed a radio station and discovered a hitherto unknown airfield.

[1] Actually, if the U.S. Joint Assessment Committee's Report is accepted the ratio was more favourable to the Americans, for the Commander-in-Chief's percentage is based on the sinking of 40 ships (a figure which happens to coincide with that given in the post-war *Japanese Report*), whereas the Joint Assessment Committee allows a total of 46.

During the night of the 15th/16th the fleet moved westward to a launching position in approximately 21° 40′ N., 116° 50′ E. for strikes against Hong Kong, Canton and Hainan Island on the 16th. Distances to Hainan varied from 250 to 290 miles and it was only possible to send two strikes and two fighter sweeps to the area. Targets were less good and plentiful than anticipated, but at Yulin harbour the 10,045-ton tanker *Harima Maru* was sunk.[1] The brunt of the assault was made against Hong Kong, where 138 aircraft attacked in three groups in the morning and a further 158 in three groups in the afternoon. Amongst the ships found in Hong Kong harbour was an important tanker convoy going from Moji to Singapore to fetch oil, which was sheltering. Ships in harbour and in the Taikoo shipyards, the nearby oil storage tanks, dockyards and wharves constituted the principal targets. The attacks met some of the most intense anti-aircraft fire experienced in the war up to that date, the description ' intense to unbelievable ' occurring in one report ; whilst the Japanese fire control and accuracy also appear to have been exceptionally good, particularly on the first attack of the afternoon, when one out of every eight of the aircraft which attacked ships was shot down. Damage to the enemy was less than had been hoped. Only three tankers and two cargo ships were sunk, but three of them were vessels of over 10,000 tons.

The total U.S. aircraft losses for the two days of operating were 61, of which 31 were operational losses ; exceptionally, these exceeded the number of enemy aircraft destroyed. Pilots and aircrew men lost numbered 48.

4

For three days following the Hong Kong strikes heavy seas and poor flying conditions limited the operations of Task Force 38. Attempts made to fuel on the 17th and 18th met with little success, and the fleet had to run inconveniently far to the southward to find a lee under Luzon, before fuelling could be completed. Japanese radio reports spoke of having ' bottled up ' the fleet in the South China Sea and broadcast dire threats of what would happen to it when it tried to withdraw. This the fleet did on the night of the 20th–21st, making use of Luzon Strait, for despite the disadvantage of unpredictable weather in the strait it afforded a better chance of escaping detection than the sheltered waters of Surigao Strait, and was more suitable strategically, since the next assignments of the fleet lay in the north. The oiler group returned via Surigao Strait.

Late in the afternoon of the 20th the fleet was heading east near Balintang Channel, with the three task groups in column and a destroyer division sweeping ahead. From 1610 onwards enemy aircraft were almost constantly on the screen, some on southerly courses and some heading north, but no attack developed. The force was apparently in the air ferry lane between Luzon and Formosa. A total of 14 enemy aircraft was shot down. By 2300, Task Force 38 had made the transit of the Strait and was proceeding to a position from which to strike Formosa next day as it ran past on the way to obtain photographic coverage of the Nansei Shoto, its final assignment before withdrawing to Ulithi to prepare for the next series of operations.

Sunrise on the 21st was at 0730, and the first strike against Formosa was launched 40 minutes earlier from a position approximately 120 miles east of Takao. Few enemy aircraft were encountered over the target, but on the

[1] Joint Assessment Committee's Report. The *Japanese Report* shows the ship as heavily damaged.

airfields of Formosa, the Pescadores, Sakishima Gunto and Okinawa a substantial number of grounded aircraft were found and over 100 were destroyed. Flying conditions were good, for the first time during the month ; and 700 sorties were made. Despite intense anti-aircraft fire, shipping in Takao, Toshien and Keelung was heavily hit, and by the end of the day, the shallow Takao harbour was full of wrecks resting on the bottom. Six tankers, two of them over 10,000 tons, four cargo vessels and a tank landing ship were sunk. For the first time in nearly two months the Japanese that day made serious air attacks on the fast carrier force. Conditions were favourable for attack. During the previous night, the force whilst passing through Luzon Strait was probably detected by one or more of the numerous enemy aircraft in the area. The U.S. attacks that day were directed against shipping rather than enemy aircraft, and the movements of the groups were limited on account of the need to top up destroyers with fuel during the day. At 1200 four of the destroyers of Admiral Sherman's Task Group 38.3 were being refuelled from two of the battleships. The group, which was more than 12 miles to the northward of the nearest task group was proceeding at a speed of 16 knots, and not zig-zagging. A little earlier, an unconfirmed enemy aircraft contact had been made 64 miles to the west ; there were many friendly aircraft returning at the time, and identification was difficult, but as a precaution, a division of fighters was vectored out to intercept. They failed to contact the enemy and at 1206 a single-engined aircraft glided out of the sun and dropped two small bombs, one of which struck the light carrier *Langley* on the forward part of the flight deck. About two minutes later, another enemy aircraft, also undetected until the last minute, glided out of the clouds and crashed through the carrier *Ticonderoga's* flight deck, starting heavy fires among the aircraft on the hangar deck. Enemy aircraft continued to approach the task groups : six were shot down but two made good their escape. At 1251, however, an aircraft gliding in without warning crashed into the *Ticonderoga's* island structure, adding to her damage. Further south, a large raid approached Admiral Radford's group (38.1). The *Cowpens* vectored out two divisions of fighters which intercepted the enemy, the eight aircraft shooting down 14 or more of the Japanese without loss. But the destroyer *Maddox* in this group, on picket duty 35 miles towards Formosa, was hit and slightly damaged by a suicide aircraft. Total personnel casualties for the day were heavy. The *Ticonderoga* had 142 killed and 202 wounded and lost 36 aircraft, the *Langley* and *Maddox*, 36 and 40 casualties respectively, and the carrier *Hancock* had 50 men killed and 75 wounded through the explosion of bombs which fell from the bomb bay of one of her aircraft when it landed on the flight deck.

The Nansei Shoto were struck next day by 682 aircraft, of which 47 were photographic. No Japanese aircraft went up in opposition, but several were destroyed on the ground. With the completion of these strikes, the fast carrier force returned to Ulithi to prepare for the next operation, the assault and capture of Iwo Jima.

5

Analysis of carrier air operations since June 1944 showed a number of significant trends. Though the average complement of aircraft of the carriers had increased, the average total of aircraft attacking targets on strike days had substantially decreased. For example, in June, off the Marianas, with an initial complement of 905 aircraft, the number attacking targets per day averaged 929 ; whereas in January, with an initial complement of 942, an average of only 565 attacked targets per strike day. The average tonnage of bombs dropped on targets daily decreased both in total and in tons per aircraft of complements as shown by the following table :—

PERIODS OF OPERATION (DAILY AVERAGES)	AIRCRAFT COMPLEMENT OF FORCE				TONS ON TARGET	TONS PER AIRCRAFT OF COMPLEMENT
	Fighters	Dive Bombers	Torpedo Bombers	Total		
12–15 June 1944 (4 days)	424	199	176	799	320	0·40
9–24 Sept. 1944 (8 days)	382	180	146	708	241	0·34
3–22 Jan. 1945 (10 days)	671	72	166	909	180	0·20

Various factors contributed to this changed condition. An increase in use of aircraft defensively was caused through the adoption of suicide operations by the Japanese which had necessitated an increase in fighters at the expense of bombers. Night carriers through the nature of their duties provided fewer sorties per 24-hour period than the carriers operating day groups. Finally, the weather in January was unfavourable for air operations.

The month had given a foretaste of the effect which the weather in the high latitudes of the Pacific was to have on future carrier operations against the home islands of Japan. Maintenance of aircraft, particularly on board the light carriers, was rendered particularly difficult through the bad weather.

'Making an engine change, changing a wing or landing gear etc., is impossible with the ship rolling and pitching as heavily as it did (over 35° at times) and more work of this nature was encountered, due to the difficulties and minor crashes involved while attempting to land on an elusive deck. Another problem encountered was that of having the night ready deck duty during periods of heavy weather. With all planes spotted forward and water breaking over the flight deck sometimes as high as the bridge structure, the pounding the aircraft took is obvious.'[1]

[1] *U.S.S. Langley, strikes and sweeps in support of reoccupation of Luzon,* M.02945/45.

CHAPTER XII

Liberation of the Philippines:

Japan abandons the South China Sea

(Plan 13)

1

THE U.S. Chiefs of Staff, in the statement of policy issued in November 1944, laid it down that the defeat of the remaining enemy in the Philippines was to be effected by such operations as could be executed without prejudice to the main object of forcing the surrender of Japan by blockade, air bombardment and invasion. Operations for the liberation of the Philippines continued. The slight opposition to the landings at Lingayen stiffened increasingly on the American left flank where the reinforced 43rd Division wheeled to the east and north, to find the enemy well deployed in depth and evidently determined to hold at all cost the approaches to the mountain passes leading to northern Luzon. In the south, however, the advance developed into warfare of free manœuvre, in which movement was limited only by the ability to keep the advancing troops supplied. By the 16th, the bridgehead was 30 miles deep and 30 miles wide. Guerilla forces lent considerable assistance throughout the campaign. The air base at Lingayen was found suitable for light aircraft, and on 17th January, Far Eastern Air Forces relieved the carrier aircraft of all troop support on Luzon. Clark and Mabalacat airfields were seized by the end of the month. An amazing scene was revealed when the U.S. troops overran Clark Field. More than 800 Japanese aircraft were counted there and at Lingayen. They lay about the airstrips and revetments in inoperable condition, despite the fact that only a few miles away were to be found ample quantities of the spare parts required to make them serviceable. Over 200 new engines, most of them still in their crates, were found in Mabalacat, never more than three or four in one place, scattered underneath houses, old rice mills, public buildings, little shacks in outlying districts, even in alleys in the villages. There were ample underground fuel stores. There was evidence leading to the belief that pilots were not lacking, and the Americans came to the conclusion that the failure to bring the aircraft into operable condition was the result of disorganization. It was not the first time during the war that such irrational conduct on the part of the Japanese had been noticed. If there actually was, however, a sufficiency of pilots it is unlikely that their training was of a high order.

In the drive to capture Manila the Americans made three minor supporting landings. On 29th January, a force of about 35,000 troops, principally of the 38th Division (reinforced) and 24th Division, were landed without opposition by Rear-Admiral A. D. Struble near San Antonio, about 15 miles north-east of Subic Bay, and quickly reached Olongapo. Next day, a battalion embarked at San Antonio occupied Grande, a fortified island at the mouth of Subic Bay. There were several coast defence guns on the island, but they were not manned by the Japanese, who did not oppose the landing. A fire support unit consisting of the light cruiser *Denver* and the destroyers *Fletcher* and *Radford* was provided for both landings, but was not required to fire a shot. Six escort carriers with screen (Task Group 77.4)[1] furnished direct air support. Enemy submarines were again active. On the morning of 30th January, the transport *Cavalier*, in a convoy returning from the San Antonio area, was torpedoed off Subic Bay by a submarine and had to be towed to Leyte. Carrier aircraft sighted an enemy submarine near the area about noon, and a hunter-killer group with an escort carrier searched for 24 hours and made three attacks, without positive results. At sunset next day, the light cruiser *Boise* made radar contact with the Japanese submarine *RO–115* on the surface in position 13° 20′ N., 119° 20′ E., about 105 miles from the previous day's sighting. Destroyers and destroyer escorts[2] attacked the submarine for some three hours with depth-charges and hedgehogs, and sank her. Three further submarines were sunk by the U.S. submarine *Batfish* (Commander J. K. Fyfe) in the space of four days. At 2250 on 9th February, the *Batfish*'s radar made contact at 11,000 yards with the enemy submarine *I–41* north of Luzon, between Camiguin and Fuga Islands (Plan 13). The night was moonless and overcast. Approaching by radar on the surface, the *Batfish* fired four torpedoes at a range of 1,850 yards, depth setting six feet. All four missed. The enemy showed no alarm. Thirty-two minutes later, the *Batfish*, having worked into position for a further attack, fired three torpedoes by radar at a range of 990 yards, with depth settings four, two and two feet respectively. The second torpedo hit and the enemy submarine sank in 18° 50′ N., 121° 40′ E., so quickly that the third torpedo passed over her.[3] At 1915 on the 11th, near Batulinao Bay on the north shore of Luzon, the *Batfish* picked up enemy radar signals. These were made by *RO–112* which was soon after sighted visually at 1,200 yards' range. The enemy dived unexpectedly but soon surfaced once more, and at 2150 the *Batfish* fired four torpedoes at her. The first torpedo blew *RO–112* apart, and as she sank two further torpedoes hit her. The third victim was *RO–113*, which the *Batfish* sank on 13th February in 19° 10′ N., 121° 23′ E., whilst the enemy submarine was proceeding from Formosa to Luzon. At 0155 that day, the *Batfish's* radar revealed the presence of a Japanese submarine at 10,700 yards range and Commander Fyfe began an attack. At 0448, at a range of 1,700 yards, he fired three torpedoes from stern tubes, for only two torpedoes remained forward. The first torpedo blew *RO–113* to pieces, the other two passing through the wreckage.[3]

On 31st January, two regimental combat teams (brigades) of the U.S. 11th Airborne Division were landed by an attack group under Rear-Admiral W. M. Fechteler, at Nasugbu, south of the entrance to Manila Bay in order to outflank the troops defending Manila, whilst the third of the three regimental combat teams of the Division landed by parachute on 3rd and 4th February, about 14 miles inland. Only 38·4 per cent of the 2,055 men landed in the correct position.[4] The same fire support unit and escort carrier group as before

[1] The organisation of the Forces is given in Appendix O.

[2] *Bell, O'Bannon, Jenkins, Ulvert M. Moore.*

[3] *See* M.03962/45, *U-boat probably sunk by U.S.S. Batfish in Balintang Channel* 18° 50′ N., 121° 40′ E.

[4] *The Army Air Forces in World War II*, Vol. V, pp. 426, 427.

were employed, and the landing was covered by a diversion by landing craft and M.T.B.s in Tayabas Bay, opposite Marinduque Island (Plan 13). The ships carried out a short preliminary bombardment, and drew no return fire. The Japanese were unprepared and offered only light opposition to the landing. This was quickly overcome, and the two forces made junction on 3rd February.

The Japanese hurriedly assembled some thirty suicide (*Hayabusa*) boats and attacked the amphibious shipping at 2245 on 31st January. Only about six of the boats reached their target. They sank the submarine chaser *PC-1129* before the screening destroyers drove them off, sinking two of them, about daylight on 1st February. U.S. light naval units that day, co-operating with land-based aircraft, searched and bombed villages along the coasts of the bays where suicide boats were reported hidden. Two small power boats only were discovered in Talin Bay, south of Nasugbu, and were sunk by gunfire by M.T.B.s. There was an unfortunate failure of recognition during the following night. Owing to the difficulty of retracting the tank landing ships from the beach, screening vessels had again remained to protect them. About 2300, the U.S. submarine chasers *PT-77* and *PT-79* approached, were not recognised, and were sunk with loss of four men of their crews.

2

By the middle of January, the troops landed at San Antonio, Nasugbu and Lingayen were converging on Manila. A few days earlier, Lieutenant-General Koyabashi, Commander of the Manila Defence Force, had withdrawn the 14 best of his 17 battalions to defensive positions east of the city. Defence of the capital was taken over by Rear-Admiral S. Iwabuchi, Commander of the Naval Defence Force. To hold Manila, Iwabuchi had a force of three army battalions and six naval battalions formed from survivors of sunken ships' crews and replacements from Japan, together with men of the 31st Special Base Force such as the Airfield Unit, Naval Construction and Repair Department, Naval Stores, Civil Engineering and Transportation Departments, Naval Office of Supplies and Accounts, the Harbourmaster's Office, and Naval Hospital. Considerable difficulty was encountered in the organisation and training of this heterogeneous naval force of 15,000 men, says the Japanese Official report.[1] When it was originally formed, during December 1944, it had been placed under General Koyabashi. However, Koyabashi had little confidence in the efficiency of the naval units in fighting on land and was not interested in them. For a long while he did not even notify their naval commander, Admiral Iwabuchi, of the defence plan when Manila was transformed from a rear base into a fortress for a last-stand battle.[2] This was typical of the attitude of the Japanese Army towards the Navy. On 1st February, after taking over the defence of the capital, Admiral Iwabuchi ordered the demolition of the wharves and other installations at Manila.

In order to open the port of Manila for the supply of the army and as a base of future Allied operations, it was necessary for the Americans to reduce the island fortress of Corregidor which blocked the entrance to Manila Bay, and to complete the capture of the Bataan Peninsula and occupation of the Cavite shore. Enemy air opposition was not expected, for Japanese air strength in the Philippines had by that time been practically eliminated. Naval opposition

[1] *Philippine Area Naval Operations, Part IV, January* 1945–*August* 1945. Japanese Monograph No. 114, p. 6. [2] *Ibid.* p. 3.

was anticipated from submarines, M.T.B.s and suicide boats. The strength of the garrison of Corregidor was quite unknown ; it was estimated at 850, but was actually 4,500.[1] At the end of September 1944 a suicide surface craft unit, with 70 suicide boats, had been sent to Corregidor. Air defence units followed, and a construction unit was sent to restore the large number of American fortress guns which had remained untouched since the Japanese seized the island in 1942. There were garrisons of 400 on Caballo Island, 373 on Carabao Island, and 100 in Mariveles. El Fraile Rocks had a garrison of about 35 members of the crew of the sunken battleship *Musashi*. Enemy forces on Bataan peninsula were estimated at 15,000 men, excluding service troops.

For the attack on the entrance to Manila Bay the Americans employed Subic Bay as their base of operations, both for assembly and embarkation of army troops, and for anchorage, replenishment and temporary repair of naval vessels. Fighter cover, air support of troops, and airborne lifts were provided by the 5th and 13th Air Forces (Far Eastern Air Force), based on Mindoro and Leyte. The Bataan–Corregidor Attack Group (Task Group 78.3) was under the command of Rear-Admiral A. D. Struble, with Rear-Admiral R. S. Berkey in command of the Fire Support Group (Task Group 77.3) consisting of five light cruisers[2] and nine destroyers[3], whose task was to cover the main sweeping operations at the entrance to the bay, protect the landings and support subsequent operations of the troops at Mariveles and on Corregidor. An additional fire support unit (77.2.5) remained in reserve at Lingayen Gulf until called on. This consisted of the *Shropshire* (Commodore H. B. Farncomb, Commodore Commanding H.M.A.S. Squadron) and two heavy cruisers[4] with the Australian destroyers *Arunta* and *Warramunga* and four U.S. destroyers.[5]

Photographic intelligence of the enemy installations was meagre, but it was believed that the many air strikes made earlier had destroyed all the former American heavy batteries that could have been made operable, as well as any new ones which might have been installed in exposed positions. In the event, it was only from medium and small calibre enemy mobile guns firing from cave positions, that serious trouble came.

The chief difficulty which the Americans expected to encounter in opening Manila Bay to shipping lay in the minefields. Extensive minefields consisting both of old U.S. and of Japanese mines, were reported guarding the entrance (*Figure 4*) : these would have to be swept within close range of such of the batteries as should survive the preliminary bombardment and the bombing by the Far Eastern Air Force which had been in progress since 22nd January. The sweepers available consisted of the six minesweepers *Saunter, Salute, Scout, Scrimmage, Scuffle* and *Sentry*, with 15 district minesweepers.

Preliminary minesweeping began at 0529 on 13th February, the sweepers working from the 100 fathoms line inwards, followed by fire support ships firing on selected targets, whilst heavy bomber strikes were made on Corregidor which soon became obscured by dust and smoke. The Japanese made no reply. Between La Monja and Corregidor Islands 28 old U.S. army electrically controlled mines were cut. Next day, minesweepers, closely supported by two destroyers, swept the channel south of Corregidor. Contact mines were thick

[1] *Philippine Area Naval Operations, Part IV, January* 1945–*August* 1945. Japanese Monograph No. 114, p. 16.

[2] *Phoenix, Boise, Denver, Cleveland, Montpelier.*

[3] *Hopewell, Nicholas, Taylor, O'Bannon, Fletcher, Radford, Jenkins, Lavallette, Abbott.*

[4] *Portland, Minneapolis.*

[5] *Conway, Eaton, Braine, Frazier.*

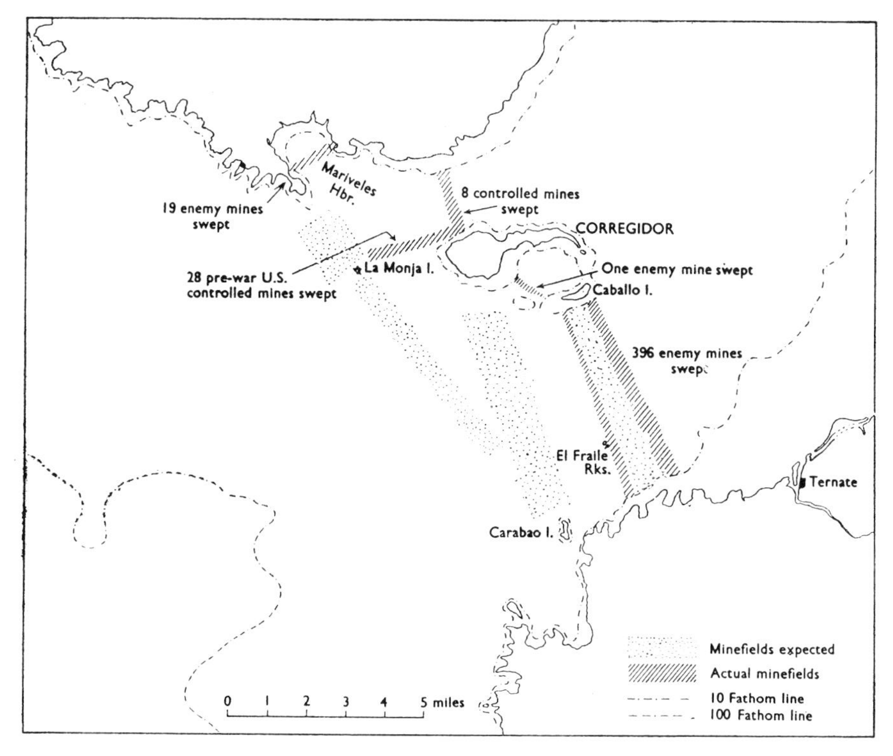

Fig. 4

there, a total of 110 being cut during the day, creating hazardous navigational problems before they could all be destroyed. The first sweep passed about 5,000 yards from Corregidor, and enemy shore batteries opened up. None of the minesweepers was hit, and their fire and that of the destroyers silenced the enemy guns. Later sweeps drew no enemy fire, though the final pass of the day came within some 1,200 yards of the Japanese guns. The narrow channel between Corregidor and Bataan Peninsula was swept in similar manner during the afternoon of the 14th. Three enemy shore batteries which most of the fire support ships had difficulty in hitting, made six or seven hits on the district minesweeper *YMS–48* damaging her so that she had to be sunk. The destroyers *Hopewell* and *Fletcher* were also hit. All ships were withdrawn, and the light cruiser *Phoenix* moved in and aided by air strikes quickly silenced the Japanese guns. Another supported group of minesweepers then went in and swept a channel into Mariveles harbour, in preparation for landings next day. No gunfire was encountered, but the destroyers *Lavallette* and *Radford* struck mines, believed to be electrically controlled. Both ships were considerably damaged, but withdrew under their own power. Mines swept numbered 452. In some cases they were so close together as to endanger considerably the minesweepers, both before and after they were cut. Disposal of the floating mines after they had been cut proved a serious problem ; all vessels in the area co-operated in the duty of sinking them by gunfire.

After another check sweep of Mariveles harbour 4,300 troops, comprising the 151st R.C.T. and the 3rd Battalion of the 34th R.C.T., landed there at 1000 on the 15th. Apart from the striking of a probable mine by a landing ship and difficulty in beaching due to the shallow approaches, the assault presented little difficulty. Supporting gunfire kept the batteries on the north side of Corregidor ineffective. Sweeping in the El Fraile–Caballo area was completed during the day, 155 more contact mines being cut, including one inside Caballo Bay (*Figure 5*) where some ineffective gunfire which was quickly silenced, was encountered. Mines continued to be formed during check sweeps in the area on the 16th, 18th and 19th, as well as in Mariveles harbour. It was evident that mines remaining in the channel north of Corregidor were electrically controlled, and the channel was closed to navigation until the control stations could be captured. One further minesweeper, the *Saunter*, struck a mine on 26th February and was badly damaged.

Though by 16th February in the course of one of the most concentrated air assaults of the war in the Pacific more than 3,000 tons of bombs in ten days had been dropped on Corregidor, which is less than one square mile in extent, the Japanese garrison remained underground almost unharmed. The Americans before the war had fortified the island as the key to the defences of Manila harbour, and it had held out for more than five months against Japanese assault in 1941–1942. The Japanese garrison was capable of active retaliation as well as defence, for in the early hours of the 16th they brought out about 30 suicide boats concealed in the ammunition magazines, and at about 0320 attacked the U.S. ICI(G)s guarding the entrance to Mariveles harbour, sinking three of them.

The island was assaulted by combined parachute troop drop and amphibious landing. The area available for parachute landings was very small. There was an airstrip called Kindley Field towards the narrow east end of the island (*Figure 5*) but this was dominated by Malinta Hill and the high ground at the west end of the island known as ' Top side '. There was a small clear, but

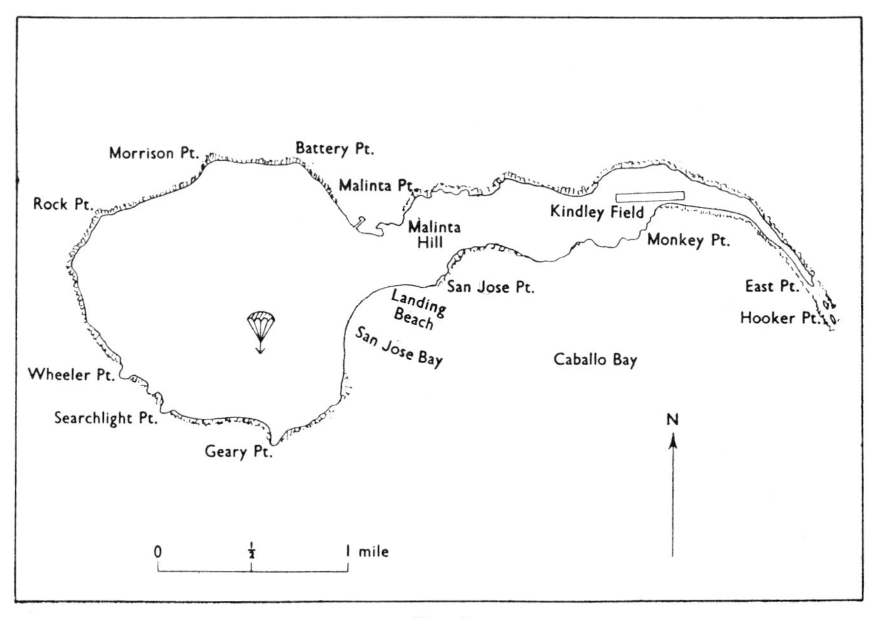

Fig. 5

obstacle studded, space on 'Top side', and it was decided to make the drop there, though the slightest miscalculation such as had been made at Nasugbu would land the paratroopers on the cliffs or in the sea.

The fire support ships returned to the area at 0500 on the 16th, and at 0839, following an hour of heavy air strikes, the dropping of the 503rd Parachute Infantry Battalion began under cover of aircraft strafing and bombing. Casualties during the day were little more than ten per cent of the men dropped. At 1000 the 3rd Battalion of the 24th RCT, brought from Mariveles in LCMs, landed at San José beach with close in support from LCS(L)s and LCI(R)s. There was some opposition at the beach and land mines were encountered, but the tactical situation was soon so favourable that the paratroopers detailed for drops on the 17th were landed instead by water at San José beach. There were some casualties to men and landing craft before opposition by machine guns and mortars was silenced. The Japanese defence plans had not taken air drop into account, and the capture of 'Top side' disorganised their defence. By 28th February when General MacArthur ordered air attacks against the island to cease, some 4,000 Japanese had been killed on Corregidor.

Meanwhile, U.S. cavalry with tanks and armoured cars had reached the north-eastern part of Manila on 3rd February, and the 11th Airborne Division entered the southern suburbs on the 5th. With the arrival of the U.S. troops, Filipino guerilla uprisings flared up throughout the city. By the 24th almost the entire garrison of more than 16,000 Japanese had been killed and organised resistance was at an end. Admiral Iwabuchi committed suicide two days later. Manila Bay was reopened to shipping on 3rd March.

3

Though Manila was secured and the Philippine Islands Leyte, Samar and Mindoro were cleared of Japanese, there still remained considerable enemy garrisons in the southern islands of the archipelago. To gain control of the straits leading into central Philippine waters in order to cut off enemy reinforcements and facilitate the ultimate reduction of the remaining Japanese strongholds in the Philippines a number of further landings were necessary on Palawan and the southern Philippine islands. These were garrisoned by the Japanese 35th Army under Lieutenant-General Suzuki who had defended Leyte. With little or no air support, and with reinforcement almost impossible to effect, each island had to depend upon its own defence.

Control was first extended south-westward through the seizure of Palawan on 28th February (*Figure 6*). Puerto Princesa, on the east coast was a good harbour, whilst Malampaya Sound in the north was one of the finest natural harbours in the Philippines. Palawan offered air bases for use in the attack on Borneo by the Australians, scheduled for the Spring, and for operations over the South China Sea. The garrison of Palawan was estimated at about 3,500, including a large number of service troops. The U.S. assault was carried out by the 86th R.C.T. reinforced to a strength of 5,322 fighting troops. More than 2,000 service troops and nearly 8,000 Air Force personnel were to be landed later for it was planned to establish a considerable air base. There were two airfields near Puerto Princesa. The landing operation, which was under the command of Rear-Admiral W. M. Fechteler, was staged from Mindoro.[1] For two days

[1] The organisation of the forces in the various operations described in this section is given in Appendix O.

preceding the landing the 5th Air Force from Leyte-Samar and the 13th from Morotai attacked Palawan. A light cruiser Covering and Support Group of three light cruisers and four destroyers under Rear-Admiral R. S. Riggs bombarded Puerto Princesa for an hour-and-a-half before the troops went ashore at 0845 on the 28th. There was no opposition to the landing. Fringing reefs, coral heads and mangrove swamps backing some of the beaches necessitated

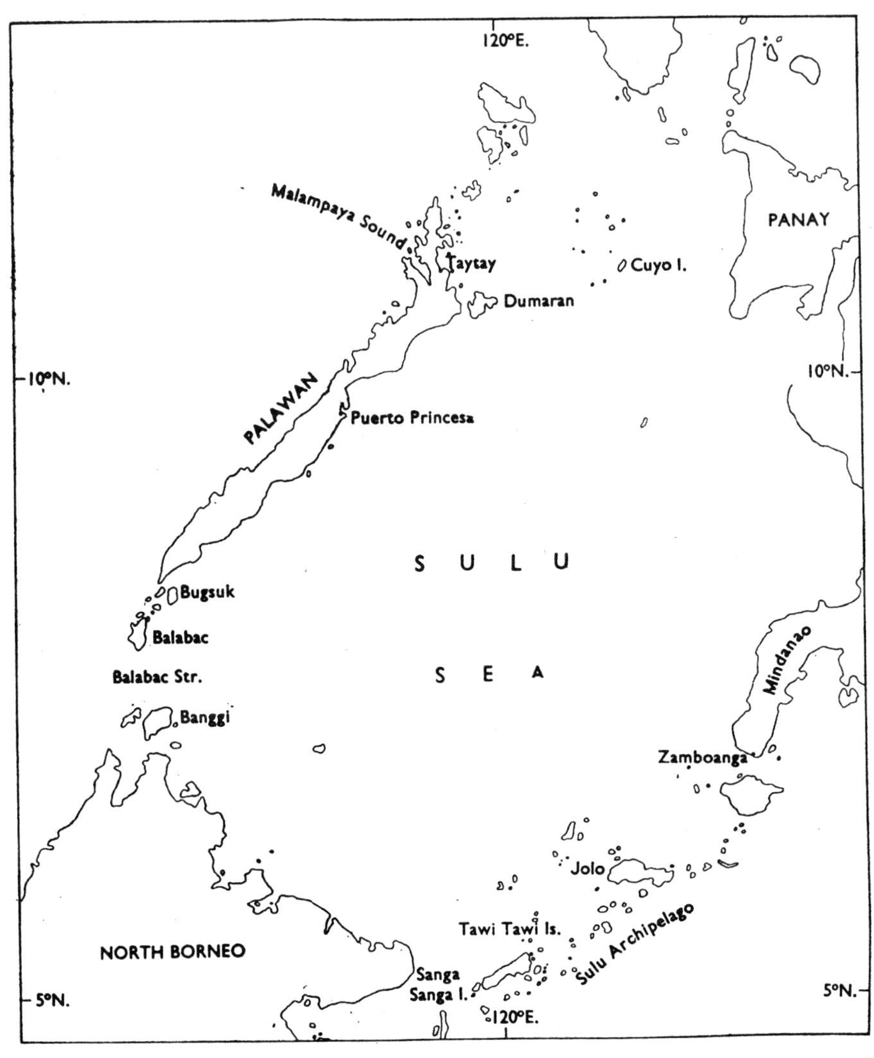

Fig. 6

the employment of amtracks (LVTs) and LCMs by the leading waves of troops, until suitable places could be found for the beaching of LSTs and LSMs. A reinforcement echelon in 19 tank landing ships arrived early next morning, with two squadrons of M.T.B.s. Fighter and night-fighter aircraft were established ashore within six days. The capture of Palawan provided an effective barrier on the west and a base for naval and air operations which controlled the Balabac Strait entrance from the South China Sea to the Subic Sea. Burias and Ticao islands were seized on 4th March and Romblon and Simara on the 12th in order to protect shipping through San Bernardino Strait and obviate the need for the roundabout route through Surigao Strait which was still subject to air attacks from the central Philippines.

In order to improve the two Japanese airfields near Zamboanga on Mindanao which were needed for the operations against Borneo, and to establish control of Basilan Strait, one of the two main passages between South-East Asia and the South-West Pacific, landings were made at Zamboanga on 10th March and Basilan Island on the 16th. Guerillas were already in occupation of most of the Zamboanga peninsula, the Japanese being confined within a defensive perimeter north of the city and nearby airfields, manned, it was estimated, by up to 8,000 troops, though actually it seems that not more than half this number was present. H.M.A.S. *Warrego* surveyed the approaches to the landing beaches.[1] The Japanese had constructed strong defences, with machine-gun nests and pill-boxes, most of which, however, were found not to be manned. Four dual purpose 10 cm. coast defence guns which had not been mounted were found after the landing. Minesweeping occupied two days prior to the assault, and was conducted under the guns of a cruiser-destroyer covering group. Extensive minefields had been reported, but few mines were swept in the waters, though naval mines were found employed as land mines ashore. In striking one of the mines an Army L.C.M. was sunk. The landing operation, which was mounted in Mindoro, was commanded by Rear-Admiral F. B. Royal and carried out by two regimental combat teams of the 41st Division. Strong M.T.B. patrols were provided to deal with expected suicide boat attacks, and Marine aircraft serviced at an airfield at Dipolog in north-western Mindanao, protected the landing. After gunfire preparation beginning at 0645 on 10th March the first wave of amtracks beached at 0915 under some enemy machine-gun, artillery and mortar fire which damaged two LSTs and two LCIs. The amtracks were unable to mount the steep bank of loose rubble near the water's edge, but LSMs and LCIs brought up bulldozers which cut lanes for vehicles to pass. Casualties in the landings were 99 for the Army and Navy together.

Land mining was extensive though much of it was ineffective, being inefficiently prepared. Booby traps had been laid and about 75 casualties to U.S. troops were caused when a great store of naval torpedoes in a tunnel were exploded by electric control. Heavily mined roads inland made tanks ineffective and as the troops approached the prepared hill positions resistance was so strong that not only Marine dive bombers and B–25s (medium bombers), but even B–24s (heavy bombers) had to be called upon to assist. Organised enemy resistance did not cease until the end of March. The 500 or so Japanese in Basilan Island were disposed of by a reinforced infantry company transported from Zamboanga on 16th March.

From Zamboanga one battalion of the 163rd Regimental Combat Team was transported to Sanga Sanga Island (Tawi Tawi) (*Figure 6*) where it landed unopposed on 2nd April, guerillas having previously cleared out the Japanese. The remainder of the 163rd R.C.T. landed on Jolo Island a week later.

Guerilla forces had practically cleared Panay Island of Japanese, except for a concentration at Iloilo (Plan 13) to deal with which Rear-Admiral Struble

[1] *Recommendations for award to surveying personnel, H.M.A.S. Warrego.* H. & A. 566/1945.

landed 14,000 combat and service troops of the 40th Division on 18th March. Only token opposition to the landing was encountered and naval gunfire preparation was withheld to save the lives of the natives. The clearance of Cebu Island called for an expedition of similar size, the America Division being employed for the landing. The beaches were well organised for defence but were found abandoned. Heavy opposition was encountered, however, inland. One of the transports, the s.s. *Michael J. Owens*, lying at the Cebu docks, had the unusual experience of being called upon to silence an enemy battery with her defensive 5-inch gun. Extensive operations were required before the island was cleared of the enemy. A landing on 1st April at Legaspi in the extreme south of Luzon, to enable the Bicol peninsula to be cleared was notable for the fact that accuracy of air support enabled 1,000 lb. bombs to be delivered whilst the troops remained no more than 400 yards from the target. Numerous other landings were made to seize coastal towns and other strongly held Japanese positions.[1] The last important amphibious operation took place on 17th April by two infantry divisions, a total of nearly 50,000 men being landed at Malabang-Parang on western Mindanao by Rear-Admiral A. G. Noble. For a week, whilst the rivers were in flood, troops made use in their advance of motor gunboats and landing craft, to circumvent blocked roads and demolished bridges. By 24th April the rivers had receded, leaving the flotilla stranded until 6th May.

By 6th July the Philippines were free of Japanese except for uninhabited mountain recesses. Out of a total of perhaps 450,000 Japanese troops in the archipelago it is believed that no more than 30,000 survived. Allied casualties in this extensive operation were approximately 12,500 killed, 500 missing, and 45,000 wounded.

4

The liberation of the Philippines, regarded by many as an end in itself, was not the real military gain which accrued from the recapture of the archipelago. The true gain was the control of the South China Sea which the Third Fleet had demonstrated in their sweep during January. The establishment of American air bases in the Philippines complicated to the point of virtual impossibility the Japanese problem of providing air cover for their convoys on the run between Singapore and Formosa. Convoys deprived of this air cover had little chance of getting through unscathed. During February 1945 no convoys sailed from Japan for the south owing to the menace of air attacks ; though convoys were resumed in March, the latter part of that month saw the final convoy pass between Japan and the south, and with it, the failure of Japan's object in going to war. Though after the fall of the Marianas Japan in the late summer of 1944 would gladly have made peace on terms, she was far from giving even momentary consideration to the unconditional surrender demanded by the Allies. The surrender of Japan was to be forced by lowering the will and capacity of the Japanese to resist, through sea and air blockade and intensive bombardment as well as by invasion. When the invasion of the Philippines was

[1] The most important of these landings were as follows :—

Guimaras Island	20th March
Pandan Point (North-Western Negros)	1st April
Masbate	3rd ,,
Busuanga Island (in the Calamian Group)	9th ,,
Tagbilaran (Bohol Island)	11th ,,
Carabao Island (south of Corregidor) (*see* Plan 13)	15th ,,

well launched in November 1944, the Americans had settled their concept of operations for the main effort in the Pacific, which up to then had remained flexible, in conformity with the object of compelling Japan to surrender unconditionally. The blockade and air bombardment were to be intensified, and bases in Okinawa, Iwo Jima and Kyushu were to be captured for the purpose, the target date of the invasion of Kyushu (Operation 'Olympic') being a twelvemonth distant. Invasion of the industrial heart of Japan through the Tokyo plain (Operation 'Coronet') was timed for 1st March, 1946. Planning was premised on on the belief that defeat of the enemy armed forces in the Japanese home islands was a prerequisite of unconditional surrender and offered the best prospect of securing the capitulation of the Japanese forces outside Japan. The possibility of a sudden collapse or surrender of the enemy was not ruled out but to the very moment of surrender the Allies remained unaware how desperate was the situation of the Japanese.

CHAPTER XIII

Assault and Capture of Iwo Jima

(Operation 'Detachment')

1

THE long debate, whether or not Formosa should be seized, had been resolved on 2nd October 1944. It was thought that casualties in capturing this large, well defended, and highly developed island might reach a prohibitive figure, and moreover the Americans found that it would be impossible to provide the necessary forces until three months after Germany should have surrendered. Accordingly, the Joint Chiefs-of-Staff, after exhaustive examination of the problem, decided to by-pass Formosa in favour of a landing in the Ryuku and Volcano Islands after Luzon had been secured.

In the Volcano Islands, a group of the Nanpo Shoto situated on the parallel of 25° N., 650 miles south of Tokyo, lies Iwo Jima, the youngest of the volcanic rocks of the Pacific. In 1945 sulphurous vapours still exuded from cracks in the pent house slabs of Mount Suribachi, the volcano at the south-west extremity of the island, which had but recently risen from the sea. Economically useless, this small island 4½ miles long by 2½ wide, was used by the Japanese as a search-plane base and a staging point for aircraft flying from Japan for the reinforcement of the Philippines. The Pacific Fleet bombed and bombarded it seven times during 1944. It was expected to be of great value in the air assault on Japan. For Iwo Jima lay midway between Japan and the great airfields of Saipan from which in the previous November Superfortresses of the U.S. 20th Air Force had begun the assault on the main Japanese islands which it was hoped would bring about surrender without the necessity for invasion. From Saipan to Tokyo the distance is 650 miles, and to Kyushu with its 63 airfields, 680 miles ; and, whilst the bombers could fly there and back, the distance was too great for fighters to do so without refuelling. On the eight square miles of flat land attached to Mount Suribachi there was ample space for airfields from which fighters could fly in company with the bombers on their missions against Japan. While the Japanese held the island, the Superfortresses based on Saipan had either to fly over the airfields of Iwo Jima, on which, on occasion, up to 175 enemy aircraft had been seen, or to take a dog-legged course which complicated navigation and entailed reducing bomb loads. 'In American hands Iwo Jima would provide a site for navigational aids, an emergency landing field for B–29s in distress, a staging field for northbound planes, a base for fighter escorts, a station for rescue activities '.[1] It would also permit medium bombers

[1] *The Army Air Forces in World War II*, Vol. V, p. 578.

to attack Japan and deprive the enemy of an important aerial lookout station. Finally, though this played no part in the decision to capture Iwo Jima, there was the question of the defence of the Marianas airfields. Between 3rd November 1944 when the Japanese, sensing the significance of the occupation of these airfields by the new B–29s began raiding them, and 2nd January 1945 when the raids ceased, 11 B–29s were destroyed and 43 damaged to a greater or lesser degree on these fields. Each of these aircraft represented a great investment of manpower, material and money. Since the intruders managed to slip in under the radar screens of Saipan and Tinian, which were ineffective in giving warning of low level attacks, Vice-Admiral Hoover stationed two of the destroyers of his Forward Area Forces as pickets in the northern Marianas.[1]

Within 48 hours, however, at 0012 on 27th November two or more Japanese naval medium bombers took the Isely Field (Saipan) defenders by surprise, destroyed one Superfortress, and damaged 11 others, two seriously, before making their escape unharmed. At noon that day the Japanese struck again in much greater strength and caused commensurate losses, though 13 of the attackers were destroyed. It was assumed—correctly—that the raiders were staging down from Japan through Iwo Jima. The decision to assault this island had, however, already been taken a month before the raids began and was independent of them.

2

In planning the assault (Operation 'Detachment') the time factor was important; for the operation, a major one entailing some 900 ships and a landing force of 70,000 U.S. Marines, had to be undertaken in the short space of time between the Lingayen landing on 9th January and the assault on Okinawa which, scheduled originally for 1st March, was eventually fixed for 1st April. The shipping used at Iwo Jima would be required again at Okinawa. The most determined resistance was expected; for Iwo Jima being the only island in the strategically important Napo Shoto group which lent itself to the construction of airfields, the Japanese had been fortifying it over a period of years. Two airfields with runways for heavy bombers were in operation (*Figure 7*) and a third was under construction. On this small island the Japanese could cover with artillery and machine-gun fire either from Mount Suribachi in the south or from the high northern area, every inch of the shore line and in particular the only two beaches on which landing was feasible. Tactical surprise was thus impossible once the preliminary bombardments to reduce the defences had begun. Similarly, U.S. artillery sited in the beach areas could reach every yard of ground on the island. The Japanese were consequently unable to carry out their policy of withdrawing into the interior which had been apparent in many operations since the American landings in the Philippines, and they were forced to adopt a mean between that policy and the earlier doctrine of fighting at the water's edge.

[1] Plans had called for the installation on Saipan of an AN/CPS–1 radar or microwave early warning set, designed to give earlier warning of air attack, particularly at low levels, though capable of picking up a bomber 200 miles away at an altitude of 30,000 ft. This radar set weighed 66 tons and to instal it would involve considerable constructional work; accordingly, installation was postponed. The incident is not without interest, for it adds yet another to the instances of the difficulties attending divided control. The Navy, which was in control in the theatre, did not want to divert manpower to installing the set; accordingly, General Arnold, who was dependent on the Navy for static defence of his Marianas airfields, failed to get the set installed until after the raids on Saipan ceased.

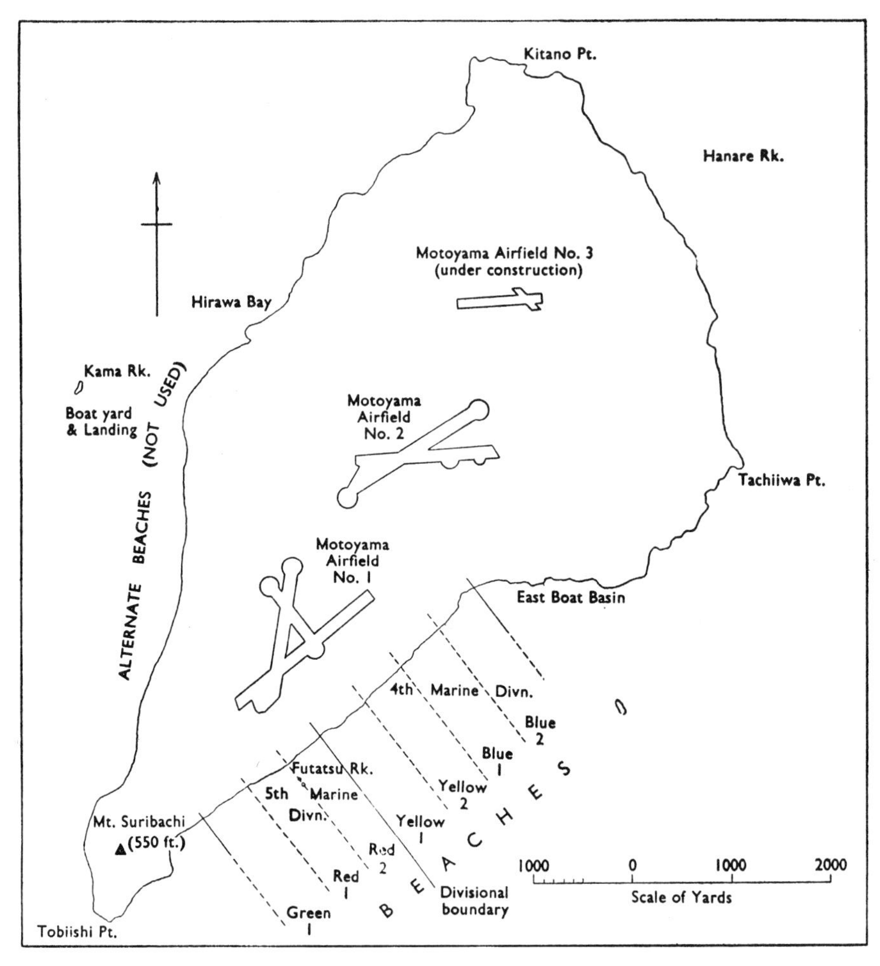

Fig. 7

Neither harbour nor protected anchorage existed at Iwo Jima, nor any barrier reef. There were no artificial beach defences, the shifting volcanic sand and the surf rendering these impossible. But immediately behind the beaches there were natural terraces which could be crossed only by tracked vehicles, and by such vehicles in many places only with difficulty, and always under fire from the defenders. The first terrace behind Red and Green beaches was mined. Inland, the defence was immensely strong, the salient features being large numbers of intricate heavily protected, interconnected underground shelters and mutually supporting blockhouses. Guns, mortars and anti-aircraft guns were skilfully sited and camouflaged ; air reconnaissance discovered 800 of the many defence positions. Land mines were extensively used. In the mountainous areas cave systems often of great extent, housed command posts, guns, equipment and supplies. Blockhouses, pillboxes and caves were constructed not only to meet a land attack but to withstand heavy naval gunfire. The marines had to take the island yard by yard with rifle, grenade and flame thrower. ' As a whole, reported the Commander of the Joint Expeditionary Force, Vice-Admiral

R. K. Turner, 'this was the best defended, most well organised, and most difficult objective this force had ever operated against. The location and organisation of the defences was the best, tactically, yet encountered.'[1] The defenders commanded by Lieutenant-General T. Kuribayshi, numbered about 20,000, nearly a third more than estimated, the original garrison of 14,000 having been reinforced with first-line troops by sea and air. The naval garrison numbered some 7,000. Part of it, at least, was organised as infantry, in addition to carrying out regular duties as air ground crews, coast defence and anti-aircraft gunners and construction and maintenance personnel.

For seven months prior to the invasion of Iwo Jima the island was subjected to aerial bombing and ship bombardment in order to reduce its value as an air base, to interfere with supply, and to destroy the defences. Beginning with an air strike on 15th June 1944, the fast carriers bombed the island five times and the U.S. Pacific Fleet and cruisers and destroyers of Admiral Hoover's Forward Force carried out four bombardments. In addition, land-based heavy bombers of the Forward Area, Central Pacific had been attacking both the airfields. The island was bombed daily for more than 70 days prior to the landing on 19th February, 1945. This high-level horizontal bombing had little effect on the enemy's defensive system. The difficulty of eliminating such targets by this means had been manifested many times during the war.

During December, rocket-firing Marine bombers based in the Marianas attacked, at night, shipping in the harbours of Chichi Jima and Haha Jima to which the enemy was in the habit of escorting merchantmen carrying equipment and supplies which he then transferred by small craft to Iwo Jima, to build up the defences of the island. In November and December, Superfortresses also went out from Saipan to attack the Iwo airfields ; whilst early in December bombers of the U.S. 7th Army Air Force, operating under control of the Strategic Air Force Pacific Ocean Areas, began daily attacks. During the latter month, 2,360 tons of bombs were dropped on the island. Yet at no time were both of the air strips rendered inoperational and no strip was out of action for an entire day ;[2] and so little was their value as staging fields affected, that one of the most destructive raids made by the enemy on Isely Field (Saipan) on Christmas Day 1944 took place after a heavy air and sea bombardment of Iwo Jima.[3]

Deep water running to within a short distance from the shore made Iwo Jima highly accessible to bombardment by surface ships, but most of the batteries were known to be carefully revetted and would require direct hits to destroy them. Many of them were mounted at elevations of 150 to 250 feet, adding to the difficulty of knocking them out. Rear-Admiral A. E. Smith on the night of 11th–12th November bombarded airfields, aircraft and installations on the island with three heavy cruisers and five destroyers (Task Group 30.2), the mean ranges used by the cruisers being 16,000 yards and by the destroyers 12,000 yards. The lesson that to bombard fixed defences with success, ships must come to within close range, took even longer of acceptance than the doctrine that to bomb successfully aircraft must come down to masthead height. On 8th December, in conjunction with an air bombardment, Task Group 94.9 comprising three heavy cruisers and six destroyers under Rear-Admiral Smith fired 7,034 rounds of 8-inch and 5-inch ammunition at the island, with Fortress aircraft spotting. The enemy batteries mostly held their fire, and smoke and

[1] *Amphibious Operations, Capture of Iwo Jima 16th February to 16th March* 1945. Cominch P–0012.

[2] *The Army Air Forces in World War II*, Vol. V, pp. 584–5.

[3] The 20th U.S. Air Force bases in the Marianas were as follows: Saipan—Isely and Kobler Fields; Tinian—West and North Fields; Guam—Harmon, North-West and North Fields.

dust prevented detailed observation of the damage caused. The bombardment was repeated on 24th and 27th December. Chichi Jima, Haha Jima and Iwo Jima were bombarded by Admiral Smith's force on 5th January 1945 in conjunction with air attacks by land-based aircraft of Vice-Admiral Hoover's Forward Area Force, and a further ship bombardment was carried out on 24th January by a force (Task Group 94.9) under Rear-Admiral O. C. Badger which included the battleship *Indiana*. ' Despite the over-optimistic reports

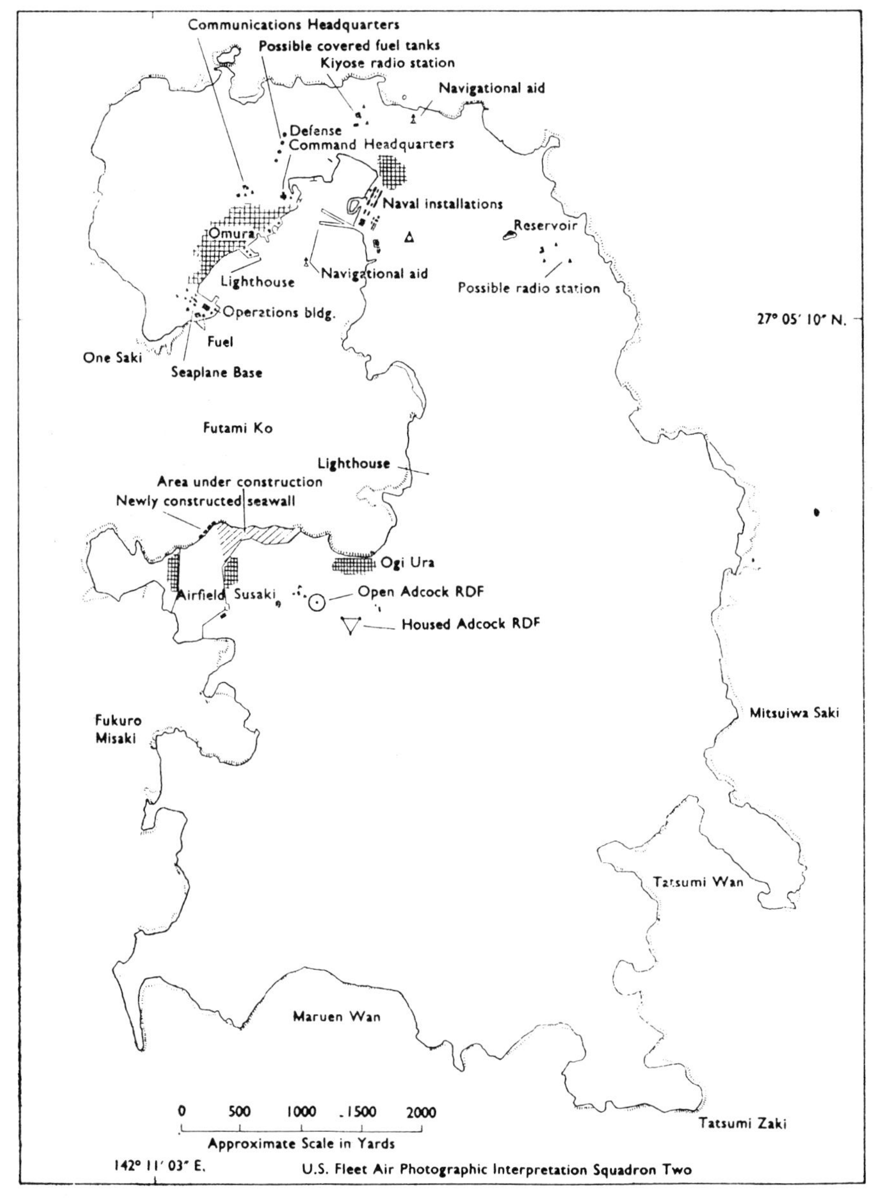

Fig. 8

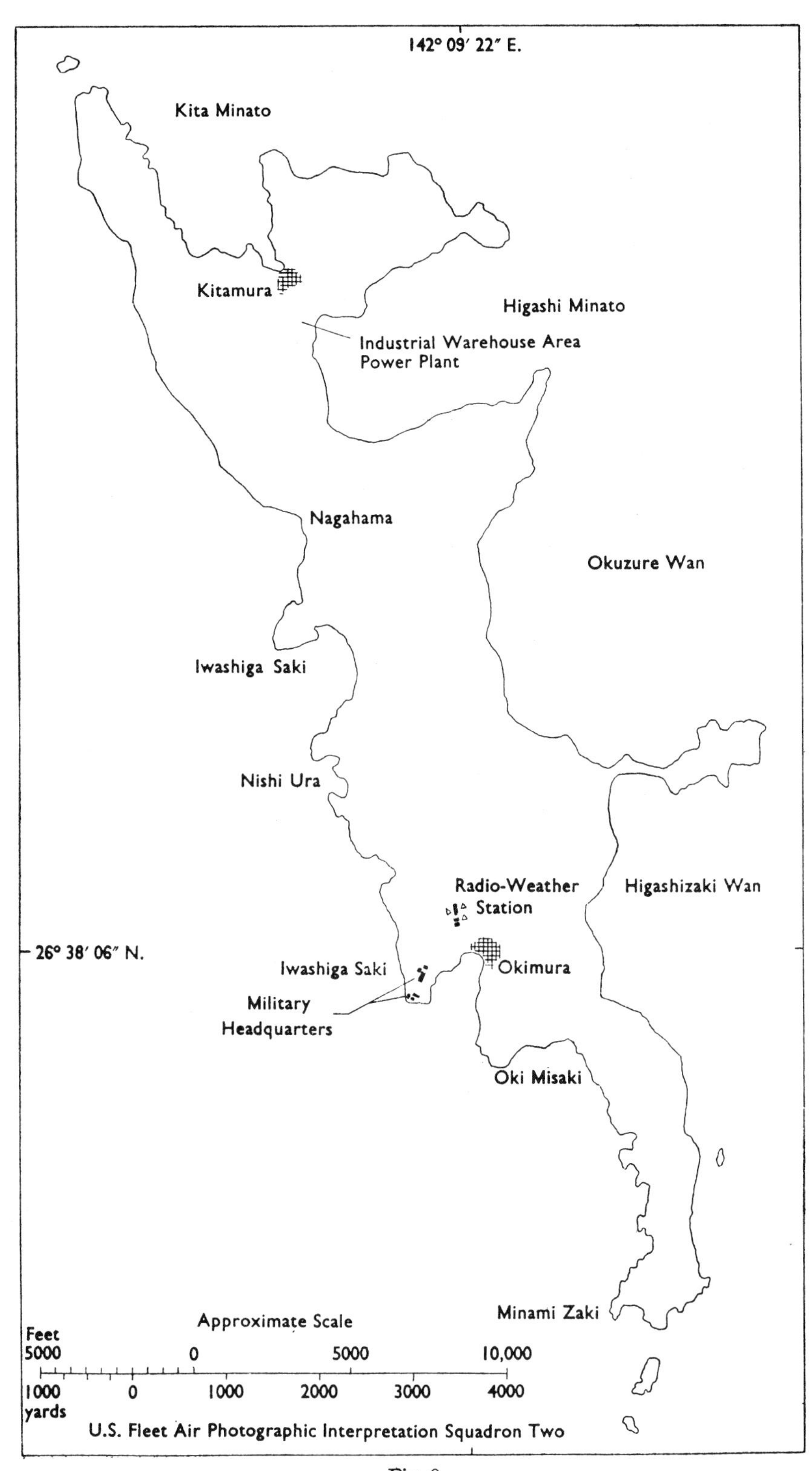
142° 09′ 22″ E.
Kita Minato
Kitamura
Higashi Minato
Industrial Warehouse Area
Power Plant
Nagahama
Okuzure Wan
Iwashiga Saki
Nishi Ura
Radio-Weather
Station
Higashizaki Wan
26° 38′ 06″ N.
Iwashiga Saki
Okimura
Military
Headquarters
Oki Misaki
Minami Zaki
Approximate Scale
Feet
5000
0
5000
10,000
1000
yards
0
1000
2000
3000
4000
U.S. Fleet Air Photographic Interpretation Squadron Two

Fig. 9

of air spotters ', reported the Commander-in-Chief, ' interpretation of photographs taken immediately after the bombardments revealed their ineffectiveness. The damage inspected after landing was caused by naval gunfire, artillery and air bombardments in support between D minus 3 and the capture of the position, and practically none was chargeable to these early bombardments '. To which Admiral Nimitz might have added ' carried out as these were at long ranges '.[1]

3

OPERATION ' DETACHMENT '—COMMAND RELATIONSHIPS

U.S. Joint Chiefs of Staff

- 20th Air Force General H. A. Arnold
- China-based Forces Lt.-General A. C. Wedemeyer
- CinCpac–CinCpoa Forces Fleet-Adm. C. W. Nimitz
  - Strategic Air Forces Pacific Ocean Areas Lt.-Gen. M. F. Harmon
  - Marshalls–Gilberts Force Rear-Adm. W. K. Harrill
  - North Pacific Force Vice-Adm. F. J. Fletcher
  - Army Forces P.O.A. Lt.-Gen. R. C. Richardson, Jr.
  - Air Force Pacific Fleet Vice-Adm. G. E. Murray
  - Service Force Pacific Fleet Vice-Adm. W. W. Smith
  - Forward Area Central Pacific Vice-Adm. J. H. Hoover
  - Central Pacific Task Forces Admiral R. A. Spruance (Com. 5th Fleet)
    - Fast Carrier Task Force Task Force 58 Vice-Adm. M. A. Mitscher (*See* Appendix P)
      - T.G. 58.1 Rear-Adm. J. J. Clark
      - T.G. 58.2 Rear-Adm. R. E. Davison
      - T.G. 58.3 Rear-Adm. F. C. Sherman
      - T.G. 58.4 Rear-Adm. A. W. Radford
      - T.G. 58.5 Rear-Adm. M. B. Gardner
    - Special Groups
      - 50.1 Fleet Flagship U.S.S. *Indianapolis*
      - 50.2 Relief Fleet Flagship U.S.S. *Missouri*
      - 50.3 Search & Reconnaissance Group
      - 50.7 A/S Warfare Group
      - 50.8 Logistic Support Group
      - 50.9 Service Squadron Ten
    - Joint Expeditionary Force Task Force 51 Vice-Adm. R. K. Turner (*See* Appendix O)
      - T.F. 52 Amphibious Support Force Rear-Adm. W. H. P. Blandy (Appendix P)
      - T.F. 53 Attack Force Rear-Adm. H. W. Hill (Appendix P)
      - T.F. 54 Gunfire & Covering Force Rear-Adml B. J. Rodgers (Appendix P)
      - T.F. 56 Expeditionary Troops Lt.-Gen. H. M. Smith, U.S.M.C.
  - South Pacific Force Vice-Adm. W. L. Calhoun
  - Submarine Force Vice-Adm. C. A. Lockwood
- South-west Pacific Forces General D. MacArthur

[1] *Battle Experience, Bombardments of Iwo Jima November* 1944–*January* 1945, pp. 79–3.

Under Fleet-Admiral C. W. Nimitz, Commander-in-Chief Pacific Fleet and Pacific Ocean Areas, control of the operations for the capture of Iwo Jima was vested in Admiral R. A. Spruance, Commander Task Force 50 and Fifth Fleet. Strategic Commanders were Vice-Admiral R. K. Turner, Commander of the Joint Expeditionary Force, and Lieutenant-General H. M. Smith who commanded the Expeditionary Troops. The tactical commanders were Vice-Admiral M. A. Mitscher, Commander of the Fast Carrier Task Force; Rear-Admiral W. H. P. Blandy (Amphibious Support Force); Rear-Admiral B. J. Rodgers (Gunfire and Covering Force), and Major-General H. Schmidt, U.S.M.C., who commanded the assault troops. The latter consisted of the V Amphibious Corps, comprising the 4th and 5th Marine Divisions with the 3rd Division in reserve; and the Garrison Force numbered some 40,000. The advanced base of the expedition was Ulithi. Here Service Squadron 10 was anchored. Comprising some 250 Auxiliary vessels of all kinds, the Squadron formed an advanced supply and repair base capable of supplying practically every form of service which would be available at any Navy Yard or Supply Depot in the U.S.A., including dry-docking.[1] Logistic support of the task forces was furnished to them while under way at sea by the Logistic Support Group, composed of fleet oilers, ammunition ships, replacement transport escort carriers loaded with aircraft for replacing losses on combatant carriers, escort carriers for the protection of the Logistic Support Group itself, general store ships, aviation supply ships carrying spare parts, towing and salvage ships, protected by a screen of destroyers and destroyer escorts. The Group remained under way in areas where it would be beyond range of probable enemy air attack, but close enough to the fighting forces for quick rendezvous when replenishments were required. Its composition was constantly changing as ships discharged their cargoes and returned to base to be filled up again, their places meanwhile being taken by ships with full loads. Both Service Squadron 10 and the Logistic Support Group were among the special groups under Admiral Spruance's direct command as was also the Anti-Submarine Warfare Group consisting of the escort carrier *Anzio* and nine destroyer escorts organised in two hunter-killer groups. Fleet Air Wing One provided a Search and Reconnaissance Group consisting of some 75 seaplanes and 72 long range land-based search aircraft. These aircraft and the co-operating air forces of the South-West Pacific Area, operating from the semi-circle of bases formed by Port Darwin, Morotai, Leyte, Mindoro, Palau, Ulithi and Saipan, covered in their daily searches from D minus 14 day a vast crescent extending from the north coast of Australia almost to the coast of China on the west and the Japanese home islands on the north. The Group also provided air-sea rescue service and offensive screens for expeditionary forces moving towards Iwo Jima and for raids by the Fast Carrier Force (Task Force 58).

Practically all the available strength of the Fifth Fleet not included in Task Force 58 and not engaged in screening the amphibious forces was included in the Gunfire and Covering Force (Task Force 54). This comprised seven of the older battleships, four 8-inch cruisers and 15 destroyers (Appendix P). The force was augmented from time to time for specific support missions, by ships detailed from Task Force 58.

---

[1] The following auxiliaries were initially assigned to Service Squadron 10:—6 AD, 6 AFD, 1 AFD(L), 3 AG, 2 AO, 6 AOG, 1 APL, 5 AR, 3 ARB, 5 ARD, 4 ARG, 1 ARH, 1 ARS, 8 ATF, 2 ATA, 3 ATD, 4 ATR, 1 DMS, 6 IX (Liberty Tankers), 12 IX (Oil Storage), 12 IX (Issuing Barges), 2 IX (Barracks Ships), 15 YC, 43 YF, 17 YO, 8 YOG, 13 YOG(L), 2 YDG, 5 YP, 4 YR, 2 YSR, 10 YW, 1 YRD(H), 1 YRD(M), 2 YSD, 9 YTB, 4 YTL, 6 LCI, 9 LCT, 3 YG.

The screening groups, known as the Transport Screen (Task Group 51.2), comprised some 24 destroyers, 18 destroyer escorts and five minesweepers. Their duty was to protect the transport groups during the forward movement and at the objective, against air, surface and submarine attack. Various elements supporting the operation as a whole or performing special tasks at the objective prior to D-day, before the arrival of Admiral Turner, were organised as Task Force 52 (the Amphibious Support Force.) This included the Support Carrier Group (Rear-Admiral Durgin), comprising eight escort carriers with a daily availability of about 350 aircraft, and a screen, which executed air support missions of all kinds at the objective and also supported air protection for the shipping there ; the Mine Group (Task Group 52.3) ; Underwater Demolition Group, (Task Group 52.4) ; Gunboat Support Group (Task Group 52.5) ; Mortar Support Group (Task Group 52.6) ; and RCM and Rocket Support Group (Task Group 52.7). The vessels of the three groups last-named were all adaptations of the original 160-foot landing craft, infantry.

The Attack Force (Task Force 53) (Appendix P) included the transports, cargo vessels and landing ships which carried the assault troops to the objective, more than 120 of these ships being required ; whilst a further 50 vessels carried personnel who performed various duties such as control and beach parties, and gear such as pontoon causeways. The Joint Expeditionary Force Reserve (Task Group 51.1, Trans. Div. 11) comprised 20 transports carrying the 3rd Marine Division. This force was kept in areas removed from the objective until after D-day, and consequently was self-contained as regards its screen of destroyers and destroyer escorts.

4

The continuing Philippine operations necessitated a reduction in the number of ships previously detailed for the capture of Iwo Jima ; and in order to provide sufficient gunfire support, two of the battleships of the Fast Carrier Task Force (Task Force 58) were loaded principally with bombardment in place of armour piercing ammunition, and certain of the cruisers also loaded additional bombardment ammunition. The Fast Carrier Force of the Fifth Fleet was commanded at this date by Vice-Admiral M. A. Mitscher. It included 16 carriers, all the eight fast battleships, 18 cruisers including the *Alaska*, classed as a ' large cruiser ', and 79 destroyers. The carriers were organised in five groups, one of which was a night group, the aggregate aircraft complement being approximately 1,170.[1] Eight of the air groups had never previously operated together in combat. Out of the 111 ships composing the force all except four had been added to the fleet since the outbreak of war. Admiral Spruance, Commander Fifth Fleet, flew his flag on board the 8-inch cruiser *Indianapolis* in Task Group 58.3. The duty of Task Force 58 was to cover the Joint Expeditionary Force against attempts at interference by Japanese air or

[1] The organisation of Task Force 58 is given in Appendix P.

surface forces. At the beginning of February the effective strength of the Japanese Fleet was as follows :—

Estimated by Allies	*Actual*[1]
3 battleships	3
2 battleship-carriers ..	2
4 aircraft carriers	4 (plus two damaged. All were in-operative through lack of air groups).
2 escort-carriers ..	1 (classed by Japanese as a carrier)
6 8-inch cruisers	6
7 light cruisers	3
42 destroyers	33 (a few of which were not yet worked up).
17 destroyer escorts	35 (Escort vessels of *Shimushu* and *Mikura* classes)
70 submarines	56 (including a few for local defence)

The proximity of enemy air bases in Japan and the Nansei Shoto made it desirable to attack these heavily, in order to give cover to the assault on Iwo Jima and as preparation for the forthcoming attack on Okinawa. Simultaneously, therefore, with the preliminary bombardment and minesweeping at Iwo Jima on 16th and 17th February, Task Force 58 carried out strikes on airfields, air installations and aircraft plants in the Tokyo area, but destruction of these targets was secondary to the primary mission of destroying aircraft, both in the air and on the ground. Some 1,500 aircraft (or dummies) were visible on the 90 airfields within 50 miles of Tokyo which were photographed during the two days.

To avoid detection in the approach to Japan, special efforts were made to destroy enemy picket boats. Fifteen destroyers operated 35 to 40 miles in advance of the leading task group, and B–29s were sent from the Marianas, with naval observers, to destroy the pickets. No more than two small craft were encountered, and were duly destroyed ; and the force arrived undetected at its launching point, 120 miles 135° from Tokyo, on the morning of the 16th. On the first day, opposition by hostile aircraft was formidable and 281 of the enemy were reported shot down and 209 destroyed on the ground. On the second day, 238 enemy aircraft were engaged, 83 being destroyed. Considerable damage was reported to have been done to Japanese aircraft plants. The large auxiliary *Yamashita Maru* (10,605 tons) (mistaken at the time for an escort carrier) was sunk in Tokyo Bay, and several picket boats and small craft were engaged and sunk during the retirement. Enemy air retaliation against the force was almost completely lacking and anti-aircraft fire was reported to be relatively ineffective and generally inaccurate. The operation of the night carrier group (Task Group 58.5) was not satisfactory ; the weather was bad and the day groups were unable to provide combat air patrols over the group which had consequently to expend nearly two-thirds of its total air effort defensively. As the complements of the night carriers *Saratoga* and *Enterprise* were only 60 per cent of those of day carriers of their class, night offensive missions were limited in scope.

[1] These figures are based on the fleet disposition list of the *Japanese Report* (Monograph No. 116) corrected by the known figures of damage and sinking, since it was apparently a practice of the Japanese to retain in the fleet list for a period vessels, especially important ones and submarines, already sunk. In the list dated 1st February 1945 ten sunken submarines are still retained, as well as the battleship *Musashi* (sunk 24th October 1944), the 8-inch cruiser *Chikuma* (sunk 25th October 1944), the carriers *Zuikaku* (sunk 25th October 1944), *Shokaku* and *Taiho* (sunk 19th June 1944).

The attack was repeated on 25th February, in co-ordination with a raid by Superfortresses of the 20th Air Force attacking from above the overcast immediately after the carriers. The night carrier *Saratoga* having been disabled by suicide air attacks four days previously whilst furnishing night fighter protection at Iwo Jima, the *Enterprise* took her place. Weather was sufficiently bad to cause minor damage to the heavy cruiser *San Francisco* and several destroyers. The force had to reduce speed and in spite of postponing the early launch of aircraft until 0730, this had to take place 175 miles from the nearest land. The approach was detected by an enemy picket vessel and the Japanese flew away as many aircraft as possible, other than fighters, from the Tokyo area. As had happened on the 16th and 17th, the weather conditions grew progressively worse as the day wore on, and little flying was done after noon. During the withdrawal about 0030 on the 26th a small enemy picket boat penetrated the screen, and before being sunk caused damage to the destroyer *Porterfield* which affected her fighting efficiency and minor damage to the light cruiser *Pasadena*. The Americans were, however, able to draw from the episode the satisfaction that their tracking procedure was good and none of their ships was hit by friendly fire in the mêlée.

Total U.S. aircraft losses in the operations against Tokyo and in photographic operations and shipping sweeps carried out on 1st March in the Nansei Shoto area were 84 in combat and 59 operationally. Submarines of the Air-Sea Rescue Service co-operated with destroyers and aircraft in life saving, but 60 pilots and 21 aircrewmen were lost. Some 650 enemy aircraft were reported destroyed in these operations. Apart from the large auxiliary sunk in Yokohama Bay on 17th February all ships destroyed, both combatant and non-combatant, were of small size. A new development in the replenishment of aircraft and pilots was adopted during these operations. Instead of embarking fighter pilots individually and thereby sacrificing their previous team training, full teams were taken aboard, the force sailing from Ulithi with 50 per cent of pilots above complement.

5

The Commander of the U.S. troops, Lieutenant-General H. M. Smith, recommended a total of nine days of preliminary bombardment, but owing to limitations of ammunition supply and time, and the subsequent troop requirements, this had to be cut down, and bombardment began on D minus 3 day, 16th February. A total of 14,250 tons of ammunition was fired, as compared with 10,965 in the capture of Saipan, the highest previous figure. Bad weather interfered with the bombardment, and some precedence had to be given to minesweeping and UDT operations. Next day, the ships moved in closer to shore, but it was difficult to spot the enemy guns, the Japanese propellant being almost smokeless ; and it was not until the fire support ships with their spotting aircraft, as well as the support aircraft, had worked at the objective for two days and become familiar with the positions and appearance of the defences, that substantial results were achieved by close range gunfire and low altitude air strikes. Return fire from the shore against the heavier ships was light, even when ships closed to less than 2,000 yards. But the 8-inch cruiser *Pensacola* sustained considerable damage from hits by shells up to 8-inch calibre, and all 12 of the gunboats supporting the UDTs were hit by shore gunfire between 1100 and 1145 on the 17th, one had to be sunk, and many had to withdraw and be replaced by reliefs. The destroyer *Leutze*, the high speed transport *Blessman*, and the minesweeper *Gamble* were damaged by air attack.

The Attack Force (Task Force 53) and other units of the Joint Expeditionary Force not already at the objective, arrived off the south-western beaches of Iwo Jima before daylight on 19th February (D-day) and began disembarking the Landing Force into their boats. Naval gunfire started at H-hour minus 140 minutes (0640 hours) and proceeded with a short break for air strikes. Towards the end, fire was restricted by Plan ' Victor ' to trajectory heights of 600 feet, to permit continuous simultaneous air support (*Figure 10*).

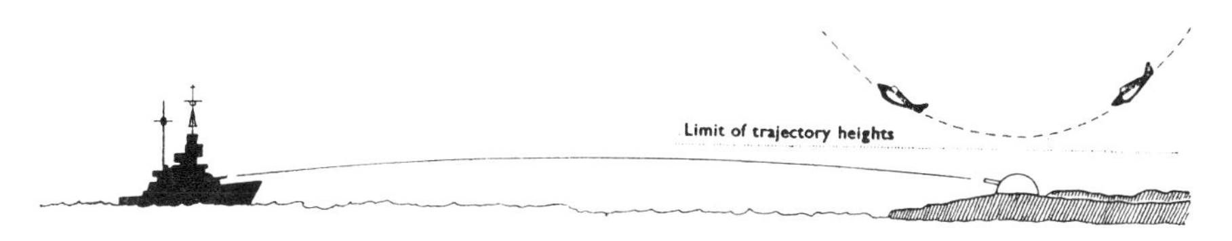

Fig. 10

Continuity of naval gunfire during the assault was achieved for the first time.[1] The pre-H-hour barrage was timed to lift by successive stages after H-hour to a line approximately 2,000 yards inland, the timing being based on expected rate of advance. Supported thus, the first waves of troops, preceded by LVT(A)s which opened fire when about 200 yards from the shore, and accompanied by the Underwater Demolition Teams on to the beaches they had reconnoitred, reached the beach at H-hour (0900), landing over practically the whole length of the south-eastern beaches on a front of about 3,000 yards. During the actual approach little gunfire was received, but heavy artillery and mortar fire soon developed on the boat lanes as well as on the beaches and on the landing ships near the line of departure which was parallel to and about 4,000 yards off the south-eastern beaches. On the right, the 4th Marine Division was unable on account of this fire to land its guns until after dark.

The unsuitable nature of the beach for a landing soon became apparent. From seaward, the dry volcanic sand or ash of which it was composed had appeared to be hard-packed, but actually it had no cohesive consistency. It flowed almost like a liquid and it was difficult to keep breech mechanisms and bolt actions in working order. The slope was steep and the surf broke directly on the beach. With each wave, boats were picked up bodily and thrown broadside on to the shore, where succeeding waves swamped and wrecked them and dug them deeply into the sand. The accumulation of wreckage piled higher and higher and extended to seaward to form underwater obstructions. Several 105-mm. howitzers loaded in DUKWs were lost *en route* in the rough seas. Some tanks stalled in the surf and were swamped. Uncollected cargo nets fouled the propellers of small craft. Troops struggled up the beach ankle-deep in the shifting sand. Wheeled vehicles bogged to their frames. Even tracked vehicles moved with difficulty ; many found it impossible to mount the slope to the first terrace. Some improvement resulted from laying steel matting on the beaches ; and later, it was found that clay hauled from a clay-pit on the island and spread over the sand formed with the latter a fairly hard surface.

LSTs and LSMs were sent in to the beaches as soon as the beachhead was secured, but they too had difficulty in keeping from broaching to. Attempts

[1] C.O.H.Q. Bulletin Y/49.

to use pontoon causeways for the most part resulted in these being damaged and sunk, or going adrift and becoming a menace to navigation in the crowded waters off the beach. The many craft required to land the large numbers of troops, and the need for bringing the transports close to the shore in order to shorten the rough water trip for the boats, resulted in numerous collisions. Finally, the beaches had to be closed to all craft smaller than LCTs, LSMs and LSTs, except for the evacuation of casualties. This task was effected by amphibious vehicles at the rate of three casualties a minute throughout the day. In the heavy swell which lifted LVTs and DUKWs to the level of the landing ships' decks, it was no easy matter to tranship the wounded. 'Although there was no problem of a fringing reef at Iwo Jima, the usefulness of the LVT and DUKW has never been more clearly shown. During periods of unfavourable surf conditions, they were the only effective carriers, and performed yeoman service in operating directly between ships in the transport area and the front line elements.'[1]

LSTs, LSMs, LCTs and smaller craft suffered extensive damage in the rough sea while alongside larger vessels. All available fenders were soon carried away. Makeshift fenders proved inadequate: those with small pressure areas caused considerable damage. Mounting lugs for causeways and pontoon barges on the sides of LSTs were a particular source of damage to vessels and small craft alongside them.[2]

The results of the first day's fighting were disappointing. The assault troops met fierce opposition behind the beaches from the onset and were pinned down a few hundred yards inland. A curtain of mortar fire on the beaches prevented artillery from landing. During the night the enemy counter-attacked on the 5th Division front and, though repulsed, dug in 300 yards away. Next day, the Marines made some progress, but very slowly. Mortar fire on the beaches caused heavy casualties to beach and shore parties and craft: seven DUKWs bringing guns ashore were wrecked. An attempt to land part of the corps reserve, the 3rd Marine Division, had to be abandoned as there was no room for the troops to deploy on shore. In the afternoon, the weather broke and heavy surf wrecked many more craft, and all except the flank beaches were almost entirely congested by wreckage. At dusk, transports and LSTs withdrew. The two LSTs acting as tenders to the Small Craft Group[3] did not arrive, and many fully loaded craft and amphibians were unable to discharge and were left cruising on the line of departure. Most of them were collected during the night, but next day some LVTs and DUKWs were found as far as 15 miles from the island.

By D plus 2 day congestion on the beaches was acute. Only LSTs and LSMs could beach and space was severely limited by wreckage. However, 31 landing craft and some DUKWs were towed off the beach, despite a lack of suitable towing lines. General unloading began on D plus 5 but not until D plus 8 were the beaches cleared of all wrecked craft; even then LVTs remained stranded.

---

[1] *Operations in the Pacific Ocean Areas during the month of February* 1945, p. 93.

[2] A breakdown of the damage sustained by the ships during the operation is given in Appendix Q.

[3] The Landing Craft Tender was a new type of logistic vessel designed to act both as a 'home' for transients and boats' crews left behind at the objective upon nightly retirement of transports, and as supply ship for small craft.

6. Iwo Jima : U.S. Marines unloading supplies.

[Facing page 162

7. Fleet Admiral C. W. Nimitz on board H.M.S. *King George V* at Guam, May 1945.

6

Heavy enemy air reaction to the amphibious assault on Iwo Jima began on the night of D-day but was of short duration. Between 1900 and 2200 on the 19th, Task Groups of the Fast Carrier Force operating some 75 miles north-west of the island were attacked in bright moonlight by about 12 to 15 enemy aircraft. The ships manœuvred into cloud cover and sent up night fighters, and the attacks were not pressed home.

Two nights later, on 21st February heavy attacks were made on the escort carriers which, pending the capture of airfields on Iwo Jima, were responsible for air support of the operation, and on the night fighter fast carrier group (Task Group 58.5) which had been left behind to reinforce the escort carriers. That evening the night fighter carrier *Saratoga* was attacked whilst operating north-west of Iwo Jima, screened by three destroyers. The ship had 14 night fighters in the air, but several enemy aircraft got through the screen. In the space of a few minutes after 1700 the ship was hit by two bombs or torpedoes and four suicide aircraft all four of which had been hit and set on fire before they crashed aboard ; a fifth aircraft was shot down in its approach. Though considerably damaged and unable to land-on her aircraft the *Saratoga* within an hour had her fires under control and was capable of 25 knots. At 1845 three enemy aircraft made a further attack. Two of these were shot down, but the third dropped another bomb on the carrier's flight deck and then crashed over the side. The *Saratoga* lost 49 aircraft and had 350 casualties, and she had to withdraw and was ultimately sent to the U.S.A. for repairs. Simultaneously, the escort carriers came under attack. The escort carrier *Bismarck Sea* cruising in the operating area about 20 miles east of Iwo Jima was attacked by two suicide aircraft. One was shot down, the other though fired at and hit until the guns could depress no further, struck the ship. Two minutes later, a third aircraft came in unseen and crashed vertically through the flight deck, rupturing the after fire main. The after part of the ship soon became an inferno of fire. After a third very heavy explosion, probably from her own torpedoes, the ship took a heavy list and finally capsized and sank about two-and-a-half hours later with the loss of 319 of her crew killed or missing and 99 wounded. In the darkness and rough sea the rescue of the survivors was difficult and went on all night. The Captain of the *Bismarck Sea* noted in his report that the percentage of loss by drowning among aircraft pilots and crews was far lower than amongst other categories ; and he attributed this to the constant exercise which had kept the airmen in good physical condition. These were the final successful enemy air attacks on the ships off Iwo Jima.

7

Japanese submarines made no successful attacks though at times there were several hundred U.S. ships anchored off Iwo Jima with no mine or net protection, and a browning shot could scarcely have failed to hit something.

Immunity was ensured by the combination of continuous air patrol designed to keep enemy submarines from approaching on the surface, and a tight double cordon of screening vessels around the entire island and the Transport and Fire Support Areas. Hunter-killer groups came into operation against any submarine contacts ; no such contact was made within 45 miles of the island. The American belief in the efficacy of hunter-killer groups was justified in the Iwo operations in so far that aircraft from the escort carrier *Anzio* operating with a group destroyed two submarines on successive days ; though it is believed this success was due in part to special intelligence.

One of the two submarines destroyed by the *Anzio* was engaged in transporting *kaitens* (' human torpedoes ') to attack the amphibious shipping off Iwo Jima. When the U.S. forces began landing, a *kaiten* unit termed *Chibaya* was formed with three parent submarines, *I–368*, *I–370* and *I–44*, which sailed from Japan on 22nd and 23rd February for the island. On the 25th, the U.S. destroyer escort *Finnegan*, part of a task unit proceeding from Iwo Jima to Saipan, sank *I–370* in 22° 45′ N., 141° 27′ E., about 200 miles south of the submarine's objective. On the same day, an aircraft from the *Anzio* sank a patrolling submarine, *RO–43*, in 25° 07′ N., 140° 19′ E. : and next day, using a special weapon, another of the *Anzio's* aircraft sunk a second of the *kaiten* parent boats, *I–368*, in 24° 43′ N., 140° 37′ E. The third parent submarine, *I–44*, succeeded in reaching Iwo Jima. Believing herself to have been sighted off the island by a destroyer, she submerged and remained down by her own account, for 46½ hours ; after which her captain abandoned the operation and returned to Japan, where he was relieved of his command.

On 1st March the *Amkitake* unit, consisting of *I–58* and *I–36*, was despatched to Iwo Jima. The first at least of these two submarines was fitted with the latest type of radar, though this was not completely efficient. *I–36* was recalled on the day after sailing, and *I–58* was ordered to return on the 8th when off the island with her *kaitens* already manned for casting loose.

This brought to an end the inglorious history of the *kaitens* on which so much research work and so many hours of skilled labour had been expended, whilst to operate these suicide craft the best remaining Japanese submarines had been diverted from their legitimate duties during the past four months.[1] Three parent submarines and every *kaiten* launched were lost, whilst their solitary achievement was the sinking of one U.S. oiler.

8

The story of the capture of Iwo Jima is a story of a month of bitter fighting on the ground and under it. General Kuribayshi conducted a static defence which was effective, intense, and notable for economy of force. There were no mobile reserves, no withdrawal through a series of defensive lines, no significant exposure of enemy troops. The defence was of the nature of a decentralised sector system self-contained and little flexible. It was conducted with the maximum number of weapons of all calibres fired from well concealed and protected positions each of which had to be destroyed. In the early stages the Japanese employed their customary infiltration tactics in considerable strength, but this activity diminished later. Once the beachhead was established, which was not until the capture of Mount Suribachi on D plus 4 day, the majority of the casualties of the U.S. Marines were caused by intense and accurate small arms fire. Total American and Japanese casualties were approximately equal : 20,845 and 21,304 respectively. The Japanese died almost to the last man ; no more than 212 prisoners of war were taken : there were no civilians amongst them.

The capture of Iwo Jima would not have been possible without the preparatory bombardment and the continued assistance of fire and support vessels and the carrier and land-based aircraft which supplemented the weapons organic to the army.[2] The enemy installations were frequently impervious to field artillery and required the destructive power of high velocity main battery naval guns.

[1] The earlier operations of the *Kaitens* are described in Volume IV of this history.

[2] *Operations in the Pacific Ocean Areas during the Month of February* 1945, p. 53.

' Napalm was tried more or less experimentally against various of these positions, but was not employed in such a manner as to prove effective. It is highly probable that a very heavy saturation of entire areas with Napalm—before ignition—would have provided the desired results which some 6,000 tons of bombs and 10,000 tons of naval gunfire failed to produce '.[1] A percentage of the ammunition of the fire-support ships had to be retained in case of action against the Japanese surface forces. To ensure that their magazines should not become depleted an unusually large number of logistic ships was used for ammunition supply. Not only were the ships of the Gunfire and Covering Force (Task Force 54) employed on day by day support of the troops, but also, as stated earlier, some of the battleships, cruisers and destroyers of Fast Carrier Force (Task Force 58) and many destroyers from the screens of other groups and units were diverted to assist. Total ammunition expenditure was 291,300 rounds of 4-inch to 16-inch.

All organised resistance on Iwo Jima ceased on 16th March. The first land-based fighters had come in to Airfield No. 1 on 6th March. Airfield No. 2 was operational ten days later. Practically no harbour development was undertaken and all unloading was across the beaches.

The principal value foreseen for Iwo when the decision was taken to capture it, was as a base for very long range fighter escorts. By the late spring of 1945, however, Japanese air strength in the home islands was deteriorating so rapidly that the bombers were again going out unescorted whilst the increasing use of B–29s in night missions also reduced the need for fighters. No more than about 1,700 escort sorties were made from Iwo.[2] Considerable use was however made of the island as an intermediate landing ground, particularly for bombers in distress. By the end of the war, 2,400 B–29s with crews aggregating 25,000 had made emergency landings on Iwo Jima's airfields. ' It is estimated ', wrote Admiral King, ' that the lives saved through this latter factor alone, subsequent to the capture of Iwo Jima, exceeded the lives lost in the capture itself '.[3]

---

[1] *Air Campaigns of the Pacific War*, USSBS, p. 44.

[2] *The Army Air Forces in World War II*, Vol. V, p. 597.

[3] Final Official Report to the Secretary of the Navy by Fleet Admiral Ernest J. King.

CHAPTER XIV

Invasion of Borneo

(Plans 18, 19, 20)

1

THE invasion of Luzon had placed the Allies in so commanding a position over the Japanese lines of communication in the China Sea, that there was no possibility of the enemy bringing home his garrisons in Malaya, Borneo and the Netherlands East Indies, though, as we have seen, he attempted to concentrate them in Malaya and Indo-China. Malaya was to be the next objective of attack by Admiral Mountbatten, but the war came to an end before the operation could be mounted. A purely military strategy on the part of the Allies might perhaps have allowed the garrisons of Borneo and the Netherlands East Indies to remain neutralized, like those of the by-passed Central Pacific islands. In many of these, as also in the Andamans which air power and the East Indies Fleet had isolated, starvation conditions prevailed. Policy dictated otherwise, however, for there were Australian and Dutch interests to be considered, which could not be ignored. After the capture of Manila there was a general Allied move southward, and the object in attacking Borneo was to establish naval and air facilities to support further clearance of the enemy from the South-West Pacific Area. Borneo was to be attacked first and Java later. In the event, Java was not attacked. The Dutch island of Sumatra also remained in Japanese hands, but had lost importance with the serious damage to its oil refineries in the ' Outflank ' operations by the British Pacific Fleet. Its ports, like those of Java, had been mined, and submarines and light forces of the East Indies Fleet were blockading it. Borneo, apart from its oil, offered air and naval bases which would increase the effectiveness of the blockade of the South China Sea. Certain ports in the island had excellent fuelling facilities, whilst Brunei Bay afforded a deep water anchorage of some 225 square miles, formerly used by the Japanese for fleet purposes. It was at one time suggested that the bay should be used as a naval base for the British Pacific Fleet ; but it was too far from the main theatre, and it was unlikely that its development could have been completed before the beginning of 1946.

Borneo (Figure 11), the third largest island in the world, is three times the size of the United Kingdom. In 1945 it was very undeveloped and there were not more than a thousand miles of metalled roads in the entire island. The oil which rendered it so valuable, was found in three main regions : on Tarakan Island off the north-east coast ; at Balik Papan in the south-east ; and at Seria in the north-west, in the British state of Brunei, with a refinery and loading point at Lutong on the coast near Miri. About half of the production of the Seria fields was suitable for bunkers without distillation. There were also oilfields at Miri, but in 1945 they were nearing the end of their life. The Balik Papan refineries had an output only less than those of Palembang which the British Pacific Fleet had recently damaged so severely. By the time the Allies invaded Borneo its oil was of little use to the enemy save for forward area operations, for he could no longer ship it away. Nevertheless, during the early part of 1945 the Japanese effected some reinforcement of western Borneo.

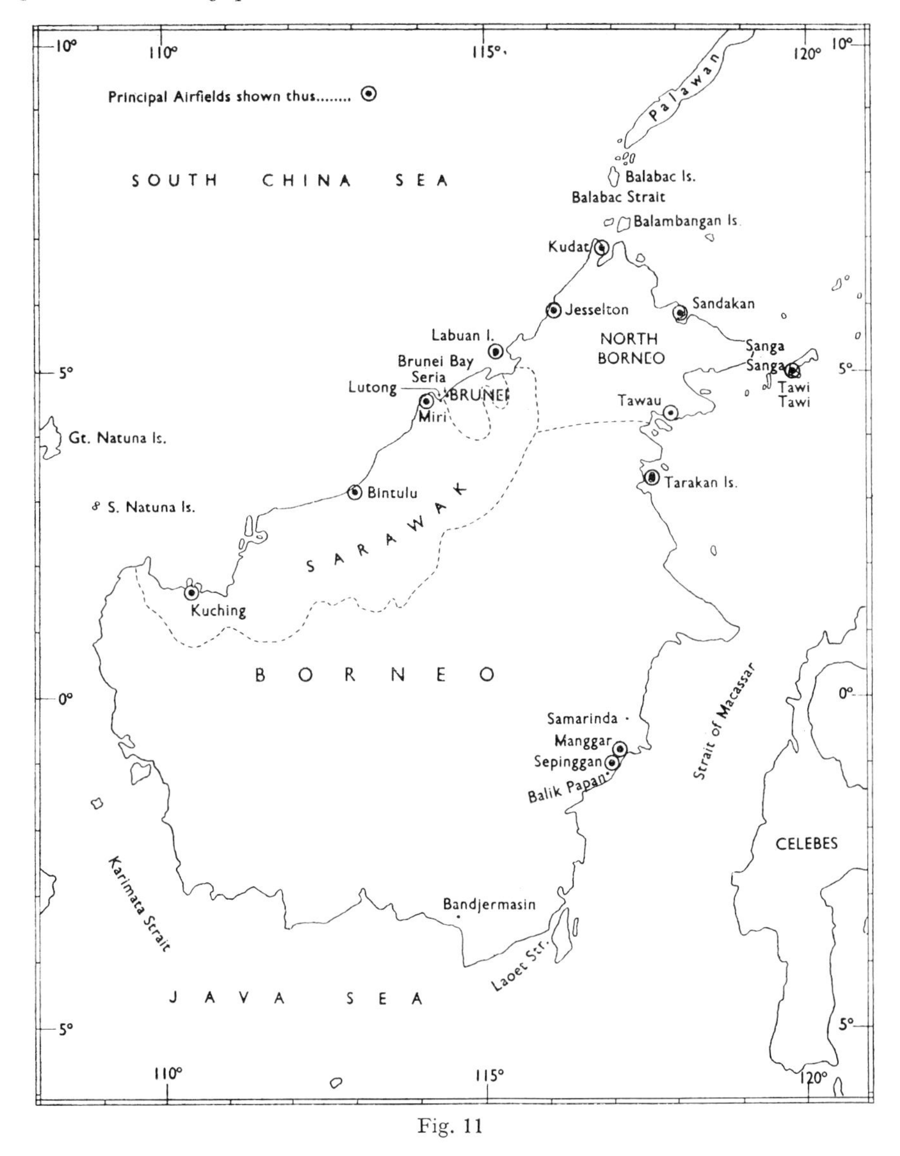

Fig. 11

There were about 25,000 enemy troops in Borneo, consisting of service troops together with locally conscripted Japanese residents incorporated into the forces. The main areas where they were stationed were Brunei–Labuan, Tarakan, Samarinda–Balik Papan, and Banjermasin. Defence was the responsibility, under Field Marshal Terauchi, of Rear-Admiral M. Kamada. The principal airfields are shown on Figure 11. U.S. Army Air Forces had bombed them in support of the Philippines campaign.

There was no intention to occupy all Borneo. The seizure of the harbours, oilfields and airfields was to be carried out as far as possible by Australian troops and air forces, together with U.S. and Australian ships of the Seventh Fleet.[1] Tarakan was to be seized first, partly for its oil, but chiefly because the airfield was to be used in support of subsequent landings at Brunei and Balik Papan. All three operations were mounted and rehearsals carried out at Morotai, Vice-Admiral D. E. Barbey being in command. The principal difficulty encountered lay in the sweeping of the minefields under enemy fire. The Australians between February and November 1944 had laid mines off all three localities selected for assault but sterilizers had not been fitted to the whole of the mines, as was done by us in the South East Asia Area to obviate the need for sweeping the approaches to prospective landing places such as Rangoon. The clearance of Allied influence mines which were still active was found most difficult ; it cost some casualties, and was not altogether successful.

The Japanese discovered by reconnaissance the assembling of amphibious vessels at Morotai, but they were uncertain where the new offensive would be carried out. Terauchi was not able to reinforce the garrisons in Borneo, but the Japanese were determined to resist stubbornly and inflict the maximum losses on the Allies before being overcome, as was inevitable.

2

Tarakan Island (Figure 12) where the first landing was to be made, is about 15½ miles long by 11 miles wide. The interior is a mountainous rain forest jungle, whilst the coast line is mostly bordered by mangrove swamps, with muddy or sandy shallow beaches. Numerous streams feed the marshy coast-line. The choice of landing beaches was conditioned by the need for capturing quickly the only airfield on the island, one of the main reasons being that there were no carriers with the expeditionary force ; these, both U.S. and those of the British Pacific Fleet, were engaged in the operation against Okinawa. This limited the position of the landing to the beaches off Linkas, the port of Tarakan city which lay one-and-a-half miles to the north-east, Linkas being connected to the port and also to the airfield and oilfields a few miles distant, by a well-built, two-way road. No other beach was connected to the airfield by road. Two beaches were used ; Red on the left and Green on the right. The approaches from seaward are extremely treacherous, with wide banks of sand and mud, which extend out for several miles. The two main channels were heavily mined, for the Japanese had laid contact mines there and the Royal Australian Air Force between 15th October and 18th November 1944 had laid 30 influence mines. The range of the tide varies from 11 feet at spring tide to three-and-a-half feet at neap tide. At high water there was no beach at all, at low water 300 yards of black mud which for the most part would not support the weight of heavy vehicles and defied later attempts to land stores from minor landing craft. The whole length of the beaches was faced from seaward with a sheer clay wall about eight feet high ; between this and the road was a space no more than 10 to 30 feet wide, with three-foot deep drains, and immediately

[1] The following Royal Australian Naval Ships took part in the Borneo operations :— Cruisers *Hobart, Shropshire ;* destroyers *Warramunga, Arunta ;* frigates *Burdekin, Barcoo, Hawkesbury ;* A/S minesweepers *Colac, Dubbo ;* surveying ship *Lachlan* (frigate) ; sloop *Swan ;* L.S.I.s *Westralia, Manoora, Kanimbla.*

beyond the road were rising slopes of soft clay heavily pitted with water-filled craters. The water table in the narrow coastal strip was no more than 12 to 18 inches below the surface of the ground.

Enemy defences in the form of coast defence and anti-aircraft guns were known to exist and the Japanese relied, largely, on a very extensive system of tunnels and land mines. It was known that the enemy had made preparations to use burning oil as a defensive measure, as the Dutch had done in 1942; and accordingly all oil tanks that could be employed in this manner were damaged or destroyed by bombing and bombardment before the landing. An effective anti-tank barrier constructed of oil pipe-line and scrap metal covered with earth and surmounted by concrete and steel pill-boxes, which, however, were not manned during the landing, had to be breached to form exits from the beaches. It was a week before these exits could be made reasonably proof against breakdown in the soft ground.

The beaches were protected by four rows of obstacles consisting, from shore to seaward of (*a*) Dutch double-apron fence in disrepair, (*b*) Double row of posts, each post mined, (*c*) Double double-apron fence (intermittent), (*d*) Double row of steel rails and iron tubes (*Figure 13*). In these, Allied engineers blew four

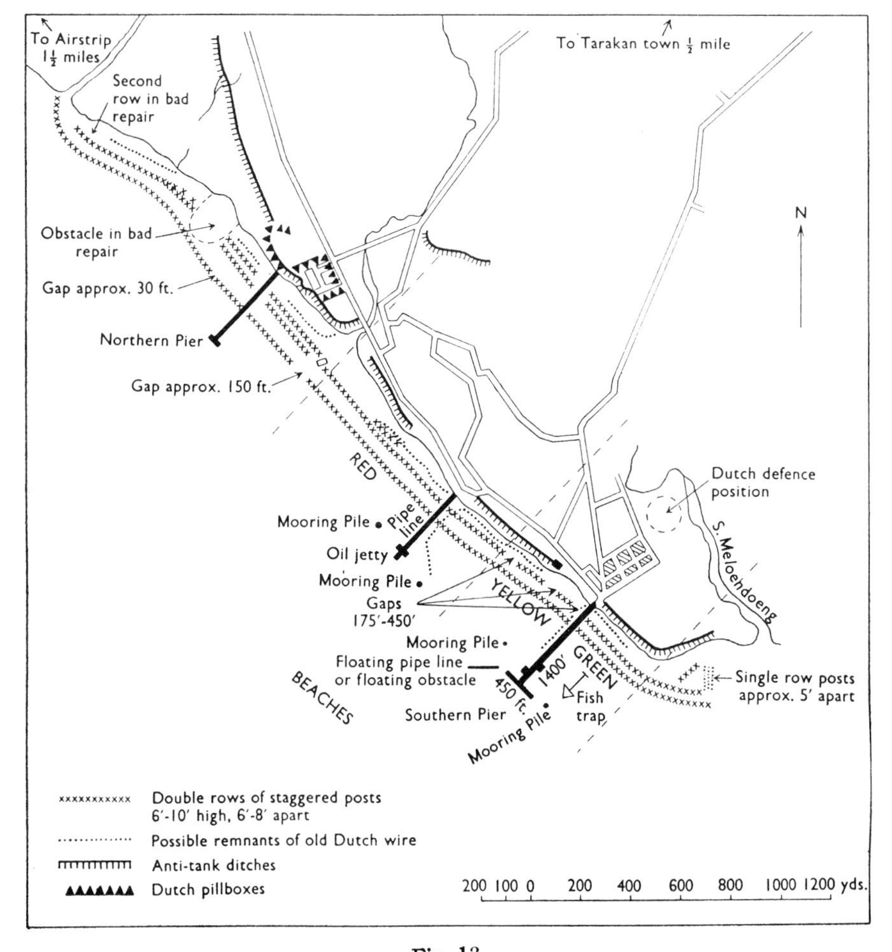

Fig. 13

30-foot gaps to provide boat lanes. The defenders numbered 1,750 Japanese troops and 350 impressed Japanese civilians, and included a good army battalion (the Tsunei Battalion) and a garrison unit 500 strong. There were no Japanese naval units nearer than Singapore, and the only enemy naval reaction was a submarine attack on the convoy, which caused no damage. In the air, the enemy reaction was very slight, U.S. and Australian air attacks having neutralised the 25 or so airstrips within flying range. The landing force under Major-General G. F. Wootten, A.I.F., consisted of the 26th Australian Infantry Brigade of the 9th Australian Division reinforced to a strength of nearly 13,000 officers and men, with 151 ships and vessels. The expedition sailed from Morotai on 27th April, with the larger transports towing loaded landing craft. The Allied air forces involved, under the command of Air Vice-Marshal W. D. Bostock, R.A.A.F., consisted of Royal Australian Air Force units in which the 1st Tactical Air Force was designated the assault force, augmented by units of the 13th U.S. Army Air Force. The aircraft operated from Tawi Tawi, Zamboanga, Palawan, Morotai and Leyte, beginning their strikes 18 days before the landing and continuing as required subsequent to the assault. Thorough preparation by pre-landing surface ship bombardment was also undertaken. The scale of support from D minus 5 to D-day (H plus 30 minutes) was :—

(*a*) Two medium bomber groups of five and four squadrons respectively.

(*b*) One dive bomber group of four squadrons.

(*c*) Two heavy bomber squadrons.

(*d*) One heavy bomber group.

The Attack Group (Task Group 78.1) (*see* Appendix R) was commanded by Rear-Admiral F. B. Royal who flew his flag in the amphibious force flagship *Rocky Mount*. The Cruiser Covering Group under Rear-Admiral R. S. Berkey included the Australian light cruiser *Hobart* and the destroyer *Warramunga*. These two ships immediately after the landing proceeded to join the *Newfoundland* and H.M.A.S. *Arunta* which with the sloop *Swan* and A/S M/S vessels *Colac* and *Dubbo* were supporting the Australian troops who landed on 11th May near Wewak in New Guinea (Operation 'Deluge') to secure the port for their own use.[1]

The support ships and craft were organised in Three Fire Support Units as follows :—

No. 1	Three light cruisers, seven destroyers.
No. 2	Six destroyers.
No. 3	Two LCI (Mortar), four LCI (Rocket), Six LCS(L).

The bombardment plan was as follows :—

(*a*) Preliminary bombardment of selected targets on D minus 3 and D minus 2 days by Fire Support Unit No. 1, the targets being oil tanks, barracks, known gun positions, suspected wireless and radar stations and supply areas. The cruisers were given prescribed targets while the destroyers were available for bombardment at the commander's discretion in co-ordination with air strikes. Safety of the support aircraft was ensured by arrangements such as Plan 'Victor' (*Figure 10*, page 161). Ships of Fire Support Unit No. 2, which was to carry out screening and patrol duties, were available to relieve the bombarding ships.

[1] *See* Vol. III of this history.

(*b*) Bombardment in support of the engineer obstacle breaching operations on D minus 1 day, by ships allotted from the same unit, plus the two LCC (Mortar) and two LCS(L).

(*c*) Bombardment in support of the landing on D-day in three stages :—

(1) From H-hour minus 95 minutes to H-hour minus 4 minutes, on targets along the beaches to a depth of 400 yards.

(2) From H-hour minus 4 minutes to H-hour plus 15 minutes, on targets between 400 and 800 yards inland. It was planned that the line of support craft would leave the line of departure so as to arrive 500 yards off-shore at H-hour minus 4 minutes. On reaching this point, as determined by radar and indicated by signal from the guide craft, and repeated by the Air Observer to the ships, the cruiser and destroyer fire was to lift.

(3) From H-hour plus 15 minutes, fire on targets of opportunity controlled by Shore Fire Control parties.

The Minesweeping Unit, consisting of 11 motor minesweepers and the high speed transport *Cofer* with four landing craft with light minesweeping gear arrived off Tarakan at 0500 on 27th April and began sweeping. This operation was rendered particularly difficult, because of the various types of mines which had to be swept (magnetic, acoustic and contact : British, American, Japanese and possibly Dutch), the strong currents, shallow depths, high tides, poor navigational markings, and shortage of time to cover the large areas involved. It had been planned to sweep the channels both north and south of Menoeloen Island (near the south end of Tarakan) (*Figure 12*) for use of the assault forces, but the preferred track, in the southern channel, had not been rendered safe at the time of the arrival of these forces. Sweeping continued for three days after the landing on 1st May (P-day). About 34 Japanese contact mines and nine or more Allied influence mines were swept. No enemy opposition to the minesweeping was encountered until the day after the landing, when five minesweepers began sweeping the channel north of Tarakan. As they neared Tanjong Juata (the north-west point of Tarakan) about six previously undetected shore batteries suddenly opened up. *YMS 481* was hit several times, blew up, and sank. *YMS 334* was badly damaged by five or six 75-mm. enemy shells, and *YMS 364* was hit once and slightly damaged. The *Cofer* and two landing craft closed the shore batteries and silenced them, and further sweeping of the channel was suspended until the Australians could seize the gun position. In the preliminary bombardment by the ships to destroy the coast defences the narrow swept channels and shallow approaches posed a problem for the larger vessels in particular, necessitating the use of extreme ranges and air spotting, whilst light units carried out the inshore missions. Scheduled bombardments were reduced in scale because of the difficulty of reaching effective ranges, until the day before the landing, when increased allowances were fired to compensate. The only casualty among the bombarding ships was the destroyer *Jenkins* which struck a mine and was damaged on 30th April in Tarakan Road, an area which had previously been swept many times.

At 0800 on 30th April, artillery and engineers landed unopposed on Sadau Island, in the channel west of Tarakan, set up 25-pounder batteries and opened fire on the Japanese positions on Tarakan. The main landings on Linkas beaches began at 0815 next day. Bombardment in support of the landings began at

H minus 95 minutes, H being the time of landing. The cruiser and destroyer fire lifted at H minus 4 minutes when the rocket and their support craft were 500 yards from the beach. These craft continued to fire on the beach area until the first wave of amphibians and assault craft passed through them. The concrete blockhouses which were set closely along the shore were not manned and there was no opposition at the beaches, though ineffective mortar and artillery fire began about two hours later. Seven LSTs carried vehicles essential to the assault waves together with pontoon causeways for landing these vehicles, mechanical equipment, guns and stores over the muddy beaches. On Green Beach on the right, the mud was shallow enough to permit the use of amphibians (LVTs), but the greater depth of mud on Red Beach required the use of L.C.V.P.s for the run-in and each L.C.V.P. towed in folding assault boats to which the troops could transfer after the landing craft grounded, for it was expected that there would be a considerable water gap to be crossed by troops disembarking even from shallow draught vessels such as L.C.V.P.s. In the event, however, the boats were not needed : the troops were able to land from the landing craft practically dryshod. To avoid swamping the folding boats the speed of the L.C.V.P.s was reduced to that of the LVTs ; and to avoid congestion on Red Beach, where conditions were bad, a smaller number of men was landed than on Green Beach. The LSTs beached on exceptionally high water. This resulted in their drying-out completely with the falling tide. The second tide of the day was about two-and-a-half feet lower, and it was not until the second day after the landing that all except seven of the LSTs, which by that time had been unloaded, were got out of the mud. The remaining seven were not retracted until the next spring tides, on D plus 10 and D plus 11 days. Fortunately, the three piers, though damaged, were available for landing stores.

From a fixed position on shore, the Japanese on the morning of the assault fired three torpedoes at the transports. One hit the U.S.S. *Rushmoor*, but failed to explode ; one of the other two passed underneath and one just ahead of an LST. Sniping at the beaches by Japanese mortars mounted on the reverse slopes of the hills began with darkness, whilst the troops advancing inland met growing opposition. Roads were mined and tanks were held up. The effectiveness of naval gunfire support was limited because much of the country was of a very close nature and the enemy did not disclose his positions by opening fire until the Australians were close. The Japanese almost everywhere fought to the death. They made many small counter attacks at night on the Australian forward positions but at no time did they make a co-ordinated counter attack. Tarakan airstrip was captured on 5th May, but required a large amount of work to put it in order. There was insufficient steel matting of good quality, most of it being 'second hand,' and moreover it was delayed in unloading. The airstrip which had been scheduled for use on D plus 6 day was not ready until 20th June, though the R.A.A.F., working from Sanga Sanga (Tawi Tawi) assumed responsibility for aerial defence on 16th May. By the end of May the oil fields were secured ; they were found badly damaged, but the Dutch Rehabilitation Service resumed oil production by the beginning of July. Japanese suicide boats were believed to be stored in a large sawmill at Sandakan harbour, and at daylight on 27th May U.S. motor torpedo boats, co-operating with R.A.A.F. Warhawks and naval Mariners raided the harbour, destroyed the sawmill and several small craft. The southern and western parts of Tarakan island were first captured and operations continued against isolated enemy strongholds in the mountainous interior. On 23rd June it was possible to announce that organised resistance had ceased.

3

The delay in getting the air garrison to Tarakan meant that the landing there failed to serve its chief immediate object, support of the landings in Brunei Bay, even though these were postponed from 23rd May to 10th June because of a delay in bringing the assault forces to the loading point at Morotai.

The great anchorage at Brunei Bay where a thousand large ships can swing at anchor over sand and mud is protected from seaward by Labuan and its associated islands (Plans 18, 19 and *Figure 14*). There are two main entrances : a deep channel south of Labuan Island and a channel east of the island five fathoms deep. There were a number of piers, mostly with limited depths alongside, situated at several small harbours around the bay. The surrounding land is generally flat, with a few isolated hills in the coastal plain. Much of the coast is bordered by swamps ; it is for the most part free of reefs, but

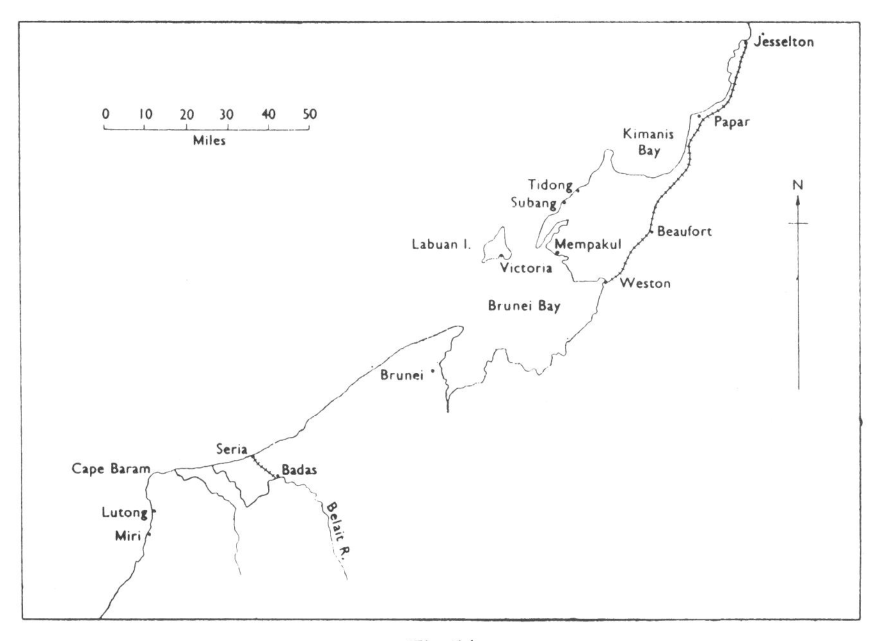

Fig. 14

extensive sand bars reach for considerable distances to seaward. Several fairly good beaches were available for landing, and little recourse to pontoon causeways was necessary. There were three airfields close by, two on Labuan Island and one about three miles from the town of Brunei. Seven other airfields were situated within a radius of 160 miles, but the Japanese air forces were depleted and air opposition was expected to be negligible. The landing force of two brigades of the 9th Australian Division, the remaining brigade being still engaged on Tarakan, and some Dutch native volunteers, under Major-General G. F. Wootten comprising nearly 23,000 troops was carried in 87 ships (Appendix R(2)). Three landing beaches were to be used, namely Brown Beach on Labuan Island, extending from Victoria town to Ramsay Point, a distance of 1,200 yards (Plan 18) ; White Beach on Muara Island, extending from Sapo Point for approximately 1,200 yards to the northward (Plan 19) ; and Green

Beach about one mile east of Brunei Bluff, running for approximately 500 yards (Plan 19). For landing on Brown and White beaches LVTs were to be used, and on Green Beach L.C.V.P.s. The shoals and channels near White Beach rendered it impossible to conduct the landing in the normal manner. Extending out from the beach for approximately 2,000 yards was a long flat underwater shelf with depths of two to 12 feet. It was consequently impossible for support craft to lead the first assault wave to the beach.

Since Labuan Island is separated by nearly 20 miles from Brunei Bluff and Muara Island the assault force was divided into three units. The Attack Group Commander exercised overall control while permitting Assault Unit Commanders to conduct the landings in their respective areas. The enemy garrison was estimated at 2,000 to 2,500. There were no underwater obstacles nor any defences on the beaches. Nothing definite was known of the defences covering the beaches or inland but it was believed there were a few coast defence and anti-aircraft guns, blockhouses, and entrenchments. These were neutralized however, by the extensive air strikes, pre-landing ship bombardment, and close support given to the troops which prevented opposition until the Australians were well inland. Between 13th May and 9th June, the day before the landing, the Royal Australian and U.S. air forces flew 2,789 sorties and dropped 3,450 tons of bombs. Not all of these were directed at pulverising the defences. More than half of the aircraft sorties had the tactical object of isolating the invasion area by attacks on troop movements, railways, barges and roads to prevent substantial reinforcement of the area.

The greatest danger to landing lay in the extensive minefields which were known to exist. The Minesweeping Group, comprising amongst other vessels 17 minesweepers, arrived off Brunei Bay at dawn on 7th June and began operations under the guns of Rear-Admiral R. S. Berkey's U.S. and Australian Cruiser Covering Group (Task Group 74.3)[1] which entered Brunei Bay on the forenoon of the 8th as soon as a channel had been swept, and bombarded the beaches to cover reconnaissance parties of underwater demolition teams. The minesweeper *Salute* struck a mine that afternoon and sank with the loss of nine men killed and 37 wounded, but this was the only casualty to the minesweepers prior to the landing. In Brunei Bay and its approaches, 69 enemy moored mines in all were swept prior to the landings and 33 further mines subsequently. On the 13th, the minesweepers began working in the Miri-Lutong area, south of Brunei Bay ; they came under the fire of shore batteries, but had no casualties. On 16th June, 338 contact mines were cut off Miri-Lutong. These had all apparently been set at depths below 40 feet as anti-submarine protection for ships while lying at the four sea-loading pipe-lines at Lutong refinery. Altogether, a total of 462 mines was swept before the operation concluded. Most of the minesweepers experienced great losses of sweeping gear, due to the heavy chains with which the contact mines were moored and to many explosions in their gear. Allied influence mines which R.A.A.F. Catalinas had laid in the area between 9th and 15th November had all been set for sterilization prior to the landings, and a number of check sweeps failed to explode any of them. The only other casualty from mines, apart from the *Salute*, was the destroyer *Caldwell* which struck a mine on the 27th and was damaged.

The naval bombardment began at 0805 on 10th June (Z-day) and was lifted just before the hour of landing (0915). Aerial bombardment by ten squadrons took place from 0840 to 0900. As the result of this thorough preparation the

[1] U.S.S. *Nashville, Phoenix, Conner, Charrette, Bell, Burns,* H.M.A.S. *Hobart* and *Arunta.*

troops landed at all points unopposed. The Muara force found the island deserted. The Brunei force captured Brooketon and advanced rapidly towards Brunei Town which was taken on the 13th, the airfield having been secured against some opposition on the previous day. The Labuan force found Victoria Town deserted and almost completely destroyed. The troops reached one of the airfields by nightfall but the island was not secured until the 15th. Major-General Wootten assumed command ashore at 1930 on Z-day. Minor landings were made at Weston on the 17th. Weston is situated about six miles up the Padas river, on the eastern side of Brunei Bay (Plan 18). To reach the landing place (Gray Beach) the assaulting battalion had to proceed up a very narrow channel in line ahead, the formation being two miles long, and then form a line of departure only 150 yards from the beach and send in the assault waves. The landing was made in LVTs launched from the parent LST seven-and-a-half miles from the beach. A landing was made on the 19th at Mempakul at the mouth of the Klias River (Plan 18). Later in the week, the Australians landed at Subang, 16 miles up the coast from Mempakul, and at Tidong, eight miles further on (*Figure 14*, page 173). Casualties amongst the troops were light. No attempt was made to penetrate the interior where certain guerilla forces were operating ; these had been raised and were led by officers of British and Australian clandestine organisations, some of whom had been introduced before the landings on 10th June. The Japanese attempted minor air attacks during the three nights following the main landing, but none of them succeeded in reaching the ships. Bombardment by the latter in support of the troops was not required subsequent to the second day after landing.

Landings were made at Lutong, (*Figure 15*) on 20th June, and at Seria on the 22nd to capture the airfields and oil refineries. Commodore Farncomb (C.T.G. 74.1) transferred his broad pendant from the *Shropshire* to the *Arunta*, which with the U.S. destroyers *Hart* and *Metcalf* carried out a preliminary bombardment, whilst the *Hobart, Shropshire* and *Warramunga* were on call at Brunei Bay. Aircraft carried out a preliminary bombing. The landings were made by the units of the 20th Brigade of the 9th Australian Division carried from Brunei Bay on board *LCI(L)546* (flagship), three LSTs, three LSMs, four LCTs and two LCMs, the LCTs and LCMs being in tow of the LSTs, LSMs and *LCI(L)546*. The *Hart* and *Metcalf* formed the screen. Close support was given by LCI-type vessels acting as gunboats, rocket ships, mortar ships, with salvage and fire-fighting LCIs. The troops landed at 0930 on Beach Crimson which extended for 1,200 yards southward from Lutong airstrip. The landing was unopposed. DUKWs and LVTs successfully negotiated 100 yards of heavy surf, but the LCVPs experienced great difficulty in landing their troops under the same conditions. Working along the coast the troops captured the oil centres of Seria and Miri by 25th June. The Australians then controlled 135 miles of the coast. No attempt was made to penetrate far inland.

" The execution of the Brunei Bay operation has been flawless," signalled General MacArthur to Vice-Admiral Barbey. " Please accept for yourself and convey to your officers and men the pride and gratification I feel in such a splendid performance."[1]

4

The third large amphibious assault on Borneo and the last one necessary to recapture the key points in the island, was made on 1st July at Balik Papan on the south-east coast (Plan 20). It was the final amphibious operation of the

[1] *Spearheads of Invasion* by W. N. Swan, p. 269.

war in the Pacific and it met by far the heaviest opposition encountered in Borneo. The place was defended by some 3,500 regular Japanese troops consisting in large part of former anti-aircraft units, whilst locally conscripted residents brought the number of the garrison up to 10,000. In the Samarinda sector, north of Balik Papan and connected to it by road (*Figure* 16) there were

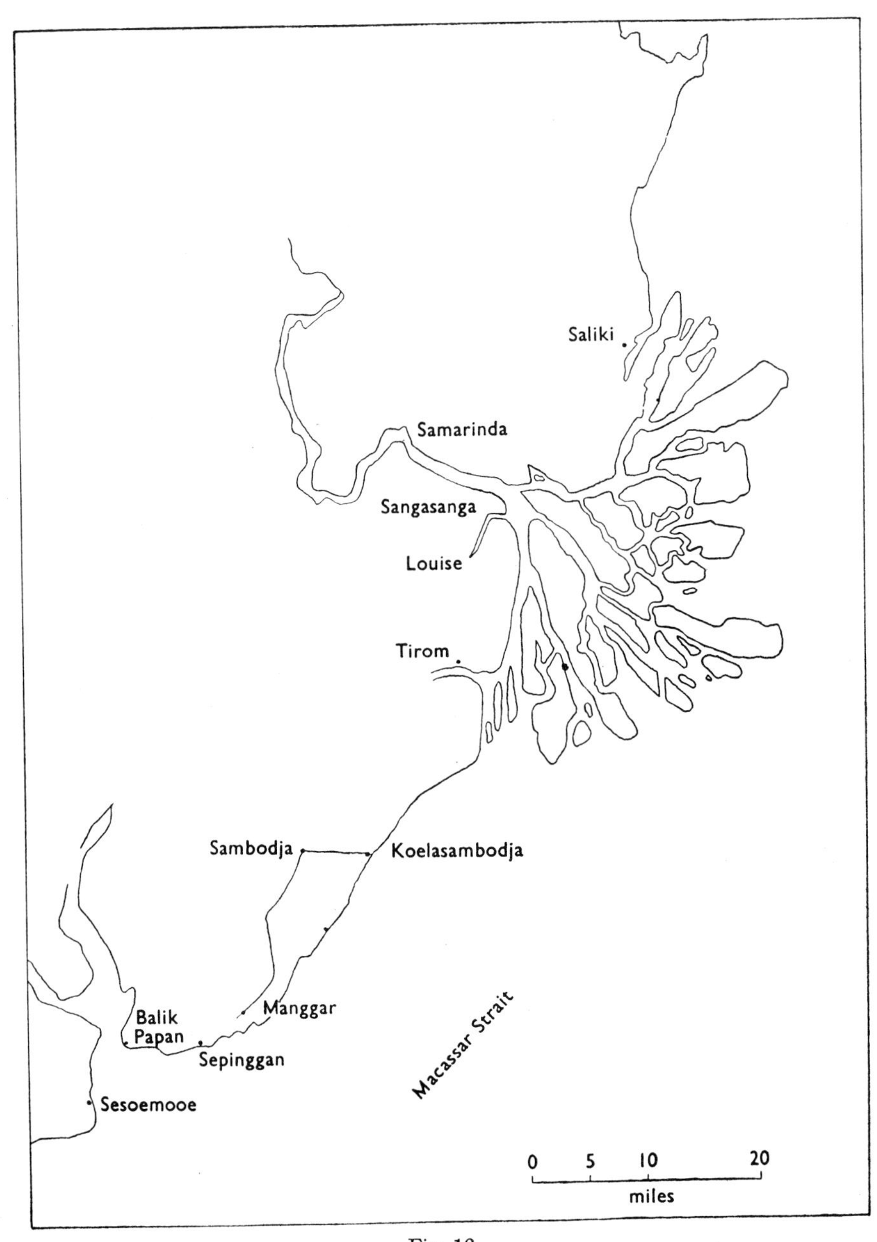

Fig. 16

a further 5,000, of whom 3,000 were locally conscripted Japanese.[1] The 7th Australian Division less one Brigade Group, comprising 25,304 troops, carried out the assault, and together with the Royal Australian Air Force Command made use of improvements in technique suggested by their experience of two previous landings, in an operation which on several counts was of extreme difficulty. For the landing had to be made only a mile from the town, where there were heavy concentrations of dual-purpose anti-aircraft guns, extensive minefields difficult to sweep, shallow water which compelled the covering ships to remain at 12,000 to 14,000 yards distance from the beaches whilst rendering counter-battery fire. In the absence of all-weather airstrips within 400 miles, close air support and cover had to be given from airfields as distant as Morotai, Palawan, Zamboanga and Sanga Sanga. Three escort carriers[2] were brought in to provide day and night combat air patrols from 30th June to 3rd July. Air support by carriers had not been contemplated in the original plan, but was necessitated by the fact that Tarakan airstrip was not completed in time to accommodate land-based aircraft for support. There was an airfield at Sepinggam and an airstrip at Manggar, but only a few Japanese fighter aircraft had survived the constant attacks made by Allied aircraft. The U.S. 5th and 13th Air Forces and Fleet Air Wing Ten and the R.A.A.F. all co-operated in land-based air support, hindered by poor flying weather. Every building near the landing area was levelled by aerial bombardment, and the Japanese anti-aircraft positions were attacked about a fortnight before the landing. The Australians had laid 118 mines off Balik Papan during 1944, and between August 1943 and January 1945 they laid 142 in the long approach through the shallow Makassar Strait. These mining operations, together with air attacks and the operations of submarines had caused the Japanese to abandon Balik Papan as a convoy assembly port in December 1944. The minelaying plan had not been integrated with the main strategic plan of the campaign which remained flexible until the last moment; and the mines had been laid unsterilized. Sixteen days of sweeping close under the guns of the enemy, protected by U.S., Australian and Dutch cruisers and destroyers, were needed to clear a passage through the Allied and Japanese minefields prior to the landing on 1st July (F-day). Surprise was consequently impossible. Fortunately, it was not necessary to carry out any preliminary survey of the approaches under the fire of the enemy, for owing to the commercial importance which Balik Papan had possessed in peacetime these were well charted.

The large and important oil refining centre of Balik Papan is situated on the Borneo side of Makassar Strait. The coastal area around the place is low and flat for a distance of about 20 miles inland, and is covered generally by a heavy growth of rain forest. Balik Papan Bay is a deep estuary of several rivers, providing adequate depth of water alongside oil loading piers, but access to the harbour by larger vessels is only possible at high tide (which ranges from about five feet to seven feet) because of a sand bar blocking the entrance, with a depth of less than four fathoms at low water. Three beaches, Red, Yellow and Green, close east of Klandasan, were used for the landing, and there was an alternative landing point off Manggar to the eastward. The beaches provided only mediocre conditions for landing craft, rendering the use of pontoon causeways necessary for the larger vessels. To seaward, the beaches were protected by numerous log barricades through which the underwater demolition teams had to blast gaps for assault amphibians and craft. The beaches were well covered by numerous

[1] Japanese Monograph No. 115.

[2] The *Suwanee, Gilbert Island, Block Island* and a screen of one destroyer and five destroyer escorts.

automatic weapons mounted in log and earth emplacements, with heavier guns up to 127-mm. (5-inch) located further inland on higher ground overlooking the assault area. The Japanese had also arranged to oppose the landing by burning oil, but this was not generally effective, except in producing smoke, owing the the pipe-line being fractured in many places by the preliminary bombardments. The increased intensity of bombing which began on 13th June and the appearance of minesweepers two days later indicated to the enemy the intentions and in a general way the landing beaches. Underwater demolition teams worked on 25th–28th and 30th June. They were covered on the first two days by bombing attacks and subsequently by close support craft. They were continuously under fire which damaged two LCS(L)s. The teams blew a gap of 1,600 yards in the obstacles at Klandasan and of 800 yards at the secondary beaches, and they brought back much information useful to the assault troops. Reconnaissance of the primary beach at Klandasan and secondary beaches off Manggar disclosed no beach mines.

On 15th June, 16 motor minesweepers with L.C.V.P.s equipped with light minesweeping gear, arrived off Balik Papan and began operations.[1] There was a lack of manœuvring room for the ships giving covering fire, due to the many navigational hazards and enemy minefields. The shallow water enabled ships to anchor, but during the first part of the minesweeping phase the supporting American light cruisers *Montpelier* and *Denver* and destroyers had to remain at ranges where neutralization or destruction of Japanese guns was difficult whilst heavy anti-aircraft fire compelled Allied bombers and cruiser spotting aircraft to remain too high for pin-point bombing and the accurate spotting necessary for destructive effect. There was, however, only a small amount of enemy large calibre coastal defence gunfire. The Dutch light cruiser *Tromp* arrived on 19th June, the U.S. light cruiser *Columbia* on the 23rd and the *Shropshire, Hobart, Arunta* and two U.S. destroyers on the 27th.

Between 16th and 23rd June *YMS 50* and *YMS 368* were damaged by Allied mines, necessitating sinking the former; whilst *YMS 10, YMS 335* and *YMS 364* were damaged by enemy gunfire.[2] Many minesweepers were forced to jettison their sweeps whilst manœuvring to avoid enemy shellfire, and other sweeps were hit and damaged. The situation improved after 24th June when the cruisers' long range fire had begun to show results and enough sweeping had been done to render it reasonably safe for destroyers to enter the southern part of the area, whilst Allied air strikes by approximately 100 aircraft daily carrying heavy napalm bombs were beginning to make themselves felt. Moreover, the cruiser-spotting aircraft had by then become more familiar with the territory and the location of the Japanese defences. From that date onwards minesweeping was only slightly hampered by gunfire, but mines continued to take their toll, *YMS 39* and *YMS 365* being lost on 26th June and *YMS 47* damaged next day. Some 15 sets of magnetic sweeping gear were lost.

At 2030 on the 25th four enemy torpedo aircraft made an attack on the minesweepers. These shot down three of the enemy without damage to themselves. At 1100 on the 27th enemy reconnaissance aircraft came over, and that night there were three raids between 2000 and 2055, by seven Japanese aircraft, but no damage was caused. During none of these attacks were there any protective fighters up, for these were based at Tawi Tawi and the distance

---

[1] The organisation of the Allied Forces is given in Appendix R (3).

[2] Admiral King's Final Official Report erroneously places the sinking of *Y.M.S. 50* off Java.

and unfavourable weather prevented their continuous presence at Balik Papan. No further molestation of the minesweepers by enemy aircraft took place. Personnel casualties in the minesweepers were seven killed and 43 wounded. Ten mental cases occurred. Mines swept numbered 34 moored and 16 influence. Some of the latter needed as many as seven passes to detonate them. The operation showed the necessity for an experienced minesweeping officer to administer and co-ordinate the operations, and for a minesweeping store supply ship in the forward area, or alternatively an immensely larger number of operational sweepers. The destroyers gave accurate navigational assistance to the small sweepers in localities where fixing their position was difficult.

The assault echelon of 121 ships carrying units of the 7th Australian Division departed from Morotai on 26th June for the objective area, 20 additional ships joining from Tawi Tawi on the 29th. At daylight (0700) on 1st July (F-Day) the scheduled pre-assault bombardment of the landing beaches and adjacent areas began by the five U.S. and Australian cruisers and six destroyers then in the area, under Rear-Admiral R. S. Griggs. This bombardment lasted for two hours, except that for 15 minutes before the second hour guns were secured whilst the first rocket barrage and low level air strike was made. Ten minutes before the hour of landing (H-hour) the bombardment increased to its maximum as the first assault waves came within 1,300 yards of the beach. Fire was then shifted to the flanks and rear areas and a second rocket barrage began. The bombardments were carried out at anchor as the minefields and navigational hazards left little room for manœuvring and the depth of water was suitable for anchoring ; no more than minor enemy attacks were to be expected, and there were few large calibre coast defence guns defending the beaches. The *Shropshire, Hobart* and *Arunta* having no aircraft, used spotting aircraft provided by the U.S. and Australian Air Forces with which communication was not entirely satisfactory.[1] More than 3,000 tons of bombs, 7,361 rockets, 38,052 rounds of 8-inch to 3-inch ammunition and 114,000 rounds from automatic weapons were fired. Examination of the area after capture definitely indicated than any less effort would have proved insufficient. The assaulting troops landed almost unopposed, the defenders having in mid-June decided to intercept the attackers not on the beaches but in the jungle, some three miles from the Samarinda road.[2]

The first wave of assault troops was despatched from the line of departure slightly ahead of schedule and landed at 0855 (H-hour being 0900).[3] All 17 assault waves were ashore by 1055 with few casualties from enemy artillery, mortars and small arms which fell among the boat waves and on the landing beaches. Aircraft from the escort carriers were also responsible for some Allied casualties.[4] Two battalions landed abreast, the 21st Brigade on the right (Green Beach) on a one-battalion front, and the 18th Brigade on the left (Yellow and Red Beaches) on a two-battalion front. Before the day ended, 10,500 assault troops, 700 vehicles and 1,950 tons of stores were landed, over very

[1] *Com Cru Div.* 15 (*T.F.* 74). *H.M.A.S. Hobart and Arunta Action Report, 26th June to 9th July* 1945, *Balik Papan.* M.1084/46.

[2] Japanese Monograph No. 115.

[3] ' Due to the error of a signalman who inadvertently two-blocked the signal on the control vessel while seeking shelter from the enemy fire from the beach ' (M.09427/45, *Com. Phib. Grp.* 8 *Action Report—Balik Papan, Manggar–Borneo, 15th June–6th July* 1945).

[4] 'Against Air (Vice) Marshal Bostock's better judgment, dive bombers from the escort carriers were also used on an F-day mission which unfortunately resulted in some Allied casualties. Later dive-bomber missions were more accurate.' (*The Army Air Forces in World War II,* Vol. V, p. 468, quoting the *History of the Far Eastern Air Force,* pp. 474–502.)

mediocre beaches with surf three to four feet high which impeded unloading. There were no beach mines to delay the construction of pontoon causeways. The first returning echelon of three LST, one AKA, one LSD and three APD was unloaded and sailed at 1930. Major-General E. J. Milford, G.O.C. 7th Australian Division, assumed command ashore at 1900. The progress of the troops ashore was rapid at first but soon met stiffening resistance. The cruisers and destroyers rendered effective fire support by day and night. The Australian communications between the ships and the troops ashore are reported to have been particularly rapid and efficient. Air observers for gunfire and strike co-ordination were flown in B–24s, but three of these were shot down by enemy A.A. fire on successive days after the landing, indicating the unsuitability of heavy bombers for such work. Sepinggam airfield was captured on 2nd July and the Manggar airstrip on the 6th.

On 5th July a ship-to-shore movement was made to Tandjong Penajam on the opposite side of the river, by which date the Balik Papan town area was completely cleared of the enemy. By the end of the month, against Japanese resistance described as desperate, the Australians had established a perimeter including the Sambodja oilfields, 28 miles from Balik Papan. Minesweepers continued operations in the approaches to the harbour until 15th July, clearing more than 200 mines, five minesweepers in all being sunk and 12 damaged, and one destroyer damaged.

CHAPTER XV

The Assault and Capture of Okinawa

(Operation 'Iceberg')[1]

(Plans 21, 22, 23)

1

WHEN, in October, 1944, the Joint Chiefs of Staff decided to drop Formosa from the list of targets for amphibious attack the assault on Okinawa in the Ryuku Islands (operation 'Iceberg') was scheduled instead for 1st March in the following year. The assault was designed to secure a forward air base for the bombing of Japan and an assembly area for the troops destined to invade the country later in the year. Operation 'Iceberg' had in the event to be postponed for a month, to 1st April. The unexpectedly stubborn resistance experienced in the Philippines had already necessitated the postponement of General MacArthur's next operation, against Iwo Jima; the assault on Okinawa had been planned on the assumption that these two earlier operations would have reached a stage when forces could be released to support Admiral Nimitz who was to conduct the Ryukus operation and would for that purpose need the assistance of troops and assault shipping from the Philippines and naval and air units from Iwo Jima.

Whilst the plans for the operation were being drawn up, the Japanese introduced in defence of the Philippine Islands their new and devastating form of air warfare, *kamikaze* or suicide operating, with what results we have seen. At Okinawa, distant only 350 miles from the airfields of Kyushu, the enemy would be able to throw against the invaders the full weight of the Formosan and the main Japanese islands' air forces in so far as he felt it safe to denude the homeland of aerial defence, together with such units as he had been able to salve

[1] A detailed description of this operation is given in Naval Staff History Battle Summary No. 47. *Naval Operations in the Assault and Capture of Okinawa, Operation 'Iceberg', March–June* 1945. *C.B.* 3081 (32).

from the Philippines. After the landing on Okinawa, the Japanese gave first priority to the disruption of the operation and the destruction of the Allied fleet. Their plan, as it revealed itself, was to use *kamikaze* units in mass suicide (*kikusui*) missions against the Allied naval units and amphibious shipping, and by this means, so isolate the invading troops that the 32nd Army which garrisoned Okinawa would be able to destroy them or drive them into the sea. The Americans felt little doubt however of the outcome of the fighting ashore on Okinawa provided command of the air could be secured. But aerial isolation of the objective area was indispensable, and to assist in achieving it land-based air forces were detailed to supplement the effort of the fast carriers and escort carriers, and the British Pacific Fleet was also assigned the role of guarding the U.S. left flank.

In an attempt to solve the problem of command in the Pacific the Americans, when the Ryukus operation was less than a week old, instituted a new command structure as a necessary preliminary to the final reorganisation of command for further operations. The rapid advances which had brought the Allies to the gates of Japan had changed the character of the operations remaining to be undertaken. On 6th April General MacArthur was appointed Commander-in-Chief of a new organisation termed U.S. Army Forces, Pacific (CINCAFPAC) and was given command of all army forces and resources in the Pacific Theatre other than those in the South-East Pacific Area and the Alaskan Department. Fleet Admiral Nimitz (CINCPOA) was given command of all naval forces and resources in the Pacific Theatre (less those in the South-East Pacific Area). MacArthur would retain operational control of the Seventh Fleet until a time agreed upon by Nimitz and himself ; and similarly, Nimitz would retain control of U.S. Army forces assigned to him, until passed to MacArthur by mutual agreement, though the Commander-in-Chief, U.S. Fleet and Chief of Naval Operations (Fleet Admiral E. J. King) retained for himself the right to re-allocate naval forces within the Central (Third/Fifth Fleet) and South-West Pacific (Seventh Fleet) Area. No Supreme Commander was appointed : the Joint Chiefs of Staff retained the direction of the war in the Pacific and announced that they would ' charge either General MacArthur or Admiral Nimitz with the overall responsibility for conducting specific operations or campaigns '. Nimitz was to complete the operations in the Ryuku Islands and MacArthur the liberation of the Philippines. Both commanders were to assist each other, Nimitz by providing naval forces to support the Commander-in-Chief South-West Pacific area (General MacArthur) and CINCAFPAC by providing the Army forces needed by CINCPOA. Outside this organisation and confusing still further the state of higher command in the Pacific there remained two air forces, one strategic and the other tactical, the 20th Air Force and the China-based forces. The former, in particular, was to play an important role in ' Iceberg '. Both Nimitz and MacArthur had, in addition, air forces of their own. CINCPOA's land-based air forces, two in number, were the Strategic Air Force, Pacific Ocean Areas (Major-General W. H. Hale) which had been created on 6th December 1944, and Admiral Hoover's Forward Area, Central Pacific ; whilst the Far Eastern Air Force under General Kenney continued to serve as CINCAFPAC'S land-based air command. The intention of the Joint Chiefs of Staff was that both Nimitz and MacArthur should retain their former areas until passed to the other command by mutual agreement or by direction of the U.S. Chiefs of Staff. Throughout Operation ' Iceberg ', however, both commanders continued to retain their areas and to rely for logistic support on a separate chain of bases. The command relationships and tasks in the Ryukus operation were as follows :—

JOINT CHIEFS OF STAFF

20th Air Force
Gen. of the Army H. A. Arnold
1. Air strikes on Formosa.
2. Air recce. and strikes on Okinawa, Kyushu, Tokyo area.

China-based Forces
Lt.-Gen. A. C. Wedemeyer
Air recce. and strikes against Hong Kong area.

CinCPAC CinCPOA Forces
Fleet Adm. C. W. Nimitz
Establish and maintain control of approaches to East China Sea by capture and defence of positions in the Nansei Shoto, in order to provide facilities for further advances towards Japan.

South-West Pacific Forces
Gen. of the Army D. MacArthur
Air attack on enemy bases in Formosa and neutralisation of airfields in Formosa.

North Pacific Force
Vice-Adm. F. J. Fletcher
Contain enemy air and naval forces in North Pacific by conducting recce. and harassing enemy positions in Kuriles.

South Pacific Force
Vice-Adm. W. L. Colhoun
Provide logistic support as directed.

Strategic Air Forces POA
Maj.-Gen. W. H. Hale
1. Neutralise enemy bases in Carolines and Nanpo Shoto.
2. Destroy enemy aircraft and air installations in Nanpo Shoto and Japan as practicable.
3. Provide fighter cover for 20th A.F. strikes on Japan.

Central Pacific Task Forces
Adm. R. A. Spruance (Com. Fifth Fleet)
1. Capture, occupy and develop air and naval bases on Okinawa Retto.
2. Gain and maintain control of Nansei Shoto area.
3. Protect air and area communications along Central Pacific area.

Forward Area Central Pacific
Vice-Adm. J. H. Hoover
Support Operation 'Iceberg' with air and naval forces under his command, this to include A/S cover, neutralisation of enemy bases by aircraft, ASR, air evacuation transport service and repair facilities.

Marshalls-Gilberts Force
Rear-Adm. W. K. Harrill
Hold positions needed for security of L. of C. and for support of air, sea and amphibious operations against Japan.

Ryukus Force
Lt.-Gen. S. B. Buckner Jr.
When released by Adm. Spruance, defend and develop captured positions in Nansei Shoto.

Submarine Force
Vice-Adm. C. A. Lockwood Jr.
1. Provide intelligence of enemy naval units.
2. Interdict sea approaches to Okinawa from Japan and Formosa.
3. Provide lifeguard services as ordered.
4. Be prepared to concentrate for the strategical or tactical support of Central Pacific Forces.

Air Force Pacific Fleet
Vice-Adm. G. E. Murray
Provide logistic support as directed.

Service Force Pacific Fleet
Vice-Adm. W. W. Smith
Provide logistic support as directed.

Army Forces POA
Lt.-Gen. R. C. Richardson Jr.
Provide logistic support as directed.

Western Sea Frontier
Adm. R. E. Ingersoll
Provide logistic support as directed.

Provide facilities for Commander Logistic Support Group (CTG50B)

Covering Forces
Adm. R. A. Spruance

Joint Expeditionary Forces
Vice-Adm. R. K. Turner

The British Carrier Force under Vice-Admiral H. B. Rawlings, operated as Task Force 57 in the Central Pacific Task Forces, using the U.S. system of signals.

The great Ryukus operation has been described in detail elsewhere.[1] Only certain salient features will be dealt with here, particularly the means adopted to ensure safety from enemy air attacks of the mass of shipping lying at open anchorage off the islands, with such introductory description of the organisation of the forces as is necessary for an understanding of the campaign, the bloodiest of the war in the Pacific, in the course of which the enemy lost nearly 8,000 aircraft and an entire Japanese army was destroyed, whilst 36 Allied ships were sunk and 371 damaged to a greater or less degree.

2

The Okinawa Gunto, a group in the Ryuku Islands, comprises a number of islands for the most part very populous, situated approximately in the centre of the Nansei Shoto chain which runs for a distance of some 500 miles south-west of Japan. Okinawa Shima is the largest and most important of these islands (Plan 23). Amongst its numerous satellites, two were to assume much importance during the operation. The Kerama Retto was seized before the main landing took place to serve as a repair base for the numerous ships and landing craft which suffered damage ; and when, shortly after the landing on Okinawa Shima the attack ran into stubborn resistance against which for a time no headway could be made the seizure of Ie Shima close-by, of immense potential value to the Americans in its possession of three airstrips, was accelerated, a division of troops was landed on 16th April and captured the island after six days.

Lying north-west and south-west, Okinawa Shima is some 60 miles long and 2 to 14 miles wide. The south-western part of the island, on which the Americans effected their landing, differs much in character from the northern part, the latter being rugged, mountainous and undeveloped, whilst the south-western part is composed of rolling country broken by scarps, and was populous and highly cultivated. In 1935, the inhabitants of Okinawa numbered 451,620, of whom 65,200 lived in the principal town, Naha, and about 19,300 in the ancient capital, Shuri, two miles to the eastward. The island offered numerous sites for airfields from which almost any type of bomber could strike Japan under fighter escort and could harry the enemy's life-lines between the home islands and the conquered territories to the south.[2] Two anchorages were capable of

[1] *See* note at commencement of chapter.

[2] Okinawa Gunto provided 26 potential airfields with an approximate capacity of five VLR wings, two fighter wings, numerous heavy and medium bombers and other types of aircraft, and a depot field.

sheltering a fleet, Nakagusuku Wan (renamed by the Americans Buckner Bay) and Chim Wan respectively, both on the east coast. Naha harbour, in the south-west, was in peacetime an open port which could accommodate destroyers in the outer harbour. It was somewhat exposed to westerly gales. The climate of Okinawa is cool and stimulating, except in late Summer, but the island lies on the track of typhoons.

The landings were planned to take place on beaches at Hagushi extending over a length of some 10,000 yards on the south-western side of the island, between Zampa Misaki and Chatan (Plan 23), which were sheltered from the easterly winds of the spring transition period. A shallow fringing reef with average depth of three feet at low water, borders the entire coast. Along much of its extent the reef approaches the character of a barrier reef, with deeper water between the lip of the reef and the shore. Gradient and surf conditions were fairly good and the terrain behind the beaches was sufficiently spacious for manœuvring a large assault force and afforded immediate access to the airfields Yontan and Katena.

The Japanese 32nd Army under Lieutenant-General M. Ushijima defended Okinawa. Admiral Spruance who was in tactical command of the Ryukus operation, estimated the garrison on L-Day, the day of the assault, at some 55,000 men,[1] but the estimate failed to give sufficient weight to the reinforcement which for some time past had been in progress from the Empire. Reinforcement from within the Nansei Shoto, by troops transported in barges or small vessels, was also feasible ; and there were reported to be between 57,000 and 62,000 enemy troops in other positions in the group. Further forces which could be flown in were 75,000 in the Shanghai area ; 84,000 in Formosa ; and 110,000 in Kyushu. The number of enemy troops actually killed before Okinawa was subdued, was 131,000.

3

The problem of air support in the assault on Okinawa, undertaken as this was beyond the range of shore-based air forces, was one which had confronted the Americans throughout their amphibious campaigns. In Operation 'Iceberg' it was accentuated through the closeness of the objective to the Empire where the main Japanese air reserves lay. The enemy air force in Okinawa was small and would probably be liquidated quickly ; but airfields in Formosa and Kyushu were within operating range of Okinawa for every category of aircraft, whilst the distance of the nearest U.S. airfields, on Luzon, was too great to permit assault support by land-based fighters. The effectiveness of the *kamikaze* system of air attack revealed during the campaigns in the Philippines and Iwo Jima, decided the Japanese to set up a definite organisation, no longer dependent

---

[1] *Commander Fifth Fleet, Action Report.* M.08112/45, p. VI—C—1.

upon volunteers, to exploit suicide tactics. The defence of the Nansei Shoto was undertaken by the 5th Air Fleet (shore-based) together with the 6th Air Army, both operating from airfields in Kyushu.

The 5th Air Fleet (Vice-Admiral Matome Ugaki) was brought up from a strength of 250 to approximately 600 aircraft. It was kept up to establishment as required by drafts from the 3rd Air Fleet (Vice-Admiral Teroka) which disposed of some 300 aircraft, and the Training Command, known as the 10th Air Fleet (Vice-Admiral Maeda) which had about 900 aircraft. Out of the 1,800 naval aircraft thus made available around Okinawa 540 are said to have been special attack (*kamikaze*) planes. The Japanese carrier-based air force had not been reconstituted after the disasters of the two Philippine sea battles. The 6th Air Army is thought to have had about 700 aircraft.

Experience had shown the Allies that command of the air could only be maintained by continuous effort, and pre-eminently through destruction of the enemy's aircraft if they could be found on his airfields or induced to rise to protect their installations. It was necessary to return day after day to crater again and again the same airfields, for within a matter of hours the enemy would have repaired those of importance to him ; whilst nothing but ceaseless surveillance could prevent reinforcement by the enemy of those of his airfields which chiefly threatened the operation in hand. The Japanese flew in aircraft to their Kyushu airfields as fast as they were destroyed.

Maintenance of control of the air by the Americans in Operation 'Iceberg' called for air forces more numerous than those under Admiral Nimitz's command. To augment these he was given permission to use the 20th (Army) Air Force.[1] Twelve months earlier, the Joint Chiefs-of-Staff had established this force to operate the new very heavy bombers (B–29s) which were being prepared for the strategic bombing of Japan. In order to avoid compromising the flexibility of operation of these long-range aircraft, since there was no unity of command either in Asia or the Pacific, the Joint Chiefs-of-Staff retained the 20th Air Force under their own control, with General Arnold as their executive agent. The 20th comprised two Bomber Commands ; the XX which operated from India, Ceylon, and from China until the Japanese advance deprived them of their airfields in January 1945 ; and the XXI which was engaged in pioneering and service testing operations against Japanese industry and cities for the purpose of preparing for the major air assault against Japan's national war structure, operating for this purpose from the airfields of the Marianas. In their original directive, the U.S. Chiefs-of-Staff had empowered Admiral Nimitz as theatre commander to direct the employment of XXI Bomber Command in a tactical or strategical emergency. It was in the interests of the XXIst that Okinawa should be captured as quickly as possible, since the chief purpose of the campaign was to secure sites for air bases near Japan ; and Major-General C. E. LeMay, Commanding-General XXI Bomber Command, on the eve of operation Iceberg empowered CINCPOA to use his Superfortresses whenever they could have a decisive effect whether an emergency existed or not.[2] For five weeks, Nimitz employed these aircraft in raids on Japan designed both to destroy the Japanese aerial offensive capacity, and to compel the enemy to retain for home defence fighters which might otherwise be used against the invaders in the Ryukus. At the end of two weeks after the landing on Okinawa the enemy's suicide air attacks against the Allied supporting fleet units had so reduced the numbers

---

[1] Known as the U.S. Army Strategic Air Forces from 1st July 1945.

[2] *The Army Air Forces in World War II*, V.630.

of the U.S. fast carriers through damage that it was actually feared all naval forces would have to retire if the situation did not improve.[1] Attacks on the Kyushu airfields, from which the *kikusui* and *kamikaze* attacks were mounted were then given first priority amongst the XXI Bomber Command missions. Between 17th April and 11th May the Command devoted about 75 per cent of its combat effort to direct tactical support of Operation 'Iceberg.' Its final operation in support of Okinawa was a heavy attack on the enemy fleet and army refuelling stations in the Inland Sea between Yawata and Kure, in which the oil storage and refining installations were destroyed. By 11th May, the Superfortresses had destroyed the principal air installations in Kyushu, and Admiral Nimitz was able to dispense with their services. Their operations are said to have confirmed the opinion of the leaders of the 20th Air Force, that the B–29 was not a tactical bomber. In the view of the U.S. official historians, its best results were obtained, not against airfields and the aircraft on them, for in the Empire the Japanese usually had sufficient warning to clear the fields, but against facilities such as storage, maintenance and repair which affected future rather than current operations. 'Specifically, it was estimated that between 17th April and 11th May, 95 per cent of the enemy's 1,405 combat sorties were flown on the same day that some of their key bases were being attacked by the Superforts.'[2] During the same period, these bombers flew 2,104 sorties against the airfields of Kyushu and Shikoku. The Fast Carrier Force also launched fighter sweeps against the Kyushu airfields in the hope of reducing opposition to the Okinawa landings, continuing these after D-day, whilst at the same time it shared with the Fifth Fleet escort carriers the duty of tactical support of the operation until the Okinawa airfields could be rendered operative. The British Carrier Force (Task Force 57) operating under Vice-Admiral H. B. Rawlings as part of the U.S. Fifth Fleet, during the first two months of the campaign covered the American left flank by neutralizing the airfields of the Sakishama Gunto alternating, whilst fuelling, with the escort carriers of the Amphibious Support Force. General MacArthur's air forces were assigned the duty of attacking and neutralizing the airfields in Formosa, the strongest and best developed Japanese base south of the home islands. Opinion in the British Pacific Fleet was that though enemy aircraft based in Formosa (29th Air Flotilla) were very much fewer in numbers than those on the fields of Kyushu, they were more skilfully handled and had been responsible for much of the damage to ships at Okinawa. 'They have scored perhaps five times more hits per sortie than their Kyushu compatriots' reported the U.S. special Naval Observer with the British Pacific Fleet.[3] The 5th Air Force, the major, or perhaps the most publicised of the formations composing General MacArthur's Far Eastern Air Force (later known as the Tactical Air Force of the Pacific Ocean Area) had been carrying out strikes on these objectives for some time past. By the end of March, lack of opposition to U.S. aircraft over Formosa caused their commander, General Kenney, to give the airfields lower priority than industrial targets. The Japanese quickly seized the opportunity to repair their air strength in the island. This was soon discovered by Admiral Nimitz who asked for heavy strikes on the airfields; but distances from Mindoro where the 5th Air Force was based, to Formosa were long and the weather was poor; and until the true state of affairs was revealed to the 5th Air Force itself by its own reconnaissance in May and June strikes were meagre; and so they remained

---

[1] *Air Campaigns of the Pacific War*, U.S.S.B.S., p. 46.

[2] *The Army Air Forces in World War II*, Vol. V, p. 634.

[3] *Operation 'Iceberg,'* B.P.F.L.O. Com. Fifth Fleet's Second Report, M.059110/45, para. 31.

despite requests for better support by Admiral Halsey who on 27th May succeeded Spruance in command of the Fleet, the official historian putting forward the explanation that 'though the conclusion that some of the suicide attacks originated in Formosa was inescapable the continuation of group strength missions against such widely dispersed targets, in accordance with Admiral Halsey's wishes, was regarded as an unnecessary waste of effort that could be profitably employed elsewhere.'[1] There was bitterness in the Fifth Fleet at what was regarded as MacArthur's failure to co-operate,[2] but the failure, if any, was but one more instance of the inadequacy of co-operation in place of unified control. On one occasion the British Carrier Force was called upon to supplement the attacks on the northern Formosan airfields which were the responsibility of XX Bomber Command operating from India. The China-Based (air) Forces under Lieutenant-General A. C. Wedemeyer, which by then had recovered some of the airfields lost to the Japanese in the previous year, were also called in to assist Admiral Nimitz by reconnaissance and strikes on the Chinese coastal area.

4

Admiral Spruance (Commander Fifth Fleet) organised his forces for carrying out the operation as the Covering Force (Task Force 50) which he kept under his own hand, and the Joint Expeditionary Force (Task Force 51) under Vice-Admiral R. K. Turner who was succeeded by Vice-Admiral H. W. Hill on 17th May when the command of the troops on shore passed to the Army. When, as already noticed, at 2400 on 27th May operational control of all naval forces then attached to the Fifth Fleet passed from Admiral Spruance to Admiral W. F. Halsey, Jr., Commander Third Fleet, all component units changed their designations by the substitution of the number '3' for '5' e.g. Task Force 57 (the British Carrier Force) became Task Force 37.

The Covering Force consisted of the Fast Carrier Force (Task Force 58) and its Logistic Support Group (Task Group 50.8); the British Carrier Force (Task Force 57) and the British Logistic Task Force (Task Force 112). These two logistic formations or fleet trains supported the fighting formations which they respectively served, in and near the combat zones. The working of the fleet trains will be described in due course. In addition, the U.S. Fast Carrier Force was ministered to afloat at its advanced bases in Ulithi and the Marianas, by a group known as Service Squadron 10 (Task Group 50.9). There were various other special groups in Task Force 50, as shown in the table overleaf.

---

[1] *The Air Army Forces in World War II*, Vol. V, p. 480. About one-fifth of the suicide air attacks are said to have come from Formosa.

[2] cf. *Admiral Halsey's Story*, p. 253.

COVERING FORCE (TASK FORCE 50) IN OKINAWA OPERATIONS

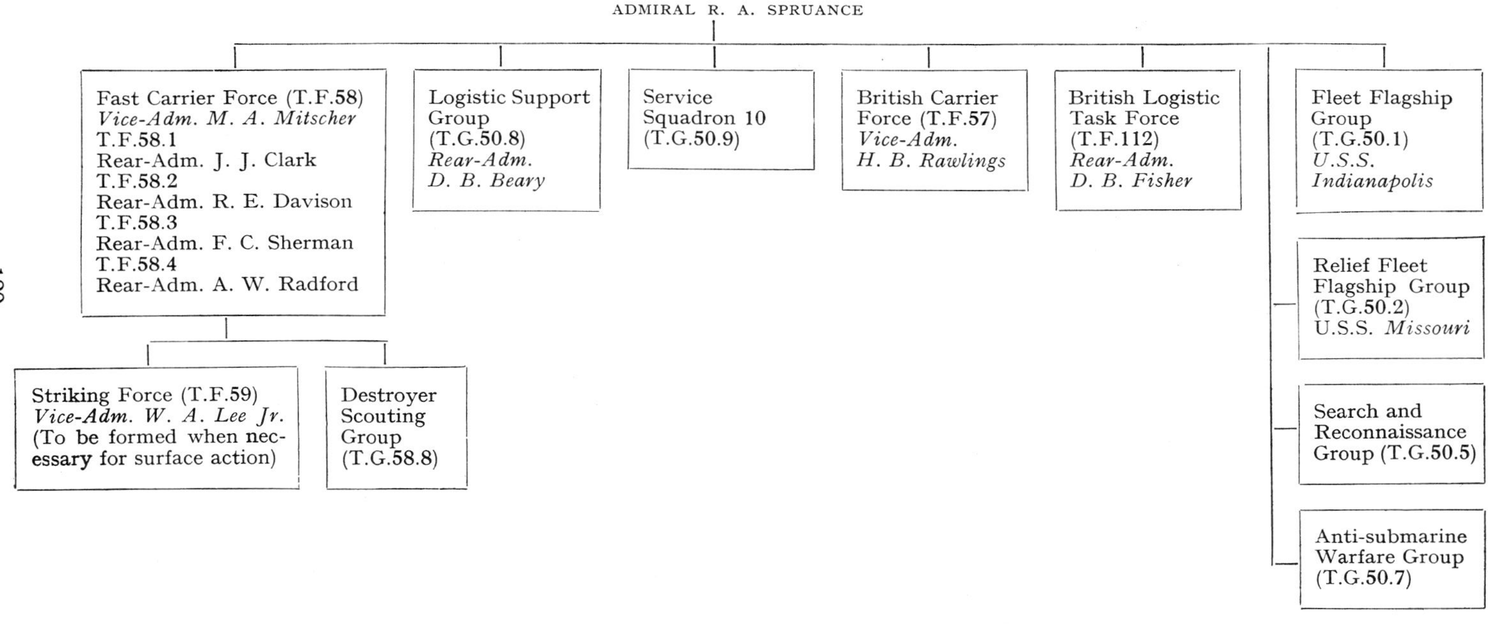

The duty of the U.S. Fast Carrier Force was to neutralise Japanese air power prior to the landings, and thereafter prevent enemy air interference with the operation. The British Carrier Force was assigned the task of neutralising the airfields of the Sakishima Gunto, a group of islands situated between Formosa and Okinawa, which the Japanese used as staging fields for attacks on the shipping at Okinawa.

Whilst Task Force 50 held the ring, the Joint Expeditionary Force (Task Force 51) under Vice-Admiral R. K. Turner carried out the assault and capture of Okinawa and the other islands of the Ryukus required by the Americans. The term 'Joint' according to American usage, indicated that forces of both the fighting services, Army as well as naval, were included in the Expeditionary Force. The troops were the 10th Army, under Lieutenant-General S. B. Buckner, Jr., consisting of the III Amphibious Corps (1st and 6th Marine Divisions) and the XXIV Corps (7th and 96th Infantry Divisions) organised as a Northern and a Southern Attack Force (Task Force 53 and 55). These included the transports and landing craft; and there was also a Floating Reserve and an Area Reserve each consisting of one Division; the Area Reserve was not however committed. The troops remained under the command of Admiral Turner until 17th May when he made over the command to General Buckner, the amphibious phase of the operation being then considered to have terminated.

The offensive power ascribed by the Allies at this date to the Japanese fleet, reduced as this was to a raiding status, was responsible for the introduction into the already complicated organisation for Operation 'Iceberg' of a force termed the Gunfire and Covering Force (Task Force 54). This powerful squadron, comprising ten of the older battleships, 13 cruisers and 29 destroyers and destroyer escorts, had two duties. It had to assign ships as necessary to the Amphibious Support Force (Task Force 52) for bombardment and secondly it was to prevent enemy surface forces from interfering with the landing operations, or in other words, to fight the Japanese fleet if it came out, a duty which also devolved on a force termed the Striking Force (Task Force 59) which would be formed if required from the 15 carriers, eight fast battleships, 15 cruisers and 48 destroyers of Task Force 58. Besides the fire support ships which C.T.F. 54 was to assign to the Amphibious Support Force (Task Force 52) this force contained also the minesweepers and underwater demolition teams for preparing for the landing and 14 escort carriers whose primary duty was to furnish air support at Okinawa. These little carriers had successfully saved the day at the Battle for Leyte Gulf, and were reported by our observers at Okinawa to have been far more efficient and assiduous in bombardment duties than the fast carriers.

A further duty of the Amphibious Support Force was the capture of a group of satellite islands termed Kerama Retto which the Americans required as a repair and logistic base and seaplane station. For this purpose the Amphibious Support Force disposed of one infantry division.

The command relationship between C.T.F. 52 (Vice-Admiral Turner from L-day) and C.T.F. 54 (Rear-Admiral M. L. Deyo) as planned, was that the Rear-Admiral was Senior Officer Present Afloat in the objective area and the Vice-Admiral was responsible for the execution of all operations at the objective. No record of any alteration in this planned relationship has been found.

The composition and duties of the various components of the Joint Expeditionary Force are shown in the table overleaf.

ORGANISATION OF JOINT EXPEDITIONARY FORCE (TASK FORCE 51) IN OPERATION 'ICEBERG'

VICE-ADMIRAL R. K. TURNER

1. Capture, occupy and defend positions in the Ryuku Islands as required.
2. Begin base development and establishment of military government at the objectives.

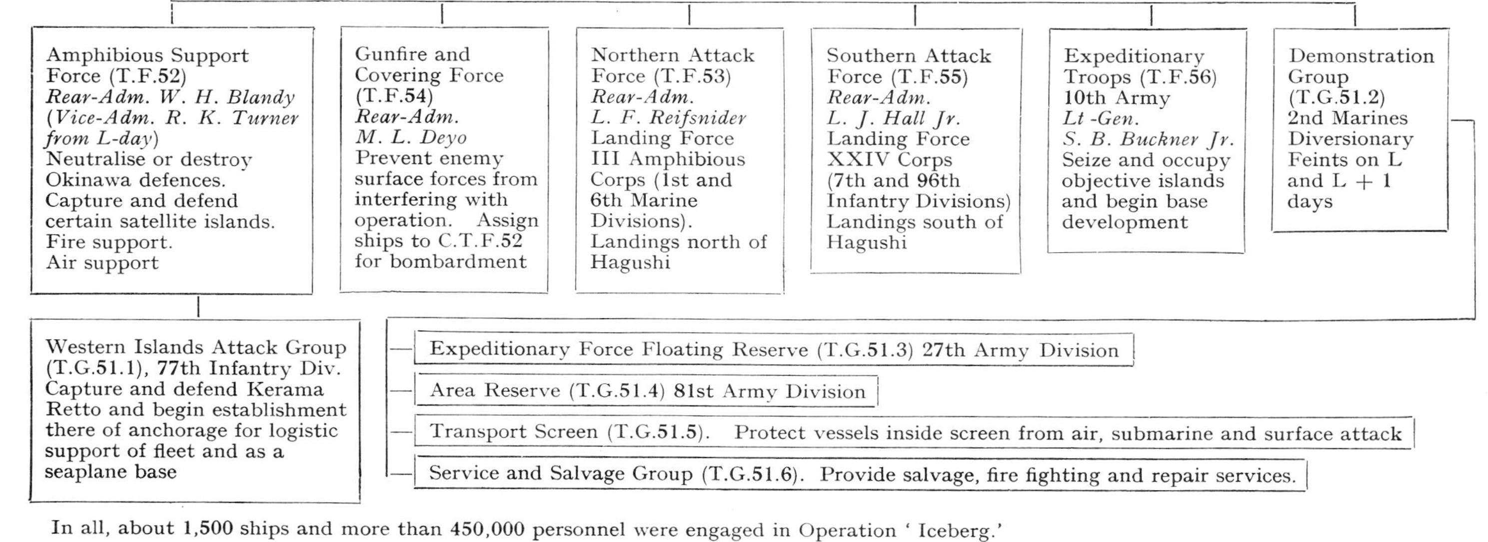

In all, about 1,500 ships and more than 450,000 personnel were engaged in Operation 'Iceberg.'

5

In order to reduce the enemy air effort against operation 'Iceberg', aircraft of the U.S. Fast Carrier Force under Vice-Admiral Mitscher raided the more important airfields in southern Japan, carrying out fighter sweeps to eliminate airborne opposition and destroy aircraft on the ground, and bombing the installations. Many of the more important of these had been put underground, and escaped damage, the abandoned buildings being left as decoys. But the bombing severed telephone wires and rendered more difficult the direction of operations by the Japanese 5th Air Fleet Command. The sailing of Task Force 58 from Ulithi on 14th March was reported by a Japanese reconnaissance aircraft from Truk. The force was reported again south of Okinawa at 2300 on the 17th and a large force of Japanese torpedo aircraft was sent off at 0350 to attack, followed by a further attack group at dawn. Deception measures by Admiral Mitscher did not deceive the enemy, most of whom found and attacked the fleet, resulting in some damage to the carriers *Intrepid* and *Enterprise*. Task Force 58, after attacking the Kyushu airfields on the 18th moved north-east next day to attack Japanese fleet units which had been located at Kure and Kobe by reconnaissance flights on the previous day. The Japanese found the American fleet that morning and Admiral Ugaki ordered out every available aircraft of the 5th Air Fleet to attack it. The *Franklin* was hit and badly damaged, and during the afternoon Admiral Mitscher retired covering the disabled carrier and launching fighter sweeps against the Kyushu airfields to prevent any organised air attacks against his slowly moving force. A late afternoon attack on the 20th resulted in damage to the destroyer *Halsey Powell* by a Japanese aircraft which had been shot down and struck the destroyer in falling, slowing her to 10 knots and causing further delay in the retirement southward. Early next day, Task Force 58 was sighted by the Japanese some 300 miles south-east of Kanoya in southern Kyushu (Plan 24), and Ugaki at 1330 despatched 18 bombers each carrying a 4,700 lb. *Oka*, or as the Americans termed it, *Baka* (' foolish ') jet-propelled bomb, this being the first operational appearance of the bomb as far as is known. This and another cumbersome missile termed ' Viper ' rendered the parent aircraft, usually a twin-engined machine, very sluggish. On this occasion no more than 30 Japanese fighters were available to protect the 18 parent aircraft. The number proved quite inadequate. Admiral Mitscher sent out 24 fighters to intercept. They met the enemy 60 miles from Task Force 58 and in a matter of minutes every one of the Japanese was shot down, with the loss of only two U.S. fighters.

The U.S. Commander-in-Chief reported that between 18th and 22nd March a total of 528 enemy aircraft was destroyed, 260 by aircraft, 46 by anti-aircraft fire from the Task Force, and 222 on the ground, the latter despite Japanese dispersal and camouflage methods. These numbers are far greater than the Japanese admit, but there is little doubt that by the 22nd the enemy's air effort was very greatly weakened.

6

On 23rd March the fast carriers began launching daily strikes against Okinawa Shima and the adjacent islands in order to prepare the area for minesweeping and the landing on Kerama Retto which was to precede the main assault. The sweeping of the mines began on 24th March, L minus 8 day, the Underwater Demolition Teams beginning work next day. The Americans considered that the minesweeping operation was probably the largest assault sweep operation ever executed. Over 3,000 square miles were swept, bringing to light 177 mines, whilst some 80 floating mines were destroyed (Plan 21).

The first day's bombardment to destroy the defences of Okinawa was carried out by the eight battleships of Task Force 58 (formed into Task Group 59.7), but the duty was taken over next day by the ships assigned from the Gunfire and Covering Force together with the Advance Support Craft (gunboats and rocket craft) (Task Group 52.25). By L minus 3 day minesweeping and under-water demolitions had advanced far enough to permit the battleships to close the range and engage the coast defences with direct fire. Air cover was provided on the first day by the fast carriers, and was taken over on L minus 7 day by the escort carriers of the Amphibious Support Force whilst the fast carriers operated principally against targets which could not be reached by naval gunfire. The Japanese withheld their fire, but most of their cleverly camouflaged and concealed coast defence guns which threatened the landing, were located and damaged or destroyed by L minus 1 day. The Kerama Retto was captured on 26th and 27th March. No less than some 400 Japanese suicide boats were found there but many others remained in various locations in the Ryukus, and until about 10th May, by which time they were for the most part destroyed, attacks on the American shipping by these craft and by midget submarines and floating booby traps took place frequently, though with success quite disproportionate to the considerable effort expended, only one ship being sunk and seven damaged.

Preceded by a tremendous bombardment and with a simultaneous feint landing on the opposite side of the island, the troops landed in face of very light opposition. The leading waves in amphibians were a few minutes late in landing, but this was immaterial, as the timing of direct gunfire support was related to the position of the first assault wave and not to a rigid timetable. Within an hour, 16,000 men landed ; by nightfall, more than 60,000 were ashore. For a few days the troops advanced rapidly and captured the two important airfields, Yontan and Katena. But about L minus 5 day their advance received a severe check, which kept them where they stood for a fortnight and was only resolved after a bloody frontal attack lasting several weeks. Simultaneously with this rally on the part of the enemy the Japanese sent down from Kyushu one of the greatest and most furious air counter attacks of the war.

7

The U.S. Tactical Air Force, consisting mainly of Army and Marine fighters under Major-General Mulcahy, assumed support duty ashore on 8th April, but the stubborn Japanese defence prevented the Americans from gaining possession of sufficient airfields for protection. Consequently, the fast carriers instead of being able to seek out and attack the enemy forces at their bases in Kyushu, had for the most part to be held close to the fleet in order to break up the Japanese suicide attacks, remaining off Okinawa after the ships were overdue for rest and repair. The Japanese were aided in their air attacks, first by an insufficiency ashore of U.S. radar sets, and secondly by the limitations of the American air search radar and aircraft identification equipment at that date. The enemy had fixed and mobile radar stations on Okinawa. He developed a receiver which enabled his aircraft to take advantage of fade areas in the U.S. radars when making their approaches ; and he employed several types of attack. The most dangerous periods were at dawn and evening twilight. The U.S. carrier task groups were accustomed to launch combat air patrols, strikes and sweeps at morning twilight. Within a few moments air within ten miles would become saturated with friendly aircraft, and it was not very difficult for the Japanese who about half an hour before first light had infested the area around the task group at all altitudes, to approach without being detected, despite IFF. The other danger period, on which fortunately the Japanese did not capitalize to the full extent, was at evening twilight when night retirement dispositions were being formed by the ships and the day's combat air patrol was landing. Most of the raids from Formosa, and the few from Sakishima, arrived in the late afternoon or night when the combat air patrol over those islands had left the area. Admiral Rawlings by late afternoon strikes on the Sakishima Gunto co-operated to lessen the weight and incidence of dusk and moonlight air attacks on the invasion shipping.

Air defence of the main attack force, the Kerama Retto area and the fighter direction and radar warning picket destroyers around Okinawa was a difficult problem. A number of protective fighters varying from 60 to 84 was kept over Okinawa Shima and other islands occupied by the Americans during the day, with a further 24 to 36 on ground alert, according to the amount of enemy air activity expected. The outlying pickets in particular suffered severely, but their effectiveness in providing air warning and in destroying enemy aircraft was amply proved. They played a vital part in the success of the operation.[1] Many of them put up very efficient anti-aircraft defence, but several were sunk. As many as 30 enemy aircraft would on occasion team up to attack a single ship.

Later, the picket stations were strengthened to a total of about two destroyer types and four landing craft in each outlying station. A minimum of nine picket stations was needed for effective cover. The picket line normally controlled two to four divisions of aircraft with four aircraft in a division.

The first heavy mass suicide attack took place on 6th April. Nearly 700 aircraft, of which 355 were *kamikazes*, left Kyushu to raid the shipping off Okinawa. Attacks began about 1500 hours. About 400 aircraft are reported to have got through the defence. The brunt of the attack fell on the pickets. The destroyers *Bush* and *Colhoun* and the high-speed minesweeper *Emmons* on picket duty were sunk, whilst nearer home three more ships were lost. The high-speed minesweeper *Rodman* was attacked by at least 11 aircraft of which three hit the ship and eight were shot down. Other ships shot down large numbers of the enemy. After a pause, air attacks began again at 1610, whilst the Night Retirement Group was forming up, and two of the screening destroyers were hit and badly damaged. In all, six ships were sunk and 18 damaged, nearly all by suicide attack. But claims of enemy aircraft destroyed ran to 300. The *Essex*'s aircraft alone reported shooting down 65.

At 2010 a signal came in from the submarine *Threadfin*, that a force was emerging at high speed from the Bungo Channel, the southernmost exit from the Inland Sea. The *Threadfin*, and the *Hackleback* which gained contact shortly afterwards, were unable to reach firing position but held on long enough to report the force as two large ships with six or more destroyers. The ships were the *Yamato* with the light cruiser *Yahagi* and eight destroyers under Vice-Admiral Ito, the only ships which in the state of the Fleet at the time and the prevailing dearth of oil could put to sea to make a traditional suicide charge with the intention of doing as much damage as possible before being sunk. They carried in their bunkers sufficient oil for the outward passage to Okinawa only, thus emphasising their suicide nature.

---

[1] Enclosure (I) *Appendix 5 to Commander-in-Chief, British Pacific Fleet's* 601/BPF/1743, 25th March 1946. M.010175/45.

A reconnaissance aircraft from the *Essex* sighted them at 0815 next day. The Japanese withdrew their air cover at 1000, but the ships put up heavy anti-aircraft fire at the U.S. tracking team which picked them up shortly after. As it was uncertain whether the enemy were making for Okinawa, Admiral Spruance, lest they should escape, ordered Vice-Admiral Mitscher to attack during the afternoon. The first strike groups reached the enemy about 1230 in rain squalls. The Japanese ships put up a great deal of anti-aircraft fire of every description, barrage, predicted concentration, and continuously pointed, and of every calibre, using red, yellow, green and purple bursts, with an abundance of white phosphorous. The *Yamato* used her 18·1-inch guns against the American aircraft at distances up to 12 or 15 miles. The history of the *Prince of Wales* and *Repulse* was repeated on this day. The *Yahagi* sank at 1405: the *Yamato* withstood ten hits with torpedoes and five with bombs before she rolled over and took to the bottom with her Admiral Ito and 2,496 officers and men. Four destroyers, one of them very badly damaged, escaped and reached Sasebo.

Taking advantage of the absence of the strike groups from the fast carriers off Okinawa, the Japanese at noon made heavy air attacks on Task Force 58. Eighteen enemy aircraft were destroyed over or near the force, but one *kamikaze*, after dropping a bomb on the *Hancock* from a height of 50 feet crashed into a group of aircraft on the flight deck, causing 80 casualties and doing damage which necessitated the ship leaving for repairs at the next replenishment day.

On the 12th there was warning of another mass suicide air attack, a total of 125 Japanese naval and 60 army aircraft being involved. The attack developed at about 1300 hours, the radar pickets again taking the brunt of it. For three hours the enemy came over in groups of ten or a dozen at heights between 18,000 and 20,000 feet. The fighters over the northern islands met them and shot down 80. Most of the remainder got through to attack Okinawa where the 72 fighters of the combat air patrol shot down a further 80 or thereabouts of them. Only a single aircraft penetrated to the transport area. But two ships were sunk and 14 damaged by suicide attacks, including two battleships seriously, whilst orthodox air attacks damaged nine more. The destroyer M.L. *Abele*, on picket duty, was subjected to a co-ordinated low-level attack by about 20 aircraft. The ship shot down two, then a suicide hit was followed almost at once by a jet-propelled bomb hit which caused her to break in two and sink immediately.

The next *kikusui* attack began on the morning of 16th April. Owing to aircraft being about, the ships were put under smoke for six hours during the previous night, and much wild shooting took place, which at 2129 evoked from Admiral Turner the signal: 'No ships will fire now except on personal orders of captains', to which the curious injunction 'Captains enforce this order,' was appended. Once more the pickets suffered severely. The destroyer *Laffey* was subjected to a co-ordinated attack by about 30 aircraft. She was hit by four suiciders and two dropped bombs, and suffered 94 casualties, but the ship survived and shot down six of the enemy. Four other ships in the picket line were hit by suicide aircraft, and the carrier *Intrepid* was damaged later in the day. Raids continued. The Japanese appeared to be capable of mounting a mass suicide attack every few days, in addition to daily raids, though the number of attackers dwindled considerably after the end of May. The first night *kikusui* attack took place during the night of 28th–29th April when more than half of the attackers were destroyed. The hospital ship *Comfort*, observing full hospital ship procedure, was crashed by a *kamikaze* at

2000 on the 28th and had 63 casualties. A heavy attack on 4th May in support of a counter attack by the 32nd Army resulted in the sinking of five U.S. ships and damage to 11, all except one by suicide air attack. For a week there was a respite, but between 11th and 14th May three U.S. flagships were hit and put out of action: first the carrier *Bunker Hill,* flagship of C.T.F. 58, then the battleship *New Mexico,* Admiral Spruance's flagship, and finally the carrier *Enterprise* to which Admiral Mitscher had shifted his flag when the *Bunker Hill* was hit. In all, between 6th April and 22nd June the Japanese mounted ten mass suicide attacks involving 1,465 aircraft; and, in addition, nearly 450 *kamikaze* attacks were made. The ratio of ships sunk, 27, and damaged, 164, to aircraft involved was almost exactly 1 in 10. Orthodox air attacks were made by about 4,800 enemy aircraft. These sank one ship and damaged 63.

For the U.S. Fifth Fleet, Japanese suicide operating made of Operation 'Iceberg' an episode which has been described as 'a continuing crisis, with the fleet including its auxiliaries, paying a price without precedent'. Fantastic as was the damage caused, from the materialistic point of view *kamikaze* suffered from the inherent defect of giving diminishing returns as losses of pilots and aircraft accumulated; it was thus a wasting asset. As practised, both in the defence of the Philippines and Okinawa, it could put out of action, but given good damage control, augmented in the British carriers by armoured flight decks, was ineffective in sinking the primary target, Allied carriers, since the power of penetration of the bomb was insufficient. Operation by the Japanese Air Command was rendered difficult because results could not be accurately evaluated, since no aircraft returned to render a report. Reconnaissance aircraft were, it is true, sent to accompany the *kamikazes* as observers, but they were far too busily occupied in avoiding Allied fighters, to be able to observe effectively.

Logically, suicide attack in any of the forms, air or sea, practised by the Japanese, differed only in kind from the last ditch defence enjoined upon the British after Dunkirk, and only in degree from such missions as the air attack on the Moehne Dam. Probably, however, the Japanese committed a cardinal error when they made suicide operating compulsory. What in the Philippines had been a crusade was at Okinawa deprived of all humanity and the virtue went out of it. Long after *kamikaze* was known to have failed, pilots, even those then under training, were herded to their death, knowing that the Emperor whom they had regarded as a Supreme Being and the country for which they were giving their lives in vain, had no longer any consideration for them as human beings.

8

Meanwhile, the British Carrier Force was operating under handicaps which were the more severe since it was operating in an American Fleet whose ships had been designed specifically for a type of work new to us, whilst the U.S. officers and men had the advantage of three years' experience in their specialised role.

Our ships had been sent to Australia for political reasons before the base was sufficiently advanced to be able to maintain them. Though considerable planning of the Australian base had taken place, the final decision that it should be set up and the Fleet engage in Pacific operations, was taken so late that much of the plan could not mature before it became necessary to send the fleet into action. The operation of the British Carrier Force in 'Iceberg' was consequently a scramble. Essential support was always a little late and there was the constant aggravation of unavoidable troubles of inexperience in the type of operation called for. The fault for deficiencies lay solely with the necessities of war ; but all difficulties were overcome, often by improvisation ; and the fact that the British Pacific Fleet played its part in the Pacific war was justification for the trials it underwent. The United Kingdom, the rear base of the Fleet, was 12,000 miles from the forward base at Sydney in Australia, which itself was 2,000 miles from the advanced anchorage at Manus and 3,500 from San Pedro Roads, Leyte Island the advanced base which was used during the first part of Operation ' Iceberg ' ; whilst Leyte itself was 800 miles from the combat area. At no time before the war ended was the Australian base able to supply and maintain the British Pacific Fleet completely without the help of U.S. bases, fuelling facilities and spare parts ; and it is unlikely that any of our ships would have remained operational for long without American help.

As far as our anti-aircraft fire was concerned our ships almost deserved to be described in the American idiom as ' unable to look after themselves '. The standard of A.A. gunnery in the ships was low.[1] The British Navy had throughout the war suffered from lack of targets and training facilities ; and it was fortunate that the British Pacific Fleet during operation ' Iceberg ' was faced with a scale of attack which was, by Pacific standards, weak. Japanese suicide aircraft scored on our carriers a higher percentage of hits than on the American fast carriers, the British sharing five hits amongst four carriers as against the same number of hits amongst 15 U.S. carriers. The armament of our ships had been designed primarily to fight ships, whereas conditions in the Pacific had shown the Americans at the very outset of the war the necessity of fitting adequate anti-aircraft armaments. Suicide air attacks introduced new complications into our anti-aircraft systems, particularly as this type of attack proved invulnerable to anything smaller than 40-mm. guns whereas the British Fleet was largely equipped with the 20-mm. gun which had proved effective against torpedo bombers. The older and well-established weapons and devices had been overtaken by events, and not all the later developments were found to be effective. A gap existed, too, between mechanical reliability and, due to the unavoidable degree of dilution in the Navy, skill in maintenance.

Nothing in the design of the U.S. carriers was permitted to interfere with their primary function of working aircraft, which called for a clear flight deck. Ship for ship, our carriers had smaller aircraft complements than the American, whether or not due to design of lifts and armoured flight decks and the restrictions in stowage space caused by higher safety precautions with the closed hangar design of our carriers. But the British armoured decks stood them in good stead under suicide air attacks ; for whereas every U.S. carrier which was hit had to withdraw to a Navy Yard for repairs, all the British carriers when hit remained operational. The short endurance of our ships was a handicap, though not a limiting factor as had generally been the case in other areas where ships normally refuelled in harbour. Fuelling during the Ryukus operation always took place at sea.

The U.S. Fleet had been gradually built up to suit the new type of naval warfare in the Pacific. This called for the employment of fast carriers armed with numbers of aircraft serviced by ample maintenance personnel and operated by air crews who, when worn out by intense striking activity over periods varying from four to six months, were taken out of the ship bodily and replaced

[1] *Report of Experience of the British Pacific Fleet from January–August* 1945, p. 15. M.01779/46.

by a fresh group. The handling parties of the British carriers were of such dimensions that the carriers which operated aircraft most successfully on deck used large numbers of officers and ratings from other departments as extra aircraft handling parties. Our own carrier force had sailed from Australia with little opportunity of working together and with an assignment to a type of warfare which under the conditions of the war against the Western Axis it had not been able to practice before.

Our aircraft left much to be desired. The multiplicity of operational types, six, nearly all of which were excluded from one or other of our carriers, was a grave hindrance. They compared unfavourably with the American equivalents in respect of non-vulnerability, range and striking power.[1] Their low endurance forced the British Pacific Fleet inshore, complicating its operations and restricting its offensive air effort. The Seafires were very nearly incapable of reaching the enemy, and during the first part of Operation 'Iceberg' their effort was entirely defensive ; whilst the American types, Avengers, Corsairs and Hellcats which constituted almost the whole of the remainder of the complement, had been so altered to 'bring them up to British standards' as to render impossible any pooling of resources with the U.S. Navy, even in this American product. Many of the aircraft received by our carriers in forward replenishments could not be flown into operations for several days, since they required extensive maintenance work on receipt.[2] The lack of air stores came nearer to causing a complete breakdown in operations than any other single factor. When the fleet carriers left Sydney in February, only ten per cent of their demands had been met, for time did not permit of sufficient stocks being accumulated and store depots organised in Australia ; supplies were short and staffs for handling air stores inadequate.

The British Carrier Force, though in aircraft complement it barely approximated to a single group in the American Fast Carrier Force, was given the status of a Force in the U.S. Fifth Fleet. The absence of sufficient ships to form more than one group resulted in a higher ratio of defensive to offensive sorties by our fighters than in the U.S. Fleet. It is, of course, a fact that fighter defensive effort is an 'overhead cost' which does not change in proportion as the ships to be defended are increased or diminished in numbers. Consequently, the greater the number of aircraft operating in any given force, the larger the proportion free to undertake offensive action. Only 42 per cent of the British sorties were offensive, compared with the U.S. figure of 65 per cent. But the greatest disadvantage of operating with a single group was that the British Pacific Fleet was prevented from playing its full part in Operation 'Iceberg', since the effort of one group, alternately striking and fuelling, was necessarily discontinuous and uneconomical of force, whilst the entire Carrier Force had to be withdrawn for repairs and major replenishment after two months at the Sakishima Gunto. The shortcoming was made good by the escort carriers of the U.S. Support Carrier Group (Task Group 52.1) under Rear-Admiral Durgin. These, in addition to continuing their close support of the troops on Okinawa after the landing, and carrying out various other duties such as providing air cover for the Service Squadron and Fleet units in the fuelling and supply area, north-west of Minami Oagari Shima, alternated with the British in rendering continuous the work of neutralizing the airfields of the Sakishima Gunto.

---

[1] A.C.1's No. 767/5/301 of 8th October 1945, *Seafire Aircraft*, M.01779/46, Appendix II.

[2] A.C.1's No. 019/16/923 of 23rd August 1945, *Final Report on Operations July/August*. Enclosure No. 2, para. 23 and Commander-in-Chief 601/BPF/1743 of 25th March 1946, Enclosure (3), p. 5, M.010175/45.

Admiral King delayed giving the executive for the assignment of the British Carrier Force to operation ' Iceberg ' and Admiral Rawlings was consequently two days late in beginning operations. Moreover, it needed the combined representations of the Commander-in-Chief Pacific Fleet and the Commander Seventh Fleet to dissuade King from withdrawing the British force, after it had become engaged in the Ryukus Operation, to cover the Australian landings in Borneo (*see* Chapter XIV) for which no U.S. carriers were available.

The striking force Task Force 113, had arrived at Sydney from the Indian Ocean on 10th February. Its initial supplies of stores, air stores, aircraft and men were still arriving from the United Kingdom even when it sailed on the 28th for its advanced anchorage, Manus in the Admiralty Islands. Here it spent several days exercising at sea, moving up to Ulithi on 18th March on receipt of the executive for its assignment to the U.S. Fifth Fleet, in which, at 0715(T) on the 23rd it became Task Force 57. The force comprised the battleships *King George V* (flagship of Vice-Admiral Rawlings (C.T.F. 57)) and *Howe*; the four fleet carriers *Indomitable* (flagship of Rear-Admiral Sir Philip Vian, A.C.1 and Second-in-Command Task Force 57), *Victorious*, *Illustrious* and *Indefatigable*; a cruiser squadron and destroyer screen (Appendix S). The Order of Battle-Aircraft at the beginning of the operation was as follows :—[1]

Indomitable	..	29 Hellcat,[2] 15 Avenger.[3]
Victorious	..	37 Corsair,[4] 14 Avenger, 2 Walrus.[5]
Indefatigable	..	40 Seafire,[4] 20 Avenger, 9 Firefly.[4]
Illustrious	..	36 Corsair, 16 Avenger.
		Total aircraft 218.

Admiral Rawlings sailed from Ulithi at 0630 on 23rd March and at 0600 on the 25th met the tanker group, which had been sent on ahead, in 18° 30′ N., 129° 08′ E. Owing to various unexpected difficulties, refuelling took nearly six hours longer than anticipated and the force had to proceed at 23½ knots through the night in order to avoid being late on their first assignment. The destroyers sailed 30 per cent short of full stowage. One, the *Wager*, remained behind to continue fuelling when the Task Force proceeded at 1530, rejoining next morning. The *Quality* and *Whelp* had to be exchanged for the *Whirlwind* and *Kempenfelt* from the screen of the fuelling group, on account of defects.

The general task of the force during this phase of Operation ' Iceberg ' was to crater the runways of Ishigaki and Miyako, on each of which islands there were three primary airfields (Plan 22). Two of these were heavily defended, and a substantial part of the effort of the strike aircraft was devoted to neutralizing the anti-aircraft gun positions. Few of the airfields appeared to be in active use; and after initial heavy bombing and machine-gunning the work of Task Force 57 consisted principally in maintaining a combat air patrol over the islands, searching for heavily camouflaged aircraft, and bombing attacks on the airfields and installations. It was somewhat thankless work, for targets were few,

[1] Figures given in Report by Flag Officer Commanding First Aircraft Carrier Squadron (Enclosure 1 to *Report of Vice-Admiral, Second-in-Command, British Pacific Fleet—Operation ' Iceberg.'* M.059159/45). Different figures are given in *Operational Research Reports by Fleet Operational Research Officer*, BPF A.01134/45.

[2] Fighter bomber.

[3] Torpedo bomber, employed as a bomber in Operation ' Iceberg.'

[4] Fighter.

[5] Amphibian Reconnaissance Bomber (Air–Sea Rescue).

apart from airfields. The flying-off positions varied between 80 and 100 miles from the target, the force withdrawing at night. The lack of fully trained and equipped night fighters was felt keenly during Operation 'Iceberg'.[1] The system of exercising tactical command was that the Vice-Admiral commanding the aircraft carrier squadron assumed tactical command when our aircraft were in the air.

During the first period of operating, which lasted 26 days, the force completed 12 days of strikes usually in periods of two days, followed by an interval of three to five days for refuelling. The average flying hours for the period were—Corsairs (fighter) and Hellcats (fighter), 45; Seafires, (fighter), 22. The scale of effort by the Hellcats, 1·22 sorties per complement aircraft per strike day, and the scale for the Corsairs, only slightly lower, were comparable with standard American carrier flying effort. The Avengers (torpedo bomber) were not extended, owing to lack of suitable targets. Our losses were 19 aircraft in combat and 28 operationally. Enemy aircraft destroyed in the air were 28 and on the ground 34 of which later, however, many were thought to be non-operational or dummies.

At 0650 on 1st April an enemy aircraft raid was detected by radar at a distance of 75 miles. Some of the attackers penetrated the protective fighter patrol and one dived into the base of the *Indefatigable's* island, causing a number of casualties and putting the flight deck temporarily out of operation. The destroyer *Ulster* was damaged by a near miss bomb and had to be towed to Leyte. No further attack occurred until the 6th when slight damage was caused to the *Illustrious* by a suicider's wing tip which struck her island. On the 12th and 13th Admiral Spruance detailed the force to supplement the efforts of Allied Air Forces South-West Pacific Area by raiding Shinchiku and Matsuyama airfields in the northern part of Formosa which the Japanese were using as fuelling fields in their attacks on the ships off Okinawa. Though pilots and aircraft were beginning to show signs of strain, as were also the maintenance and handling personnel, strikes were made with every available aircraft, launched from a point some 50 miles from Formosa, involving 50 miles of flying over enemy territory. On the first evening, the Japanese made a sortie from Ishigaki; it was intercepted by fighters and failed to reach the Fleet, eight of the enemy being shot down. On the second day, four enemy aircraft got through and ineffectually attacked the *Indomitable*. After three more strike days in the Sakishima Gunto the fleet retired, anchoring in San Pedro Roads, Leyte, 32 days out from Ulithi, to undertake a short replenishment. With its few slow small tankers and inadequate Fleet Train the force had exhausted its effort for the time being. It was unfortunate that when the fleet carrier squadron began operating no less than three fighter wings were near, at or beyond the end of an operational tour of accepted limits and had to be relieved at this first replenishment period.

From the beginning, it was apparent that however thoroughly the airfields were neutralized by day, the Japanese were determined and able to effect repairs under cover of darkness; the need for night intruders to slow down repairs was keenly felt. The enemy anti-aircraft positions on Miyako remained unsubdued to the last and continued to inflict casualties on British aircraft, for the high explosive bombs with which the Fleet was provided proved unsuitable for their reduction.

[1] A.C.1s No. 0109/12/867 of 14th May 1945, *Report on Iceberg 7 and 8*, paras. 2, 3. (*Report of Experience of the British Pacific Fleet from January–August* 1945, M.01779/46.)

At Leyte, the ships found themselves many miles from the shore, with virtually no boats, and the few days' stand-off was a less thorough restorative of stamina and moral for the aircrews, than might have been expected. The fleet sailed again at 0630 on 1st May with the *Formidable* replacing the *Illustrious*, to continue the neutralization of the Sakishima Gunto, operations being planned with a cycle of two days of strikes followed by two for replenishment.

On the first strike day, 4th May, a bombardment of the Japanese airfields and anti-aircraft positions on Miyako was carried out by the battleships and cruisers, as well as air strikes, partly for the benefit of the young and untried members of the ships' companies. The carriers remained some 30 miles away to the southward, and the Japanese seized the opportunity of the heavy ships' absence to bring them under air attack by some 16 to 20 aircraft working with decoys. There were no enemy on the radar screen however when at 1131 a Zeke was seen diving from a great height on to the *Formidable* and was taken under fire. Hit by the *Formidable's* close-range weapons, the suicide aircraft nevertheless crashed into the ship's flight deck near the island structure, starting a large fire in the deck park of aircraft, killing and wounding 55 men and damaging 11 aircraft beyond repair, holing and denting the flight deck to a depth of two feet. However, by 1700 the ship was again flying-on aircraft. Three minutes later, another Zeke hit the *Indomitable* but bounced over the side, doing no damage except to the ship's radar. A few minutes later a third Zeke dived on the ship. Hit hard and often, it burst into flames and crashed into the sea ten yards off without doing any damage. By 1450 the heavy ships had returned to the carriers and taken station. During the afternoon several enemy aircraft were shot down, though it was not until the fleet was withdrawing for the night that another attack developed. This was satisfactorily broken up by our fighters.

On the evening of 9th May the *Formidable* was hit again by a suicider which dived into her after-deck park, putting 18 aircraft out of action but causing little damage. Fifty minutes later the ship was once more fit to land-on aircraft but she had only four bombers and 11 fighters serviceable. Meanwhile, the *Victorious* had been hit by a suicider aided by decoys which crashed on her flight deck near the forward lift, where its bomb detonated. The resulting fire was quickly brought under control, but the explosion holed the flight deck and damaged one motor. Five minutes later, a suicider made a shallow power glide on the *Victorious*. Though hit hard by gunfire and on fire, it struck the flight deck a glancing blow and passed over the side damaging four Corsairs beyond repair but doing little other harm. Another suicider attacked the *Howe*, but was hit at long range and continued to be hit until it crashed in flames 100 yards off, after passing over the battleship's quarter deck.

When Task Force 57 resumed action on 12th May, Admiral Rawlings moved the launching position further eastward. The change proved effective, and no further serious attacks were made on the force. The low approach adopted by the suiciders during their later attacks in lieu of their previous practice of high approach greatly reduced the warning period, and to overcome this, radar pickets, each consisting of a 6-inch cruiser and a destroyer, were stationed 12 miles north-west and south-west of the fleet, to increase the range of detection.

On 18th May whilst fuelling and exchanging aircraft the *Formidable* suffered a serious fire when a Corsair in the hangar accidentally fired her guns into an Avenger, which exploded. About 30 aircraft were damaged or destroyed. By evening, the ship was capable of operating once more. On the 20th, in dense fog, the *Quilliam* was badly damaged in collision with the *Indomitable* and had to be towed to the fuelling area. The *Formidable* was detached on the 22nd to Sydney via Manus to expedite repairs in order to ensure that four carriers would be available for the final operations against the main Japanese islands which were to take place after Okinawa was secured. After final strikes on the 25th the fleet followed her to Manus, where the ships were to disperse to their rear bases for major storing for the final operations. Two days later when Admiral Spruance relinquished command of the Fifth Fleet to Admiral Halsey he signalled to Admiral Rawlings, 'I wish to express to you and to the officers and men under your command, my appreciation of the fine work you have done and the splendid spirit of co-operation in which you have done it. To the American portion of the Fifth Fleet, Task Force 57 has typified the great traditions of the Royal Navy'. In his report, Admiral Spruance stated that the British Pacific Fleet had gained sufficient experience to undertake operations with the U.S. Fast Carrier Force.[1]

Over the whole period of its employment in Operation 'Iceberg' Task Force 57 was at sea for 62 days, broken by eight days re-storing at Leyte. On the 23 strike days the carriers flew 4,691 sorties, dropped 927 tons of bombs and fired 950 rocket projectiles. The number of enemy aircraft destroyed was probably less than the estimate of 100 made by the force. Various other targets than airfields, such as shipping and W/T Stations, were attacked. Our aircraft losses totalled 160, including 26 shot down in combat and 72 destroyed operationally. Suicide attacks accounted for 32 destroyed on board their carriers and 30 were lost in the *Formidable's* hangar fire. Deck-landing crashes were responsible for the loss of 61 aircraft, a higher total than that caused by the efforts of the enemy. Flying casualties numbered 41 killed and missing, non-flying casualties 44 killed and 83 wounded.

In two respects, the operating statistics of the U.S. (so far as available) and British carrier forces compared unfavourably. Proportionately, our aircraft losses operationally were nearly double the American, as the following table shows:—

	OPERATIONAL LOSSES	NUMBER OF COMPLEMENT AIRCRAFT	DAYS AT TARGET	AIRCRAFT DAYS ‡ PER AIRCRAFT LOST OPERATIONALLY
U.S.	231*	919	80	318
British	72†	218	54	163

* Excludes 15 lost in typhoon.
† Excludes 30 lost in *Formidable's* hangar fire.
‡ Number of complement aircraft X number of days at target.

Most of the 61 British aircraft destroyed in deck landing crashes were Seafires, whose proportion of crashes per sortie was some 50 per cent. higher than that of the Fireflies and during Phase I of Operation 'Iceberg' nearly three times as great as those of the Avengers and Corsairs.[2]

Secondly, the immense disparity between the 1908 enemy aircraft claimed destroyed by Task Force 58, and the 75 allowed by U.S. Commander-in-Chief to Task Force 57, needs explanation. The conditions under which the two forces operated differed greatly. The particular part played by Task Force 57 was one

[1] *Action Report, Ryukus Operation through 27th May* 1945. VI–A–2. M.08112/45.
[2] Figures based on replacements as percentage of sorties.

which offered little opportunity of inflicting heavy losses on the enemy, though on the other hand it must be borne in mind that part of the American effort was expended in direct support of the land forces and gave no return in aircraft destroyed. The majority of the Japanese aircraft destroyed by the Americans were brought down in the air—two-and-a-half times as many as were destroyed on the ground. In the British Fleet the numbers destroyed in each manner were equal. The few air attacks on Task Force 57 never offered a large group of enemy aircraft at which to fire. No *kikusui* or massed suicide air attacks were made on the British comparable with the ten such raids made on Task Force 58 and the shipping at Okinawa which the U.S. fast carriers were defending. The extent to which the massed attacks contributed to swell the figures of Japanese losses is clear from a comparison between the figures of the first part of the operation, when such attacks were of frequent occurrence, and the second part, when far fewer Japanese aircraft offered themselves to the Americans as targets. In the first period the ratio of enemy aircraft destroyed in the air to those destroyed on the ground was $3\frac{1}{2}$ to 1 ; in the second part of the operation it was little more than $1\frac{1}{4}$ to 1.

9

At the start of our operations in ' Iceberg ' it was found that events in the war against Japan had overtaken planning in so far as the composition of the Fleet Train was concerned. The unexpectedly rapid advance into the Philippines had placed our advanced anchorage rather more than twice as far ahead of our shore bases as had originally been contemplated, and in the absence of shore facilities, this naturally had a direct effect on the number of ships required to keep the fleet supplied at the advanced anchorage. The comparatively new American policy of replenishment at sea had to be provided for, whilst the few attendant tankers originally allocated to deal with the old type of warfare with ships based on harbours, were inadequate to deal with a type of operating in which the fleet, virtually based at sea off the enemy coast, was entirely dependent on its tankers. The British striking force had to adopt this policy or content itself with no more than spasmodic raids.

Rear-Admiral Fisher, who commanded the Fleet Train, was responsible to Admiral Rawlings for keeping the Fleet directly supplied, including the transport of supplies from the supply bases to the Fleet ; arrangements for the evacuation of sick and wounded by sea ; mails and amenities for the Fleet ; chart offices afloat ; and salvage. (*See* Appendix Z). The ships composing the Fleet Train included oilers, armament store issuing ships capable of transferring at sea bombs and all types of projectiles including 14-inch, victualling store issuing ships, hospital ships, repair ships, a tug, a collier, a water boat. Sixty-nine vessels in all, including the screen, were employed on Fleet Train duties during Operation ' Iceberg '. (*See* Appendix T). The Fleet Train ferried supplies from Leyte to the fuelling area, a distance of some 700 miles each way, to which the striking force returned approximately every third or fourth day. Three or four Logistic Support Groups were formed to perform the duty of ferrying, the total number of vessels employed in the Logistic Support Groups being nine tankers, five escort carriers, and one armament store issuing ship, a hospital ship and a tug. Fifteen escort vessels were used as screens. Combat air patrol and anti-submarine duties were performed by an escort carrier and screen which operated under the orders of the Commander Logistic Support Group. Ferry carriers were required for transporting reserve aircraft from Australia to the advanced anchorage, whilst the new sea-based type of warfare made it necessary to provide replenishment carriers to transfer aircraft to the fuelling area off the enemy coast and fly them across to the fleet carriers operating from there. For these duties, six fighting escort carriers were reduced to the role of ferry or replenishment carriers. The duties of the replenishment carriers included maintenance of all types of operational aircraft, for during the early days, while the British Fleet was operating from Leyte, adequate air facilities did not exist. This entailed sending forward from Australia aircraft in fully serviceable condition, and the subsequent care of five—and later six—types of aircraft imposed a great strain on the maintenance ratings in the replenishment carriers. These carriers also performed a variety of tasks in connection with the transfer at sea of stores and casualties, as there was no other means of performing them. The Fleet Train anchorage was largely fixed by the question of fuel tankers, but the replenishment carriers were tied to their airfields and replenishment ports, which might or might not be at the same place so that these carriers might very well have to operate from a different anchorage from the remainder of the Fleet Train. Subsequently, therefore, the Air Logistics Groups were separated from the Fleet Train under the title Air Train, which was placed under the command of a Commodore (COMAT) who was himself responsible to Rear-Admiral, Fleet Train.[1]

Most of the ships in the Fleet Train were manned by merchant seamen, for the shortage of trained naval personnel in the British Commonwealth rendered it impossible to replace their crews by naval officers and ratings. Many of the ships were entirely foreign manned: Dutch, French, Belgian, Norwegian, Danish, Lascar and Chinese seamen were all represented in this heterogeneous assembly of foreign merchantmen, H.M. Ships, and red and blue ensign ships. The administration of such a force was in itself a most difficult problem, even before taking into consideration the diverse functions performed by each of these ships. It was carried out by a Commodore, Second-in-Command, Fleet Train (COFT).

At the outset, the Fleet Train comprised 65 vessels. By the end of Operation 'Iceberg' it had grown in number to 109. Most of the ships composing it had not originally been intended for the purpose. This threw a great strain on the Fleet Train. The flagship, the *Lothian*, had been fitted out as a Headquarters Ship for combined operations in northern latitudes; she was seriously overcrowded and, in the tropical heat of the Pacific, conditions were very bad. The limitations in endurance imposed by the construction of the merchant ships constituting the majority of the Fleet Train, their inadequate complements, the poor state of repair which delayed several in joining and necessitated an abnormal amount of maintenance, and the heterogeneity of ships within types and classes both as to speeds and loads, rendered planning and operation difficult. At the beginning of the operation the replenishment carriers were not worked up for the duties they were called upon to perform. Their complements of air maintenance ratings were inadequate and had to be made up by drafting men, many of whom had never been to sea. All ships had a most limited range of air stores and had to maintain operational aircraft for far longer periods than had been expected.

It was in refuelling at sea, however, that the deficiencies of the Fleet Train were chiefly felt and, incidentally, that the importance of co-ordination between operations and logistics was most clearly apparent. Apart from the all too small

[1] COMAT hoisted his broad pendant on 10th June. His duties are defined in Appendix ZA.

number of tankers available (three for the first two fuellings and thereafter five, with a sixth on one occasion) the tankers had insufficient pumping capacity and lacked adequate means of transferring fuel and aviation spirit. Some tankers could only pass through one hose astern, others carried no aviation spirit, hoses for aviation spirit were too small, and so forth. The method adopted for fuelling big ships astern was much slower than the United States Navy method of fuelling all ships alongside. Both H.M. Ships and tankers had had insufficient practice, resulting in bad station keeping and slow handling of gear. Oiling gear, hoses and fittings were in bad condition, and there was lack of spare hoses. The expenditure of hoses was so greatly in excess of anything anticipated, that at one time Admiral Rawlings signalled to the Commander-in-Chief that the shortage might become the deciding factor in the length of time he could continue operations ; and hoses had to be flown from Australia to enable the fleet to continue to operate. During the first part of Operation ' Iceberg ' delays were caused by bad weather and heavy swell. In the second part of the operation supplies were sufficient but with no margin whatever. But through great exertions and makeshifts the result was attained, that no fleet operation was ever curtailed or postponed on account of delay in delivery of fuel.

The striking force of the British Pacific Fleet, on arrival at Manus on 7th March to undertake fuelling and provisioning before moving up to the combat area, found awaiting it such vessels—27 in all—of the Fleet Train as the Admiralty had been able to provide, and the authorities to load and despatch from Sydney in the intervals between the incessant waterfront strikes which made working to a date so difficult when loading ships in Australia. The necessity for fleet training during this period added to the difficulties of replenishment. The Fleet was ill-provided to meet the conditions prevailing in the huge anchorage. Small gales blew. The swell made large and strong catamarans a necessity for fuelling heavy ships ; but the British had none. The great distances over water called for numerous harbour service craft ; but these were in short supply, for although the requirement for boats had been forecast with a high degree of accuracy the lack of suitable shipping to move them forward resulted in their not being where they were needed. There were difficulties of communication with the fleet auxiliaries anchored miles away from the Fleet. Refrigerated stores were affected by the heat. The Fleet was short of 179,000 gallons of water per day, but there was little water at Manus and the Fleet had no proper waterboat.

As the decision to employ the British Pacific Fleet in Operation ' Iceberg ' was taken only a few days before the striking force had to sail from Manus, no planning of air replenishment was possible, and with only two available replenishment carriers, the *Striker* and the *Slinger*, the supply of aircraft to Task Force 57 was very much on a hand to mouth basis.

On 23rd April, on the conclusion of the first part of Operation ' Iceberg ', Task Force 57 arrived at Leyte, in order to replenish with stores, provisions, fuel and ammunition. Owing to postponement of about a week in the anticipated date of arrival, half the perishables went bad before they could be issued. This replenishment was easier than the former one, at Manus. The distances in harbour were less long and the climate was better. The Fleet was fortunate in that the weather was good, for had there been any swell the work might not have been completed on time, for lack of suitable fenders. Once again, there was an acute shortage of harbour craft. In order to make every boat of the Fleet Train available all shore leave was stopped. The Americans lent landing craft, and in terms of lift, 54 per cent. of the boats were American. The tankers were overworked and had little rest or opportunity for repairs.

The escort carriers *Striker* and *Ruler* sailed from Leyte on 3rd May, two days after Task Force 57 sailed to begin the second part of Operation 'Iceberg'. The *Ruler* carried 18 Hellcats and four Avengers for Combat Air Patrol duties. Of these, six Hellcats and one Avenger were lost while landing or taking-off, three pilots losing their lives. Six of the Hellcat pilots had not previously deck-landed this type of aircraft and had had no deck-landing training apart from that provided during their initial training. Unlike the U.S. replenishment carriers, those of the British Pacific Fleet (entirely American-built escort carriers) were not fast enough to fly-off certain types of aircraft under 'no wind' conditions. Their catapults could not be used to launch British type aircraft: thus when there was insufficient wind a large proportion of the aircraft could not be transferred to the fleet carriers at sea.

The weather during the second part of Operation 'Iceberg' was ideal for fuelling at sea, and it was possible by placing small working parties on board the tankers to complete fuelling the Task Force in one day, though a second day in the fuelling area was always necessary in order to give the limited maintenance crews of the carriers time to carry out normal upkeep and overhaul work on their aircraft as well as to keep pilot fatigue down to an acceptable minimum.

During the operation about 180,000 tons of oil fuel were supplied to Task Force 57, as well as over 2,000 tons of aviation fuel and 140 aircraft. The two repair ships H.M.S. *Artifex* and H.M.S. *Resource,* with the destroyer depot ship *Tyne* successfully effected all necessary repairs to the Fleet that did not require docking; and they also carried out much light construction work, such as fenders for harbour fuelling of carriers, and considerable remodelling and alteration work. The biggest task was the repair of the *Indefatigable's* battle damage which was carried out in six working days, and the ship sailed fully operational. The floating docks were still on passage at the time of the operation, and such dockings as were necessary were carried out by the U.S. Navy.

On completion of the second part of Operation 'Iceberg' the Striking Force underwent a major replenishment and rehabilitation from 1st to 24th June. During this period the greater part of Task Force 37, as it had become with the change of U.S. Command on 27th May, together with some of the ships of the Fleet Train, went to Australian ports to replenish. Those ships of the Fleet for which there was no room at Australian ports had to undergo their replenishment from the Fleet Train at Manus. During this major replenishment period Okinawa Gunto was declared secured (21st June) and the next assignment of the British Pacific Fleet was in the assault on the Japanese homeland.

10

Whilst the British Pacific Fleet was undertaking major replenishment and repairs Admiral Rawlings formed Task Group 111.2 to neutralise the air installations on Truk (Figure 17) in order to decrease the threat of air attack on Allied forces near that area, another object of the raid being to give battle experience to units newly reporting to the Fleet. At 1700 on 12th June Rear-Admiral E. J. P. Brind took out from Manus Task Group 111.2, organised as follows:—

Task Unit 1: Fleet carrier *Implacable* (Flag of C.T.G. 111.2) (21 Avengers, 11 Fireflies, 48 Seafires).

Task Unit 2: *Swiftsure* (CL), *Ruler* (CVE), *Termagant* (DD).

Task Unit 5: Light cruisers H.M.C.S. *Uganda,* H.M.N.Z.S. *Achilles,* H.M.S. *Newfoundland.*

Task Unit 15: Destroyers *Troubridge, Tenacious, Terpsichore, Teazer.*

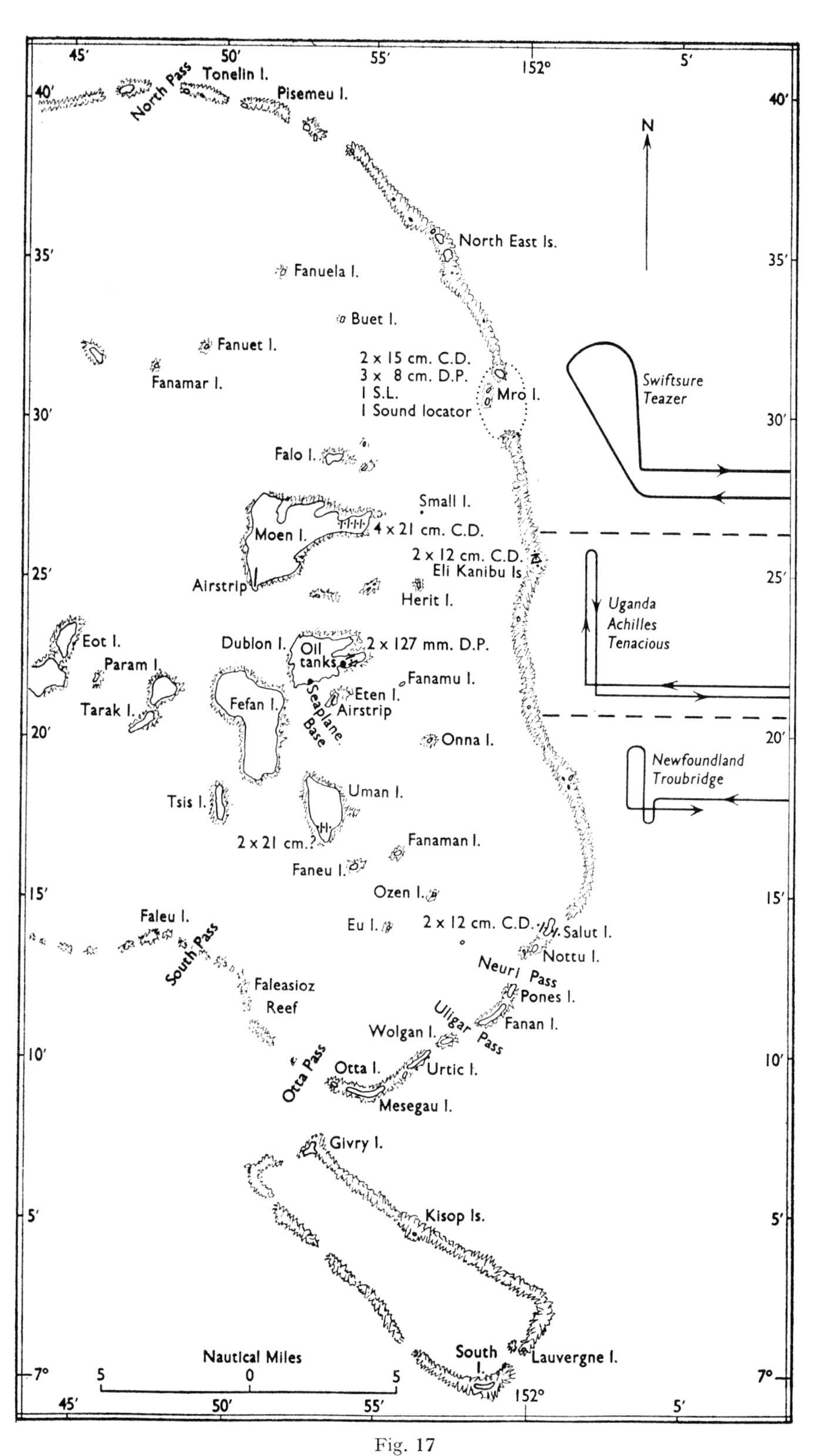

Tonelin I.
North Pass
Pisemeu I.
North East Is.
Fanuela I.
Buet I.
Fanuet I.
Fanamar I.
2 x 15 cm. C.D.
3 x 8 cm. D.P.
1 S.L.
1 Sound locator
Mro I.
Swiftsure
Teazer
Falo I.
Small I.
Moen I.
4 x 21 cm. C.D.
2 x 12 cm. C.D.
Eli Kanibu Is
Airstrip
Herit I.
Uganda
Achilles
Tenacious
Eot I.
Param I.
Tarak I.
Dublon I.
Oil tanks
2 x 127 mm. D.P.
Fanamu I.
Fefan I.
Seaplane Base
Eten I.
Airstrip
Onna I.
Newfoundland
Troubridge
Tsis I.
Uman I.
2 x 21 cm.
Fanaman I.
Faneu I.
Ozen I.
Eu I.
2 x 12 cm. C.D.
Salut I.
Nottu I.
Faleu I.
South Pass
Faleasioz
Reef
Neuri Pass
Pones I.
Fanan I.
Uligar Pass
Wolgan I.
Otta Pass
Otta I.
Urtic I.
Mesegau I.
Givry I.
Kisop Is.
South I.
Lauvergne I.
Nautical Miles
5
0
5
45′
50′
55′
152°
5′
40′
35′
30′
25′
20′
15′
10′
5′
7°
N

Fig. 17

None of the force except the *Swiftsure* had had any extensive gunnery experience with the British Pacific Fleet ; the *Implacable* and *Newfoundland* had none, but the former had experience in Norway and the latter had recently participated in a bombardment at Wewak in New Guinea. After the ships were under way, they received word from Manus that in addition to air attack bombardment should be included as part of the raid, and the necessary procedure was therefore practised *en route*. The group arrived in the launching area in the early evening of the 13th. Task Unit 3[1] was detached to be within 20 miles of the flying-off position (85 miles, 205° from Doublon Island) at dawn next day and to close the main body as soon as convenient later. The remainder of the Task Group increased speed to reach the flying-off position at 0530 on the 14th.

At the time of launching the first strike, H-hour, 0540, the force was on the northern edge of the inter-tropical front and encountered heavy rain squalls but it appeared the weather would be satisfactory over the target, and the first strike and photographic reconnaissance flight were flown-off. The value of a second flight deck was shown when the *Ruler* landed-on six Seafires which might otherwise have been in difficulties reaching and landing-on the *Implacable* which was in a heavy squall and had aircraft ranged for the next strike. The weather improved during the day, and the *Implacable* continued to strike at intervals of about 2¼ hours, whilst maintaining during daylight a combat air patrol of eight Seafires over the Task Group. All strikes were escorted. The force operated during the day between 80 and 60 miles from Doublon. Task Unit 3 and the *Ruler* remained conveniently close to the main body during daylight, ready for emergency landings and sharing the combat air patrol. A U.S. submarine and Catalinas stood by for Air-Sea Rescue, but were not called upon. Destroyers rescued several aircrews ditched near the fleet. Suitable targets were difficult to find owing to the heavy and frequent raids already made by the U.S. air forces.

At daylight on the 15th, the main body made rendezvous with Task Unit 3, some 80 miles east of Doublon. The bombardment group of four cruisers and three destroyers, with Rear-Admiral Brind on board the *Uganda*, separated from the remainder of the force and proceeded towards Truk, the carriers following ten miles to the eastward in order to provide combat air patrol. The approach was designed to achieve surprise if possible. The bombarding positions were chosen to enable as many as possible of the targets to be engaged by direct fire in the event of a failure of communications. The bombarding force was divided into three groups. The *Troubridge* was attached to the *Newfoundland*, the *Teazer* to the *Swiftsure*, and the *Tenacious* to the *Uganda* and *Achilles*, for counter battery fire and smoke cover if required. The *Implacable* flew off six Seafire spotters. In the centre, the *Uganda* and *Achilles*, 1,500 yards apart, carried out a simultaneous shoot at Doublon seaplane base at a range of about 20,000 yards, with 30 rounds per gun, whilst the *Swiftsure* and *Newfoundland*, acting independently, engaged coast defence batteries. Since the *Newfoundland's* target batteries made no reply, the ship engaged her alternative target, Eten airstrip. Except for the *Newfoundland*, the results of the bombardment were not up to the standard required, mainly owing to lack of practice. The operation of the *Uganda* and *Achilles* was a tale of communications disasters, one spotter attempting to control two ships, with technical failures superadded. The bombarding force withdrew at 1110, to rejoin the carriers. The *Implacable* continued to make air strikes until dusk, and carried out a night strike with six Avengers.

---

[1] The organisation of Task Unit 3 was as follows :—*Newfoundland, Swiftsure, Uganda Troubridge, Teazer, Tenacious.*

The force flew 103 day and 10 night offensive sorties and 103 defensive sorties. Seafires were used as fighter bombers and Fireflies used rockets. All strikes were escorted. Two enemy aircraft were destroyed. In addition, damage was caused to shipping, a floating dock, harbour installations, radio and radar equipment and shore batteries. The only opposition encountered was light A.A. fire which damaged three of our aircraft. Night intruders were operated. At 0600 on the 16th the force assembled and set course for Manus.

11

After 81 days of fighting Okinawa was secured, its garrison, the Japanese 32nd Army numbering 131,000, being killed or taken prisoners to the last man. The casualties of the U.S. Army and Marines were 7,213 killed and missing, and 31,081 wounded. Amongst the killed was the Army Commander, Lieutenant-General S. B. Buckner, Jr.

The U.S. Fifth/Third Fleet, including the British Task Force, suffered heavy casualties. In supporting the operations the American Fleet lost 539, the British 160 aircraft. U.S. Naval personnel casualties were 4,907 killed and missing and 4,824 wounded ; British 85 killed and missing and 83 wounded.

In the British force no ships were sunk, but three carriers and two destroyers were damaged. A fourth carrier was hit by a suicide aircraft which, however, caused practically no damage. In the American Fleet, out of 525 fighting ships which at the outset comprised the fleet 22 were sunk and 254 damaged. Amongst landing craft and auxiliaries 14 were sunk and 117 damaged. In no previous operation had the American naval losses in ships and men been so high, both in sum and in relation to those of the ground forces. Nearly half the damage and three out of four of the losses of ships were caused by suicide air attacks : the severity of these losses was due to the immobilisation of the fleets off Okinawa for nearly 12 weeks within range of an effective shore-based air force. This role was not one for which the carriers had been designed. It was forced on them by the stubborn Japanese defence which for long prevented the U.S. troops from obtaining airfields where they could base sufficient aircraft for their own protection ; in these circumstances, defence by evasion was not feasible, and active defence was prejudiced by the incomplete technical development of U.S. warning apparatus at that date. But their attacks cost the Japanese nearly 8,000 aircraft and destroyed their extra-metropolitan air forces.

The Okinawa campaign created a new, or at least an intensified problem in morale and well-being of the ships' crews. For nearly three months officers and men were subjected to almost daily air attacks and night nuisance raids ; they were seldom free from the menace of suicide boats—about 1,000 of which were destroyed—and submarines. They responded with alertness, skill and determination. The value of amenities in maintaining morale under difficult conditions was decisively proved at Okinawa, though to American and British crews the word amenities may well have had different meanings.

The capture of the islands provided the U.S. forces with air and naval bases within 350 miles of industrial Kyushu. A major fleet anchorage and a large number of potential airfields became available for the final assault on Japan.

CHAPTER XVI

The Final Air Assault on Japan

(Plans 24, 25.)

1

WITH the liberation of the Philippines and the capture of Iwo Jima and Okinawa the Americans stood on the threshold of Japan. A year earlier, the Joint Chiefs of Staff had faced and accepted the fact that unconditional surrender, on which the Allies insisted, might involve invasion of Japan as well as maritime (sea-air) blockade which had been in existence since the early days of the war. Before the assault on the Japanese home islands, or, indeed, any further major amphibious operation could be undertaken, there had to be a pause while U.S. air strength was being built up in the Ryukus and troops redeployed from the Philippines and elsewhere, including Europe where Germany had surrendered unconditionally on 8th May. In the Ryukus, on Okinawa and Ie Shima, the latter 'the most valuable eleven square miles of land in the Western Pacific', no less than 25 miles of paved airstrips were being constructed. Though there was a general belief at the highest naval and military levels that Japan could be brought to unconditional surrender by the pressure of maritime power,[1] nevertheless invasion preparations, which would need many months to complete, had to go on. On 25th May the Joint Chiefs-of-Staff issued the directive for a landing on Kyushu (Operation 'Olympic') to take place on 1st November, and three weeks later President Truman approved the directive.[2]

---

[1] The views of President Roosevelt on the possibility of forcing surrender by maritime power alone, with which General MacArthur and Admiral Nimitz finally agreed at a meeting with the President at Honolulu in July 1944, are given in *I Was There*, by Fleet-Admiral W. D. Leahy (pp. 291–6). Admiral Halsey's views are given in *Admiral Halsey's Story*, p. 261, and General Arnold's in *The Army Air Forces in World War II*, Vol. V, pp. 17, 26, 27, *inter alia*. The views of Admiral Spruance, who alternated with Halsey in operational command of the U.S. Fleet in the central Pacific, are not known.

[2] On 9th August 'Majestic' was substituted for 'Olympic' because of possible compromise of the latter code name through its publication in a restricted document.

The Americans had not yet solved the question of supreme command in the Pacific theatre. Primary in the operation of invading Japan was the land campaign, and consequently primary responsibility for the landing was assigned to General MacArthur. This included control of the actual amphibious assault through appropriate naval commanders, but MacArthur was directed to ' co-operate ' with Admiral Nimitz in planning the amphibious phase of the operation. For this phase Nimitz would bear the responsibility, and he was to ' correlate ' his plans with MacArthur.[1] The Ryukus, where the operation was to be mounted, were transferred to General MacArthur on 31st July, 1945.

Meanwhile, already defeated though the Japanese were, it was necessary to exert unremitting pressure on them, in order if possible to bring them to the state of mind to admit defeat without invasion. This was to be effected by air assault. In the Ryukus, at the beginning of July 1945, a new army air force was formed independent of General MacArthur, Commander-in-Chief, Army Forces in the Pacific. Known as the U.S. Army Strategic Air Force in the Pacific (USASTAF) it was constituted from the 20th Air Force (B–29s) and the 8th Army Air Force re-deployed from Europe and re-equipped with B–29s.[2] Its commander, General C. A. Spaatz, fresh from victory in Europe and enjoying unequalled prestige in the field of strategic bombardment, was given the task, under General Arnold,[3] of carrying out strategic air operations against Japan with the object of accomplishing the progressive destruction and dislocation of the country's military, industrial and economic systems to a point where her capacity for armed resistance to invasion would be fatally weakened. It may be noticed, however, that a number of the urban area targets chosen by the Field Command of the 20th Air Force, were more consistent with the object of securing a decision by air power alone.[4] In Okinawa, the Philippines, Marianas and Iwo Jima a new Tactical Air Force of the Pacific was formed from the 5th, 7th and 13th Army Air Forces with naval and marine Privateers and Mariners (patrol bombers, both) of Fleet Air Wing One. On 13th July, General G. C. Kenney, Commander of the former Far Eastern Air Force, was given command of this force under General MacArthur. This was the force which would support the landings in Japan. Meanwhile, the aircraft were conducting operations against air power in the Japanese Empire on a wide assignment, attacking enemy shipping lanes in order to isolate Japan from the Asiatic mainland, interrupting land communications in Kyushu and Western Honshu, destroying or neutralising military concentrations and vital installations in those areas, conducting aerial reconnaissance and photography ; whilst as from 20th July they were to attack air installations, rail, road and water communications, industries and port facilities in north China and Korea ; and after neutralizing enemy air power, to blockade the Yangtze river, destroying port facilities on the Korean coast, and knock out rail repair facilities.[5] From the Marianas, B–29s of the 20th Air Force were conducting an intensive minelaying campaign of Shimonoseki Strait and the Inland Sea (Operation ' Starvation ')[6] to supplement the submarine and air blockade ; and to add to the ceaseless harrying of the Japanese, at the end of May U.S. submarines penetrated into the Sea of Japan, the last waters in which Japanese merchant shipping sailed without molestation by underwater craft.

---

[1] *The Army Air Forces in World War II*, Vol. V, p. 686.

[2] The 8th A.A.F. did not actually become operational in the Pacific before the surrender of Japan.

[3] General Arnold reported direct to the Joint Chiefs of Staff.

[4] *The Effects of Strategic Bombing on Japan's War Economy*, p. 36.

[5] *The Army Air Forces in World War II*, Vol. V, p. 695.

[6] *See* Volume V of this History.

These operations were now to be supplemented by aerial bombing and surface bombardment of Japan by the U.S. Third Fleet, including the British Pacific Fleet, with cruiser and destroyer sweeps in order to increase the pressure on the enemy already being exerted by the 15,000 Allied naval and 7,000 U.S. army first line combat aircraft based in the Pacific Theatre. To oppose these, the Japanese had probably little more than 10,000 first line aircraft, of which half were suicide planes. There was evidence of a general shortage of aviation fuel in Japan, and training groups had been ordered to use an absolute minimum and to store all possible for operational needs.[1] Mindful of the fantastic losses caused by suicide air attacks on the Fifth/Third Fleet in the Philippines and Ryukus, the Joint Chiefs-of-Staff laid down as one of the tasks of the Far Eastern Air Force to provide air protection for the Fleet whilst engaged in carrier strikes against Japan, as requested by the Commander-in-Chief, Pacific, by concentrating attacks on the Kyushu airfields.

2

The Fast Carrier Force of the British Pacific Fleet was released from Operation 'Iceberg' on 25th May and the U.S. Third Fleet on 10th June. The British ships retired to their rear base Sydney in Australia for major replenishment and training for the air assault on Japan, those for whom there was no room at Australian ports going to Manus to replenish from the Fleet Train, whilst the Americans retired to San Pedro harbour, Leyte. The objects of the assault were to reduce the tactical air strength of the enemy, to destroy any strategic targets which directly supported the Japanese war effort, and to assess the enemy war potential in northern Honshu and Hokkaido which were out of practical range of the land-based aircraft.[2] The objectives of the Third Fleet were modified during the course of the operations; the remnants of the Japanese Navy and Japanese shipping were made the primary target rather than the remaining Japanese air strength. The combined U.S. and British forces formed the U.S. Third Fleet under the command of Admiral Halsey. In this Fleet, Task Force 38, the U.S. Fast Carrier Force, was commanded by Vice-Admiral J. S. McCain. His force comprised at the time three task groups, two of which each contained three fleet and two light carriers, and the third four fleet and two light carriers, a larger number than the Americans had previously operated in a single group (*see* Appendix V). The total aircraft complement was 1191. Each group was screened as usual by battleships, cruisers and destroyers capable of keeping station with 33-knot carriers. The British force, Task Force 37, comprised four fleet carriers with screen (Appendix W). The total aircraft complement was 255. Tactical control of Task Force 37 was reserved to Admiral Rawlings, who, however, worked in close tactical co-operation with Task Force 38, conforming to their movements, and, in fact, acting to all intents and purposes as a Task

---

[1] General Signal, 3rd June 1945, by Chief of Staff of Combined Naval Forces (Admiral Toyoda, former Commander-in-Chief Combined Fleet). The Combined Naval Forces was an organisation formed in April 1945. It comprised the Combined Fleet, China Area Fleet, and all base forces as far south as Takao. Its first commander, Admiral Toyoda, was succeeded in May as Supreme Commander, by Admiral Ozawa.

[2] *Operations in the Pacific Ocean Areas during the Month of July* 1945, p. 4.

group of Task Force 38.[1] The British were to take part in battleship and cruiser bombardment as well as in surface sweeps. All replenishment with fuel and stores was to be done at sea. Japanese submarines were still operating, but no attacks were made on the Fleet. Precautions against attack were taken, but it seems probable that had the Japanese submarines showed enterprise the method of replenishing would have been very risky.

One of the stipulations of the agreement N–F1 which was the outcome of the conference between Admirals Nimitz and Fraser at Pearl Harbour prior to the operations (page 18) was that to the maximum practicable extent the British ships would constitute a separate task force with no more tactical co-ordination with the U.S. task forces than the situation required. ' I myself did not mean this to preclude the possibility of a British task group operating in an American force ', wrote Admiral Fraser, ' but the C.-in-C. Pacific appears to have taken it to mean that, and during the July operations he counterordered Com. Third Fleet's expressed intention to operate the British Task Group as a part of the American Fast Carrier Task Force '.[2] Actually, Admiral Halsey disregarded this restriction in practice, and operated the British Task Force as a group, as part of his own Task Force.

The operations, like those of the Strategic and Far Eastern Air Forces were mainly strategic, directed towards reducing Japan's capacity to resist invasion. It was not feasible from carriers' decks to mass the great air effort required to neutralize an industrial complex, but pointed at Japanese air power the role of the carriers was to destroy enemy aircraft, on the ground and in the air. The refusal of the Japanese to commit their aircraft in strength against any attacks short of invasion rendered it impossible, however, to destroy any considerable number in the air. On the ground, too, it was difficult to make substantial killings. Dispersal and camouflage had been carried to great lengths rendering good photographic reconnaissance essential. Aircraft were dispersed up to five miles from their airfields, cleverly camouflaged and concealed in every conceivable place, so that the Japanese air commander later told Halsey he could neither scramble his aircraft in reasonable time nor even communicate with them. Dispersal also diminished their anti-aircraft defence.

---

[1] Admiral Halsey in his memoirs, *Admiral Halsey's Story*, p. 261 gives the following account of the manner in which this co-operation was arranged.

> ' When I was informed at Pearl Harbour that the British Pacific Fleet would report to me, I naturally assumed that I would have full operational control, but when I re-read the plan at Leyte, I discovered that tactical control had been reserved. This would force me to present Admiral Rawlings with three alternatives, and I did so now :
>
> 1. T.F. 37 would operate close aboard us, as another task group in T.F. 38 ; it would not receive direct orders from me, but it would be privy to the orders that I gave T.F. 38 ; these it would consider as " suggestions " to be followed to our mutual advantage, thereby assuring us a concentrated force with concentrated weapons.
>
> 2. T.F. 37 would operate semi-independently, some 60 or 70 miles away, thereby preserving its technical identity at the cost of a divided force. (I stipulated that I would consent to this choice only if the request were put in writing.)
>
> 3. T.F. 37 would operate completely independently, against soft spots in Japan which we would recommend if so desired.
>
> Rawlings did not hesitate. He said, " Of course I'll accept Number 1." My admiration for him began at that moment.'

Admiral Rawlings in his Report (M.010175/45, Appendix No. 1, p. 1) says : ' The principal points which were settled forthwith were the desire of the British Task Force to work in close tactical co-operation with T.F. 38, conforming to their movements, and that we should take part in Battleship and Cruiser bombardments as well as in surface sweeps.'

[2] *Commander-in-Chief BPF Despatches, November* 1944–*July* 1945, M.059378/45, p. 95.

At the outset of the operations Admiral Halsey asked for maximum co-operation from the Far Eastern Air Force and the Strategic Air Force. In the event, co-operation was only moderately effective. Whilst various factors connected with the existing commitments of the land-based air forces and the distance of their airfields from the targets contributed largely to this,[1] the fundamental reason was, without doubt, the lack of a supreme commander in the Pacific.[2]

The Fleets achieved complete superiority in the air above their ships: no large scale attack was launched on the Fleets, but an extensive fighter direction and air warning organisation was employed in anticipation of attacks. In addition to the usual problems of air warning and interception the number of separate formations operating many miles apart, called for a central control which went far beyond anything previously required. A number of Japanese search aircraft and small parties of suiciders provided an ample test of the fighter defences of the Fleets, for suicide attacks on the radar pickets continued up to the end. Enemy aircraft that closed within 50 miles of any unit and escaped were the rare exception. The meagre total of 48 Japanese aircraft shot down by the combat air patrol in the neighbourhood of the Fleets shows how weak was the Japanese reaction. The most successful disposition of combat air patrol was found to be 20 fighters stacked up to 30,000 feet over each task group, with eight fighters at medium altitude and four more at 30,000 feet, over each radar picket group. More than half the kills resulted from interceptions through fighter direction in radar pickets. Three pickets, each composed of at least four destroyers were employed and were normally stationed 40–60 miles from the Fleet guide so as best to provide remote cover over 180° in the general direction of expected attack. The pickets were specially fitted and manned for their primary function, the control of aircraft. In the British Pacific Fleet, lacking destroyers fitted with any adequate equipment, strenuous efforts were made to train cruisers to the necessary standards and their aircraft direction room complements were increased accordingly. For the purpose of force control and reporting the British Task Force 37 acted as a group of Task Force 38 and accepted the directions of Task Force 38 Fighter Direction Officer. It is probable that the British did not reap the full benefit of all the information available owing to unfamiliarity with the organisation and the difficulties in relating air and surface plots.

3

Though the war with Germany ended in May, the resources necessary for rehabilitation at home left less for the Pacific than had been available earlier in the year. Expected reinforcements of ships and men were not forthcoming, and resources were even tighter than before.

The inferiority, compared with the Americans, of our ships, aircraft and equipment imposed a great strain on the crews of the British Pacific Fleet and

[1] *Report by BPF Liaison Officer to Com. Third Fleet, Third Fleet Operations, 1st July–15th August* 1945. M.09042/45.

[2] H.S. opinion. The inquisitive reader is referred to *The Army Air Forces in World War II*, Vol. V, pp. 695–96, where a rare official sidelight is given on the desire of the army air forces to knock out Japan by themselves.

jeopardised the part of the Fleet in the final operations leading to the surrender. The deficiencies which manifested themselves in the Ryukus, were still more afflictive, whilst others were superadded, now that we were working in company with the Americans and striking blow for blow with them. The U.S. carriers were faster, had clearer and larger flight decks, and better servicing and maintenance facilities on board. It has been said that had the British Fleet experienced very light winds during the strikes against Japan operations would have been hampered by the inadequate speed of our fleet carriers compared with the American ; whilst neither the *Formidable* nor the *Victorious* could have maintained their rate of striking for more than two successive strike days, owing to their limited fuel capacity. The U.S. aircraft were newer and of longer endurance. The lack of a night carrier was felt by us, even if only to provide a spare deck by day in case of an emergency landing whilst all carriers had aircraft ranged.

The greatest difficulty was experienced in keeping our ships supplied with fuel and certain essential stores, chiefly radar equipment. Shortage of stores was due in part to transport difficulties, but basically to the fact that ships were not adequately stored before leaving base. The difficulties of fuel supply arose from other reasons. Despite every contrivance and a fair measure of good fortune the inadequacy of our too few and slow tankers, their low rate of pumping (about half that of the American oilers), and the poor quality of their new British hoses finally defeated our efforts to stay the full course with the Americans, possessing as our Allies did, a sufficient number of large, fast fleet oilers with a high rate of pumping. Our bulk fuel points were at Eniwetok and Manus, distant from 5 to 14 days' steaming from the operating areas : whilst the areas of striking and consequently the fuelling positions, might be changed by 500 miles or more without warning, the British Pacific Fleet was working on no margin with tankers ; the number and speed of those available did not allow enough to be kept permanently close to the operating area ; and a very serious situation was developing when the end of the war provided a breathing space. That the British force never missed a day's operations between 17th July and 10th August, must be ascribed in the main to the typhoons which by requiring many changes in the Commander Third Fleet's plan, gave Admiral Rawlings invaluable time. Even so, on 6th–7th August two escort carriers of the Fleet Train were used to supply fuel, and Task Force 37 was compelled on two occasions to borrow oil from the American Fleet. Most of our ships had to haul out through lack of oil before the conclusion of operations, leaving a token force to continue to operate in the U.S. Third Fleet.

The aircraft complements of the British carriers had been increased to figures not greatly below those of the U.S. carriers of comparable age.[1] Replacements brought out by ferry cruisers ultimately met all the Fleet's requirements, largely owing to the cancellation of part of the strike programme due to a typhoon. The intensity of flying of the fighter aircraft both absolutely and relatively was more than four times as great as during the Ryukus operation, and that of the Avengers nearly one-fifth greater. Our aircraft were still inferior to the American as in Operation ' Iceberg '. On one occasion, the attack on the Japanese battleship *Nagato*, our forces did not take part, (primarily), reported our liaison officer with the Third Fleet, ' because of the shorter range

[1] The average complement of the ten U.S. fleet carriers and six light fleet carriers used in the final operations was about 74. The complements of the four British fleet carriers were as follows :—*Formidable*—54, *Victorious*—53, *Implacable*—78, *Indefatigable*—70 ; average—66.

of their aircraft '.[1] The short endurance of the Seafires continued to be a source of anxiety. The U.S. Fleet struck normally at ranges between 150 and 230 miles from the target. Strikes by Avengers and Corsairs from the *Formidable* and the *Victorious* were launched at an average of 185 miles distance, though the former ship records one strike travelling approximately 300 miles to its target. Strikes by Seafires, Fireflies and Avengers from the *Implacable* and *Indefatigable* were launched at ranges between 85 and 195 miles. By fitting the Seafire L.III with 89-gallon jettison tanks the *Implacable* (Captain C. C. Hughes-Hallett) was able to send these aircraft to the nearer targets, but they could carry no bombs. As the Seafire could not be effectively operated above 15,000 feet, they were not even available for the upper flight of the combat air patrol. Nevertheless, there had been a great increase in their efficiency since March, and they flew about twice as many sorties and about three times as many hours per aircraft per day as in March and April.

The British Pacific Fleet continued to employ the U.S. system of signals, but our equipment was inadequate. A normal day's traffic was about 250 messages by V/S, 350 in Bridge Receiving Room, and 650 on the foxes[2], the latter representing about 60,000 groups, of which 50 per cent was normally broken down. The number of VHF circuits for communications generally which were required when working with the Americans was far more than had been allowed for, and had the Americans not loaned sets, the force would have been hard put to maintain satisfactory communication. The Americans themselves were none too well off in this respect. 'New ships continue to report to the active war zone with antiquated communication facilities', reported Commander Task Force 38. 'The Navy afloat is forced to "muddle on" with phones and radio installations that were old prior to the outbreak of war'.[3] The Americans used R/T for all purposes. In the British ships, R/T had not been universally adopted and taught, and a high standard of R/T operating could only be maintained in most ships provided not more than one or two circuits were manned. Very little use was made of flag signalling as, in large circular dispositions, that method of manœuvring was too slow. Our daylight signalling lamps were not sufficiently powerful for ships on the screen to read them.

For air defence, complete reliability and flexibility of communications were essential. These we did not have. Much anxiety was caused by material failures in ships' radio equipment working aircraft. The sets were too few and were overworked. The HF equipment failed to maintain the necessary communications at ranges up to 60–70 miles, while the tedious process of tuning the transmitters was an offence to the Force as a whole. With regard to fighter direction and air warning, Admiral Rawlings reported: 'Whereas in the matter of Radar Equipment, the superiority of the Americans was only a matter of degree[4], and the British had little difficulty in maintaining a tolerable standard of warning at all times, the communications were a constant anxiety and at all times threatened the organisation with complete break-down.[5]

---

[1] Report of Commander C. E. A. Owen, B.P.F.L.O. to C.T.F. 38, dated 26th August 1945, para. 30. But see p. 223, where the reasons for Halsey's decision that the British should not participate in attack on Japanese major fleet units, are given.

[2] Broadcast method of communication not requiring an answer from the stations addressed.

[3] *T.F.* 38. *Action Report Operations against Japan 2nd July–15th August* 1915, M.0957/45, Encl. (E), p. 2.

[4] The British radar equipment was superior to the U.S. from the point of view of high cover. With low cover and fighter direction radar the position was reversed.

[5] *Report of V.A. 2nd i/c BPF and FOC 1st Aircraft Carrier Squadron in BPF*, M.010175/45.

4

JULY

10th	Aircraft strikes by Task Force 38 (Third Fleet Fast Carrier Force) against airfields on Tokyo plain.
14th	Surface bombardment of Japan Ironworks, Kamaishi, by Task Unit 34.8.1.
14th–15th	Aircraft strikes by Task Force 38 against Kushiro, Muroran and Aomori; destruction of Hokkaido–Honshu railway ferry system.
15th	Surface bombardment of Japan Steel Co. and Wanishi Iron and Steel Mfg. Co., Muroran by Task Unit 34.8.2.
17th	Surface bombardment by Task Unit 34.8.2 and Task Unit 37.1.6. (*King George V*, *Quality*, *Quiberon*) of industrial area in and around Hitachi and Mito.
17th–18th	Aircraft strikes by Task Force 38 and Task Force 37 (British Pacific Fleet) on Tokyo airfields. (Weathered out after two strikes).
18th	Aircraft strikes by Task Force 38 and Task Force 37 against Yokosuka Naval Base and airfields.
Night, 18th–19th	U.S. light cruiser/destroyer bombardment of radar installations at Cape Nojima, followed by anti-shipping sweep across entrance to Sagami Bay.
23rd	Anti-shipping sweep by Destroyer Squadron 61 off Sagami Bay.
24th–25th	Aircraft strikes by Task Force 38 and Task Force 37 on remaining units of Japanese Fleet in the Inland Sea and on airfields and shipping in the area south and West Honshu, Shikoku and Kyushu.
24th	Anti-shipping sweep by U.S. light cruisers and destroyers across Kii Suido.
25th	The above force bombarded Kushimoto Seaplane Base and Shionomisaki Landing Field.
28th	Second series of aircraft strikes by Task Force 38 and Task Force 37 on Japanese naval units in the Inland Sea. Final destruction of Japanese Fleet.
Night, 29th–30th	Task Unit 34.8.1 and Task Unit 37.1.2 (*King George V*, *Undine*, *Urania*, *Ulysses*) bombarded Hamamatsu.
	Strikes by Task Force 38 and Task Force 37 against Central and South-West Honshu and the Inland Sea.
31st	Anti-shipping sweep of Suguru Gulf and bombardment of Shimizu by Destroyer Squadron 25.

AUGUST

9th	Strike by Task Force 38 and Task Force 37 aircraft on airfields and shipping in Northern Honshu–Hokkaido. Task Unit 34.8.1 and Task Unit 37.1.8 (*Newfoundland*, *Gambia*, *Terpsichore*, *Termagant*, *Tenacious*) bombarded Kamaishi.
10th	Aircraft strikes by Task Force 38 and Task Force 37 on airfields in Northern Honshu and Tokyo areas.
13th	Task Force 38 (including British group) aircraft attacked airfields in Tokyo area.
15th	Strikes against Tokyo airfields by Task Force 38 halted at 0700.

5

The U.S. Fast Carrier Force under Vice-Admiral S. McCain in the fleet carrier *Shangri-La* made its first strike on 10th July, Admiral Halsey being present in the battleship *Missouri*. The first aircraft strikes were chiefly exploratory, directed against airfields in the Tokyo plain where the Japanese still maintained considerable air strength, for the most part fighter interceptors for use against B–29s, and new aircraft awaiting assignment. There were also numerous primary and intermediate trainers which had been converted into suicide bombers and were being saved for use against the expected invasion.

Extensive preliminary reconnaissance for Japanese pickets and minefields had been made by aircraft and submarines, the Americans having in the Spring introduced a sonar device which enabled their submarines to plot minefields successfully. In the advance towards Japan air barriers were flown to prevent discovery and a secret anti-picket sweep of seven submarines preceded Task Force 38, the submarines afterwards assuming positions in the air-sea rescue organisation ; the Japanese had, however, withdrawn the flotillas of small craft which formerly infested the waters within 300 miles from their main islands. Tactical surprise was achieved. There was almost no air opposition and only two enemy aircraft were destroyed in the air, though 340 were claimed destroyed on the ground ; the Task Force was not attacked. Admiral Halsey made public the names of some of the attacking ships, and no attempt was made to conceal the position of Task Force 38.

After replenishing at sea the force moved northward for attacks against northern Honshu and Hokkaido. Fog prevented further strikes being launched until the 14th and 15th. The airfields which were the primary target were weathered in and targets of opportunity were consequently attacked. The most important damage was the destruction of the Hakodate–Aomori railway ferry system. Of the 12 railway ferries eight were sunk, two were beached and flooded, and two under repair were damaged, whilst numerous cargo vessels engaged in transporting coal between Hakodate and Aomori were sunk. The most important immediate effect of the strike was a reduction of half to two-thirds of the monthly coal shipments between Hokkaido and Honshu, which were essential to Japanese industry, in addition to cutting off important agricultural supplies of the northern island. The Japanese possessed no suitable replacements for these ferries and were unable at that stage of the war to build new ones expeditiously.

On 14th July, while the air strikes were in progress, a small battleship and cruiser force, Task Unit 34.8.1 (Appendix V), formed from Task Force 38, carried out from a point off the coastal city of Kamaishi the first surface bombardment of the Japanese homeland, the target being out of practicable range of B.29s based in the Marianas. The primary target was the Kamaishi Iron Works. Fire was opened at 1210, range 26,000 yards, closing. At 19,000 yards reduced charges were used instead of service charges. The bombardment continued for two hours, the lack of minesweepers compelling the ships to remain outside the 100-fathom curve, for the minesweepers were carrying out a minesweeping operation in the East China Sea.[1]

No shore batteries replied and no aircraft rose to retaliate. Severe damage resulted. This was the first industrial target to which photographic interpretation had been applied in order to analyse the damage caused. It failed to reveal

[1] T.F. 39, comprising 121 minesweepers with supporting vessels, swept 7,300 square miles and destroyed 404 mines without casualty to any ship. The operations lasted from 5th to 30th July. The minesweepers remained, however, under Third Fleet control until 17th July. A further minesweeping operation took place between 11th and 25th August, 578 mines being destroyed.

the true extent of the damage. Hits were spread over the whole target but density was insufficient to destroy any major building, and structural roof damage, as revealed by photographs, was subsequently found to be an unsatisfactory index for estimating physical damage or production losses caused by base-detonating projectiles. Accordingly, the works were bombarded again in the following month, as will be described in due course.

During the night, another battleship and cruiser Task Unit, 34.8.2[1] was detached from Task Force 38 and at dawn on the 15th bombarded Muroran for four hours, the primary targets being the Wanishi Iron Works and the Japan Steel Company's works. Fire was opened at 28,000 yards.

The weather was hazy and the sky overcast which rendered spotting and accurate observation of damage difficult. Here, too, examination of aerial photographs resulted in an underestimate being made of the damage done to the Wanishi Iron Works. The importance of good intelligence of targets was shown by the fact that the second primary target attacked, the Japan Steel Company's works, had already declined greatly in importance. Intelligence failed to indicate this.

6

The system of command in the British Fleet was similar to that used in Operation 'Iceberg' (*see* page 182). U.S. lifeguard submarines and aircraft were used.

The following ships formed Task Force 37 in the early stages. Owing to the failure of all the air compressors fitted in the *Indefatigable* only three carriers were available for the first strikes.

1st Battle Squadron	*King George V* (Flag of C.T.F. 37).
1st Aircraft Carrier Squadron	*Formidable* (Flag of Second-in-Command and A.C.1).
	Victorious.
	Implacable.
4th Cruiser Squadron ..	*Newfoundland* (Flag of C.S.4).
	Black Prince.
	Euryalus.
	Achilles.
	H.M.C.S. *Uganda*.
	H.M.N.Z.S. *Gambia*.
4th Destroyer Flotilla ..	*Grenville* (Captain D.4).
	Undine.
	Urania.
	Urchin.
	Ulysses.
	Undaunted.
	H.M.A.S. *Quiberon*.
	H.M.A.S. *Quickmatch*.
	Quality.
	Quadrant.
24th Destroyer Flotilla ..	*Troubridge* (Captain D.24).
	Tenacious.
	Termagant.
	Terpsichore.
	Teazer.

[1] *See* Appendix V. The *North Carolina*, *Alabama* and *Wadleigh* did not take part in the bombardment.

The *Indefatigable* joined on 20th July, with the destroyers *Wakeful, Wrangler* and *Barfleur* (Flag of R.A.D.). The *Uganda* left for Esquimalt on the 27th, on relief by the *Argonaut* which had joined on the previous day. After 12th August, a token force, consisting of the *King George V, Indefatigable, Gambia, Newfoundland, Troubridge, Termagant, Tenacious, Teazer, Terpsichore, Barfleur,* H.M.A.S. *Napier,* H.M.A.S. *Nizam, Wakeful* and *Wrangler* remained with the Third Fleet. Owing to lack of oil, the remainder of the British Pacific Fleet returned to base.

The British Pacific Fleet (Appendix W) sailed from Sydney on 28th June on its road northwards to rendezvous with the U.S. Third Fleet and take its share in the Allied operations against Japan. The Fleet fuelled at Manus and again between 13th and 15th July in position 34° 10′ N., 155° 30′ E. Owing to the inadequacies of the tankers, fuelling, even without the *Indefatigable* and three destroyers, was only completed in time thanks to a 24-hour postponement by the Commander Third Fleet, on account of bad weather, of the scheduled strikes. The *King George V*, after repeated partings of messengers and burstings of buoyant hoses, was forced to fuel alongside an oiler, although she was not fitted for this purpose. Fuelling was successful and set a precedent in the Royal Navy for battleships fuelling alongside at sea during operations. The Fleet joined the Third Fleet at 0645 on 16th July in 39° 10′ N., 148° 30′ E., where the method of tactical co-operation was settled at a meeting between the two Commanders-in-Chief on board the *Missouri*. The combined Fleet was formed in four groups in the order from north to south Task Force 37, Task Group 38.1, Task Group 38.4, Task Group 38.3, and proceeded to the flying-off position in approximately 37° N., 143° E., for the attack next day on airfields, installations and shipping in the area north of Tokyo. The weather was bad and the Americans flew off only two strikes, neither of which were able to find their targets. Our own aircraft found the weather over their targets slightly better, and four out of the six strikes launched were successful.[1] As the day progressed the weather deteriorated and Admiral Halsey cancelled the remaining strikes. Bombs dropped in the British strikes were 83 × 500 lb., together with 28 × 60-lb. rocket projectiles. We destroyed nine enemy aircraft on the ground and damaged nine. Anti-aircraft fire shot down three of our aircraft, but the pilots were saved.

At 1430 on the 17th the *King George V*, screened by the *Quality* and *Quiberon* as Task Unit 37.1.6, detached from the main body and joined a U.S. battleship and cruiser bombarding group under Rear-Admiral Oscar Badger (Task Unit 34.8.2 *see* Appendix V) for attack on the heavily industrialised area in and around Hitachi and Mito. For this first combined U.S.-British bombardment of Japan the *King George V*, operating independently with her screening destroyers, was assigned targets similar to those of the U.S. battleships.[2] One SP picket destroyer was stationed ten miles or more on the disengaged side, where there was freedom from echoes. The raid was carried out in rain and fog by night with light air cover. A night combat air patrol was employed for the first time in the war by us. Due to the low foreshore, the navigational problem was difficult. The weather was too bad for the spotting aircraft to fly, consequently flare ranging was impracticable. Firing began at 2310 and continued

[1] Launchings were as follows: *Formidable*—28 Corsairs (two strikes); *Implacable*—eight Fireflies, 12 Seafires; *Victorious*—28 Corsairs (two strikes), Total 78, of which 16 Corsairs and 12 Seafires failed to find their targets. The targets attacked were Masuda, Sendai, Matsushima, and Niigata airfields.

[2] The *King George V*'s targets were an unidentified industry (97 × 14-inch rounds), Hitachi Engineering Works ' Densen ' (91 × 14-inch), and the Hitachi Engineering Works ' Taga ' (79 × 14-inch).

for about an hour, shooting entirely by radar and loran navigation nearly 2,000 tons of shells being fired at ranges between 28,800 and 26,000 yards. Poor visibility made it impossible to determine immediately the damage caused. Subsequent photographic reports showed that three out of the nine target areas assigned, were hit. Damage in the industrial area was slight. There were in the area several works of the Hitachi Manufacturing Company concerned with the electrical equipment, copper refining and armament industries. The largest works the Kaigan Plant, which produced 25 per cent. of the total Japanese heavy electrical power generating equipment, had been heavily damaged by a B–29 high explosives' attack prior to 17th July, and was consequently not a target for surface bombardment. The built-up area and essential services were considerably damaged. The damage was increased by a B–29 incendiary attack some 24 hours later: many people had evacuated the city after the bombardment and were consequently not available to fight fires; and as a result about 78 per cent. of the built-up area was destroyed or damaged.

The *King George V* was released to rejoin Task Force 37 at 0715 on the 18th, and as the weather was unsuitable for flying Admiral Halsey turned the whole Fleet south to search for better weather. At 1130, the weather having improved, strikes were ordered to be flown-off. The last minute changes in target assignments rendered necessary by the weather, coupled with the delay incidental in passing the originator's orders by R/T through another Task Group to our force on an overcharged line, left insufficient time for briefing, but delay in departure of the strikes was unacceptable. The striking power of Task Group 37 was seriously impaired through the leakage of salt water into the petrol system of the *Victorious*, which resulted in the ship being able to despatch no more than one strike of six Corsairs during the day. The *Formidable* flew-off two strikes of 16 and eight Corsairs respectively, and the *Implacable* eight Fireflies and 20 Seafires in three strikes, to attack various airfields in the Tokyo area.[1] The primary target of Task Force 38 was the battleship *Nagato* at Yokosuka naval base. She was badly damaged but the Americans were using bombs, for due to the position of the ship it was not possible to launch torpedoes against her; and the *Nagato*, though damaged, remained afloat. As already mentioned, the British strikes were given a different target, on the ground of the short range of their aircraft. Twelve aircraft were destroyed and 18 damaged by our aircraft. Anti-aircraft fire was very heavy, the Americans lost 12 aircraft and 16 crew. Two of our Corsairs were lost with their pilots; and Seafires were near lost on two occasions whilst endeavour was made to find conditions clear enough in the fog, to land these low endurance aircraft.

7

That evening, while the Fleet retired to the fuelling area, a force of four U.S. light cruisers and a squadron of destroyers was detached and bombarded radar installations near Nojima Saki, the cruisers each firing five full salvos from their main batteries. Following the bombardment, the force carried out a sweep across the entrance to Sagami Bay, which drew blank. Destroyer Squadron 61 returned to Sagami Bay for another sweep in the early morning of the 23rd. Contact was made with a convoy of four ships, two of which the destroyers damaged. Another force of light cruisers and destroyers made a high-speed sweep across Kii Suido on the 24th, and bombarded Kushimoto Seaplane Base and Shionomisaki landing field and the radio station early on the following

[1] Nobara, Naruto, Chosi, Konoike, Natori, Kitakawa Airfields and Kitaura Seaplane Station.

morning. Destroyer Squadron 25 carried out a sweep of Suguru Gulf and a bombardment of Shimizu on the early morning of the 31st. These tactical bombardments were secondary to the sweeps, and the material damage caused by the brief shelling—seven minutes at Shimizu, five minutes at Nojima Saki, four minutes at Shionomisaki—was slight. The operation of Kushimoto Seaplane base was not affected. No aircraft were on the landing field at Shionomisaki and no significant damage was caused ; the wireless station was not hit. The radar station at Nojima Saki remained unhit. Some damage was caused by the bombardment of the Shimizu area, but intelligence had failed to discover that one of the two targets, the Japan Light Metals Company's works, had already virtually ceased operation owing to shortage of raw materials and other causes.

8

The weather was too bad for flying on the 19th. The Fleet was due to refuel by noon on the 21st but Admiral Halsey shifted the fuelling rendezvous nearer to the next flying-off position and, fortunately for our ships, extended the replenishment period by 24 hours in order to re-ammunition his ships. The *Indefatigable* and three destroyers joined the Fleet on the 20th with the British oiling group which was located about 0430 after an Avenger had been flown-off to search for it. The oilers were 2,500 tons short, for the *Indefatigable* had come up from Manus at high speed and hence required more fuel than anticipated ; and Admiral Rawlings was compelled to ask Halsey to fuel three of our cruisers, a request which the latter readily granted. Aircraft replenishment was carried out by the *Arbiter*. Again burst hoses and low pumping rates so reduced the rate of fuelling that the Task Force would not have been in time for the next strike had not the oiling course been westerly, that is, approaching the launching position. The future programme of the Fleets was by then sufficiently clear to show that it was essential that the pumping capacity of our tankers should be augmented by some means or other. Accordingly, the Rear-Admiral Fleet Train was instructed to fit the *Arbiter* with buoyant hose astern so that she could be used as an auxiliary oiler. Fuelling was completed by 1900 on the 21st. For the Americans, this was probably the largest replenishment ever carried out by a Fleet at sea. Task Force 38 took aboard about 55,000 tons of fuel oil, besides ammunition, stores and provisions, replacement aircraft and personnel.

The next replenishment on 26th and 27th July took place more than 700 miles from the position originally planned. With half the oiling force of four tankers never having oiled heavy ships before there was little hope for a quick fuelling. One of the oilers had been hurriedly converted at Sydney for abeam oiling only and was making her first appearance as a Fleet attendant oiler ; whilst another, which proved able to fuel from one side only and with a single hose astern, had been repaired in 48 hours at Manus after arriving from Colombo via Torres Strait with speed down to 7½ knots owing to a foul bottom and engine defects. The overall pumping rate was so slow that Admiral Rawlings had to ask Halsey to fuel the *Newfoundland* and *Achilles*, as there was otherwise no possibility of their being ready to leave on time. The practice of fuelling heavy ships alongside became firmly established on this day. After fuelling on the 26th the *King George V* successfully embarked 14-inch shells for trial.

9

By the 24th, the weather had improved sufficiently to enable air strikes to be resumed. The three-hour sortie was obligatory on us, this being the limit of Seafire endurance : the timing cycle had to be related to the American plan, rather than to convenience, in order that, as far as was practicable, the British force should be in wind with the U.S. force flying four-hour sorties. This was necessary for station-keeping purposes.

The target for Task Force 38 was Kure, where the principal remaining units of the Japanese Fleet lay under camouflage. The ships were immobilised through lack of fuel and some of them which were damaged, were reduced to an A.A. status only, though this may not have been known to the Americans ; and their powerlessness to interfere with any amphibious landing on the Japanese mainland had been demonstrated at Iwo Jima and Okinawa. But their destruction was a necessary prelude to invasion. In Halsey's view there were three reasons why the Japanese Fleet had to be destroyed. American self-respect demanded this, the only appropriate retaliation for Pearl Harbour. If, when Russia entered the war a supply line had to be established, it would run between Kamchatka and Hokkaido, a route so exposed that a few cruisers could dominate it. Finally, the Japanese must not be left with a fleet to be used as a bargaining asset after the war.[1] The enemy ships generally were anchored in non-torpedo water and the lines of attack and retreat of dive-bombers were covered by heavy concentration of anti-aircraft guns. Only the use of variable time-fuzed bombs saved the Americans very heavy losses. For the first time during these operations strong enemy airborne opposition was encountered. Complete destruction of the Fleet was not achieved on the 24th, though much damage was caused. There was for once good co-ordination with shore-based air power. Six hundred B–29s attacked aircraft industries and installations in the Tokyo–Nagoya area, 100 P–51s (fighters) from Iwo Jima attacked the Nagoya airfields, and various aircraft from Okinawa ranged over the whole of Kyushu. The aircraft carrier *Amagi* was seriously damaged and capsized, the battleship *Hyuga* and the heavy cruiser *Tone* were sunk, and numerous other ships were damaged. Strikes against the ships remaining afloat continued next day, but had to be cancelled at 1309, on account of the weather. Not until the 28th could action be resumed. The battleships *Ise* and *Haruna*, the heavy cruiser *Aoba*, the light cruiser *Oyodo*, flagship of the Commander-in-Chief, Combined Naval Forces, the old heavy cruisers *Iwate* and *Izumo*, and some lesser units were sunk, and many other ships were damaged. On the same day 79 B–24s (Liberators—heavy bombers) of the Far Eastern Air Force also attacked the remnants of the Japanese Fleet in an un-co-ordinated attack[2] in which the only results recorded by the Japanese were four bomb hits on the *Aoba*, whilst two B–24s were lost and 14 others damaged by flak. By the end of the day, the Japanese Navy had ceased to exist.

The British Pacific Fleet was not allowed to participate in the destruction of the Japanese Fleet. 'It was imperative', wrote Admiral Halsey, 'that we forestall a possible postwar claim by Britain that she had delivered even a part of the final blow that demolished the Japanese Fleet'.[1] The targets assigned to the British on the 24th were for the most part airfields, but included also Osaka, where there were no warships of prime importance, and shipping in the Inland Sea. Here an escort carrier (apparently the *Kaiyo*) received several hits with bombs and the frigates *C.D. No. 4* and *C.D. No. 30* were sunk and various minor vessels were damaged or sunk, in addition to destruction caused ashore. Fifteen enemy aircraft were destroyed. We flew-off 15 strikes, including

[1] *Admiral Halsey's Story*, p. 265.

[2] 'A mission understandable only as competition with the Third Fleet.' (*The Army Air Forces in World War II*, Vol. V, p. 698.

five combined strikes, a total of 261 aircraft, of which 227 made attacks. Our total sorties that day were 416. We lost four aircraft in combat.

Task Force 37 attacked similar targets next day, flying-off beginning at 0430. Before bad weather caused air operations to be cancelled in the afternoon we launched 155 aircraft, of which 118 found and attacked their targets. One Avenger was lost. Three groups of enemy torpedo bombers threatened the Fleet at dusk whilst day fighters were being landed-on. The first group closed straight in and was intercepted by four British dusk Hellcats of the *Formidable*, the only British aircraft in the air. They reported four enemy aircraft carrying torpedoes, of which they shot down three but the fourth escaped. The second group broke up after being engaged by U.S. night fighters and gunfire from the picket destroyers. The third group turned away at 65 miles. We lost no aircraft in combat that day.

On the 28th Task Force 37 flew-off ten individual and four combined strikes, a total of 260 aircraft, in addition to 135 for defensive duties and four for photographic reconnaissance and search, targets being shipyards and shipping in the eastern part of the Inland Sea and the Kii Suido and aircraft and air installations on the mainland. Much damage was done in shipyards and factories, but only minor vessels were found, many of which were sunk or damaged. Strong enemy airborne opposition was again encountered and we lost eight aircraft in combat, the Americans 27.

10

No air strikes were planned for the 29th, but the *King George V*, with *Undine*, *Urania* and *Ulysses*, forming Task Unit 37.1.2, detached from the main body to join an American bombarding group of battleships and heavy cruisers under Rear-Admiral J. E. Shafroth in the *South Dakota* for bombardment of Hamamatsu. The *Urania* and *Ulysses* collided in fog, but were able to continue in operation.

Widespread damage had been inflicted on the Hamamatsu area by air attacks prior to the surface bombardment. The production of the Japan Musical Instrument Company, at that time manufacturing aircraft propellers, which was the *King George V*'s target, had fallen to about 3 per cent. of peak production in consequence. It was, however, still a good target on account of the potential importance of its facilities. The *King George V*, operating independently, opened fire at 2319, range 20,075 yards, in good bright moonlight with a clear sky, enabling the air spotter to be employed successfully. To fix her position, the *King George V* made use of a transit between Kakezuka lighthouse and the centre of the target area, resulting, it was reported, in an accurate opening salvo. The remaining salvos were well grouped, but outside the target, owing evidently to an error of identification by the spotting aircraft. Only 265 out of 300 rounds of 14-inch H.E. (reduced charges) were expended, due to failure of tubes. The total firing time was 27 minutes. There was no opposition, either from enemy aircraft or from shore batteries, though the *Undine* twice opened fire on what was believed to have been groups of small craft, probably fishing craft. Though some destruction was caused ashore all of the important propeller production plant escaped serious injury, and consequently direct effects of the bombardment upon production were negligible.[1]

[1] The *Massachusetts*, which fired at Musical Instrument Plant No. 1, put nine out of 109 discovered hits on the target, the *King George V* (apparently) seven out of 179 on Plant No. 2. (Vide *Ships Bombardments of Japan* 1945, *Comments and Data on Effectiveness of Ammunition and Accuracy of Firings*, Enclosure J, Part IV, Figure 4.)

The indirect effects, however, such as labour absenteeism and idleness, and disruption of essential services, caused a total stoppage of production. Such buildings and equipment of the Imperial Government Railway Hamamatsu Locomotive works as had survived bombing, were attacked by the American ships and were put out of operation for about three months. Three other industrial works were also attacked: two of them had already practically ceased production, and the third was not hit. Other targets which were not hit, were the Tenryu and Bentenjima bridges on the Tokaido main railway line, whose destruction would have paralysed industry in the Nagoya-Tokyo area. The line was, however, cut in Hamamatsu and traffic brought to a standstill for 65 hours.

11

During the 29th, the Fleet moved to a fresh launching position. The targets of next day's strikes were shipping in the Maizuru area and Nagoya Bay and airfields in south-west Honshu. The first two strikes were weathered out. At Maizuru, the frigate *Okinawa* was reported sunk by us,[1] and shipping sunk by the Americans included the freighters *Tatsumiya Maru* and *Kashi Maru*. Two Seafires and a Corsair, with their pilots, were lost in combat. We launched 216 aircraft on offensive missions, of which 192 reached their targets, and 130 defensive aircraft went up, before the weather deteriorated. As the planned fuelling programme allowed only 24 hours for the next replenishment Admiral Rawlings was given permission to disengage and retire independently to the fuelling area, which was more than 700 miles from the position originally planned.

Fuelling began at 1000 on the 31st from four oilers, two of which were without any experience. The logistic group also included two ammunition ships, one VSIS, the radar maintenance ship *Arbutus* whose lack of stores and repair facilities, however, prevented her from undertaking any radar repairs at all and limited her usefulness to transferring stores which could be made available between ships of the Task Force. The whole oiling programme was disrupted and the carriers' burdens considerably increased through the fact that the best oiler was not immediately ready to supply aviation fuel by the alongside method. One oiler arrived 750 tons of aviation fuel short, having sailed from Sydney in haste; and she was consequently able to supply only one carrier. Her new British made hoses were of inferior quality and frequently parted, bursting if full pressure was put on, and her gear was not up to its work, whilst her cargo had been loaded so that far too high a proportion of it was diesel oil, which ships were not prepared to receive. The *King George V* embarked 14-inch shell from the *Robert Maersk*. The operation was carried out in a swell big enough to give the ammunition ship, which was not much more than one-twentieth of the size of the *King George V*, considerable motion. Her small number of hands thus had great difficulty in controlling such heavy weights. The *Victorious* next day attempted to bomb up from the same ammunition ship, but the vessel was too small for the existing swell conditions. She had no gyro compass and her magnetic compass was dangerously affected by the heavy ship alongside, varying from 7 to 15 degrees with the roll and pitch. On 2nd August the swell had gone down sufficiently for the ship to complete bombing

[1] Claimed, however, by the Americans.

up from the *Robert Maersk*. The whole operation of replenishment was carried out in a long and unpleasant typhoon swell which ran at right-angles to the wind and sea. As oilers became lighter, they developed a considerable roll, at times lifting forefoot and most of the screw clear of the water, though all ships succeeded in accomplishing their oiling by 1650 on 2nd August.

On the previous day, with a typhoon threatening the fuelling area, Admiral Halsey ordered all groups to proceed to Area Hurricane (25° N., 137° E.) and to remain there, replenishing as necessary, until further orders. The next operations were scheduled for 5th August, but for a week the weather prevented further flying operations. Changes of fuelling positions and strike plans, caused through the weather, made it very difficult for the British destroyers to keep topped-up with fuel from the heavy ships and yet keep reasonable station in the Fleet. At one time it was thought that before the next fuelling on 8th August some of the destroyers would be on their diesel and the *Napier* burning cordite.

Meanwhile, on the 7th the Fleets worked north, and on 9th August were off north-east Honshu. The move was made at the request of General MacArthur, for reconnaissance had indicated that the Japanese had massed the greater part of their remaining aircraft on the northern Honshu–Hokkaido fields for an attack on Okinawa which had recently been placed under his command. Two previously untouched and apparently stockpile airfields were discovered. Strikes were made that day against airfields and shipping in northern Honshu from a position in 37° 43′ N., 144° 51′ E. Hokkaido was fog-bound. The British force launched 267 strike and photographic reconnaissance aircraft, of which all except nine found and attacked their targets. We lost seven aircraft in combat and four pilots. There was no enemy opposition over the target, but heavy attacks were aimed at the Fleets. Most of the attacks were repulsed by the picket groups and combat air patrol, which destroyed 12 enemy aircraft. Suicide aircraft came from the Tokyo airfields at intervals all day. McCain had received orders not to strike in the Tokyo area. He was forced to launch his strikes, however, from a position south of the weather line (actually 30 miles from heavy fog), or not at all. This put the Task Forces within easy range of the suicide squadrons on the Tokyo airfields. The four destroyers on the southern picket stations were under almost continuous attack, and finally the destroyer *Borie* was hit by a suicide aircraft and badly damaged, with 49 killed and 34 wounded. She was the only ship of the combined fleets to suffer serious damage during the final operations against Japan. No less than 720 Japanese aircraft were claimed destroyed or damaged on 9th and 10th August.

Whilst the air strikes were in progress, Rear-Admiral Shafroth took the battleship and cruiser bombarding group 34.8.1 towards Kamaishi, to complete the destruction of the Japan Iron Works which were believed not to have been sufficiently damaged in the bombardment on 14th July. The force was joined by the *Gambia* and *Newfoundland*, with the *Terpsichore*, *Termagant* and *Tenacious*. This second and more effective attack on the Japan Iron Works so increased the damage caused that the total loss of pig iron, had the Japanese planned to continue full-scale production, would have sufficed for the steel requirements of 100 ships of 4,000 tons each. The battleships and cruisers opened fire at 1254 with their main batteries, and continued to shell the target for nearly two hours, firing, as on 14th July, about 750 tons of projectiles from mean range of 14,000 yards. The *South Dakota* and *Indiana* provided air spotters for the British cruisers, with success. Several enemy aircraft were chased by the combat air patrol, and one or two destroyed.

12

The plan of operations under which the Fleets were working, called for retirement of the ships early in August. As a result, however, of Russia's declaration of war Admiral Halsey decided to continue his attacks on 10th August, fuel on the 11th, and strike on the 12th and 13th ; and he asked Admiral Rawlings to what extent his force could co-operate. It had been Admiral Rawlings' intention, after the strike on the 10th, to withdraw Task Force 37 to base, to refit and replenish prior to Operation ' Olympic '. Tanker movements to implement this were already under way and the refitting and replenishing programme had no time margin. The targets lay many miles to the north, but feeling that it was incumbent upon us to do all we could to sustain the full effort at this juncture, though knowing that the U.S. oil position precluded our fuelling from their oilers in any quantity, Rawlings offered his entire force for one more strike day, after which he would have to retire. It was at first hoped to retain the *King George V* and three cruisers with destroyers for a bombardment arranged for the 13th, though this introduced the risk that half the destroyers would only make Manus under tow ; but this was nullified through machinery defects of long standing affecting two shafts in the *King George V*.

On the 10th, all strikes were flown-off on schedule in poor weather, but conditions over the targets were much better. Shipping at Okkaichi and Onagawa Wan, and airfields were again attacked. Two hundred and twenty-seven out of 236 or our aircraft attacked the targets ; six aircraft with four pilots and two aircrewmen were lost in combat ; two vessels, listed by the Japanese as an auxiliary minesweeper and an auxiliary patrol vessel,[1] were sunk in Onagawa harbour.

The Fleets oiled next day, and at Admiral Halsey's suggestion the two fleet flagships *Missouri* and *King George V* oiled from the *Sabine* simultaneously, one each side, forming a notable sight. All strikes scheduled for the 12th were cancelled on account of a typhoon threat.

The Japanese peace feelers were now approaching a climax, and it was arranged that a token British force should remain with the U.S. Fleet and be incorporated in Task Force 38 for the naval occupation of Japan. The *King George V*, *Indefatigable*, H.M.N.Z.S. *Gambia*, the *Newfoundland*, *Troubridge*, *Termagant*, *Tenacious*, *Teazer*, *Barfleur*, H.M.A.S. *Napier* and *Nizam*, and the *Wakeful* and *Wrangler* formed Task Group 38.5, the northerly group of the Fleet under the direct orders of Admiral McCain.

On the 13th, from positions about 35° N., 142° E., the Fleet attacked targets in the Tokyo area. The Japanese air forces made a concerted effort to damage the carrier force. Two hundred and fifty-four of their aircraft were destroyed on the ground and a further 149 were damaged. During daylight and after dusk 21 enemy aircraft approached the Fleet. All were intercepted and shot down by the patrols directed by the pickets ; none succeeded in getting nearer than 25 miles from the force. ' The precisions of the interceptions and speed at which the bogies were shot down was remarkable ', reported Admiral Rawlings. ' The whole was a most finished performance '.[2]

For the oiling the next day all fuel requirements of the British Task group were met from the U.S. logistic group. The *Indefatigable* on the 15th launched

[1] *Kongo Maru No.* 2 and *Takunan Maru No.* 6 (*Japanese Report*).

[2] M.010175/45.

her first strike at 0400 against targets in the Tokyo area from a position 34° N., 142° E. The target was weathered in, but a camouflaged factory was successfully bombed. The strike was intercepted by 12 Zekes (Mitsubishi Zero minus three fighters), of which four were shot down and the remainder probably shot down by the escorting fighters. One Seafire was lost and one Avenger shot up and had to ditch. At 0700, on instructions from the Commander-in-Chief, Pacific, all strikes were cancelled. The signal to cease offensive operations against Japan was hoisted at 1100. Twenty minutes later, whilst the signal was flying, a Judy (dive bomber), which by some means eluded discovery, dived on the *Indefatigable* and dropped two bombs close to her. Corsairs of Task Group 38.1 shot the enemy down. A few more Japanese aircraft attempting to attack were shot down by the pickets and patrols during the afternoon. They may have failed to receive word of the cease fire. These were the final offensive acts in the maritime war.

13

In most respects, except that of combat and operational losses, the British air effort compared well, proportionally as the number of their aircraft, to the American. For a standard strike day the Americans scheduled an average of 2·03 sorties per first line aircraft establishment to the British 1·7 sorties, though the British obtained 85 per cent. successful sorties, that is, sorties which reached the target, to the U.S. 80 per cent.[1] The British figures showed a slightly higher number of enemy aircraft destroyed and damaged per offensive sortie than the American, but this may have been due to the exclusion of the British from attacks on important enemy warships, and their consequent proportionately greater employment in attacking airfields. The figures of shipping sunk and damaged by both U.S. and British are not considered sufficiently reliable for comparison. Too few of the British claims were backed by photographic assessment to enable a useful analysis to be made of shipping attacks.

British combat losses were nearly 50 per cent. higher than U.S. though on the whole the Americans probably attacked the more heavily defended targets, whilst British Seafires were not sent on individual strikes to heavily defended targets, nor were the Seafire units of our combined strikes allowed to go down and strafe. The higher British losses were probably due to the smaller average size of British sweeps and strikes ; to the fact that the British had no variable time-fuzed flak-bursting bombs (used for the first time by the Americans in these operations), and that we did not employ jamming or radar counter-measures. Despite the fact that the smaller sweeps on the average attacked airfields less well defended than those attacked by the combined strikes composed of large numbers of aircraft figures show that strikes of the latter type can more than compensate for the otherwise greater flak risk involved in attacks on heavily defended airfields. The advantages of saturating defences was exemplified in the Pacific as in the European theatre of air warfare.

British operational losses, expressed as a percentage of offensive sorties were nearly four times as great as the U.S., which if the figures are correct seems to show that there must have been a great improvement on the part of the

[1] *Report of the Flag Officer Commanding First Aircraft Carrier Squadron, BPF* (Enclosure 3 to Report of V.A. 2 i/c BPF, M.010175/43). In the *Analysis of British Pacific Fleet in Operations against Japan*, M.010312/45, p. 24 the British total sorties per complement aircraft per strike day is shown as exactly equal to that of the Americans, both being given as 1·39. It is noted by the Commander-in-Chief BPF that the *Analysis* 'does not necessarily represent the views of the Commander-in-Chief.'

Americans since the January strikes on Formosa when up to 16 aircraft were lost operationally in a single day. Available data are insufficient to furnish a satisfactory explanation of this. In particular, it is not possible to discover whether the British for reasons of operational necessity tended to ditch or return for repair a higher percentage than the Americans of old or damaged aircraft, or whether a higher proportion of replenishment aircraft supplied proved unsatisfactory. There seems to be some evidence of a general deterioration in British deck landing performance after Operation ' Iceberg '. Replacements needed on account of deck landing crashes exceeded in number those required on account of aircraft lost to flak or in combat (50 as compared with 46). The very high flying effort of the Seafires—two of the four carriers were Seafire carriers—combined with their high deck landing loss rate (37·1 per cent. of first line aircraft establishment) was a minor contributory cause. More than three times as many Seafires were lost in deck landing crashes as to flak and in combat.

14

It was perhaps fortunate that the Japanese air reaction to the bombardments by surface ships during the July–August air strikes on Japan was so slight, for the bombardments entailed temporary reduction of the anti-aircraft protection of the Fleet during the absence of the bombarding ships with their combat air patrol and screen. They also caused complications to the strike programme through the additional commitments of providing CAP and spotting aircraft. The Commander, Task Force 38, was of the opinion that more damage could have been inflicted on the industrial plants attacked, by the combat air patrol flown to cover the bombarding groups during their absence from the Task Force.[1] A decision on this point depends not only upon a comparison of the damage which can be effected by bomb and projectile respectively, but also upon other factors. To state, as post-war examination of the various targets attacked enables us to do, that the average amount of structural damage caused by a hit from a 16-inch high capacity projectile on a heavy steel-framed building is about 1,400 square feet, whilst the equivalent figure for the 2,000 lb. general purpose bomb is 8,800 square feet : or that the mean area of effectiveness of a similar projectile for serious damage (destroyed plus heavy damage) against machine tools is 4,900 square feet as contrasted with 8,500 square feet for a 1,000-lb. bomb, is an incomplete reply to a question which should rightly be answered in a special study rather than in a general operational history. It is perhaps sufficient to state here, that choice of weapon—bomb or projectile—against heavy industrial targets, would seem to be governed largely by deciding whether, in specific circumstances, sufficient hits can most easily be delivered by ships or aircraft, and weighing the relative risk involved.[2] In July, 1945, the risk of bombarding ships remaining close to the enemy's coast was very small, whilst the bombardments had a stimulating effect on the crews of the bombarding ships.

Much of the effect of the July–August strategic bombardments on production, other than in the iron and steel industry where direct physical destruction was caused, appears to have been due to the morale factor, especially labour

[1] BPF Liaison Officer to 2nd Carrier Task Force *Report on Second Carrier Task Force Operations 1st July–15th August* 1945, M.09889/45.

[2] Conclusion arrived at by the USSBS, vide *Report of Ships' Bombardment Survey Party Report*, No. BIOS/JAP/PR/1722, p. 2.

absenteeism and reduced labour productivity.[1] The Yamate Plant of the Hitachi Works, for example, ceased production entirely for a month following bombardment, though no more than four shells fell within the plant boundaries ; but persistent absenteeism resulted. At Hitachi, too, after short bombardment which caused little physical damage there was a fall in output of copper ore from 40,000 tons a month to 1,500 tons, caused, it is reported, through the refusal of the miners to enter the mines, for fear that a subsequent bombardment might cause breaks in the pipes which would flood the mines. It must be noticed, however, that at two Japanese plants the bombardments are said to have resulted in an upsurge of morale and an extra effort to get production going again.

Admiral Rawlings rated high the effect of the bombardments on the morale of an enemy ' who must feel there is no knowing where the next one will come '.[2] This was borne out by post-war investigation. People who had been subjected to both heavy bombing and gunfire feared the latter more than either high explosive or incendiary bombing.[3] This agrees with statements made during the war by prisoners-of-war who had experienced both bombing and gunfire attacks during the campaigns in the Central Pacific. The effect on morale of shelling by surface ships was due to its unexpectedness and unpredictability, the longer duration of the attack and the impossibility of estimating how long it would last, in contradistinction to aerial bombing of which there was usually prior warning whilst its conclusion was indicated by the departure of the aircraft. The effect on civilian morale of the brief tactical ' Scarborough Raid ' bombardments by cruisers and destroyers firing 6-inch and 5-inch shells was in no way comparable to that of the sustained attacks carried out on strategic targets by heavy units.

It is improbable that there was sufficient time for the economic effects of the strategic bombardments to be felt on the fighting fronts before the war ended.

A comparison of the vastly greater number of hits on target in gunnery exercises at short range as compared with those obtained in the July bombardments where the mean ranges at which the 16-inch battleships fired were 23,300 yards during day and 24,740 yards in night firings, seems to indicate that surface ship bombardments of industrial targets can be effective and economical of ammunition expenditure and effort, provided they are carried out at short ranges at which accuracy of firing is such as to ensure adequate concentration on the target of a sufficient amount of heavy ammunition.[4] But destruction of heavy industrial plants by such attacks is not to be expected unless either a very large amount of ammunition is allotted to the task or much greater accuracy is obtained than was the case in July–August, 1945. The damaging effect of 8-inch and smaller projectiles against heavy steel-framed buildings appears to be minimal compared with that effected by 16-inch.[5] In the bombardments under review the average accuracy of heavy cruiser fire was slightly less than the average accuracy obtained by battleships.

The fire-raising effect of H.E. projectiles against industrial targets was found to be surprisingly small, though incendiary ammunition, even in small calibres, should produce results comparable to those obtained by incendiary bombing,

---

[1] *Effects of Surface Bombardment on Japanese War Potential*, Report No. BIOS/JAP/PR/1721.

[2] *Reports of Vice-Admiral i/c and F.O.C. 1st A.C. Squadron, BPF*, M.010175/45.

[3] *Reports of Ships' Bombardment Survey Party*, Report No. BIOS/JAP/PR/1722, p. 5.

[4] The Americans report that gunnery exercises indicate that at least 90 per cent of hits on individual large buildings is to be expected at short ranges, as compared to an average of something less than 1 per cent in the July bombardments. (*Ibid.*, p. 2.)

[5] The USSBS investigation reported it as nil (i.e. no serious damage).

if used against urban areas or other inflammable targets. Examples have already been cited, to show how vital is the role of intelligence in strategic bombardments, both by surface ships and aircraft, and how necessary the maintenance of an organisation capable of identifying key industries in the enemy's war economy, designating the most vulnerable points of attacks, providing detailed information on targets of bombardment, and assessing results. Before the July–August bombardments took place, certain of the industrial targets had already lost their value through having ceased production, owing to shortage of raw materials or prior damage by aerial bombing. Intelligence of the two most important targets attacked, the Kamaishi Iron Works and the Wanishi Iron Works was relatively good. The coke batteries were correctly designated as the most vital parts of the works. It was believed, however, that production both of coke as well as iron and steel at these works was much below capacity and that consequently it would be necessary to cut through a heavy cushion of idle capacity in order to effect significant reduction in production. Actually, all, or nearly all, the coking capacity was required to maintain production, and there was little or no idle capacity.

To the extent that two of the most important targets in the vital Japanese iron and steel industry suffered severe damage, the bombardments may be said to have been successful.

CHAPTER XVII

Surrender of Japan

(Plan 2)

1

THE Japanese Government had for some months been trying to find a way to end the war on their own terms. By the early weeks of 1945 it had become clear to the senior statesmen that the country was facing certain defeat and should seek peace without delay. In the previous July, following the loss of Saipan, the xenophobe government of General Tojo had fallen, to be replaced by one headed by Kunikai Koiso, a retired Army General who was known as a critic of Tojo. In the following month the basis of war direction was broadened with the formation of a new Inner Cabinet with right of access to the Emperor. Known as the Supreme Council for the Direction of the War, it comprised six regular members: the Prime Minister, Foreign Minister, Minister of War, Minister for the Navy, and the Chiefs-of-Staff of the two fighting services, together with a secretariat which had no direct responsibility for anything that took place in the meetings of the Council. Any other Cabinet Minister could be brought in as a regular member when necessary, and the two Deputy Chiefs-of-Staff attended the meetings but did not vote.[1] The purpose of the Council was to formulate policy for directing the war and to 'co-ordinate the combined strategy for politics and war.' Though where operations were concerned the Imperial General Staff remained the more influential body the importance of the step lay in the harnessing of the military to the political, economic and civilian requirements of the country; whereas formerly the two Chiefs-of-Staff had not merely been responsible for executing operational plans but also almost automatically capable of formulating strategic plans and setting them in train without the knowledge of the Cabinet.[2] Nevertheless, though appointment of a new government under Koiso broke the grip of the ruling military faction, there was no change of heart towards the war, and the decision was taken to continue to fight with greater vigour and to make further sacrifices. Meanwhile the Allies continued to draw closer to the main Japanese islands as one defensive position after another fell.

The first three months of 1945 witnessed a fundamental deterioration in Japan's position. It was a period of disasters without precedent. On 3rd March

[1] This custom arose when the Chiefs of Staff were imperial princes and needed assistants.

[2] Admiral Yonai, a former Prime Minister and Minister for the Navy in the Koiso administration, considered however that the Supreme Council for the Direction of the War was a misnomer and that it was really more of the nature of a liaison organ between the military and the 'Government' (Interrogation of Admiral Mitsumasa Yonai, Nav. No. 76).

General MacArthur opened Manila harbour to shipping, on the 16th Iwo Jima fell, and on the 20th General Slim's Order of the Day registered the winning of the battle for Central Burma which foreshadowed the fate of Rangoon. During that month the China Sea was abandoned by Japanese shipping and no more oil would thenceforth enter Japan. Between 9th and 19th March more than 30 square miles of the capital and three other great Japanese cities, Osaka, Kobe and Nagoya were added to those already burnt out by Superfortress raids. A week later U.S. aircraft began mining the home ports of Japan. On 1st April the Americans landed on Okinawa and on the 5th Russia gave notice of abrogation of the Neutrality Pact.[1] This was a likely presage of war. Three days later, the Government of Koiso resigned and the aged Baron Kantaro Suzuki took office as Premier with instructions from the Emperor to arrange an end to hostilities. The surrender of Germany now at length rendered it possible to discuss the subject in open Cabinet. There was no longer in the minds of the civilian and less militaristic members of the Japanese Cabinet any question whether or not to stop the war: the question was by what means and how quickly could it be ended. Specific peace overtures, using China as an intermediary, had been under consideration even before the fall of the Koiso Administration but were not pursued; and early in May negotiations for Russia to intercede began in both Tokyo and Moscow. Konoye, the intended emissary to the U.S.S.R., whilst ostensibly he was to negotiate, received direct and secret instructions from the Emperor to secure peace at any price, notwithstanding that the terms might be severe. The Russians however procrastinated and refused to give a definite reply; and Stalin, at a meeting in July with the Allies, who had already become cognisant of the earlier Japanese request to Russia to intercede on their behalf in August of the previous year,[2] minimised the importance of the Japanese approach. In Japan, the Ministers in the National Council were divided on the subject of ending the war. Suzuki, Shigenori Togo (Foreign Minister) and Admiral Yonai (Minister for the Navy) were determined on peace. The War Minister General Anami and the two Chiefs of Staff, Admiral Toyoda and General Umezu, wished to continue to fight in the hope of establishing a better position from which to negotiate terms. The Emperor did not immediately come into the open despite his instructions to Konoye and his cryptic injunction to Koiso on taking office in July of the previous year, which it appears was intended as a direction to bring the war to an end. Though the official Japanese propaganda line was that the surrender of Germany would make no difference to Japan's war policy of resistance, nevertheless, from early May until the surrender in August the principal problem of the peace party was to give effect to the decision to end the war against the wishes of the powerful military Junta. The aged Suzuki's house was burnt down and he himself narrowly escaped assassination for proposing to open negotiations for peace. The Potsdam Declaration had not at that date been issued and the army persuaded itself that the unconditional surrender terms of the Cairo Conference would not actually be applied but might be mitigated through negotiation and the threat of exacting heavy sacrifices from the Allies if insisted upon.

---

[1] The Pact, which was signed on 13th April 1941, expired on 25th April 1946, and under its provisions if either of the contracting parties did not wish to continue it in effect after its expiration date notice of abrogation had to be given, one year before that time. The pact, as the Russian Foreign Minister, Mr. Molotov, recalled in a note to the Japanese Ambassador in Moscow was concluded before Germany attacked Russia and before the outbreak of war in the Pacific. Since then Japan had been lending assistance to Germany in the war against the USSR, and was herself at war with Great Britain and the U.S.A. The Pact had consequently lost meaning and its continuance had become impossible.

[2] *See* p. 2.

2

By July, Japan was in chaos, and a position was rapidly being reached in which resistance to invasion would literally be reduced to an affair of sticks and stones, to such a state of stagnation had output of war equipment and supplies been reduced through shortages of food and raw materials caused by the blockade, together with the destruction of stocks and disruption of means of distribution resulting from increasingly heavy air raids. Output of war material had been declining for several months and in July stood at less than 50 per cent. of the peak reached in the previous autumn; in the aircraft industry, which had been subjected to intensive attack, it was lower still. There had been no leather for shoes since 1944. Wool and cotton cloth had almost completely disappeared. The food situation was menacing; the available supplies gave the civilian population less than minimum requirement.[1] On the black market, the price of food stood at an average of 4,000 per cent. of the official price. Yet so bad was the situation with regard to imported raw materials, that foodstuffs were being converted to industrial uses. The sweet potato and apple crops produced aircraft fuels; vegetables and sugar gave lubricants; milk provided glue, and salt industrial chemicals. The waste products of many such processes were being reclaimed and offered as food. Fertilisers, on which Japanese agriculture was heavily dependent, were at 45 per cent. of requirements. This short-fall, together with the draining of man-power from the land resulted in the rice crop, Japan's staple, falling in 1945 to no more than 63 per cent. of the 1930–40 average. By the end of March 1945 the reserve of rice was exhausted, and the deficit was only in part made good by increasing grain imports from Manchuria; and, indeed, by August these too had almost stopped. Requisition of fishing vessels for naval and cargo carrying purposes, lack of fuel and of material for fish nets, together with restriction of fishing grounds as the Allies drew closer to Japan, brought consumption of the other staple food, fish, to 15 per cent. of its 1939 level. There was a definite threat of famine in 1946. Air defence was stultified by shortages of aircraft and aircraft fuel; there was a decline of 75 per cent. in aircraft engine production, 60 per cent. in air frame output, over 90 per cent. in aluminium production and 85 per cent. from peak in oil refining. The impact of bombing on the social organisation was intense. About 13,000,000 people had lost their homes, and owing to general shortages and the poverty of Japanese organising ability, the orderly rehousing and feeding of these millions and the replacement of a minimum of household goods and clothing had not been undertaken.

An estimate of Japan's fighting capabilities called for by Suzuki and presented in June, showed the conclusion that Japan could not continue to fight on account of the inability to produce aircraft, losses and damage to shipping, the precarious food situation, and the anti-war feeling among the people. Already as early as February 1945 Konoye who had been three times Premier and held other high offices, warned the Emperor that more to be feared than defeat was a communist revolution which might take place in the event of defeat: conditions, internal as well as external, pointed to the danger of such a revolution. Incessant air bombardment, added to the long endured shortage of food, clothing and shelter, was driving more and more of the people to despair. Though public morale might never have reached such a low ebb as to render the prosecution of the war impossible[2] continuance of resistance presupposed the continued functioning

[1] The minimum requirement of the Japanese was considerably less than that of western nations and averaged 2,160 calories a day. The civilian rations gave about 1,800 calories.

[2] USSBS opinion.

of central government. But there was a prospect that this would shortly break down in consequence of the attack on the railways which, as the Japanese knew, was about to begin. Japan's railway system was unusually vulnerable to air attack. There were 1,200 tunnels and on the lines linking important shipping and manufacturing centres, an average of nearly four bridges per mile. Disruption of transport would have rendered the defending forces immobile in face of invasion and promised actual starvation of the civilian population in the deficit food areas such as western Honshu through inability to distribute food stocks; for the alternative means of transport by coastal shipping and road were overstrained, the one through the hindering effect of Allied bombing and mining, and the other through the inadequate mileage of heavy duty surfaced roads and the undeveloped state of heavy road transport. The aviation fuel needed for the suicide air attacks which formed part of the 'Ketsu' Plan—the operation to resist invasion—had been hoarded to that end, but the stocks had been dispersed when the air attacks on the homeland began and redistribution would not have been feasible. In the opinion of the Japanese authorities responsible for economic planning and supply the forthcoming effective interruption of railway transport by air attack, which it has been estimated was entirely within the capacity of the Allies, would have rendered further resistance impossible.

3

On 18th July, Mr. Harry Truman, who had become President of the United States after the death of President Roosevelt on 12th April, met in conference ('Terminal') at Potsdam with Mr. Winston Churchill and Generalissimo Chiang Kai-Shek, President of the National Government of the Republic of China. Marshal Stalin was present, but since the U.S.S.R. was not at that time at war with Japan, he did not sign the declaration regarding that country which resulted from the Conference.[1] Allied forces for the invasion of Japan were already being assembled at Okinawa, where on 8th August a new command was created under General MacArthur. As far as could be foreseen, it was only through invasion of their homeland that the Japanese could be brought to submit to unconditional surrender terms, and the decision to invade Kyushu in November had already been taken at Washington, though the Combined Chiefs-of-Staff at Potsdam decided that the present methods of blockade and aerial bombardment should be continued and intensified. The Prime Minister's position was not easy, for he felt he should abstain from saying anything which would make us seem reluctant to go on with the war against Japan for as long as the United States thought fit.[2] He did, however, in the course of talks with Mr. Truman at Potsdam, dwell upon the tremendous cost in Allied lives which the enforcement of unconditional surrender would entail. It became clear there was no need to press the President on the subject; whilst the Secretary of War, Mr. Stimson, and the Chief-of-Staff, General G. C. Marshall were also of his view.

---

[1] The United Kingdom Parliament had been dissolved on 15th June. The General Election, which resulted in a change of Government, had been held on 5th July, but in order to give time for the soldiers' votes to be included, the counting of the votes did not begin until three weeks later. Mr. Attlee, who in the event became Prime Minister in the new Government accompanied Mr. Churchill to Potsdam but had no official responsibility to the Crown otherwise than as a Privy Councillor. The last meeting of the 'Terminal' Conference which Mr. Churchill attended was on 25th July. Mr. Attlee became Prime Minister next day and returned to Potsdam on 28th July as the representative of the United Kingdom.

[2] Churchill, *The Second World War*, Vol. VI, 1954, p. 555.

The difficulty of the Allies as well as those factions in Japan which desired peace, was how to achieve this end. It was known that the Japanese Army was almost intact, and the Allies believed that the enemy were determined and were preparing to resist desperately against invasion of their homeland. As to the true state to which the blockade and bombing had brought Japan, there was no certainty. Stalin on arrival at Potsdam had told Mr. Churchill that as he was leaving Moscow he received a somewhat irregular message delivered to him through the Japanese Ambassador. The message, which was from the Emperor, stated that Japan could not accept unconditional surrender but might be prepared to compromise on other terms. With gross dissimulation Stalin did not mention that for several weeks the Japanese had been trying to persuade the U.S.S.R. to intercede and that they were now desperate. Not until 28th July did he inform the Conference that he had received a more definite request that the Soviet Union would intercede for peace, to which he was giving a negative reply. By that time, the President, the Prime Minister and Generalissmo Chiang Kai-Shek had decided to send an ultimatum calling for immediate unconditional surrender, not of the Government, but of the armed forces of Japan, a distinction which since the Army did not consider themselves servants of the State, would seem to have encouraged the peace party in that country to hope that the position of the Emperor would not be affected. The danger in dissolution of the monarchy, as Ismay had earlier pointed out to the Prime Minister, was that there would be no one in authority to order cease fire in outlying areas, and fighting might continue for long in British and Dutch territories and China.

The document (*see* Appendix X) was published on 26th July. It made clear the determination of the Allies to continue the war until Japan ceased to resist. It cited the devastated state of Germany as an example to the people of Japan of the consequences of continued senseless resistance; demanded the elimination for all time of the authority and influence of the irresponsible Japanese militarists; limited Japan's sovereignty to her home islands; insisted for the Japanese people on future freedom of speech, religion and thought; and promised access to, but not control of, raw materials, and eventual participation by Japan in world trade. No reply nor comment had been evoked from Japan when the Potsdam Conference ended on 2nd August, and with the conclusion of the Conference went the expectation of any reply.

About a fortnight earlier, the Americans had secretly and successfully tested the first nuclear bomb by explosion. It was hoped that demonstration of the power of this engine of unprecedented destruction would induce the Japanese Government to accept the Potsdam terms forthwith and thus save further bloodshed. Accordingly, after due warning, on 6th August a so-called atom bomb was dropped by U.S. aircraft on Hiroshima, one of the larger cities of Japan which, though its industries for the most part contributed to the war effort, had not yet been heavily bombed. This was followed three days later by a similar bomb on Nagasaki, another relatively undamaged city, where there were important Mitsubishi plants. These bombs, though they expedited acceptance of the Allied demand for unconditional surrender, did not, by the testimony of Japan's leaders, persuade her to accept the terms on which the Allies insisted.

The delivery to the Marianas of fissionable material for the bombs resulted in the loss of the U.S. heavy cruiser *Indianapolis*. After being damaged by a suicide aircraft off Okinawa on 31st March, whilst the ship was flagship of Admiral Spruance, Commander Fifth Fleet, the *Indianapolis* was repaired on

8. U.S.S. *Indianapolis,* sunk 30th July 1945.

9. The *Nagato* : only Japanese battleship afloat (heavily damaged) at the end of the war.

[*Facing page 236*

10. H.M.S. *Formidable*, crashed by a Japanese suicide aircraft, 4th May 1945.

the west coast of the U.S.A. and afterwards carried atomic material from San Francisco to Guam. From Guam she proceeded to Leyte unescorted at 17 knots. The ship had ceased zigzagging some four hours previous to the disaster. About midnight on 29th–30th July, when 420 miles from Leyte, she was hit on the starboard bow by two torpedoes fired by the Japanese submarine *I–58*, though the submarine was not seen. The ship sank in 13 minutes, three minutes after the order to abandon ship was given. No distress signal was made, and the failure of the ship to arrive at Leyte was not noticed until she was 60 hours overdue. It is estimated that of the 1,196 persons on board, some 700 got off the ship alive. The chance sighting of the survivors in the water by a U.S. patrol aircraft resulted in the rescue of 318, but 878 perished.

4

On 8th August the U.S.S.R. hurriedly declared war on Japan. Six months earlier, on 11th February, at the Conference known as 'Argonaut', held at Yalta between President Roosevelt, Mr. Winston Churchill and Marshal Stalin, an agreement had been signed detailing the conditions on which the U.S.S.R. would declare war against Japan.[1] At the time, the surrender of Germany was not in sight, and the American military authorities estimated that after her surrender a further 18 months would be needed to defeat Japan. They expected to land an army of a million men. We ourselves should also make a contribution of troops in addition to employing our fleet in the Pacific, together with an air force (Force 'Tiger') to take part in the bombing of Japan. The Japanese army was believed to be fanatically determined to fight to the last, even though this would entail the ruin of the country. So little knowledge had the Allies of the reduced capacity of Japan to resist, that it was thought the country would have to be conquered yard by yard, and the casualty list would be long. The naval and military authorities at Potsdam estimated that the total Allied casualties might reach one million, with an equal number of the enemy[2]; whilst the Prime Minister expected that we ourselves should suffer at least half a million.[3] Up to date, the U.S. casualties had been moderate, less than a quarter of the English relative to the size of the populations of the two countries,[4] but Tarawa and other incidents had shown how sensitive was American opinion on the subject of losses. It was thought that Russian help would reduce the casualties, whereas the considerable Japanese army in Manchuria, if Russia remained neutral, might be thrown against the Allies in the battle for Japan. This gave Stalin much bargaining power which he used to extort concessions. Actually, this bargaining power was bogus, for Russia's interests in the Far East would assuredly have brought her into the war against Japan without any urging.

[1] The purpose of the Yalta Conference was to secure the peace of Europe after the war. It resulted in a Declaration of Liberated Europe in which the three signatories promised the establishment of free elections and democratic governments in countries then occupied by their troops.

[2] Letter dated 12th January 1953 from President Truman reproduced in facsimile in *The Army Air Forces in World War II* by U.S.A.F. Historical Division of Research Studies.

[3] Churchill, *The Second World War*, VI, p. 552.

[4] At that date, the death rate for England was one in 165, for New Zealand one in 175, for the other Dominions an average of one in 372, and for the United States one in 775. Churchill, *op. cit.*, p. 624.

Russia's conditions for entering the war were as follows :

(*a*) Preservation of the *status quo* in Outer Mongolia ;

(*b*) Restoration of the Russian rights lost at the Treaty of Portsmouth (signed 5th September, 1905 and later affirmed in the Treaty of 1925) namely : (i) Karafuto (South Sakhalin) and the islands adjacent to it to be returned, (ii) the commercial port of Dairen to be internationalised with safeguards for the preponderant interests of the U.S.S.R., and Port Arthur to be leased to the Soviet Union as a naval base : (iii) The Chinese Eastern Railway and the South Manchuria Railway (giving an outlet for Dairen) to be joint-operated by a Sino-Soviet company, on the understanding that the paramount interests of the U.S.S.R. would be safeguarded. China to retain full sovereignty in Manchuria.

(*c*) The Kurile Islands to be acquired by the U.S.S.R.

Great Britain was not consulted in the making of this agreement. Mr. Churchill, as our representative, was asked by the Americans to approve it and did so. 'To us the problem was remote and secondary,' he wrote. 'It would have been wrong for us to get in their way unless we had some very solid reason.'[1]

In the belief that Russian help would save Allied lives the U.S.A. bid high for Stalin's support, though not without misgivings amongst certain of the President's advisers, as their later writings show. The agreement has been criticised since the war, mainly because Russian aid proved superfluous and an embarrassment to U.S. policy in the Far East. It was the consequence of failure to correlate the known facts bearing on Japan's position, together with a tragic failure to link Russia's aspirations to her acts. The U.S.S.R. had already given ample evidence, by her subversive intrigues in Italy and the Balkans and by her treacherous behaviour at the time of the Warsaw rising in July 1944, that it was totally lacking in humanity and considered no interests or rights other than its own. With the ink of Stalin's signature on the Declaration of Liberated Europe barely dry Russian tanks and troops were deploying in the streets of Bucharest and establishing by force the rule of a Communist minority in Rumania. Russia had become a mortal danger to the free world.

On 8th August the U.S.S.R. declared war on Japan.[2] Though the Soviet Union made no contribution towards victory, Stalin claimed full belligerent rights.

The Russian army at once advanced into Manchuria, where the Japanese garrison of some 900,000 men had been weakened by withdrawals for the defence of the homeland. A Russian flotilla operated on the Amur river, and occupation of the country was substantially completed by 23rd August.

The Russian Pacific Fleet, based at Vladivostok, Sovetskaya Gavan and Petropavlovsk (*see* Plan 2) was commanded by Admiral Ivan S. Yumashev. Under him, Rear-Admiral Ivan Ivanovich Baykov, Commander of the Kamchatka Flotilla, after three weeks of hostilities occupied Karafuto and the Kurile Islands. He also occupied the Habomai Islands, off Hokkaido, claiming them as part of the Kuriles, a claim which the United States did not recognise. Shortly before the surrender of Japan the Russian Pacific Fleet landed marines

[1] *Op. cit.*, p. 342.

[2] Churchill, *op. cit.*, p. 136, says that at the inter-Allied Conference in Teheran in November 1943 Stalin had volunteered a solemn undertaking that Russia would enter the war against Japan on the day Germany was beaten.

to seize Chongjin (Seishin), the Japanese supply base in north-eastern Korea; and on 25th August marines from the Pacific Fleet were landed at Wonsan (Gensan) in an operation designed to cut off the units of the Japanese Kwantung Army retreating down the peninsula before the Russian advance. The Americans later landed troops in Korea and accepted the surrender of all Japanese troops south of the parallel of 38° North, the Russians accepting the surrender of those north of that latitude.

Russian submarines operated in the northern part of the sea of Japan. The Russians are credited with sinking two Japanese frigates, the *C.D. No. 82* (9th August) and the *Kanju* (15th August), both in the Sea of Japan, probably by aircraft, together with two merchant ships in the Sea of Okhotsk.[1]

5

The Russian declaration of war found Japan unprepared to fight the U.S.S.R. and the Japanese Army incapable of forming any effective counterplan to the Russian advance into Manchuria. For the first time the Army, which so far had suffered no more than local defeats, faced disaster. The industries of Manchuria were quite inadequate to support a large scale campaign on the mainland of Asia, whilst the home industries could not even provide for the defence of the homeland. Yet the Army still remained stubborn in its opposition to acceptance of the Potsdam Declaration. The Inner Cabinet remained deadlocked on two opposing opinions as before. The Prime Minister, the Foreign Minister and the Minister for the Navy wished to accept the Declaration, provided the Emperor's position was not affected. The War Minister and the two chiefs-of-staff made a further condition that the Allied forces would not occupy Japan, that Japan should be allowed herself to withdraw, disarm and demobilise her armed forces abroad, and that the prosecution of war criminals should be undertaken only by the Japanese Government itself. In the early hours of the morning of 9th August the Emperor gave his decision to stop the war. The full Cabinet decided to accept the Potsdam terms, provided the Emperor retained his prerogatives. This decision was cabled to the United States through the Swiss Government early on the 10th. The American reply made no direct statement of the Emperor's position but said his powers and those of the Japanese Government would be subject to the authority of the Supreme Commander for the Allied Powers. On this basis the Emperor on the 14th issued an Imperial rescript to stop the war, and the Cabinet formally accepted unconditional surrender. Apart from a few minor incidents this was accepted by the armed forces. The war was at an end.

[1] The *Kasado Maru* on 8th August, probably sunk by aircraft, and the *Ryutto Maru No. 2* on the 10th, by agent unknown.

CHAPTER XVIII

Appraisal

1

IT should now be clear that the defeat of Japan was brought about primarily by maritime power and its air component.[1] Though the surrender coincided with the climax of an effective bombing offensive against the Japanese homeland, this must not be interpreted to mean that the defeat of Japan was effected by air power, either alone or primarily. Japan's economy and her ability to fight a war were basically dependent upon the possession of sufficient shipping to bring home the imports she needed. Maritime power, by destroying her merchant marine and interdicting her sea routes was overwhelmingly responsible for reducing food below subsistence level and depriving the country of the necessary materials for continuance of resistance. Maritime power exerted further, though less readily measurable pressure in its effect on the morale of the Japanese through insufficiency of food, deprivation of all luxuries, most of the amenities and many of the necessities of life. Finally, air attacks on the homeland causing heavy casualties, loss of homes, and vast displacements of the population, had an effect out of all proportion to the weight of attack, to so desperate a state had blockade reduced the country. One and one-third million tons of bombs were dropped on Germany before she surrendered. On Japan, less well defended and more vulnerable owing to the preponderant use of timber as building material, little more than one-tenth of that weight, about 160,000 tons was employed.

There can be little doubt that the blockade would of itself have proved decisive before much longer. Food shortage would have compelled Japan to surrender, even if no invasion had been planned, if Russia had not entered the war, and if the nuclear bombs had not been employed. But U.S. Intelligence appraisals of political and morale factors were so uncertain that the Chiefs-of-Staff could not rule out the possibility that ground force action might be necessary. It was not until after the nuclear bombs had been dropped, that the primary mission of securing an independent decision was explicitly accepted for the Strategic Air Force.[2] Accordingly, whilst continuing to exert pressure at sea and in the air the Allies considered it necessary to make preparations also

[1] This was not the opinion, however, of the Military Analysis Division of the U.S. Strategic Bombing Survey, which found 'little point in attempting precisely to impute Japan's unconditional surrender to any one of the numerous causes which jointly and cumulatively were responsible for Japan's disaster.' USSBS *Summary Report*, p. 26.

[2] *The Effects of Strategic Bombing on Japan's War Economy*, Report No. BIOS/JAP/PR/1589, p. 63.

for a continental war. In the First World War, by fighting on the Continent of Europe in addition to pursuing the traditional maritime strategy adapted to our genius we had lost a generation of our young men. Already, to finance the Second World War we had parted with our heritage and become for an unforeseeable period in the future pensioners of the United States. Another Cadmean victory gained on the fields of Japan might well have made the United Kingdom one with Nineveh and Tyre. Japan, closer, however, to collapse than the Allies were aware, surrendered before the preparations for invasion were complete.

2

The demand for the unconditional surrender of Japan emerged from the Cairo Conference in December, 1943 (' Sextant '). The danger of driving an adversary to desperation had long been a tenet of British military thinking; and the implications of insistence upon unconditional surrender and the consequences likely to result from the ruin of Japan were not lost upon the English. Policy in the Pacific conflict was, however, a matter for the Americans to decide. Pursuing on the one hand maritime strategy, allied during the later months of the war to a policy of bombing designed to pave the way for invasion, though in practice it exerted its major effect upon the civilian population rather than upon those industries which supported the armed forces, the United States employed her great resources in preparing to subjugate Japan by invasion. There was never at any time amongst the leaders of the nation unanimity on the necessity for such a policy, since the object of the Allies was the limited one of preserving world peace and future security; they required no territorial acquisitions and had no wish to destroy the Japanese nation. The two Commanders, MacArthur and Nimitz, who divided the Pacific between them, are said both to have come to the conclusion, 12 months or more before the surrender, that Japan could be forced to submit to the Allied terms by the application of sea and air power without invasion,[1] a belief which was also shared by the United States Strategic Bombing Survey, the advisory body perhaps in the best situation of all to form a correct judgment.[2] The air leaders, not unnaturally, seem to have been in no doubt as to the ability of the great precision bomber, the B-29, to compel surrender.

There was, however, a widespread feeling in the United States that Japan deserved to be punished for the treacherous attack on Pearl Harbour in 1941. The highest naval authority in the U.S.A. has placed on record his particular satisfaction in the devastation caused by the raid on Truk in February 1944, as ' partial payment for the debt incurred at Pearl Harbour '.[3] On the threshold of the Nuclear Age the language of the Age of Elegance is outmoded; nevertheless, though the basic injunction is the same in each case there is a world of difference between Halsey's signal to his Fleet on the last New Year's Eve of the war: ' Keep the bastards dying ' and Nelson's requirement: ' Not victory, but annihilation.'

Military tradition in the United States had always assigned to the Army the major role in war, even though by reason of her geographical situation the Navy

---

[1] Fleet Admiral William D. Leahy, *I Was There*, pp. 291-96.

[2] Representatives of the USSBS were called to Washington in June 1945 for consultation, *see* USSBS *Summary Report*, pp. iii, 16, 26. The USSBS had been established with a civilian business man at its head by Presidential directive in November 1944, to conduct an impartial study of the effects of strategic bombing of Germany for use, amongst other purposes, in connection with air attacks on Japan.

[3] Admiral King's *Second War Report*.

constituted the country's first line of defence. The idea that sea power and its air component could win wars, was not, as with us, firmly based. Yet as the American aircraft carriers spearheaded the spectacular advance across the Pacific to the very shores of Japan ; as huge naval bases sprang into being almost, it seemed, overnight it became more and more evident that the role of the U.S. Army in the war against Japan was a supporting one. There were not wanting in the United States proponents of what in certain circles in that country were designated, perhaps somewhat contemptuously, 'relatively painless methods of winning the war' ; but finally the majority, even of those who at one time had been in favour of a policy of *delenda est Carthago* were persuaded that the cost in blood, time, and treasure, of invasion would be almost unbearably heavy. Eventually, after the maritime strategy of the Allies had brought Japan to the verge of collapse, the nuclear bomb, foreseen forty years earlier,[1] made a timely appearance to underline the consequences that would follow further resistance.

3

The difficulty under which the Americans laboured in deciding whether invasion would be necessary to defeat Japan, was that of obtaining reliable intelligence of conditions in the enemy country. The ability of the Americans to read certain Japanese coded messages, though it served them on various occasions, was of little use in assessing Japan's economic position and capacity for resistance. Some years previous to the war the Japanese Government had ceased to publish certain of those statistics on which economists are accustomed to base their assessment of a country's economic position and potential, with the result that no certainty existed as to Japan's capability to sustain a major war. It was not generally appreciated that by mobilising the whole of her resources Japan could deliver some heavy initial blows but thereafter must fight largely on the defensive with dwindling resources. As third amongst the world's maritime powers, a large producer of steel, and the world's greatest exporter of textiles she gave the appearance of possessing considerable industrial potential and thus capacity for war. The best intelligence of Great Britain and the United States had been unable, by the time war broke out, to assess her petroleum position, already suspected and now known to have been, with the raw material of aluminium, her Achilles heel ; with the result that it was not until more than two years after the outbreak of hostilities that the Allies began the concerted attacks on her oil imports which almost of itself would in time have deprived her of all power of offence or defence.[2] Economic conditions in the country continued during the war to be largely unknown to the Allies. This explains why, towards the end of the war, the Americans were bombing Japanese factories which had already ceased production through lack of raw materials or whose plant had been removed to a safe position, and why it was thought necessary to lay the cities of Japan one after another in the dust.

4

In a war of so vast a scope as that against Japan the Americans found it impossible to solve the problem of unity of control. It is believed that they never seriously looked beyond the conflicting claims of the two equally successful

[1] By H. G. Wells in *The War of the Worlds*.

[2] The United States Strategic Bombing Survey considered that 'an intensive submarine and mining campaign against the Sumatran oil sources, could have been undertaken in 1944, which would probably have hastened Japan's collapse.' (*The Effects of Strategic Bombing on Japan's War Economy*, p. 80.)

commanders who controlled the two main theatres into which the Pacific was divided; and so they failed to achieve the solution adopted by us in the South-East Asia Area, of disregarding seniority and appointing as Supreme Commander the officer held to be most suitable for the post.[1] It would perhaps have been unseemly, and indeed during the first three-and-a-half or more years it was unnecessary to give to a junior officer command of both Admiral Nimitz's great armada and General MacArthur's veteran divisions. The question was bedevilled for the American Chiefs-of-Staff because by the time the campaigns in the Pacific Ocean Areas and the South-West Pacific Area impinged upon one another and the B–29 had appeared and, operating from bases in three separate commands, was ranging across theatre boundaries, rendering a solution urgent, General Eisenhower had been appointed to the supreme command in Europe and there may have been a certain delicacy in appointing an American also to the supreme command in that other theatre in which United States and British forces were soon to fight side by side.

The expedient of functional in lieu of territorial division of command in the Pacific, to which the Americans finally resorted, had whilst the fighting lasted, no effect in practice. Throughout the war, dual command functioned for the most part in a fairly satisfactory manner. There were, it is true, overlapping lines of communication and un-coordinated air operations; whilst the support of one commander by another was not always an unqualified success. The more nearly the actual fighting was approached, however, or in other words, the more junior the personnel concerned, the more complete was the co-operation. Yet the constant recurrence in U.S. directives of such expressions as 'co-operate', 'correlate plans', 'primary responsibility' and the like bear witness to the difficulties of planning frequently encountered by the Joint Chiefs-of-Staff.

5

The Japanese contributed to their own defeat, or, at least, they failed to stave-off defeat for as long as they might have succeeded in doing, for defeat by resolute adversaries as powerful as the United States and the United Kingdom was, of course, inevitable. Nevertheless, despite the mistakes arising from defects in the Japanese character it is unquestionable that given the limitations under which Japan laboured, faced as she was from the outset with lack of resources necessary to raise her economic production to the level called for by the scale on which the war was fought, hers was a definite achievement in

[1] Admiral King, in his Final Official Report to the Secretary of the Navy on the Second World War states, however :—

> 'There can be no hard and fast rule for setting up commands in the field. . . . The War Department and the Navy Department working together for many years . . . before the war began, had correctly diagnosed what was likely to occur and had instituted, not rigid rules, but a set of principles for joint action in the field which proved sufficiently flexible to meet the varying conditions that were encountered during the war.'

Admiral King's next paragraph leaves it in doubt, however, whether he is referring to theatre command or planning, for he continues :—

> 'We now have before us the essential lessons of the war. . . . The most definite and important lesson is that to attempt unity of command in Washington is ill-advised in concept and would be impracticable of realisation.'

This, if we substitute Tokyo for Washington, is precisely what occurred in the Korean War 1950–53. For the first six months until December 1950 there was no co-ordinating commander in the field between General MacArthur in Tokyo and the commanders of the 8th Army and 10th Corps respectively in Korea. So quickly are the lessons of a war forgotten.

defying for nearly four years an adversary with potential twice her own.[1] Had she not committed the errors of failing both to conduct a vigorous campaign against Allied shipping on the lines of communication across the Pacific and of failing to provide for the protection of her own merchant marine she might much longer have survived the strategical error of over-extending her defensive perimeter in the Spring of 1942 which led to the Battle of Midway, the passing of the initiative to the Allies, and the ceaseless drain on resources of the operations in New Guinea and the Solomons. This mistake, which was rendered possible through the manner in which decisions on naval strategy were taken, was, however committed in the flush of victory.[2] Lack of understanding of the full meaning of maritime power was responsible for Japan's failure to employ her submarines to prevent the transference of the huge American war potential across thousands of miles of sea to the area of active operations where alone it could be applied. Despite the exhortations of their Axis partner, Germany, the Japanese Navy refused to reconsider their doctrine of employing submarines as a closely integrated arm of the Fleet, arguing that the shipbuilding capacity of the United States was so great as to render nugatory a campaign on the trade routes. Submarine raids were indeed made on the U.S.A.–Australia route during 1942 and again in 1943 but they were merely half-hearted.

It is less easy to explain why Japan, with the lesson before her of the plight to which the United Kingdom was at one time reduced during the First World War, failed to make provision for the protection of her own merchant shipping. The subject has already been discussed[3] but there are certain pointers worth pondering. The first is that Japan in 1941 was not alone in being unconvinced of the value of convoy which is arguably a defensive measure, whereas Japan's predilections were for offence. Such protection as could be given to her merchant shipping, was, however, given from the first. In the course of planning for war the probable losses of ships, year by year, were estimated, but were seriously miscalculated,[4] perhaps because the planners expected the Allies to employ their submarines not against communications, but in a manner similar to themselves. Failure to take effective measures was just one more *lacuna* in the organisation for war of a desperately poor country. In their dependence upon imported raw materials every ship sunk reduced their capacity to replace both ship and cargo. When the danger was at length grappled with the drain on her strength had gone so far that she was unable to remedy it. Thus was Japan defeated.

---

[1] Actually, U.S. production at peak was ten times that of Japan, but only one-fifth was employed in the Pacific, four-fifths being allotted to the war against Germany. Japan surrendered whilst the forces employed against Germany were still in process of re-deployment.

[2] Throughout this history, for obvious reasons it has not been feasible to describe the effect on the course of the war exercised by the personalities of those taking part. The Historical Section feels justified, however, in citing one outstanding instance which resulted in the turning point of the war. The attempted extension of the Japanese perimeter to Midway in June 1942, which had such disastrous consequences for Japan, was decided upon by the Commander-in-Chief, Combined Fleet, Admiral Yamamoto. This man was, even for a Japanese, unusually devoted to the Emperor. The U.S. air raid on Tokyo on 18th April 1942 made Yamamoto fearful of danger to the Emperor's person, and to prevent a repetition he decided to keep the U.S. bombers at Hawaii at arm's length. It needs but a cursory examination of Yamamoto's physiognomy (*see* Illustration in Vol. I of this history) to see that he was of a markedly maternal type, which enables us to understand how his devotion to Hirohito and determination to protect him could outweigh his brilliant strategical judgment and involve him in this unsound adventure.

[3] In Volume V of this History.

[4] *See* Japanese documents reproduced in *Japan's Struggle to end the War*, Report No. BIOS/JAP/PR/1618.

The Japanese Government began to organise the country for total war too late. The ease with which the early conquests were effected conduced to public belief, at least, that the whole war would be as easy, a belief fostered by Government propaganda which until the loss of the Marianas and the breaching of the defensive perimeter turned everything into an apparent advantage to Japan. Disasters such as Midway were concealed not only from the general public, but as far as possible from everyone not intimately concerned. There was consequently no general sense of urgency but almost a disinterested attitude towards the war. In the fifth decade of the twentieth century the old Japan of cherry blossom no longer existed ; Tojo had made of the country a police state, and the urge of patriotism had weakened.

When Japan began hostilities in December 1941, her economy was organised for the war in China. This called for no extraordinary effort, and priorities in war material were given chiefly to munitions and equipment for the Army. The great increase in shipping losses which occurred in October and November 1942, brought the authorities face to face with reality. It was no longer a question of the short war for which they had planned, and they began to reorganise the country for total war. This took time, and it was not until the following spring that output began to rise ; the increase in the gross national product during the two previous years had been no more than two per cent. During the next 18 months, progress was extremely rapid. But it had begun too late, and by the time maximum output was reached, which for basic industry was the summer of 1944 and for the munitions industry some months later, the foundations upon which this output was based were already crumbling : shipping was short, raw materials could no longer be brought through the blockade in sufficient quantities and the factories were living on stockpiles. In many materials the position became critical even before the end of 1944.

So many and grave mistakes were made in the organisation of Japan's economy, even after the need to organise for total war was recognised, as to raise doubts whether the authorities possessed the necessary administrative ability to wage such a war. The production of coal, for example, basic need of almost every Japanese factory and one of the few raw materials found in the country, instead of being kept in step with the requirements of industry, was allowed to decline some months before the peak production of the factories was reached. The Japanese recognised the need to rationalise the coal mining industry through working, whilst the war lasted, the most efficient and highest quality mines ; but like various other desirable objects this was never achieved. Again, in 1944, when the output of steel was falling and was much below the needs of the war, the authorities actually stiffened the specifications for finished steel ; whilst over-allocations caused disorganisation of plans through chronic failures of scheduled deliveries. Whilst the backlog of ship repairs was mounting three of the largest shipbuilding yards which specialised in the repair of ships, laid down new ways and organised themselves for an increased amount of new building, instead of concentrating on repairs. They thus lost the advantages of specialisation, for they completed in 1943 only one-fifth of their scheduled repairs, whilst their shipbuilding extensions were still not all completed when the war ended.

It was not only in the sphere of organisation and administration that mistakes were made. Materials and research badly needed in other directions were devoted to the evolution of the *kaiten* (human torpedo) and midget submarines ; and towards the latter part of the war Japan's few remaining effective submarines in the Pacific were diverted to the duty of carrying to distant areas a few of these unreliable, and as events proved, ineffective suicide weapons which at best could have exerted no decisive effect on the course of the war. Most inept was the building of three gigantic submarines to carry aircraft to bomb America ; and the fiasco of the Army's attempt, refusing naval assistance, to build their own submarines to carry supplies to their by-passed garrisons in the south.

War production suffered from the handicap that the country had emerged from an agrarian state too recently for there to exist an adequate reserve of workers with sufficient aptitude for operating the engineering processes called for by modern war. When furnished with a prototype German submarine, for example, the Japanese were forced to conclude that the type was too complicated for them to copy. Japan had, however, certain achievements to her credit. Her contact-firing torpedo was far superior to any possessed by the Allies during the first half of the war, whilst her destroyers carried reloads and were proficient in reloading their tubes in action. Japan built the two largest and most heavily gunned battleships afloat. Both were sunk during the war, before examination of them was possible ; but they were almost certainly remarkable for nothing but their size, a novel but not particularly effective arrangement of their armour, and the calibre of their main armament guns ; in technical devices the ships were probably not the equals of the modern Allied battleships. Excluded during the war from the exchange of ideas with other countries, Japan, starting on a technological level almost equal to that of her enemies, was unable to keep abreast of modern inventions and developments. Nevertheless, where certain devices were concerned, as for example counter-measures to Allied mining, the Japanese were defeated, not so much by the complexity of the devices called for, as by the shortages of material and trained personnel which prevented their technicians from recommending the adoption of the most effective counter-measures.

In the war at sea, possession by the Allies of efficient means of communication stultified Japan's advantage in holding interior lines. Many of her operational difficulties stemmed from imperfect development of communications. Signalling within the Fleet was inefficient : communication between naval and army air forces or even between carrier and naval land-based forces was in general possible only at headquarters level. Communication to aircraft involved in convoy protection was mainly via the bases of the aircraft ; and ship to aircraft communication was not very satisfactory.[1] For an aircraft to be able to communicate directly with a submarine was exceptional ; such signals had to be routed through a shore station.

The side of the naval war against Japan which came to the notice of the public in Great Britain and the U.S.A. was largely a contest of air power. Little news of the operations of the American, British and Dutch submarines was permitted to reach publication, and the gradual strangulation of Japan which they were bringing about remained unknown whilst the aggressive campaigns in which the U.S. Navy won great victories in the air were publicised. The Allies discovered that without incurring an unacceptable ratio of loss they were able to operate their aircraft carriers wherever they chose, even off Japan's home islands where the enemy's main air reserves lay, though it must be borne in mind that the war

[1] Statement in Interrogation by Rear-Admiral S. Horuichi, C.O.S. 1st Escort Fleet from May–December 1944 ; C.O. 901 Air Group January–September 1945. (Interrogation Nav. No. 47.) ' Only twice in my experience has any communication (from ship to aircraft) worked.' (Lieut.-Commander S. Yasumoto, Captain of escort vessel *Shiokaze* and subsequently Staff Officer 103rd Convoy Escort Squadron. Interrogation Nav. No. 45.)

did nothing to show that carriers could operate their aircraft except by evasion, in an area within range of effective land-based air forces. The Japanese never evolved nor copied from the Americans the tactical organisation which enabled the Allies to operate in this manner, with their surface ships grouped around the aircraft carriers and giving these the support of their anti-aircraft armaments, and in two of the three great battles which destroyed Japanese naval power, the Marianas and Leyte Gulf, her main battleship strength was many miles distant at the time when the carriers they might have helped to protect were being destroyed.[1] It may never again be feasible for great assemblages of ships to lie off hostile coasts in support of landing operations nor for fleet trains to crawl across the sea or wait at open rendezvous for the fighting ships to come to take fuel and stores from them. But in the particular circumstances of the war against Japan the method of naval air operating evolved by the Americans, with balanced groups built around fast carriers and based on the supply train, served its purpose perfectly.

The beginning of Japan's downfall in the war is usually ascribed to the ill-advised extension of the war plan in the summer of 1942, when the defensive perimeter was pushed outwards to include Midway, New Guinea and the Solomons. But the failure of the expanded war plan was a failure of carrier-based air power; and this had its origins in the losses incurred in the successive carrier raids carried out in the first four months of the war, on Allied bases extending from Pearl Harbour to Darwin and from Darwin through the Netherlands East Indies to Ceylon, when Japan paid too high a price in the wastage of trained airmen. Her losses in those early strikes were not excessive, and even the high figure of loss reached soon afterwards in the fighting in the air above the Solomons and Bismarcks would not have crippled a force with adequate reserves. Actually, Japan soon increased her aircraft production to a figure exceeding her losses; but personnel were short, for her reserve of trained airmen was very small and in the belief that the war would be short the training facilities provided were of the most meagre description. In his report on the Midway operation the Commander-in-Chief Combined Fleet describes how he was compelled to sail with pilots most of whom had no more than basic training.

With the best of Japan's carrier aircraft pilots lost in the early raids the Battle of Midway destroyed her carrier air force. Incompletely reconstituted, the groups were disembarked to operate from shore bases in the south and were destroyed again in defending the southern conquests. Once more the Japanese laboured to rebuild. By June 1944, however, when the Combined Fleet was committed in defence of the Marianas the new carrier pilots were still incompletely trained, with the result that of every ten aircraft which took off from the carriers' decks in that battle nine were destroyed by the experienced U.S. airmen. The shore-based naval air flotillas fared little better. Committed piecemeal in the Solomons, they too by early 1944 had lost much of their first-line strength and were consequently unable at Leyte in October to support the fleet in the battle which saw the Japanese fleet at sea for the last time and reduced it to a strictly auxiliary status. By that date the Army Air forces also had lost much of their early strength and were unable to fill the breach. With

[1] In the first of the three battles, Midway, although the main battle fleet was far away the carrier force was accompanied by a numerically adequate force of battleships and heavy cruisers. Their failure to give efficient support to the carriers was due, in so far as it did not result from ineffective A.A. gunnery, to faulty tactical disposition, namely, too loose initially, and disorganised through taking evasive action to repel the torpedo aircraft attacks which preceded the damaging bombing attacks.

control of the air precarious even over the home islands, Japan could think of no better plan than by suicide tactics to do as much damage as possible to the Allies in the hope of postponing the hour of surrender and ameliorating the terms of peace.

6

For Japan the war had been a gamble. With resources minimal by comparison with those of the nations she provoked Japan was incapable of a sustained war effort against an alliance of two such great powers as the United States and the United Kingdom. She staked everything on a single damaging blow, relying thereafter upon building around her conquests a strong defensive perimeter in the expectation that this would gain for her a negotiated peace. There were not amongst the Japanese many able to differentiate between the character of Angle-Saxon and Oriental sufficiently clearly to recognise that it was not within the power of an aggressor to set his own chosen limits to a war in which the Americans and the English were provoked to take up arms in defence of interests vital to them. There is foreboding in the words ascribed when war broke out to Admiral Yamamoto, Commander-in-Chief of the Japanese Fleet, whose death was worth a major victory to the Allies. ' We can carry on for one year somehow, but after that, I don't know.' Admiral Toyoda, last Commander-in-Chief of the Combined Fleet, and Admiral Yonai, Navy Minister in the two final administrations of the war, both thought that hostilities could have been avoided. ' If I had been Prime Minister at the time, we probably should not have had this war,' said Yonai ; but unfortunately he was forced from office nearly 18 months before Pearl Harbour on account of his far-seeing opposition to the adherence of Japan to the Tripartite Pact. Whether, given Japan's aspirations and the mistrust which her banditry of late years had engendered in the Western Powers Yonai could have kept the country from embarking on that disastrous adventure, is open to question. For so great a conflict Japan had neither the material nor the moral stamina required. Once war was joined the end might be far distant, but could never be in doubt.

APPENDIX A

Organisation of Japanese Fleet

September 1944

(1)

OPERATIONAL ORGANISATION

Admiral S. Toyoda, Commander-in-Chief, with flag in the light cruiser *Oyodo* at Kure

MOBILE FORCE

MAIN BODY OR 'A' FORCE
(Vice-Admiral J. Ozawa)

Fleet carrier
Zuikaku

Light carriers
Chitose
Chiyoda
Zuiho

Heavy cruiser
Mogami

10th Destroyer Flotilla
Yahagi (light cruiser)
Asagumo
Michisio
Nowake
Maikaze
Urakaze
Isokaze
Hamakaze
Yukikaze
Shimozuki
Fuyuzuki
Akizuki
Suzutsuki
Hatsuzuki
Wakatsuki

SECOND DIVERSION ATTACK FORCE
(Vice-Admiral K. Shima)

Battleship carriers
Ise
Hyuga

Heavy cruisers
Nachi
Ashigara

1st Destroyer Flotilla
Abukuma (light cruiser)
Kasumi
Shiranuhi
Hatsuharu
Hatsushimo
Wakaba

'B' FORCE

Fleet carrier
Junyo

Light carrier
Ryuho

FIRST DIVERSION ATTACK FORCE
(Vice-Admiral T. Kurita)

Battleships
Musashi (18-inch)
Yamato (18-inch)
Nagato (16-inch)
Kongo (14-inch)
Haruna (14-inch)
Fuso (old 14-inch)
Yamashiro (old 14-inch)

Heavy cruisers
Atago
Maya
Takao
Chokai
Haguro
Myoko
Kumano
Tone
Suzuya
Chikuma
Aoba

Light cruisers
Kitagami
Kinu

2nd Destroyer Flotilla
Noshiro (light cruiser)
Kiyoshimo
Akishimo
Hayashio
Shigure
Samidare
Okinami
Kishinami
Naganami
Asashimo
Hamanami
Fujinami

APPENDIX A

(2)

ADMINISTRATIVE ORGANISATION

SECOND FLEET

1st Battle Squadron
Musashi (18-inch), *Yamato* (18-inch), *Nagato* (16-inch).
2nd Battle Squadron
Fuso (14-inch)[1], *Yamashiro* (14-inch)[1].
3rd Battle Squadron
Kongo (14-inch), *Haruna* (14-inch).
4th Cruiser Squadron (8-inch)
Atago, Maya, Takao, Chokai.
5th Cruiser Squadron (8-inch)
Haguro, Myoko.
7th Cruiser Squadron (8-inch)
Kumano, Tone, Suzuya, Chikuma.
2nd Destroyer Flotilla
Noshiro (light cruiser).
2nd, 27th, 31st, 32nd Destroyer Divisions
Kiyoshimo, Akishimo, Hayashio, Shigure, Samidare, Okinami, Kishinami, Naganami, Asashimo, Hamanami, Fujinami, plus *Shimakaze.*

THIRD FLEET

1st Aircraft Carrier Squadron
Unryu (Fleet carrier), *Amagi* (Fleet carrier).
3rd Aircraft Carrier Squadron
Zuikaku (Fleet carrier), *Chitose* (light carrier), *Chiyoda* (light carrier), *Zuiho* (light carrier).
4th Aircraft Carrier Squadron
Ise (battleship carrier), *Hyuga* (battleship carrier), *Junyo* (Fleet carrier), *Ryuho* (light carrier).
Attached
Mogami (8-inch cruiser), *Taiho* (Fleet carrier), *Shokaku* (Fleet carrier).
10th Destroyer Flotilla
Yahagi (light cruiser).
4th, 17th, 41st, 61st Destroyer Divisions
Asagumo, Michisio, Nowake, Maikaze, Urakaze, Isokaze, Hamakaze, Yukikaze, Shimozuki, Fuyuzuki, Akizuki, Suzutsuki, Hatsuzuki, Wakatsuki.

FIFTH FLEET

21st Cruiser Squadron
Ashigara (8-inch), *Nachi* (8-inch).
1st Destroyer Flotilla
Abukuma (light cruiser).
7th, 18th, 21st Destroyer Divisions
Kasumi, Shiranuhi, Hatsuharu, Hatsushimo, Wakaba.

SIXTH FLEET[2]

15th Submarine Division
I–16, I–26, I–29[3], *I–36, I–37, I–38, I–41, I–44, I–45, I–53, I–54, I–55*[3].
34th Submarine Division
I–10[3], *I–177, RO–41, RO–43, RO–46, RO–47, RO–48*[3].
7th Submarine Flotilla
I–361, I–362, I–363, I–364.
8th Submarine Flotilla
I–8, I–52, I–165, RO–113, RO–115, RO–501.
11th Submarine Flotilla
Chogei (submarine tender), *I–12, I–46, I–47, I–48, I–56, I–365, I–366, I–367, I–368, I–370, RO–49, RO–50.*
Kure Submarine Flotilla
Jingei (submarine tender), *I–121, I–122, I–155, I–156, I–157, I–158, I–159, I–162, RO–62, RO–63, RO–64, RO–67, RO–109, RO–112, RO–68, RO–500.*
6th Submarine Division
RO–57, RO–58, RO–59.

---

[1] From 10th September.
[2] As on 15th September 1944.
[3] Already sunk, but still retained in the list.

SOUTH WEST AREA FLEET

16th Cruiser Squadron
Aoba (8-inch), *Kitagami* (6-inch), *Kinu* (6-inch).

19th Destroyer Division
Uranami, Shikinami.

COMBINED FLEET

Oyodo (light cruiser), flag of Commander-in-Chief, Combined Fleet.

Ships working up
Hosho (old light carrier).

11th Destroyer Flotilla
Light cruisers
Tama, Nagara, Natori.
Destroyers
Kuwa, Maki, Kiri, Sugi, Momi.
Attached destroyers
Yukaze, Hibiki.

APPENDIX B

British Pacific Fleet

State on 26th January, 1945

Admiral Sir Bruce Fraser, Commander-in-Chief

TASK FORCE 118 (Vice-Admiral Sir (H) Bernard Rawlings, Vice-Admiral Commanding 1st Battle Squadron and Second-in-Command, British Pacific Fleet).

Battleships .. .. .. *King George V, Howe.*

Fleet carriers .. .. .. *Indefatigable* (Rear-Admiral Sir Philip Vian, Flag Officer Commanding Aircraft Carriers, British Pacific Fleet), *Illustrious, Victorious, Indomitable.*

Cruisers .. .. .. *Swiftsure*, H.M.N.Z.S. *Gambia, Black Prince, Argonaut, Euryalus.*

Destroyers .. .. .. 4TH DESTROYER FLOTILLA
H.M.A.S. *Quickmatch*, H.M.A.S. *Quiberon, Quality, Queenborough.*

25TH DESTROYER FLOTILLA
Grenville, Ulster, Undine, Ursa, Urania, Undaunted.

27TH DESTROYER FLOTILLA
Kempenfelt, Wessex, Wager, Whelp, Whirlwind, Wakeful.

Total: 2 B.B., 4 C.V., 2 C.L., 3 C.L., A.A., 16 D.D.

(2) SUPPORT FORCES

Escorts.. .. .. .. 21ST MINESWEEPING FORCE (R.A.N. manned)
Ballarat, Maryborough, Lismore, Whyalla, Goulburn, Kalgoorlie, Toowoomba, Bendigo.

22ND MINESWEEPING FORCE (R.A.N. manned)
Geraldton, Cessnock, Cairns, Ipswich, Tamworth, Woolongong, Pirie, Launceston.

FRIGATES AND SLOOPS
Crane, Redpole, Pheasant, Woodcock, Whimbrel, Barle, Helford, Parret.

(3) THE FLEET TRAIN (Task Force 117)

Advanced anchorage.	
Replenishment carriers (CVE)	*Slinger, Speaker.*
Repair ships (ARB)	*Resource.*
Aircraft repair ship (ARV) ..	*Unicorn.*
Victualling store issuing ship (AF).	*Fort Edmonton.*
Hospital ship (AH)	*Oxfordshire.*
Tugs (ATA)	2.
Oilers (AO) and (AOG) ..	*Brown Ranger, Dingledale, San Ambrosio, Cedardale, Arndale, San Adolfo, Wave King, Aase Maersk.*
Naval store issuing ship (AKS)	*Bacchus.*
Destroyer depot ship (AD) ..	*Tyne.*

INTERMEDIATE BASE

Air store ship (AKS) ..	*Fort Colville*
Victualling store issuing ship (AF).	*Denbighshire, Fort Albama, City of Dieppe.*
Hospital ship (AH)	*Tjitjalengka.*
Tugs (ATA)	2.
Distilling ship (AW)	*Stagpool.*
Repair ship (ARH)	*Artifex.*
Netlayer (AN)	*Guardian.*

Divided between advanced anchorage and intermediate base

Armament store issuing ship (AE).	*Corinda, Darvel, Hermelin, Heron, Kheti, Pacheco Prince de Liège, Princess Maria Pia, Robert Maersk Thyra S.*

On passage between advanced and rear bases

Ferry carriers (CVE) ..	*Striker, Fencer.*
Armament store carriers (AE)	*Gudrun Maersk, Kistana, Kola.*
Naval store carrier (ARS) ..	*Bosphorus.*

APPENDIX C

East Indies Fleet

Established in January, 1945

Admiral Sir Arthur Power, Commander-in-Chief

3rd Battle Squadron ..	*Queen Elizabeth* (flag of Vice-Admiral H. T. C. Walker, Commanding 3rd B.S.), *Valiant, Renown.*[1]
5th Cruiser Squadron ..	*Newcastle* (flag of Rear-Admiral A. D. Read, Rear-Admiral Commanding 5th C.S.),[2] *London, Cumberland, Suffolk, Nigeria, Kenya, Phoebe,* H.M.N.S. *Tromp.*
Escort Carriers	
1st Division	*Begum* (A/S), *Empress, Shah* (A/S).
2nd Division	*Ameer* (Flag).
Assault carriers	*Khedive, Slinger, Speaker.*
Ferry Carrier	*Battler.*
16th Destroyer Division ..	*Paladin, Pathfinder, Penn, Petard.*
7th Destroyer Flotilla ..	*Napier, Nepal, Norman, Nizam.*
10th Destroyer Flotilla ..	*Ashanti, Eskimo, Nubian, Tartar.*
26th Destroyer Flotilla ..	*Saumarez, Venus, Verulam, Vigilant, Virago, Volage.*
11th Destroyer Flotilla ..	*Rotherham, Raider, Rapid, Relentless, Rocket, Roebuck, Racehorse, Redoubt.*
24th Destroyer Flotilla ..	*Troubridge, Teazer, Tenacious, Termagant, Terpsichore, Tumult, Tuscan, Tyrian.*

[1] Relieved by F.S. *Richelieu* on 20th March.
[2] Succeeded on 11th March by Rear-Admiral W. R. Patterson.

APPENDIX D

Composition of the U.S. Third Fleet

10th October, 1944

Admiral W. F. Halsey, Jr. Commander-in-Chief
Task Force 38

Vice-Admiral M. A. Mitscher

Task Group 38.1
(Vice-Admiral
J. S. McCain)

Carriers
- *Wasp* (flag)
- *Hornet*

Light carriers
- *Cowpens*
- *Monterey*

Heavy cruisers
- *Boston*
- *Canberra*
- *Wichita*

Destroyers
- *Izard*
- *Charrette*
- *Conner*
- *Bell*
- *Burns*
- *Boyd*
- *Brown*
- *Cowell*
- *Mc Calla*
- *Grayson*
- *Woodworth*

Task Group 38.2
(Rear-Admiral
G. F. Bogan)

Carriers
- *Intrepid* (flag)
- *Bunker Hill*
- *Hancock*

Light carriers
- *Cabot*
- *Independence*

Battleships
- *Iowa*
- *New Jersey* (flag of Commander-in-Chief Third Fleet)

Light cruisers
- *Vincennes*
- *Houston*
- *Miami*
- *San Diego* (A.A.)
- *Oakland* (A.A.)

Destroyers
- *Owen*
- *Miller*
- *The Sullivans*
- *Stephen Potter*
- *Tingey*
- *Hickox*
- *Hunt*
- *Lewis Hancock*
- *Marshall*
- *Cushing*
- *Halsey Powell*
- *Uhlmann*
- *Benham*
- *Yarnall*
- *Stockham*
- *Wedderburn*
- *Twining*
- *Colahan*

Task Group 38.3
(Rear-Admiral
F. C. Sherman)

Carriers
- *Essex* (flag)
- *Lexington* (flag of CTF 38)

Light carriers
- *Princeton*
- *Langley*

Battleships
- *Massachusetts*
- *South Dakota*
- *Alabama*

Light cruisers
- *Santa Fé*
- *Mobile*
- *Birmingham*
- *Reno* (A.A.)

Destroyers
- *Porterfield*
- *Callaghan*
- *Cassin Young*
- *Irwin*
- *Preston*
- *Laws*
- *Longshaw*
- *Morrison*
- *Pritchett*
- *Clarence K. Bronson*
- *Cotten*
- *Dortsch*
- *Gatling*
- *Healy*
- *Cogswell*
- *Caperton*
- *Ingersoll*
- *Knapp*

Task Group 38.4
(Rear-Admiral
R. E. Davison)

Carriers
- *Franklin* (flag)
- *Enterprise*

Light carriers
- *San Jacinto*
- *Belleau Wood*

Heavy cruiser
- *New Orleans*

Light cruiser
- *Biloxi*

Destroyers
- *Maury*
- *Grindley*
- *Helm*
- *McCall*
- *Mugford*
- *Ralph Talbot*
- *Bagley*
- *Patterson*
- *Swanson*
- *Nicholson*
- *Wilkes*

APPENDIX E

Organisation of Allied Forces for the Landings on Leyte

(1) AMPHIBIOUS FORCE

(Vessels employed by the Attack Forces and early Reinforcement Echelons)

Northern Attack Force	*Type*	*Southern Attack Force*
1	Headquarters ships (AGC)	3
2	Reserve headquarters ships (RAGC)	—
17	Assault transports (APA)	21
3	Landing ships, infantry (LSI)	—
4	Transports (AP)	5
1	Assault troop carrier (converted minelayer) (CM) (H.M.S. *Ariadne*)	—
5	Transports (high speed) (APD)	—
4	Assault M.T. transports (AKA)	6
2	M.T. transports (AK)	2
—	Landing ships, vehicle (LSV)	2
5	Landing ships, dock (LSD)	5
95	Landing ships, tank (LST)	48
12	Landing ships, medium (LSM)	6
16	Landing craft, infantry, large (LCI(L))	—
29	Support LCI	50
—	Landing craft, tank (LCI)	12 (on board LST)
10	Control craft	?
40	Liberty ships (up to D plus 15)	?

(2) NAVAL FORCES

BOMBARDMENT AND FIRE SUPPORT GROUP

Northern Attack Force	*Type*	*Southern Attack Force*
3	Old battleships	3
—	Heavy cruisers	3
—	Light cruisers	3
3	Destroyers	13
	LCI (Rocket), LCI(G), LCI (Mortar) and LCS.	

CLOSE COVERING GROUP

2 heavy cruisers (Royal Australian Navy).
2 light cruisers.
7 destroyers (2 Royal Australian Navy).

ESCORT CARRIER GROUP

18 escort carriers.
9 destroyers.
18 destroyer escorts.

ESCORTING DESTROYERS (for attack force and reinforcing echelons)

MINESWEEPING GROUP

M.T.B.s

(3) MILITARY FORCES

	Troops
(*a*) SIXTH ARMY HEADQUARTERS	
X CORPS (Northern Landing Force)	48,400
1st Cavalry Division (Infantry) (two R.C.T. only).	
24th Infantry Division (less one R.C.T.).	
21st Regimental Combat Team (24th Division) (Panaon).	
2nd Engineer Special Brigade.	
XXIV CORPS (Southern Landing Force)	52,900
96th Infantry Division.	
7th Infantry Division.	
(*b*) SIXTH ARMY TROOPS	23,400
381 R.C.T. (Floating Reserve).	
6th Ranger Battalion (Dinagat-Homonhon).	
(*c*) SIXTH ARMY SERVICE COMMAND	44,700
Garrison troops (Special)	900
Approximate total	170,300

(*d*) IN RESERVE

32nd Infantry Division at Hollandia with one R.C.T. at Morotai.
77th Infantry Division at Guam.

(4) AIR FORCES

(*a*) THIRD FLEET

16 carriers with a total of 986 aircraft (fighters, night fighters, torpedo-bombers).

(*b*) ESCORT CARRIER GROUP

18 escort carriers with a total of 448 aircraft of same type as (*a*) ; 16 of these carriers were in direct support of the operation.

(*c*) FAR EASTERN AIR FORCES

Approximately 1,974 aircraft, mainly of the following types : heavy bombers 432 ; light medium and other bombers 422 ; fighters (all types) 673) ; troop carriers 336.

(*d*) LAND-BASED ALLIED AIR FORCES

Carried out long range bombing against strategic targets.

(5) FORCES CO-OPERATING

THIRD FLEET

8 Fleet carriers.
9 light carriers.
6 battleships.
4 heavy cruisers.
8 light cruisers.
3 light cruisers (A.A.).
5 destroyers.

SUBMARINES OF THE PACIFIC AND SEVENTH FLEETS

APPENDIX F

Battle for Leyte Gulf

23rd–26th October, 1944

ORGANISATION OF U.S. SEVENTH FLEET

(Vice-Admiral T. C. Kinkaid)

(1) TASK FORCE 77 (Covering Force) (Vice-Admiral Kinkaid)

Task Group 77.2 (Fire Support and Bombardment Group—Rear-Admiral J. B. Oldendorf, U.S.S. *Louisville*)

BATTLE LINE (Rear-Admiral G. L. Weyler)

Battleships *Mississippi* (flagship), *Maryland, West Virginia, Tennessee, California, Pennsylvania.*

Destroyers *Aulick, Cony, Sigourney, Claxton, Thorn, Welles.*

LEFT FLANK FORCE (Rear-Admiral Oldendorf)

Heavy cruisers *Louisville* (flagship), *Portland, Minneapolis.*

Light cruisers *Denver* (flagship), *Columbia.*

Destroyers *Newcomb, Leutze, Bennion, Heywood L. Edwards, Richard P. Leary, Robinson, Albert W. Grant, Bryant, Halford.*

RIGHT FLANK FORCE

TASK GROUP 77.3 (Close Covering Group—Rear-Admiral R. S. Berkey, U.S.S. *Phoenix*)

Light cruisers *Phoenix* (flagship), *Boise.*

Heavy cruiser H.M.A.S. *Shropshire* (Captain C. A. G. Nichols, R.N.).

Destroyers *Hutchins, Bache, Daly, Beale, Killen,* H.M.A.S. *Arunta* (Commander A. E. Buchanan, R.A.N.).

SPECIAL ATTACK GROUP 79.11

Eastern attack group (destroyers) *Remey, McGowan, Melvin.*

Western attack group (destroyers) *Monssen, McDermut.*

Patrol (destroyers) *McNair, Mertz.*

(2) ESCORT CARRIER GROUP

TASK GROUP 77.4 (Rear-Admiral T. L. Sprague, U.S.S. *Sangamon*)

77.4.1 PANAON CARRIER GROUP

Escort carriers 77.4.11 *Sangamon* (flagship), *Suwannee, Santee, Chenango.*

77.4.12 *Saginaw Bay* (flagship of Rear-Admiral G. R. Henderson), *Petrof Bay.*

Screen 77.4.13 *McCord* (destroyer), *Trathen* (destroyer), *Hazelwood* (destroyer), *Richard S. Bull* (destroyer escort), *Richard M. Rowell* (destroyer escort), *Eversole.*

77.4.2 SOUTHERN CARRIER GROUP (Rear-Admiral F. B. Stump)

Escort carriers 77.4.21 *Natoma Bay* (flagship of Rear-Admiral F. B. Stump), *Manila Bay.*

77.4.22 *Marcus Island* (flagship of Rear-Admiral W. D. Sample), *Kadashan Bay, Savo Island, Ommaney Bay.*

Screen 77.4.23 *Haggard* (destroyer), *Franks* (destroyer), *Hailey* (destroyer), *Richard W. Suesens* (destroyer escort), *Abercrombie* (destroyer escort), *Leray Wilson* (destroyer escort), *Walter C. Wann* (destroyer escort).

77.4.3 NORTHERN CARRIER GROUP (Rear-Admiral C. A. F. Sprague)

Escort carriers 77.4.31 *Fanshaw Bay* (flagship of Rear-Admiral C. A. F. Sprague), *Saint Lo, White Plains, Kalinin Bay.*

77.4.32 *Kitkun Bay* (Rear-Admiral R. A. Ofstie), *Gambier Bay.*

Screen 77.4.33 *Hoel* (destroyer), *Heerman* (destroyer), *Johnston* (destroyer), *Dennis* (destroyer escort), *John C. Butler* (destroyer escort), *Raymond* (destroyer escort), *Samuel B. Roberts* (destroyer escort).

APPENDIX G

Battle for Leyte Gulf

ORGANISATION OF U.S. THIRD FLEET UNTIL 0240 25TH OCTOBER

(Admiral W. F. Halsey Jr., U.S.S. *New Jersey*)

(1) TASK FORCE 38

(FIRST CARRIER TASK FORCE, PACIFIC FLEET)

(Vice-Admiral M. A. Mitscher, U.S.S. *Lexington*)

TASK GROUP 38.1 (Vice-Admiral J. S. McCain)

Carriers	*Wasp, Hornet, Hancock.*
Light carriers	*Monterey, Cowpens.*
Cruisers	*Chester, Salt Lake City, Pensacola.*
Light cruisers, A.A.	*Oakland, San Diego.*
Destroyers	*Case, Cassin, Downes, Dunlap, Fanning, Cummings, Izard, Conner, Brown, Cowell, McCalla, Grayson, Woodworth.*

TASK GROUP 38.2 (Rear-Admiral G. F. Bogan)

Carrier	*Intrepid.*
Light carriers	*Cabot, Independence.*
Battleships	*Iowa, New Jersey.*
Light cruisers	*Vincennes, Biloxi, Miami.*
Destroyers	*Owen, Miller, The Sullivans, Tingey, Hickox, Hunt, Lewis Hancock, Marshall, Cushing, Colahan, Halsey Powell, Uhlmann, Yarnall, Twining, Stockham, Wedderburn.*

TASK GROUP 38.3 (Rear-Admiral F. C. Sherman)

Carriers	*Essex, Lexington.*
Light carriers	*Langley, Princeton.*
Battleships	*Massachusetts, South Dakota.*
Light cruisers	*Santa Fé, Mobile, Birmingham.*
Light cruiser (A.A.)	*Reno.*
Destroyers	*Clarence K. Bronson, Cotten, Dortch, Gatling, Healy, Cogswell, Caperton, Porterfield, Callaghan, Cassin Young, Preston, Laws, Longshaw, Irwin, Morrison.*

TASK GROUP 38.4 (Rear-Admiral R. E. Davison)

Carriers	*Franklin, Enterprise.*
Light carriers	*San Jacinto, Belleau Wood.*
Cruiser	*New Orleans.*
Light cruiser	*Biloxi.*
Destroyers	*Maury, Gridley, Helm, McCall, Mugford, Patterson, Bagley, Ralph Talbot, Swanson, Nicholson, Wilkes, Ingersoll, Knapp.*

(2) TASK FORCE 34

(Heavy Striking Force)

(Formed 0430 25th October)

(Vice-Admiral W. A. Lee Jr., U.S.S. *Washington*)

TASK GROUP 34 (BATTLE LINE) (Vice-Admiral Lee)

Task Unit 34.1.1 (Bat. Div. 7)	*Iowa, New Jersey.*
Task Unit 34.1.2 (Bat. Div. 8)	*Massachusetts, Washington.*
Task Unit 34.1.3 (Bat. Div. 9)	*South Dakota, Alabama.*

TASK GROUP 34.2 (RIGHT FLANK) (Rear-Admiral F. E. M. Whiting)

Task Unit 34.2.2 (Cru. Div. 14)	*Vincennes* (flagship), *Miami, Biloxi.*
Task Units 34.2.3, 34.2.4 (destroyers)	*Tingey, Owen, Miller, Hunt, The Sullivans, Hickox, Lewis Hancock, Marshall.*

TASK GROUP 34.3 (CENTRE) (Rear-Admiral C. T. Joy)

Task Unit 34.3.1 (Cru. Div. 6)	*Wichita* (flagship), *New Orleans.*
Task Unit 34.3.3 (destroyers)	*Cogswell, Caperton, Ingersoll, Knapp.*

TASK GROUP 34.4 (LEFT FLANK) (Rear-Admiral L. T. Du Bose)

Task Unit 34.4.2 (Cru. Div. 13)	*Santa Fé* (flagship), *Mobile.*
Task Unit 34.4.3 (destroyers)	*C. K. Bronson, Cotten, Dortch, Healy, Patterson, Bagley.*

(3) SPECIAL TASK GROUP 34.5 (Rear-Admiral O. C. Badger)
(Former 1620 25th October)

Battleships	*Iowa* (flagship), *New Jersey.*
Cruisers	*Vincennes, Biloxi, Miami.*
Destroyers	*Tingey, Owen, Miller, The Sullivans, Hickox, Hunt, Lewis Hancock, Marshall.*

APPENDIX H

Battle for Leyte Gulf

ORGANISATION OF JAPANESE FLEET, 23RD–26TH OCTOBER 1944

NORTHERN FORCE

(Main Body of Mobile Force or Attack Group—Kd MB)
(Vice-Admiral J. Ozawa)

Aircraft carrier ..	*Zuikaku** (Fleet flagship).	Fighter aircraft	52
Light Carriers ..	*Chitose*, Chiyoda*, Zuiho**.	Fighter bombers	28
		Torpedo bombers	25
		Bombers	7
		Attack (torpedo aircraft) ..	4
			116
		Float reconnaissance aircraft	2

Battleship carriers	*Hyuga****, *Ise**** (flagship) (eight 14-inch guns, sixteen 5·5-inch guns, eight 5·1-inch H.A. guns).
Light cruisers ..	*Tama** (seven 5·5-inch guns, three 3-inch H.A. guns, six Q.R.T. (24-inch)).
	Oyodo (six 6·1-inch guns, two 4·7-inch H.A./L.A. guns, 1 Q.R.T.)
Destroyers ..	*Isudzu* (light cruiser) (seven 5·5-inch guns, three 3-inch H.A. guns, 6 Q.R.T. (24-inch)).
	Hatsutsuki, Wakatsuki, Akitsuki*, Shimotsuki, Kuwa* (eight 4-inch H.A./L.A. guns, 1 Q.R.T. (24-inch)).
	Maki (three 5-inch H.A./L.A. guns, 1 Q.R.T. (24-inch)).
	Sugi, Kiri (? Armament).

Ships marked * were sunk.

Ships marked *** were damaged.

APPENDIX H

CENTRE FORCE

1st and 2nd Night Combat Units or 1st Diversion Attack Force (1 – YB)
(Vice-Admiral T. Kurita)

Battleships .. *Yamato**** (flagship), *Musashi*** (nine 18·1-inch guns, twelve 6-inch guns, twelve 5-inch. A.A. guns).

*Nagato**** (eight 16-inch guns, eighteen 5·5-inch guns, eight 5·1-inch H.A. guns).

Kongo, Haruna (eight 14-inch guns, fourteen 5·9-inch guns).

Cruisers .. .. *Atago*** (Fleet flagship), *Takao***, *Maya***, *Chokai** (ten 7·87-inch guns, four 4·7-inch H.A. guns, four Q.R.T. (24-inch)).

*Myoko*** (flagship), *Haguro, Kumano**** (flagship), *Suzuya** (ten 7·87-inch guns, eight 5·1-inch. H.A. guns, 4 Q.R.T. (24-inch)).

*Chikuma**, *Tone* (eight 7·87-inch guns, eight 5·1-inch H.A. guns, four Q.R.T. (24-inch)).

Destroyers .. *Noshiro** (light cruiser) (six 6·1-inch guns, two 4·7-inch H.A./L.A. guns, one Q.R.T. (24-inch)).

*Hayashimo**, *Akishimo, Asashimo, Kishinami, Okinami, Naganami* (six 5-inch guns, two Q.R.T. (24-inch)).

Hamanami, Fujinami (six 5-inch guns, two P.R.T. (24-inch)).

Shimakaze (six 5-inch guns, three P.R.T. (24-inch).

*Yahagi**** (light cruiser) (six 6·1-inch guns, two 4·7-inch H.A./L.A. guns, one Q.R.T. (24-inch)).

*Isokaze, Urakaze, Hamakaze, Yukikaze, Kiyoshimo****, *Nowake** (six 5-inch H.A./L.A. guns, two Q.R.T. (24-inch)).

SOUTHERN FORCE

C Force, 3rd Night Combat Unit or 3rd Section
(Vice-Admiral S. Nishimura)

Battleships .. *Yamashiro** (flagship), *Fuso** (twelve 14-inch guns, sixteen 5·5-inch guns, eight 5·1-inch H.A. guns).

Cruiser .. .. *Mogami** (ten 7·87-inch guns, eight 5·1-inch guns).

Destroyers .. *Michisio**, *Yamagumo**, *Asagumo** (six 5-inch H.A./L.A. guns, two Q.R.T. (24-inch)).

*Shigure**** (five 5-inch H.A./L.A. guns, two Q.R.T. (24-inch)).

SECOND DIVERSION ATTACK FORCE

(Vice-Admiral K. Shima)

Cruisers .. .. *Nachi**** (Fleet flagship), *Ashigara**** (ten 7·87-inch guns, four Q.R.T. (24-inch)).

Destroyers .. *Abukuma** (light cruiser) (seven 5·5-inch guns, three 3-inch H.A. guns, six Q.R.T. (24-inch)).

Shiranuhi, Kasumi (six 5-inch H.A./L.A. guns, two Q.R.T. (24-inch)).

Ushi, Akebono (six 5-inch H.A./L.A. guns, three T.R.T. (24-inch)).

Ships marked * were sunk.

In the Centre Force, ships marked ** were sunk, or were damaged and turned back, before taking part in the Battle off Samar. Certain destroyers escorted the damaged ships and only 11 took part in the Battle.

Ships marked *** were damaged.

Another destroyer of the Centre Force, the *Fujinami*, was sunk on 27th October (after the battle was ended) by carrier aircraft south of Mindoro Island in 12° 00′ N., 122° 30′ E., whilst escaping from the battle area.

APPENDIX J

Nominal List of Ships Sunk and Damaged

by Suicide Air Attack During the Philippines Campaign

LEYTE—SAMAR OPERATION

Name of Ship	*Type of Ship*	*Date of Attack*	*Nature of Damage*
H.M.A.S. *Australia*	Cruiser	21st October	Minor.
LCI 1065	Landing craft	24th October	*Sunk.*
Sonoma	Ocean tug	24th October	*Sunk.*
Augustus Thomas	s.s.	24th October	Extensive.
St. Lo	Escort carrier	25th October	*Sunk.*
Santee	Escort carrier	25th October	Extensive.
White Plains	Escort carrier	25th October	Minor (near miss).
Kalinin Bay	Escort carrier	25th October	Extensive (two hits).
Sangamon	Escort carrier	25th October	Minor (near miss).
Kitkun Bay	Escort carrier	25th October	Minor.
Suwanee	Escort carrier	25th October	Extensive.
Suwanee	Escort carrier	26th October	Extensive.
California	Battleship	27th October	Minor.
Benjamin Wheeler	s.s.	27th October	Extensive.
Denver	Light cruiser	28th October	Minor (near miss).
Intrepid	Carrier	29th October	Minor
Franklin	Carrier	30th October	Extensive.
Belleau Wood	Light carrier	30th October	Extensive.
Abner Read	Destroyer	1st November	*Sunk.*
Ammen	Destroyer	1st November	Extensive.
Claxton	Destroyer	1st November	Extensive.
Anderson	Destroyer	1st November	Extensive.
Lexington	Carrier	5th November	Minor.
Thomas Merritt	s.s.	12th November	?
Unidentified	LST	12th November	?
Jeremiah Daily	s.s.	12th November	Extensive.
Achilles	Repair ship	12th November	Extensive.
Egeria	Repair ship	12th November	Extensive.
Five unidentified	s.s.	12th November	?
Silvestre Almirante	s.s.	18th November	Extensive.
Alpine	Transport, attack	18th November	Extensive (near miss).
Alcoa Pioneer	s.s.	19th November	Extensive.
James O'Hara	Transport, attack	24th November	Minor.
Cabot	Light carrier	25th November	Extensive.
Intrepid	Carrier	25th November	Extensive (two hits).
Essex	Carrier	25th November	Extensive.
Hancock	Carrier	25th November	Minor (near miss).
Montpelier	Light cruiser	27th November	Minor.
Colorado	Battleship	27th November	Extensive.
St. Louis	Light cruiser	27th November	Extensive.
ARD 19	Floating dock	27th November	Extensive.
Maryland	Battleship	29th November	Extensive.
Saufley	Destroyer	29th November	Minor.
SC 744	Submarine chaser	29th November	*Sunk.*
Aulick	Destroyer	29th November	Extensive.

ORMOC OPERATION

Name of Ship	*Type of Ship*	*Date of Attack*	*Nature of Damage*
Mugford	Destroyer	5th December	Extensive.
Drayton	Destroyer	5th December	Extensive.
LSM 34	Landing ship, medium	5th December	Minor (near miss).
LSM 20	Landing ship, medium	5th December	*Sunk.*
LSM 23	Landing ship, medium	5th December	Extensive.
Marcus Daly	s.s.	5th December	Extensive.
Mahan	Destroyer	7th December	*Sunk* (three hits).
Ward	Destroyer	7th December	*Sunk.*
Lamson	Destroyer	7th December	Extensive.

ORMOC OPERATION—*continued*

Name of Ship	Type of Ship	Date of Attack	Nature of Damage
Liddle	High speed transport	7th December	Extensive.
LST 737	Landing ship, tank	7th December	Minor.
LSM 318	Landing ship, medium	7th December	*Abandoned.*
LSM 18	Landing ship, medium	7th December	Minor (near miss).
William S. Ladd	s.s.	10th December	*Extensive (later sunk).*
Hughes	Destroyer	10th December	Extensive.
PT 323	Motor torpedo boat	10th December	*Extensive (total loss).*
LCT 1073	Landing craft, tank	10th December	*Sunk.*
Reid	Destroyer	10th December	*Sunk.*
Caldwell	Destroyer	11th December	Minor (near miss).
Caldwell	Destroyer	12th December	Extensive.

MINDORO OPERATION

Name of Ship	Type of Ship	Date of Attack	Nature of Damage
Haraden	Destroyer	13th December	Extensive.
Nashville	Light cruiser	13th December	Extensive.
H.M.A.S. *Bishopdale*	Oiler	14th December	Extensive.
Marcus Island	Escort carrier	15th December	Minor (two near misses).
Howorth	Destroyer	15th December	Minor.
LST 472	Landing ship, tank	15th December	*Sunk.*
LST 738	Landing ship, tank	15th December	*Sunk.*
PT 84	Motor torpedo boat	17th December	Minor (near miss).
Liddle	High speed transport	18th December	Extensive.
Gatling	Destroyer	18th December	?
PT 300	Motor torpedo boat	18th December	*Sunk.*
LST 749	Landing ship, tank	21st December	Extensive.
LST 460	Landing ship, tank	21st December	Extensive.
Juan de Fuca	s.s.	21st December	Extensive.
Somiel Dick	s.s. (Dutch)	26th December	Extensive.
William Sharon	s.s.	28th December	Extensive.
John Burke	s.s.	28th December	*Sunk.*
Unidentified LCI or LCM	Landing craft	28th December	*Sunk.*
Orestes	M.T.B. tender	30th December	Beached (later salvaged).
Porcupine (IXI 26)	Unclassified	30th December	*Sunk.*
Pringle	Destroyer	30th December	Extensive.
Gansevoort	Destroyer	30th December	Extensive.
Cargo Ship No. 125	Cargo ship	30th December	?

LINGAYEN OPERATION

Name of Ship	Type of Ship	Date of Attack	Nature of Damage
Cowanesque	Oiler	3rd January	Minor.
Ommaney Bay	Escort carrier	4th January	*Sunk.*
Unidentified	Ammunition ship	4th January	*Sunk.*
H.M.A.S. *Arunta*	Destroyer	5th January	Minor (near miss).
Manila Bay	Escort carrier	5th January	Extensive (two hits).
H.M.A.S. *Shropshire*	Cruiser	5th January	Minor.
Savo Island	Escort carrier	5th January	Minor.
Helm	Destroyer	5th January	Minor.
LCI (G) 70	Landing craft, infantry gunboat	5th January	Minor.
Apache	Ocean tug, fleet	5th January	Minor.
Stafford	Destroyer escort	5th January	Extensive.
YMS ?	District motor minesweeper	5th January	*Sunk.*
Louisville	Heavy cruiser	5th January	Extensive.
Orca	Seaplane tender	5th January	Minor (near miss).
H.M.A.S. *Australia*	Cruiser	5th January	Extensive.
H.M.A.S. *Australia*	Cruiser	6th January	Extensive.
California	Battleship	6th January	Extensive.
New Mexico	Battleship	6th January	Extensive.
Minneapolis	Heavy cruiser	6th January	Minor (near miss).
Louisville	Heavy cruiser	6th January	Extensive.

LINGAYEN OPERATION—*continued*

Name of Ship	*Type of Ship*	*Date of Attack*	*Nature of Damage*
Columbia	Light cruiser	6th January	Extensive (two hits).
R. P. Leary	Destroyer	6th January	Minor.
A. M. Sumner	Destroyer	6th January	Extensive.
Southard	Minesweeper (converted destroyer)	6th January	Extensive.
Long	Minesweeper (converted destroyer)	6th January	*Sunk* (two hits).
Walke	Destroyer	6th January	Extensive.
O'Brien	Destroyer	6th January	Extensive.
Newcomb	Destroyer	6th January	Minor (near miss).
Brooks	High speed transport	6th January	Extensive.
Lowry	Destroyer	6th January	Minor (near miss).
LST 918	Landing ship, tank	6th January	Minor (near miss).
LST 912	Landing ship, tank	8th January	Minor.
Calloway	Transport, attack	8th January	Minor.
H.M.A.S. *Westralia*	Landing ship, infantry	8th January	Minor (near miss).
Kitkun Bay	Escort carrier	8th January	Extensive.
Leedstown	Transport, attack	8th January	Minor.
H.M.A.S. *Australia*	Cruiser	9th January	Extensive.
Kadashan Bay	Escort carrier	8th January	Extensive.
Columbia	Light cruiser	9th January	Extensive.
H.M.A.S. *Australia*	Cruiser	9th January	Minor.
Mississippi	Battleship	9th January	Extensive.
Republic	Transport (Naval)	9th January	Extensive.
Hodges	Destroyer escort	9th January	Minor.
Dupage	Transport, attack	10th January	Minor.
Leray Wilson	Destroyer escort	10th January	Extensive.
Belknap	High speed transport	12th January	Extensive.
Gilligan	Destroyer escort	12th January	Minor.
Richard D. Suesens	Destroyer escort	12th January	Minor (near miss).
LST 700	Landing ship, tank	12th January	Extensive.
Otis Skinner	s.s.	12th January	Extensive.
Kyle Johnson	s.s.	12th January	Extensive.
Elmira Victory	s.s.	12th January	Minor (near miss).
LST 778	Landing ship, tank	12th January	Minor (near miss).
D.D. Field	s.s.	12th January	Minor (near miss).
Zeilin	Transport, attack	13th January	Extensive.
Salamaua	Escort carrier	13th January	Extensive.

Note.—Action reports from which the foregoing table was compiled were in some cases incomplete and lacking in detail, especially as to minor units, of which several, in addition to those listed, were reported as having been hit.

APPENDIX K

U.S. Landing on Mindoro

15th December, 1944

ORGANISATION OF FORCES

ATTACK FORCE

(Rear-Admiral A. D. Struble)

Task Group

78.3 MINDORO ATTACK GROUP (Rear-Admiral Struble)

Nashville (flag) (light cruiser).

12 destroyers, 9 transports (high speed), 30 landing ships, tank, 12 landing ships (medium), 31 landing craft, infantry (large), 9 minesweepers, 7 district motor minesweepers, 4 landing craft, personnel (ramp), 14 small control craft.

Task Group

77.3 CLOSE COVERING GROUP (Rear-Admiral R. S. Berkey)
Phoenix (flag), *Boise* (light cruisers), *Portland* (heavy cruiser).
Destroyers *Barton, Walke, Laffey, O'Brien, Allen, Sumner, Moale, Ingraham.*

70.1 MOTOR TORPEDO BOAT GROUP (Commander C. E. Dowling)
23 M.T.B.s.

HEAVY COVERING AND CARRIER GROUP

(Rear-Admiral T. D. Ruddock, Jr.)

77.12 Battleships .. .. *West Virginia, Colorado, New Mexico.*
Light cruisers .. *Denver, Columbia, Montpelier.*
Escort carriers .. *Natoma Bay, Manila Bay, Marcus Island, Kadashan Bay, Savo Island, Ommaney Bay.*
Destroyers .. .. *Waller, Renshaw, Conway, Cony, Eaton, Robinson, Conner, Sigourney, Bennion, Remey, Mertz, McDermut, Patterson, Haraden, Twiggs, Stembel, Ralph Talbot, Braine.*

APPENDIX L

U.S. Fast Carrier Force as Reorganised

1st December, 1944

TASK FORCE 38 (Vice-Admiral J. S. McCain)

TASK GROUP 38.1 (Rear-Admiral A. E. Montgomery)
Carriers .. .. *Yorktown, Wasp.*
Light carrier .. *Cowpens.*
Battleships .. *Massachusetts, Alabama.*
Heavy cruisers .. *San Francisco, Baltimore.*
Light cruisers .. *Astoria, San Diego, Oakland.*
Destroyers .. *Buchanan, Hobby, Welles, Dyson, Spence, Thatcher, Colahan, Halsey Powell, Benham, Yarnall, Stockholm, Wedderburn, Hailey, Franks, Cushing.*

TASK GROUP 38.2 (Rear-Admiral G. F. Bogan)
Carriers .. .. *Lexington, Hancock, Hornet.*
Light carriers .. *Independence, Monterey.*
Battleships .. *Iowa, New Jersey.*
Light cruisers .. *Vincennes, Miami, Pasadena, San Juan.*
Destroyers .. *Capps, D. W. Taylor, Evans, J. D. Henley, Boyd, Brown, Cowell, Hazelwood, Trathen, Owen, Miller, The Sullivans, Stephen Potter, Tingey, Hickox, Hunt, Lewis Hancock, Marshall.*

TASK GROUP 38.3 (Rear-Admiral F. C. Sherman)
Carriers .. .. *Essex, Ticonderoga.*
Light carrier .. *Langley.*
Battleships .. *North Carolina, Washington, South Dakota.*
Light cruisers .. *Santa Fé, Mobile, Biloxi.*
Destroyers .. *C. K. Bronson, Cotten, Dortch, Gatling, Healy, Cogswell, Caperton, Ingersoll, Knapp, Porterfield, Callaghan, Cassin Young, Preston, Laws, Long, Longshaw, Prichett.*

APPENDIX M

Organisation of the Luzon Attack Force

TASK FORCE 77 (Vice-Admiral T. C. Kinkaid)

Task Group

77.1 FLAG GROUP
1 amphibious force flagship, 1 light cruiser, 4 destroyers, Commander support aircraft.

77.2 BOMBARDMENT AND FIRE SUPPORT GROUP (Vice-Admiral J. B. Oldendorf)
77.2.1 *San Fabian Fire Support Unit* (Rear-Admiral G. L. Weyler)
3 battleships, 2 heavy cruisers, 1 light cruiser, 10 destroyers, 3 underwater demolition teams and supporting landing craft.
77.2.2 *Lingayen Fire Support Unit* (Vice-Admiral J. B. Oldendorf)
3 battleships, 3 heavy cruisers, 9 destroyers, 3 underwater demolition teams and supporting landing craft.

77.3 CLOSE COVERING GROUP (Rear-Admiral R. S. Berkey)
3 light cruisers, 6 destroyers.

77.4 ESCORT CARRIER GROUP (Rear-Admiral C. T. Durgin)
17 escort carriers, 16 destroyers, 6 destroyer escorts.

77.5 HUNTER—KILLER GROUP (Captain J. C. Cronin)
1 escort carrier, 5 destroyer escorts.

77.6 MINESWEEPING AND HYDROGRAPHIC GROUP (Commander W. R. Lond)
2 light minelayers, 1 minelayer, 10 minesweepers (converted destroyers), 10 minesweepers, 43 motor minesweepers, 1 frigate, 1 coastguard cutter, 1 surveying ship, 1 harbour defence motor launch, 1 high speed transport.

77.7 SCREENING GROUP (Captain J. B. McLean)
5 destroyers.

77.8 SALVAGE AND RESCUE GROUP (Commander Huie)
6 Fleet tugs, 3 salvage vessels, 8 landing craft, infantry (large), 2 repair ships, landing craft, 2 ocean tugs (old).

77.9 REINFORCEMENT GROUP (Rear-Admiral R. L. Conolly)
1 amphibious force flagship, 8 destroyers, 6 destroyer escorts, 16 transports (attack), 3 transports (operated by Navy), 5 cargo ships (attack), 11 transports (high speed), 50 landing ships (tank).

77.10 SERVICES GROUP (Rear-Admiral R. O. Glover)
Forces assigned plus 6 destroyer escorts, 2 landing ships, tank (ammunition).

78 SAN FABIAN ATTACK FORCE (Vice-Admiral D. E. Barbey)
27 destroyers, 13 destroyer escorts, 1 amphibious force flagship, 1 coastguard cutter, 1 R.A.G.C., 1 oiler, 16 transports (attack), 6 transports (operated by Navy), 1 hospital transport, 3 cargo ships (attack), 30 cargo ships (auxiliary), 5 landing ships (dock), 1 landing ship (vehicle), 82 landing ships (tank), 20 landing ships (medium).

79 LINGAYEN ATTACK FORCE (Vice-Admiral T. S. Wilkinson)
19 destroyers, 6 destroyer escorts, 3 amphibious force flagships, 18 transports (attack), 3 transports (operated by Navy), 1 hospital transport, 3 landing craft (infantry), 6 cargo ships (attack), 4 landing ships (dock), 2 landing ships (vehicle), 38 landing ships (tank), 31 landing ships (medium), miscellaneous small craft.

APPENDIX N

Composition of U.S. Fast Carrier Force (TF38) and Service Groups, January, 1945

TASK FORCE 38 (Vice-Admiral J. S. McCain)

TASK GROUP 38.1 (Rear-Admiral A. W. Radford)

Carriers	*Yorktown, Wasp.*
Light carriers ..	*Cabot, Cowpens.*
Battleships ..	*South Dakota, Massachusetts.*
Heavy cruisers ..	*San Francisco, Baltimore, Boston.*
Light cruiser (A.A.)	*San Diego.*
Destroyers.. ..	*Colahan, Benham, Yarnall, Stockham, Wedderburn, Cushing, Mansfield, De Haven, Lyman K. Swenson, Collett, Maddox, Blue, Brush, Taussig, Samuel N. Moore, Uhlmann, Twining.*

TASK GROUP 38.2 (Rear-Admiral G. F. Bogan)

Carriers	*Lexington, Hancock, Hornet.*
Battleships ..	*New Jersey, Wisconsin.*
Light cruisers ..	*Pasadena, Astoria, Wilkes-Barre, San Juan* (A.A.).
Destroyers ..	*Owen, Miller, The Sullivans, Stephen Potter, Hunt, Lewis Hancock, Marshall, English, Sperry, Ault, Waldron, Haynsworth, Weeks, Hank.*

TASK GROUP 38.3 (Rear-Admiral F. C. Sherman)

Carriers	*Essex, Ticonderoga.*
Light carriers ..	*Langley, San Jacinto.*
Battleships ..	*Washington, North Carolina.*
Heavy cruisers ..	*Santa Fé, Vincennes, Miami, Biloxi.*
Light cruiser (A.A.)	*Flint.*
Destroyers ..	*Gatling, C. K. Bronson, Cotten, Dortch, Healy, Cogswell, Caperton, Ingersoll, Knapp, Porterfield, Callaghan, Cassin Young, Preston, Laws, Longshaw, Prichett, Halsey Powell.*

TASK GROUP 38.5 (Rear-Admiral M. B. Gardner)

Night carrier ..	*Enterprise.*
Light night carrier	*Independence.*
Destroyers.. ..	*McCord, Trathen, Hazelwood, Franks, Buchanan, Haggard.*

TASK GROUP 30.8 (Captain J. T. Acuff)

Escort carriers ..	*Nehenta Bay, Rudyerd Bay, Cape Esperance, Sargent Bay, Kwajalein, Altamaha, Shipley Bay.*
Destroyers.. ..	*Welles, Evans, Gatling, Hickox, Macdonough, Farragut, Thorn, Hobby, Trathen.*
Destroyer escorts ..	*Hilbert, Lamons, Crowley, Samuel S. Miles, O'Neill, Stern, Lake, Weaver, Thatcher, Reynolds, Wesson, Mitchell, Bangust, Swearer, George, Riddle, Lyman, Kyne.*
Oilers	*Atascosa, Aucilla, Cache, Caliente, Chicopee, Chikaskia, Cimarron, Escalante, Guadalupe, Kankakee, Kennebago, Manatee, Marias, Merrimack, Millicoma, Monongahela, Nantahala, Neches, Neosho, Niobrara, Pamanset, Patuxent, Saugatuk, Taluga, Tomahawk.*

TASK GROUP 30.7 (Captain G. C. Montgomery)

Escort carrier ..	*Anzio.*
Destroyer escorts ..	*Lawrence C. Taylor, Oliver Mitchell, Robert F. Keller.*

APPENDIX O

Minor U.S. Landings in the Philippines, 1945

Organisation of Allied Forces

(1)

SAN ANTONIO (29TH JANUARY)

GRANDE ISLAND (30TH JANUARY)

ATTACK GROUP (Rear-Admiral A. D. Struble)
1 AGC, 13 APA, 4 AP, 7 AKA, 2 AK, 1 LSV, 5 APD, 35 LST, 6 LSM, 10 AM, 20 YMS, 19 miscellaneous small craft.
Escort: 7 destroyers, 7 destroyer escorts.

FIRE SUPPORT UNIT
Light cruiser *Denver*, destroyers *Fletcher*, *Radford*.

DIRECT AIR SUPPORT (Task Group 77.4) (Rear-Admiral W. D. Sample)
Escort carriers *Natoma Bay*, *Marcus Island*, *Savo Island*, *Steamer Bay*, *Petrof Bay*, *Tulagi*, 6 destroyers, 4 destroyer escorts.

ASSAULT TROOPS
San Antonio—38th Infantry Division (reinforced), 34th R.C.T. of 24th Infantry Division.
Grande Island—one battalion of 38th Infantry Division.

(2)

NASUGBU (31ST JANUARY)

ATTACK GROUP (Rear-Admiral W. M. Fechteler)
1 CGC, 4 APD, 35 LCI, 8 LSM, 6 LST, 27 miscellaneous small craft.
Escort: 6 destroyers, 3 destroyer escorts.

FIRE SUPPORT UNIT
Light cruiser *Denver*, destroyers *Fletcher*, *Radford*.

DIRECT AIR SUPPORT
As for San Antonio and Grande Island.

ASSAULT TROOPS
Two R.C.T.s of 11th Airborne Division landed by sea, one R.C.T. by parachute.

(3)

MARIVELES (16TH FEBRUARY)

CORREGIDOR (16TH FEBRUARY)

ATTACK GROUP (Task Group 78.3) (Rear-Admiral A. D. Struble)
1 CGC, 6 LCI(L), 5 LST, 6 LCT, 20 LSM, 25 LCM.
Inshore support: 2 PC, 6 LCI(R), 6 LCS(L).
Escort: 6 destroyers.
Salvage craft.

FIRE SUPPORT GROUP (Task Group 77.3) (Rear-Admiral R. S. Berkey)
Light cruisers *Phoenix*, *Boise*, *Denver*, *Cleveland*, *Montpelier*.
Destroyers *Hopewell*, *Nicholas*, *Taylor*, *O'Bannon*, *Fletcher*, *Radford*, *Jenkins*, *Lavallette*, *Abbott*.

RESERVE FIRE SUPPORT UNIT
Heavy cruisers H.M.A.S. *Shropshire* (flag of Commodore Commanding Australian Squadron), *Portland*, *Minneapolis*.
Destroyers *Conway*, *Eaton*, *Braine*, *Frazier*, H.M.A.S. *Arunta*, H.M.A.S. *Warramunga*.

ASSAULT TROOPS
Mariveles—151st Infantry, R.C.T., 3rd Battalion of 34th R.C.T.
Corregidor—503rd Parachute Infantry Battalion (by parachute), 3rd Battalion of 24th R.C.T.

(4)

PALAWAN (28TH FEBRUARY)

ATTACK GROUP (Task Group 78.2) (Rear-Admiral W. M. Fechteler)
1 CGC, 4 APD, 1 LSD, 10 LCI(L), 20 LSM, 6 LST, 7 LCI(R), 3 LCI(M), 4 LCS(R), 1 PC, 3 SC, 4 YMS, 1 LCI(D), 1 ATF.

COVERING AND SUPPORT GROUP (Task Group 74.2) (Rear-Admiral R. S. Riggs)
Light cruisers *Denver* (F), *Cleveland, Montpelier.*
Destroyers *Fletcher, Jenkins, O'Bannon, Abbott.*

ASSAULT TROOPS
186th R.C.T. (reinforced) of 41st Division.

(5)

ZAMBOANGA (10TH MARCH)

BASILAN ISLAND (16TH MARCH)

ATTACK GROUP (Task Group 78.1) (Rear-Admiral F. B. Royal)
1 AGC (flagship), 23 LST, 21 LSM, 32 LCI, 4 APD, 1 LSD.
Screen: destroyers *Waller, Saufley, Philip, Sigourney, Robinson, McCalla, Bancroft, Bailey*, destroyer escorts *Rudderow, Chaffee.*
Support craft unit: 1 LCI, 7 LCS(L), 5 LCI(R), 2 LCI(M), 2 LCI(D).
Control unit: 2 PC, 2 SC.
Minesweeping unit: 11 YMS.
Service unit: 1 ATF, 1 ATR, 1 AGS, 1 AN.

COVERING GROUP
Light cruisers *Phoenix, Boise*, destroyers *Taylor, Nicholas, O'Bannon, Fletcher, Jenkins, Abbott.*
M.T.B. unit: 1 AGP, 21 M.T.B.s.

ASSAULT TROOPS
Zamboanga—41st Infantry Division (reinforced) less 186th R.C.T.
Basilan Island—one reinforced infantry company of 41st Division.

(6)

ILOILO (18TH MARCH)

ASSAULT GROUP (Task Group 78.3) (Rear-Admiral A. D. Struble)
1 CGC, 16 LST, 10 LSM, 13 LCI, 1 ATR, 2 SC, 4 LCI(R), 1 LCI(M), 1 LCI(D), 16 LCM.
Escort unit: destroyers *Charles Alsburne, Claxton, Converse, Thatcher, Dyson.*
Minesweeping unit: 5 YMS.
Surveying vessel H.M.A.S. *Warrego.*

COVERING AND FIRE SUPPORT UNIT (Task Unit 74.2.2)
Light cruiser *Cleveland*, destroyers *Conway, Eaton, Stevens.*

ASSAULT TROOPS
40th Division (reinforced) less one R.C.T.

(7)

CEBU (26TH MARCH)

ATTACK GROUP (Task Group 78.2) (Captain A. T. Sprague Jr.)
1 AGC, 4 APD, 15 LCI(L), 11 LSM, 17 LST, 3 LCT, 5 LCI(R), 4 LCS(L).
2 PC, 8 YMS, 1 LCI(D), 1 ATA.
Screen: destroyers *Flusser, Shaw, Conyngham, Drayton, Smith.*

COVERING GROUP (Task Group 74.3) (Rear-Admiral R. S. Berkey)
Light cruisers *Phoenix, Boise*, H.M.A.S. *Hobart*, destroyers *Nicholas, O'Bannon, Taylor, Abbott, Fletcher, Jenkins.*

ASSAULT TROOPS
The Americal Division less 134th R.C.T.

(8)

CABALLO ISLAND (27TH MARCH)

TRANSPORT UNIT
LCM.

SUPPORT UNIT
Destroyers *Conway, Cony,* 3 rocket-equipped M.T.B.s.

(9)

LEGASPI (1ST APRIL)

ASSAULT GROUP
Landing craft : 4 AM, 2 L.C.V.P.s equipped with light sweeping gear.

ASSAULT TROOPS
158th R.C.T.

(10)

SULU (2ND APRIL—SANGA SANGA ISLAND (TAWI TAWI), 9TH APRIL—JOLO)

ASSAULT GROUP
Miscellaneous landing craft, YMS.

SUPPORT UNIT
3 destroyers.

ASSAULT TROOPS
One battalion landing team of 163rd R.C.T.

(11)

MALABANG-PARANG (MINDANAO) (17TH APRIL)

ATTACK GROUP (Rear-Admiral A. G. Noble)
1 AGC, 1 CGC, 5 APD, 45 LCI, 4 LCS(L), 16 LSM, 66 LST, 8 XAK, 17 LCT, 7 YMS, 10 PT, 1 AGS, 1 AO, 2 PC, 2 SC, 4 PGM, 1 AFT, 1 ATR, 2 AGP, 1 PCE(R).
Screen : 9 destroyers, 2 destroyer escorts.

COVERING AND FIRE SUPPORT GROUP (Rear-Admiral R. S. Riggs)
Light cruisers *Denver, Cleveland, Montpelier,* 6 destroyers.

APPENDIX P

Assault on Iwo Jima

Organisation of U.S. Forces

JOINT EXPEDITIONARY FORCE, TASK FORCE 51 (Vice-Admiral R. K. Turner).

AMPHIBIOUS SUPPORT FORCE, TASK FORCE 52 (Rear-Admiral W. H. P. Blandy)

Amphibious force flagship *Estes.*

GUNFIRE AND COVERING FORCE, TASK FORCE 54 (Rear-Admiral B. J. Rodgers)

Old battleships .. *Nevada, Idaho, Tennessee, Texas, New York, Arkansas, West Virginia.*
8-inch cruisers .. *Tuscaloosa, Chester, Pensacola, Salt Lake City.*
Destroyers .. . *Newcomb, Heywood L. Edwards, Richard P. Leary, Bennion, Terry, Halligan, Hall, Stembel, John D. Henley, Paul Hamilton, Bryant, Mullany, Twiggs, Capps, Leutze.*
Light minelayer .. *Hawley.*

The following vessels from Task Force 58 (fast carrier force) joined Task Force 54 temporarily while engaged in fire support :—
Battleships .. *Washington, North Carolina.*
8-inch cruisers .. *Indianapolis, Boston, San Francisco.*
Light cruisers .. *Vicksburg, Santa Fé, Pasadena, Biloxi, Astoria, Wilkes-Barre.*

SUPPORT CARRIER GROUP (Task Group 52.2) (Rear-Admiral C. T. Durgin)

52.2.1 (Rear-Admiral C. A. F. Sprague)

Escort carriers .. *Natoma Bay, Sargent Bay, Wake Island, Petrof Bay, Steamer Bay.*
Destroyers .. .. *Bagley, Ralph Talbot.*
Destroyer escorts .. *Richard S. Bull, Grady, O'Flaherty, Wesson.*

52.2.2 (Rear-Admiral C. T. Durgin)

Escort carriers .. *Makin Island, Lunga Point, Bismarck Sea, Anzio.*
Destroyers .. .. *Daly, Hutchins, Helm.*
Destroyer escorts .. *Lawrence C. Taylor, Melvin R. Newman, Oliver Mitchell, Tabberer, Robert F. Keller.*

52.2.3 (Rear-Admiral G. R. Henderson)

Escort carriers .. *Saginaw Bay, Rudyerd Bay.*
Destroyers .. .. *Stockton, Patterson.*
Destroyer escorts .. *J. C. Butler, Edmonds.*

52.2.4 (Captain L. A. Moebus)

Escort carrier .. *Saratoga.*
Large cruiser.. .. *Alaska.*
Destroyers .. .. *Bagley, Helm.*

MINE GROUP (TASK GROUP 52.3) (Rear-Admiral A. Sharp)

Minelayer .. .. *Terror* (flagship).

52.3.1 Minesweepers .. .. *Hopkins, Dorsey, Howard, Hogan, Chandler, Hamilton.*
Minelayer .. .. *Breese.*
52.3.3 Minesweepers .. .. *Signet, Skirmish, Staunch, Scurry, Spectacle, Spector.*
Minelayer .. .. *Lacy.*
52.3.4 Minesweepers .. .. *Serene, Shelter, Strategy, Strength, Success, Rebel.*
Patrol vessel .. .. *PC 800.*
52.3.5 Minesweepers .. .. *Champion, Ardent, Defense, Devastator, Gamble.*
52.3.6 7 district motor minesweepers.
Minelayer .. .. *Lindsey.*
52.3.8 6 district motor minesweepers.

UNDERWATER DEMOLITION TEAMS (TASK GROUP 52.4)

Transports (high speed).. *Gilmer, Waters, Bates, Barr Bull, Blessman*

GUNBOAT SUPPORT GROUP (TASK GROUP 52.5)

52.5.1 1 LCI(C), 6 LCI(G).
52.5.2 6 LCI(G).
52.5.3 1 LCI(G), 6 LCS(L).
52.5.4 6 LCS (L).

MORTAR SUPPORT GROUP (TASK GROUP 52.6)

Landing craft, flotilla flagship 679.

52.6.1 Mortar Support Unit 1, 6 LCI(M).
52.6.2 Mortar Support Unit 2, 6 LCI(M).
52.6.3 Mortar Support Unit 3, 6 LCI(M).
52.6.4 Mortar Support Unit 4, 1 LCI(M).
52.6.5 Mortar Support Unit 5, 6 LCI(M).

RCM AND ROCKET SUPPORT GROUP (TASK GROUP 52.7)

52.7.1 9 LCI(R).
52.7.2 3 LCI(G).

ATTACK FORCE, TASK FORCE 53 (Rear-Admiral H. W. Hill)

ASSAULT TROOPS (TASK FORCE 56)

V Amphibious Corps (Major-General H. Schmidt, U.S.M.C.).
4th Marine Division (Major-General C. B. Cates, U.S.M.C.).
5th Marine Division (Major-General K. E. Rockey, U.S.M.C.).
Garrison Force (Task Group 10.16) (Major-General J. E. Chaney, U.S. Army).
Expeditionary Troops Reserve.
3rd Marine Division (Major-General C. B. Erskine, U.S.M.C.).
Air Support Control Unit (Task Group 52.10).
Transport Group Able (Task Group 53.1) (Trans. Ron. 16).

ATTACK FORCE, TASK FORCE 53—*continued*

53.1.1 Trans. Div. 46.
Transports, attack .. .. *Cecil, Deuel, Darke, Hocking.*
Cargo ships, attack .. .. *Thurston, Tolland, Whiteside.*

53.1.2 Trans. Div. 47.
Transports, attack .. .. *Rutland, Highlands, Sandoval, Hansford, Carteret.*
Cargo ships, attack .. .. *Whitley, Yancey.*

53.1.3 Trans. Div. 48.
Transports, attack .. .. *Talladega, Missoula, Lubbock, Dickens, Lenawe.*
Cargo Ships, attack .. .. *Athene, Stokes.*
Landing ship, dock .. .. *Gunston Hall.*

56.2.1 Able Landing Group (Major-General K. E. Rockey, U.S.M.C.).
5th Marine Division, plus attached units, corps and garrison force troops, assigned for transportation.

Transport Group Baker (Trans. Ron. 15).

53.2.1 Trans. Div. 43.
Transports, attack .. .. *Bayfield, Mellette, Hendry, Sibley, Berrien.*
Cargo ships, attack .. .. *Shoshone, Artemis.*
Landing ship, vehicle .. .. *Ozark.*

53.2.2 Trans. Div. 44.
Transports, attack .. .. *Hinsdale, Pickens, Sanborn, Napa, Bladen.*
Cargo ships, attack .. .. *Southampton, Starr.*
Landing ship, dock .. .. *Belle Grove.*

53.2.3 Trans. Div. 45.
Transports, attack .. .. *Logan, Newberry, Mifflin.*
Cargo ships, attack .. .. *Leo, Muliphen.*
Landing ship, dock .. .. *Ashland.*

56.2.2 Baker Landing Group (Major-General C. B. Cates, U.S.M.C.).
4th Marine Division, plus attached units, corps and garrison force troops, assigned for transporation.

Tractor Flotilla (Task Group 53.3).

Flotilla flagships .. .. *Gregory* (destroyer), LCI(L) 994.
53.3.1 Tractor Group Able.
Group flagships .. .. *Little* (destroyer), LCI(L) 995.
53.3.2 LST Unit 1, 7 LSTs.
53.3.3 LST Unit 2, 7 LSTs.
53.3.4 Tractor Group Baker.
53.3.5 LST Unit 3, 7 LSTs.
53.3.6 LST Unit 4, 7 LSTs.
53.3.7 Tractor Group Charlie.
Group flagships. .. .. *Rooks* (destroyer), LCI(L) 998.
53.3.8 LST Unit 5, 9 LSTs.
53.3.9 LST Unit 6, 9 LSTs.

Control Group (Task Group 53.5).

53.5.1 Central Control Unit, 1 PCE, 2 PC(S).
53.5.2 Control Unit Able, 2 PC(S), 2 SC.
53.5.3 Control Green, 1 PC, 1 SC.
53.5.4 Control Red, 1 PC, 1 SC.
53.5.5 Control Unit Baker, 2 PC, 3 SC.
53.5.6 Control Yellow. 1 PC.
53.5.7 Control Blue, 1 PC, 1 SC.

Beach Party Group (Task Group 53.6).

Group flagship, SC 724.

53.6.1 Beach Party Unit Able, Trans. Ron. 16.
53.6.3 Green Beach Party, Trans. Div. 48.
53.6.4 Red Beach Party, Trans. Div. 47.
53.6.2 Beach Party Unit Baker, Trans. Ron. 15.
53.6.5 Yellow Beach Party, Trans. Div. 45.
53.6.6 Blue Beach Party, Trans. Div. 44.

ATTACK FORCE, TASK FORCE 53—*continued*

Pontoon Barge, Causeway and LCT Group (Task Group 53.7).
Group flagship, LCI(L) 772.
53.7.1 Pontoon Barge Unit Able, sixteen 3 × 12 barges.
53.7.2 Pontoon Barge Unit Baker, twelve 3 × 12 barges.
53.7.3 Causeway Unit Able, 3 causeway sets.
53.7.4 Causeway Unit Baker, 3 causeway sets.
53.7.5 LCT Unit Group Flagship, LCI(L) 423.
53.7.6 LCT Unit Able, 6 LCT.
53.7.7 LCT Unit Baker, 6 LCT.

Small Craft Group.
1 LCI(L), 2 LCI(G), 2 LST(M).
53.8.1 Small Boat Unit, small boats assigned.

MISCELLANEOUS TASK GROUPS OF TASK FORCE 51 (Vice-Admiral R. K. Turner)

Joint Expeditionary Force Reserves (Task Group 51.1).
51.1.1 Trans. Ron. 11.
Transports, attack .. .. *Fremont, Fayette, Knox, Leedstown, Harry Lee.*
Cargo ships, attack .. .. *Almaack, Warrick.*
51.1.3 Trans. Div. 32.
Transports, attack .. .. *Pres. Jackson, Pres. Adams, Doyen, Bolivar.*
Transport .. .. .. *Cape Johnson.*
Cargo ship, attack .. .. *Libra.*
Cargo ship, auxiliary .. .. *Jupiter.*
51.1.4 Trans. Div. 33.
Transports, attack .. .. *Callaway, Fred Funston, James O'Hara, Feland.*
Cargo ship, attack .. .. *Alhena.*
Cargo ship, auxiliary .. .. *Hercules.*
56.3 Landing Force Reserve (Major-General C. B. Erskine, U.S.M.C.).
3rd Marine Division plus attached units.
51.1.5 Screen.
Destroyers .. .. .. *Anthony, Bush, Wadsworth, Boyd, Bradford.*
Destroyer escorts .. .. *Swearer, Stern, O'Neill.*

Transport Screen (Task Group 51.2).
Amphibious force flagship .. *Biscayne.*
Destroyers .. .. .. *Hyman, Mannert L. Abele, Evans, Calhoun, Putnam, Fullam, Guest, Bennett, Hudson, Pringle, Stanly, Howorth, Gregory, Little, Van Valkenburgh, Halford, Rooks, Wadsworth, Anthony, Mullany, Boyd, Bradford, Bush.*

Destroyer escorts .. .. *Samuel S. Miles, Wesson, Elden, Halloran, William C. Miller, Cabana, Cionne, Deede, Canfield, Rall, Connolly, Finnegan, Grady, McClelland, Riddle, Swearer, Stern, O'Neill.*

Light minelayers .. .. *Robert H. Smith, Thomas E. Fraser, Shannon, Harry F. Bauer.*

Service and Salvage Group (Task Group 51.3).
Repair ship, landing craft .. *Agenor.*
Repair ship, battle damage .. *Oceanus.*
Salvage vessels .. .. *Clamp, Gear, Shackle.*
Ocean tugs, Fleet .. .. *Tawasa, Munsee.*
2 ocean tugs, rescue.
6 LCS(L) (3).
1 LST.

Hydrographic Survey Group (Task Group 51.4).
2 PC(S) (H).

APPENDIX P

FAST CARRIER FORCE, TASK FORCE 58 (Vice-Admiral M. A. Mitscher)

TASK GROUP 58.1 (Rear-Admiral J. J. Clark).

Fleet carriers	*Hornet* (F), *Wasp*, *Bennington*.
Light carrier	*Belleau Wood*.
Battleships	*Massachusetts* (F), *Indiana*.
Light cruisers	*Vincennes* (F), *Miami*, *Vicksburg*.
Light cruiser (A.A.)	*San Juan*.
Destroyers	*De Haven*, *Mansfield*, *Lyman K. Swenson*, *Collett*, *Maddox*, *Blue*, *Brush*, *Taussig*, *Samuel N. Moore*, *John Rodgers*, *Stevens*, *Harrison*, *McKee*, *Murray*, *Ringgold*, *Schroeder*, *Sigsbee*, *Dashiell*.

TASK GROUP 58.2 (Rear-Admiral R. E. Davison)

Fleet carriers	*Lexington* (F), *Hancock*.
Light carrier	*San Jacinto*.
Battleships	*Wisconsin* (F), *Missouri*.
8-inch cruisers	*San Francisco* (F), *Boston*, *Pittsburgh*.
Destroyers	*Owen*, *Miller*, *The Sullivans*, *Stephen Potter*, *Tingey*, *Hickox*, *Hunt*, *Lewis Hancock*, *Marshall*, *Cushing*, *Halsey Powell*, *Colahan*, *Uhlmann*, *Benham*, *Yarnall*, *Twining*, *Stockham*, *Wedderburn*.

TASK GROUP 58.3 (Rear-Admiral F. C. Sherman)

Fleet carriers	*Essex* (F), *Bunker Hill* (FF).
Light carrier	*Cowpens*.
Battleships	*New Jersey* (F), *South Dakota*.
Light cruisers	*Pasadena* (F), *Springfield*, *Astoria*, *Wilkes-Barre*.
8-inch cruiser	*Indianapolis* (Fleet flagship).
Destroyers	*Ault*, *English*, *Charles S. Sperry*, *Waldron*, *Haynsworth*, *Wallace L. Lind*, *John W. Weeks*, *Hank*, *Borie*, *Porterfield*, *Callaghan*, *Cassin Young*, *Irwin*, *Preston*.

TASK GROUP 58.4 (Rear-Admiral A. W. Radford)

Fleet carriers	*Yorktown* (F), *Randolph*.
Light carriers	*Cabot*, *Langley*.
Battleships	*Washington* (F), *North Carolina*.
Light cruisers	*Santa Fé* (F), *Biloxi*, *San Diego*.
Destroyers	*Barton*, *Laffey*, *Lowry*, *Ingraham*, *Moale*, *McCord*, *Trathen*, *Hazelwood*, *Hermann*, *Haggard*, *Franks*, *Clarence K. Bronson*, *Cotten*, *Dortch*, *Gatling*, *Healy*.

TASK GROUP 58.5 (Rear-Admiral M. B. Gardner)

Fleet carriers (night fighter) ..	*Enterprise* (F), *Saratoga*.
Large cruiser	*Alaska*.
8-inch cruiser	*Baltimore* (F).
Light cruiser	*Flint*.
Destroyers	*Remey*, *Norman Scott*, *Mertz*, *Monssen*, *Melvin*, *McDermut*, *McGowan*, *McNair*, *Laws*, *Longshaw*, *Morrison*, *Pritchett*.

APPENDIX Q

Nominal List of Ships Damaged and Sunk

in Capture of Iwo Jima

Date	*Ship*	*Type*	*Damage*
	BY SUICIDE AIR ATTACK		
18th February	*Gamble*	Light minelayer	Major.
21st February	*Bismarck Sea*	Escort carrier	Sunk.
21st February	*Saratoga*	Fleet carrier	Major.
21st February	*Lunga Point*	Escort carrier	Minor.
21st February	*Keokuk*	Net cargo ship	Minor.
21st February	*LST 477*	Landing ship, tank	Major.
	BY BOMB		
18th February	*Blessman*	High speed transport	Major.
	BY SHORE BATTERIES		
17th February	*Leutze*	Destroyer	Major.
17th February	*Tennessee*	Battleship	Minor.
17th February	*Pensacola*	Heavy cruiser	Major.
17th February	*LCI(G) 474*	Landing craft, infantry (gunboat)	Sunk.
17th February	*LCI(G)s 438, 441, 449, 450, 457, 466, 469, 473*	Landing craft, infantry (gunboat)	Major.
17th February	*LCI(G)s 346, 348, 471*	Landing craft, infantry (gunboat)	Minor.
23rd February	*LSMs 46, 47*	Landing ship, medium	Minor.
25th February	*LCI 760*	Landing craft, infantry	Minor.
26th February	*Hamlin*	Seaplane tender	Minor.
27th February	*Leo*	Cargo ship, attack	Minor.
27th February	*LST 884*	Landing ship, tank	Minor.
28th February	*Terry*	Destroyer	Major.
1st March	*Colhoun*	Destroyer	Minor.
2nd March	*Biloxi*	Light cruiser	Minor.
	MORTAR FIRE WHILE BEACHED		
19th February	*LSMs 74, 145, 211, 323*	Landing ship, medium	Major.
20th February	*LSM 216*	Landing ship, medium	Minor.
23rd February	*LSMs 46, 47*	Landing ship, medium	Minor.
27th February	*LSM 792*	Landing ship, medium	Minor.
28th February	*LST 42*	Landing ship, tank	Minor.
	COLLISION		
14th February	*Halford*	Destroyer	Major.
	H. E. Stephenson	Cargo ship	Minor.
16th February	*Barton*	Destroyer	Major.
	Ingraham	Destroyer	Minor.
19th February	*Estes*	Amphibious Force flagship	Minor.
	Chester	Heavy cruiser	Major.
20th February	*LSM 59*	Landing ship, medium	Minor.
	LCI 54	Landing craft, infantry	Minor.
21st February	*Napa*	Transport, attack	Major.
	Logan	Transport, attack	Minor.
23rd February	*LST 390*	Landing ship, tank	Minor.
	LST 807	Landing ship, tank	Minor.
24th February	*LSM 49*	Landing ship, medium	Minor.
	LCI 356	Landing craft, infantry	Minor.
24th February	*Fuller*	Transport, attack	Minor.
24th February	*H. L. Edwards*	Destroyer	Minor.
	Bryant	Destroyer	Minor.
26th February	*LST 121*	Landing ship, tank	Minor.
	LSM 140	Landing ship, medium	Minor.

COLLISION—*continued*

Date	*Ship*	*Type*	*Damage*
27th February	*Colhoun*	Destroyer	Minor.
	Libra, Knox	Cargo ships, attack	Minor.
2nd March	*LST 224*	Landing ship, tank	Minor.
	LCS 52	Landing craft, support	Minor.
4th March	*Yarnall, Ringgold*	Destroyers	Major.
	STRIKING REEF OR OBSTRUCTION		
20th February	*Bradford*	Destroyer	Minor.
22nd February	*Nawman*	Destroyer escort	Minor.
2nd March	*Hercules*	Cargo ship	Minor.
	ALONGSIDE OTHER VESSELS		
18th February	*Washington*	Battleship	Minor.
	Hailey	Destroyer	Minor.
20th February	*Indianapolis*	Heavy cruiser	Minor.
	Shasta	Ammunition ship	Minor.
21st February	*LSM 43*	Landing ship, medium	Minor.
22nd February	*LSM 145*	Landing ship, medium	Minor.
24th February	*Williamson*	Destroyer	Minor.
24th February	*PC 578*	Patrol vessel	Minor.
27th February	*LSM 779*	Landing ship, medium	Minor.
28th February	*President Adams*	Transport, attack	Minor.
2nd March	*Berrien*	Transport, attack	Minor.
6th March	*Yancey*	Cargo ship, attack	Minor.
	DAMAGED BY SEA		
21st February	*LSM 43*	Landing ship, medium	Minor.
24th February	*Moale*	Destroyer	Major.
24th February	*LSMs 202, 241*	Landing ships, medium	Minor.
26th February	*Preston*	Destroyer	Minor.
26th February	*Stephen Potter*	Destroyer	Minor.
26th February	*J. W. Weeks*	Destroyer	Minor.
26th February	*Colahan*	Destroyer	Minor.
26th February	*Benham*	Destroyer	Minor.
26th February	*Halsey Powell*	Destroyer	Minor.
26th February	*San Francisco*	Heavy cruiser	Minor.
	OPERATIONAL DAMAGE		
19th February	*Uhlmann*	Destroyer	Minor.
19th February	*Starr*	Cargo ship, attack	Minor.
23rd February	*LST 716*	Landing ship, tank	Minor.
23rd February	*LSM 92*	Landing ship, medium	Minor.
23rd February	*YMS 361*	District motor minesweeper	Minor.
23rd February	*PC 877*	Patrol vessel	Minor.
23rd February	*Solace*	Hospital ship	Minor.
24th February	*SC 1027*	Submarine chaser	Minor.
24th February	*Howard*	Minesweeper	Minor.
27th February	*LST 775*	Landing ship, tank	Minor.
27th February	*LSMs 60, 44, 47, 140, 261*	Landing ships, medium	Minor.
1st March	*LSM 59*	Landing ship, medium	Major.
2nd March	*LST 634*	Landing ship, tank	Minor.
3rd March	*New York*	Battleship	Major.
	MISCELLANEOUS		
15th February	*LSM 169* (mined)	Landing ship, medium	Major.
17th February	*Waldron* (rammed Japanese picket boat)	Destroyer	Minor.
19th February	*Patuxent* (internal explosion)	Oiler	Major.
19th February	*Samaritan* (friendly shell hit)	Hospital ship	Minor.
22nd February	*Dewey* (increase of damage from December typhoon)	Destroyer	Minor.
25th February	*Porterfield* (fire from Japanese picket boat)	Destroyer	Minor.
25th February	*Pasadena* (fire from Japanese picket boat)	Light cruiser	Minor.
2nd March	*Bennett* (blind bomb or torpedo)	Destroyer	Minor.

APPENDIX R

Organisation of Allied Forces in
Operations Against Borneo

Vice-Admiral D. E. Barbey in command

(1) TARAKAN ATTACK FORCE

ATTACK GROUP (78.1) (Rear-Admiral F. B. Royal)
Rocky Mount (AGC)
(H.M.A.S. *Westralia* and *Manoora*).
2 LSI, 1 AKA, 1 LSD, 21 LST, 12 LCI, 4 LSM, 12 LCT.
Support : 6 LCS, 4 LCI(R), 2 LCI(M), 2 LCI(D) with 4 demolition units.
Screen : destroyers *Waller, Bailey, Bancroft, Philip, Drayton, Smith, Caldwell,* 3 frigates, 2 destroyer escorts, 1 M.T.B. tender, 21 M.T.B.s.
Landing craft control unit : 1 PC, 1 LCI(L), 2 LCS.
Minesweeping unit : 1 APD, 11 YMS.
Service unit : 1 AGS, 1 AN, 1 ATR, 1 ATO, 4 LCI(L) equipped for salvage and fire fighting.
Press unit.
Beachmaster unit.

COVERING GROUP (74.3) (Rear-Admiral R. S. Berkey)
Light cruisers *Phoenix, Boise,* H.M.A.S. *Hobart.*
Destroyers *Taylor, Nicholas, O'Bannon, Fletcher, Jenkins,* H.M.A.S. *Warramunga.*

(2) BRUNEI ATTACK FORCE

ATTACK GROUP (78.1) (Rear-Admiral F. B. Royal)
(H.M.A.S. *Westralia, Manoora* and *Kanimbla.*)
1 AGC, 3 LSI, 1 AKA, 1 LSD, 5 ADD, 34 LST, 22 LCI, 20 LSM.
Close Support : 1 LCI(L), 7 LCS(L), 6 LCI(G), 6 LCI(R), 3 LCI(M).
Screen : 10 destroyers, 6 destroyer escorts, 2 frigates.
Demolition unit : 1 APD, 2 LCI(D).
Landing craft control unit : 2 PC, 4 SC, 1 LCI(L).

COVERING GROUP (74.3) (Rear-Admiral R. S. Berkey)
Light cruisers *Boise, Phoenix, Nashville,* H.M.A.S. *Hobart.*
7 destroyers.

(3) BALIK PAPAN ATTACK FORCE

ATTACK GROUP (78.2) (Rear-Admiral A. G. Noble)
1 AGC, 1 CGC, 3 LSI (H.M.A.S. *Westralia, Manoora* and *Kanimbla*), 1 AKA, 1 LSD, 5 APD, 1 LCF(F), 22 LSM, 35 LST, 16 LCI(L), 2 PC, 3 SC.
Close support : 10 LCS(L), 8 LCI(R), 6 LCI(G).
Screen : 10 destroyers, 5 destroyer escorts, 1 frigate.
Service, salvage and miscellaneous units.
Minesweeping Group : 1 APD, 5 AM, 12 YMS, 1 LSM.

COVERING GROUP (74.2) (Rear-Admiral R. S. Riggs)
Light cruisers *Montpelier, Denver,* 4 destroyers (from 15th June), H.N.M.S. *Tromp* (from 19th June) ; light cruiser *Columbia,* high speed transport *Schmidt* (from 23rd June) ; H.M.A.S. *Shropshire, Hobart,* 3 destroyers (from 27th June) ; light cruisers *Phoenix, Nashville* (4th to 6th July).

APPENDIX S

British Carrier Force (Task Force 57)

(Vice-Admiral Sir H. Bernard Rawlings)

TASK.—Neutralize airfields in the Sakishima Gunto.

1st Battle Squadron (Task Unit 1)	*King George V*	(Captain T. E. Halsey (flag of C.T.F. 57)).
	Howe	(Captain H. W. U. McCall).
1st Aircraft Carrier Squadron (Task Unit 2)	*Indomitable* (29 Hellcat[1], 15 Avenger[2])	(Captain J. A. S. Eccles (flag of A.C.1 and Second-in-Command Task Force 57 Rear-Admiral Sir Philip L. Vian)).
	Victorious (37 Corsair[3], 14 Avenger, 2 Walrus[4])	(Captain M. M. Denny).
	Illustrious (36 Corsair, 16 Avenger)	(Captain C. E. Lambe).
	Indefatigable (40 Seafire[3], 20 Avenger, 9 Firefly[3])	(Captain Q. D. Graham).
4th Cruiser Squadron	*Swiftsure* (nine 6-inch, ten 4-inch)	(Captain P. V. McLaughlin (flag of C.S.4 Rear-Admiral Sir E. J. P. Brind)).
	H.M.N.Z.S. *Gambia* (twelve 6-inch, eight 4-inch)	(Captain R. A. B. Edwards).
	Black Prince (eight 5·25-inch)	(Captain G. V. Gladstone).
	Argonaut (eight 5·25-inch)	(Captain W. P. McCarthy).
25th Destroyer Flotilla (Task Unit 8)	*Euryalus*[5]	(Captain R. Oliver-Bellasis (flag of R.A.(D.) temporarily Rear-Admiral J. H. Edelsten)).
	Grenville	(Captain H. P. Henderson (Captain D.25)).
	Ulster	(Lieutenant-Commander R. J. Hanson).
	Undine	(Commander T. C. Robinson).
	Urania	(Lieutenant-Commander D. H. P. Gardiner)
	Undaunted	(Lieutenant-Commander C. E. R. Sharp).
	Note.—Ursa was docking at Manus.	
4th Destroyer Flotilla	(R.A.N.) *Quickmatch*	(Commander O. H. Becher (Captain D.4).
	(R.A.N.) *Quiberon*	(Lieutenant-Commander G. F. E. Knox).
	Queensborough	(Commander P. L. Saumarez).
	Quality	(Lieutenant-Commander The Viscount Jocelyn).
27th Destroyer Flotilla	*Whelp*	(Commander G. A. F. Norfolk).
	Wager	(Lieutenant-Commander R. C. Watkin).

Note.—Kempenfelt (Captain E. G. McGregor (Captain D.27)) was attached to Task Unit 112.2.5, the group remaining in the replenishing area.

Whirlwind (Commander W. A. F. Hawkins) and *Wessex* (Lieutenant-Commander R. Horncastle) were attached to Task Unit 112.2.1 and Task Unit 112.2.2 respectively, the Tanker Group proceeding between Leyte and the replenishment area.

---

[1] Fighter bomber.

[2] Torpedo bomber fighter employed throughout the operation almost exclusively as bombers.

[3] Fighter.

[4] Amphibian reconnaissance bomber.

[5] Joined the 4th C.S. on 29th March, when R.A.(D) proceeded to Leyte.

APPENDIX T

State of Fleet Train (Task Force 112)

British Pacific Fleet

MANUS–LEYTE, MARCH–MAY 1945

Rear-Admiral D. B. Fisher, H.M.S. *Tyne*

Escort carriers	*Striker*[1] (Captain W. P. Carne, Commodore 2nd Class). *Speaker*[1] (Captain U. H. R. James (Acting)). *Ruler*[1] (Captain H. P. Currey). Arrived Leyte 1st May. *Slinger*[1] (Captain B. L. Moore). *Fencer*[2] (Commander A. M. Harris (Acting) (Emergency)). Arrived Leyte 10th April. *Chaser*[1] (Captain R. G. Poole). Arrived Leyte 11th May.
Destroyers	*Napier*[3] (Captain N. L. Buchanan (Captain D.7)). *Nepal*[3] (Lieutenant-Commander C. J. Stephenson). *Nizam*[3] (Commander C. H. Brooks). *Norman*[3] (Commander J. Plunkett-Cole).
A.A. sloops	*Crane* (Lieutenant-Commander R. G. Jenkins). *Pheasant*[4] (Commander J. B. Palmer (Acting)). *Woodcock* (Lieutenant S. J. Parsons). *Whimbrel* (Lieutenant-Commander N. R. Murch).
Frigates	*Avon* (Lieutenant-Commander P. G. A. King). *Findhorn* (Lieutenant-Commander J. C. Dawson). *Parret* (Lieutenant-Commander T. Hood, R.N.R.).
Minesweepers	*Pirie*[3] (Temporary Lieutenant D. S. Thomson, R.A.N.R.). *Whyalla*[3] (Commander N. R. Read (Acting)). *Launceston*[3] (Temporary Lieutenant-Commander E. J. Barron (Acting), R.A.N.R.). *Burnie*[3] (Lieutenant-Commander E. M. Andrewartha, R.A.N.R.)). *Ipswich*[3] (Temporary Lieutenant R. H. Creasey). *Bendigo*[3] (Lieutenant W. Jackson, R.A.N.V.R.). *Woollongong*[3] (Temporary Lieutenant J. Hare, R.A.N.R.). *Cairns*[3] (Temporary Lieutenant N. G. Webber, R.A.N.R.). *Kalgoorlie*[3] (Lieutenant E. J. Peel). *Ballarat*[3] (Commander F. B. Morris). *Lismore*[3] (Lieutenant L. C. G. Lever, R.A.N.R.).
Destroyer depot ship ..	*Tyne*[5] (Captain S. Boucher (flag of R.A.(D), B.P.F., Rear-Admiral J. H. Edelsten)).
Landing ship headquarters (large).	*Lothian*[5] (Captain G. C. F. Branson (Acting) (Retired)).
Landing ships, infantry (large).	*Empire Spearhead*[5] (Lieutenant A. F. Benton, R.N.R.). Base ship. *Glenarm*[5] (Captain C. A. G. Hutchinson (Retired)). Transport. *Lamont*. (Captain R. W. Lundy (Acting) (Retired)). Departed Manus 2nd May.

[1] Replenishment carrier.

[2] Ferry escort carrier.

[3] On loan to Royal Australian Navy.

[4] S.O. escort group.

[5] At Leyte for Fleet replenishment.

Repair ships	*Artifex*[5] (Captain C. C. Fleming (Acting)).
	Resource[5] (Captain D. B. O'Connell (Retired)).
Aircraft repair ship	*Unicorn*[5] (Captain G. M. Merewether (Acting)).
Aircraft component repair ship.	*Deer Sound*[5] (Captain R. H. Johnson (Acting) (Retired)). Arrived Leyte 15th April.
Netlayer	*Guardian*. Departed Manus 5th April.
Tankers	*Arndale*.[5-6]
	Brown Ranger.[5]
	Wave Emperor. Arrived Manus 24th May.
	Dingledale.[5-6]
	San Adolfo.[5-6]
	San Ambrosio.[5-6]
	Loma Nova. Arrived Manus 20th May.
	Wave King.[5-6]
	Wave Monarch.[5-6] Arrived 15 March.
	Cedardale.[5-6]
	Aase Maersk.[5-6]
	San Amado.[5] Arrived 29th March.
Armament store issuing ships and armament store carriers.	*Gudrun Maersk*.[5] Arrived 6th April.
	Hermelin.[5]
	Corinda. Arrived Manus 25th April.
	Darvel. Arrived Manus 25th April.
	Kistna. Arrived Manus 13th April.
	Heron.[5]
	Kheti.[5]
	Robert Maersk.[5-6]
	Thyra S.[5]
	Pacheco.[5] Arrived Leyte 6th April.
	Prince de Liège.[5] Arrived Manus 1st April.
	Princess Maria Pia. Arrived Manus 19th April.
Air store issuing ship	*Fort Colville*.
Naval store issuing ship	*Bacchus*.[5] Also used as distiller.
N.S.I.S./V.S.I.S.	*City of Dieppe*.[5]
Victualling store Issuing ships.	*Denbighshire*.[5]
	Fort Edmonton.[5]
	Fort Alabama.[5] Arrived Manus 1st April.
	Fort Dunvegan. Arrived Manus 25th May.
Naval store carriers	*Bosphorus*.[5] Arrived Leyte 15th April.
	Slesvig. Arrived Manus 1st May.
Distilling ship	*Stagpool*.[5] Arrived Manus 21st March.
Hospital ships	*Tjitjalenka*.[5] Arrived Leyte 20th April.
	Oxfordshire.[5]
	Maunganui.[5] Arrived Leyte 10th April.
Tugs	*Weasel*[5] (Temporary Acting Sub-Lieutenant D. P. Budge). Arrived Leyte 25th April.
	Empress Josephine. Arrived Manus 20th April.
Deperming ship	*Springdale*. Arrived Manus 20th April.
Collier	*Atlas*. Arrived Leyte 6th April.
Destroyer repair ship	*Montclare*. Arrived Manus 22nd May.

[5] At Leyte for Fleet replenishment.

[6] Served in logistic support group.

APPENDIX U

State of Fleet Train (Task Force 112)

British Pacific Fleet

MANUS, JULY–AUGUST 1945
(Rear-Admiral D. B. Fisher)

Destroyer repair ship ..	*Montclare.*
Repair ships	*Artifex.* *Resource.* Refit 7th July.
Escort maintenance ship ..	*Flamborough Head.* Arrived 18th July.
M/S maintenance ship ..	*Kelantan.*
Radio maintenance ship ..	*Arbutus.*[1]
Boom vessel	*Barbain.* Arrived 1st August.
Tankers	*Olna.*[1] Arrived 23rd July. *Arndale.* Refit completed 10th September. *Dingledale.*[1] *San Adolfo.*[1] *San Ambrosio.*[1] *Wave King.*[1] *Cedardale.*[1] *Wave Monarch.*[1] *Aase Maersk.* *San Amado.*[1] *Wave Emperor.*[1] *Eaglesdale.*[1] *Carelia.*[1] *Wave Governor.*[1] Arrived 25th July.
Water tankers	*Brown Ranger.* *Green Ranger.* *Seven Sisters.* Arrived 26th July. *Loma Nova.*
Small tankers	*Rapidol.* *Ieve.* *Serbol.* *Darst Creek.*
Armament store carriers ..	*Kistna.* *Kola.* *Pacheco.* Refit completed 15th July. Arrived 30th July.
Armament store issuing ships.	*Corinda.*[1] *Darvel.* *Hermelin.* *Heron.* *Kheti.* Refit completed August. *Gudrun Maersk.* Refit 12th July. *Prince de Liège.* *Princess Maria Pia.* *Robert Maersk.*[1] *Thyras.*
Naval store issuing ship ..	*Bacchus.*

[1] Served in logistic support group.

N.S.I.S./V.S.I.S.	*City of Dieppe.* Refit.
Victualling store issuing ships.	*Fort Dunvegan.* *Fort Edmonton.* *Fort Wrangel.*[1] *Glenartney.*[1]
Naval store carriers ..	*Bosphorus.* *Jaarstroom.* *Marudu.* *San Andres.* *Slesvig.*
Accommodation ships ..	*Lothian.* Refit completed 20th August. *Glenearn.* *Empire Spearhead.* *Lancashire.* *Aorangi.* Arrived 10th July.
Deperming ship	*Springdale.*
Salvage ships	*Salvestor.* Arrived 9th July. *Salvictor.*
Distilling ship	*Stagpool.* Refit completed 10th October.
Hospital ships	*Tjitjalengka.*[1] *Oxfordshire.* *Gerusalemme.* Arrived 29th July. *Maunganui.*
Tugs	*Weazel.*[1] *Empress Josephine.* *Lariat.* *Empire Sam.* *Integrity.* Arrived 28th July.
Colliers	*Atlas.* Left 6th August. *Edna.* Arrived 1st August, replaced *Atlas.*
Floating docks	*AFD 20.* *AFD 18.*
Aircraft maintenance ship	*Pioneer.*
Aircraft repair ship ..	*Unicorn.*
Aircraft component repair ship.	*Deer Sound.*
Aircraft store issuing ship	*Fort Colville.* Arrived 15th July.
Escort carriers.	*Striker.*[1] *Slinger.*[1] *Speaker.*[1] *Ruler.*[1] *Arbiter.*[1] *Chaser.*[1]
Escort vessels	37 (23 of these served in logistic support group).
Destroyer depot ship ..	*Tyne.*
Total Task Force 112 ..	121 ships, 2 floating docks.

[1] Served in logistic support group.

APPENDIX V

Composition of U.S. Task Force 38

During the Final Operations Against Japan

In Command: Vice-Admiral J. S. McCain in *Shangri-La*

	Task Group 38.1 (Rear-Admiral T. L. Sprague)	Task Group 38.3 (Rear-Admiral G. F. Bogan)	Task Group 38.4 (Rear-Admiral A. W. Radford)
Carriers	*Bennington* *Lexington* *Hancock*	*Essex* *Randolph* *Ticonderoga*	*Yorktown* *Shangri-La* *Bonhomme Richard* *Wasp*
Light carriers ..	*San Jacinto* *Belleau Wood*	*Monterey* *Bataan*	*Independence* *Cowpens*
Battleships	*Massachusetts* *Indiana* *South Dakota*	*North Carolina* *Alabama*	*Iowa* *Wisconsin* *Missouri*
Heavy cruisers ..			*Quincy* *Chicago* *Boston* *St. Paul*
Light cruisers ..	*Topeka* *Duluth* *Atlanta* *Dayton* *Oklahoma City* *Amsterdam* *San Juan*	*Pasadena* *Springfield* *Astoria* *Wilkes-Barre* *Oakland* *Tucson*	*San Diego* *Flint*
Destroyers	*De Haven* *Mansfield* *Lyman K. Swenson* *Collett* *Maddox* *Samuel N. Moore* *Blue* *Brush* *Taussig* *John Rodgers* *Harrison* *McKee* *Murray* *Ringgold* *Schroeder* *Dashiell* *Cogswell* *Caperton* *Ingersoll* *Knapp* *Higbee*	*Erben* *Walker* *Abbot* *Hale* *Stembel* *Black* *Chauncey* *Bullard* *Heermann* *Southerland* *Benner* *English* *Ault* *C. S. Sperry* *Waldron* *J. W. Weeks* *Hank* *Borie* *W. L. Lind*	*Remey* *Norman Scott* *Wadleigh* *Mertz* *Monssen* *McDermut* *McGowan* *McNair* *Melvin* *Cushing* *Colahan* *Uhlmann* *Benham* *Stockham* *Twining* *Wedderburn* *Rowe* *Smalley* *Watts* *Wren* *Frank Knox* *Stoddard*

	TASK UNIT 34.8.1 (Rear-Admiral J. F. Shafroth)	TASK UNIT 34.8.2 (Rear-Admiral O. C. Badger)
(Temporarily formed from Task Groups 38.1, 38.3 and 38.4 for special duties during July)		
Battleships	*Massachusetts*	*Wisconsin*
	Indiana	*Missouri*
	South Dakota	*Iowa*
		North Carolina
		Alabama
Heavy cruisers	*Quincy*	
	Chicago	
Light cruisers		*Atlanta*
		Dayton
Destroyers..	*Erben*	*Remey*
	Walker	*Wadleigh*
	Abbot	*Norman Scott*
	Hale	*Mertz*
	Stembel	*Monssen*
	Black	*McGowan*
	Bullard	*McNair*
	Chauncey	*Melvin*
	Heermann	*Frank Knox*

TASK UNIT 34.8.1
(Rear-Admiral J. F. Shafroth)
(Formed for the bombardment of Kamaishi on 9th August 1945)

Battleships .. .. *Indiana, Massachusetts, South Dakota.*
Heavy cruisers .. *Quincy, Chicago, St. Paul, Boston.*
Destroyers .. .. *Erben, Walker, Hale, Stembel, Bullard, Chauncey, Heermann, Ingersoll, Southerland.*

APPENDIX W

Composition of British Task Force 37

During the Final Operations Against Japan

In Command : Vice-Admiral Sir Bernard Rawlings

Fleet Carriers .. *Formidable* (flag of AC1 Vice-Admiral Sir Philip Vian) (6 Hellcat[1], 36 Corsair[1], 12 Avenger[2], Total 54), *Victorious* (37 Corsair, 14 Avenger, 2 Walrus[3], Total 53), *Implacable* (48 Seafire[1], 12 Firefly[1], 18 Avenger, Total 78), *Indefatigable* (40 Seafire, 12 Firefly, 18 Avenger, Total 70).

Battleship .. .. *King George V* (flag of VABPF).

Light cruisers .. *Newfoundland* (flag of C.S.4 Rear-Admiral Sir E. J. P. Brind), H.M.N.Z.S. *Gambia*, H.M.N.Z.S. *Achilles.*

Light cruisers (A.A.) *Euryalus, Argonaut*[4], *Black Prince.*

Destroyers .. .. *Quadrant, Tenacious,* H.M.A.S. *Quiberon, Quality,* H.M.A.S. *Quickmatch, Grenville* (Captain D.4), *Urania, Ulysses, Undine, Urchin, Troubridge* (Captain D.24), *Terpsichore, Teazer, Termagant, Undaunted, Wakeful, Wrangler, Barfleur* (flag of R.A.D. Rear-Admiral J. H. Edelsten).

TASK UNIT 37.1.6
(VABPF)
(Formed for bombardment of Hitachi 17th–18th July 1945)

Battleship .. .. *King George V.*
Destroyers .. .. *Quality, Quiberon.*

[1] Fighter.
[2] Torpedo bomber.
[3] Amphibian Reconnaissance Bomber (Air Sea Rescue).
[4] Joined the force after the first strike period.

APPENDIX X

The Potsdam Declaration, 26th July 1945

26th July 1945.

We, the President of the United States, the President of the National Government of the Republic of China and the Prime Minister of Great Britain, representing the hundreds of millions of our countrymen, have conferred and agree that Japan shall be given an opportunity to end the war.

2. The prodigious land, sea and air forces of the United States, the British Empire and China, many times reinforced by their armies and air fleets from the West, are poised to strike the final blows upon Japan. This military power is sustained and inspired by the determination of all the Allied nations to prosecute the war against Japan until she ceases to resist.

3. The result of the futile and senseless German resistance to the might of the aroused free peoples of the world stands forth in awful clarity as an example to the people of Japan.

The might that now converges on Japan is immeasurably greater than that which, when applied to the resisting Nazis, necessarily laid waste the lands, the industry, and the methods of life of the whole German people. The full application of our military power, backed by our resolve, will mean the inevitable and complete destruction of the Japanese forces, and just as inevitably the utter devastation of the Japanese homeland.

4. The time has come for Japan to decide whether she will continue to be controlled by those self-willed militaristic advisers whose unintelligent calculations have brought the Empire of Japan to the threshold of annihilation, or whether she will follow the path of reason.

5. The following are our terms. We shall not deviate from them. There are no alternatives. We shall brook no delay.

6. There must be eliminated for all time the authority and influence of those who have deceived and misled the people of Japan into embarking on world conquest, for we insist that a new order of peace, security and justice will be impossible until irresponsible militarism is driven from the world.

7. Until such a new order is established and until there is convincing proof that Japan's war-making power is destroyed points in Japanese territory designated by the Allies will be occupied to secure the achievement of the basic objectives we are here setting forth.

8. The terms of the Cairo declaration shall be carried out, and Japanese Sovereignty shall be limited to the islands of Honshu, Hokkaido, Kyushu, Shikoku and such minor islands as we determine.

9. The Japanese military forces after being completely disarmed shall be permitted to return to their homes, with the opportunity of leading peaceful and productive lives.

10. We do not intend that the Japanese shall be enslaved as a race nor destroyed as a nation but stern justice will be meted out to all war criminals, including those who have visited cruelties upon our prisoners. The Japanese Government shall remove all obstacles to the revival and strengthening of democratic tendencies among the Japanese people. Freedom of speech, of religion, and of thought, as well as respect for fundamental human rights, shall be established.

11. Japan shall be permitted to maintain such industries as will sustain her economy and allow of the exaction of just reparations in kind, but not those industries which would enable her to rearm for war.

To this end access to, as distinguished from control of, raw materials shall be permitted. Eventual Japanese participation in world trade relations shall be permitted.

12. The occupying forces of the Allies shall be withdrawn from Japan as soon as these objectives have been accomplished, and there has been established, in accordance with the freely expressed will of the Japanese people, a peacefully inclined and responsible Government.

13. We call upon the Government of Japan to proclaim now the unconditional surrender of all the Japanese armed forces, and to provide proper and adequate assurance of their good faith in such action. The alternative for Japan is complete and utter destruction.

APPENDIX Y

Speech Broadcast to the Third Fleet

by Vice-Admiral Rawlings, 16th August, 1945

Admiral Halsey, Flag Officers, Commanding Officers, Officers and men of the Third Fleet. Yesterday, after hearing Admiral Halsey's inspiring words to the Third Fleet, of which we have the honour to be part, I asked him if I might come to his Flagship to say a few words to you all. I was not sure that with our voice transmission gear, we could carry sufficiently far to reach all units of the Third Fleet and if I may so put it, I decided to take the bull by the horns, and so I asked him if I might come over to speak from his Flagship in the centre of his Fleet.

A great deal seems to have happened since March, when I received orders to report for duty to Admiral Nimitz. The words I used then in placing my ships under his orders were that it was ' With feelings of great pride and pleasure that the British Pacific Fleet joins the United States Naval Forces under your command.'

Nothing that has happened since makes me wish to change one word of what I then said ; the story of how the two Fleets have come together is quite simple and straightforward, which is as things should be among sailors.

It begins with Task Force 57 as we then were, operating under the orders of Admiral Spruance and we took it as a compliment that he just told us what he wanted and left us to get on with it. We look back on those decisive days in the battle for Okinawa with a feeling of pride. We never met our Admiral but we felt he understood us. Perhaps on the whole it was as well that we were then operating on our own as it gave us the chance to get used to an unaccustomed way of manœuvring and signalling which was to stand us in good stead later.

With that behind us we joined the Third Fleet not only with keen anticipation but, I believe, with a little confidence that we knew enough to take our place in the line with the famous Fighting Third ; and so what Admiral Halsey said yesterday meant much to us.

The story is, perhaps, reaching its end in the last few days, when we have passed under the direct command of Vice-Admiral McCain as Task Group 38.5 and so became an integral part of those Fast Carrier Task Forces which have fought their way from the black days of 1941 to their present victory. It may not perhaps be fantastic to feel that the way our two navies have come together, welded and integrated, may point the manner in which our two great democracies will now move forward together. In their amalgamation, neither Navy I hope, has lost its own character or individuality. It would be the greatest pity if they did so, for when all is said and done everything in the story of sea warfare shows that character and individuality are in the end the only things that really count. But with them today must go that spirit of co-operation which these months have shown to be within our reach.

Perhaps I might add that I share to the full with Admiral Halsey the conception that the Navy is still the first line of defence for both our countries, and I believe, also, that the day when either of us abandon his sage advice to keep the naval sword sharp, will bring us the nearer to being again attacked by such evil forces as those we have now subdued.

In so thinking may I quote to you the opening sentence of the message sent by the Board of Admiralty to the British Fleet when Germany was broken ; it began—' For the second time since the Battle of Trafalgar sea-power, relentlessly applied, has preserved and sustained our nation and Commonwealth and led to the decisive defeat of Germany.'

The story of the Third Fleet in which we have been privileged to lend a hand, provides during the last six weeks the perfect picture of the result of sea-power relentlessly applied in the waters of the Pacific.

Very many of us in both our navies will in the future be returning to civil life. To those who remain may I say that I can conceive of no greater contribution to the future of the world than that our two navies should make a habit of meeting and working together from time to time. Perhaps those of you who will be leaving the sea will help to bring that about.

But to each one of you, whatever you may feel about that conception, whatever happens and whatever the future holds, I suggest that each will be able to say to himself, " I fought in the Third Fleet under Halsey," and, so saying, face up with a greater courage to whatever tomorrow shall bring.

APPENDIX Z

Duties of the Rear-Admiral, Fleet Train

(*a*) OPERATIONS.—The Rear-Admiral, Fleet Train, is responsible for the operation of the Fleet Train as a whole. He will transfer to the Operational Task Force Commanders the detailed operational control of the Fleet Train groups while employed on servicing their Task Forces at sea.

(*b*) ADMINISTRATION.—The Rear-Admiral, Fleet Train, is responsible to the Commander-in-Chief for the administration of the ships of the Fleet Train.

(*c*) LOGISTICS.—The Rear-Admiral, Fleet Train, is responsible to the Vice-Admiral, Second in Command, British Pacific Fleet, for :—

(i) Keeping the Fleet directly supplied. This includes the detailed logistic planning for each specific operation and the transport of supplies from the supply bases to the Fleet, in ships of the Fleet Train ;

(ii) the maintenance and repair of H.M. Ships, auxiliaries, and aircraft (in accordance with the policy promulgated by the Flag Officer, Naval Air Stations (Australia)) of the Fleet within the capacity of the Fleet Train ;

(iii) arrangements for the evacuation of sick and wounded by sea ;

(iv) mails, distributing authorities, chart offices afloat ;

(v) amenities for the Fleet ;

(vi) salvage and tugs.

After the appointment of the Commodore, Air Train (10th June, 1945), the responsibilities of R.A.F.T. were amended as follows :—

THE REAR-ADMIRAL, FLEET TRAIN

(*a*) LOGISTICS

(i) The Rear-Admiral, Fleet Train, is responsible to the Commander-in-Chief for keeping the Fleet directly supplied. This includes the detailed logistic planning for each operation and the transport of supplies from the Supply Bases to the Fleet.

(ii) The maintenance and repair of H.M. Ships and auxiliaries of the Fleet within the capacity of the Fleet Train.

(iii) Arrangements for the evacuation of sick and wounded by sea and air.

(iv) Mails, distributing authorities, Chart Offices afloat.

(v) Amenities afloat for the Fleet.

(vi) Salvage and floating docks.

(*b*) ADMINISTRATION.—The Rear-Admiral, Fleet Train, is responsible to the Commander-in-Chief for the general administration of the Fleet Train.

(*c*) OPERATIONS

(i) The Rear-Admiral, Fleet Train, is the operating authority for the whole of the Fleet Train forward of Australia, including the operation of the Air Train, as advised by the Commodore, Air Train. He will transfer to the operational Task Force Commander the detailed operational control of Fleet Train Groups while employed on servicing Task Forces at sea.

(ii) The Rear-Admiral, Fleet Train, will also be responsible for informing the Vice-Admiral (Q) of his requirements for movements of Fleet Train ships in Australian waters.

APPENDIX ZA

Duties of the Commodore, Air Train

(*a*) LOGISTICS.—The Commodore, Air Train, is responsible to the Rear-Admiral, Fleet Train, for the air logistic support of the Fleet in the Forward Area, including :—

(i) Supplies of aircraft, air crews, maintenance personnel and airstores ; and

(ii) Maintenance and repair of aircraft in the Forward Area, both by Fleet Air Maintenance Groups and ashore, in conformity with the policy of the Flag Officer, Naval Air (Pacific).

(*b*) LOGISTIC PLANNING.—The Commodore, Air Train, is responsible to Flag Officers Commanding Aircraft Carrier Squadrons for detailed logistic planning for each specific operation, the plans being framed in accordance with the policy of the Flag Officer, Naval Air (Pacific). After they have been concurred in by the Rear-Admiral, Fleet Train, he will co-ordinate them with the general logistic plan.

(*c*) ADMINISTRATION.—The Air Train will form a sub-command of the Fleet Train and will consist of the following categories :—

Ferry and Replenishment Carriers (administered by A.C. 30).
Aircraft Maintenance Ships.
Aircraft Engine Repair Ships.
Aircraft Repair Ships.
Aircraft Component Repair Ships.
Air Store Issue Ships.

The Commodore, Air Train, will be responsible to Rear-Admiral, Fleet Train, for the administration of the Air Train, except Ferry and Replenishment Carriers.

The Commodore, Air Train, will administer reserve air crews and the Forward Air Drafting Pool, communicating direct with the Flag Officer, Naval Air (Pacific) and the Commodore R.N. Barracks, Sydney.

The Commodore, Air Train, is authorised to deal direct with :—

(i) Flag Officer, Naval Air (Pacific) on technical matters.

(ii) Monabs in the Forward Area, with regard to the provision of reserve aircraft and pools and aircraft reserve.

OPERATIONAL CONTROL OF THE AIR TRAIN.—The Rear-Admiral, Fleet Train, will have operational control of the Air Train in the Forward Area (including C.V.E.'s) disposing ships in accordance with the policy of the Flag Officer, Naval Air (Pacific) and the requirements of the Commodore, Air Train.

APPENDIX ZB

East Indies Fleet: State on VJ-Day

15th August, 1945

Battleships

Nelson	Captain C. Caslon.
French Ship *Richelieu*	

Cruisers

Nigeria	Captain H. A. King.
Ceylon	Captain K. L. Harkness.
Cleopatra	Captain B. I. Robertshaw.
Cumberland	Captain P. K. Enright.
London	Captain S. L. Bateson.
Phoebe	Captain S. M. Raw.
Sussex	Captain A. F. De Salis.
Royalist	Captain W. G. Brittain.
Glasgow[1]	Captain C. P. Clarke.
Jamaica[1]	Captain J. Hughes-Hallett.
Norfolk[1]	Captain J. G. Y. Loveband.
Dutch Ship *Tromp*[1] (A.A. Ship).	Captain F. Stam, R.Neth.N.
Dutch Ship *Jacob Van Heemskerck*[1]	

Assault Carriers

Ameer	Acting Captain P. D. H. R. Pelly.
Attacker	Captain G. F. Renwick.
Emperor	Acting Captain Sir Charles E. Madden, Bt.
Empress	Captain J. R. S. Brown.
Hunter	Captain A. D. Torlesse.
Khedive	Acting Captain D. H. Magnay.
Pursuer	Captain T. L. Bratt.
Searcher	Captain J. W. Grant.
Stalker	Captain L. C. Sinker.
Trouncer[1]	Acting Captain G. A. Rotherham.

General Purpose Carriers

Shah	Captain W. J. Yendell.
Smiter	Acting Captain L. G. Richardson.
Trumpeter	Captain C. B. Alers-Hankey.

Ferry Carriers

Activity	Acting Captain E. J. R. North, R.N.R.
Fencer	Lieutenant-Commander A. M. Harris.

Deck-landing Training Carrier

Begum	Acting Captain C. L. Howe.

Fighter-direction Ships

Ulster Queen	Acting Captain M. H. J. Bennett, R.N.R.
Palomares[1]	Acting Captain C. L. de H. Bell, R.N.R.

Destroyer Depot Ship

Woolwich	Captain (retired) W. B. Hynes.
Scout	Tender to *Woolwich*.

[1] (Non-operational, off station or on passage).

APPENDIX ZB

Destroyers

Myngs	Captain J. H. Allison.
Zenith[1]	Lieutenant-Commander R. W. B. Lacon
Zambesi[1]	Lieutenant-Commander J. M. Palmer.
Zealous[1]	Commander R. F. Jessel.
Zebra[1]	Lieutenant-Commander E. C. Peake.
Zephyr[1]	Lieutenant-Commander C. R. Purse.
Zest[1]	Lieutenant-Commander R. B. N. Hicks.
Zodiac[1]	Lieutenant-Commander H. R. Rycroft.
Carysfort[1]	Commander A. L. Hobson.
Cassandra[1]	Lieutenant C. C. Anderson.
Roebuck[1]	Commander C. D. Bonham-Carter.
Eskimo[1]	Lieutenant-Commander E. N. Sinclair.
Tartar	Captain B. Jones.
Nubian	Lieutenant-Commander F. C. Brodrick.
Paladin	Acting Lieutenant-Commander H. R. Hewlett.
Penn	Lieutenant-Commander A. H. Diack.
Petard	Lieutenant-Commander R. L. Caple.
Rotherham	Captain H. W. Biggs.
Racehorse	Commander G. E. Fardell.
Raider	Lieutenant-Commander J. C. Cartwright.
Redoubt	Lieutenant-Commander F. W. M. Carter.
Rapid	Lieutenant-Commander F. P. Baker.
Relentless	Lieutenant-Commander G. B. Barstow.
Rocket	Lieutenant-Commander B. M. D. I'Anson.
Saumarez	Captain M. L. Power.
Venus	Commander H. G. D. DeChair.
Verulam	Lieutenant-Commander D. H. R. Bromley.
Vigilant	Lieutenant-Commander L. W. L. Argles.
Virago	Lieutenant-Commander A. J. R. White.
Volage	Commander L. G. Durlacher.
Farndale	Commander E. G. Roper.
Bicester	Commander R. W. F. Northcott.
Blackmore	Acting Lieutenant-Commander J. S. Kerans.
Bleasdale	Temporary Acting Lieutenant-Commander T. G. Clarke, R.N.V.R.
Brecon	Acting Lieutenant-Commander N. R. H. Rodney.
Calpe	Acting Lieutenant-Commander N. F. R. Gille, R.N.R.
Chiddingfold	Lieutenant-Commander F. G. Woods.
Cowdray	Lieutenant D. J. Beckley.
Eggesford	Lieutenant G. H. Evans.

Unallocated

French Ship
Le Triomphant
Dutch Ships
Tjerk Hiddes, Van Galen

Monitors

Abercrombie	Acting Captain C. F. H. Churchill.
Roberts	Captain C. B. Tidd.

Gunboats

Aphis[1]	Lieutenant J. E. Dyer.
Cockchafer[1]	Lieutenant E. A. Tyrer.
Scarab[1]	Acting Lieutenant-Commander B. J. Anderson.

Submarine Depot and Accommodation Ships

Wolfe	Acting Captain J. E. Slaughter.
Wuchang	Temporary Acting Lieutenant-Commander J. H. L. McCarter, S.A.N.F.(V).

[1] (Non-operational, off station or on passage).

Submarines

Scorcher	Lieutenant K. S. Renshaw, R.N.R.
Scythian	Temporary Acting Lieutenant-Commander C. P. Thode, R.N.V.R,
Seadog	Lieutenant E. A. Hobson.
Shalimar	Lieutenant W. G. Meeke.
Sibyl	Lieutenant H. R. Murray.
Spur	Lieutenant P. S. Beale.
Statesman	Lieutenant R. G. P. Bulkeley.
Subtle	Lieutenant B. J. B. Andrews.
Thrasher	Lieutenant-Commander M. F. R. Ainslie.
Torbay	Lieutenant-Commander C. P. Norman.
Trident	Lieutenant A. R. Profit.

A/S Training Submarines

Vigorous	Lieutenant N. R. Wood.
Visigoth	Lieutenant C. H. Hammer.
Vivid	Lieutenant J. C. Varley.

Sloop

Italian Ship *Eritrea*

A/S Sloops

R.I.N. *Cauvery, Godavari, Kistna, Narbada, Sutlej, Jumna*[1]

Sloops

Falmouth	Lieutenant-Commander N. E. Cutler.
Shoreham	Lieutenant-Commander R. J. Tadhunter, R.N.R.

Frigates

Awe	Lieutenant-Commander H. P. Carse, R.N.V.R.
Dart	Acting Lieutenant-Commander A. G. Scott, R.N.R.
Evenlode	Temporary Acting Lieutenant-Commander W. F. McAusland, R.N.V.R.
Inver	Temporary Acting Lieutenant-Commander W. R. Seward, R.N.V.R.
Jed	Lieutenant-Commander R. S. Miller, R.N.R.
Kale	Lieutenant-Commander G. W. Houchen, R.N.R.
Lochy	Lieutenant-Commander W. J. P. Roberts, R.N.R.
Lossie	Lieutenant-Commander A. F. MacFie, R.N.R.
Rother	Temporary Acting Lieutenant-Commander B. H. C. Rodgers, R.N.V.R.
Taff	Lieutenant-Commander M. E. Impey.
Teviot	Lieutenant D. Welsh, R.N.—in Command until 11th June, 1945 (no further C.O. appointed).
Halladale[1]	Lieutenant-Commander J. E. Woolfenden, R.N.R.
Ness[1]	Temporary Acting Lieutenant-Commander R. S. Steel, R.N.R.
Tay[1]	Acting Lieutenant-Commander R. Atkinson, R.N.R.
Loch Craggie	Temporary Acting Lieutenant-Commander C. L. L. Davies, R.N.V.R.
Loch Fyne	Temporary Acting Lieutenant-Commander R. F. J. Maberley, R.N.V.R.
Loch Glendhu	Lieutenant-Commander E. G. P. B. Knapton.
Loch Gorm	Temporary Acting Lieutenant-Commander H. Vernon, R.N.R.
Loch Katrine	Temporary Acting Lieutenant-Commander R. A. Cherry, R.N.R.
Loch Lomond	Commander S. Darling, R.A.N.V.R.
Loch More	Lieutenant-Commander R. A. D. Cambridge, R.N.R.
Loch Quoich	Temporary Acting Lieutenant-Commander J. E. B. Healey, R.N.V.R.
Loch Ruthven	Acting Lieutenant-Commander R. T. Horan, R.N.R.
Loch Scavaig	Acting Lieutenant-Commander C. W. Leadbetter, R.N.R.
Loch Tarbert	Temporary Acting Lieutenant-Commander W. S. Thomson, R.N.R.

[1] (Non-operational, off station or on passage).

FRIGATES—*continued*

Natal	Lieutenant-Commander D. A. Hall, S.A.N.F.(V).
Deveron (Nominated for transfer to R.I.N.)	Temporary Acting Lieutenant-Commander W. P. Bush, R.N.V.R.
Nadder (Nominated for transfer to R.I.N.)	Temporary Acting Lieutenant-Commander P. E. Kitto, R.N.R.
Test (Nominated for transfer to R.I.N.)	Acting-Commander T. S. L. Fox-Pitt.
Bann[1]	Acting Lieutenant-Commander R. H. Jameson, R.N.R.
Shiel[1]	Lieutenant H. P. Crail, R.N.R.
Trent[1]	Lieutenant-Commander C. D. Smith, R.N.R.
Loch Eck[1]	Acting Lieutenant-Commander W. McInnes, R.N.R.
Loch Insh[1]	Temporary Acting Lieutenant-Commander E. W. C. Dempster, R.N.V.R.
Loch Killisport[1]	Temporary Acting Lieutenant-Commander G. Butcher, R.N.V.R.
Loch Achray[1]	Temporary Acting Lieutenant-Commander C. J. Alldridge, R.N.R.

CUTTERS

Banff	Temporary Acting Lieutenant-Commander J. D. Nesbitt, R.N.R.
Fishguard	Acting Lieutenant-Commander C. A. Woods, R.N.Z.N.R.
Gorleston	Commander J. H. Eaden.
Lulworth	Commander R. C. S. Woolley, R.N.R.
Sennen	Lieutenant B. M. Skinner.

CORVETTES

R.I.N. *Assam, Sind*	
Charlock (Nominated for transfer to R.I.N.)	Lieutenant J. S. Hough, R.N.R.

A/S VESSELS

R.I.N. *Kalavati, Sonavati.*	

CORVETTES

Freesia	Temporary Lieutenant W. L. Hancock, S.A.N.F.(V).
Meadowsweet	Temporary Lieutenant C. G. Jackson, R.N.R.
Monkshood	Lieutenant O. R. B. Stephen, S.A.N.F.(V).
Rockrose	Temporary Lieutenant E. A. King, R.N.V.R.
Rosebay	Temporary Acting Lieutenant-Commander G. R. E. Southwood, R.N.R.
Smilax	Lieutenant A. Branson, R.N.R.
Snowflake	Lieutenant E. J. Powell, R.N.R.
Thyme	Temporary Acting Lieutenant-Commander F. E. Eastman, S.A.N.F.(V).
Tulip	Lieutenant J. H. Merriman, R.N.R.
Violet	Temporary Lieutenant A. R. J. Tilston, S.A.N.F.(V).
Honesty	Temporary Lieutenant M. J. Rowlands, R.N.V.R.
Jasmine[1]	Temporary Lieutenant E. C. Leaver, R.N.R.
Nigella[1]	Temporary Acting Lieutenant-Commander J. B. Campbell, R.A.N.V.R.

FLEET MINESWEEPERS

Friendship	Commander D. L. Johnston.
Gozo	Acting Commander T. T. Euman.
Lennox	Temporary Acting Lieutenant-Commander C. H. Walton, R.N.R.
Lightfoot	Lieutenant-Commander A. S. Drysdale, R.N.V.R.
Melita	Temporary Acting Lieutenant-Commander G. R. May, R.N.R.
Pelorus	Lieutenant-Commander F. J. Bourgat.
Persian	Lieutenant-Commander J. L. Woollcombe.
Postillion	Temporary Acting Lieutenant-Commander W. E. Halbert, R.N.R.
Immersay (attached danlayers)	Temporary Acting Lieutenant-Commander J. H. A. Winfield, R.N.R.
Lingat (attached danlayers)	Temporary Lieutenant P. W. Jequier, R.N.V.R.
Pickle	Commander C. P. F. Brown

[1] (Non-operational, off station or on passage).

FLEET MINESWEEPERS—*continued*

Chameleon	Temporary Acting Lieutenant-Commander D. P. Richardson, R.N.V.R.
Pincher	Temporary Acting Lieutenant-Commander C. B. Blake, R.N.V.R.
Plucky	Temporary Acting Lieutenant-Commander G. Wallis, R.N.V.R.
Recruit	Acting Commander A. E. Doran.
Rifleman	Lieutenant-Commander C. L. Carroll, R.N.R.
Jewel[1]	Temporary Acting Lieutenant-Commander B. A. Breeze, R.N.V.R.
Serene[1]	Temporary Acting Lieutenant-Commander R. M. Ritchie, R.N.V.R.
Scaravay[1] (attached danlayers)	Temporary Lieutenant J. W. Monaghan, R.N.Z.N.R.
Sandray[1] (attached danlayers)	Temporary Lieutenant J. E. Freestone, R.N.R.

R.I.N. *Baluchistan, Bihar, Carnatic, Deccan, Kathiawar, Khyber, Konkan, Kumaon, Orissa, Oudh, Rajputana, Rohilkhand, Bengal, Bombay, Punjab.*

DEPOT SHIP

Lucia	Acting Commander G. H. Stapleton.

DOCKYARD SHIP

Wayland	Acting Captain W. G. A. Shuttleworth.

REPAIR SHIP

Ausonia	Acting Captain J. M. Scott.

HULL REPAIR SHIP

Mullion Cove	Commander J. E. Evans, R.N.R.

ESCORT DEPOT SHIP

Caradoc	Captain A. J. Baker-Cresswell.

ESCORT DEPOT AND MAINTENANCE SHIP

Gombroon	Commander J. E. Fenton.

ESCORT MAINTENANCE SHIP

Beachy Head	Acting Captain C. K. Adam.

M/S MAINTENANCE SHIP

Corbrae	Lieutenant-Commander C. H. Pollock.

MOTOR CRAFT MAINTENANCE SHIP

Mull of Galloway	Commander E. C. Hicks, R.N.R.

COASTAL FORCE WORKSHOP TENDER

Derby Haven[1]	Commander T. A. Sergeant.

SURVEY VESSELS

Challenger	Commander C. W. Sabine.
Nguva	Lieutenant-Commander C. J. Wood.
Virginia	Temporary Lieutenant P. P. O'Sullivan, R.N.R.
White Bear	Lieutenant-Commander K. W. Hay
H.D.M.L. 1238	Temporary Lieutenant T. E. Powell, R.N.V.R.
H.D.M.L. 1288	Sub-Lieutenant W. A. Bailey, R.N.V.R.
H.D.M.L. 1376	Temporary Sub-Lieutenant C. M. Ockleford, R.N.V.R.

AIRCRAFT TARGET SHIP

Italian Ship *Carabiniere*

[1] (Non-operational, off station or on passage).

APPENDIX ZB

Boom Carriers

Devon City	Acting Commander A. McD. Harvey.
Ethiopian	Acting Commander K. A. S. Phillips, R.N.R.

Anti-boat Net Layer

Brittany	Temporary Lieutenant S. R. Berry, R.N.R.

Controlled Minelayers

Dabchick	Temporary Acting Lieutenant-Commander P. E. Martin, R.N.R.
Redshank	Temporary Lieutenant L. Punnett, R.C.N.V.R.
Sandmartin	

Salvage Vessels

Ocean Salvor	
Salviola (off-station)	

Base Ships

Lanka (Colombo)	Captain J. F. W. Mudford.
Highflyer (Trincomalee)	Acting Captain A. O'Leary.
Maraga (Addu Atoll)	Temporary Lieutenant J. F. Humphreys, R.N.V.R.

Depot Ships

Landguard	Temporary Lieutenant R. O. Tyrer, R.N.V.R.
Mayina	Acting Captain W. R. G. Reid.
Ying Chow	Acting Commander A. G. D. Bagot.

Deperming Ships

Bushwood	Temporary Lieutenant C. C. Boxall, R.N.R.
Springtide	Temporary Sub-Lieutenant F. W. Treves, R.N.R.

Base Ships

Tana (Kilindini)	Commander Sir P. Bowyer-Smyth.
Ironclad (Diego Suarez)	
Sambur (Mauritius)	Commander W. Pennefather.
Sangdragon (Seychelles)	Acting Commander L. P. Lane.
Sheba (Aden)	Acting Commander E. A. Aylmer.
Jufair (Bahrein)	Lieutenant-Commander J. Irvin, R.N.R.

Tenders to *Jufair*

Euphrates (Persian Gulf)	Captain J. W. Whitehorn.
Oman (Khor Kuwai)	

R.N. Bases in India

Braganza (Bombay)	Captain A. R. Farquhar.
Amzari (Vizagapatam)	Acting Captain G. I. S. More.
Chilwa (Calcutta)	Temporary Lieutenant R. J. Evans, R.N.R.
Chinkara (Cochin)	Captain P. C. W. Manwaring.
Pangkor (Bombay)	Temporary Lieutenant R. Warren, R.N.R.
R.N. Base (Madras)	
Tengra (Mandapam)	Acting Captain J. N. Sheffield.

R.N. Air Stations

Bambara (Trincomalee)	Acting Captain H. M. Spreckley.
Bherunda (Colombo)	Captain A. F. Campbell.
Garuda (Coimbatore)	Acting Captain E. R. G. Baker.
Kalugu (Cochin)	Acting Temporary Commander (A) E. K. Lee, R.N.V.R.
Rajaliya (Puttalam, Ceylon)	Acting Commander J. C. Cockburn.
Ukussa (Katukurunda, Ceylon)	Captain J. S. Crawford.
Vairi (Sular)	Acting Commander G. R. Brown.
Valluru (Tambaram—Madras)	Acting Captain H. M. S. Mundy.

APPENDIX ZB

ROYAL INDIAN NAVY

BASE AND DEPOT SHIPS

Adyar (Madras)
Circars (Vizagapatam)
Dalhousie (Bombay)
Hoogli (Calcutta)
Monze (Karachi)
Moti (Bombay)
Patunga (Chittagong)
Sita (Ceylon)
Venduruthi (Cochin)

TRAINING VESSELS, ETC. (R.I.N.)

SLOOP

Clive, Hindustan (Survey Vessel)

A/S VESSELS

Lawrence, Ramdas

TRAINING VESSELS

Dipavati, Hira, Investigator, Lal, Nilam, Madras (Radar Training Ship)

A/S PATROL VESSELS

Agra, Baroda, Berar, Karachi, Lahore, Nasik, Patna, Poona, Ahmedabad, Calcutta, Cuttack, Madura, Shillong, Travancore.

CORVETTE

Gondwana

L.S.H.(L)

Bulolo — Acting Captain H. R. Conway.
Largs — Captain A. A. Martin, R.N.R.

L.S.H.(S)

Nith — Lieutenant-Commander W. A. Grinham, R.N.V.R.
Waveney — Temporary Acting Lieutenant-Commander B. T. Whinney, R.N.V.R.

L.S.I.(L)

Glengyle — Captain B. B. Grant, R.N.R.
Glenroy — Acting Captain R. M. Archdale.
Persimmon — Acting Commander W. E. Gelling, R.N.R.
Rocksand — Commander (Retired) H. W. D'Arcy-Evans.
Sanfoin — Commander A. Longmuir, R.N.R.
Sansovino — Acting Commander A. S. Winton, R.N.R.
Sefton — Lieutenant-Commander F. A. C. Bishop, R.N.R.

L.S.I.(M)

Prinses Beatrix — Acting Commander J. Stretch, R.N.R.
Queen Emma — Acting Commander T. L. Alkin.

L.S.I.(S)

Prins Albert — Acting Lieutenant-Commander E. C. St. A. Coles, R.N.R.

L.S.C.

Empire Elaine (Red Ensign)

L.S.D.

Highway — Acting Commander C. Edgecombe, R.N.R.
Northway — Acting Commander K. S. Munro, R.N.R.

L.S.G.

Dewdale
Ennerdale

L.S.I.(L)

Barpeta (Red Ensign)
R.I.N. *Llanstephen Castle*

APPENDIX ZC

British Pacific Fleet: State on VJ-Day

August 15th, 1945

Battleships

Ship	Commanding Officer
Duke of York (C.-in-C., B.P.F.)	Captain A. D. Nicholl.
King George V (V.A., 2nd in Command)	Captain B. B. Schofield.
Anson	Captain A. C. G. Madden.
Howe[1]	Captain H. W. U. McCall.

Aircraft Carriers

Ship	Commanding Officer
Formidable	Captain W. G. Andrewes.
Indefatigable	Captain Q. D. Graham.
Indomitable	Captain J. A. S. Eccles.
Colossus	Captain G. H. Stokes.
Glory	Captain A. W. Buzzard.
Venerable	Captain W. A. Dallmeyer.
Vengeance	Captain D. M. L. Neame.
Illustrious[1]	Captain W. D. Stephens.
Implacable[1]	Captain C. C. Hughes-Hallett.
Victorious[1]	Rear Admiral M. M. Denny.

Replenishment Carriers

Ship	Commanding Officer
Striker	Captain W. P. Carne.
Arbiter	Captain D. H. Everett.
Chaser	Captain R. G. Poole.
Ruler	Captain H. P. Currey.
Slinger	Lieutenant-Commander J. G. Hopkins.
Speaker	Acting Captain U. H. R. James.

Ferry Carriers

Ship	Commanding Officer
Vindex	Acting Commander J. D. L. Williams.
Fencer[1]	Lieutenant-Commander A. M. Harris.
Reaper[1]	Acting Commander I. T. Clark.

Cruisers

Ship	Commanding Officer
Bermuda	Captain J. S. Bethell.
Belfast	Captain R. M. Dick.
Euryalus	Captain R. S. Warne.
Gambia (New Zealand manned)	Captain R. A. B. Edwards.
Achilles (New Zealand manned).	Captain F. J. Butler, R.N.Z.N.
Swiftsure	Captain P. V. McLaughlin.
Argonaut	Captain W. P. McCarthy.
Newfoundland	Captain R. W. Ravenhill.
Black Prince[1]	Captain G. V. Gladstone.
Ontario[1] (R.C.N. manned).	Captain H. T. W. Grant.
Uganda[1] (R.C.N. manned)	Captain E. R. Mainguy, R.C.N.

[1] (Non-operational, off station or on passage).

APPENDIX ZC

FAST MINELAYERS

Apollo	Captain L. N. Brownfield.
Ariadne	Captain F. B. Lloyd.
Manxman	Captain G. Thistleton-Smith.

AUXILIARY A/A SHIP

Prince Robert (R.C.N. manned)	Captain W. B. Creery, R.C.N.

DESTROYER DEPOT SHIPS

Tyne	Captain S. Boucher.
Montclare	Captain G. W. Hoare-Smith.

DESTROYERS

Quadrant	Lieutenant-Commander P. C. Hopkins.
Quality	Commander The Viscount Jocelyn.
Queenborough	Commander P. L. Saumarez.
Quiberon (R.A.N. manned)	Commander G. S. Stewart, R.A.N.
Quickmatch (R.A.N. manned)	Lieutenant-Commander O. H. Becher, R.A.N.
Quilliam[1]	Lieutenant J. R. Stephens.
Napier (R.A.N. manned)	Acting Captain H. J. Buchanan, R.A.N.
Nepal (R.A.N. manned)	Lieutenant-Commander C. J. Stephenson, R.A.N.
Nizam (R.A.N. manned)	Commander C. H. Brooks, R.A.N.
Norman (R.A.N. manned)	Lieutenant-Commander J. Plunkett-Cole, R.A.N.
Barfleur	Commander M. S. Townsend.
Troubridge	Captain G. F. Burghard.
Teazer	Lieutenant-Commander T. F. Taylor.
Tenacious	Lieutenant-Commander G. C. Crowley.
Termagant	Lieutenant-Commander D. C. Beatty.
Terpsichore	Commander R. T. White.
Tumult	Lieutenant-Commander A. S. Pomeroy.
Tuscan	Lieutenant-Commander P. B. N. Lewis.
Tyrian	Commander R. H. Mills.
Trafalgar[1]	Captain A. F. Pugsley.
Armada[1]	Lieutenant-Commander R. A. Fell.
Camperdown[1]	Lieutenant-Commander J. J. S. Yorke.
Hogue[1]	Commander A. St. Clair-Ford.
Grenville[1]	Captain R. G. Onslow.
Ulster[1]	Lieutenant-Commander R. J. Hanson.
Ulysses[1]	Lieutenant-Commander B. G. B. Bordes.
Undine[1]	Commander T. C. Robinson.
Undaunted[1]	Lieutenant-Commander C. E. R. Sharp.
Urania[1]	Lieutenant-Commander D. H. P. Gardiner.
Urchin	Lieutenant-Commander A. F. Harkness.
Ursa	Commander D. B. Wyburd.
Kempenfelt	Captain E. G. McGregor.
Wager	Lieutenant-Commander R. C. Watkin.
Wakeful	Lieutenant-Commander G. D. Pound.
Wessex	Lieutenant-Commander R. Horncastle.
Whelp	Commander G. A. F. Norfolk.
Whirlwind	Commander W. A. F. Hawkins.
Wizard	Lieutenant-Commander R. H. Hodgkinson.
Wrangler	Lieutenant-Commander E. G. Warren.

OFF-STATION

Algonquin (R.C.N. manned)	Acting Lieutenant-Commander D. W. Piers.

ESCORT (Command and H.Q. Ship)

Enchantress	Acting Lieutenant-Commander A. J. Clemence, R.N.R.

[1] (Non-operational, off station or on passage).

APPENDIX ZC

A.A. Sloops

Pheasant	Acting Commander J. B. Palmer.
Crane	Lieutenant-Commander R. G. Jenkins.
Redpole	Lieutenant-Commander E. J. Lee.
Whimbrel	Lieutenant-Commander N. R. Murch.
Woodcock	Acting Lieutenant-Commander S. J. Parsons.
Avon	Acting Commander P. G. A. King, R.N.R.
Findhorn	Temporary Acting Lieutenant-Commander J. P. Burnett, R.N.V.R.
Parret	Lieutenant-Commander T. Hood, R.N.R.

Frigates

Helford	Commander C. G. Cuthbertson, R.N.R.
Barle	Temporary Acting Lieutenant-Commander J. Duncan, R.N.R.
Derg	Lieutenant-Commander N. B. J. Stapleton, R.N.R.
Odzani	Acting Lieutenant-Commander J. N. Burgess, R.A.N.V.R.
Plym	Acting Lieutenant-Commander A. Foxall, R.N.R.
Usk	Temporary Acting Lieutenant-Commander G. B. Medlycott, R.N.R.
Widemouth Bay	Acting Lieutenant-Commander J. H. MacAlister, R.N.V.R.

A.A. Sloops

Alacrity[1]	Lieutenant-Commander J. Clutton Baker.
Amethyst[1]	Lieutenant-Commander N. Scott-Elliott.
Black Swan[1]	Lieutenant-Commander A. D. C. Inglis.
Erne[1]	Lieutenant-Commander P. S. Evans.
Hart[1]	Acting Commander H. F. G. Leftwich.
Hind[1]	Lieutenant-Commander A. D. White, R.N.R.
Cygnet[1]	Lieutenant-Commander A. H. Pierce, R.N.R.
Flamingo[1]	Lieutenant A. Traill, R.N.R.
Opossum[1]	Lieutenant-Commander W. F. Hollins.
Starling[1]	Temporary Acting Lieutenant-Commander G. C. Julian, R.N.Z.N.V.R.
Stork[1]	Lieutenant-Commander D. E. Mansfield.
Wren[1]	Commander S. R. J. Woods, R.N.R.

Frigates

Highbury Bay	Acting Lieutenant-Commander G. P. D. Hall.
Veryan Bay	Lieutenant J. S. Brownrigg.
Whitesand Bay	Acting Lieutenant-Commander B. C. Longbottom.

Submarines (Depot Ships)

Adamant	Captain B. Bryant.
Maidstone	Captain L. M. Shadwell.
Bonaventure	Acting Captain W. R. Fell.

Submarines

Taciturn	Lieutenant-Commander E. T. Stanley.
Tapir	Lieutenant J. C. Y. Roxburgh.
Taurus	Lieutenant P. E. Newstead.
Thorough	Lieutenant A. G. Chandler, R.N.R.
Thule	Lieutenant-Commander A. C. G. Mars.
Tiptoe	Lieutenant R. L. Jay.
Totem	Lieutenant-Commander M. B. St. John.
Trenchant	Lieutenant J. C. Ogle.
Trump	Lieutenant A. A. Catlow.
Turpin	Lieutenant J. S. Stevens.
Scotsman	Lieutenant A. H. B. Anderson, R.N.R.
Seascout	Lieutenant J. W. Kelly.
Selene	Lieutenant-Commander H. R. B. Newton.
Sidon	Lieutenant H. C. Gowan.
Sleuth	Lieutenant K. H. Martin.
Solent	Lieutenant J. D. Martin.
Spearhead	Temporary Lieutenant R. E. Youngman, R.N.R.
Stubborn	Lieutenant A. G. Davies.
Supreme	Lieutenant T. E. Barlow.

[1] (Non-operational, off station or on passage).

SUBMARINES—*continued*

Sanguine[1]	Temporary Lieutenant P. C. S. Pritchard, R.N.R.
Sea Devil[1]	Lieutenant D. W. Mills.
Seanymph[1]	Lieutenant M. I. Usher.
Spark[1]	Lieutenant D. G. Kent.
Stygian[1]	Lieutenant G. S. C. Clarabut.
Terrapin[1]	Lieutenant R. H. H. Brunner.
Tudor[1]	Lieutenant S. A. Porter.

A/S TRAINING SUBMARINES

Voracious	Lieutenant D. R. Wilson, R.A.N.V.R.
Vox	Temporary Lieutenant W. E. I. Littlejohn, R.A.N.V.R.
Virtue	Non-operational. Lieutenant I. G. Raikes.

MINESWEEPERS

Temporarily Allocated

Coquette[1]	Commander R. W. D. Thomson.
Rowena[1]	Lieutenant-Commander G. C. Hogart, R.N.R.
Mary Rose[1]	Lieutenant D. H. Edelston.
Moon[1]	Lieutenant J. B. Lamb.
Providence[1]	Lieutenant E. G. Mason.
Seabear[1]	Lieutenant-Commander W. A. C. Harvey, R.N.R.
Thisbe[1]	Acting Commander F. A. I. Kirkpatrick.
Courier[1]	Commander (Retired) E. S. Jerome.
Felicity[1]	Acting Lieutenant-Commander H. R. Richards.
Hare[1]	Temporary Acting Lieutenant-Commander J. K. M. Warde, R.N.V.R.
Liberty[1]	Temporary Commander J. S. Roe, R.N.R.
Michael[1]	Acting Lieutenant-Commander J. D. Jones.
Minstrel[1]	Lieutenant-Commander E. B. Cutlack, R.N.R.
Wave[1]	Acting Lieutenant-Commander D. C. Salter.
Welcome[1]	Temporary Acting Lieutenant-Commander T. Gentle, R.N.R.

ATTACHED DANLAYERS

Shillay	Temporary Lieutenant R. P. Rodriquez, R.A.N.V.R.
Trodday	Temporary Lieutenant H. S. Chisholm, R.N.V.R.

CORVETTES (R.A.N. manned)

Ballarat	Acting Commander N. R. Read, R.A.N.
Bendigo	Lieutenant W. Jackson, R.A.N.V.R.
Burnie	Lieutenant-Commander E. M. Andrewartha, R.A.N.R.
Goulburn	Lieutenant E. K. Connor, R.A.N.R.
Maryborough	Lieutenant-Commander M. W. Lancaster, R.A.N.
Toowoomba	Lieutenant H. F. Goodwin, R.A.N.R.
Whyalla	Lieutenant G. L. B. Parry, R.A.N.V.R.
Cessnock	Lieutenant A. G. Chapman, R.A.N.R.(S).
Gawler	Lieutenant-Commander J. H. P. Dixon, R.A.N.R.
Geraldton	Acting Commander A. J. Travis, R.A.N.
Ipswich	Temporary Lieutenant R. H. Creasy, R.A.N.R.(S).
Launceston	Acting Temporary Lieutenant-Commander E. J. Barron, R.A.N.R.(S).
Pirie	Lieutenant G. K. Mackenzie, R.A.N.V.R.
Tamworth	Lieutenant M. B. Gale, R.A.N.R.
Woolongong	Temporary Lieutenant J. Hare, R.A.N.R.(S).
Kalgoorlie[1]	Temporary Lieutenant-Commander J. S. McBryde, R.A.N.R.(S).
Lismore[1]	Lieutenant K. S. Sutherland, R.A.N.V.R.
Cairns[1]	Lieutenant C. M. Callow, R.A.N.V.R.

AIRCRAFT TARGET SHIPS

Lewes[1]	Temporary Acting Lieutenant-Commander M. H. Grylls, S.A.N.F.(V).
Penn[1]	Lieutenant-Commander A. H. Diack.

BOOM CARRIERS

Fermoor	Temporary Acting Lieutenant-Commander E. R. Crone, R.N.R.
Leonian[1]	Acting Commander R. F. Graham, R.N.R.

[1] (Non-operational, off station or on passage).

APPENDIX ZC

Base Depots

Beaconsfield (Melbourne)	Acting Temporary Lieutenant M. Gibbs, R.N.V.R.
Furneaux (Brisbane)	Commander J. F. Steemson.
Golden Hind (Sydney)	Captain H. B. Crane.
Pepys (Manus)	No record.
Woolloomooloo	Acting Commander J. D. Stevenson.

H.Q. Ship

Lothian (L.S.H.)	Captain G. C. F. Branson.

Transport

Glenearn (L.S.I.(L))	Captain C. A. G. Hutchison.

FLEET TRAIN

Accommodation Ships

Aorangi
Lancashire

Heavy Repair Ships

Artifex	Captain C. C. Fleming.
Resource	Captain (Retired) D. B. O'Connell.

Hull Repair Ship

Dullisk Cove	Lieutenant-Commander G. B. Herbert-Jones, R.N.R.

Auxiliary Repair Ships

Assistance	Acting Captain J. H. Young.
Diligence	Acting Captain E. H. Hopkinson.

Escort Maintenance Ships

Berry Head	Commander K. M. Drake, R.N.R.
Flamborough Head	Lieutenant-Commander J. F. Denman.

Maintenance Ship (Minesweepers)

Kelantan	Commander S. P. Herivel, R.N.V.R.

Radio Repair Ship

Arbutus (N.Z. manned)	Temporary Lieutenant N. D. Blair, R.N.Z.N.R.

Command Ship Logistic Supply Group

Aire (C.L.S.G.)	Acting Lieutenant-Commander H. I. S. White, R.N.R.

Fleet Attendant Tanker (Fast)

Olna	Captain (Retired) P. L. Williams, R.N.R.

AIR TRAIN

Aircraft Maintenance Ship

Pioneer (C.O.M.A.T.)	Commodore (2nd Class) H. S. Murray-Smith.

Aircraft Repair Ship

Unicorn	Acting Captain C. M. Mereweather.

Aircraft Component Repair Ship

Deer Sound	Acting Captain R. H. Johnson.

Air Stores Issuing Ships

Fort Colville
Fort Langley

APPENDIX ZC

FLEET ATTENDANT TANKERS (RED ENSIGN)

Aese Maersk, Arndale, Bishopdale, Carelia, Cedardale, Dingledale, Eaglesdale, San Adolfo, San Amado, San Ambrosio, Wave Emperor, Wave Governor, Wave King, Wave Monarch.

SMALL TANKERS (RED ENSIGN)

Brown Ranger, Darst Creek, Golden Meadow, Green Ranger, Ieve, Loma Navia, Rapidol, Serbol, Seven Sisters.

WATER CARRYING TANKERS

Empire Crest, Vacport

NET LAYER

Guardian Captain R. D. Binks, R.N.R.

DEPERMING SHIP

Springdale Lieutenant (Retired) J. S. Seal, R.N.R.

COLLIER

Edna (Red Ensign)

SALVAGE VESSELS

King Salvor, Salvestor, Salvictor

Temporary Lieutenant R. H. A. Adams, R.N.V.R.
Temporary Acting Lieutenant-Commander W. J. Harvey, R.N.R.

HOSPITAL SHIPS

Empire Clyde, Gerusalemme, Maunganui, Oxfordshire, Tjitjalengka, Vasna.

ISSUING SHIPS (RED ENSIGNS)

ARMAMENT STORES

Corinda, Darvel, Hermelin, Heron, Kheti, Kistna, Pacheco, Prince De Liege, Princess Maria Pia, Robert Maersk, Thyra S., Hickory Burn, Hickory Dale, Hickory Glen, Hickory Stream.

NAVAL STORES

Bacchus, City of Dieppe (Also V.S.I.S.)

VICTUALLING STORES

City of Dieppe (Also N.S.I.S.)
Fort Alabama, Fort Constantine, Fort Dunvegan, Fort Edmonton, Fort Providence, Fort Wrangell, Glenartney.

MINE ISSUE SHIP

Prome

DISTILLING SHIPS

Bacchus (also N.S.I.S.), *Stagpool*

ARMAMENT STORES

Gudrun Maersk, Kola

NAVAL STORES

Bosphorus, Jaarstroom, Marudu, San Andres, Slesvig

APPENDIX ZD

U.S. Intelligence

Report of United States Strategic Bombing Survey (vide Air Campaigns of the Pacific War)

INTELLIGENCE

The most outstanding feat of American military intelligence in connection with the war against Japan was the breaking of the Japanese code. This permitted forewarning our forces of Japanese intentions in many instances and permitted making advance preparations for countering Japanese operations.

Three major factors, however, adversely affected our military intelligence throughout the war. These were :—

(*a*) *First.*—An artificial barrier existed between the intelligence services of the Army and Navy. Throughout the war, lacking unified command in the Pacific we operated without an intelligence system capable of meeting the requirements of co-ordinated land, sea and air warfare. In numerous cases, at all levels of command down to and including the squadron and company, essential intelligence available to one service was not necessarily available or expeditiously forwarded to another participating service. At all levels of command, however, co-operation and co-ordination was attempted in the exchange of intelligence information, many times with outstanding success. However, a system was not established during the war which ensured the timely production of balanced, objective intelligence and the timely dissemination of that intelligence to all those who needed it in the performance of their tasks.

(*b*) *Second.*—American intelligence, prior to World War II, had not been objective. As a result, much basic information which was essential to military operations was not available when needed. Such basic geographical information as weather, tides, winds, topography, depth of waters, location of roads, trails, swamps, mountain passes and so forth was inadequate and wholly lacking in many cases. Similarly, specific information on man-made features in such form as to facilitate selection of target systems was wholly inadequate. Much of the essential information was available in hundreds of different businesses, books, documents, and other sources, but a gigantic task was faced in its collation for military use.

Combat intelligence, initially underestimating enemy capabilities, swung to the opposite extreme and became over-cautious, consistently over-rating the enemy's forces and capabilities. Improvement in combat intelligence, however, was steady throughout the war as experience with the enemy increased, and as aerial reconnaissance and other sources of information provided a constantly increasing measure of the enemy's deployment and capabilities.

(*c*) *Third.*—The American national viewpoint has traditionally abhorred the spy. Consequently, our national intelligence, including our espionage organization, was not adequate to satisfy our national security requirements. Traditionally, we were prepared to accept the first blow before obtaining essential objective intelligence and before taking up arms to defend ourselves. This abhorrence of national intelligence work and this willingness to learn that a war is in progress only after we have been attacked can be disastrous in a future war. Our national security demands that our intelligence organization of the future, beginning today, be aware of the plans, capabilities, and probable intentions of possible future enemies at all times. Only by having such information can our military forces have an even chance of protecting our nation.

Bibliography

Principal sources used generally throughout this Volume and in the preparation of Chapter I

OFFICIAL

(*a*) BRITISH

Naval War Diary. Historical Section, Naval Staff, Admiralty.

'*Pink List*'. Operations Division, Naval Staff, Admiralty.

Particulars of War Vessels and Naval Aircraft, British Commonwealth of Nations. C.B. 01815 (B) Series.

Particulars of United States War and Auxiliary Vessels. C.B. 01815 (U) Series.

Particulars of Foreign Vessels. C.B. 1815 Series.

German, Italian and Japanese U-boat Casualties during the War, Particulars of Destruction. Cmd. 6843. H.M.S.O., London.

British and Foreign Merchant Vessels Lost or Damaged by Enemy Action during the Second World War. B.R. 1337.

Far East and Pacific Intelligence Reports. Naval Intelligence Division, Admiralty.

Monthly Anti-Submarine Report, April–May 1945. C.B. 04050/45 (4) (5).

Commander-in-Chief Ceylon, War Diary 1*st July* 1944–8*th January* 1945. M.059073/44.

Commander-in-Chief East Indies, War Diary 22*nd November* 1944–*August* 1945. Record Office Case WHS.8957.

Commander-in-Chief British Pacific Fleet, War Diary 4*th February* 1945–23*rd March* 1945. T.S.D. 3157/45.

(*b*) UNITED STATES

Admiral E. J. King's Second and Final Official (War) Reports to the Secretary of the Navy. Government Printing Office, Washington, D.C.

Publications of the United States Strategic Bombing Survey (Pacific), Naval Analysis Division. Government Printing Office, Washington, D.C.

Interrogations of Japanese Officials. Volumes 1 and II.

Summary Report (*Pacific War*) 1946.

The Campaigns of the Pacific War.

Japan's Struggle to End the War. Report No. B.I.O.S./J.A.P./P.R./1618. Reprint. H.M.S.O., London.

German, Japanese and Italian Submarine Losses, World War II. Opnav–P–33–100 Nav. 5–48. Chief of Naval Operations, Navy Department.

Japanese Naval and Merchant Ship Losses during World War II. Prepared by the Joint Army-Navy Assessment Committee. Government Printing Office, Washington, D.C. February 1947.

Operations in the Pacific Ocean Areas. Series of monthly reports by Commander-in-Chief U.S. Pacific Fleet and Pacific Ocean Areas, September 1944–August 1945.

The Army Air Forces in World War II. Volume V. *The Pacific : Matterhorn to Nagasaki, June* 1944 *to August* 1945. Ed. W. J. Craven and J. L. Cate. U.S. Air Force Historical Division of Research Studies. University of Chicago Press. 1953.

Japanese Defence against Amphibious Operations. Military Intelligence Division, War Department, Washington, D.C. 1945.

(*c*) JAPANESE

The Imperial Japanese Navy in World War II. Japanese Monograph No. 116. A graphic presentation of the Japanese Naval Organisation and list of combatant and non-combatant vessels lost or damaged in the war. Prepared by G.H.Q. Far East Command, February 1952, initially prepared by former officers of the Japanese Navy under American supervision.

Ship and Related Targets : *Japanese Submarine Operations.* U.S. Naval Technical Mission to Japan. S–1/BIOS/JAP/PR/1280. February 1946.

UNOFFICIAL

The Second World War. Volume V. *Closing the Ring.* Winston S. Churchill. Cassell & Co., Ltd., London, E.C. 1952.

Spearheads of Invasion. By W. N. Swan. Angus and Robertson, London, W.C.1. 1953.

United States Submarine Operations in World War II. T. Roscoe. U.S. Naval Institute, Annapolis, Maryland. (Based on official sources.)

Sink 'em All—Submarine Warfare in the Pacific. Vice-Admiral C. A. Lockwood (Retired). Based on official sources. Admiral Lockwood was Commander, Submarines, Pacific Fleet during the war.

General Kenney reports. By George C. Kenney. Duell, Sloane & Pearce, New York. *n.d.* (General Kenney commanded the Allied Air Forces in the South-West Pacific and the Far Eastern Air Force. The claims of enemy aircraft losses which he makes bear little relation to the facts.)

History of United States Naval Operations in World War II. Volume VIII. S. E. Morison.

Principal sources used in preparing Chapter II

History of the Fleet Train. Captain R. F. Leonard, R.N. (In Ms.).

Basing of R.N. Forces on Australia for Intensification of War Effort. Record Office W.H. Cases 8733–46.

Australia as Rear Base for British Pacific Fleet. Communication Arrangements. M.012661/44.

Intermediate Fleet Base in Pacific. Plan Dropped. M.059006/45 and other papers bound up in the same volume.

Establishment of Main Base for BPF at Sydney. M.012748/44, M.01563/45, M.01670/45, M.02732/45.

Commander-in-Chief BPF. Appointment. M.011926/44.

Basing of BPF on Australia. M.057556/44, M.058190/44, M.058105/44.

Australia as Base for British Operations against Japan. Cabinet Committee. 328.

Northbridge Military Mission to Australia &c. R.O. Case 00 253.

Proposal to Abandon Intermediate Base. M.058551/45.

Principal sources used in preparing Chapter III

Operation 'Robson'. Air Strike on Belawan, 17–22nd December 1944. M.02627/45, A.0132/45 (behind A.0366/45).

Operation 'Lentil'. Air Strike on Targets in Sumatra, 31st December 1944–*7th January* 1945. M.02816/45 (behind M.02627/45), A.0109/45, A.0335/45, A.0137/45, A.0366/45 (behind A.0132/45), H. & A. 157/45.

Operation 'Meridian'. Attack on Oil Refineries at Palembang,24th–29th January 1945. M.03320/45, H. & A. 312/45.

Report of Proceedings, 13th January–4th February 1945. M.03026/45.

Enemy Air Attacks, 29th January 1945. M.02279/45.

Euryalus Report, 29th January 1945. M.03496/45.

Air–Sea Rescue Operations. U.S. Submarine Patrol Report. NID.02503/45.

Interrogation of Major Kurokawa. NID.6508/47.

Air Reports. A.0737/45, A.0273/45, A.0657/45, A.0329/45, A.0301/45.

Seatic Air Historical Bulletin. Publication No. 248. *22nd April*, 1947. NID.03353/47.

Commander-in-Chief East Indies, *War Diary.* (In Record Office Case WH.8957.) 22nd November–31st December, 1944. Part I. T.S.D. 4443/44 ; 22nd November–31st December 1944. Part II. T.S.D. 3188/45 ; January 1945. T.S.D. 3183/45.

Principal sources used in preparing Chapter IV

Commander-in-Chief East Indies, *War Diary.* November 1944–July 1945. Record Office Case WH.8957.

Operations 'Suffice' and 'Training'. Anti-Shipping Sweep and Bombardments by Force 68, *21st–25th February* 1945 *and 27th February–4th March.* M.058924/45.

Operation 'Transport'. Sweep by Force 70 *and Bombardment of Port Blair, 14th–19th March.* M.05090/45, M.059109/45, H. & A. 775/45.

Operation 'Onboard'. Sweep by Force 70, *25th–29th March.* M.04434/45.

Operations 'Penzance' and 'Passbook'. Sweeps by Force 62, *1st–4th April and 9th–11th April.* M.059165/45.

Operation 'Gable'. Patrol in Gulf of Martaban by Force 62, *27th April–4th May.* M.05555/45, M.06436/45, M.06682/45.

Operation 'Stacey'. Photographic Reconnaissance of Kra Isthmus, Penang and North Sumatra by Force 62, *26th February–4th March.* M.058869/45.

Operation 'Sunfish'. Photographic Reconnaissance of Port Swettenham and Port Dickson Areas and Bombardment of Sabang by Force 63, *8th–20th April.* M.05853/45, M.06968/45.

Operation 'Balsam'. Photographic Reconnaissance of Southern Malaya and Strikes against Sumatran Airfields by Force 63, *18th–23rd June.* M.07309/45, H. & A. 1017/45.

Operation 'Clearance Baker'. 12th–13th April. H. & A. 779/45, 1351/45 (H.M.S. *Torbay*).

Operation 'Cattle'. 15th–16th April. H. & A. 779/45, 1351/45 (H.M.S. *Torbay*).

Operation 'Dukedom/Mitre'. Sinking of the Haguro, 16th May. M.06514/45, M.06887/45, M.07923/45, M.07066/45, A.0941/45, H. & A. 576/45, H. & A. 912/45.

Operation 'Bishop'. Covering Operations for Assault on Rangoon, 29th April–9th May. M.05523/45.

Operation 'Irregular'. Attack on Shipping by Force 65, *5th–15th June.* M.059166/45, H. & A. 798/45.

Operation 'Collie'. Sweeping of Enemy Minefield and Bombardment of Car Nicobar, 5th–11th July. M.08439/45.

Operation 'Livery'. Minesweeping off Phuket Island, 24th–26th July. Loss of the Squirrel and Vestal. M.01366/46, M.09220/45, M.09034/45, H. & A. 1294/45, M. 3019/46.

Operation 'Livery'. Reports of Suicide Attacks by Enemy Aircraft on H.M. Ships Nelson, Sussex, Ameer and Empress. M.3989/45.

Sinking of the Ashigara 8th June. M.0768/45 ; *H.M.S./M. Trenchant Report of Sixth War Patrol.* H. & A. 1016/45 ; *H.M.S. Stygian Patrol Report 29th May–27th June* 1945. M.07931/45 ; *Interrogation of Captain Yamanoue and Commander Ino.* NID.0721/46.

Principal sources used in preparation of Chapters V, VI, VIII and IX

C.O.H.Q. Bulletin Y/46. *Combined Operations against Leyte, October* 1944.

Leyte (Philippines) Operations, British Combined Operations Observers' Report. M.012980/44.

H.M.A.S. Australia, Warramunga, Shropshire, Bombardment of Leyte, 20th October 1944. M.04528/45.

H.M.A.S. Arunta, Action Report, 13th–29th October 1944, *covering Leyte Operation.* M.01977/45.

Carrier Strike on Luzon, 5th and 6th November 1944. B.N.L.O.s Report. NID.0051371/44.

Amphibious Operations, Invasion of the Philippines, October 1944 *to January* 1945. Cominch P–008. U.S. Fleet. Headquarters of Commander-in-Chief. 30th April 1945.

Sho One. From Formosa to Lingayen. U.S. Strategic Bombing Survey. The O.N.I. Review, Volume I, No. 13. November 1946.

Recommendations for Improvement of Future Operations (Leyte, October 1944). M.013376/44.

Commander Third Fleet, Operational Summaries of Carrier Strikes, 28th October–22nd November. M.0508/45.

CTF 38 *Action Report of Operations in Support of Central and Northern Philippines, 30th October–26th January* 1945. M.M.03191/45 (behind M.06562/45).

Carrier Division 27, *Operations, 12th August* 1944–*4th February* 1945, *Palau and Philippines.* M.03229/45.

C.T.G. 38.1 *Action Report.* M.0411/45.

C.T.G. 38.3 *Report on Battle of Formosa, 12th–14th October* 1944. M.0633/45.

Action Report of Nansei Shoto Strike, U.S.S. Essex. M.01565/45.

U.S.S. New Orleans, Western Pacific Report, 10th–21st October 1944. M.0638/45.

U.S.S. Princeton, Action Report, 10th October 1944. M.02142/45.

U.S.S. Princeton, Action Report, 12th–14th October. M.01814/45.

U.S.S. Lexington, Action Report. M.0965/45.

U.S.S. Wichita, Action Report, 2nd–13th October. M.02377/45.

U.S.S. Lexington, Action Report of Attacks on the Visayas and Southern Luzon, 21st October 1944. M.01596/45.

U.S.S. ***Santa Fé****, Action Report, 21st October.* M.02313/45. (Air strikes in Visayan area.)

U.S.S. Santa Fé, Action Report, 27th October. M.02314/45. (Strike by *Essex* and *Lexington* against damaged cruiser and two destroyers off Mindanao.)

Report of Action against Luzon and Ormoc Bay, 2nd–24th November. M.0629/45. (Covers attack on Japanese reinforcement convoy, 11th November 1944.)

U.S.S. Boston, Action Report, 2nd–21st November. M.0641/45 (behind M.0629/45).

Report of Torpedoing of U.S.S. Reno, 3rd November. M.0126/45.

U.S.S. Reno, Torpedoing of, 3rd November 1944. *Passage to Ulithi.* M.06203/44.

Com. Cru. Div. 13, *Action Report.* M.01556/45.

U.S.S. Wichita, Action Report, 5th–20th November, Leyte Area. M.01566/45.

U.S.S. Santa Fé, Action Report Air Strikes on Luzon Area, 5th–6th November 1944. M.01600/45.

U.S.S. Santa Fé, Action Report, 5th and 6th November 1944, *Manila.* M.02137/45.

U.S.S. Lexington, Action Report of Attacks on Luxon Island on 5th and 6th November 1944. M.0962/45.

U.S.S. Langley, Action Report, 2nd–14th November 1944. M.01548/45.

C.T.G. 38.3 (*Com. Car. Div.* 1), *Action Report, Manila Strikes, 5th and 6th November* 1944. M.0857/45.

C.T.G. 38.2, *Action Report, 5th–6th November* 1944, *Luzon.* M.08330/45.

C.T.G. 38.2, *U.S.S. Cabot, Strikes against Southern Luzon and Bicol Area, 1st November–9th November* 1944. M.08308/45.

U.S.S. Monterey, Action Report Operations against Luzon, 10th–20th November. M.0511/45.

U.S.S. San Jacinto, Action Report Operations against Luzon, 10th–20th November. M.0627/45.

C.T.G. 38.4, *Action Report Operations against Luzon, 10th–20th November.* M.0127/45.

U.S.S. Enterprise, Action Report Operations against Luzon, 10th–20th November. M.0262/45.

T.G. 38.3, *Report of Ormoc Bay Strike, 11th November.* M.0640/45.

U.S.S. Bunker Hill, Action Report, 5th–17th November, Ormoc and Leyte. M.0415/45.

U.S.S. Wasp and Carrier Group 81 *in Central Luzon Area, 11th–24th November.* M.0631/45.

U.S.S. Yorktown, Action Report Philippine Islands, 11th–15th November 1944. M.0214/45.

T.G. 38.3, *Com. Car. Div.* 1 *in U.S.S. Essex, Manila Strikes, 13th–14th November* 1944. M.02355/45.

U.S.S. Cabot, Action Report, 14th–27th November 1944, *Southern Luzon.* M.013403/44.

Air Strike by U.S.S. Bunker Hill on Shipping in and near South Harbour, Manila Bay. M.0415/45.

U.S.S. Intrepid, Operations against South Luzon and Sibuyan Sea Shipping, 14th–27th November 1944. M.0634/45.

U.S.S. Cowpens, Air Attack on Luzon Area, 19th November. M.0626/45.

U.S.S. Minami, A.A. Action Reports on19th and 25th November, Luzon. M.0860/45.

U.S.S. Yorktown, Action Report of Operations against Enemy Airfields in Central Philippines, 19th November 1944. M.01569/45.

U.S.S. Mobile, Report of Carrier Air Operations of Task Groups 38.2 *and* 38.3 *against Luzon, 25th November.* M.0628/45.

U.S.S. Intrepid Damaged. M.02341/45 (behind M.02317/45).

U.S.S. Iowa, Action Report, 25th November. M.0507/45.

Com. Car. Div. 4, *U.S.S. Intrepid, Action Report, 14th–27th November* 1944. M.02354/54.

U.S.S. Essex, Report of Action off Luzon, 25th November 1944. M.01158/45.

U.S.S. Ticonderoga, Action Report, 25th November. M.01560/45.

U.S.S. Independence, Action Report, 14th–30th November, Luzon. M.01561/45.

U.S.S. Colorado, A.A. Action Report, 23rd–29th November, Leyte Gulf. M.0967/45.

South Dakota, Action Report, 22nd November–2nd December 1944, *Luzon.* M.02312/45.

Combat Div. 7, *Action Report, 25th November.* M.01572/45.

U.S.S. Maryland, Damaged by Suicide Plane Attack, 29th November 1944. M.01138/45.

Combat Div. 4, *Bombardment and Fire Support for Assault and Capture of Leyte Island, 19th–29th October.* M.01816/45.

Com. Cru. Div. 4, *Action Report, Bombardment and Capture of Leyte, 16th–24th October* 1944. M.07099/45.

BIBLIOGRAPHY

Leyte, Action Report Commander Amphibious Group 8. M.042/45.

U.S.S. Mississippi (*C.T.U.* 77.2.11), *Action Report, 19th–24th October* 1944, *Leyte.* M.0410/45. *Endorsements.* M.06324/45.

Action Report, Bombardment in Support of Leyte Landing Operations. M.01809/45.

U.S.S. Boise, Bombardment in Support of Leyte Landing Operations, 20th–24th October. M.0316/45.

U.S.S. Nashville, Action Report, 20th October 1944. M.01557/45.

Action Report, 5th October–4th November 1944, *Leyte, LST Group* 42. M.01801/45.

Action Report (*Boise*), *Bombardment of San Ricardo Area, Leyte.* M.01809/45, M.0316/45.

U.S.S. Pennsylvania, A.A. Actions, 17th October–25th November 1944, *Leyte Area.* M.0650/45. *Endorsements.* M.0963/45.

U.S.S. Alabama, Action Report, 25th October–24th November. M.0714/45.

U.S.S. Massachussetts, Action Report, 25th October–24th November. M.02325/45.

U.S.S. Denver, A.A. Action, Reports for 26th and 28th October, and 24th, 27th, 29th November, Leyte. M.01804/45.

U.S.S. Phoenix, Action Report, Leyte Gulf, 1st November 1944. M.01558/45. (The *Phoenix* was flagship of Rear-Admiral R. S. Berkey.)

U.S.S. Honolulu, Action Report, Bombardment of Leyte, 12th–29th October 1944. M.02144/45.

U.S.S. Savo Island, Action Report, Air Protection of Shipping. M.01568/45.

U.S.S. Marcus Island, Action Report, Leyte Operation, 19th–27th November. M.01552/45.

C.T.U. 77.4.6, *Operations in Threatened Area to East of Leyte Gulf, 23rd–27th November.* M.0712/45.

U.S.S. Montpelier, A.A. Actions in Leyte Gulf, 27th and 29th November. M.0506/45.

U.S.S. St. Louis, Action Report, A.A., 27th November 1944, *Leyte Gulf.* M.0861/45.

C.T.G. 77.2, *Action Report, 16th November–2nd December* 1944, *Leyte Gulf.* M.03010/45.

U-Boat known sunk by U.S.S. Scabbardfish, 28th November. M.01934/45. (The submarine was *I*–365.)

T.G. 77.12 (*Combat Div.* 4 *in U.S.S. West Virginia*), *Action Report, 2nd–14th December* 1944. M.01788/45.

Com. Min. Ron. 13, *Action Report, 6th–8th December, Ormoc Bay Landing.* M.01802/45 (Minesweeping).

C.T.G. 78.3 *in U.S.S. Hughes, Ormoc Landing, 7th December* 1944. M.01790/45.

Amphibious Landing Operation in Ormoc Bay, Report by C.T.U. 78.3.5 (Commander Destroyer Squadron 60). M.01644/45.

Com. 7th Fleet, Action Report, 12th–17th December, Mindoro. M.06475/75.

Escort Carriers (*T.U.* 77.12.7), *Action Report covering Operations in Connection with Occupation of Mindoro, 10th–19th December* 1944. M.0505/45.

C.O., U.S.S. Cowpens, Action Report, Operations against Enemy in Manila Area during Occupation of Mindoro Island, 10th–16th December. M.01803/45.

U.S.S. Hornet, Action Report, Central Luzon, 10th–23rd December 1944. M.02381/45.

U.S.S. Essex, Support of Mindoro Landing Operations, 14th–16th December 1944. M.01690/45.

U.S.S. Monterey, Action Report, 10th–21st December 1944, *Luzon.* M.02356/45.

U.S.S. Wisconsin, Action Report, 11th–24th December 1944. M.0116/45.

U.S.S. Boston, Action Report, 10th–24th December 1944. M.01267/45.

U.S.S. Wasp, Action Report, 10th–21st December 1944. M.0961/45.

C.T.U. 38.2.2, *Action Report, 1st–24th December* 1944. M.01645/45. (The above five papers describe the Typhoon of 18th December in which U.S.S. *Hull, Monaghan* and *Spence* were sunk. Times in M.01645/45 are apparently K Zone.)

U.S.S. Independence, Strikes on Luzon in Support of Landings on Mindoro, December 1944. M.02357/45. (Night fighter carrier.)

C.T.G. 38.3, *Luzon Sweeps, 14th–16th December* 1944. M.03185/45.

U.S.S. Iowa, Action Report, 1st–24th December 1944. M.0236/45.

U.S.S. Langley, Sweeps in Support of Airborne and Amphibious Landing on Mindoro Island, 14th–16th December 1944. M.03197/45.

C.T.G. 38.2, *Action Report, Central Luzon, 11th–24th December* 1944. M.03186/45.

Report on Operations of Third Fleet, 1st–29th December 1944. M.01690/45. (Admiral Halsey's report.)

BIBLIOGRAPHY

U.S.S. Kabashan Bay, Action Report, Escort of Mindoro Assault group through Sulu and Mindanao Seas, 13th–17th December. M.01805/45.

C.T.G. 27.12, *Action Report, 2nd–14th December* 1944. M.03237/45.

Task Unit 78.3.5, *Re-occupation of Mindoro, 12th–18th December.* M.01141/45. (U.S.S. *Nashville* damaged.)

U.S.S. Santa Fé, Action Report, Air Strikes in Support of Landings on Mindoro, 14th–16th December. M.01792/45.

U.S.S. Mobile, Action Report, Air Strikes in Support of Landings on Mindoro, 14th–16th December. M.01263/45.

U.S.S. Manila Bay, Action Report in Support of Occupation of Mindoro, 10th–17th December 1944. M.01264/45.

U.S.S. Marcus Island, Report of Action, 10th–19th December 1944. M.01160/45.

U.S.S. Montpelier, Action Report of Operations in Support of Landing on Mindoro, 12th–17th December. M.01806/45.

Com. Min. Div. 13, *Action Report of Operations in Support of Landing on Mindoro 12th–17th December.* M.01815/45.

U.S.S. Columbia, Action Report, 13th–17th December 1944. M.02320/45. (Effect on morale of shortage of fresh provisions and mails.)

U.S.S. Natoma Bay (T.U. 77.12.7), *13th–17th December* 1944. M.02358/45.

U.S.S. Denver, Action Report, Mindoro. M.01813/45.

U.S.S. Requisite, Action Report, Mindoro Landing, 12th–18th December 1944. M.01815/45 (Minesweeping Report.)

Action Report, 27th December 1944 *to 1st January* 1945, *Leyte to Mindoro.* M.01807/45 (second Mindoro re-supply echelon).

C.T.U. 78.3.15, *Action Report, Leyte to Mindoro, 27th December* 1944–*3rd January* 1945. M.03224/45 (second Mindoro re-supply echelon).

U.S.S. Yorktown, Support of Landings on Mindoro, 14th–16th December 1944. M.01266/45.

U.S.S. San Diego, Action Report, 10th–24th December 1944, *Mindoro.* M.02319/45.

Destroyer Squadron 60, *U.S.S. Barton, Action Report, Mindoro, 12th–18th December* 1944. M.02382/45.

German U-Boat probably Sunk by U.S.S. Flounder. M.01405/45.

U-Boat probably Sunk by U.S.S. Lawrence C. Taylor and Aircraft from U.S.S. Anzio. M.01405/45. (The submarine was *I–26*, sunk 17th November.)

U-Boat known Sunk by U.S.S. Waller, Renshaw, Saufley, Pringle, off Davao Gulf. M.01934/45. (The submarine was *I–46*.)

Battle Experience, *Bombardments of Iwo Jima, November* 1944–*January* 1945. *Third Fleet Operations in Support of Central Luzon Landings—including the South China Sea Sweep, 30th December* 1944–*23rd January* 1945. Secret Information Bulletin No. 23. T.S.D. 279/45.

Amphibious Operations, Invasion of the Philippines, October 1944 *to January* 1945. U.S. Fleet, Headquarters of Commander-in-Chief. Cominch. P–008.

Marine Aviation in the Philippines. Major C. W. Boggs, Jr., U.S.M.C., Historical Division, Headquarters, U.S. Marine Corps, U.S. Government Printing Office, Washington, D.C. 1951.

Philippine Area Naval Operations, Part IV, January 1945–*August* 1945. Japanese Monograph No. 114.

Principal sources used in preparation of Chapter VI

The official sources are listed in C.B. 3081 (30) Naval Staff History Battle Summary No. 40, *Battle for Leyte Gulf, 23rd–26th October* 1944.

An additional (unofficial) source (not available when Battle Summary No. 40 was prepared) is *Admiral Halsey's Story* by Fleet-Admiral William F. Halsey, U.S.N., and Lieutenant-Commander J. Bryan III, U.S.N.R. McGraw-Hill Book Company, Inc. New York, London. Second Printing, 1947.

Principal sources used in preparation of Chapter X

Lingayen Gulf Landing, December 1944–*January* 1945 (*Operation Musketeer*). M.03235/45 (this is the best report), M.06586/45, M.03198/45 (passage to objective).

H.M.A.S. Shropshire, Action Report, 1st–18th January 1945—*Lingayen.* M.06463/45.

H.M.A.S. Australia, Action Report, 6th–9th January, Lingayen Gulf. M.06469/45.

Guns v. Suicide Bombers, Narrative by Officer of H.M.A.S. Australia. M.03498/45.

H.M.A.S. Warramunga, Action Report, 3rd–18th January 1945, *Lingayen.* M.06461/45.

H.M.A.S. Arunta, Action Report, 2nd–12th January, Lingayen. M.06467/45.

H.M.A.S. Kanimbla, Action Report, 31st December 1944–*10th January* 1945. M.09184/45.

C.T.G. 77.3, *Action Report, Luzon.* M.06172/45.

U.S.S. San Francisco, Operations in Support of Conquest of Luzon. M.03233/45.

C.T.G. 79.2, *Action Report of Amphibious Attack on Lingayen.* M.02718/45.

U.S.S. Leon, Appling, Adair, Luzon, 23rd November 1944–*15th January* 1945. M.03222/45.

U.S.S. Lunga Point, Lingayen Gulf, 27th December 1944–*23rd January* 1945. M.03200/45.

C.T.U. 77.2.1, *Bombardment of and Fire Support for Landings, Lingayen Gulf, 1st–18th January* 1945. M.03011/45.

C.T.G. 77.9, *Reinforcement Group.* M.03012/45.

U.S.S. Manila Bay, Operations in Support of Landing at Lingayen, 1st–19th January 1945. M.02346/45.

U.S.S. West Virginia, Bombardment and Fire Support for Landings, Lingayen. M.02978/45.

U.S.S. Ommaney Bay, Action Report, Lingayen, 1st–4th January 1945. M.02997/45.

C.T.G. 79.2, *Amphibious Attack on Lingayen, Attack Group B.* M.02710/45.

Task Unit 77.4.4, *Action Report, Lingayen, 29th December* 1944–*17th January* 1945. M.02473/45.

U.S.S. Louisville, Action Report, Seizure and Occupation of Luzon Area, 2nd–12th January 1945. M.01969/45.

Commander Battleship Squadron 1 (*C.T.G.* 77.2), *Action Report, 3rd–18th January* 1945. M.06126/45.

U.S.S. Kitkun Bay, Action Report, South China Sea, 31st December 1944–*9th January* 1945. M.02472/45.

U.S.S. Kabashan Bay, Action Report, 29th December 1944–*12th January* 1945, *Luzon.* M.02348/45.

U.S.S. Hoggatt Bay, Action Report Covering Lingayen Gulf Operations, 1st–23rd January 1945. M.01968/45.

C.T.U. 77.4.2, *Action Report, 1st–17th January* 1945, *Lingayen Operation.* M.02998/45.

U.S.S. Knox, Report of Assault on Lingayen, 24th December 1944–*9th January* 1945. M.02990/45.

U.S.S. Ticonderoga, Operations in Support of Lingayen Assault, 3rd–21st January 1945. M.02422/45.

U.S.S. New Mexico, Bombardments and Close Cover, Lingayen Assault, 3rd–18th January 1945. M.02308/45.

C.T.G. 79.4, *U.S.S. Cambria, Action Report, 9th–12th January* 1945, *Lingayen Operation.* M.03235/45.

C.T.U. 78.1.2 *and* 78.1.22, *Lingayen Gulf, Action Report, 9th–10th January* 1945. M.03204/45.

Transport Division 26, *Action Report.* M.02370/45.

U.S.S. Braine, Action Report. M.03199/45 (sinking of enemy destroyer).

Action Report, 5th–17th January, Philippines Support Aircraft. M.03182/45.

C.T.U. 79.3.3, *Lingayen Operation, 6th–14th January* 1945. M.03203/45.

U.S.S. Shamrock Bay, Action Report, 31st December–23rd January 1945. M.03221/45.

C.T.U. 79.6.1, *Lingayen Attack, 9th–10th January* 1945. M.03232/45.

U.S.S. Fayette, Action Report, 8th, 9th, 10th January 1945, *Lingayen Operation.* M.02983/45 (flagship of Commander Transport Division 6).

U.S.S. Colorado, Action Report, 1st–18th January 1945, *Lingayen Gulf Operation.* M.02944/45.

U.S.S. Boise, Operations Incidental to Amphibious Assault and Landings on Luzon Island. M.03656/45.

Amphibious Operations, Invasion of the Philippines, October 1944 *to January* 1945. Cominch P–008. United States Fleet, Headquarters of the Commander-in-Chief.

Philippine Area Naval Operations, Part IV, January–August 1945. Japanese Monograph No. 114.

BIBLIOGRAPHY

Principal sources used in preparation of Chapter XI

Report on Operations of Third Fleet, 30th December 1944–*23rd January* 1945. M.03190/45 (Commander Third Fleet's report.)

C.T.F. 38, *Action Report, Formosa.* M.03191/45.

C.T.G. 38.3, *Action Report, 30th December* 1944–*26th January* 1945. M.03236/45.

U.S.S. Lexington, Action Report, 30th December 1944 *to 22nd January* 1945, *Formosa, Luzon, Indo China, Hong Kong, Okinawa.* M.02977/45.

Com. Cru. Div. 13, *C.T.U.* 38.3.3, *Carrier Air Strikes on Luzon, 6th–7th January* 1945. M.03017/45.

Com. Cru. Div. 13, *C.T.U.* 38.3.3, *Carrier Air Strikes on Formosa, 9th January* 1945. M.0365/45 (behind M.0302/45).

U.S.S. Cowpens, Air Strikes on Formosa, 8th–9th January. M.03210/45.

U.S.S. San Jacinto, Action Report, Formosa, Luzon, Saigon, Camranh Bay, South China Coast, Hong Kong, Nansei Shoto. M.03189/45.

C.T.G. 38.1, *Action Report, Formosa, Luzon, Indo China and China Coast, 30th December* 1944–*26th January* 1945. M.02988/45.

U.S.S. Yorktown, Report of Action, Luzon, Formosa, French Indo China, Japanese held China, Nansei Shoto, 30th December 1944–*23rd January* 1945. M.03214/45.

U.S.S. Cowpens, Action Report, 10th–20th January 1945, *Indo China, China, Formosa.* M.03218/45.

U.S.S. Wasp, Action Report, 30th December 1944–*25st January* 1945, *Philippine Islands.* M.01964/45.

U.S.S. Enterprise, Operations in Support of Landings on Luzon, 8th–23rd January 1945 (Night Operating Carrier). M.03192/45.

C.T.U. 38.2.2, *Action Report, 30th December* 1944–*26th January* 1945. M.03205/45.

Cru. Div. 10, *Action Report, 30th December* 1944-*23rd January* 1945. China Sea Sweep. M.03220/45 (behind M.03020/45).

Com. Cru. Div. 13, *C.T.U.* 38.3.3, *Action Report.* M.03020/45.

U.S.S. Langley, Strikes and Sweeps in Support of Re-occupation of Luzon. M.02945/45.

C.T.G. 38.2, *Support of Lingayen Landing, 30th December* 1944–*26th January* 1945. M.03223/45.

Cru. Div. 2, *Action Report, 1st–31st January* 1945. M.05016/45.

Operation Mike I, C.T.G. 38.5, *Action Report, 5th–22nd January, Lingayen Gulf, P.I.* M.09808/45.

C.T.G. 34.5, *Action Report.* M.02987/45.

Com. Bat. Div. 8, *Action Report.* M.03209/45.

U.S.S. Washington, Action Report, 30th December 1944–*23rd January* 1945, *Ryukus, Formosa, China Coast, North Luzon Area and Nansei Shoto.* M.02927/45.

China Sea Sweep, 30th December 1944–23rd January 1945: Reports of Task Group Commanders: *C.T.G.* 1. M.02988/45. *C.T.G.* 2. M.03223/45. *C.T.G.* M.03236/45.

U.S.S. Hancock, Action Report, 30th December 1944—*25th January* 1945, *Formosa, Luzon French Indo China, the China Coast and Nansei Shoto.* M.02946/45.

U.S.S. Hornet, Action Report, 1st–23rd January 1945, *Ryukus, Formosa, Luzon and South China Sea.* M.03024/45.

C.T.G. 38.3, *Action Report, 30th December* 1944–*23rd January* 1945, *Ryukus, Formosa, China Coast, North Luzon and Nansei Shoto.* M.08299/45.

Com. Cru. Div. 13, *Carrier Air Strikes on Formosa, Hainan and Indo China Coast, 15th–16th January* 1945. M.03019/45 (behind M.03020/45).

Com. Cru. Div. 13, *Carrier Air Strikes on Formosa, Hainan and Indo China Coast, 21st–22nd January.* M.03018/45 (behind M.03020/45).

U.S.S. Santa Fé, Report Covering 30th December 1944–*26th January* 1945. M.02995/45 (behind M.03020/45).

C.T.U. 38.3.3, *Carrier Air Strikes on 21st January* 1945, *Formosa.* M.03225/45.

U.S.S. Cowpens, 21st–26th January, Formosa and Nansei Shoto. M.03202/45 (behind 03210/45).

Battle Experience. *Third Fleet Operations in Support of Central Luzon Landings—including the South China Sea Sweep, 30th December* 1944–*23rd January* 1945. Secret Information Bulletin No. 23, U.S. Fleet, Headquarters of Commander-in-Chief.

BIBLIOGRAPHY

Principal sources used in preparation of Chapter XII

H.M.A.S. Shropshire, Action Report, 16th February (Bombardment of Corregidor). M.06468/45.

H.M.A.S. Warramunga, Action Report, 16th February 1945, *Corregidor.* M.09176/45.

Recs. for Awards to Surveying Personnel, H.M.A.S. Warrego. H. & A. 566/45.

C.T.G. 78.3, *Action Report, 29th–31st January* 1945, *Amphibious Landings in Zambales Province, Luzon.* M.06321/45.

C.T.G. 78.2, *Action Report, 25th January–5th February, Nasugbu (Luzon) Landing.* M.05641/45.

U.S.S. Montpelier, Action Report, Landings at Mariveles Bay and Corregidor Island, 13th–16th February 1945. M.04762/45.

U.S.S. Boise, Action Report, Bataan and Corregidor, 13th–17th February 1945. M.05011/45.

C.T.G. 77.3, *Action Report, 13th–18th February, Mariveles, Corregidor.* M.06316/45.

U.S.S. Minneapolis, Action Report, 16th February 1945, *Corregidor.* M.06174/45.

Cru. Div. 12, *Action Report, Puerto Princesa, Palawan, 27th–28th February* 1945. M.03746/45.

Action Report, Zamboanga Operations, 4th–14th March 1945 (*C.T.G.* 74.3, *Com Cru. Div.* 15). M.06205/45.

U.S.S. Boise, Action Report, 8th–12th March, Zamboanga. M.06212/45.

C.T.U. 74.2.2, *U.S.S. Cleveland, Action Report, 17th–20th March, Operations in Support of Amphibious Occupation of Iloilo, Panay.* M.06139/45.

C.T.G. 76.10, *Action Report, 30th March–5th April, Sanga Sanga and Jolo (P.I.).* M.06243/45.

C.T.U. 76.10.2, *Action Report, 31st March–3rd April and 8th–11th April, Attacks on Sanga Sanga, Jolo, Sulu Archipel, Philippine Islands.* M.06098/45.

U.S.S. Montpelier, Denver, Cleveland, Sigourney, Young, Stevens—Malabang, Parang, Cotabaito (Philippines), 14th–24th April 1945. M.06479/45.

C.T.U. 78.2.2, *Action Report, 17th April, Mindanao.* M.06501/45.

LCI(R) 224 *and LCI(R)* 331, *Action Reports, 15th–16th April, Carabao I.* M.06472/45.

C.T.G. 74.3, *Action Report, 24th–28th March* 1945, *Cebu City Operations.* M.06168/45.

U.S.S. Phoenix, Action Report, Cebu. M.04527/45.

Principal sources used in preparation of Chapter XIII

British Combined Operations, Observer's Report of Operations against Iwo Jima. M.05613/45.

C.O.H.Q. Bulletin Y/49, *Iwo Jima and Okinawa.*

Amphibious Operations, Capture of Iwo Jima, Cominch P–0012. M.08472/45.

C.T.F. 54, *Action Report, 10th February–10th March, Iwo Jima.* M.06325/45.

Report by Commander of U.S. Joint Expeditionary Force. M.04768/45.

C.T.G. 94.9, *Action Report, Bombardment of Iwo Jima, 24th and 27th December* 1944. M.02342/45.

C.T.G. 58.4, *Action Report, 10th February–1st March* 1945, *Tokyo and Iwo Jima.* M.05004/45.

C.T.G. 94.9, *Action Report, Part of Combined Air and Ship Operation.* M.0964/45.

U.S.S. Salt Lake City, Bombardment of Iwo Jima, 24th and 27th December 1944. M.02146/45.

U.S.S. Pensacola, Action Report, Bombardment of Iwo Jima, 8th December 1944. M.01811/45.

Action Report, Com. Cru. Div. 5, *Iwo Jima, 16th February–12th March* 1945. M.08336/45.

U.S.S. Bunker Hill, Action Report, 10th February–5th March 1945, *1st and 2nd Strikes on Tokyo and Support and Capture of Iwo.* M.05646/45.

U.S.S. Essex, Action Report, Iwo Jima, 10th February–4th March 1945. M.03745/45.

C.T.U. 52.2.1, *Action Report, Iwo Jima, 10th February–11th March* 1945. M.06167/45.

U.S.S. Enterprise, Action Report, 10th–23rd February 1945, *Iwo Jima, Phase* 1. M.05630/45.

U.S.S. Enterprise, Action Report, 23rd February–9th March, Iwo Jima. M.03663/45.

U.S.S. Tennessee, 1st and 2nd Endorsement to Action Report, 16th–19th February 1945, *Iwo Jima.* M.08200/45. *Action Report, 16th February–7th March* 1945. M.03615/45.

Com. Cru. Div. 13, *Action Report, 19th–22nd February* 1945, *Iwo Jima, 1st and 2nd Endorsements.* M.08653/45.

U.S.S. Alaska, Action Report, Iwo Jima, 23rd February–9th March 1945, *Operations in Support of Capture of Iwo Jima.* M.05013/45.

U.S.S. West Virginia, Action Report, 19th February to 1st March 1945, *Bombardment of and Fire Support for Landings, Iwo Jima.* M.05002/45.

Cru. Div. 13, *Iwo Jima, 16th–26th February* 1945. M.03612/45 (behind M.08653/45).

U.S.S. North Carolina, Bombardment of Iwo Jima, 19th–22nd February 1945. M.05643/45.

U.S.S. Nevada, 16th February–7th March 1945, *Iwo Jima.* M.05629/45.

U.S.S. San Juan, 10th February–1st March 1945, *Operations in Support of Occupation of Iwo Jima.* M.05644/45.

Com. Bat. Div. 5, *C.T.U.* 54.9.1, 54.1.3, 54.9.12, *Arkansas, Texas, 10th February–12th March, Iwo Jima.* M.06127/45.

Com. Bat. Div. 5, *C.T.U.* 54.9.1, 54.1.3, 54.9.12, *Arkansas, Texas, 10th February–12th March, Iwo Jima. 5th Endorsement.* M.08337/45.

U.S.S. Salt Lake City, Action Report, 16th February–12th March, Iwo Jima. M.06208/45.

U.S.S. Vincennes, Invasion of Iwo Jima, 10th February–5th March 1945. M.05008/45.

U.S.S. Tuscaloosa, 10th February–12th March, Iwo Jima Operation. M.03658/45.

U.S.S. Randolph, Action Report, Tokyo, Iwo Jima, 10th–28th February 1945. M.05007/45.

C.T.G. 51.17, 51.26, *C.T.U.* 52.2.3, *Action Reports, 10th February–14th March, Iwo Jima.* M.06133/45.

U.S.S. Idaho, Action Report, 16th February–7th March, Iwo Jima. M.06133/45.

U.S.S. Washington, Action Report, 19th–22nd February, Iwo Jima. M.06173/45.

Com. Bat. Div. 6, *Action Report, 19th February–22nd February, Iwo Jima.* M.06204/45.

U.S.S. South Dakota, Action Report, 10th February–5th March, Iwo, Tokyo, Okinawa. M.06176/45.

C.T.U. 52.4.3, *U.S.S. Bull, Bates, Barr, Waters, 10th February–8th March, Iwo Jima.* M.06238/45.

Com. Fire Support Unit 4, *Action Report, 16th–28th February, 1st–12th March, Iwo Jima.* M.06230/45.

U.S.S. Vicksburg, Action Report, 14th February–5th March 1945, *Iwo Jima.* M.06095/45.

C.T.G. 53.2 (*Com. Transport Sqn.* 15), *Action Report, 19th February–4th March* 1945, *Iwo Jima.* M.06100/45.

Com. Cru. Div. 13, *U.S.S. Biloxi, Action Report, 19th–21st February, Bombardment of Iwo Jima.* M.08313/45.

U.S.S. Santa Fé, Action Report, 19th–22nd February 1945, *Fire Support, Iwo Jima.* M.06318/45.

U.S.S. Pensacola, Action Report, 16th February–1st March 1945, *Gunfire and Covering Support.* M.05642/45.

C.T.U. 58.2.2, *Action Report, Tokyo, Iwo Jima, Nansei Shoto, 10th February to 1st March.* M.03613/45.

U.S.S. New York, Action Report, Bombardment of Iwo Jima, 16th–18th February 1945. M.05638/45.

Task Force 58, *Com. Cru. Div.* 14, *Action Report, 10th February–3rd March* 1945, *Iwo Jima, Okino Daito Jima.* M.05014/45.

Support Carrier Unit 4, *U.S.S. Saratoga, Air Attack off Iwo Jima, 21st February* 1945. M.03648/45.

Cru. Div. 10, *23rd February–5th March* 1945, *Iwo Jima.* M.03654/45.

U.S.S. Birmingham, Action Report, 28th February–5th March, Iwo Jima. M.06209/45.

Naval Gunfire Support, Iwo Jima. M.08937/45.

Principal sources used in preparing Chapter XIV

H.M.S. Taciturn, Patrol Report, 13th May–27th June 1945. M.07598/45.

Borneo Area Naval Operations 1945. Japanese Monograph No. 115, Headquarters Far East Command.

TARAKAN OPERATION

H.M.A.S. Hobart, Report of Proceedings, Borneo. M.09165/45.

H.M.A.S. Westralia, Action Report, 1st May 1945, *Tarakan Operation.* M.09186/45.

H.M.A.S. Manoora, Action Report, 1st May 1945 *Tarakan Operation.* M.09138/45, M.09172/45.

H.M.A.S. Warramunga, Action Report, 24th April–15th May 1945, *Tarakan.* M.09182/45.

Task Group 78.1, *Action Report, 1st–3rd May* 1945, *Tarakan.* M.06815/45 (Commander Amphibious Group 6).

U.S.S. Boise, Action Report, 24th April–5th May 1945, *Tarakan I., Borneo.* M.07291/45.

C.T.U. 78.1.16, *Action Report, 25th April–1st May, Tarakan.* M.06816/45.

U.S.S. Phoenix Supporting, 24th April–5th May 1945. M.06924/45.

C.T.G. 74.3, *Action Report, 27th April–5th May* 1945, *Tarakan.* M.08662/45.

U.S.S. Taylor, Action Report, 24th April–5th May 1945, *Operations in Support of the Seizure of Tarakan Island, Dutch Borneo.* M.09157/45.

U.S.S. Philip, Action Report, 30th April–3rd May 1945, *Sadan and Tarakan Operations.* M.01094/46.

C.T.U. 78.1.5 [Minesweeping Unit], *Action Report, Minesweeping Operations, Tarakan I., NEI.* M.08609/45.

U.S.S. Titania, Action Report, 26th April–9th May 1945, *Tarakan.* M.09179/45.

U.S.S. Nicholas, Action Report, 24th April–5th May 1945, *Tarakan.* M.08667/45.

C.O.H.Q. Bulletin Y/50, *Tarakan, Borneo, 1st May* 1945.

BRUNEI BAY OPERATION

H.M.A.S. Shropshire, Action Report, Brunei Bay, 17th–22nd June 1945. M.09426/45, M.01081/45.

H.M.A.S. Arunta, Action Report, Brunei Bay, 5th–12th June 1945. M.01089/46.

H.M.A.S. Arunta, Action Report, Miri-Lutong, 23rd June 1945. M.01080/46.

H.M.A.S. Lachlan (*C.T.U.* 78.1.6), *Action Report, 7th–12th June* 1945, *Brunei Bay.* M.01088/46.

C.T.G. 78.1, *Action Report, 10th–17th June* 1945, *Brunei Bay, Borneo.* M.08090/45.

C.T.G. 74.3, *Action Report, 5th–17th June* 1945. M.09155/45, M.09955/45.

C.T.U. 76.2.20 (*C.O., LSM Flotilla* 7), *Action Report, 14th–17th June* 1945, *Borneo* (Western Landing, 17th June). M.08611/45.

U.S.S. LST 637, *Action Report, 22nd May–12th June* 1945, *Labuan I.* M.09158/45.

U.S.S. Cleveland, Action Report, 7th–15th June 1945, *Operations in Support of Amphibious Occupation of Brunei, Muria and Victoria Town in North Borneo.* M.08603/45.

C.T.U. 78.1.2, *Action Report, 4th–12th June* 1945, *Brunei Bay.* M.08322/45.

C.T.U. 74.3.3, *Action Report, 5th–17th June* 1945, *Brunei Bay.* M.08607/45.

Com. LCI(L) Group 72, *Action Report, 2nd–12th June* 1945, *Brunei Bay.* M.08612/45.

U.S.S. Charrett, Action Report, 8th–17th June 1945, *Brunei Bay.* M.08665/45 (Fire support).

Com. LST Flot. 15, *Action Report, 10th–12th June* 1945, *Brunei Bluff, Muara Island.* M.08606/45.

U.S.S. Nashville, Action Report, 9th–10th June 1945, *Brunei Bay.* M.08360/45, M.01095/45 (Bombardment).

U.S.S. Shields, Action Report, 26th–27th June 1945, *Miri, Sarawak, Borneo.* M.01083/46 (Bombardment).

U.S.S. Rocky Mount, Action Report, 4th–12th June 1945, *Brunei Bay.* M.09181/45.

U.S.S. Cleveland, Action Report, 7th–15th June 1945, *Brunei Bay, Muria and Victoria Town.* M.09145/45.

U.S.S. LCS(L)(3) 45, *Action Report, 2nd–12th June* 1945, *Brunei Bay.* M.09961/45.

U.S.S. Y.M.S. 160, *Action Report, 7th–12th June* 1945, *Brunei Bay.* M.09170/45.

C.T.U. 76.2.20 (*C.O. LSM Flot.* 7), *Action Report, 14th–17th June* 1945. M.08611/45.

C.T.U. 76.2.50 (*Com. LCI(L) Flot.* 8), *Action Report, 20th June* 1945, *Lutong.* M.08608/45.

U.S.S. Phoenix, Action Report, 9th–15th June 1945. M.08356/45 (Cruiser Covering Group).

U.S.S. Conner, Action Report, 5th–16th June 1945. M.08361/45, M.08666/45 (Fire Support and Covering Operations).

U.S.S. Boise, Action Report, 8th–11th June 1945. M.08357/45 (Cruiser Covering Group).

C.T.U. 78.1.16 (*Com. LST Flot.* 24), *9th–12th June, Labuan.* M.01082/46.

Com. Des. Ron. 1, *Action Report, 8th–17th June* 1945. *Brunei Bay.* M.01077/46.

C.T.U. 78.1.3 (*C.O. LCS(L) Flot.* 1), *Action Report, Brunei Bay.* M.01087/46.

UDT 11, *Action Report, 8th June* 1945, *Labuan I.* M.01068/46.

U.S.S. Hart, Action Report, 7th–25th June 1945, *Brunei Bay.* M.01076/46, M.09143/45.

BIBLIOGRAPHY

BALIK PAPAN OPERATION

Com. Des. Div. 15, *H.M.A.S. Hobart and Arunta, Action Report, 26th June–9th July* 1945, *Balik Papan.* M.01084/46.

H.M.A.S. Shropshire, Action Report, 26th June–9th July 1945, *Balik Papan.* M.09177/45.

C.T.G. 74.2, *U.S.S. Colombia, Montpelier, Denver, Action Report, 13th June–2nd July* 1945, *Balik Papan.* M.01074/46.

Com. Phib. Grp 8, *Action Report, Balik Papan, Manggar, 15th June–16th July* 1945. M.09427/45.

UDT 18, *Action Report, 25th–28th June and 1st July* 1945, *Klandasan and Manggar-Ketjil Beaches, S.E. Borneo.* M.09222/45.

C.T.G. 78.2, *Action Report, Balik Papan, Manggar, 15th June–6th July* 1945. M.09965/45, NID.08369/45.

U.S.S. Denver, Action Report, 15th June–2nd July 1945, *Balik Papan.* M.09156/45.

U.S.S. Eaton, Action Report, Balik Papan, 13th June–2nd July 1945. M.08660/45.

U.S.S. Montpelier, Action Report, 12th June–2nd July 1945, *Balik Papan.* M.09101/45.

U.S.S. Charette, Action Report, 28th June–9th July 1945, *Balik Papan.* M.09154/45, M.09140/45.

Com. Des. Div. 102, *Action Report, Seizure of Balik Papan Area, 28th June–9th July* 1945. M.01078/46.

Com. Des. Div. 44, *U.S.S. Conway, Cony, Stevens, Hart, Metcalf, Action Reports, Operations at Balik Papan, 13th June–2nd July* 1945. M.01079/46.

C.T.G. 74.2, *Action Report, 13th June–2nd July* 1945, *Balik Papan, Borneo.* M.09147/45, M.08613/45, M.01074/46.

U.S.S. Conyngham, Action Report, 1st–3rd July 1945, *Balik Papan.* M.09970/45.

U.S.S. Y.M.S. 392, *Action Report, Balik Papan, 11th June–1st July* 1945. M.01092/46.

Beachmaster, Naval Beach Party No. 2, *Action Report, 1st–9th July* 1945, *Balik Papan Area.* M.01069/46.

Com. Phib. Grp. 8, *Action Report, Balik Papan, Manggar, Borneo, 15th June–6th July* 1945. M.09427/45, M.09965/45.

C.T.U. 78.2.2, *H.M.A.S. Manoora, Kanimbla, Westralia, U.S.S. Titania, Carter Hall, Action Report, 1st July* 1945,*Balik Papan.* M.01096/46.

U.S.S. Eaton, Action Report, Balik Papan, 13th June–2nd July 1945. M.08660/45 (Support and Covering Group).

Com. Des. Ron. 5, *Action Report, 26th June–4th July* 1945, *Balik Papan.* M.08604/45.

Com. Des. Ron. 5, *Action Report, 15th–17th July* 1945. M.09180/45.

U.S.S. Hart, Action Report, 26th June–1st July 1945, *Balik Papan.* M.08610/45 (behind M.08604/45). (Task Group 74.4, H.M.A.S. *Shropshire* (flag), *Hobart, Arunta,* U.S.S. *Metcalf, Hart.*)

Com. Car. Div. 22, *Action Report, 26th June–6th July* 1945, *Balik Papan.* M.09425/45.

C.T.G. 74.3 (*Com. Cru. Div.* 15), *Action Report, 28th June-9th July* 1945, *Balik Papan.* M.01075/46.

U.S.S. Phoenix, Action Report, 28th June–10th July 1945, *Balik Papan, Manggar.* M.09107/45.

U.S.S. Nashville, Action Report, 26th June–7th July 1945, *Balik Papan.* M.09963/45.

C.T.U. 78.2.15, *Action Report, 26th June–15th July* 1945, *Balik Papan.* M.09979/45.

U.S.S. Conway, Cony, Stevens, Hart, Metcalf, Action Report, Balik Papan. M.09146/45.

U.S.S. Albert W. Grant, Action Report, 30th June–9th July 1945, *Balik Papan.* M.09175/45, M.09141/45.

U.S.S. Burns, Action Report, 28th June–11th July 1945, *Balik Papan.* M.09178/45.

U.S.S. Cleveland, Action Report, 27th June–3rd July 1945. M.09686/45.

U.S.S. Bell, Action Report, 22nd June–7th July, Balik Papan. M.09173/45.

U.S.S. Columbia, Action Report, 21st June–2nd July 1945. M.09100/45.

U.S.S. LCS(L) 29, *Action Report, 20th June–2nd July* 1945, *Manggar, Balik Papan.* M.09171/45.

U.S.S. LST 1017, *Action Report, 1st–4th July* 1945, *Balik Papan.* M.09166/45.

BIBLIOGRAPHY

Principal sources used in preparation of Chapter XV

The principal reports on Operation ' Iceberg ' are listed in the Naval Staff History Battle Summary No. 47, *Naval Operations in the Assault and Capture of Okinawa, March–June* 1945, C.B. 3081(32). An additional source is *Report of Experience of the British Pacific Fleet from January–August* 1945. M.01779/46.

The report on Operation ' Inmate ' is in M.07669/45, *Operation ' Inmate ', Neutralisation of Air Installations in Truk Atoll, 12th–17th June* 1945. *Task Group* 111.2, *H.M.S. Implacable.* The War Diary of the Vice-Admiral British Pacific Fleet covering the period 5th–28th June 1945, is numbered T.S.D. 3159/45 (in Record Office Case WH.8957).

Principal sources used in the preparation of Chapter XVI

(*a*) British

Note.—To ensure quick circulation within the Admiralty certain reports were circulated in multiple copies. Where important minutes are contained in the different copies, registered numbers of all such copies are given below.

C.-in-C. BPF. *Reports of Naval Operations against Japan, 17th July–2nd September* 1945. (Includes report of V.-A. Second-in-Command BPF and F.O.C. 1st Aircraft Carrier Squadron BPF.) M.010175/45.

C.-in-C. BPF. *Despatches, November* 1944 *to July* 1945. M.010453 (copy in M.059378/45), M.0406/46, M.083/45.

C.-in-C. BPF. *Despatches, July* 1945 *to November* 1945. M.0405/46, M.0407/46.

C.-in-C. BPF. *Report of Experience of the British Pacific Fleet from Janaury–August* 1945 M.01779/46.

C.-in-C. BPF. *The British Pacific Fleet in Operations against Japan* (Analysis). M.010312/45.

BPF Liaison Officer to 2nd U.S. Carrier Task Force. *Report on Second Carrier Task Force Operations, 1st July–15th August* 1945. M.09889/45.

Report by BPF Liaison Officer to Com. Third Fleet. Third Fleet Operations, 1st July–15th August 1945. M.09042/45.

King George V, Report of Bombardment of Hitachi, E. Honshu, 17th July 1945. M.09198/45.

King George V, Bombardment of Hamamatsu, Honshu, 29th July 1945. M.09196/45.

H.M.S. Newfoundland and H.M.N.Z.S. Gambia, Report of Operations from 28th July–12th August 1945 *in Southern Honshu.* M.010345/45.

Commander-in-Chief and Vice-Admiral British Pacific Fleet War Diaries. (Record Office Case WH.8957.)

4th February–23rd March 1945. TSD.3157/45.
26th May–5th June 1945. TSD.3158/45.
5th–28th June 1945. TSD.3159/45.
28th June–6th July 1945. M.09437/45.
6th–16th July 1945. M.010283/45.

(*b*) United States

Com. Third Fleet, 1st July–15th August 1945, *Japan.* M.01070/46.

Brief of Action Report, C.T.F. 38, *Operations off Japan for the Period from 2nd July to 15th August* 1945. M.0283/46.

*Brief of CAG*6, *Memorandum No.* 3 *CM*–14 *on Japan Operations, 10th–18th July* 1945. M.09888/45.

U.S.S. Randolph, Report on Fighter Direction in U.S. Fleet, 1st July–10th August 1945. M.09436/45.

Action reports

Com. Third Fleet, 1st July–15th August 1945, *Japan.* M.01070/46.

Task Force 38, *Operations against Japan, 2nd July–15th August* 1945. M.09579/45.

Com. Second Carrier Task Force (*C.T.F.* 38), *2nd July–15th August* 1945, *Japan.* M.09809/45.

C.T.G. 38.1, *Com. Car. Div.* 3, *1st July–15th August* 1945, *Japan.* M.09737/45.

C.T.G. 38.3, *Com. Car. Div.* 4, *1st July–15th August* 1945. M.09815/45.

U.S.S. Wasp, 21st July–15th August 1945, *N. Honshu, S.W. Honshu and Tokyo Plains Area.* M.09275/45.

Com. Bat. Div. 9, *1st July–15th August* 1945, *Japan.* M.09986/45.

U.S.S. Independence, 1st July–15th August 1945, *Japan.* M.09951/45.

U.S.S. Monterey, Honshu, Hokkaido, 1st July–15th August 1945. M.09794/45.

U.S.S. Essex, 2nd July–15th August 1945, *Japan*. M.09800/45.

U.S.S. Alabama, 1st July–13th August 1945, *Japan*. M.09752/45.

U.S.S. Wilkes-Barre, 1st July–15th August 1945, *Japan*. M.09753/45.

Com. Cru. Div. 17, *C.T.U.* 38.3.4, *2nd July–15th August* 1945, *Japan*. M.09739/45.

U.S.S. Springfield, 2nd July–15th August 1945, *Japan*. M.09749/45.

U.S.S. North Carolina, 8th July–15th August 1945, *Japan*. M.09821/45.

U.S.S. Topeka, 1st July–15th August 1945, *Japan*. M.09683/45.

U.S.S. Pasadena, 1st July–15th August 1945, *off Japan*. M.09788/45.

Com. Des. Div. 96, *2nd July–15th August* 1945, *Japan*. M.09927/45.

U.S.S. Missouri, 2nd July–15th August 1945, *Honshu, Hokkaido, Kyushu*. M.09748/45.

U.S.S. Cowpens, 1st July–15th August 1945, *Honshu, Shikoku, Hokkaido*. M.09828/45.

U.S.S. Shangri-La, 2nd July–15th August 1945, *Honshu, Hokkaido*. M. 09798/45.

U.S.S. Hancock, 1st July–15th August 1945, *Japan*. M.09952/45.

U.S.S. Lexington, 1st July–15th August 1945, *Japan*. M.09924/45.

U.S.S. Bennington, 2nd July–15th August 1945, *W. Honshu to E. Hokkaido*. M.09996/45.

U.S.S. Topeka, Anti-Shipping Sweep across E. Entrance of Sagami Nada and Bombardment of Najima Saki, Night 18th–19th July 1945. M.09810/45.

U.S.S. Massachusetts, 1st July–15th August 1945, *Japan*. M.09826/45.

U.S.S. Belleau Wood, 2nd July–15th August 1945, *Japan*. M.09967/45.

U.S.S. Bon Homme Richard, 2nd July–15th August 1945, *Japan*. M.09968/45 (Night Carrier in Task Group 38.4).

U.S.S. Iowa, 2nd July–15th August 1945, *Japan*. M.09972/45.

U.S.S. Indiana, 1st July–15th August 1945, *Japan*. M.09973/45.

U.S.S. Boston, 20th July–15th August 1945, *Japan*. M.09974/45.

U.S.S. Duluth, 21st July–15th August 1945, *Japan*. M.09976/45.

U.S.S. Dayton, 2nd July–15th August 1945, *Japan*. M.09984/45.

U.S.S. Yorktown, 2nd July–15th August 1945, *Japan*. M.09989/45.

U.S.S. San Jacinto, 1st July–15th August 1945, *Japan*. M.09990/45.

U.S.S. Oklahoma City, 2nd July–15th August 1945, *Japan*. M.09995/45.

Com. Cru. Div. 18, *Anti-Shipping Sweep, E. Entrance Sagami Nada and Bombardment Nojima Saki, 18th–19th July* 1945. M.09384/45.

U.S.S. Ticonderoga, 1st July–15th August 1945, *Japan*. M.09283/45.

U.S.S. Wilkes-Barre, Anti-Shipping Sweep across Kii Suido, 24th–25th July 1945. M.09284/45.

U.S.S. Astoria, 24th–25th July, Bombardment of Honshu Coast near Shiono Misaki. M.09287/45.

Com. Bat. Div. 9, *Night Bombardment of Hitachi Area, Honshu, Japan, 17th–18th July* 1945. M.09419/45.

U.S.S. Indiana, 14th July 1945, *Bombardment of Kamaishi*. M.09420/45.

U.S.S. Massachusetts, 14th July 1945, *Bombardment of Kamaishi*. M.09394/45 (behind M.09420/45).

U.S.S. Chicago, 14th July 1945, *Bombardment of Kamaishi*. M.09391/45 (behind M.09420/45).

U.S.S. Indiana, Bombardment of Hamamatsu, 29th–30th July 1945. M.09960/45.

U.S.S. South Dakota, 29th–30th July 1945, *Hamamatsu, Honshu*. M.09811/45.

Com. Cru. Div. 17, *C.T.F.* 35, *Anti-Shipping Sweep by T.G.* 35.3 *across Kii Suido and Bombardment of Kushimoto and Shionomisaki Night 24th–25th July*, 1945. M.09807/45.

U.S.S. Oklahoma City, Anti-Shipping Sweep of Sagami Nada and Bombardment of Nojima Saki, 18th–19th July 1945. M.08856/45.

C.T.U. 34.8.2, *Com. Bat. Div.* 7, *Bombardment of Hitachi Industries, Mito Area, Honshu, 17th July* 1945. M.09164/45.

U.S.S. Atlanta, 17th–18th July, Bombardment of Hitachi Area. M.09386/45.

U.S.S. Alabama, 17th–18th July, Bombardment of Hitachi Area. M.09168/45.

U.S.S. Dayton, 17th–18th July, Bombardment of Hitachi Area. M.09169/45 (includes also bombardment of 15th July).

BIBLIOGRAPHY

Com. Bat. Div. 9, *Shore Bombardment of Muroran, Hokkaido,* 15*th July* 1945. M.09424/45.

U.S.S. Iowa, Shore Bombardment of Muroran, Hokkaido, 15*th July* 1945. M.09421/45 (behind M.09424/45).

U.S.S. Missouri, Shore Bombardment of Muroran, Hokkaido, 15*th July* 1945. M.09418/45 (behind M.09424/45).

C.T.F. 31, *Com. Bat. Div.* 7, 19*th August–8th September* 1945, *Japan.* M.09682/45. (Details of damage to *Nagato.*)

Com. Bat. Ron. 2, *C.T.F.* 34, *C.T.G.* 34.8 *and C.T.U.* 34.8.1, *Bombardment of Kamaishi,* 14*th July* 1945. M.0393/46.

Com. Bat. Ron. 2, *C.T.U.* 38.1.2, *and Com. Bat. Div.* 8, *C.T.U.* 38.1.3, *Operations from* 1*st July to* 15*th August* 1945, *Japan.* M.010741/45.

U.S.S. South Dakota, 14*th July* 1945, *Honshu.* M.08855/45.

U.S.S. Pasadena, Anti-Shipping Sweep along East Coast of Honshu, Japan, 14*th*–15*th July,* 1945. M.09513/45.

Com. Cru. Div. 17, *Anti-Shipping Sweep along East coast of Honshu, Night of* 14*th*–15*th July* 1945. M.09515/45.

Anti-Shipping Sweep of East China Sea

C.T.F. 95, *Com. Bat. Ron.* 1, 4*th*–30*th July* 1945. M.09813/45.

Com. Cru. Div. 16, *Operations in East China Sea by T.G.* 95.2, 25*th July–7th August* 1945. M.09790/45.

C.T.G. 95.2, 13*th*–23*rd July* 1945. M.09396/45.

Com. Cru. Div. 16, 13*th*–23*rd July* 1945. M.09393/45.

U.S.S. Montpelier, 13*th*–23*rd July* 1945. M.09387/45.

U.S.S. Columbia, 13*th*–23*rd July* 1945. M.09398/45.

U.S.S. Denver, 21*st July* 1945. M.09389/45.

United States Strategic Bombing Survey Reports

Report of Ships' Bombardment Survey Party, Shionomisaki, 24*th*–25*th July, Nojima Saki (Radar Station),* 18*th*–19*th July.* Report No. BIOS/JAP/PR1738 (NID.623/48).

Effects of Surface Bombardment on Japanese War Potential. Report No. BIOS/JAP/PR/1721 (NID.6207/47).

Reports of Ships' Bombardment Survey Party. Report No. BIOS/JAP/PR/1722 (G.02928/48).

The Effects of Strategic Bombing on Japan's War Economy. Report No. BIOS/JAP/PR/1589.

Principal sources used in preparation of Chapter XVII

The Effects of Strategic Bombing on Japan's War Economy, Appendix A.B.C., U.S.S.B.S., London—H.M.S.O.

Japan's Struggle to End the War. U.S.S.B.S., London—H.M.S.O.

UNOFFICIAL

The Second World War, Volumn VI, *Triumph and Tragedy.* W. S. Churchill. Cassell & Co., Ltd. 1954.

The Memoirs of Harry S. Truman, Volume I, *Year of Decisions.* Hodder & Stoughton. 1955.

JAPANESE

Naval Operations against Soviet Russia. Japanese Monograph No. 106.

Index

References are to pages
(n = footnote)

INDEX

INDEX

Printed in the United Kingdom for HMSO
Dd 0296898 C15 1/95 9091